CARSCAPES

CARSCAPES

The Motor Car, Architecture and Landscape in England

KATHRYN A. MORRISON AND JOHN MINNIS

To Peter

Kathryn Morrison

John Minnis

Published by

YALE UNIVERSITY PRESS

New Haven and London

for

THE PAUL MELLON CENTRE FOR STUDIES IN BRITISH ART

in association with

ENGLISH HERITAGE

Designed by Gilllian Malpass

Printed in China

Library of Congress Cataloging-in-Publication Data
Morrison, Kathryn.
Carscapes : the motor car, architecture and landscape in England / Kathryn A
Morrison, John Minnis.
p. cm.
Includes bibliographical references and index.
ISBN 978-0-300-18704-5 (cl : alk. paper)
1. Automobiles–Social aspects–England–History. 2. Transportation,
Automotive–Social aspects–England–History. 3. England--Social life and customs.
4. Architecture and society–England–History. 5. Cultural
landscapes–England–History. I. Minnis, John. II. Title.
HE5664.A6M655 2012
306.4'6--DC23

2012022079

Page i Typical car wheels of the period are carved in relief on the pilasters of the
Neo-Classical Bristol Motor Co. showroom of 1929–30, designed by Charles White,
at Ashton Gate, Bristol. When this photograph was taken, in 2008, the premises were
disused.

Page ii A metropolitan traffic policeman conducting traffic on Fleet Street, London,
circa 1960, photographed by John Gay.

CONTENTS

ACKNOWLEDGEMENTS

THE ORIGINS OF THIS BOOK — with its emphasis on England rather than Britain — lie in a study of road transport buildings undertaken by the Royal Commission on the Historic Monuments of England (RCHME) for English Heritage (EH) in 1997 (see Calladine and Morrison 1998). This short desktop exercise highlighted the paucity of information on such buildings, and stressed the need for a proper survey. It was recommended that this be based on fieldwork, as much as on documentary research, to gauge levels of survival and, generally, to assess the condition of this aspect of the historic environment. At the time, resources were lacking, and this recommendation could not be taken forward. But ten years later — some years after the merger of RCHME and EH — 'The Car Project' was launched, with an intensive programme of national fieldwork and research (carried out 2008–10). This now forms the basis of our understanding of a number of twentieth-century building types, and has informed guidelines on how to measure their significance and determine their potential for listing. Preparing this book has been a crucial part of that analytical process, but it also represents an attempt to stimulate general interest in — and awareness of — aspects of our historical surroundings that are often disregarded.

'The Car Project' was overseen and carried out by the authors, but a very substantial part of the fieldwork and research was undertaken with our colleague Matthew Whitfield, to whom we owe an especially large debt of gratitude. The country house garage was researched by another colleague, Pete Smith, to whom we are also immensely grateful. Katie Carmichael undertook research and fieldwork on motorway service areas and Hannah Waugh carried out research on roadside catering. Magnus Alexander produced a study of road-related archaeology.

Many other friends and colleagues at English Heritage have contributed their specialist skills and expertise to this publication. For ground photography we must thank Steve Cole and his team: Keith Buck, Alun Bull, Nigel Corrie, James O. Davies, Mike Hesketh-Roberts, Derek Kendall, Pat Payne, Bob Skingle and Peter Williams. Aerial photography — the only way to illustrate some of the vast sites covered in this book — was undertaken by Damien Grady and Dave MacLeod. The graphics were prepared by Andy Donald, except for the drawings of motorway junctions, which are by Philip Sinton. Those who have drawn our attention to buildings of interest, sent us snippets of information, or simply provided much-needed support include: Allan Adams, Peter Barlow, Allan Brodie, John Cattell, Wayne Cocroft, Emily Cole, Andrew David, Dale Dishon, Geraint Franklin, Emily Gee, David Grech, Peter Guillery, Elain Harwood, Julian Holder, Edward Impey, Anne Locke, Sarah Newsome, Treve Rosoman, Susan Skedd, Jo Smith, Simon Taylor, Pete Topping, June Warrington and Gary Winter.

Although this is a co-authored work, John Minnis was the lead author for Chapters 3, 4, 5, 8, 10 and 11, while Kathryn Morrison took the lead for Chapters 1, 2, 6, 7, 9, 12 and 13. We share responsibility for the Introduction and Conclusion. The text was much improved following the intervention of several diligent and well-informed readers, who made numerous constructive suggestions and spotted some shameful howlers. In particular, we must thank Andrew Saint, Head of the Survey of London, who cheerfully undertook the Herculean task of reading the text from start to finish. Other chapters or sections were read at different stages by Alun Howkins, Malcolm Jeal, David Jeremiah, David Lawrence, Michael Ware, Mike Worthington-Williams and an anonymous reader for Yale

University Press. We are deeply grateful to them all and, if some errors remain, we accept full culpability ourselves.

In addition to those who read parts of the text for us, we have depended heavily on the knowledge and expertise of other motoring historians, many of them members of the Society of Automotive Historians in Britain, who were most generous with their knowledge and provided access to their private collections. In particular, we should like to acknowledge input from John Banner, the late Tony Beadle, Tony Clark, Bryan Goodman, John Harrison, Allan Lupton, Jocelyn Martin, Nic Portway, John Tarring, John Warburton and Jonathan Wood.

Many archives and libraries lent us invaluable assistance. Foremost amongst these is the Library of the Veteran Car Club of Great Britain at Ashwell in Hertfordshire (with special thanks to their librarian, Simon Moss, and to their past chairman, Chris Ashton, and past secretary, June Cutchie), which allowed us full access to their collections. Other libraries and archives which provided us with a particularly helpful service include: British Motoring Heritage Trust, Gaydon; British Newspaper Library, Colindale; BP Archive (Bethan Thomas); Cambridge University Library; Getty Images; London Metropolitan Archives; RIBA; Coventry Transport Museum; The National Archives, Kew; the National Monuments Record (Ian Leith, Nigel Wilkins and the library team); the National Motor Museum, Beaulieu (Jonathan Day); Shell Archive; and the City of Westminster Archives Centre (Alison Kenny). Other organisations (and individuals within them) that have lent support and help to the project include: Jonathan Rishton at *The Automobile*; Charles Ambrose of Charles Trent Ltd; George Demidowicz of Coventry City Council; Kathy Chaney at David Salomons House; Philip Heath of South Derbyshire District Council; the Federation of British Historic Vehicle Clubs; Janet Messenger of Jet Petroleum; Andrew Lidster, Stephen Oliver and James Rothwell of the National Trust; Simon Bradley and Charles O'Brien of the Pevsner Architectural Guides; Peter Cobley of Sevenoaks District Council; and Denis Dunstone of the Transport Trust.

We should also like to thank the following for helpful advice and information at various stages: G. Adams, Keith Adamson, Dave Anscombe, Nicholas Antram, Chris Baglee, Linda Bagwell, Anne Baker, Peter Barnett, Valerie Bayliss, David Bell, Vivien Bellamy, Michael Bennett, Christopher Bentley, Diana Bevan, Norman Bird, Geoff Brandwood, Robert Bridson, Clive Bromson, David Brown, Josef Brown, Peter Brown, Mathewson Bull, Ian Burt, Paul Camp, Ian Cater, Kathleen Clarke, J. W. Clitherow, John Colverd, David Coney, Tim Cornall, Clive Dalton, Phil d'Arcy, John L. Day, Barry Dent, William Dent, Bruce Dowell, Howard Duckworth, J. Dunphy, Alexandra Edwards, Steven Edwards, David Elsom, Anna English, Emlyn Evans, Beryl Finbow, Andy Foster, Andrew Foyle, Michael Freisman, A. D. George, Geoffry J. Grayson, Dave and Rita Green, Kevin Happs, Angela Harley, Judith Harrall, Ray Harrington, Guy Harrison, Clare Hartwell, Trevor Heaton, Peter Hemmings, Keith Hills, Robert Hornung, Peter Howard, Bob Hughes, Rob Hurn, Peter Iles, Christopher Jeal, Gordon Jones, Steve Jones, Dr Gerry Kennedy, Peter Kindon, Stephen Kitching, Steve Knight, G. Lambert, Sharon Langford, John Lawson, Stuart C. Lindsey, Sandra Lynn, Grace McCombie, Harry W. McFarlane, Sue McGlennon, Gerard Marsden, Ian Maxwell, Judith May, Alan Mayor, Roger Mills, Pansy Mitchell, Marian Mollett, Donald Monk, Chris Moxey, Geoff Mullett, Peter Nickson, Geraldine O'Farrell, Stanley Paine, James Paling, Neil Parkhouse, Gillian Pearce, David Peckham, Martin Pellatt, Alison Pinto, Francis Plowden, Peter Plumridge, Jonathan Radgick, Stuart and Gail Rayne, Raymond M. Rayner, John Reynolds, Peter and Jean Rix, Catherine Roberts, Christian Robinson, Chris Rogers, Peter Rumsey, Robin Sawers, Karen Sayer, H. Schofield, John Selby, Peter Selby, Jackie Shipley, Iain Simm, Graham Simpson, Rory Sinclair, George Skuse, Mike Sloan, Melvin Spear, Ivar Stav, Ron Stock, Sarah Sullivan, Anne-Marie Sutcliffe, Victor Sutcliffe, Michael Swerdlow, Jerome Tait, Christopher Taylor, Gordon Taylor, Carough Thuring, Leigh Travail, Jonathan Turley, Chris Wakeling, Denise Walecka, Brian Walker, Rob Walker, Ian Wallace, Sue Wallace, Mary Walsham, Chris Welch, Helen Wells, Bob Westlake, John Wettem, Brett Wilde, Dave Whitehead, Sarah Whittingham, Ray Whitworth, Leon Winnert, Gary Woodward, David Wordley, Sharon Wort, James Yardley and Anna Zakharova.

We extend particular thanks to Gillian Malpass of Yale University Press for having faith in this project from the outset and seeing it through to fruition. We are especially grateful to Gillian for producing the design with such skill and attention to detail. Delia Gaze made an impeccable job of copy-editing, making sensible suggestions and helping us to refine our prose. We thank also Jacquie Meredith for proof-reading and Susan Tricklebank for the index. We also wish to express our profound gratitude to the Paul Mellon Centre for Studies in British Art for their most generous support.

Finally we thank our spouses, Kate Minnis and Ron Baxter, not just for being supportive, but also for joining in with the research, fieldwork and photography, and for acting as soundboards for many of our ideas.

1 Park Lane Garage, a vast underground car park in central London, opened in October 1962.

INTRODUCTION: LIVING WITH CARS

WHEN THE FIRST PETROL-POWERED motor cars stuttered and spluttered onto English roads in 1895, spewing clouds of dust and astounding passers-by, they entered a world that had been created by and for a society heavily dependent on horse-drawn vehicles. This was true for local transportation at least, since the railway – with its then extensive network of main and branch lines – offered a far superior means of travelling long distances.

In both town and country, the existing infrastructure proved ill suited to the new machines, to the frustration of pioneering motorists. Slowly but surely, over the next century new building types emerged, existing building types were modified, plots and streets were redesigned, pedestrians were restrained as never before, tram and railway lines were scrapped, and new bypass and cross-country routes were devised. This did not just feed the seemingly insatiable demands of cars and drivers, it also acknowledged their superiority as users of public space. Visionaries dreamt that the car might inaugurate a utopian environment, a 'Motopia' or 'Autopia',[1] and by the end of the twentieth century the rural and urban landscape of England had certainly been reshaped around the car. Carscapes had come into being, but few would describe the results as utopian. In particular, one might deplore how traditional towns have been turned inside out – with their shopping and office complexes positioned on the edge rather than in the centre – primarily for the convenience of motorists. This type of carscape, sometimes named 'exurbia', has been repeated, with variation, in developed countries around the world.

Carscapes sets out to illuminate the century-long process that saw the world around us re-engineered for cars. Given the genesis of this book (see Acknowledgements), the world in question is restricted by and large to England, rather than Great Britain as a whole. The book poses a series of questions. Just why and when and how did the car become such a powerful catalyst for change? And to what extent can it be held responsible for how entrepreneurs, politicians, planners, architects and engineers have opted to arrange the towns and cities we live in today? The approach is thematic, with each theme treated chronologically, creating its own free-standing narrative.

The structure of Part I, 'The Life Cycle of the Car' (Chapters 1–8), is dictated by the cradle-to-grave life-cycle of the motor car, with individual chapters looking at manufacture, buying and selling, garaging, servicing, filling-up, parking and, finally, scrapping. The buildings and spaces created for each stage in the cycle are examined, together with their geographical locations, which are seen to shift over time. Part II, 'Driving Around' (Chapters 9–13), considers the experience of driving around, whether in the country or in the town. It is devoted to places and spaces as well as buildings: examining how road networks and roadscapes have evolved; how the car and the motorist have interacted with the countryside; and how towns and cities have adapted their streets for motor traffic. Finally, the Conclusion considers the heritage of carscapes. It contemplates futurism and future trends: the encroachment of exurban forms (such as retail sheds) on urban centres, questions over the future availability and affordability of fuel, and the potential of the electric car. We may not yet be poised on the brink of the next transport revolution, but we can anticipate it in the not-too-distant future. First trains, then cars – what next?

Environmental concerns may prove, eventually, to be the greatest agents of change. It has long been believed that vehicle emissions trigger respiratory and other illnesses; that dependence

2 Burton Street, Melton Mowbray, photographed by John Gay during a snowfall, *circa* 1954.

on fossil fuel is depleting finite natural resources; and that fumes contribute to acid rain and general pollution. Since the 1980s the notion that cars are causing serious damage to the natural environment has gained mainstream credibility. In particular, vehicles are known to produce a large proportion of the so-called greenhouse gases (especially CO_2) that are thought to contribute to climate change: essentially, a potentially dangerous increase in the temperature of the land, the sea and the atmosphere.

One of the first legislative responses to these environmental concerns was the introduction of lead-free petrol in 1986, with all new cars being built with catalytic converters from 1993, and leaded petrol being banned from 1 January 2000. Initiatives to reduce regulated emissions, since 1992, have imposed pressure on manufacturers to design cars to cleaner standards. The problem of old cars with high emissions diminishes as these are, gradually, scrapped: many were disposed of under the Government's 'scrappage scheme' of 2009, which offered incentives to those who, Aladdin-like, acquired new cars for old. In the context of collective environmental guilt, all kinds of businesses now display 'green' credentials in order to attract custom by projecting a responsible and eco-friendly corporate image. Although it might seem an oxymoron, this extends to businesses connected with cars, and examples will be found in this book of superficially 'green' car parks and car factories. Otherwise, the greatest impact of environmentalism on the physical environment, as dictated by cars, has been on road schemes. Opposition to these accelerated in the early 1990s, notably with the battle to prevent the M3 ploughing its way through Twyford Down in Hampshire. Although the M3 was completed on the planned alignment, the anti-road campaign was, ultimately, victorious, since many major road schemes were subsequently abandoned.

The authors – both drivers, if not avid motorists – have attempted to remain objective: neither to criticise nor to applaud the car and its diverse impacts. Yet throughout *Carscapes* we consider how the legacy of the car, in terms of the physical environment, has been perceived and valued. The historic significance of increasing numbers of buildings and structures erected for cars is now recognised by listing; the demolition of so-called landmark car parks, such as the 'Get Carter' car park in Gateshead (see pl. 244), has attracted as much wrath as delight; old road signs are appreciated and retained; and many museums recreate the ephemeral clutter of the country garage (see pl. 429). Nostalgia surrounding cars and driving clearly extends to the historic environment, even stretching, at times, into the 1970s. This reflects the way in which cars have defined our lives: everyone alive in England today has some childhood memory of cars.

Car-related experience and behaviour has been the subject of many academic and popular studies, by geographers, historians and cultural commentators, often drawing on the evidence of cinema, literature, television, art and pop songs.[2] While this discourse lies largely beyond the scope of *Carscapes*, the social context inevitably informs the story. One cannot ignore how cars have widened people's geographical and cultural horizons, enabling the exploration of the countryside, of monuments and country houses. Owning a family car – and, perhaps, also a caravan – opened up new possibilities for weekend trips and annual holidays. From being largely the prerogative of the well-to-do at the beginning of the twentieth century, this lifestyle was available to the multitude by the 1960s. Pride in one's car spawned rituals, such as washing and polishing the beloved family car on the front drive on a Sunday morning, in full view of the neighbours. One's choice of car was expressive of social and financial status, or at least aspirations. The dangers associated with cars also put paid to some age-old practices, such as children congregating to play, unsupervised, in the street. More fundamentally, cars gave people more choice in terms of where they lived and worked. It became possible to settle some considerable distance from the workplace and, eventually, from shops. Today, many of us think nothing of travelling – encapsulated in our comfortable, air-conditioned cars, equipped with sound systems and 'sat navs' – for a couple of hours a day, whether to go to work or to visit a mall. A great proportion of our lives is spent on bituminous surfaces, often stuck at roadworks or in traffic jams, where we have ample opportunity to study and absorb the roadscape.

The tension between public and private transport surfaces periodically in the course of *Carscapes*, but this book attempts to retain a tight focus on the privately owned motor car. Public and commercial transportation has been excluded from this study. Taxicabs and cycles, too, have featuring rather than starring roles. The inclusion of all aspects of road transport – horses, carriages, trams, omnibuses, cabs, bicycles, motor cycles, lorries and vans – would have over-diluted the story, and prevented the landscape of the car from being explored in depth. Each of these forms of transport has its own distinct story, which is worth telling elsewhere. Despite their exclusion from *Carscapes*, many of the phenomena discussed in the ensuing chapters relate to the development of motor traffic in general, rather than the private car in particular, and will thus be of broader interest. The creation of the arterial road network, for example, triggered the growth of road haulage, which has largely superseded rail freight, causing the relocation of industry from its old heartlands beside railways and canals, and witnessing the growth of logistics, with huge storage warehouses lining the country's main traffic arteries and intruding into the English scenery (see pl. 311).

Although the heavy goods vehicle, or HGV, plays a minor part in this book, the pedestrian – often cast as the weak adversary of the motorist – looms large. Cars are undoubtedly part of the universal experience of modern life, whether one drives or not.

We all live with their noise and fumes, and are alert to their potential dangers. This book describes the growth of motor traffic from the point of view of the pedestrian, as well as the motorist. Having enjoyed complete freedom on the slow-moving roads of the 1890s, those on foot were being rigidly controlled by guardrails, crossings, footbridges and subways by the 1930s, and were segregated completely from cars by the 1960s. The motoring lobby repeatedly demanded fines, or even prosecutions, for pedestrians who dared to disobey the rules. But after being subservient to the motorist for the last eighty years, as we write, in 2011, the pedestrian might just be gaining the upper hand in some urban centres through 'Shared Space' schemes.

The motor car, now well into its second century, is here to stay. Public transportation may be improving, but it is highly unlikely to threaten private transport in the foreseeable future. If, however, certain improvements can be achieved – for example, manufacturing batteries that will run for 300 rather than 100 miles, and installing a comprehensive network of rapid recharging (or battery exchange) points – electric power may at last supersede internal combustion. Regardless of how it is powered, the car will continue to shape and reshape aspects of the historic built environment, in ways that are currently unimaginable.

1: THE LIFE CYCLE OF THE CAR

3   A mechanic at work in an unidentified garage in Padstow, Cornwall, in 1956. This photograph was taken by John Gay.

4 A series of archive photographs records Morris's factory at Cowley, Oxford, *circa* 1925. Here we see the continuing use of wooden trestles. They support wooden bodies while they are being rubbed down in preparation for painting.

1: MAKING CARS

Since 1896 motor cars have been manufactured at nearly 1,000 sites in England – some of them tiny workshops, others enormous factories.[1] Most car manufacturers started out in second-hand buildings, adapted and enlarged for the purpose. Amongst those who went on to capture a large share of the market and develop huge industrial complexes were Austin at Longbridge, Morris at Cowley, Vauxhall at Luton, and Ford, first at Trafford Park and later at Dagenham. None of these key sites survives intact, but in their heyday they exercised massive economic, social and cultural sway within their respective regions. The city most dependent on the motor industry for its prosperity and growth, from the earliest days, was Coventry in the West Midlands, where Daimler, Standard, Hillman, Singer and many other well-known makes were manufactured (pl. 5). Today, Coventry's pre-eminence has faded, and England's surviving car factories are geographically scattered. Amongst them are 'shadow factories' built in preparation for the Second World War, complexes erected by Japanese manufacturers in the 1980s and 1990s, and smaller modern factories making luxury marques.

This complicated industry – with branches embracing coach-building and components manufacture as well as car assembly – has shrivelled since the 1950s, in the face of mounting global competition, and most of its historical sites have been cleared. Despite this, some motor cars of British design and construction, such as Rolls-Royce, Jaguar and Aston Martin, remain highly esteemed the world over.

•

Building a Customer Base, 1896–1914

A successful automotive industry could not develop in Britain until conditions allowed motoring, as an activity, to thrive. The advantages of the 'self-propelled carriage' had to be proved to the public, and especially to those with the wherewithal to indulge what was, initially, an expensive hobby. Furthermore, existing legislation – especially stringent speed restrictions – had to be modified before motoring could become a realistic proposition on British roads. For factories to succeed, substantial capital had to be invested and engineers had to master the new technology. Less predictably, manufacturing had to be wrestled from the stranglehold of certain entrepreneurs who sought to make their fortune by manipulating this fledgling industry.

In the development of petrol-powered motor cars, Britain lagged behind Europe, and even the U.S.A., but over the years native engineers had built a number of vehicles powered by electricity, steam or gas.[2] Indeed, road steamers, including steam coaches and agricultural traction engines, had trundled along British roads since the beginning of the nineteenth century.[3] Commitment to steam power – encouraged by the availability of coal – may have deterred experimentation with alternative fuels. By 1890, however, vehicles powered by petrol internal combustion engines, designed by Carl Benz and Gottlieb Daimler in Germany in 1885 and 1886 respectively, were attracting widespread admiration. They were being manufactured and sold in France (i.e., Benz designs by Emile Roger and Daimler designs by Panhard et Levassor), as well as in Germany. In 1891 the English engineer Frederick R. Simms (1863–1944) negotiated the patent rights to Daimler engines in the U.K., and subsequently fitted them to motor boats. He formed the Daimler

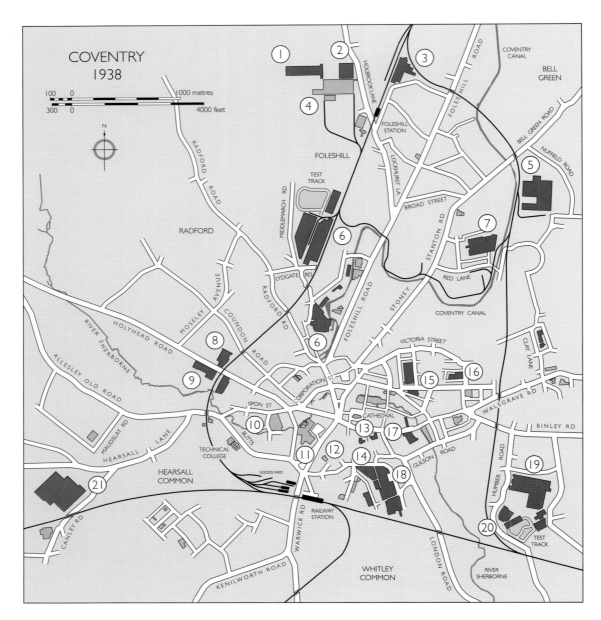

5   A map of Coventry ('the Metropolis of Motordom'), showing the locations of the main motor manufacturers in 1938.

KEY: 1=SS Cars; 2=Triumph (Gloria); 3=Riley; 4=Dunlop; 5=Morris (Foundry); 6=Daimler; 7=Rover (New Meteor); 8=Carbodies; 9=Alvis; 10=Rudge; 11=Corner-croft; 12=Climax; 13=Lea Francis; 14=Maudslay; 15=Singer; 16=Caton and Co.; 17=Morris Engine; 18=Armstrong Siddeley; 19=Humber; 20=Hillman; 21=Standard.

Motor Syndicate in 1893 to develop this work. It was only after the petrol engine had demonstrated its superiority in a series of keenly scrutinised Continental road trials, however, that pioneering motorists such as Evelyn Ellis (1843–1913) and Sir David Salomons (1851–1925) began to import motor cars.[4] In November 1895, with few cars yet daring to make outings on British roads, Simms sold the Daimler patent rights to the company promoter Harry J. Lawson (1852–1925), who then formed the British Motor Syndicate. Lawson retained Simms as his consulting engineer.

Lawson is a pivotal, if disreputable, figure in the history of British motoring. While he has been allowed some credit for developing the safety bicycle in the 1870s, his claims to have invented the motor car in 1880 were ludicrous.[5] His goal was to monopolise the emergent British motor industry by controlling every significant patent (notably Daimler, De Dion, Bollée and Pennington, though never Benz) relating to car and cycle manufacture. In the course of 1896 Lawson floated four manufacturing companies: the Daimler Motor Co., the Great Horseless Carriage Co., the New Beeston Cycle Co.[6] and the Coventry

Motor Co.[7] All these were based in Coventry and, although they employed a large workforce and produced some cars over the next few years, they are generally regarded as shell companies, set up to cream capital from investors.[8] Lawson, however, did not enjoy a completely clear field, since several other companies had been set up to manufacture motor cars by the end of 1896. By and large modelling their products on the Benz, rather than the Daimler, to avoid falling foul of Lawson's patents, these included William Arnold's Motor Carriage Co., based in East Peckham, Kent;[9] L'Hollier Gascoine and its successor, the Anglo-French Motor Carriage Co., which planned to manufacture – or, more precisely, modify – the Roger-Benz car in Maidstone, Kent, and, later, in Digbeth, Birmingham;[10] and the Yeovil Motor Car & Cycle Co. in Somerset, which was reputedly fitting up a 'new and commodious' factory.[11] These ventures produced few cars and were of short duration. Rather longer-lived was the Star Motor Co. of Wolverhampton, which made its first Benz-type car in 1899. A number of other companies that formed in the 1890s, such as Walter Bersey's Universal Electric Carriage Syndicate, were absorbed by Lawson's British Motor Syndicate. Lawson's activities, however, were strongly opposed. By the end of 1896 the press was rounding on him, rumours about the stability of his ventures spread and his companies lost value. Furthermore, his patents were becoming outdated. An action by a successor company for patent infringement was thrown out of court in 1901, and Lawson's career terminated ignobly in 1904 with a conviction for fraud.[12]

Despite Lawson's brazen self-aggrandisement, it must be acknowledged that he helped to whet an appetite for motor cars in England. In January 1896 he and Simms formed the Motor Car Club (MCC), which organised exhibitions and pressed for the repeal of the 'Red Flag Act'. The Locomotive Act of 1865 – drafted with agricultural vehicles in mind – had specified that a pedestrian with a red flag must walk in front of any motorised vehicle to warn of its approach, and imposed a maximum speed limit of 4mph.[13] Although an amendment Act of 1878 had dropped the statutory requirement to display a red flag, some local authorities continued to insist on this, and the flag assumed symbolic value for motoring pioneers. At the first exhibition of the MCC, held in February 1896 and attended by the Prince of Wales, four self-propelled carriages were tested on the smooth surfaces of the galleries and courts of the Imperial Institute in London.[14] A wooden slope with a gradient of 1 : 10 was erected in the quadrangle to demonstrate the vehicles' climbing ability. The MCC's second exhibition, which opened at the same venue on 9 May 1896, conflicted with the *London International Exhibition of Horse-Drawn and Horseless Carriages*. This had opened on 2 May at Crystal Palace in south London, where routes through the grounds were staked out with red flags and notices, warning visitors of the presence of cars.[15] The Crystal Palace exhibition

was co-organised by Sir David Salomons, Lawson's rival as the chief propagandist of motoring in Britain. Salomons had held the very first British motor exhibition at Tunbridge Wells in Kent in October 1895,[16] and had founded the Self-Propelled Traffic Association in December of that year.[17] His respectability allowed him to lobby more convincingly than Lawson for the repeal of the Locomotive Act. Taken together, however, Lawson's and Salomons's competing exhibitions of 1896 brought a wide range of vehicles – mostly of foreign manufacture – to the attention of the public. The few British-made exhibits included a petrol car made for John Henry Knight at the Elliot Reliance Works in Farnham, Surrey.[18] The two exhibitions also served to illustrate the pros and cons of the available technologies: the oil or petrol motor such as Daimler (efficient, despite its offensive smells and vibrations), the electric motor such as Bersey's Victoria (clean, but with a limited geographic range and heavy batteries), and steam cars like Serpollet (fast, with a weighty boiler and visible vapour). In autumn 1896 the Locomotives on Highways Act abolished the need for a pedestrian to precede a car, and established a maximum speed limit of 12mph.[19] Lawson greeted this landmark Act by holding the Emancipation Day Run from London to Brighton on 14 November, generating a great deal of publicity for the motor car despite unfavourable weather and a certain amount of organisational chaos (pl. 6).[20] Salomons, predictably, shunned the event.

6   The Emancipation Day Run was held on 14 November 1896 to celebrate the passage of the Locomotives on Highways Act. Here, Harry J. Lawson and his wife sit on their Panhard-Levassor outside the Metropole Hotel in Brighton.

7 The Motor Exchange driving school in Notting Hill, London, in 1905 had a training track with dummy figures of a dog and a chicken. Since reports of early motoring are littered with incidents involving the death or mutilation of dogs and livestock, this training track was surely set up in an attempt to remedy the situation.

Emerging from Lawson's shadow, Frederick Simms formed the Automobile Club of Great Britain (and later Ireland) in August 1897.[21] This incorporated Salomons's Self-Propelled Traffic Association in 1898 and became the Royal Automobile Club (RAC) in 1907. It has been pointed out that few early members were engaged in motor manufacture.[22] Nevertheless, the Thousand Miles Trial of 1900, like subsequent trials organised by the club, had great value in advertising newfangled motoring beyond London and the South. Likewise, manufacturers gleaned publicity from wins in trials and races, for example, when Napier's agent Selwyn F. Edge won a silver medal in the Thousand Miles Trial and went on to lift the Gordon Bennett trophy in 1902.[23] The motor industry had nothing to do with the opening of the world's first motor racing circuit, at Brooklands, Surrey, in 1907, yet it benefited from technological advances designed to improve the performance of racing cars, just as road builders would learn from Brooklands' super-elevated curves and use of concrete.

Simms's Automobile Club was responsible for the formation of the Motor Union, which merged with the existing Motor Vehicle Users' Defence Association in 1901.[24] This provided legal defence for members – who often became embroiled in disputes – and pressed for legislative change to favour motorists. Some of its demands were met by the Motor Car Act of 1903, which raised the speed limit to 20mph, whilst also imposing driving licences and compulsory car registration. By 1 April 1904, 13,302 private cars were registered in England and Wales (see Appendix). As traffic increased, so did accidents, largely because traffic was still unregulated.[25] Indeed, there was resistance to regulation, and the Automobile Association (AA) was formed in 1905 principally to organise cycle patrols to warn motorists of police speed traps.[26] Motoring could be a hair-raising escapade for travellers and pedestrians alike, and there was a great demand for properly trained chauffeurs. Until 1935 there was no driving test, or even compulsory tuition, yet some motoring schools existed by the turn of the century, one of the earliest being William Lea's in Liverpool, based from 1899 in an old ice-skating rink.[27] In 1905 the Motor Exchange in Notting Hill in London set up a private 'course' for novices, featuring a greasy 'side-slip patch' that would accustom learners to slippery road conditions, and a training area with dummy animals that ran on tracks (pl. 7).[28] Many alumni of motoring schools became chauffeurs or commercial drivers.

Before long, demonstrations and shows were being arranged by provincial organisations throughout the country, often with associated trials. Commercial shows assumed increasing importance for car manufacturers: for example, Cordingley & Co.'s exhibitions at Agricultural Hall, Islington, London, which included cars from 1897. Simms organised the first annual trade show to be held by the Society of Motor Manufacturers and Traders at Crystal Palace from 30 January to 7 February 1903. In subsequent years, this took place at Olympia in Kensington, usually in November.[29] It launched the busiest season of the year for manufacturers and distributors alike.

In 1904 there were 14,887 cars registered in Great Britain, a figure that had risen to 218,556 by 1913 (see Appendix). Having got off to a slow start, British manufacturers had to persuade car owners to give up their foreign vehicles, which they ordered through the plush showrooms that Henry Hewetson, C. S. Rolls, Charles Friswell and other dealers had opened in city centres (see Chapter 2). In 1906 the country was reportedly importing 400 cars each month from France (many as bare chassis, to be bodied in Britain), whilst exporting just two in the opposite direction.[30] The Liberals won the election of that year on a platform of free trade, yet the British Empire Motor Trades Alliance bluntly accused those who bought foreign cars of being 'unpatriotic and unwise'.[31] Nevertheless, the home industry produced just 10,500 cars and commercial vehicles in 1908, rising to 34,000 by 1913.[32] Only when protectionist policies were introduced during the First World War could a British car-manufacturing sector thrive properly.

The Industry and its Products, 1896–1914

The first cars made in the U.K. were one-offs, built in outbuildings and small workshops by men drawn to explore the possibilities of motor manufacture. Engineers such as Frederick Lanchester (1868–1946), Herbert Austin (1866–1941) and Henry Royce (1863–1933) dismantled foreign cars to uncover their secrets, and undertook many experiments before they were capable of building a prototype, let alone producing vehicles for a commercial market. For these men, their inability to run their machines at speed on public roads was a considerable drawback.

Against this backdrop, the first British car factory was extraordinarily ambitious. This was Motor Mills ('birthplace of the British motor industry'),[33] a former cotton-spinning mill at Foleshill on the outskirts of Coventry, bought in March 1896 to house Harry J. Lawson's manufacturing companies. The site had easy access to railway sidings and a canal, suggesting that practical considerations were to the fore in choosing the location.[34] The four-storey mill, owned by the Great Horseless Carriage Co., was of cast-iron construction, with a vast central atrium under a glass roof (pl. 8). It was surrounded by single-storey workshops occupied by Daimler, which became productive in March 1897.[35] For much of 1896 – ostensibly while Lawson's businesses were being organised and equipped – most of the

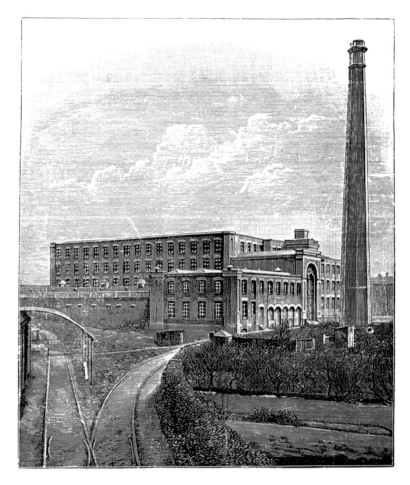

8 This image shows Motor Mills in Coventry in 1896, at the time it became England's first car factory.

floor space in the mill itself was let to tenants, including Humber, whose Coventry cycle factory had burnt down in July 1896. A condition of Humber's tenancy was that it manufacture a British version of the Léon Bollée tandem tricycle, known as the Coventry Motette, on the understanding that the Great Horseless Carriage Co. would take over its plant once the premises were vacated. By the time this came about, in early 1897, only five Bollées had been built.

In March 1897, to counter rumours that Motor Mills was an unproductive sham,[36] the Coventry-based magazine *The Autocar* published an article about the factory.[37] While the accompanying photographs demonstrate that this account was not entirely fictitious, it must be read with caution, since the editor, Henry Sturmey, was one of Lawson's closest business allies. The article conveyed an impression of activity. The Great Horseless Carriage Co. was split into two departments under a single manager, occupying at least two floors of the mill. The ground floor, recently recovered from Humber, housed a large smiths' shop for heavy forging, but was otherwise in the throes of conversion for the construction of Panhard-style cars and Bollée tandems. The company's most established manufacturing space was on the second floor. Completed cars were lowered by hoist to the ground floor, but it was noted that a 'huge carriage lift' was in the course of erection. The first floor, under separate management, was devoted to cars built by the American Edward J. Pennington, who is considered an even greater charlatan than Lawson. This included a trial room of 'just sufficient size to allow a carriage being run in a circle'. The unvisited third floor may have been occupied by another of Lawson's concerns, the Beeston Pneumatic Tyre Co. (established 1893), which aimed to supply tyres to the group's various manufacturing companies.

With a handful of exceptions (such as Daimler and the Motoring Manufacturing Co., which superseded the Great Horseless Carriage Co. in 1898), British car manufacturers continued for some years to make cars on a one-by-one basis. By 1900, however, at least twenty firms – including Humber and Wolseley – were engaged in some level of volume production.[38] Most of those who built chassis had branched out from established areas of engineering, for example, making sewing machines, bicycles and stationary engines. Indeed, the prevalence of engineering skills and properly equipped workshops in the west Midlands helps to explain why motor-car manufacture took root so quickly in Coventry, Birmingham and Wolverhampton. Another factor was the state of the cycle industry, which peaked in 1896, leaving premises vacant or under-utilised. The cycle industry itself was of relatively recent origin, starting in 1868 when James Starley of the Coventry Sewing Machine Co. decided to diversify. Prior to concentrating on sewing machines and cycles, Coventry had been an established centre of watch, clock and silk manufacture.

The job of building a car for the commercial market was immensely complicated, but the main processes soon became clear: to amass (i.e., buy or manufacture) all the required component parts; to assemble a chassis from parts; to paint the chassis, fit it with temporary wheels and seats, and take it out for a road test; to add the body, the final wheels and seats; and to dispatch it to the customer or agent. Obtaining components was not easy: apart from a few established firms that made parts for cycles, British manufacturers were – it is often argued – seldom capable of producing standardised, or interchangeable, parts for cars.[39] In many cases, the only options for car manufacturers were to import parts from continental Europe or to set up their own foundries and machine shops. Under these circumstances, the process of building a car involved wildly varying degrees of assemblage, since some manufacturers bought in more pre-assembled components (for example, complete engines, gear boxes and radiators) than others. This affected the time taken to build a car, but, as a rough guide, in 1897 Daimler – which could now produce four cars each week – considered that it took at

least two to three months from start to finish.[40] This may not have factored the body into the equation, since this alone could take months to build.

Despite the existence of a body shop at Motor Mills from 1897,[41] in the first decade of the industry there was an almost complete separation of chassis building (making the frame and the mechanical parts) and coachbuilding (making the body). Although manufacturers struggled to source mechanical components, when it came to bodies they could turn to any number of established British coachbuilders, whose skills were internationally admired. Proximity to a canal or railway line was desirable for the transportation of chassis to coachbuilders located in other cities, with strong communication links favouring north and west London. The construction of composite bodies was specialised, labour-intensive work involving a variety of trades and materials: the carpenters who made the wooden frames, floorboards and panels; the metal workers who hammered steel panels into shape; the painters who applied multiple coats of paint and varnish to the finished bodies; and the upholsterers and trimmers who made and fitted the seating, padding and pockets. Painting and varnishing required a roomy, well-lit workshop, with walls glazed to reduce dust, since each coat was applied by hand and took twenty-four hours to dry. Initially, most motor manufacturers had neither the skills nor the space to undertake coachbuilding themselves. The process adopted by Napier – which manufactured its luxury cars on a backstreet site in Lambeth, south London (from 1899), before moving to a new factory in Acton, west London (from 1902) – was typical. The firm's chassis were tested before being sent to the Regent Carriage Works in Fulham, west London, to be bodied, then returned to Napier for a trial run of 200 miles before, finally, being delivered to the customer by Napier's sole agent, Selwyn F. Edge (see Chapter 2).[42]

Between 1900 and 1906 productivity increased. By 1906 Napier could complete two cars per week; Herbert Austin was turning out four; and the more established Daimler now managed thirty.[43] Humber was to the fore in the volume-production of cars, notably with the Humbrette, introduced in 1903. When the company opened a new assembly/finishing works on Far Gosford Street, Coventry, in 1906, it hoped to produce thirty cars weekly.[44] Once its new works off Folly Lane opened in 1908, however, Humber's potential output soared to 100–120 per week.[45] Not all companies were successful. Of the 393 firms known to have engaged in motor manufacture – often briefly, as a sideline – between 1896 and 1913, many were under-financed and collapsed. Just 113 existed in 1914.[46]

By 1914 British factories had produced motor cars of various shapes, sizes and prices. At the top end of the market, Daimler, Lanchester, Maudslay, Napier and Rolls-Royce produced luxurious cars with a large profit margin. During the Olympia show of 1905, Daimler reduced the price of its cheapest car from £700 to £590, citing the standardisation of parts and the extension of its works (now occupying the whole of Motor Mills) as a crucial reason. Daimler's most expensive car was reduced from £1,050 to £890.[47] To put this in context, a newly built semi-detached house in south-east England could be bought for about £300 to £400. Many cars, however, were much cheaper. As one might have expected, former cycle manufacturers – such as Humber, Rover, Singer, Sunbeam and Swift – were responsible for developing motorised cycles and smaller models of car (such as the strange, diamond-shaped Sunbeam Mabley of 1901, costing £130). By imposing a penalty on large engines, the Finance Act of 1909 sparked a boom in cyclecars and light cars. Cyclecars – which ranged in price from around £70 to £125 – were a cheap, low-powered compromise between the motorcycle and the motor car and were of poorer quality than the light car, which was defined as having an engine no larger than 1500cc.

By 1914 several manufacturers were specialising in the high-volume production of affordable cars with greatly improved comfort and performance. Foremost amongst these was the Model T Ford (1908, £125 to £135), followed by the Morris Oxford (1913, £175, reduced in 1914 to £113) and the Singer 10 (1912, £195). Interestingly, few British firms emulated Ford's successful single-model policy (building only the Model T from 1909, and offering it only in black from 1912), exceptions being Rover, with the Rover 12 of 1912, and – at the other end of the scale – Rolls-Royce, which concentrated on the Silver Ghost from 1908. The adoption of a single model, usually on an annual basis, made it easier for a factory to maintain regular production and to retain its workforce throughout the year.

Car Factories, 1896–1914

The factories that had characterised England's Industrial Revolution were typically multi-storeyed buildings in tight urban situations, brick-clad with cast-iron columns, metal-framed windows and double-pitched roofs. Many coachworks, such as that belonging to Salmons in Newport Pagnell, Buckinghamshire (1844; pl. 9), were of this type, as were engineering works like the Elliot Reliance Works in Farnham, where John Henry Knight's petrol-driven car was built in 1895.[48] While multi-storey factories were still being built in the 1890s, many manufacturers in diverse industries had relocated to more spacious single-storey works, sprawling over larger sites that were often on the edges of towns. These factories could be lit naturally through sawtooth roofs, angled to the north in order to obtain a diffused light. The cycle manufacturer Singer, for example, erected a single-storey factory with north lighting on Canterbury Street, Coventry, in 1891.

9   Salmons Coachworks on Tickford Street, Newport Pagnell, Buckinghamshire, was built in 1844, and a new building (lying at right angles, to the rear) was added in 1912. From 1955 to 2007 this factory was occupied by Aston Martin Lagonda, which retains a depot across the street.

Thus, two distinct architectural approaches to factory layout were available to those preparing to enter motor manufacture in the 1890s and early 1900s, regardless of whether they decided to convert existing premises or build anew. Inevitably, manufacturing processes had to be arranged in a very different way, depending on which factory type was adopted. Some of the earliest purpose-built car factories followed the long-established multi-storeyed model, which should not necessarily be regarded as outmoded since the multi-storey concrete-frame 'daylight' factory – admittedly, having wider spans and larger windows than factories of traditional construction – became favoured in the early twentieth century by car producers in America, where it was pioneered by the architect Albert Kahn, working with the Trussed Concrete Co. (later known as Truscon) for Packard, Pierce and Ford.[49] Whether they had a framework of reinforced concrete, iron or steel, multi-storey buildings had some undeniable advantages: they required smaller sites and were cheaper to build. Their chief disadvantage was a reliance on hoists or lifts to transport chassis and heavy parts from floor to floor. In such buildings, cars were usually made by moving processes upwards sequentially, with the assembled – sometimes even bodied – chassis being completed on the upper floor and brought down by hoist or ramp. In 1902 Dennis Bros. moved into a new three-storey factory of this type, on Bridge Street in the heart of Guildford in Surrey (pl. 10).[50] Another surviving example, with a U-shaped or courtyard plan, was built in 1902 by the Star Motor Co. on Frederick Street in Wolverhampton.[51]

Some multi-storey car factories were conversions rather than new build. The Gardner-Serpollet steam car, for example, was built – in small numbers – by the British Power Traction & Lighting Co. in an extended cycle factory in York,[52] from 1900 until the firm's bankruptcy in 1903. More significantly, in 1912 William Morris (1877–1963) acquired a dormitory wing of the empty Military College at Cowley, outside Oxford, as his first factory (pl. 11). Adapting it in the now-standard manner, he moved production up the building, floor by floor, with machining on the ground floor, chassis assembly on the first floor, body fitting on the second floor, and painting and storage in the loft.[53] It was in the Military College that Morris assembled his first car, the bullnose Morris Oxford, buying as many components as possible in bulk from a range of suppliers based throughout the Midlands: for example, engines from White & Poppe (Coven-

10 (*left*) Rodboro Buildings, Guildford, Surrey, was built for Dennis Bros., to designs by J. Lake, in 1901, and is probably the earliest surviving purpose-built car factory in England. Though extended in 1903, it soon proved inadequate, and in 1905 Dennis Bros. moved its manufacturing processes to a new site, retaining this building as offices until 1919.

11 (*below*) By *circa* 1925, when this photograph was taken, the upper floor of William Morris's original factory in Cowley – the former Oxford Military College of 1877 – was being used for body mounting.

12 The Sunbeam Works on Upper Villiers Street, Wolverhampton. The original works, which began as a bicycle factory, are to bottom left, while the new purpose-built motor-car works of 1905–7 (the 'Moorfields Works' designed by Joseph Lavender) are centre picture. Although car production ceased here in 1935, the buildings survive.

try), wheels from Sankey (Shropshire), axles from Wrigley (Birmingham), tyres from Dunlop (Coventry and Birmingham) and bodies from either Raworth (Oxford) or Hollick & Pratt (Coventry). It has been observed that the roads connecting these suppliers became 'part of the factory production lines'.[54] On the eve of war, impressed by Henry Ford's achievements, Morris began to search out suppliers of cheaper and more standardised components in the U.S.A., where he must have visited concrete-frame daylight factories. Few such factories were ever built for motor manufacture in England, though they were adopted by Arrol Johnston in Dumfries, Scotland (1912–13), and by Fiat in Turin, Italy (1916–20). Ultimately, multi-storey factories fell out of favour because they could not easily accommodate long assembly lines.

From the turn of the century, British car manufacturers preferred single-storey works, typically with a two-storey office block along the frontage, concealing vast expanses of north-lit sheds to the rear. Many such factories already existed, in differ-ent branches of industry, and were easily adapted for car manu-facture. Thus, in 1901 the Wolseley Tool & Motor Car Co. moved into the empty Adderley Park Works (demolished) in Birming-ham.[55] Wolseley's manager, Herbert Austin, who had built the company's first car in 1896, took responsibility for organising the factory.[56] In 1905, however, Austin left Wolseley and set up on his own. Drawing on his experience of establishing Adderley Park, he acquired – and quickly extended – a single-storey tin-box printing works at Longbridge, outside Birmingham. The original buildings survived until 1998.

One of the first single-storey factories to be purpose-built for car manufacture was Thorneycroft's in Basingstoke, Hampshire (1898, demolished), which later concentrated on commercial vehicles. Others were erected by Napier in Acton, London (1902–7, part demolished), Clement Talbot in Ladbroke Grove, London (1903–4, part demolished), Sunbeam in Wolverhampton (1907; pl. 12), Vulcan in Crossens, Lancashire (1907; pl. 13), Humber in Coventry (1908, demolished; pl. 14) and Rolls-Royce

13   The Vulcan Motor Works in Crossens, near Southport, Lancashire, were designed by Prescott & Bold and built in 1907. By 1927, when the firm stopped making cars, the works had expanded greatly. Today, the factory houses Dorman Traffic Products, which makes hazard-warning equipment. From *Building News*, 13 December 1907, p. 835.

14   Humber's new factory on the east side of Coventry was built in 1908 to designs by the architects Harrison & Hattrell. This shows the vast Machine Shop.

in Derby (1908, demolished).[57] The chief benefit of these factories was that heavy machinery and finished products were confined to ground level. Their sites, however, often stood some distance from residential centres, where the workforce lived: workers had to cycle to work, or make use of public transport, and to compensate for this inconvenience employers began to provide canteens and recreation rooms. Over time, suburban housing grew up around these factories – usually, before the First World War, in the form of brick terraces. Occasionally, public buildings betrayed the community's dependence on the motor industry. In 1904, for example, a three-storey red brick public house called the 'Motor Hotel' was built on the corner of Dorset Road in Coventry, close to Motor Mills and to the homes of its car-worker clientele. It is still there today.

Superficially, single-storey car factories resembled those erected for other industries, but, inevitably, they had peculiarities unique to vehicle manufacture. Initially, they were arranged as workshops that undertook discrete tasks, often separated from one another by movable glass screens, rather than solid walls, allowing them to expand or contract as necessary.[58]

Although Morris made few, if any, of his own parts, the largest section of many car factories was the machine shop, where metal tools and components were made by cutting, drilling, grinding and milling. The machine shop built by Humber in Coventry in 1908 (pl. 14) occupied 71,400 square feet and employed 700 hands. Filled with seemingly endless (340ft long) rows of machines, powered by belts run from overhead line shafts attached to the roof trusses, it was divided into departments producing items such as cylinders, crank shafts and gear wheels. Wolseley (which never made a great profit) was well known for manufacturing just about all of its own components, and in 1911 it was noted that most of the machinery and components in use by Wolseley's former manager Austin, if not imported, were designed and made at Longbridge.[59] Austin's machine shop, like Humber's, was vast.

At the heart of most single-storey factories was an erecting or assembly hall, where sub-assemblies were brought together to create complete chassis. This often loomed over surrounding workshops because it was fitted with overhead hoists or cranes that could raise and move chassis, without disturbing surrounding workers (pl. 15). Vauxhall's Luton plant of 1907 had an overhead travelling crane to bring the chassis frame into the erecting shop, as did Daimler's, Humber's and Rolls-Royce's works, all built in 1908. The engineer Henry Royce, perhaps significantly, had manufactured cranes – including travelling cranes for docks and mills – before forming his partnership with Rolls. Initially, each chassis was assembled on the floor or on a trestle, to which the required components were brought (pl. 16). The assembly line, however, was already in its infancy, although it was not yet motorised. In America, in 1908, Henry Ford had started to fit

chassis with skids and pull them along with a towrope. In England, some manufacturers were beginning to fit the chassis with dummy wheels and push it from one fitter to the next, at first along the floor, but later on metal rails.[60] Rolls-Royce's main workshops, for example, were connected by an internal rail network with turntables.[61] Many erecting shops were tall enough to incorporate mezzanines or galleries around their periphery, generally accommodating stores or upholstery shops. These produced two-storey elevations for what were, in essence, tall single-storey sheds.

Another huge – but, in this case, optional – department was the body shop. Manufacturers were reluctant, at first, to undertake laborious coachbuilding, but it is notable how many firms – including Austin, Lanchester, Daimler, Sunbeam and Humber – set up their own coachworks in the years 1905–7.[62] Lanchester explained that traditional coachbuilders would not adhere to his templates, with the result that when the body was delivered, it would not fit the chassis.[63] Daimler's manager claimed that his company would never have undertaken its own coachbuilding 'had they been able to get their bodies manufactured exactly as they wanted them and when they wanted them'.[64] Coachbuilders, of course, retorted that measurements sent by chassis-makers proved unreliable. Wherever the blame lay, the end result was that manufacturers began to set up their own coachbuilding shops: in 1906 Daimler employed 300 men in coachbuilding,[65] and in 1908 Humber employed 350.[66] These manufacturers faced a recurring taunt that 'generally speaking, the engineer does not make a good designer of bodies'.[67] Bodies were usually built one by one, on body horses that were mounted on castors for easy transfer to the next process. Once the carpenters had constructed a basic body, it was transferred to the coachsmiths' shop for the addition of metal elements such as hinges and handles. Coachsmiths' shops had individual workstations, each with its own furnace (pl. 17). Composite bodies, like chassis frames, were jig drilled (i.e., within a wooden armature) to ensure the precise positioning of their various elements.

Smiths' shops and foundries, with their risk of catching fire, were often detached, as were fire stations and water towers, and engine or power houses, with their distinctive tall chimneys. Sawmills were positioned beside timber-seasoning sheds and stores, and were isolated because they generated so much noise and dust. For respite and cleanliness, canteens and kitchens, too, were detached.

Once a chassis was completed, it had to be tested.[68] The compact Clement Talbot factory in west London (1903–4) was neatly ringed by a continuous roadway, while an oval test track with banked corners was created behind Rolls-Royce's factory in Derby (pl. 18).[69] For the first few years Austin, like Morris, sent his chassis and completed cars (like 'bees entering and leaving a hive') onto public roads for test drives,[70] but in 1913

16   Chassis being built on trestles in Austin's erecting shop at Longbridge around 1913.

17   The forge in Vauxhall's factory at Luton, Bedfordshire, in 1910. Note the line of furnaces.

15 (*facing page*)   A chassis being raised out of the way by travelling crane in Daimler's chassis assembly shop in 1908. The factory was built in 1906–7 on a new site at Radford, Coventry.

18 The banked oval test track behind Rolls-Royce's Derby factory was added in 1911. This was mostly surfaced in tarmacadam, but the banked end was covered in granite setts. Here the firm's chassis were tested before being sent to the coachbuilders. The road on the bridge was the main route into the works, rather than part of the test track.

he created a new circular test track on the brow of Cofton Hill at Longbridge, to 'obviate unwelcome attentions of the police'.[71] The outline of this track can still be made out within the boundary of the present Nanjing Automotive works (see pl. 27). Specially built test tracks usually had a variety of surfaces, with a steep slope and sometimes a water splash.

19 Clement Talbot built its Motor Works on Barlby Road, London, in 1903–4. The architecturally elaborate entrance block contained offices and an engine room. Though this still stands, the workshops to the rear were replaced, in the mid-1990s, by a residential development with apt street names, such as Shrewsbury Street and Humber Drive.

Whatever their layout, most pre-1914 English car factories had little architectural pretension. Even the office building that fronted the factory floors was usually plain. England had nothing so grandiose or extravagant as Argyll's factory, built in Glasgow in 1906, with turrets and a domed clock tower. The frontage of Clement Talbot's in London, however, came close. This factory, financed by the Earl of Shrewsbury and Talbot, was designed by William T. Walker and built in 1903–4. The reinforced-concrete office block (pl. 19) was given a red brick and ashlar façade in a heavy Edwardian Baroque style. Projecting from the main entrance was a *porte cochère*. Cars were displayed on the marble floor of the entrance hall, whilst a sweeping staircase led up to offices. Another factory office intended to impress was Vauxhall's in Luton, Bedfordshire, designed by H. B. Cresswell in 1907 in a Queen Anne style.

In the years preceding the First World War, the volume and speed of production in car factories improved enormously. This was largely down to Henry Ford, who opened his first foreign assembly plant on the Trafford Park Industrial Estate, outside Manchester, in October 1911. A former electric tramcar factory, of the single-storey type, was adapted and extended by its original architect, Charles Heathcote. This was not the first time that Heathcote — a local architect responsible chiefly for factories and warehouses — had been engaged by a U.S. company, since he had worked alongside American engineers and contractors on Westinghouse's Trafford Park plant between 1899 and 1903.[72] As one of the first architects to ensure that his practice was able to draw

20   This archive photograph of Ford's first British assembly plant at Trafford Park, Manchester, dating from 1914, shows its powered assembly line on the far right.

up plans for steelwork, as well as the architectural shell of a building,[73] he continued to serve Ford for decades to come. At Trafford Park, a right-hand-drive version of the Model T was assembled from American components, with just about everything supplied from Ford's own factories, except for bodies. These were made initially by a nearby coachbuilder, Scott Bros., but this proved slow, and in 1912 Ford took over Scott's. Otherwise, parts were shipped across the Atlantic to Liverpool, then transported to Trafford Park via the Manchester Ship Canal, which had opened in 1894. This approach saved a great deal on freight – because fully built cars took up more space than com-

pactly packaged components – and resulted in enhanced British sales, which rose from 1,485 in 1911 to 6,139 in 1913.[74]

A radical innovation was gradually introduced at Trafford Park in 1912–13. From this time, chassis were made using a powered endless chain assembly line, raised to trestle height (pl. 20). This was the first moving assembly line to be installed in a British factory, of any kind. Great efficiency was obtained by placing components close to this line, or by feeding items such as wheels directly to the line by conveyors. This system had been implemented recently at Ford's American plant, Highland Park, an extremely long multi-storey daylight factory built in the years

1908–14 in the outskirts of Detroit to designs by Albert Kahn, working with Ford's construction engineer, Edward Gray.[75] The moving assembly line marked a considerable advance on the dummy wheels used to push cars along tracks in some British factories. In the early 1920s Ford's plant was described by an insider as

> a wheel, the hub of which was the final assembly conveyor. Or perhaps a better illustration would be a spider's web, with all the radial strands representing paths of gradually growing parts and all the cross strands representing minor assemblies, the ultimate object being the final assembly conveyor. The lay-out of the plant, the lay-out of the shop, was entirely subject to that consideration.[76]

By 1916 Henry Ford realised that the single-storey steel-framed factory accommodated a moving assembly line much better than the multi-storey concrete-framed factory. The outcome was the huge Ford River Rouge plant in Michigan, designed by Kahn and begun in 1916.[77] Future Ford assembly plants in England would also be mostly on one storey.

Specialists: Coachbuilders and Component Manufacturers, 1896–1914

In 1897 Daimler was poised to receive orders for engines from coachbuilders, who would surely count amongst its most important customers.[78] But in the event, it was Daimler that began to order bodies from coachbuilders, thus assuming the lead role in producing finished cars. This turn of events was down to the conservatism of coachbuilders: they applied craft-based technologies that had scarcely changed in 100 years and – according to many of those observing the trade at the time – were loath to cooperate with the engineers who made motor cars, unable to believe that the age of the horse-drawn carriage was ending.[79] They hoped that automobiles would be a passing fad, and persisted in making carriages for a dwindling market. Not all coachbuilders shared this outlook, however: some clearly understood the inevitability of the motor car and entered into profitable working relationships with car manufacturers. In 1908 Lord Montagu observed that 'coachbuilders are now building more bodies for motor-cars than horse vehicles'.[80] Despite this, continuity with the past was emphasised by the adaptation of broughams, landaulets, phaetons and other conventional forms of horse-drawn carriage to the motor chassis. It was some time before car design broke free from this tradition.

One of the first coachbuilders to venture into this new line of business was Thrupp & Maberly of Oxford Street, London, which is known to have bodied an electric Victoria for the Queen of Spain, along with four other cars, in 1896.[81] Working

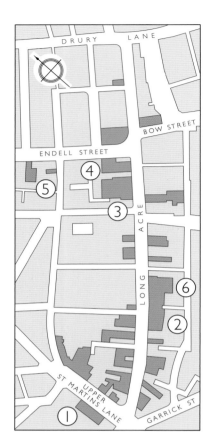

KEY 1896
1 Aldridge's Repository
2 Windover's
3 Morgan and Co.
4 Henry J. Hall and Co.
5 Coulson's Livery Stables
6 Victoria Carriage Works

Horse and Carriage trade

21 Throughout the nineteenth century Long Acre was the metropolitan centre of the horse and carriage trade. In the late 1890s it was represented by forty to fifty businesses, with many more in the surrounding streets.

on a larger scale, Arthur F. Mulliner of Northampton had built 150 bodies, mostly on Daimler chassis, by 1900. In 1907 he ceased making carriages altogether, enlarging his works on Bridge Street in Northampton and opening a new factory and sales office at 132–135 Long Acre, London (see pl. 56), which had been the centre of coachbuilding in London since the eighteenth century.[82] Joseph Cockshoot & Co. of New Bridge Street, Manchester (demolished), made its first bodies in 1903 for the Stanley Steam Car, Rex and Velox, but went on to undertake work for a wide range of other marques, including Rolls-Royce. Even when car manufacturers began to undertake their own coachwork, increased demand enabled new specialist coachbuilders to emerge.

Some coachbuilders rebuilt or extended their existing factories to suit the demands of the new industry, often gravitating to north or west London from their traditional city-centre sites. Hooper & Co., an old firm whose carriages were made by royal appointment, extended its works on King's Road, Chelsea, in 1911, while Barker & Co., one of several firms that made bodies for Rolls-Royce, moved its factory from Chandos Street/Bedford Street in Covent Garden to vast premises in Olaf Street,

22 Fort Dunlop at Erdington, north of Birmingham, became the largest factory in Britain in the 1920s. This building originally belonged to a much larger complex. Derelict for twenty years, and used as little more than an advertising hoarding, it became a landmark for motorists on the M6. In 2006, however, it was redeveloped by Urban Splash as a Travelodge, with adjoining office and retail space, under a grass roof.

Shepherd's Bush, in 1909. These firms also maintained West End showrooms: Hooper's on the corner of St James's Street and Bennett Street, and Barker's in South Audley Street. By 1913 Hooper was claiming the ability to make, sell and repair motor cars.[83] Mulliner in Long Acre, too, was advertising chassis, proving that, just as chassis manufacturers could buy in bodies, so coachbuilders could buy in chassis and, indeed, market a complete new car.[84] Their lack of mechanical knowledge, however, made aftercare a problem, and such initiatives ceased after the First World War.

Coachbuilders clung to the multi-storeyed factory model longer than car manufacturers. In 1905 the Regent Carriage Co. in Fulham rebuilt part of its premises especially for the manufacture of motor bodies.[85] This company made customised composite bodies for Napier, Daimler, Crossley and Renault. Its new two-storey factory (demolished) was designed and built under

the supervision of the general manager, Mr H. Arkell. It was equipped with a large timber store, a forge, woodworking machinery and a gas-heated stove for hardening varnishes and paint. The body shop was on the ground floor, while delicate work, such as trimming and painting, was carried out on the upper floor, beneath a pitched steel-framed roof with glazing along the ridge. Similar factories erected outside London included an addition to Salmons of Newport Pagnell (see pl. 9), built in 1912.

Other coachbuilders moved into single-storey complexes. Particular thought was invested in the new motor bodybuilding works of Brown, Hughes & Strachan (demolished), built on the Park Royal estate in west London in 1911.[86] While assuming the usual form of parallel sheds covered by a sawtooth roof, it had two-storey elevations, explained by the fact that galleries ran around three sides of a full-height central area. These galleries contained the offices, stores and upholstery shop, while the central space accommodated the main workshops: primarily woodwork and erection bays, but also dust-excluding cubicles for painting. This was an example of the galleried design so often adopted for chassis-erection shops in car factories, suggestive of cross-fertilisation between the two industries.

Numerous firms that supplied the cycle industry, such as Lucas (lamps), Dunlop (tyres) and Smith (speedometers), adapted existing products for cars, while others emerged to meet new requirements. Many of these firms were based in the west Midlands, with a concentration in Coventry, mirroring the distribution pattern of car manufacturers themselves. These included White & Poppe (engines), Wrigley (axles), the Motor Radiator Manufacturing Co. (radiators) and Rudge-Whitworth (wheels). Some components that seem crucial today were optional accessories in the early days of motoring. These included hoods, windscreens and wipers, as well as horns, mirrors, locks and trunks. The largest component and accessory manufacturers operated from huge wholesale depots in London, the most famous being the Michelin Building (see pl. 123).

Wheels and tyres were elements of cars that manufacturers happily left to specialists, some of whom earned an international reputation. Joseph Sankey & Sons became the largest manufacturer of motor-car wheels in Europe. In the nineteenth century this company had made metal trays and hollow ware, but in the age of the motor car it developed the pressed steel wheel. In 1910 Sankey's acquired the Castle Car Works, a single-storey tramcar factory of 1900, in Hadley, near Wellington, Shropshire, which still exists as GKN (Guest, Keen & Nettlefold).[87] As far as tyres were concerned, Dunlop (taken over by Harvey Du Cros senior in 1889) was the leader in the field, despite fierce competition from the likes of Continental, Michelin, Pirelli, Goodyear and Firestone. Set up in 1896 to manufacture pneumatic tyres for bicycles, Dunlop made car tyres from 1900.[88] Pneumatic tyres had quickly become standard for cars, since they absorbed shocks from the road more efficiently than solid rubber tyres. Dunlop's first factories were located in Coventry (Alma Street) and Birmingham (Para Mills, Aston Cross), but in 1913 Fort Dunlop was established at Erdington, north-east of Birmingham, with access to both canal and railway.[89] As Dunlop's principal manufacturing base, this was hugely extended by the architects Sidney Stott and Walter W. Gibbings in the early 1920s, becoming, reputedly, the largest factory in England.[90] A small part survives today (pl. 22).

•

Motor-car Manufacture, 1914–1945

The First World War provided impetus for the motor industry by training thousands of new drivers and mechanics. For five years, however, the production of private cars was severely restricted, since most factories were requisitioned to manufacture munitions, aircraft or military vehicles (pl. 23). In the course of the war, Austin, at Longbridge, turned out 8 million shells, 650 guns, more than 2,000 aeroplanes and nearly 500 armoured cars.[91] In 1917, to house the workforce, the Longbridge Village Estate was built with 250 dwellings – including prefabricated wooden bungalows shipped over from Michigan – laid out as a

23 Like Wolseley, the Electrical & Ordnance Accessories Co. was a subsidiary of Vickers. Its factory on Drews Lane in Ward End, Birmingham, by J. J. Hackett, was built in 1914 to manufacture the Stellite car, but turned immediately to war work upon completion. Wolseley transferred its main operations to this site after the war. The sheds were repaired following aerial bombardment during the Second World War.

24 The Longbridge Village Estate, or garden suburb, was built to house workers at Austin's factory in 1917

garden suburb (pl. 24).[92] In addition, hostels were provided, and fleets of buses brought workers to the factory each day from outlying areas. Many factories acquired extensions – including timber munitions sheds and steel-framed aircraft hangars – built for war work with capital provided by the Ministry of Munitions, but later purchased by the occupying firms and adapted for car manufacture. Few firms were able to maintain car production during the war, a situation that gave American marques a strong advantage. In response to pressure from Associated British Manufacturers, the budget of September 1915 (the McKenna Duties, named after the Chancellor of the Exchequer, Reginald McKenna) imposed a tax of 33⅓ per cent on imported vehicles and components. This effectively eliminated foreign competition from the home market, although cars from Canada and other outposts of empire attracted lower duties, opening up an indirect route for American imports. Despite being lifted briefly in 1924–5, these stringent taxes remained in place until the 1960s.

After the Armistice in 1918, demand for cars surged. Numbers of licensed private cars in the U.K. had dropped dramatically during the war, but quickly recovered (see Appendix). With the introduction of a 'horsepower tax' in 1921 (£1 per unit of horsepower), light cars became very popular, while large American vehicles were discouraged. Many new firms entered the industry, but a strike in 1919–20, and an economic slump in 1920–22, put many out of business. Thereafter, small-scale manufacturers struggled to match the prices set for mass-produced cars by companies such as Austin (with the Austin 7 of 1922, £225) and Rover (with the Rover 8 of 1922, £180 to £190). Between 1920 and 1929 the overall number of British car manufacturers fell from 130 to 50, but many more came and went throughout this uncertain and competitive decade.[93]

Annual factory output of private cars rose from 71,396 in 1923 to 165,352 in 1928 and 341,628 in 1938, while over the same period the price of cars dropped by half.[94] At the same time, the aesthetics and technology of cars changed enormously, and elec-

25 Bean's factory in Tipton, Staffordshire, had been built by German prisoners in 1916 for wartime manufacture and was adapted in 1919–20 for chassis making. Twin powered assembly lines were installed for the volume production of a mid-range car. The moving chain is visible through the chassis in this photograph.

tric accessories such as self-starters, mechanical windscreen wipers and dipping headlamps became the norm rather than optional extras. In 1920 the typical British car was a four-seated open-topped tourer, but by 1930 this was being ousted by the closed saloon. The gradual adoption of the all-steel body, and eventually integral construction, which dispensed with the separate chassis, had a great impact on the styling of cars. In general, new models became increasingly streamlined.

Throughout the inter-war period, the industry was dominated by Morris, Austin and Ford, followed by the Rootes Group (see below), Vauxhall and Standard. High import tariffs encouraged foreign manufacturers to set up factories (or, perhaps more accurately, assembly plants) on British soil, rather than import fin-

ished vehicles. Thus, Citroën opened a factory at Slough, Buckinghamshire (1926),[95] Renault at Acton, London (1927),[96] and Fiat at Crayford, Kent (1928). As for American firms, Ford was joined on this side of the Atlantic by Hudson, which set up in Brentford, London (1922), and by Chrysler at Kew, London (1924), while General Motors took over Vauxhall (1925). New firms such as Alvis (1919), Bentley (1919), MG (1924), Triumph (1923) and SS (i.e., Jaguar, 1931) made a significant impression, while others vanished from the scene for ever – including well-established firms like Clyno (1929). Some big names were rescued from difficulties: Austin had to be restructured (1921), and the bankrupt Wolseley (1927) was bought up by William Morris, now Lord Nuffield. Other mergers and takeovers further

26   Standard installed this static U-shaped assembly line in its Canley factory in 1920. From *The Motor*, 26 January 1921, p. 1303.

transformed the industry. Armstrong and Siddeley-Deasy got together (1919); Sunbeam formed an alliance with Talbot and Darracq (1920); Singer bought Calcott (1926), Rolls-Royce bought Bentley (1931) and Morris bought Riley (1938). The largest organisation to emerge was the Rootes Group. Hitherto distributors rather than manufacturers, Rootes absorbed Humber (1928), Hillman (1929), Sunbeam and Talbot (1935), as well as the coachbuilders Thrupp & Maberly (1925). By 1939 there were only thirty-three car manufacturers left in the U.K., representing twenty corporations.

Ford's rivals were aware of its powered chassis assembly line (see above),[97] and had learned much about flow production from their experience of munitions and aircraft manufacture during the war years of 1914–18. The challenge of arranging the work as efficiently as possible led to the widespread adoption of open-plan interiors for flow production, and the creation of an assembly line, whereby the item itself was moved from workman to workman, or gang to gang, each of whom was restricted to a specific task. Sub-assemblies were produced on the same principle, feeding products through to the final assembly line. Few factories had powered assembly lines before the mid-1920s. One

exception was Harper Bean Ltd, an established iron founder that had entered vehicle manufacture in 1919 with a car named the Bean. The factory at Tipton, Staffordshire, was placed in the hands of an American production manager who introduced messenger boys on roller skates, as well as two electrically powered assembly lines (pl. 25).[98] Set at floor level and measuring 150 feet in length, these moved at the rate of 12 inches per minute. Few other factories could afford this kind of machinery – indeed, just a year after starting manufacture Bean was embroiled in financial trouble – yet they did their best to rationalise production in an innovative manner. In 1920, for example, Standard installed a new system in its Canley factory (demolished; pl. 26) on the edge of Coventry, a site comprising spacious A-frame sheds that had been erected in 1916 for aircraft production and were extended immediately after the war. Standard's new line was regarded as a compromise between the American moving assembly line and 'the ordinary British method'.[99] A U-shaped railway was laid down in the erecting shop, and the chassis was gradually assembled on trolleys, which were pushed manually along the rails. At any one time, the rail could accommodate ten to twelve frames, and a chassis could be built in eight hours. This

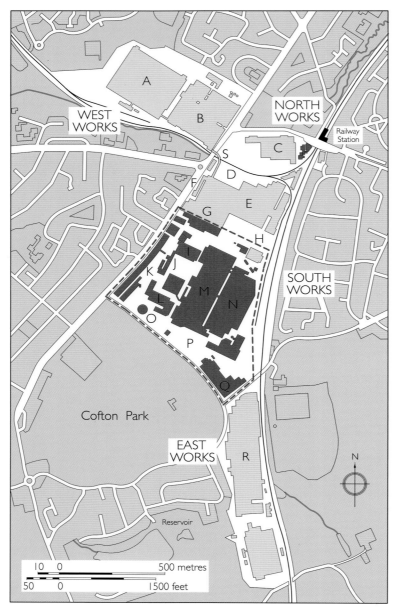

WEST
WORKS

NORTH
WORKS

Railway
Station

SOUTH
WORKS

EAST
WORKS

Cofton Park

Reservoir

N

10   0   500 metres

50   0   1500 feet

KEY

☐ Demolished 2006 - 2009   [⌐] Area occupied by Nanjing Automotive 2009

A Metro Works (1976-1977)
B West Works (1916-1917, later used as body shop)
C North Works (1916-1917, including steel works)
D Site of original White & Pike's factory (1893, much
   extended by Austin after 1905)
E Machine Shop (1957)
F Offices (1957)
G Press Shop (1919-1922; extended 1927-1928)
H Dalmuir Building
I Design Block (1962)

J "The Kremlin" offices (1948)
K Service Department (1932)
L Exhibition Hall and Canteen (1955)
M CAB 1 (1951-1952)
N CAB 2 (1960-1961)
O Commercial Vehicle Showroom (mid-1960s)
P Site of Car Park (1961)
Q Flight Shed (1936-1937)
R East Works (1936)
S Conveyors

27   The layout and scale of Austin's factory at Longbridge, near Birmingham, is shown in this block plan. After undergoing various corporate transformations, Austin eventually became MG Rover. When this entered administration in 2005, Nanjing Automotive bought its assets and restarted production of the MG TF on part of the South Works. The remainder was sold for re-development and demolished in the years 2006–9.

approach led to the development of assembly lines that looped or zigzagged through buildings, maintaining continuity over a great length. These lines were often reorganised and updated when new models were introduced. In addition to modernising production flow lines, throughout the 1920s all the major factories invested in expensive new technologies, such as heavy metal presses and spray paint installations, for which the spacious wartime sheds proved well suited. Much machinery was now powered by individual electric motors rather than overhead line shafting, permitting more flexible floor layouts.

Though Austin struggled to reassert itself immediately after the war, its market was secured in 1922 with the 'baby Austin', which accounted for about half of the company's production through the mid- to late 1920s; its output in 1932 was 42,520, but this had almost doubled by 1937.[100] The efficiency of Longbridge was greatly improved. Compressed air sprays were used for painting by 1919,[101] and heavy steel presses were introduced in 1921. Soon afterwards, the site was reorganised as three subfactories: chassis erection, foundry and machine shops, and coachbuilding (pls 27 and 28). These became known, respectively, as South Works (the original factory), North Works (built for munitions 1916–17; demolished) and West Works (built for munitions 1916–17; demolished). Constantly updated and reorganised through the 1920s, each of the Works operated an assembly line that delivered the main units of cars to the erecting shop. By 1928, however, the factory had yet to introduce a moving line for chassis assembly.[102]

Morris became the largest supplier to the home market in 1924 (pls 4 and 29). To secure regular stock, the company began to buy up its suppliers, including the engine manufacturer Hotchkiss & Cie (1923) and the coachbuilders Hollick & Pratt (1923), both of Coventry. Like its rivals, Morris was preoccupied with refining the assembly line. Just after the war, chassis were still pushed manually from one workstation to the next. In 1926 a huge new chassis assembly shop known as Block C was completed. Measuring 500 by 250 feet, this had a single static assembly line, used for both Cowley and Oxford models, fed by sub-assemblies and capable of producing, on average, 2,000 cars per week. In 1928–9 a new erecting or body-mounting shed was added. This was where the chassis was united with its engine and body. It measured approximately 1,000 feet, and comprised three lines: one each for the Cowley, Oxford and Minor models.[103] The tracks were fitted with dollies, or 'transveyors', each capable of accommodating a single chassis, onto which cranes with grabs dropped engines and bodies from overhead bridges (pl. 30). After being fitted with its engine, the chassis was sprayed black in a tunnel, in which it was rotated in a cradle; it then travelled through a second tunnel to be dried, or hardened. Only after being tested was it partnered with its body.

28   This aerial view of Longbridge, from the south, shows the flight shed of 1936–7 in the foreground. The photograph dates from August 2005, just four months after MG Rover went into administration, and shows the site intact.

29 A view inside Morris's factory at Cowley, Oxford, *circa* 1925, showing painted bodies entering a drying tunnel.

The adoption of the all-steel welded body was a major development at Cowley.[104] William Morris had studied the production of such bodies in America in 1925 and, convinced of their advantages, played a lead role in setting up the Pressed Steel Co., beside his own factory, in 1926–7. In the high sheds of the new Pressed Steel Works (pl. 31), giant presses operated by compressed air stamped out wings, doors, rear panels and even entire sides, which were then electrically welded together to make a shell, before being welded to a steel frame. Although this technology did away with the need for timber frames, it was not immediately embraced by every manufacturer: even Morris continued to produce composite bodies for certain models.

Ford remained under the thumb of its American parent for some time, but in 1928 was reorganised under the auspices of its British manager, Percival Perry, and in 1931 began to produce its own British models (for example, the Ford Model Y 8hp,

launched in 1932 for £120). Meanwhile, Ford had been searching for a location with good waterside access that would supersede Trafford Park. In 1923 the firm discovered a marshy site by the Thames to the east of London, and it was here that its new Dagenham factory (pl. 32) was built in 1929–31, although some elements of the scheme were not completed until 1935.[105] As well as being the most significant car factory to be built from scratch in the U.K. between the wars, this was the largest automobile factory in Europe, producing 100,000 cars each year. Inspired by Ford's River Rouge plant in America, Dagenham was certainly the most self-reliant car plant in the U.K., equipped with its own wharf, blast furnace, sinter plant, coke ovens, foundry and power station. The last (1935, demolished), with its four funnel-like chimneys and gigantic Ford script logo, became a landmark for shipping on the River Thames. Ford did, however, depend on Briggs Motor Bodies to make the steel engine shop, body shop and upholstery shop) zigzagged from north-east to south-west; it was centred on a single assembly line fed by a monorail conveyor, terminating in a dispatch bay by the wharf. To the east lay the power station, coke ovens and blast furnace. The power station, designed to consume London rubbish as well as conventional fuel, had its own jetty.

Ford had thrown down the gauntlet, and in 1934 Morris's Managing Director, Leonard Lord, reorganised chassis assembly at Cowley. Five parallel chassis assembly lines – now powered – moved at 4 feet per minute and were fed by various types of mechanical handling equipment.[107] These provided for fifteen different models of car. The engines came from Morris Engines, the former Hotchkiss & Cie, which relocated to a new factory and foundry at Courthouse Green (demolished, see pl. 5) in north-west Coventry in 1937. Morris reinforced its market lead with the Morris 10 (1933, £165 or £169 10s.) and Morris 8 (1934, £132 10s.), but faced intense competition from other manufacturers, whose factories also grew at this time. Vauxhall, for example, expanded its Luton site in 1932–3. Rover reorganised in 1933, quitting its Meteor Works for a new factory on Helen Street to the north-west of Coventry. Austin remodelled its South Works in 1936, raising its annual output to 80,000 vehicles.[108] The atmosphere in the car factories in the early 1930s was captured by J. B. Priestley, who visited Daimler's factory in 1933:

> All these sheds were the same: a long vista of blue electric-light shades, a misty perspective of flywheels above and brown-overalled men below. They were all hard at it and most of them were having a smoke too, for they are allowed to smoke for three-quarters of an hour in the morning and in the afternoon: a wise rule.[109]

Since car factories increasingly brought coachbuilding in-house and went over to all-steel bodies, specialist coachbuilders faced a bleak future. Some (e.g., Carbodies) concentrated on high-volume contracts for major manufacturers, others (e.g., Avon) took on low-volume contracts making special bodies for principal manufacturers, while a few (e.g., Hooper and Gurney Nutting) made custom-built bodies for wealthy customers. Outside the bespoke trade, the craft skills involved in coachbuilding were overtaken by technology. Painters were made redundant by the spread of mechanised application and drying techniques, and the introduction, from 1925, of quick-drying cellulose paints. The work of the manual panel beater was threatened by presses, while the carpenter's role diminished as wooden frames were abandoned. Composite bodies produced by traditional firms seemed increasingly heavy and inflexible, and in 1936 even the top-end coachbuilder Park Ward developed a steel-frame system for its Bentleys. The next big step in mass production, however, was the integral or monocoque body, initiated in France by Citroën in 1934, and in Germany by Opel in 1935.

30   Morris's new body-mounting shed of 1929, drawn by Gordon Crosby for *The Autocar*. Engines and bodies were lowered onto the chassis from overhead gantries or bridges. From *The Autocar*, 22 March 1929, p. 572

bodies for its cars and the Kelsey-Hayes Wheel Co. to make its wheels. The factories of both these American companies were designed by Wallis, Gilbert & Partners.[106]

In the 1930s tourists could sail from Westminster for tours of the Ford factory, arriving at a floating pontoon attached to the west end of the wharf. This projected into the river in front of the factory, and was used for the shipment of cars and the delivery of raw materials. It was fitted, at its east end, with two mobile unloaders and a high-line track to the ore yard. Facing the wharf was a four-storey office block (demolished), behind which lay a great expanse of single-storey sheds arranged east–west, representing the main production area. The sheds, designed by Charles Heathcote & Sons, the Manchester architects who had acted for Ford since 1911, had double pitched roofs with steel trusses, corrugated iron cladding, long glazing strips and electrically operated ventilators. Production (divided mainly into machine shop,

31 Although the Morris factory at Cowley has been demolished, the Pressed Steel Works, set up in 1926–7, still stands. Photographed in 2005, this is now a BMW plant, used to manufacture the Mini.

The Pressed Steel factory in Cowley was extended for the construction of such bodies in 1937, and in the following year it supplied integral bodies to both Morris and Vauxhall, which adapted their assembly lines accordingly. Inevitably, British coachbuilders dwindled in number, with surviving firms becoming increasingly specialised in their output.

In this context, it is perhaps surprising that several coachbuilding factories of architectural note were built in the 1930s. One of the most distinctive was Hooper's (demolished), located on Western Avenue, London, by Park Royal Station.[110] This was built in 1933 in the streamlined moderne style that became common for factory offices facing the new arterial roads, reflecting the growing shift from railways to road haulage.[111] These buildings were advertisements for the brand, as much as functional buildings. In *English Journey* (1934), J. B. Priestley claimed that they were 'tangible evidence, most cunningly arranged to take the eye, to prove that the new industries have moved

south'.[112] Examples of car-related factories on the Great West Road (pls 33 and 34) included John Charles & Co. (1933–4) and the Firestone Tyre & Rubber Co. factory (Wallis, Gilbert & Partners, 1928, extended 1933), the latter famously demolished on the eve of listing in 1980.[113]

In 1936, with war imminent, the Air Ministry proposed to fund a 'shadow' scheme whereby motor manufacturers would erect, equip and manage new factories for the production of aero-engines, supplementing (or 'shadowing') existing plant. Several major firms – including Austin, Daimler, Rover, Singer, Standard and Rootes – signed up to this, and construction work began on a number of new factories, some on greenfield sites, others adjoining existing factories. These shadow factories – such as Rolls-Royce at Crewe, Cheshire (1938, now Bentley), and in the west Midlands Rootes at Ryton (1939, demolished; pl. 35), Rover at Acocks Green (1936–7, demolished) and Solihull (1939–40, now Jaguar Land Rover), and SS/Jaguar at Browns

32   This aerial photograph of Ford's Dagenham factory, 'the Detroit of Europe', built in the years 1929–31, was taken from the south in 2006. Note the jetty to the right.

Lane, Coventry (mostly demolished) – were built as single-storey, top-lit sheds, with long office frontages. The committee set up to oversee the scheme was chaired by Lord Austin, whose own factory at Longbridge was enlarged by the erection of the East Works, or Aero Factory (1936–7, demolished; see pl. 27, bottom of picture), comprising a huge building with high sawtooth roofs and an underground aircraft factory. All that survives today is the flight shed, or hangar. One of the largest of all shadow factories was set up in 1938 by Lord Nuffield at Castle Bromwich, near Solihull, to manufacture Spitfires, but production was initiated so slowly that it was taken off his hands by Lord Beaverbrook, Minister for Aircraft Production. In later years, Fisher & Ludlow made car bodies in this factory, which is now a Jaguar Land Rover plant.

Repeating the experience of 1914–18, civilian car production ground to a halt during the Second World War. Existing factories were converted for wartime production, mostly of aircraft and aero-engines, although military cars were also manufactured. Some sites, such as Vauxhall at Luton and Rover at Coventry, sustained considerable bomb damage, despite the extensive camouflaging of buildings. The experience of Wolseley at Ward End, Birmingham (see pl. 23), was typical. At the outbreak of war the introduction of a new model, the Wolseley 8, was cancelled; air-raid shelters were built for the workforce, and a fire brigade and air-raid wardens were recruited. In winter 1940–41 the site was camouflaged, being painted as an extension of the adjoining housing estate, with roads continued in paint across the factory roofs. This was of little use, however, because the Luftwaffe had taken clear aerial photographs of the site in August 1940, and subjected the factory to heavy bombardment in April 1941. Although just one man was killed, it was reported that 20 per cent of the buildings and 40 per cent of the roofs were destroyed. Like other bombed factories, it was rebuilt quickly so that war work could resume.

33   Numerous factories were erected along this stretch of the Great West Road, in Brentwood, west London, in the late 1920s and early 1930s. To top right in this photograph of 1963 is the Firestone tyre factory, built in 1928 to designs by Wallis, Gilbert & Partners, and demolished in 1980.

34   This map of the Great West Road shows the locations of motor-related businesses, including factories, in the late 1930s.

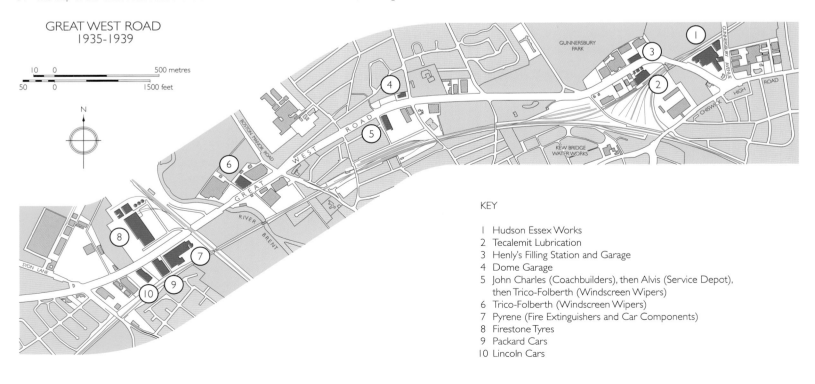

GREAT WEST ROAD
1935-1939

KEY

1   Hudson Essex Works
2   Tecalemit Lubrication
3   Henly's Filling Station and Garage
4   Dome Garage
5   John Charles (Coachbuilders), then Alvis (Service Depot),
    then Trico-Folberth (Windscreen Wipers)
6   Trico-Folberth (Windscreen Wipers)
7   Pyrene (Fire Extinguishers and Car Components)
8   Firestone Tyres
9   Packard Cars
10 Lincoln Cars

Sunbeam-Talbot and, from 1956, Singer), Standard (including Triumph from 1945) and Vauxhall (i.e., the American company General Motors). Amongst the strongest of the smaller companies were Rover, Jaguar and Rolls-Royce, whilst new arrivals included Lotus and Healey.

By and large, car design picked up where it had left off in 1939, with a preference for bulbous, streamlined forms inspired by American vehicles. Amongst the first new models were the Standard Vanguard (1947), the Morris Minor (1948, created by Alec Issigonis) and the rather more aerodynamic Jowett Javelin (1947, designed by Gerald Palmer), which was made at Idle, near Bradford.[115] Javelins were manufactured by adding mechanical parts to bodies, ready-made by Briggs of Dagenham, that were rolled over in cradles whilst the engines were fitted from above.[116] Mechanical handling devices of this nature became increasingly common throughout the industry. In tandem with this, however, a few companies, such as the Morgan Motor Co. – which has occupied the same site in Malvern, Worcestershire, from 1919 to the present day – prided themselves on maintaining traditional, craft-based techniques (pl. 37).

The use of large sheds remained standard after 1945, sometimes with basements and mezzanines, but alongside this several multi-storeyed factories were built. Architectural form and treatment remained relatively untouched by the mechanisation and computerisation of manufacturing processes, though cladding, lighting, heating and ventilation evolved over time. Not surprisingly, given the relatively recent introduction of monocoque

36   The interior of CAB1, the new car assembly building, at Longbridge in November 1951. The sign reading 'the ships are waiting' reminds the workforce of the importance of the post-war export drive.

35   The Rootes 'shadow factory' at Ryton was built in 1939. It was photographed from the air in 2007, shortly before its demolition.

Car Production since 1945

Once car manufacture recommenced in 1946, it was directed by Labour Government policy ('export or die') on foreign markets: in 1951, for example, 506,000 vehicles were manufactured for export and 419,000 for the home market.[114] As well as imposing export targets (pl. 36), the Government restricted steel supplies and taxed new cars heavily. By now, the industry had coalesced around the 'Big Six' manufacturers, though another twenty smaller producers existed, as well as several independent motor body builders. The 'Big Six' – responsible for producing 90 per cent of British cars in the immediate post-war period – were Austin, Ford, the Nuffield Organisation (i.e., Morris, Wolseley, Riley and MG), the Rootes Group (i.e., Hillman, Humber,

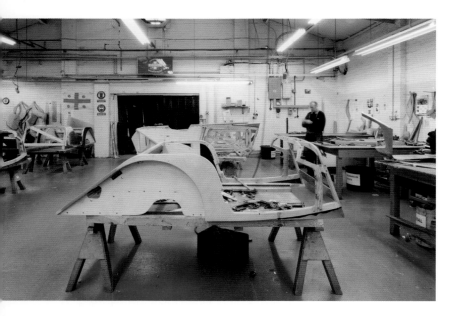

37 Traditional coachbuilding still being undertaken at the Morgan factory in Malvern, Worcestershire, in 2011.

bodies, some of the first major developments in post-war car factories concerned body plants. In the years 1954–8 Vauxhall added a huge L-shaped multi-storeyed building (AC, demolished) with a press shop, panel store, body shop and final assembly area. In the press shop, 225 presses were arranged in twenty-six lines; pressings were fed from here to the body shop by six overhead conveyors.[117] The body shop, together with final assembly, occupied most of the ground floor, while trimming took place on a looped assembly line on the first floor, and part of the paint shop – as ever, situated at the top of the building to reduce dust – was located in a second-floor 'penthouse'. Beneath all this, a basement was devoted to stores, seat and spring manufacture, and to wheel and tyre assembly.

It was now possible to rust-proof metal bodies, inside and out. The first 'Rotodip' plant in the country, developed by the Carrier Engineering Co., was installed in 1948 at the press plant of Fisher & Ludlow at Castle Bromwich, for the manufacture of Standard Vanguard bodies.[118] This was followed a year later by Morris at Cowley.[119] In each case, the plant involved a 300-foot-long tunnel, in which a body revolved on its horizontal axis, as if impaled on a spit, as it passed through tanks of rust-proofing solution, before being dried, primed and baked. Morris also introduced 'Rotospray', a method of painting bodies by rotation. A decade later, a new glass-fronted paint plant (1957, demolished) at Cowley was described as 'a modern miniature Crystal Palace'. Every week 3,000 gallons of paint were dispensed from a central 'dairy' – comprising a battery of fifty-two 100-gallon containers, in twenty-six colours – to automatic spray booths with air conditioning where bodies, already rust-proofed and primed, were

painted.[120] Two huge water tanks below the factory floor received the waste; operatives wore protective clothing, and walls were lined with asbestos.

Steel shortages, and the expense of steel presses, led to the adoption of alternative materials for car bodies. Aluminium was used a great deal, and wood-framed estate cars, such as the Morris Traveller (1950), were introduced with some success. In the mid-1950s glass fibre bodies – pressed in moulds then heated and 'cured' – were adopted by some low-volume producers. Throughout this period, many of the remaining specialist coachbuilders were absorbed by major manufacturers: Park Ward had been purchased by Rolls-Royce in 1939; Vanden Plas was acquired by Austin in 1946; BSA bought Carbodies in 1954; David Brown (owner of Aston Martin-Lagonda) acquired Tickfords (i.e., the former Salmons) in 1955; Mulliner of Birmingham became part of Standard-Triumph in 1958, and H. J. Mulliner was purchased by Rolls-Royce in 1959, creating Mulliner Park Ward (whose premises are now Car Giant, Willesden, north London). In the course of 1953 two companies that made steel pressings rather than traditional coachwork were taken over: Fisher & Ludlow by the British Motor Corporation (BMC) and Briggs Motor Bodies by Ford. This left Pressed Steel as the last large-scale independent motor body builder in the country – until its merger with BMC in 1965.

Longbridge continued to expand after 1945, with new buildings going up on the site of the Cofton Hill test track and First World War flying ground, situated between the South Works and East Works (see pls 27 and 28). An office block nicknamed 'The Kremlin' was added in 1948. Then, in 1951, a new car assembly building (CAB1; pl. 38) was built.[121] Since the original South Works, to the north of CAB1, had a lower ground level, a conveyor bridge and 1,000-foot tunnel were needed to feed axles, engines, bodies and other parts to this building. A Hollerith punch-card system ensured that the correct engines and bodies were delivered for each model.[122] From an underground marshalling yard, these were hoisted through the floor and lowered onto one of four assembly tracks. CAB1 admitted a great deal of daylight through its glazed sides and two parallel monitor roofs. The monitor roof was a form of clerestory pioneered by Albert Kahn and used in the American motor industry since the First World War.[123] It was also adopted for additions made in 1956 to Rover's former shadow factory in Solihull, and for a new body plant built for Pressed Steel in 1955, just outside Swindon, Wiltshire. This was designed by Harry Weedon & Partners.[124]

Harry Weedon & Partners had been appointed consultant architect to Austin in 1950 and, after Austin merged with Morris in 1952 (turning the Big Six into the Big Five), continued to work for the newly created BMC, which was chaired by Morris's former manager, Leonard Lord. Harry Weedon (died 1970) was

38 The exterior of CAB1 at Longbridge, designed by the American architect Charles Howard Crane and built in 1951. This type of monitor roof had been popular for some time in the American car industry.

a Birmingham architect who had specialised in cinema design between the wars,[125] then became involved in the dispersal of industrial plant in 1940. He may have worked alongside the architect of CAB1, Charles Howard Crane (1885–1952), an American who also specialised in cinemas, and had designed the Earls Court Exhibition Centre in the 1930s. Under Weedon's auspices, various additions were made to the South Works at Longbridge through the 1950s and 1960s. In 1955 the company's design department moved into a new Styling Studio behind 'The Kremlin', then in 1962 to a much larger Design Block, run by Alec Issigonis, the designer of the Mini (1959).[126] Storage space for finished cars was always a problem, and in 1961 a 3,300-space multi-storey car park (demolished) was built (see Chapter 7). CAB2 went up in 1961–3, and in 1965 a circular exhibition hall

(the 'Elephant House') was built as a 'showcase for export' to display vans and lorries; it survives, albeit in a heavily altered condition.

Despite the glass walls of CAB1, the advent of cheap electric lighting made the natural illumination of the workplace less vital and, following American precedent, a number of plants now relied entirely on artificial light and air conditioning. Ford, for example, built a multi-storey assembly plant at Dagenham in the late 1950s with an artificially lit assembly line on the ground floor and a flat roof.[127] Another multi-storey development was the so-called rocket range (demolished) built at Canley for the Triumph Herald (1958–9).[128] This stood three storeys high, with bodies and chassis combined on the top floor, assembly lines on the middle floor and stores in the basement. In assembly halls,

39   This factory at Ellesmere Port on the Mersey was built by Vauxhall in the years 1960–65, reflecting the expansion of the company in the post-war period. The Viva was made here in the 1960s, the Chevette in the 1970s and the Astra in the 1980s. Looking at the factory from the south-east, this shows block EC to front left, EA to front right and ED to rear left.

the overhead cranes with grabs, so familiar before the war, were gradually dispensed with, freeing up roofs for industrial services and catwalks. In their stead, items were moved around the workplace using a combination of conveyors and fork-lift trucks, with components stacked on pallets.

From the early 1960s further mergers took place. BMC acquired Jaguar (1966; Jaguar itself had bought Daimler in 1960), while Leyland Motors acquired Standard-Triumph (1961), Rover (1967) and BMC (1968), to form the British Leyland Motor Corporation (BLMC). Chrysler acquired control of Rootes between 1964 and 1967. This placed British Leyland and Chrysler at the top of the field, alongside Ford and Vauxhall. Despite foreign incursions, the home market was growing and car ownership had become a reasonable aspiration for working-class families: there were 3,525,858 cars in Britain by 1955, and 7,732,000 by 1965 (see Appendix). To capitalise on this growing market, several manufacturers wished to build new modern works in regions of established motor-car manufacture, where they were guaranteed a source of skilled labour, as well as access to suppliers and transport networks. As part of a general dispersal policy, however, the Government exerted pressure on companies to locate new factories in areas of high unemployment, generally in the North, far removed from traditional car-making centres. Thus Vauxhall built a factory at Ellesmere Port, Cheshire (1960–65; pl. 39); Ford built at Halewood on Merseyside (1960); Standard-Triumph built two factories at Speke (Speke No. 1, 1960–69, demolished; Speke No. 2, 1960–69), also on Merseyside; and Rootes built at Linwood in Scotland. Owing to their remoteness from the existing centres of the industry, these factories became heavily – and expensively – dependent on road haulage. More adventitiously, because they occupied greenfield sites they could adopt ideal layouts, built in planned phases. Ellesmere Port, for example, was designed with three interconnected blocks: EA, the machine shop, built in 1961; EC, a manufacturing block, built in 1963; and ED, a combined body press shop and car assembly building, completed in 1965. Some elements of these new-generation car factories had basements (usually stores or workshops) and mezzanines (usually paint shops), but they were mostly one storey high, with roof lights and metal-clad elevations.

40   General Motors' Millbrook Proving Ground in Bedfordshire (1969–70) is dominated by a circular high-speed track, 2 miles long with five lanes and a total width of 85 feet.

As well as building new plant, manufacturers updated and extended existing sites for the production of particular models. Rootes' former shadow factory at Ryton (see pl. 35), for example, was remodelled in 1967–8 for the Hillman Avenger. The assembly line was ¾ mile long and incorporated the so-called carousel and gate line systems.[129] The carousel was a continuous line for the manufacture of under-body assembly, while gate line involved the use of vertical jigs to assemble the sides of bodies. Automatic control was overseen by a closed-circuit television system.

Between the wars there was a tendency to minimise the testing of finished cars outside factories, while workshops were provided for the testing of component parts, such as engines. After the Second World War, however, extensive vehicle proving grounds, or test tracks, were created. Bearing little resemblance to early factory test tracks, these were more like race circuits, and had an impact on the landscape equivalent to miles of

motorway. The first was built by the Motor Industry Research Association (MIRA, founded 1946) at Lindley, near Nuneaton in Warwickshire, in 1951. Others – largely to preserve the secrecy surrounding prototypes and new production models – were constructed by the motor manufacturers themselves, starting with General Motors at Chaul End near Luton, in 1957,[130] then Ford, at Dunton in Essex, in 1969.[131] Dunton was a fully fledged automobile research centre, where both cars and components were subjected to thorough testing.[132] In 1969–70 General Motors created the Millbrook Proving Ground at Lidlington near Ampthill in Bedfordshire, for Vauxhall, Opel (its German sister company), and Bedford trucks (pl. 40). The layout was based on General Motors' proving ground at Milford in Michigan: it spread over 700 acres, had 13½ miles of roads, and cost £3.5 million to build.[133] Test facilities included a circular speed track, a hill circuit, a wind tunnel, troughs containing salt and fresh water, a variety of road surfaces, a safety engineering building

41 An aerial view of British Leyland's plant at Longbridge, photographed from the south-west in August 2005. This was specially built for the Metro in 1976–7, and demolished *circa* 2009.

where seats, seat belts and other components were tested, and an impact barrier. Not to be outdone, Rootes purchased Bruntingthorpe airfield in Leicestershire for use as a proving ground in 1972, and British Leyland acquired the former RAF bomber base at Gaydon, Warwickshire, in 1976. Extensive testing of components was still undertaken within factories: the new Metro, for example, received thorough checking in Longbridge's specially built Customer Validation Building (CVB) from 1980.[134]

From 1932 until 1955 Britain ranked as the largest car producer in Europe, and the second in the world, behind the U.S.A. But in 1956 the success of the Volkswagen Beetle enabled West Germany to overtake Britain. By 1970 Britain had slipped to sixth place globally, and in 1974 imports overtook exports for the first time since 1913. With the patriotic 'buy British' ethos of the post-war period evaporating, cars were now being imported from Japan, as well as from Europe. British factories struggled with low investment and productivity, while antagonistic relationships between management and the workforce triggered damaging strikes. The industry had suffered from strikes between the wars, but these were minor in comparison with the series of disputes that started with layoffs at BMC in 1956, and endured through subsequent decades. While desperation to retain labour saw a transfer of power from managers to shop stewards, unpopular models like the Morris Marina (1971) and Austin Allegro (1973) failed to impress customers. These systemic problems resulted in the contraction of the industry and the demise of many familiar British marques: Riley (1969), Singer (1970), Wolseley (1975), Humber (1976), Sunbeam (1976), Hillman (1978), Morris (1983), Triumph (1984) and Austin (1989).

In 1974 both Chrysler (i.e., the former Rootes) and BLMC approached Harold Wilson's Government for help. Chrysler received a loan, but sold its European interests to Peugeot in 1977, when the British operation became Peugeot-Talbot. BLMC, on the other hand, was nationalised as British Leyland (BL) in 1975, and renamed Rover Group in 1986. BL made efforts to introduce commercially appealing models, adding a new building to the West Works at Longbridge to build bodies for the new Mini Metro. This small car was launched in 1980 with a strongly patriotic advertising campaign. The Metro Building of 1976–7 (demolished; pl. 41), designed by the Harry Weedon Partnership, was a typical steel-framed shed with corrugated metal sides and ribbon windows. To reduce its visual impact in what was now a suburban area to the north-west of Longbridge, its height was lowered by excavating the ground by 14 metres, and the sides of the building were painted dark green. Excavated soil was used to create a landscaping of hills, planted with trees. In the first significant application of robotics in the U.K. industry, automated welding equipment with a value of £20 million was purchased from the German company KUKA. Robotic welding had been introduced by Nissan in Japan in

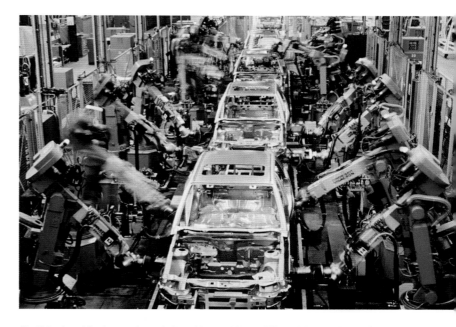

42 Robotic welding became increasingly sophisticated from 1980: this is Vauxhall's body-framing line at Ellesmere Port in 1992.

1970, and was already in use in progressive Continental factories. It involved computer-controlled mechanical arms that reached inside car bodies to weld elements together. Once completed, the Metro body was lowered onto its mechanical parts in CAB1, which was adapted for the purpose.

Expensive robotic welding gradually replaced traditional hand welding, controlled by jigs. When Vauxhall decided to manufacture the Astra at Ellesmere Port in 1981, it installed robotic welding for the first time. By 1992 Collins and Stratton were able to view three generations of robot welders at work in this factory, observing how they had become 'much lighter and more nimble' over the years (pl. 42).[135] The latest generation of high-tech equipment, such as computer-controlled Kobra 'pick and place' equipment and the tri-axis press, was adopted to carry, transfer and manipulate pressings, bodies and cars. The most significant Japanese innovation was probably the cradle type of assembly line, with cars 'stuffed up' into the suspended body: the reverse of the approach on the Metro line, where bodies had been dropped onto the mechanicals. It was also a Japanese idea to fit doors last of all, to ensure easy access to interiors.

With Japanese innovation showing the way forward for Western car makers, it seemed the logical next step when three new car factories were built in England in the 1980s and 1990s by Japanese manufacturers. These circumvented quotas set for imports by the EEC, and took advantage of incentives offered by the Conservative Government. All three were built on former airfield sites, where they could make use of existing runways to test cars. First of all, Nissan opened a new assembly plant for the

43 Toyota built a factory on a former airfield near Burnaston, Derbyshire, in 1990–92. This view from the west shows the original production facility: three linked blocks, from right to left, the body shop, the paint block and the chassis assembly line, with a plastics moulding shop to the rear. These have been greatly extended since 1992. The first car built here was the Carina E; the most recent is a hybrid version of the Auris, which switches between electric motors and a petrol engine.

Datsun on the former Sunderland airport site, near Washington New Town in Tyne and Wear, in 1986. Toyota then opened a factory of similar size at Burnaston, near Derby, in 1992 (pl. 43), and Honda built on the outskirts of Swindon in 1992. These factories were characterised by the great bulk of their linked blocks, their all-over metal cladding and their flat roofs.

Apart from the advent of the Japanese, the story of motor manufacture in England since the 1990s reads as a litany of factory closures, site clearance and redevelopment. Of course, the troubles of the motor-manufacturing sector can be traced back to the 1960s, when foreign imports began to attack the home market. Government interference in the growth strategies of major companies played its part, as did the production of unappealing cars, but it was unionisation that made it impossible for factories, run by huge conglomerates, to adapt quickly to new technologies and working conditions. As a reminder of past con-

flicts within the industry, purpose-built union offices from the 1960s and 1970s still stand on the edges of sites such as Dagenham. Regardless of this history, the rapidity of the destruction of the indigenous industry and its physical fabric since the 1990s has been startling. Coventry works closed and demolished in the late 1990s included the former Standard factory at Canley, Daimler's at Radford and Alvis's on Holyhead Road. Other parts of the country also suffered. Ford ceased producing cars in this country in 2002, though diesel engines continue to be made at Dagenham and transmissions at Halewood. Vauxhall stopped car manufacture at Luton in 2003: the surviving part of the factory, formerly Bedford Vehicles, now GM Manufacturing Ltd, produces vans. MG Rover – the last of Britain's high-volume producers – closed its Longbridge plant in 2005, and although the South Works was taken over by Nanjing Automotive, owned by the Chinese state, the rest of the site was cleared.

44   The cleared Hillman (south) and Humber (north) site, photographed from the south in 2010, has left a great (if temporary) gap on the east side of Coventry. All that remains of the Recreation Ground is a bowling green, showing up as a pocket-handkerchief of green.

In the new millennium – although car ownership in Britain continued to rise from 23,196,000 in 2000 to 27,018,000 in 2010 (see Appendix) – the closure and subsequent demolition of car factories in Coventry continued apace, with the erasure of Jaguar's Browns Lane factory (2008), Peugeot's Ryton factory (2006) and Peugeot's site at Stoke (2010), formerly occupied by Hillman and Humber (pl. 44). As seen at the start of this chapter, Coventry had witnessed the birth of motor manufacture in Britain and thrived on the back of the industry throughout the twentieth century, becoming the British equivalent of Detroit, Turin or Wolfsburg. Today the only vehicles produced in the town are black London cabs, made by London Taxis International (formerly Carbodies) on Holyhead Road. Coventry's components industry has also declined.[136] Just as watches once yielded to sewing machines, sewing machines to cycles, and cycles to cars, so cars have, in their turn, ceded the economy of

the city to a mixture of business and financial services, design and development, creative industries and logistics.

In Coventry, as elsewhere, the closure of car factories has upset the social and economic equilibrium of communities that were created three or more generations back for car workers. Employment opportunities have been lost, as have communal facilities, such as the cricket grounds, bowling greens and social clubs that manufacturers provided in patriarchal fashion for their workforce. The demolition of the factories themselves has removed prominent local landmarks, further eroding the community's sense of its distinctive identity and united purpose. A faint echo of what once existed is sometimes provided by the street names of new developments on former factory sites, drawn from well-known models or designers of cars. While many factories have succumbed to housing estates, others have become business or technology parks. In some instances, production sheds have been

45 Sir Nicholas Grimshaw & Partners' Rolls-Royce factory at Goodwood, West Sussex, opened in 2003 with green aspirations. The 35,000-square-metre roof is planted with sedum, and in 2006 attracted nesting skylarks.

retained as industrial units, while more flexible office blocks have been converted into apartments, hotels or even university accommodation.

Against this backdrop, it is notable that a handful of small new car factories have bucked the trend of the characterless, giant shed. Shortly after Rolls-Royce was bought by BMW and separated from Bentley, Sir Nicholas Grimshaw & Partners were commissioned to design a small L-shaped factory on the Goodwood estate in Sussex, where the racetrack could be used to test cars. Taking landscaping much further than the Metro building of 1977, this factory (2001–3) was built in a former gravel pit and landscaped by Grant Associates. It was partially sunk into the ground, screened by 400,000 trees and shrubs, and covered by a 'green' roof designed to harvest rainwater (pl. 45). Although only five cars were made here each day, this was car production as theatre: visitors outside the building could watch the assembly line through glazed walls, whilst inside production could be viewed from mezzanine walkways. Another interesting development took place at Gaydon in Warwickshire, where Aston Martin relocated in 2003. This new site included headquarters, showrooms, a studio and a production facility, designed by the Weedon Partnership but built by an Austrian company. With its 'drawbridge', moat and sheer curved sandstone elevation, it has invited comparisons with castles. It, too, makes concessions to the green movement, with intentions to plant a sedum roof. Finally, McLaren's Production Centre (2010; Foster + Partners)

– for high-performance sports cars – is located next door to its Technology Centre (1999–2004; Foster + Partners) in Woking, Surrey, to which it is connected by an underground walkway. One of the most recent facilities of its kind in the U.K., it is characterised by light, bright, uncluttered workspaces.

Surveying the British car manufacturing scene in 2010, factories with the largest outputs are Nissan (Sunderland), Jaguar Land Rover (Halewood, Castle Bromwich and Solihull),[137] Honda (Swindon), BMW/Mini (Cowley), Toyota (Burnaston), Vauxhall (Ellesmere Port) and MG (Longbridge). A number of other factories produce small quantities of specialist or luxury cars.[138] The next chapter in the story of British car manufacture may involve electric vehicles (EVs), which are eligible for Government subsidies. Nissan will manufacture the Leaf, its new EV, at Sunderland from 2013. If these do well, other plants may be set up to manufacture the accoutrements of EVs, such as batteries and charging points.

The heritage of British car manufacture is celebrated in numerous transport museums. Although it is commonly claimed that the world's first motor museum was created by Ford in 1929 at Dearborn, Michigan, a motor museum opened at 175–179 Oxford Street, London, as early as 1912, with a collection of forty vehicles amassed by Edmund Dangerfield, editor of *The Motor*.[139] This transferred to the Crystal Palace in March 1914.[140] Between the wars, private, municipal and national museums began to display cars, but today the principal motor museums are at

46   The National Motor Museum, Beaulieu (Leonard Manasseh & Partners, with Sir Hugh Casson to advise on the interior design, 1970–72). The square structure was given sawtooth façades with 'arrow slit' windows, and was covered by pitched roof lights in the form of an 'X'. Its green monorail and orange tubular steelwork add to its bustling atmosphere. This museum displays many of the historic products of British car factories.

Beaulieu, Hampshire, and Gaydon, Warwickshire. That at Beaulieu originated in 1952, when Lord Montagu began to show a small collection of historic vehicles in the hall of Beaulieu Abbey, in honour of his father. By 1956 this was named the Motor and Motor Cycle Museum (though generally known as the Montagu Motor Museum), and had grown to a collection of twenty-four cars and forty-one motorcycles, now displayed in large sheds in the garden. A more substantial building with space for 100 cars was erected in 1959. The museum continued to expand, and in 1965 the architects Leonard Manasseh & Partners were commissioned to create a much larger museum, named the National Motor Museum, within a carefully planned setting. This project is regarded as the partnership's masterpiece (pl. 46).[141] It included

woodland car parks and a restaurant. By the time it opened in 1972, several European manufacturers (such as Renault, Fiat and Daimler-Benz) had built their own museums. Their example, and that of Lord Montagu, persuaded British Leyland to create a museum of historic vehicles at Donington Park near Derby in 1976. Much of this collection transferred to Syon Park, Isleworth, in 1980, where it continued to grow as other manufacturers became involved. In 1993 it moved to a purpose-built museum, the Heritage Motor Centre, at the former RAF Gaydon.

At Beaulieu, Gaydon and many other sites, historic British vehicles are enjoyed by thousands of visitors each year, although in most cases the factories that produced them have vanished.

47   The interior of Argyll's showroom, 17 Newman Street, London, photographed *circa* 1905.

2: SELLING CARS

HAVING MADE CARS, MANUFACTURERS had to encourage the public to buy them, whether through the intermediary of dealerships, or through their own directly owned retail outlets, or a combination of both approaches. Architecturally, some of the most striking showrooms were undoubtedly the 'headquarter' – or, in modern parlance, 'flagship' – showrooms of the main manufacturers. At first, showrooms were positioned in urban centres, later relocating to suburban arterial routes and, more recently, to edge-of-town retail parks. Over time, many dealerships expanded to enjoy a regional or national presence. Whether large or small, they offered service – or 'aftercare' – facilities, and many also reconditioned cars traded in by customers for sale in their own used-car department. To this day, the standard – but by no means universal – layout for this type of business comprises a new-car showroom on the frontage and a repair garage to the rear, but there might also be a separate department for the sale of second-hand cars – nowadays generally on a forecourt – and provision for garaging, refuelling or hiring. Regardless of how they fit into the kaleidoscopic business model of the English garage, it is the treatment of sales areas for cars that provides the focus of this chapter.

Early Car Dealers and their Showrooms, 1896–1914

Initially, motor manufacturers did not have the resources to set up their own retail networks and had to rely on existing businesses to sell their cars for them. One might reasonably have expected carriage repositories to be the first established retail outlets to add cars to their stock. After all, they already specialised

in the supply of vehicles to private customers and possessed spacious premises in city-centre locations. But many such businesses also made carriages or sold horses, and these vested interests caused them to underestimate, or disregard, the motor car. Cycle dealers, perhaps because they were mechanically minded, were more eager to sell cars, though this usually necessitated relocation to larger shops. It is remarkable how many of the men who set themselves up as agents for motor-car manufacturers in the late 1890s had previous experience not just of selling, but also of making and racing bicycles. Whatever their origins, car dealers quickly acquired a reputation for untrustworthiness. Some made frequent court appearances – for dangerous driving, for speeding, for defrauding the public or, indeed, defrauding one another – thus tarnishing the reputation of their entire profession. Customers were particularly anxious about being swindled when conducting business with used-car salesmen.

Although horse and carriage repositories were too mired in tradition to welcome the motor car with open arms, their influence can be discerned in some car showrooms. Moreover, by the early 1900s their increasingly redundant premises – and those of city-centre coachbuilders – were being taken over by expanding motor dealerships. This was a significant shift. Since the late sixteenth century the horse and carriage had been favoured by the well-to-do for both local and – until the advent of the train – long-distance travel. By the time that motor cars began to challenge the traditional pattern of the horse and carriage trade, every large town in England possessed at least one substantial horse and carriage 'repository', 'depository', 'mart' or 'bazaar'. These had come into existence in the mid-eighteenth century, superseding long-established horse markets and fairs. Some specialised in horses, others in carriages, but most combined the

48   Aldridge's on St Martin's Lane, London, was rebuilt for street widening in 1843 (architect, Charles Hatchard) and extended in 1883 (architect, Spencer Chadwick). This view of 1883 shows the newly covered horse run and the carriage gallery, or 'loft'. The firm offered motor cars from 1907, but continued to sell horses here until 1926. It was demolished in 1955. From the *Illustrated London News*, 30 June 1883, p. 657.

two, and might also sell harnesses and saddles. Repositories did not have a monopoly: each town had its share of private horse dealers and livery stables, and it was always possible to order a new carriage direct from a coachbuilder, made to one's own specifications.

Though spacious, the premises of horse and carriage dealers were not ideal for the sale of motor cars. They included a ride, or horse run, often covered by a roof, where horses could be put through their paces before an audience of would-be buyers. Other requirements were extensive stabling, a large feed store, and a display space for carriages, often on galleries. Few carriage galleries survive, although plenty are documented, such as Mr Leader's 'spacious showshop, elegant gallery [and] showrooms' on Oxford Street in the 1820s.[1] Also in London, new carriage galleries were erected at Tattersall's in 1865 and at Aldridge's in 1883 (pl. 48).[2] Vehicles were transported from floor to floor by hoists or, less commonly, by ramps.

Some of the first car showrooms were set up in carriage repositories. In November 1896, coinciding with the introduction of the Locomotives on Highways Act, a new company, Ramsay's 'Horse, Carriage, Cycle & Auto Car Repository', was formed to build an auction house at 223 Hammersmith Road,

London, with showrooms on the frontage.[3] According to its prospectus, Ramsay's hoped to sell 150 horses a week, 20 vehicles and 20 sets of harness. Although nothing came of this project, in 1897 the established horse trader James Cooper built a 'Horse, Carriage, Cycle & Auto Car Repository' – adopting identical phrasing to Ramsay's – on Westgate Road, Newcastle upon Tyne, to a design by the local architect, T. Dawson.[4] From the outset, the second floor was devoted to the sale of carriages, cycles and 'auto cars' (pls 49 and 50). This sales floor assumed the traditional form of a top-lit carriage gallery, arranged around a light well. It could be reached either by carriage lift or by a narrow wooden ramp. The wrought-iron trusses of the roof spanned between 40 and 50 feet without intermediary supports, leaving a clear circuit of 140 feet with a wooden floor. Remnants of pipes reveal that this showroom was lit by gas, supplementing the natural light admitted through the skylights and windows. The design of the lower floors suggests that Cooper had no notion of how quickly the car would supersede the horse: here was the usual horse run, where auctions took place, overlooked by a two-tier viewing gallery, while the remainder of the space was taken up by stabling. By the 1920s, like so many other carriage repositories, this business had been transformed into a

49 The top floor of Cooper's Repository, Westgate Road, Newcastle upon Tyne. Dating from 1897, this is the earliest known purpose-built car showroom in England. The premises had become a garage by the 1920s. Since this photograph was taken in 2005, the building has been redeveloped as Cooper's Studios.

'motor mart'. Similarly, Aldridge's eventually became one of the main motor auction houses in central London.

But the most successful early car showrooms, rather than being tucked away on the upper-floor galleries of carriage repositories, were set up in conventional city-centre shops. Even before the Locomotives on Highways Act was passed in November

50 Cooper's second-floor auto-car showroom of 1897 was arranged around a light well – illuminating the galleried horse-auction room below – with a carriage lift to the rear. Based on Tyne and Wear Archives TWAS/T186/17382.

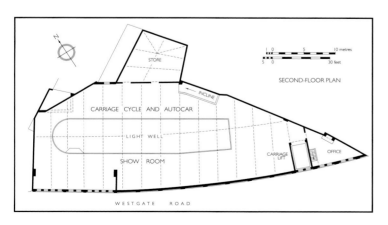

1896, enabling motoring to take off in England, several agents had opened for business, primarily in London and Birmingham. One of the most precocious was Rootes & Venables, who were offering the three-wheel 'Rootes Petrocar or Petroleum carriage' for £180 from their premises on Westminster Bridge Road, London, in November 1895.[5] Most dealers imported cars from France or Germany, sometimes modifying and rebranding them for British customers. Thus, in spring 1896, Leon L'Hollier of Bath Passage, Digbeth, Birmingham – a French-born perambulator manufacturer – was offering Benz cars imported from the French agent of the make, Emile Roger of Paris, and adapted by his partner, Edmund Gascoine, the manager of an ironworks in Maidstone, Kent.[6] In June 1896 the cycle dealer Charles Friswell of Holborn Viaduct, London – a street where cycle shops, such as Humber, Swift, Singer and Triumph, clustered – restructured his business and began to sell imported Peugeot cars.[7] Around the same time a former tea trader, Henry Hewetson, set himself up at 59 Mark Lane, London, as the agent for the Acme or Arnold Motor Carriage, a vehicle based on the Benz and 'made' in East Peckham in Kent, selling at around £125.[8] Harry J. Lawson of the British Motor Syndicate (see Chapter 1) kept premises at 366 Euston Road, London, where

51 No. 124 Holland Park Avenue (in the background) was occupied successively in the 1890s by a cycle shop, the Automobile Association and – as shown here – Friswell Ltd. The cars are Peugeots.

52 Inspecting cars in the yard of Friswell's Great Motor Repository at 1 Albany Street, off Euston Road in London. In the early 1900s this was one of the largest car showrooms in the capital.

'there could be found motor vehicles of all kinds'.[9] Another man who entered the business prior to November 1896 was Julius Harvey, an engineer with works at 11 Queen Victoria Street, London: he began selling cars in July 1896,[10] and supplied the first motor vans for the delivery of the Royal Mail in winter 1897.[11] After November 1896 car showrooms opened with increasing frequency.

Typical of the earliest car showrooms was a shop at 1 Prince's Road/124 Holland Park Avenue in London. In June 1898 the Automobile Association – not to be confused with the later organisation of the same name – was established here as the London agency for several French and German marques.[12] By February 1900 the premises had expanded into mews at the rear, becoming a parking and repair garage, with a dressing room and reading room, as well as a showroom.[13] In March 1901 it was announced that Charles Friswell was to open at this site (pl. 51).[14] Friswell remained in Holland Park for a very brief time, moving on to set up his 'Great Motor Repository' in much larger premises at 1 Albany Street, just off Euston Road, around 1903 (pls 52 and 60).[15] This was a car showroom on a hitherto unimagined scale, occupying a building that seems to have been erected around 1863 as a furniture pantechnicon and auction house. Meanwhile, by 1901 a former associate of the Automobile Association, Daniel Weigel, had opened his own agency, the British Automobile Commercial Syndicate Ltd, at 97–98 Long Acre in Covent Garden, in the former premises of the coachmaker Henry J. Hall & Sons.[16] Within a decade, car dealers would colonise Long Acre, the one-time bastion of London's carriage trade (pl. 53; compare pl. 21).

A number of car dealers, like Friswell, quickly made their mark in this new line of business. Around 1899 – at the instigation of his manager Selwyn F. Edge (an Australian cyclist who later became a racing driver) – Harvey Du Cros junior, the chairman of the Dunlop Pneumatic Tyre Co., set up the Motor Vehicle Co.[17] This was the sole British agent for the French manufacturers Gladiator and Clement-Panhard, selling their cars from Dunlop's premises at 14 Regent Street. In 1900 Edge obtained the exclusive agency for Napier cars – then manufactured in Lambeth – with financial backing from Du Cros. Meanwhile, other dealers were licensed by Du Cros to sell both Panhard and Mercedes cars. Charles S. Rolls, for example, began to sell French-made cars, including Panhards, under licence from Du Cros, on Brook Street, Mayfair, in 1903, a year before he met the engineer Henry Royce and Rolls-Royce was formed. Another important figure was Percival Perry, who began his long career by working for Harry J. Lawson, then set up an agency selling Ford cars on Long Acre in 1904.[18] In Oxford, William Morris started out as a bicycle manufacturer, not opening his first car showroom until 1909, then selling various marques before moving into car manufacture in 1912. From this point, the main London dealer for Morris was Gordon Stewart (the head of Stewart & Ardern), who ordered 400 Morris cars before any were actually built, and sold them from his small showroom at 18 Woodstock Street, off Oxford Street.[19] By this time department stores were selling cars. One of the first was Harrods, which opened a galleried showroom in a former tabernacle in Lancelot Place, Knightsbridge, in 1902.[20] Gamages, Barkers, the Civil Service Co-op and many other London department stores followed this lead. In 1911 Harrods opened new showrooms, and two years later *The Motor* reported that Selfridges had doubled the size of the motoring department on its lower ground floor.[21]

Dealers generally took a deposit from the customer and, having taken a cut, paid this to the manufacturer in advance of delivery, at which time the remainder was paid in cash. Agents could receive as much as 9 per cent of the value of a car. The deposit system helped to fund car manufacture and development.[22] But manufacturers exerted control over their agents through the Motor Traders' Association, formed in 1910. Members of the Association effectively discouraged retail price-cutting by boycotting offending agents.[23] Sometimes, manufacturers chose to sell direct from their own retail premises, appointing a manager to run the showroom. One of the first to do this was Daimler, which had opened a showroom at 219–229 Shaftesbury Avenue, London, around 1898. The French manufacturer Mors opened a showroom and garage at 55–59 Shaftesbury Avenue, a traditional terraced building with an ornate shopfront, in 1905.[24] In 1909 these relatively capacious premises were taken over by Henry Ford as his first U.K. showroom, managed by the former Ford agent, Percival Perry.[25] Rover had acquired premises on New Oxford Street in 1907, at which time its Coventry factory was producing thirty-four cars per week.[26] As well as stocking vehicles ready to be test-driven in the London traffic, Rover displayed cylinders, axles, gear boxes and a stripped chassis, in order to impress customers with the inner workings of its cars. Other manufacturers' showrooms in London included Argyll on Newman Street (1905; see pl. 47), Lanchester on Oxford Street (*circa* 1905), Iris on Bird Street (1907)[27] and Ariel on New Bond Street (1907).[28]

Very few showroom frontages or interiors survive from this period, and it is only through historical accounts and photographs that we can glean some idea of their appearance. Most were simply adapted shops, with one or two cars displayed behind a plate-glass window. Since few existing shopfronts had sufficiently low sills, a new one usually had to be installed. Inside, these showrooms were generally long, narrow spaces, which invited the display of cars parallel to party walls, to either side (or, sometimes, just to one side) of an aisle. Although contemporary cars were quite light and narrow, this was far from ideal since customers could not walk around the vehicles to inspect them from all angles. Turntables were occasionally fitted to aid manoeuvring in very crowded showrooms. If possible, cars were displayed on more than one floor, transported vertically by hydraulic lift. Photographs reveal that these were seldom protected by anything more substantial than a simple metal balustrade, and took up relatively little floor space.[29] Cars needed to be driven or pushed in and out of showrooms on a regular basis, usually through a back entrance, but sometimes through display windows that could open like doors. Differentials

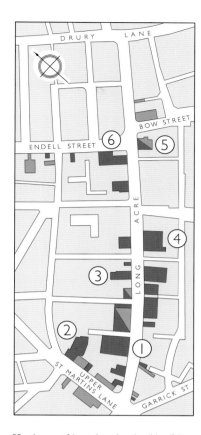

53 A map of Long Acre, London, identifying coachbuilders and car dealers *circa* 1916 (compare pl. 21). This illustrates the degree to which motor cars had superseded the carriage trade. Buildings shown as green/red accommodated businesses relating to motor cars *and* to the horse and carriage trade.

between floor and pavement levels introduced problems that were dealt with in various ways. Portable wooden boards offered a temporary solution. Sometimes a permanent slope was built, but, ingeniously, at De Dietrich's new Regent Street showroom of 1908, the floor could be tilted by means of a screw mechanism in the basement.[30] An account of Burgess & Harvey's Oxford Street showroom in *The Motor* in 1908 suggests that the rear entrance was at mid-floor level: 'the floor is sloped upwards to make a run-way for cars, and a part of the floor can be lifted bodily, so as to open up a similar sloped run-way that leads to the basement, the latter being detachable and only fitted in place when a car is being run in or out from the basement'.[31] Two years later, cars could exit Keele's showroom on New Bond Street via a slope with a 1 : 8 gradient, considered steep enough to test a car.

Efficient lighting was difficult to achieve, and electricity was supplemented by daylight whenever possible. Since the rear sections of showrooms were often just one storey high, they could be lit from above, through skylights or roof lanterns. The showroom of the Benz dealer Henry Hewetson, at 6–8 Dean Street, Soho, was particularly bright and spacious, illuminated by rows

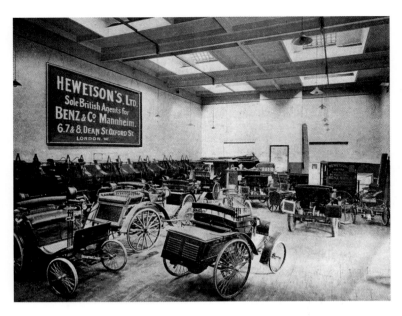

54 Henry Hewetson's Benz showroom – located to the rear of the Soho Bazaar, at 6–8 Dean Street, London – in April 1900.

55 Austin's Oxford Street Club Room in 1912.

of roof lights (pl. 54).[32] In 1900, to make as much use of the available space as possible, and to prevent tyres from developing a 'flat', most of Hewetson's machines were upended against the perimeter walls and fitted with wheels and chains only when required by a potential customer. Indeed, dealers frequently had to complete the assembly of vehicles themselves, after taking delivery from manufacturers.

Although the story of the first car showrooms is largely one of adaptation rather than new build, interiors were often designed by established retail architects or professional shopfitters. The target customer group was wealthy and male, despite the condescending notion, frequently expressed in the trade literature, that it was usually the woman – as ever associated with conspicuous consumption – who chose the car. Not surprisingly, showrooms had the air of a gentleman's club: centrally heated, often panelled, and equipped with comfortable leather sofas and armchairs. In 1905 the Argyll showrooms at 17 Newman Street, just off Oxford Street, were fitted out with elegant furniture, potted plants, chandeliers and carpeted gangways (see pl. 47).[33] Selwyn F. Edge opened a showroom at 14 New Burlington Street in 1907, selling Napier cars, which then led the British luxury car market.[34] Edge's premises – recalled with nostalgia in 1927 as 'the most elegant in Europe'[35] – had an electric lift and an impressive staircase leading up to a first-floor showroom where cars were positioned on a chequered floor of green and white marble, lit by a large roof lantern.

In the years preceding the First World War it is evident that the Britishness of certain marques was reflected in showroom design, appealing to customers' innate patriotism. In 1912, for example, Rolls-Royce's showrooms at 15 Conduit Street, London (which Rolls had occupied since 1905), were redecorated by the architect Edward Keynes Purchase in a style considered 'thoroughly British', that of the late seventeenth century, complete with carved English oak panelling.[36] In the same year Herbert Austin took over the former premises of the coachbuilders Holland & Holland, on Oxford Street, as a fully fledged headquarters with a Neo-Jacobean club room and library (pl. 55) for Austin owners and an Adam-style showroom.[37]

Although some early garages – for example, The London Motor Garage Co. of 1902–3 on Wardour Street, London (see Chapter 6) – had a small motor accessories shop at the front, new buildings that were erected primarily for the sale of cars did not appear in significant numbers until around 1906.[38] One of the first purpose-built car showrooms in London was created in that year after fire destroyed 132 Long Acre, a building that had accommodated the Ariel Motor Co. and Messrs Slatters, coachbuilders. Its replacement (pl. 56) housed Du Cros-Mercedes (later Milnes-Daimler-Mercedes) on the ground floor and the works of the coachbuilder Alfred F. Mulliner on the upper floors.[39] The showroom had a two-tier arcaded frontage clad in glazed tiles. Notably larger than those contrived in older buildings, it took up the entire ground floor and had to be divided by a party wall to meet fire regulations. Cars were taken in from a side street to an hydraulic lift: they could then be transported to the desired floor, or run through to the showroom, where several turntables helped manoeuvre them into position.

New fireproof showroom and office buildings for car sales now began to appear in major cities throughout England, some-

56 Nos. 132–142 Long Acre, photographed in 1923. With fire acting as a catalyst, this was one of the earliest purpose-built car showrooms in London, dating from 1905–6. The British Motor Trading Corporation was a short-lived company controlling the production of Bean, Swift and Vulcan vehicles.

57 The imposing concave façade of Minerva House (1912–13) – built close to Tottenham Court Road, London, for the Belgian motor manufacturer – was topped by a statue of the eponymous goddess. This later became Dex House.

O. Type) in John Bright Street was designed in a precocious Neo-Georgian style for George Heath Motors, while Daimler erected premises (1911; A. Gilbey Latham) in Paradise Street.[41] In Coventry, the centre of motor-car manufacture, Rover built a three-storey showroom in Warwick Row in 1911.[42] Seaside towns were advanced in the provision of showrooms, with both of Caffyn's Eastbourne premises, built in 1906 and 1911, including lower-floor showrooms (see pl. 118). London, however, remained at the heart of the retail trade. Here, Minerva, the Belgian manufacturer, erected a large building designed by George Vernon on North Crescent, near Tottenham Court Road, in 1912–13 (pl. 57), while the French firm Darracq built a showroom on New Bond Street in 1914 (demolished; pl. 58). Standing in the heart of the West End shopping district, this was designed by Robert Frank Atkinson, an architect who specialised in commercial architecture, including Selfridges department store on Oxford Street and the Adelphi Hotel in Liverpool.

By 1913, realising that architectural interest in this new building type was gathering pace, *Building News* ran a competition to design 'an automobile show-house'. This produced rather indifferent results, but it did expose the prevailing influence of mainstream retail architecture.[43] This was evident in Darracq's, and also in the showroom of the Olympia Garage, built in Newcastle upon Tyne in 1910 for Rossleigh's, a company named after its proprietors, Messrs Ross and Sleigh, who had started out around 1890, somewhat predictably, as cycle dealers. The Olympia was designed by the local architects Marshall & Tweedy, established designers of retail buildings – including Fenwick's department store – who were appointed to the job following a competition.[44] Their building comprised a very wide central bay, surmounted by a long, low arch and flanked by square turrets containing vehicle entrances. The plate-glass display windows of the central showroom dominated the design, and incorporated a deep lobby entrance to entice window-shoppers: a form of shopfront particularly popular at this time with retailers such as drapers, who were just discovering the benefits of letting customers peruse extensive window displays that funnelled them into the shop.[45] This modern retail method was now applied to the purchase of cars.

Most of the purpose-built showrooms hitherto mentioned occupied the ground floors of multi-storey, multi-functional buildings. The Olympia was different, since the two-storey showroom took up the full height of the frontage: the garage lay to the rear. Single-storey showrooms were also being erected, a notable early example being that of the coachbuilder and motor agent John Clayton Beadle in Dartford, Kent. This was designed by Robert Frank Atkinson in 1910, and represents an approach that would become increasingly popular as the twentieth century progressed (pl. 59). It obviated the need for hoists or expensive car lifts.

times associated with workshops, sometimes with office headquarters, and occasionally with both. In Manchester, J. Cockshoot & Co. – an established carriage builder, now turning out motor bodies as well as undertaking the agency of several marques – erected splendid new workshops and offices, including two floors of showrooms with plate-glass display windows, in 1906.[40] In Birmingham, Borough Buildings (1909–10; Marcus

58 This purpose-built car showroom at 150 New Bond Street, London, was designed by the prominent retail architect Robert Frank Atkinson – the architect of Selfridges – for the French firm Darracq in 1914. Two pairs of headlamps may be seen in the first-floor windows.

Discount Motor Car Co. was based at 145–147 Euston Road, but after 1903 he traded as Dunhill's Motorities (slogan: 'everything but the motor') from 359–361 Euston Road (see pl. 60).[48] As well as this wholesale depot, the firm opened two West End retail outlets on Conduit Street, in 1902 and 1905. These shops sold clothing and accessories to chauffeurs and their employers, with women 'automobilists' catered for at No. 2 and men at No. 5. The existence of a shop dedicated to female motorists might suggest that they were more numerous at this time than social historians believe, but this more probably reflects the necessity of being properly attired and equipped, even as a passenger. In 1905 Dunhill set up branch establishments in Edinburgh and Manchester, and in the new Argyll showrooms on Newman Street. One of Dunhill's inventions, however, patented in 1904, caused his business career to change direction: this was a smoking pipe fitted with a windshield that enabled it to be puffed in an open car without sparks flying out. Following the success of this pipe, Dunhill developed a national chain of tobacconists' shops, whilst maintaining his 'Motorities'. This spawned many competitors. London's department stores prided themselves on their motoring accessory departments, as did certain car showrooms, such as Burgess & Harvey's at 463 Oxford Street and Warwick Wright's on Marylebone High Street.[49]

Dunhill was not alone on Euston Road (see pl. 60), since this area attracted second-hand car dealers as well as accessory manufacturers. These businesses often occupied larger premises than West End car showrooms, and held greater stocks. In 1905, for example, the Grand Maison d'Automobiles (the Motor House) supplemented its original building at 366–368 Euston Road with new premises at Nos. 314–316, which were thoroughly remod-

The provision of a works department, with a large stock of spare parts, was expected of dealerships from the outset, and in later years this 'aftercare' side of the business would carry traders through periods when sales of new cars were slack. Even if this were co-located with the showroom, however, the Edwardian car salesman would not have sullied himself with the repair and maintenance of cars. Despite his dodgy reputation, considerable refinement was expected of him. He was assumed to be a 'superior tradesman . . . dealing with a varied class of people, comprising the aristocracy, the upper classes, and certain sections of the middle class'; he should have 'a gentlemanly bearing combined with the suavity and aplomb of a Bond Street or Oxford Street shopwalker'.[46] Often, he would have been trained to sell motoring accessories – coats, goggles, baskets, trunks, waterproof rugs, foot muffs – as well as cars. This was a significant branch of the trade. One of the principal accessories dealers was Alfred J. Dunhill, who had inherited a business manufacturing products such as shop blinds, tents and horse clothing.[47] From 1900 his

59 John Clayton Beadle's showrooms in Dartford, Kent, were designed by Robert Frank Atkinson in 1910; they are now a pub.

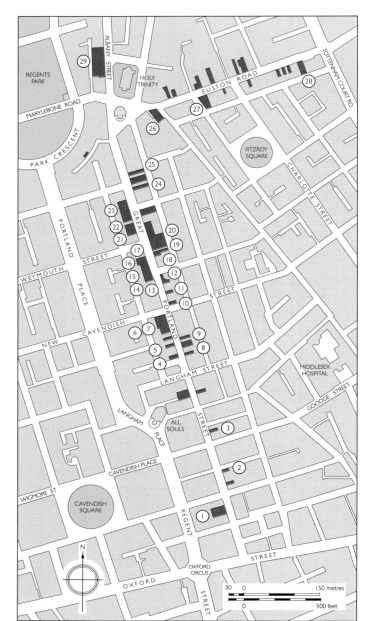

60 This map shows the extent to which the motor trade had infiltrated Great Portland Street and Euston Road in London by 1914.

elled.[50] Large cars were displayed at Nos. 314–316, small cars at Nos. 366–368: together, these buildings could show 300 cars. The market in second-hand cars was already thriving.

In the years leading up to the First World War, London's Great Portland Street (pls 60 and 61) was transformed into 'a veritable motordom', and in 1914 a Great Portland Street Motor Club was set up over Bayard's new showroom at Nos. 155–157.[51] A decade earlier, this had been a typically mixed metropolitan thoroughfare, although the carriage-builder W. & F. Thorn had been based at No. 19 since 1824; Righton & Cundy, cycle makers, occupied No. 161 by 1895; and Mrs Rhoda Mebes & Co. had opened as a bicycle maker at No. 214 by 1899.[52] In the early twentieth

century Great Portland Street – and especially the northern end of the street – attracted a great variety of car-related businesses, perhaps seeking proximity to the great motor emporiums of Friswell's, Mann Egerton and the Car Mart on nearby Euston Road. The diverse businesses on the street included Trevor's motor school (No. 162), The Klaxon Co. (selling horns, at No. 41),[53] S. Smith & Sons (at 'Speedometer House', Nos. 179–185)[54] and the Warland Dual Rim Co. (at No. 111).[55] Much of Great Portland Street was rebuilt in the early twentieth century, often by or for motor firms, providing spacious modern showrooms. One of the first of the street's new motor palaces was Thorn's, which was rebuilt after a fire in 1907–8 (pl. 61).[56] The company

61 W. F. Thorn's Great Portland Street showrooms were designed by Frank M. Elgood and built in 1907–8. This business made the transition from horse-drawn carriages to motor cars around this date; both were sold from these premises.

– as with Cockshoot's of Manchester, coachbuilders who had diversified into motor body-building and acted as agents for many makes of car – appointed Frank M. Elgood as its architect.[57] The main show spaces on the two lower floors were visually connected, not just by a two-tier shopfront, but also by a sweeping central staircase that led up to a gallery surrounded by a sinuous balustrade, reminiscent of the elegant bazaars of the previous century or contemporary Oxford Street department stores – in fact, not unlike Cockshoot's Manchester premises, completed a year earlier. Every floor, except the attic, was reputedly 'designed for exhibiting purposes'. At the time of opening, forty 'horse vehicles' were displayed on the first floor, but these were quickly phased out. At the outbreak of the First World War one of the newest and most modern showrooms on Great Portland Street, at Nos. 117–123, on the corner of New Cavendish Street (see pl. 60), had been designed by H. O. Cresswell, with the lower two floors devoted to the showrooms and offices of the Studebaker Motor Car Co., which shipped its vehicles from the U.S.A. and Canada.[58] Much of the trade enjoyed by Great Portland Street, naturally, fell away during the war, and the street struggled to maintain its predominance through the 1920s. Today, this thoroughfare retains only fragmentary reminders of its motoring heyday.

Selling Cars Between the Wars

Between 1918 and 1939 cheaper cars came on the market, average incomes grew, and car ownership expanded from around 100,000 to 2 million (see Appendix). Dealers had to broaden their appeal and extend their geographic reach to attract first-time owners from the suburban middle classes. To do this they set up showrooms – and service depots – alongside new bypasses and suburban arterial routes. By 1939 many working men also had cars, but these were usually bought second-hand. Women still experienced bias from dealers, who often failed to treat them seriously as motorists, for example, by refusing to authorise hire-purchase agreements.[59] Showrooms were still aimed, squarely, at prosperous men.

Immediately after the war, top-end car dealers congregated close to London's Clubland. Bond Street, where Humber opened in 1922 and Rover in 1924, was a favourite spot: *Car and Golf* magazine even suggested that it could become the centre of the London car trade.[60] Architecturally, the most impressive new venture was Wolseley's splendid headquarters showroom on nearby Piccadilly (1922; W. Curtis Green). Green was awarded a RIBA bronze medal for the street frontage, with giant Corinthian columns framing plain cast-iron panelling. Below

62 The luxurious interior of Wolseley's Piccadilly showroom, which later became a bank and is now a restaurant. From *Motor Owner*, June 1923.

this, the principal show windows were framed by three solid arches fitted with decorative wrought-iron grilles at tympanum level. The central arch contained the main entrance. This opened into a vast interior, 25 feet high, which was divided into nine square bays defined by Doric columns (set at 20ft spacings and coated in red lacquer) carrying arches (pl. 62). The inspiration was reportedly Brunelleschi's church of Santo Spirito in Florence, and cars were certainly displayed reverentially. Within each bay, a single car stood on the marble floor, under a dome. According to the *Architects' Journal*: 'it is just a noble showroom, where the cars look their best and where the soundness of the building and the refinement of the detail convey a subtle suggestion of the quality of the wares'.[61]

The reconstruction of Devonshire House, opposite the Ritz Hotel on Piccadilly, as a block of flats (1925–6, by the American architect Thomas Hastings, with Professor C. H. Reilly) provided a prestigious new home for several established dealers. Within months of one another, Rootes (by now the country's largest car distributor) and Citroën opened new showrooms here.[62] The monumental interior of the Citroën showroom involved an ambitious remodelling of the ground and mezzanine floors of the building, supposedly based on the Tomb of Napoleon at the Hôtel des Invalides, Paris, with a balustraded balcony and central vault. The car lift was inconspicuous: 'when not in operation, no lift can be seen, but only two guides'.[63] The platform rose from its resting place on the lower floor and fastened itself by grappling hooks to the underside of a movable section of the ground floor, 'with which it becomes one'. After descending with a car, it rose again automatically, replacing the flooring in its proper position, before returning to the lower floor. This showroom had lettering lit by tubular electric lighting ('voltalux'), something that would quickly become commonplace. Two years after opening on Piccadilly, Citroën erected the extremely modern Garage Marbeuf (1928–9; Laprade & Bazin) off the Champs-Elysées in Paris, which, despite being one of the best-known car showrooms in the world, was demolished in 1952.[64] Here, a gigantic plate-glass display window (measuring 68ft by 62ft) revealed cars on five stacked balconies, as if set on shelves in a Brobdingnagian glass cabinet. Flanking this, the lateral bays of the façade were treated with thin bands of windows in the moderne style that was just beginning to impinge on English commercial architecture.

The second-hand trade was active all over London, but still clustered around Euston Road. It spread parallel to Warren Street and down Tottenham Court Road, where Smallman Brothers' Motor Auction Mart was built in 1921.[65] Warren Street became something of a street market for cars, largely because so many car-related businesses on Euston Road backed onto it.[66] One of the biggest businesses, dealing in new as well as second-hand cars, was the Car Mart. This had been established in 1908 on Euston Road, expanded rapidly after 1918, and in 1923–4 acquired and altered one of the most imposing showrooms in London, on the corner of Park Lane and Piccadilly (pl. 63).[67] In 1927 the company acquired Macy's Garage on Balderton Street (see Chapter 6), and in 1933 opened 'Europe's largest showrooms', Stanhope House, at 320 Euston Road.[68] Its neighbour, Henly's, started around 1918, occupying a series of ever-larger showrooms on Great Portland Street, with a service station in nearby Foley Street. In 1927 the company joined Rootes and Citroën in Devonshire House, and a year later opened Henly House at 385–387 Euston Road, which laid a new claim to be the 'largest showroom in Europe'.[69] Thorn's was still going strong and in 1929 it was announced that they would extend their Great Portland Street premises by building a 'roof-garden showroom . . . a kind of Crystal Palace', where cars could be displayed under ideal light conditions.[70] This was an unusual solution to

down Neo-Classicism, often faced in off-white Portland or Empire (i.e., reconstituted) stone. Typical examples were T. D. Morison's Alfa Romeo showroom at 1 Baker Street, London (1927; Gordon Jeeves),[74] and Stewart & Ardern's in Acton (1929; Arthur H. Davis & Partners).[75]

Eye-catching displays became increasingly important. The façade of William Vincent's garage in Reading, Berkshire (1926–8), with its tall, arched central entrance, appeared (or, according to the *Architect and Building News*, pretended) to stand one storey high, but, in fact, screened two levels, the floor being disguised by strips dividing the plate-glass display windows.[76] Inside, the upper floor was treated as a gallery, where second-hand cars were displayed. One novel feature of this showroom was the installation in the display windows of electric turntables, each capable of taking four cars, which were floodlit at night. Other showrooms adopted similar tactics. In summer 1929, during 'Citroën Week', R. Cripps & Co. on Parliament Street, Nottingham, displayed a six-cylinder Citroën car that revolved on its axis, and was explained to customers by means of an electrically operated gramophone, positioned close to the chassis.[77] Cox's new Leeds showroom opened in 1929 with a display of a

the perennial problem of lighting showrooms. In general, between the wars there was a strong tendency to locate used-car departments on upper floors. This was the arrangement at, for example, the Morris Garage in Oxford of 1932 (see pl. 226), where the top floor was of light steel construction.

In the mid-1920s showrooms indulged in a short-lived fashion for mock timber framing, reflecting the contemporary fondness for motoring jaunts into the English countryside. Easton's showrooms of 1924 at 5 Warwick Street, London, sold American marques yet adopted a half-timbered style, with walls 'embellished with scenes, the work of a prominent artist', who remained unnamed, despite his or her prominence.[71] This Old English style was adopted for Skurray's Ford dealership in Swindon (1927; H. Fisher), on a site that had once been occupied by a horse repository.[72] It reappeared at Cox's on Magdalene Street, Cambridge (1925; pl. 64), and at English Motor Agencies of Southsea, Hampshire.[73] Nationally, however, the favoured architectural style for new showrooms in the mid- to late 1920s was a neutral, pared-

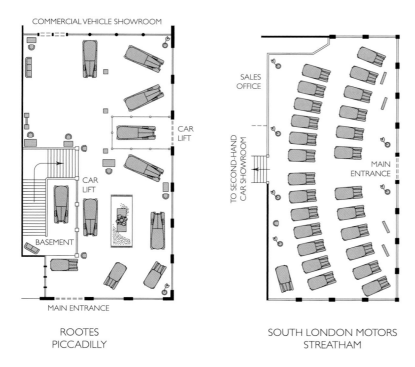

COMMERCIAL VEHICLE SHOWROOM

CAR LIFT

CAR LIFT

BASEMENT

MAIN ENTRANCE

ROOTES
PICCADILLY

SALES OFFICE

TO SECOND-HAND CAR SHOWROOM

MAIN ENTRANCE

SOUTH LONDON MOTORS
STREATHAM

65a and b   Two contrasting approaches to the layout of car showrooms. In the first, Rootes' palatial showroom on Piccadilly, cars were positioned at different angles around a central table that stood on a Persian carpet and was adorned with a vase of flowers. In the second, the Streatham showroom of South London Motors, cars were arranged in serried ranks facing the windows. Salesmen hovered in the background until a customer appeared.

working model of an Essex Challenger, showing all the parts in motion.[78] Much thought was also devoted to the layout of cars in the main showroom, beyond the window display. Space permitting, cars were grouped as attractively as possible, in a way that allowed the customer to view them from different angles. In Rootes' tasteful showroom on Piccadilly (pl. 65a), cars were disposed artistically around a table, revealing different aspects of the models on show and encouraging browsing, whilst at South London Motors on Streatham High Road, the entire showroom (1930–31; pl. 65b) was arranged with regimented symmetry as an enormous window display.[79] Window displays were at their most imaginative at Christmas and New Year, when synthetic snow was used to create tableaux, perhaps in an attempt to drum up trade at a quiet time of year. Most car sales were clinched in the late spring or after the Motor Show in October and November, and dealers were constantly looking for ways to diversify. Around 1930 some followed the lead of the big department stores by trying to sell light aircraft: the Hygienic Garage in Leeds, for example, secured the dealership for the Blackburn Bluebird IV and fully expected to reap a 'golden harvest', like that enjoyed by pioneers in the motor trade before the First World War.[80] Others, such as Coppen Allen of 205–207 Great Portland Street, sold motor boats.[81]

Shopfitters like Frederick Sage,[82] Parnall & Sons and E. Pollard & Co. became increasingly involved in designing car showrooms. Cars were now generally brought in and out through the front windows, and so it was important that these could be opened quickly and easily. By the early 1920s folding doors with metal frames, manufactured by firms such as Crittall's and Hope's, became common. In 1927 Parnall's advertised a new type of plate-glass window that dropped out of sight into a slot below ground, rather than swinging in or out.[83] This was used at the premises of Coppen Allen.[84] The showroom opened at Easter 1927, but a few months later was taken over by William Whiteley's, which had come under the control of Selfridges.[85] Whiteley's object was 'to introduce to the public their new system of car purchase on the easy-hire system without any initial deposit'.

Hire purchase ('HP'), though commonplace in America, was offered by relatively few British car dealers before the 1920s.[86] A number of finance houses, such as the United Dominions Trust, specialised in this business after the First World War. In 1921 a group of British dealers – wishing to keep the benefits of such schemes within the trade – formed the United Motor Finance Company at 201 Great Portland Street, to finance sales by instalments under the HP system. Considering themselves pioneers, they financed manufacturers and dealers who, in turn, financed their customers. Most of the vehicles bought with their assistance were made by Ford, Morris or Austin. In 1924 Ford extended its own 'Weekly Purchase Plan' to the U.K.,[87] while the Austin Finance Co. was formed in 1928.[88] Despite the take-up of such schemes, HP was distrusted by many British dealers and was abhorred by the middle and upper classes. Surprisingly, the availability of financing agreements was seldom deployed as an advertising tool to encourage the less wealthy sectors of society to buy cars.[89] In fact, HP carried such stigma that people preferred to travel to London to buy impersonally, rather than risk it becoming known locally that they had acquired their car on the never-never. Consequently, in 1938, 34 per cent of cars sold in London were bought by people living outside the area.[90] The sensitivities surrounding HP explain the appearance, from the 1920s through to the 1960s, of small private offices opening off showrooms, where paperwork could be completed with the utmost discretion.

Ford, with its economical assembly-line production (see Chapter 1), was largely responsible for extending motoring to the middle class. The company was also responsible for taking showroom design to new theatrical levels, in April 1930, with the opening of its new 'London Exhibition Salon and head offices' at 88 Regent Street, close to Piccadilly Circus (pl. 66).[91] Ford's long-standing architects, Charles Heathcote & Son, collaborated with Messrs G. & A. Brown of Hammersmith on the shopfront and main showroom; the chairman, Sir Percival Perry,

66   The highly decorative interior of Ford's new showroom on Regent Street, London, in 1930.

vated the problem of reflections from across the street or from passing traffic. They permitted a clear view into the main Ford showroom, which was bathed in different colours of light at night. This type of window, though expensive and initially incapable of opening to let vehicles in and out, was taken up by other dealers, for example by A. R. Atkey on Parliament Street in Nottingham[93] and Woodcote Motors in Epsom, Surrey.[94] It was only in the mid-1930s that Pollard's developed a non-reflective window that could be opened. The curved glass was held within a deep box frame that was hinged to open inwards and moved on rollers. An example was installed at Armstrong Siddeley's showroom at 10 Old Bond Street.[95] This introduced a new problem, however, since the cars on display had to be set well back from the glass to enable the window to swing open.

In 1929 *The Builder* bemoaned the fact that the motor industry had hitherto made so few demands on the services of architects, suggesting that a time may come 'when . . . all firms will combine to show their products in one fine central building'.[96] In fact, large exhibition halls specifically for motor vehicles had already been built on the Continent: for example, in Milan in 1923,[97] and in Paris in 1925.[98] There was no equivalent in Britain, where the largest annual displays were held at Olympia, which was a multi-purpose exhibition hall. A comparable scheme, however, was proposed in 1932 for a futuristic 'Motor Centre' that would occupy an (unidentified) island site in central London (pl. 67). This was conceived by William Glass, originator of Glass's Guides (the bible of the used-car trade to this day), who was credited with introducing the notion of used-car shows in 1916.[99] Its architect was Charles Ernest Elcock (1878–1944), perhaps better known for his hospital designs. Firmly in the streamlined moderne fashion, Elcock's building had cantilevered 'motor roads', or 'gallery-roads', 20 feet wide, that projected from the exterior of the four principal upper floors and from the smaller recessed top floors, which were bisected by a central vertical accent containing a lift, while further verticals were provided by masts. The motor roads were linked to a curved ramp at the rear of the building, of the type built about the same time in the Piccadilly Circus Garage (see Chapter 6). Thus, one could drive from the street to the roof, a distance of 1¼ miles. This road was abutted by glazed shopfronts (2½ miles of them), fronting car showrooms. Customer parking was provided on the roadway and in the basement car park. Perhaps unsurprisingly, Elcock's Motor Centre was never built.

Rather than congregate together, motor dealers cherished their differences, cultivating an individual identity through distinctive signage and shopfront design. A typical multiple dealership was South London Motors. Between 1921 and 1933 the company expanded from a single repair shop into a business with a headquarters in Streatham in south London (see pl. 65b), a cen-

officiated at the opening. The entrance and display windows were contained within one of the massive rusticated arches of the Quadrant. The main showroom, which could be surveyed from a shaped balcony with a glass floor, was decorated with a seascape executed in coloured marbles and mosaic and set within arcading, presenting the illusion that this air-conditioned space was an open-sided pavilion in an Arcadian landscape. The high, coffered ceiling was covered with silver metal leaf. Other showrooms in the same building were treated more conventionally, with oak or mahogany panelling and decorative plasterwork. The upper floors were devoted to offices, with a conference room at the top that could hold a gathering of eighty members of Ford sales staff, or Ford dealers. Two years after opening, Ford's windows were refitted with the first examples of concave non-reflective windows – invented by Gerald Brown and installed by E. Pollard & Co. – of a type that survives today (2011) at the former Simpson's (now Waterstone's) on Piccadilly, and Heal's (latterly Habitat) on Tottenham Court Road, but unfortunately not at 88 Regent Street.[92] These windows were especially suited to car showrooms, since the display of large glossy objects aggra-

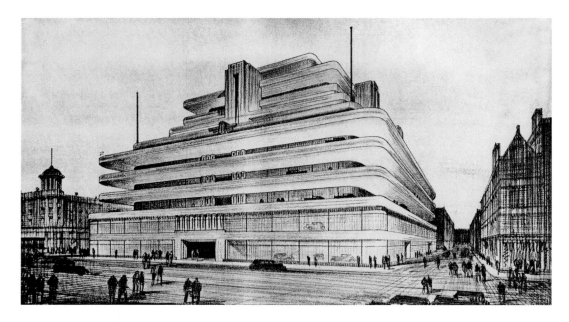

67   A 'Proposed Motor Centre for London' designed by Elcock & Sutcliffe in 1932. *The Builder* claimed that this extraordinary building was a purely functional design, with no attempt to make the building look 'original' or 'modern'. If erected, it would have accommodated 5,000 cars. From *The Builder*, 23 Sepember 1932, p. 503.

tralised service station, and fourteen agencies concentrating on car sales. South London Motors developed a house style for its frontages (e.g., at Beckenham, Wallington and Morden) that seems to have taken inspiration from Montague Burton, 'the Tailor of Taste'.[100] The showrooms occupied corner sites and had distinctive transom lights displaying the names of the various marques stocked.[101] In suburban locations, or lining new bypasses, dealers wanted to attract those driving past, not just pedestrians, and so they positioned themselves by major junctions, where drivers might pause at traffic lights. To capture attention from a distance, they began to favour a brazenly modern architectural style, with eye-catching moderne styling, towers and neon lettering. Furthermore, in such situations, an open forecourt positioned directly outside the showroom could provide extra display space. Forecourts, however, were not, as yet, particularly common – an early example being Mead's in Taplow, Buckinghamshire (1935; Rix & Rix)[102] – and most showrooms maintained traditional building lines.

The vacillations of Stewart & Ardern, the largest distributors of Morris cars in south-east England, illustrate the general drift towards suburban retailing. When the company opened at 103 New Bond Street in 1923, it was probably selling the least expensive cars on the street. This was the tip of the Stewart & Ardern iceberg: the company ran depots on Great Portland Street (1923) and later on Euston Road (1926), handling stocks and repairs, and reconditioning old cars for the second-hand market. Eventually, these activities were centralised in a massive new depot at Acton in west London (just as Appleyard, another

Morris dealer, centralised its operation in Leeds in 1927). Here, as well as a stand-alone showroom, there was a vast stockroom where hundreds of new Morris cars were stored and prepared for sale. A few years later, an imposing headquarters was created in a new building (1934; Wimperis Simpson & Guthrie) on the corner of Berkeley Square, an area fast becoming a centre for the car trade.[103] Morris House contained Stewart & Ardern's main showrooms and a special lecture theatre where technical instruction was offered to owner-drivers. In the meantime, however, economic depression had caused a slump in new-car sales, and Stewart & Ardern decided to open branches in locations that would be more convenient for its customers – or potential customers – who could not all be expected to travel to Acton or Berkeley Square.

Some of the most appealing and influential modern showrooms of the 1930s were built by Stewart & Ardern. By 1939 their chain included 'regional depots' in Croydon, Harrow, Catford, Golders Green, Ilford, Sutton, Southend-on-Sea, South Tottenham and Staines. Most of these occupied old buildings, but those at Staines (demolished), Ilford (pl. 68) and Catford (demolished; pl. 69) were purpose-built in 1934–5 to designs by the architect Cameron Kirby. They adopted an accomplished moderne style, with pale reconstituted stone or smooth veneers that concealed the brick skin of the underlying steelwork, high parapets masking pitched roofs, strong curves, carefully positioned neon lettering and vertical accents.[104] Each showroom had an unusually wide glass frontage, fitted with a folding door that enabled cars to be taken onto a forecourt. The door, or

68   The tall glass doors of Stewart & Ardern's Ilford showroom (1934–5) opened concertina-fashion to reveal a sleek modern interior, with light fittings flush with the ceiling. This building survives, in a much-altered state.

69   The interior of Cameron Kirby's showroom on Bromley Road, Catford (1934–5), for Stewart & Ardern. This shows the effective use of mirror glass on the walls.

70   William Watson & Co. Ltd, on Bold Street, Liverpool, was built (1939) with large windows so that displays of cars on three floors would be visible from the street. The canopy over the ground-floor windows acted as a sunblind to suppress reflections, and as an arcade to shelter window shoppers. Furthermore, it was strong enough to support the ladders required for window cleaning. The company's architect, who developed Watson's house style, was D. A. Beveridge.

screen, at Staines was said to be the largest of its kind in Europe.[105] The interiors of the showrooms were lit by flush circular panels of sandblasted plate glass set into the ceilings.[106] The floors were laid in maple strips: despite concerns about oil spillage, this was quite common, with wooden showroom floors often contrasting with harder materials, such as granolithic, in workshops. One wall of the showroom at Catford was mirrored, and a far corner accommodated a glazed office with a curved front. This was an ideal vantage point for a salesman to watch for potential customers, and it offered a private place to seal a deal. By the mid-1930s Morris had developed a network of hundreds of showrooms all over the country: George Kenning, for example, dominated Derbyshire and south Yorkshire (see pl. 142) in the same way that Stewart & Ardern ruled the South-East.

Glamorous photographs of Cameron Kirby's service stations were published in the architectural and motoring press, inspiring much emulation. In the mid- to late 1930s, throughout the country, new garages were built with smooth, white facings, flat rooflines, curved corners, sharp verticals (with towers used for clocks, water tanks or storage) and electrically lit signs, usually bright red in colour (see Chapter 4). A typical example was Jessups of Romford (1936; J. Amott), a building enlivened by red geraniums planted along the roofline, matching the colour of the neon lettering on the central water tower, which supplied the requisite vertical accent.[107] In Jessups' showroom, the 'shadowless' top lighting – recessed into the ceiling like Cameron Kirby's showrooms for Stewart & Ardern, and lined by reflectors – aspired to emulate daylight. The vehicle doors between the showroom and the repair garage were 'invisible'; they hung on horizontal trunnions and lifted upwards rather than outwards. Most garages of this type have been demolished or altered beyond recognition. One that retains its character is Rootes's garage in Maidstone (1938–9; Howard & Souster; see pl. 137), where the showroom occupied a double-height space with a curved mezzanine viewing gallery.[108]

One preoccupation of dealers and their architects in the 1930s was the creation of well-lit window displays that remained undisturbed by reflections. The concave windows adopted by Ford on Regent Street were expensive and, ultimately, impractical. A cheaper, if less effective, solution was a permanent canopy (pl. 70). The curved canopy of the Cresta Garage in Worthing, West Sussex (circa 1935; A. J. Seal), was of 'Glas-crete', small glass bricks that admitted light.[109] At Great Northern Motors' new premises of 1936 in Finchley, north London, one of the largest showrooms of the decade,[110] the show windows were recessed behind a low-roofed veranda, 6 feet deep, with a completely solid roof that ensured no direct sunlight could fall on the glass. Reducing reflections would remain a major issue in the second half of the century.

Selling to a Mass Market since 1945

Restrictions on building materials and labour, as well as delays in getting car factories up and running following war work, discouraged the construction of new-car showrooms immediately after 1945. There were exceptions, however, such as the 'home-made' showroom built in 1947–54 by Higlett & Duncan on a bombed site on Paynes Road/Park Road in Southampton, using odds and ends of materials, and their own labour.[111] It was only in the mid- to late 1950s, as car ownership accelerated beyond the most optimistic pre-war predictions, that the building of new-car showrooms resumed apace. The urban multi-storeyed showroom with lifts was relegated to the past, except for a few pre-war survivors, and the single-storey (although often double-height), flat-roofed, glass-box showroom became the dominant form, whether located on the fringes of urban centres, in suburbs, or on arterial routes. Some were even mass-produced, using prefabricated systems designed for car showrooms.[112] Such showrooms stood in stark contrast to attached repair shops, which had very different structural and aesthetic requirements. For example, at Lincolnshire Motors in Lincoln (1958–9; Denis Clarke Hall, Sam Scorer and Roy Bright), the garage was covered by an eye-catching hyperbolic paraboloid roof, while the adjoining showroom occupied a more conventional glass-fronted cylinder (pl. 71). The reception area for garages was now often located in the showroom, so that customers were exposed to new models, whether actively seeking a replacement car or not.

During the late 1950s dealerships expanded as never before: by 1962 Kennings had 175 branches and by 1964 Caffyns had 58 branches. Appleyard's, founded in 1919 in Leeds, spread through the West Riding, with purpose-built outlets in towns such as Bradford and Huddersfield; by 1964 its central depot stocked 1,000 new cars.[113] This all sparked a great deal of new building. Some of the most interesting showrooms to survive from this time, however, were built by independent garages in out-of-the-way locations (pl. 72).

From the late 1950s there was a pronounced fashion for curvilinear forms. Convex ground plans, especially on corners, had the benefit of presenting a display of cars to oncoming traffic in each direction. Thus Turnbull's Garage (1958; William Roseveare), opened by the racing driver Stirling Moss, had a circular form overlooking the Charles Cross roundabout and viaduct on Plymouth's inner ring road. This had a concrete folded plate roof supported on ten columns, very similar in design to Charles Barber's showroom in Northwich, Cheshire (1963; pl. 73), which also stood at a junction.[114] Another classic example of this arrangement was Dawnier Motors (1961; William Ahrend & Son), now Ewell Honda, a fan-shaped showroom facing onto a junction of the Ewell Bypass in Surrey. This had a radial portal frame structure, with tapered brackets cantilevered out from each

71 The Lincolnshire Motor Co. showroom rotunda and garage, Lincoln, built in 1958–9. Circular and polygonal showrooms, which showed cars from all angles, were especially popular around 1960. The façade of the garage was recessed below the over-arching roof, the central piers of which formed the focal point of a pump island.

portal to support a canopy that shaded inclined display windows.[115] Curves were also introduced into elevations. E. J. Baker & Co's Vauxhall showroom in Staines, Middlesex (1959; Westwood, Sons & Partners), was quadrant-shaped,[116] with a tall upright frontage parallel with the main road. Another variant on this theme was the showroom designed by the architect and cartoonist Frank Hoar for the racing driver Jack Brabham, and built in Woking, Surrey, in 1966.[117] The high concave frontage was fitted with an inclined, curved canopy.

Angular monopitch and butterfly roofs were also popular in the years around 1960, producing a jagged outline, aesthetically akin to the new Ford Anglia. R. H. Patterson & Co's (now Arnold Clark's) Ford garage on Scotswood Road, Newcastle (1964; Ryder, Yates and Partners), had a butterfly-shaped roof, rising to the front, with the showroom ceiling suspended beneath lattice girders, all revealed to the eye by a long stretch of glazing. At the back of the showroom was a Formica mural designed by Peter Yates, emblazoned with names of models such as 'Cortina' and 'Zephyr'. The site was opened by the Minister of Transport, Colin Buchanan, and, as part of the celebrations,

the television presenter Michael Miles hosted a game of 'Take Your Pick', the prize being a Ford Cortina.[118] A 'central pylon' by the road concealed the exhaust from the central heating and the intake for the air conditioning, and also displayed the word FORD.

Inside, showrooms required more fittings than ever before for catalogues and leaflets, while many opened integral accessories shops, with counter service. American influence surfaced in several experimental designs. Shaw & Kilburn's remodelled showroom in St John's Wood (1964), for example, opened as London's first 'drive-in' showroom. Up to twelve customers could drive in, inspect cars, and drive out, all under cover. A playground was provided for children, who were cared for by a female member of staff while their parents looked at cars. As far as design was concerned, showroom lighting continued to be the main preoccupation. It had been discovered that the ideal approach, when dealing with cars, was flat, indirect lighting, combined with matt or textured walls, ceilings and floors. Fluorescent tubes were used widely, often set into false ceilings that hid wiring and held flush fittings in place. The full gamut

72   The small but stylish Drome Garage in Watton, near Thetford, Norfolk, was designed in 1964 by a local architect. It had an inwardly sloping end window and a sloping roof, which was clad on the underside with polished aluminium to reflect light onto the display area. It held just two cars.

73   Charles Barber & Sons' showroom on Station Road in Northwich, Cheshire, opened in 1963. It is pentagonal in plan, with projecting gables forming pointed canopies over each bay. The woodwork, originally exposed, has been painted white.

74 This eye-catching showroom rotunda formed the centrepiece of the Tower Garage at Alderley Edge in Cheshire (built in 1962 for Total). The glazing is inclined and sheltered by a solid canopy, to reduce reflections. The cantilevered saucer-like roof also protected petrol pumps, though these have long gone.

of lighting possibilities was explored at Cripps & Co.'s new showroom on Parliament Street, Nottingham, which was remodelled by R. W. Cooper in 1955, with electrical work by R. G. Baker. Here, the ceiling was lit by tubes hidden in a suspended fibrous plaster tray or trough: in addition, flush lights were set in recesses fitted with 'egg-crate' louvres in the undersides of the tray; pendant lights were suspended on rigid rods; and recessed lights were set into the ceiling at the front of the window display.[119]

The form of display windows was still a matter for serious consideration. Glazing bars were made as slender as possible and – as can be seen at the Tower Garage, Alderley Edge, Cheshire (1962; Moir & Bateman; pl. 74)[120] – the glass itself was often inclined and shaded by a solid canopy to reduce reflections. Inclined glazing had been adopted by high street shops in the

early 1950s,[121] and was quickly taken up for car showrooms.[122] As with the concave non-reflective windows pioneered by Ford in the 1930s, inclined windows were not easily opened to drive cars in and out. At Kays on Ashbourne Road in Derby (1959; Samuel Morrison & Partners),[123] a complicated opening mechanism was invented, with lifting gear concealed in the space above the showroom ceiling. More straightforward sliding or folding doors were the commonest solution, permitting the showroom to communicate with a forecourt. Almost universally, following American precedent, the forecourt became the preserve of the second-hand car.

The forecourt allowed prospective buyers to browse in freedom, without being badgered by salesmen. In 1962 Leeds Autocars in Harrogate created a 'used car garden', with flower-beds, shrubs and paths, sufficiently wide to display sixty cars.[124]

Forecourts remained the norm, however, and were often covered by free-standing canopies with soffit lighting. These protected cars and customers in bad weather, and provided some illumination at night; in addition, their fascias could display signs. Where these structures might interfere with the visibility of new-car displays, they were raised above the showroom roof, but – space permitting – they were located to one side of the site. An early example of a basic forecourt canopy was erected by South London Motors in Streatham (1958; C. W. Lowe).[125] Regarded as a temporary structure, this had a monopitch steel roof, with simple fluorescent tubes on the soffit. The canopied forecourt of Endeavour Motors in Brighton (1964) communicated with the new-car showroom during the day, but the latter was sealed off by armour-plated glass at night.[126] Sometimes the distinction between exterior and interior spaces was deliberately blurred. In Barnsley in Yorkshire, in 1968, Appleyard's erected a wide garage with a double-pitched roof, the open-fronted central section being penetrated by a used-car area beneath a projecting canopy.[127] Canopies could be very large: that of the American-style Autodrome (G. S. Oscroft & Co.'s Vauxhall dealership), Castle Boulevard, Nottingham (1965), sheltered forty cars.[128]

Auctions played a large part in the disposal of second-hand vehicles, often to the trade. The premises of Central Motor Auctions at Rothwell near Leeds, with a saleroom capable of accommodating 600 cars, were advertised in 1961 as 'the first purpose-built motor auction in the country'.[129] The seventeenth branch of British Car Auctions, built at Brighouse, Yorkshire, in 1972 (by Huddersfield architects, Arthur Quarmby Associates), claimed to be the 'most modern' car auction centre in the world.[130] Its two auction halls had automatic doors and elevated seating. The building included open-plan offices, a restaurant and a snack bar; there was public parking for 600 cars, sheltered by an extension of the main roof. In 1971 Birmingham City Council developed a 'car supermarket', the Cardrome, which was still considered Britain's 'largest car supermarket' in 1977.[131] A lull in the sale of new cars from the early 1970s into the 1980s signalled golden years for the second-hand trade. Today, one of the country's biggest used-car complexes is Car Giant, occupying the former Mulliner Park Ward site in Willesden, north London.

Since the 1970s the standard new-car showroom has been little more than a glass-sided room tacked onto the front of a vast servicing shed, usually of steel with a pitched roof and aluminium cladding (pl. 75). Typically, this was surrounded by an array of used cars on an open forecourt littered with banners and bunting: the under-lit forecourt canopy was all but abandoned, in favour of powerful lighting standards. Showroom clusters were encouraged by planning regulations, as well as the needs of retailers, and can be seen on the approach roads of

75 The shed-front showroom is a ubiquitous arrangement, recurring up and down the country since the 1970s. This example is positioned at the front of the repair garage of Robins & Day Peugeot, on the Canterbury ring road, photographed from the city walls.

towns or on industrial/retail estates. Most grew piecemeal, but a planned and landscaped retail village for cars, the Meadowhall Automotive Scheme, was developed by Bond Bryan Architects for British Land in 2007 for a site next to a major out-of-town shopping mall on the outskirts of Sheffield. This is the present-day equivalent of Elcock's Motor Centre (see pl. 67), and no doubt other developments of this type can be anticipated.

Against the mundane backdrop of the ubiquitous shed-front showroom, a handful of high-quality designs have stood apart since around 1980. Some of these can be categorised as high tech. One of the first was Norman Foster & Partners' Renault Distribution Centre in Swindon (1981–2; pl. 76), where Team 4 – Foster and his partners of the time – had designed what may be the first high-tech building, the Reliance Controls Electronics Factory, fifteen years earlier.[132] The Renault building included a double-height car showroom, or gallery. This was contained within a festive framework ('exoskeleton') of yellow masts and arched braces, and its PVC-membrane canopy roof was sufficiently high for cars to be suspended above the ground. This industrial style was especially suited to buildings erected for the sale of a technologically advanced product like the car, and a more mainstream version of high tech was adopted by the trade, for example, at Marshall's Car Centre, which was built close to Cambridge Airport in 1995. This was laid out like a retail outlet village, with eight showrooms – each dedicated to a different marque – arranged in an arc around a customer car park, with a tubular canopy over the display fronts. From the 1990s until the mid-2000s many garages erected showrooms that can be described as 'tented pavilions'. The silver-coloured conical

76 Architectural interest in car showrooms was revived around 1980. The high-tech Renault Distribution Centre (Spectrum) in Swindon was designed by Norman Foster & Partners and built in 1981–2.

roof of Gates's used-car saleroom in Stevenage (2002–4; Architen Landrell; pl. 77), for example, is of PVC-coated polyester fabric and is supported by a central steel mast. The imagery of the tent seems most appropriate for edge-of-town used-car showrooms, since it evokes the impermanent nature and low prices of the urban market stall.

High-end manufacturers have increasingly advised on the design of new-car showrooms: sometimes on their structure, as well as more superficial branding, fixtures and fittings. Audi's concept – 'One Name, One Standard, Everywhere' – demands a certain level of uniformity, and in recent years a distinctive type of two-storey Audi showroom with a glazed frontage and curved roof has made its appearance on the outskirts of many British towns. Porsche is also notable for its consistent modern house style, with grey metallic cladding and curved frontages display-ing bold, red lettering. BMW/Mini dealerships also comply with strict aesthetic guidelines – in this case, glossy black veneers – as at Halliwell Jones in the Wirral, Merseyside (Taylor Design; pl. 78). Many of the architects designing modern car showrooms are generalists, but some specialise almost entirely in this type of

work. To pick just one random example, Scaramanga Designs (established 1979) had responsibility for implementing Peugeot's retail concept – memorable for its bright blue surfaces – in the U.K., acting as the middleman between dealer and manufacturer. As well as working for Peugeot, it produced dozens of designs for Skoda.[133]

The high-tech 'pavilion' style has, by and large, been ousted by a more refined neo-modern styling for car showrooms. This is sometimes a conscious reinterpretation of the streamlined moderne style that was so popular in the late 1930s. The effec-tiveness of curves and subtly coloured night-time illumination has been rediscovered, but the smooth white finishes of the classic modern era have been replaced by matt grey metallic cladding. Double-height show spaces are popular, ideally with full-height tinted glazing fitted in panels without visible glazing bars. Behind the glass façade, the brightly lit interior often includes a mezzanine gallery. With so much glass, even with pro-tection from extended eaves, interiors have to be air conditioned. The ultimate modern showroom is the seven-storey Audi show-room (Wilkinson Eyre; pl. 79) that opened beside the elevated section of the M4 in west London in 2009, in the midst of a recession, having cost £45 million to build. This has the now-requisite fully glazed façade: curved, inclined, and topped by an S-shaped roof with projecting eaves, supposedly inspired – in the sort of language so often adopted for projects harbouring 'iconic' ambitions – by the manta ray fish, or the wings of a B2 stealth bomber. Three floors contain showrooms, with space for 116 cars.

England – not even the West End of London – possesses nothing quite like Citroën's stunning showroom on the Champs-Elysées (2002–7; Manuelle Gautrand), where eight cars are stacked on turntables behind a glass showfront, faceted like crystal, incorporating the firm's double chevron logo.[134] The way forward, however, may be pointed by a Mercedes showroom (Ayshford Sansome), situated next door to Audi on the M4 at Brentford. In 2009–10 this was remodelled with one of first glass display towers to be erected in England, a Wöhr Parksafe 580 holding sixteen cars on eight levels.[135] Another eye-catching display tower was built in autumn 2010 by Hodgson Mazda in Gateshead, with visibility from the A1 as it bypasses the west side of the city (pl. 80). Designed by Autopod Solutions and prefabricated in Germany, this rectangular tower stands eight storeys high and holds thirty-one cars, which are moved about by computer-controlled lifts and can be retrieved for a customer in under one minute. Vertical showrooms allow architecture to resume its role in the spectacle of car sales, something that has been largely absent for more than a generation. In fact, many installations of this type now exist on the Continent, where the supreme example remains the well-known Volkswagen Autoturme, built in Wolfsburg in 1994. These two glass-sided nineteen-storey towers stand in a pool and are filled with cars that are delivered to and from their stalls by robotic arms. Like Audi's site at Ingolstatt, this is actually an automotive theme park rather than a conventional showroom: perhaps the closest English equivalent is Mercedes-Benz World at Brooklands, Surrey.

Nowadays, internet cafés are sometimes provided by so-called prestige showrooms. The World Wide Web enables people to cut out the middleman when selling or buying a car, but it is being used to great effect by dealers themselves, as well as by private individuals. Yet motorists still like to inspect and test-drive a vehicle before buying. More ominous threats to the future well-being of the English car dealership derive from environmental concerns, which are likely to impact on motoring in all its aspects. A recent incentive scheme, however – a £2,000 reward for disposing of any car more than nine years old and buying anew – has demonstrated the British Government's continuing willingness to support what is left of the indigenous motor industry, including its distributive arm, through thick and thin.

77   The used-car sales office located in the middle of the forecourt of Gates's Ford dealership in Stevenage, Hertfordshire, with tented canopies and the new car showroom behind.

78   Halliwell Jones' two-storey BMWMini showroom on the A50 in the Wirral, by Taylor Design. Like many car manufacturers, BMW/Mini impose a distinctive livery and architectural approach on dealers, without insisting on a standardised off-the-peg building.

79 (*facing page*) West London Audi is a 'landmark' building, with upper-level showrooms that can be viewed fleetingly from the elevated section of the M4. This is one of the largest and most expensive showrooms to be built in England in recent years.

80 (*right*) The display tower of Hodgson Mazda, Gateshead, which is highly visible from the A1. This Continental fashion is beginning to catch on in England.

1st September, 1929

Your garage problem
Solved

SHUFFREY

MC 1930

MORRIS

MORRIS MOTORS LTD. MOTOR HOUSE DEPARTMENT COWLEY, OXFORD

Catalogue B

81 Morris garage brochure, *circa* 1930.

3: KEEPING THE CAR AT HOME

Having purchased a motor car, the owner had to house it. As their alternative name, 'horseless carriages', suggests, early motor cars had much in common with their horse-drawn predecessors, and they were often built by the same coachbuilders (see Chapter 1). Built largely of wood and painted in the traditional coachbuilder's manner – using a great many coats of enamel, sometimes as many as twenty, each one rubbed down – they would very soon deteriorate if left out in the rain. It was even recommended that, on return from each journey, they were thoroughly washed down, cleaned and dried, necessitated largely by the state of the roads.

Their accommodation was initially referred to as a 'motor house' and this was the term most widely used until 1914, with 'motor stables' as an alternative for the larger complex. 'Garage' tended to be used to describe a public car park, and then a place where cars were sold, repaired and maintained. It was certainly used in that sense in 1902, when the *Car Illustrated* stated that '"garage", an unfortunate word borrowed like many of our automobile terms from our friends across the Channel . . . signifies a motor-car store-house' and went on to describe parking and repair and maintenance garages.[1] Already the distinction was becoming blurred when the Arts and Crafts architect C. Harrison Townsend noted in 1908 that, 'for the home of the car, we very largely use the French word "garage", alternatively with what I think the more desirable English equivalent of "motor house"'.[2] In a paper delivered to the Architectural Association, he went on to use 'garage' to mean a public storing place for cars.

In the earliest days of the motor car, certainly prior to 1900, the purchasers were generally wealthy men who would already have extensive stabling. The car was simply kept in part of the building currently occupied by horse-drawn vehicles. Other than plenty of space to house the tools and spares that were required in such large quantities by pioneer motorists, there were few special requirements. These early cars were also quite small. The one thing unique to the car was a need to find somewhere to store its fuel. The highly inflammable petrol (usually called 'benzene' in this period) was stored away from the car and other objects of value in a benzene house, usually a small ventilated shed, but sometimes an underground store.

The Earliest Motor Houses

The motoring magazines had much to say on almost every aspect of motoring, but they were uncharacteristically silent on the question of housing cars, the only reference being to a French architect's suggestion that new houses in Paris ought to be fitted up with 'coach-houses for autocars'.[3] It was not until 1899 that the first example was illustrated, with the publication of an article on Dr W. W. Barrett's motor house at 39 Park Avenue, Southport. Dr Barrett, one of the first doctors in the north to use a car on his rounds to visit patients, designed a two-storey addition to his house to accommodate his two Daimlers (pl. 82). The exact date of construction is not known, but it was certainly complete by April 1898, when the first of the cars was acquired. The motor house was centrally heated, as was Dr Barrett's residence, and he was able to go to his car via a corridor from his dining room without leaving the warmth, important for a man who had to go out in all weathers. Above the ground-floor garage was a billiard room and a room where Barrett could indulge his mechanical interests.[4] Dr Barrett's

82 Dr W. W. Barrett's motor house at Southport, Lancashire, in 1899.

83 Dr Barrett's motor house today, converted into residential accommodation.

84 The exterior of Sir David Salomons's motor stables at Broomhill, Kent, photographed *circa* 1906.

85 Sir David Salomons's motor stables: the inspection pits.

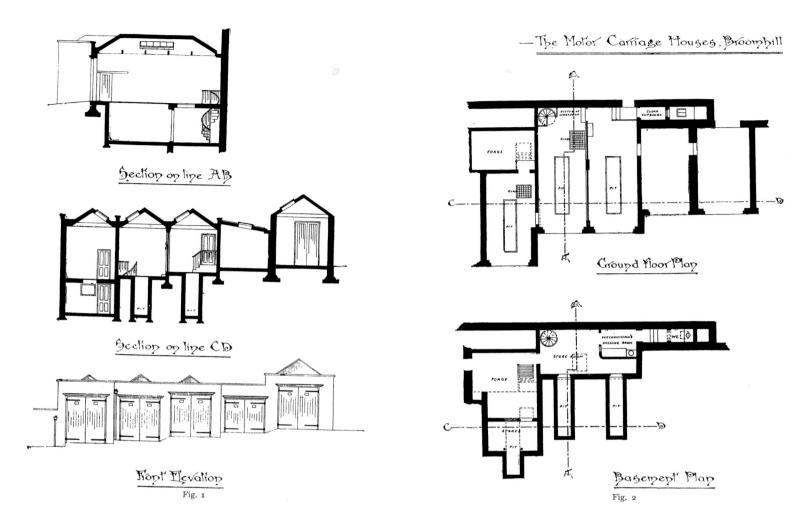

Section on line AB

Section on line CD

Front Elevation

Fig. 1

Ground Floor Plan

Basement Plan

Fig. 2

86 Plan of Sir David Salomons's motor stables, from *Motors and Motor-driving*, ed. Alfred C. Harmsworth, 1902.

motor house is now in residential use but has a claim to be the earliest surviving domestic garage in England (pl. 83).

Dr Barrett had an examination pit of two levels (2ft and 4ft deep) in his garage and this reflected the rapidly developing technology of the motor car. Some of the earliest examples had their engines largely exposed at the rear, but by the end of the 1890s they were less accessible in many cases, mounted lower and hidden under the bonnet. A pit became an absolute requirement for the car owner. The need to incorporate pits led to Sir David Salomons rebuilding the motor stables at his house, Broomhill, at Southborough, Tunbridge Wells, Kent (pl. 84).

Salomons had a good claim to have introduced the motor car to Great Britain, organising the first motor exhibition at Tunbridge Wells in 1895 (see Chapter 1). The date of his original stables is not known, but they may well date back to 1895 when he bought his first car, which would make them the earliest examples of a domestic garage in England. These stables consisted of individual garages linked together and backing on to the large private theatre that Salomons had erected at Broomhill.

At some time before 1902, as cars became larger and the need to incorporate pits became evident, Salomons reconstructed the motor stables slightly to the north of their predecessors. He must have been happy with the basic design since they resembled the original motor houses closely, built in the same buff brick and with similar lintel mouldings. The fronts were faced in stone to match the house. Salomons acted as his own architect and described the design of the stables – the result of considerable thought – in detail in one of the most influential of early motoring books, intending it to be an exemplar (pl. 86).[5] Despite this, they are quite modest in appearance, especially when they are compared to the magnificent range of stables provided by Salomons for his horses and carriages in the years 1890–94. Here again, he had largely designed the stables himself, although he had instructed a local architect, William Barnsley Hughes, to prepare the drawings. But, unlike the motor stables, which are hidden away at the side of the house, the horse stables are in a commanding position on the main drive, where they are visible to all visitors. The contrast between the two displays their rela-

87   The motor house, Trevin Towers, Eastbourne, built for J. J. Hissey in 1898 or early 1899.

tive hierarchical positions, even in the hands of a man who was one of the leading advocates of motoring.

The most significant features of the motor stables were the inspection pits, reached through doors at basement level and of sufficient depth for a man to stand upright (pl. 85). The building also accommodated a small forge, a 'mechanicians' dressing room and a lavatory, while above was a workshop and clothing store. Shelves and cupboards lined the walls; central heating was provided; and lighting was through electric bulbs and skylights. The building was constructed to an exceptionally high standard, with much use of pitch pine and panelled doors throughout. Few subsequent changes were made, other than the lengthening of some of the garages to cater for larger cars, probably immediately before 1914 or during the early 1920s. Today, it survives remarkably intact, including much original signage, fittings and even the original wooden electrical conduit, complete with the sockets for inspection lamps, mentioned by Salomons in his description.

Two other motor houses are known to pre-date 1900. One was that constructed for Evelyn Ellis at Rosenau, his house at Datchet in Buckinghamshire.[6] In July 1895 Ellis was the first

person to import a petrol-driven motor, a Daimler-engined Panhard-Levassor, and he took the Prince of Wales on his first drive in a car. He was the first to drive a petrol-powered motor car on the roads in England when, on 6 July 1895, he took possession of his first motor from the railway station at Micheldever; he and his mechanic, Frederick Simms, drove the vehicle back to Datchet. The motor house there consisted of little more than a detached rectangular structure with a flat roof and four garages in a row. There was hard-standing in front and an external inspection pit; to one side stood an earlier building that appears to have contained the workshop.

Another known pre-1900 motor house was constructed in late 1898 or early 1899 for the travel writer James John Hissey at his house, Trevin Towers, in Eastbourne, Sussex (pl. 87).[7] This is not only extant, but is also still used for its original purpose today. Hissey had a considerable input in the design of the house, which was constructed in 1894, and it is likely that the motor house owes much to him as well. Built in an Arts and Crafts style adjacent to the stables, it employed an unusual plan with two garages almost forming a right angle with their doorways adjoining. Both had a pit, and walls lined with timber matchboarding.

88   The motor house at Rounton Grange, Yorkshire, built in 1904 to the design of George Jack.

At the Country House, 1900–1914

Although Sir David Salomons had outlined what he felt was the ideal way to house motor cars, most country houses had a ready-made solution to the problem in the form of existing carriage houses. Conversion of these was by far the most popular way of housing cars. The modifications necessary generally included concreting the floor, putting in an inspection pit, adding heating pipes and replacing the existing doors. Initially, motor houses were often a simple addition to the existing stable court and then, as the car began to take over, equine accommodation was converted, leaving sufficient only to cater for hunting and riding. Purpose-built accommodation tended to be limited to newly built houses or to those that were extensively rebuilt.[8]

The country house garage reflected, on a larger scale, the development of the domestic garage, but with some significant differences. These include the extent of accommodation provided for chauffeurs; the spatial and stylistic relationship between the motor house and the country house it served; and much more generous provision of workshops, generators and washing shelters. The internal divisions seen at Ellis's and Salomons's motor houses were soon phased out in favour of large open areas designed to take a number of cars, while the pits approached from a basement that Salomons had employed at Broomhill were not adopted elsewhere.

The most elaborate motor houses were those that included chauffeurs' accommodation. At Rounton Grange in the North Riding of Yorkshire, a motor house was added in 1904 to the designs of George Jack, chief assistant to Philip Webb, who had built the house in 1871–6 (pl. 88).[9] It consisted originally of a row of four garages with the chauffeurs' accommodation above, but was extended to the south by Jack in 1913 with two longer garages and a sleeping-platform on the first floor. Perhaps the most impressive example and one that achieved extensive publicity at the time of its construction was that at Ewelme Down in Oxfordshire, which was designed, together with the house, by Walter Cave in 1905 (pls 89 and 90).[10] It was arranged as a courtyard, similar in form to a stable block, with the cars entering via an archway, topped by a prominent gable, in the west range. The chauffeurs lived in the north range, with further bedrooms in the attic of the west range, and had a mess room on the ground floor.

89 Ewelme Down, Oxfordshire. The comprehensive facilities provided by Walter Cave, photographed on completion in 1905.

The courtyard layout was also employed at Tylney Hall in Hampshire, where R. Selden Wornum constructed a large and imposing motor court situated between the service and stable courts between 1899 and 1901.[11] The motor house was entered through a pilastered gateway, and had a tall water tower at one corner and garages on either side. In front of these garages were colonnades supporting an almost continuous balcony providing washing places for the cars underneath.[12] In contrast, the new stables and motor house built at Tandridge Court in Surrey to the designs of F. S. Brereton in 1904 were circular in form and incorporated a tower over the entrance gateway.[13] Six motor houses with chauffeurs' accommodation occupied a third of the circular court, the remainder being taken up with stables. By 1915, when the motor house at Horton Priory in Kent was built by George Hornblower, as part of his restoration of the priory, only a small riding stable was provided, reflecting the change seen elsewhere from horses to motorised transport.[14]

The location of country house garages, away from mains supplies, meant that they needed to have independent arrangements for the provision of power and water. Many incorporated a generator (usually powered by a gas or oil engine) for lighting, to provide power for machine tools in the workshop and to charge car batteries, while water towers supplied the water required for both heating and washing. Glazed washing canopies were not

entirely new, having been used to shelter carriages, but their use expanded considerably. An extensive one was provided at Sandringham, Norfolk, for Edward VII as a later addition to the large motor house added to one end of the stable court in 1902.[15] Like most of them, it was constructed using light steel trusses. These canopies tend to be of plain appearance, although that at Tandridge Court is supported on elaborate brackets sprung from the walls.

The style of the motor house often differed from that of the house. At Ewelme, the motor house was rendered in the Arts and Crafts manner of Voysey, quite unlike the house, which was of stone and broadly Neo-Elizabethan, while that at Rounton was built in clapboarded timber, simple in appearance and again bearing no resemblance to the austere Queen Anne style of Philip Webb's stone-built house. Possibly the distance of both buildings from the house – both were out of sight of it – was a factor, since at some houses, such as Great Chalfield Manor in Wiltshire, which was restored by Sir Harold Brakspear, the motor house, built in 1908, was carefully designed to match the house and other existing service buildings.[16] Examination of surviving motor houses on country estates reveals a wide variety of styles, with some owners willing to put up only the most utilitarian structures, devoid of any decorative treatment. These included the Duke of Beaufort, who, before 1905, erected a pair of simple

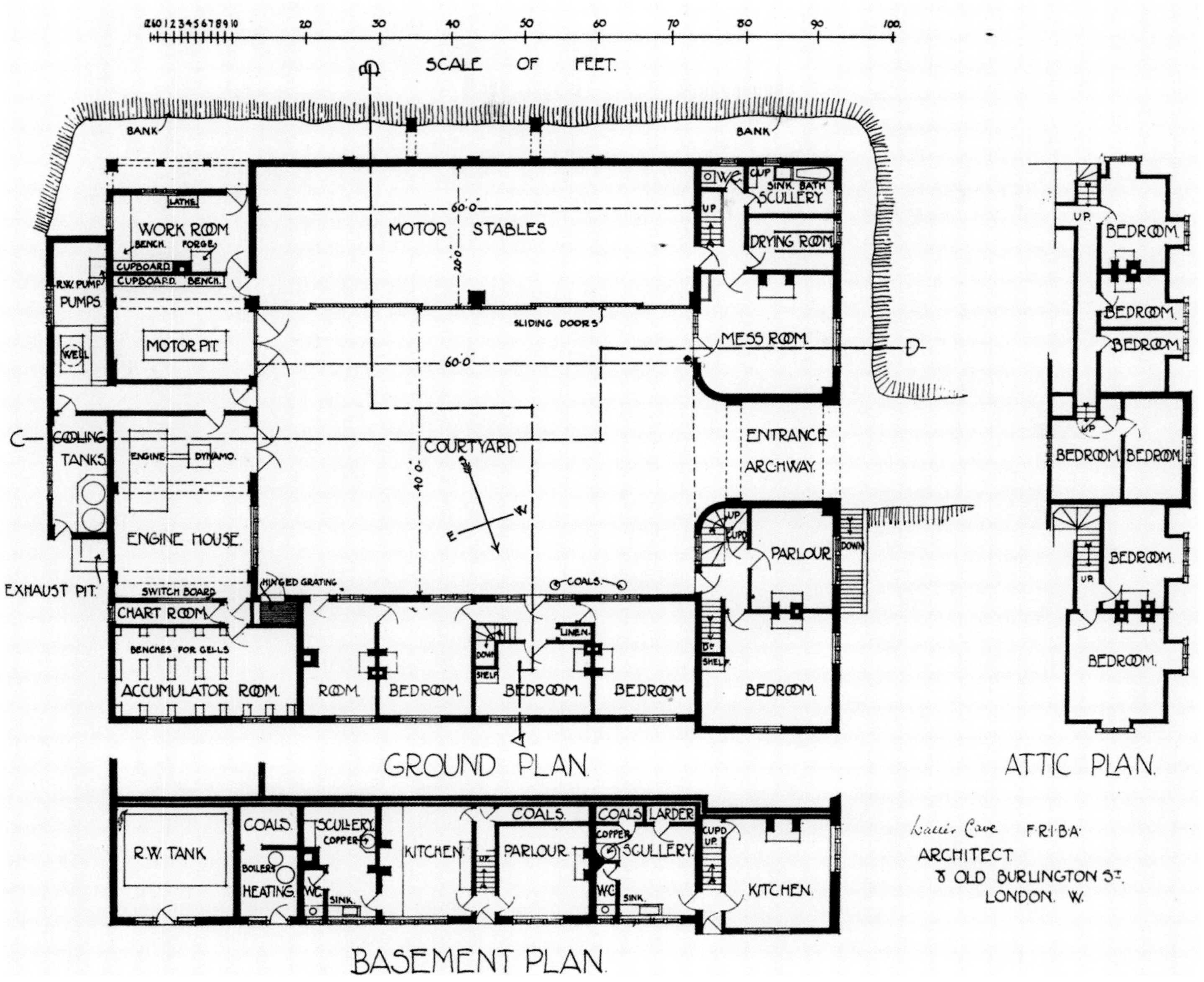
SCALE OF FEET
BANK
BANK
WORK ROOM
LATHE
BENCH. FORGE
CUPBOARD
CUPBOARD. BENCH.
R.W. PUMP
PUMPS
WELL
MOTOR PIT
MOTOR STABLES
60'0"
20'0"
SLIDING DOORS
60'0"
COOLING TANKS
ENGINE
DYNAMO.
ENGINE HOUSE.
COURTYARD.
40'0"
EXHAUST PIT.
SWITCH BOARD
HINGED GRATING
COALS.
CHART ROOM.
BENCHES FOR CELLS
ACCUMULATOR ROOM.
ROOM.
BEDROOM.
BEDROOM.
BEDROOM
LINEN.
SHELF
W.C.
CUP
SINK. BATH
SCULLERY.
DRYING ROOM
UP
MESS ROOM.
ENTRANCE ARCHWAY.
UP
CUPD
PARLOUR
DOWN
BEDROOM.
GROUND PLAN.
BEDROOM.
BEDROOM.
BEDROOM.
BEDROOM.
BEDROOM.
BEDROOM.
BEDROOM.
ATTIC PLAN.
R.W. TANK
COALS.
BOILERS
HEATING.
W.C.
SCULLERY.
COPPER
SINK.
KITCHEN.
UP
PARLOUR.
COALS.
COALS.
LARDER
COPPER
SCULLERY.
W.C.
SINK.
CUPD. UP.
KITCHEN.
F.R.I.B.A.
ARCHITECT
8 OLD BURLINGTON ST.
LONDON. W.
BASEMENT PLAN.

90 Plan of the motor house at Ewelme Down. From *Car Illustrated*, 10 October 1906, p. 318.

stone garages (later expanded to six) at Badminton House in Gloucestershire.[17] An equally plain, flat-roofed pair of garages was added to the stable court at Somerleyton Hall in Suffolk at about the same time.[18] On the whole, the motor house never became the showpiece that was the stable block, and it was often located some distance from the house, or, if adjacent to it, was tucked away in as unobtrusive a position as possible. The contrast between provision for cars and for horses observed at Sir David Salomons's house at Broomhill was to be widely repeated.

•

The Suburban and Domestic Motor House, 1900–1914

In the early days of motoring, motorists were interested in cars not primarily as a means of transport but as an end in themselves. Engineering was their hobby. In an interview with Leonard Williamson, a trained electrical engineer, the *Car Illustrated* noted: 'his interest in the mechanical side is greater than his interest in driving'.[19] In five and a half years as a motorist, he had owned eighteen machines. At his home at 28 Albert Road, Southport, he had a comprehensive workshop with numerous power tools, and in the grounds was a circular test

91 Leonard Williamson drives his dog around his banked test track in Southport on a curved dash Oldsmobile in 1902.

track with sharp curves banked up, on which he achieved a maximum of 25mph (pl. 91).

A second-hand market was in existence as early as 1898, and by the early 1900s modestly priced cars were appearing, leading to many more car owners among the middle classes. In the more prosperous suburbs of major cities, motor cars began to take their place as a means of transport, and accommodation had to be provided for them. Many home owners simply converted an existing stable. Others built relatively small motor houses beside their dwellings. Sometimes the two are hard to distinguish, especially since the building of domestic stables continued until around 1910.

Aldersbrook, a middle-class suburb in north-east London, illustrates the process of transition from horse-drawn to motorised transport. 'Birchdale', 76 Aldersbrook Road, was built in 1902. A plan for a stable to comprise a coach house, two stalls and a harness room was submitted in April 1908.[20] By April 1911 a revised plan was deposited to cater for motor cars.[21] While the original two stalls in the stable remained largely unchanged, the coach house was adapted for use as a garage through an extension to the west with access via a rolling shutter and the addition of a gated drive. A service pit was added in the space between the garage and the horse stalls. But second thoughts

prevailed and on 27 April a further amended plan was submitted that removed one stall completely, replaced by the pit, reduced the size of the harness room and enlarged the space available for the car.[22] Thus, within three years, the horse was marginalised, a phenomenon that was taking place across England.

In Birmingham, new garages are recorded in the building plans register. In Chantry Road, Moseley, there are many early garages. Some, such as that at No. 20, were probably converted from stables, because they have prominent openings, circular in this case, giving access to the hayloft. No. 34 has a purpose-built motor house of 1904, built directly on to the house (pl. 92).[23] It is quite shallow, and its style, with a half-timbered gable incorporating a louvred ventilator, complements that of the house.

By 1902 companies that made prefabricated buildings, of which Boulton & Paul were the best known, were advertising a variety of timber motor houses, covering a wide range of styles and prices. In general, they were much more ornate than post-1918 designs and included half-timbering, elaborate bargeboards, decorative cupolas, small paned windows and thatched roofs. The Portable Building Co. of Manchester offered motor houses with 'rustic-jointed weatherboarding' halfway up the exterior walls and half-timbering above, the interiors fully matchboarded and

with corrugated iron roofs, at prices from £21 10s. to £75, plus erection charges (pl. 93).[24]

One particularly elaborate example came from Sweden, with the Country Gentleman's Association acting as the British agents.[25] Another, having gablets and a Venetian window to the side elevations, was offered by A. G. Quibell of West Green, London.[26] Such structures were expected not to detract from the appearance of the house. Boulton & Paul also advertised steel-framed fireproof buildings for the storage of petrol.[27] A surviving petrol store has been identified on the Rothschild estate at Ashton Wold, Northamptonshire (pls 94 and 95). It has vents both low down and below the eaves, a lowered floor that could be filled with sand to absorb spillages, and slate shelves on iron supports to reduce fire risk. These precautions, however, were to some extent negated by the reed-thatched roof of the store, enabling it to harmonise with other estate buildings.

In 1906 houses on the Hale Estate, Edgware, Middlesex, were advertised as 'having room for motor', and motor houses were included in some speculatively built houses in the London area from about 1912.[28] But these were very much the exceptions and the car owner was generally left to fend for himself. Much

92 (*left*) Motor house at 34 Chantry Road, Moseley, Birmingham, built in 1904.

93 Prefabricated garages from the Portable Building Co. catalogue cover, *circa* 1909.

Artistic Designs to harmonize with your residence.

94 and 95   Exterior and interior of the petrol store on the Ashton Wold estate, Northamptonshire. Built in the early 1900s by William Huckvale for Charles Rothschild, it survives in original condition.

advice concerning the basic requirements for a successful motor house was given in the columns of motoring journals and in the many motoring manuals that were published. The first factor was size: the building had to be large enough to accommodate a car, and in particular of sufficient length to house any car that the owner might acquire in the future. It needed to be wide enough to enable the doors to be opened, and high enough to allow a spare tyre or two to be carried on the car roof. The walls should be faced with glazed bricks or tiles so that they could be washed down, and the junction of the walls with the floor should be coved to avoid the accumulation of dirt. Air gratings should be placed low down to expel petrol fumes, which are heavier than air. Drains should be open, half-round channels rather than underground pipes to prevent the build-up of explosive gases. Heating the garage was essential, since the motor house 'cannot be too dry'.

By 1908 the provision of a pit was not considered crucial since car manufacturers were making mechanical parts both more accessible and more reliable. If a pit was considered essential, it should be 6 feet by 3 feet by 4 feet 6 inches deep. Access should be by wooden steps, and ideally, like the garage, it should be lined with a washable surface and covered by 2-inch-thick boards when not in use. A covered washing space outside was essential, and sometimes over an exterior pit. The covering usually took the form of an iron and glass canopy; very few have survived, at least in a suburban setting.

While motor-house design was discussed extensively in the motoring press, it seemingly failed to engage the architectural profession. It was raised on two occasions in papers read before the Architectural Association, the first in 1906 by M. G. Pechell and the second in 1908 by C. Harrison Townsend. Townsend's paper concentrated on technical necessities and mentioned all those features that occur in most early motor houses. He was concerned with practical arrangements rather than style, which is hardly mentioned.[29] The subject otherwise rarely arose in the architectural press prior to 1914, although *The Builder* commented: 'the country garages now being erected looked like stables, which they were not, and the town garages looked like anything from a restaurant to a private house . . . an entirely new development like motor cars must bring in its train a new form of architecture'.[30]

Ingenious solutions proliferated. One motor house in Surrey was disguised as a tennis pavilion, complete with a veranda containing a bench and a darkroom catering for one of the owner's other interests.[31] At Tunbridge Wells, Elliott Alves used the falling land behind his house to conceal a garage for three cars, hewn out of solid sandstone below a conservatory. The garage is still used today, retaining the ebonised tile surface of its courtyard, although the conservatory and the chauffeur's dressing room below it have gone.[32] Converting the conservatory was itself seen as an ideal solution by Captain M. Bowman-Manifold: it had drainage, ventilation and heating, and while it needed 'stout brown paper' affixed to the glass roof to keep down the effect of the sun, this was done 'without seriously interfering with its floral utility'.[33]

By 1910 in London the motor car had begun to replace the horse, at least for the well-to-do, and the conversion of mews to accommodate cars rather than horses was rapidly gathering pace. In 1914 it was reported that cars far outnumbered horses in the mews of Belgravia, Mayfair and the area around Harley Street. In one large mews in Belgravia, more than eighty cars were being kept in the partly converted stables, in contrast to only twelve horses.[34]

After 1910 the motor house became less imposing. In 1912 W. H. Knight of Bromley Common advertised examples constructed of asbestos panels, described as 'the latest substitute for brick', in addition to those of corrugated iron or wood.[35] From around 1910 there was a vogue for a new type of car aimed at those with much less to spend, the cyclecar. As its name suggests, this was a somewhat spindly affair, small and very lightly constructed with cycle-type wheels and accommodating one or two people, generally in extreme discomfort; some of the tandem type, where the passenger sat behind the driver, could be driven through a front gate (pl. 96). They could fit in a structure no larger than 11 feet by 6 feet 6 inches, and garages began to be advertised that in many cases had more in common with a garden shed than a motor house.[36]

In England, the motor car was still seen as something to be kept at arm's length from the house. Notwithstanding Dr Barrett's heated passage from dining room to garage, attempts to integrate the housing of the car with that of its owner remained rare. In France, however, integral garages began to appear relatively early. The *Car Illustrated* gave examples, chiefly located on the ground or basement floors of three- and four-storey houses, and berated the conservative English for their failure to do likewise.[37] In the U.S.A., Frank Lloyd Wright included an integral garage at the Robie House, Chicago, in 1909. Two accounts of garage design, one French, the other American, include some attractive structures of considerable architectural elaboration, and many of the ground plans include turntables, something not seen in contemporary British domestic garage descriptions.[38] Overall, however, developments in America seem to have followed a similar pattern to England, with the same mixture of converted stables, purpose-built or prefabricated motor houses and elaborate structures with accommodation for chauffeurs, together with the use of large public garages in cities.[39]

•

QUITE FEASIBLE. Some types of cyclecars, notably the tandem type, can be driven through many front gates, especially those of country houses, and of houses built on "Garden City" principles.

96 The cyclecar inaugurated a new era in motoring. Much was made of the way that its narrow width enabled it to fit much more easily into the environs of the average house. From *The Cyclecar*, 27 November 1912, p. 4.

Motor House to Garage, 1918–1939

Integral domestic garages finally began to appear in the early 1920s, although they were still very much the exceptions. Perhaps inevitably, an early instance was Coventry, where in 1920 it was reported that several houses being built along Warwick Road, where many of the city's industrialists lived, had integral garages. An example illustrated in the press – a gable-ended building added at one end of the house but abutting a wing at the rear – suggested that little trouble had been taken to integrate the garage fully into the design.[40] Exactly how the garage should be integrated into the overall design of the house remained a subject for discussion. A suggested design in *The Motor* posited a house on falling land with the garage at the rear, at basement level, underneath the hall and scullery.[41] Sometimes the integral garage was a little tentative, one example being fitted with a fireplace so that it could be converted into an additional room if

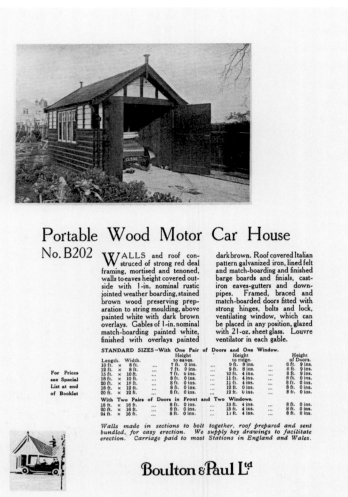

Portable Wood Motor Car House
No. B202

WALLS and roof constructed of strong red deal framing, mortised and tenoned, walls to eaves height covered outside with 1-in. nominal rustic jointed weather boarding, stained brown wood preserving preparation to string moulding, above painted white with dark brown overlays. Gables of 1-in. nominal match-boarding painted white, finished with overlays painted dark brown. Roof covered Italian pattern galvanized iron, lined felt and match-boarding and finished barge boards and finials, cast-iron eaves-gutters and down-pipes. Framed, braced and match-boarded doors fitted with strong hinges, bolts and lock, ventilating window, which can be placed in any position, glazed with 21-oz. sheet glass. Louvre ventilator in each gable.

For Prices see Special List at end of Booklet

STANDARD SIZES—With One Pair of Doors and One Window.

Length.	Width.		Height to eaves.		Height to ridge.		Height of Doors.
10 ft.	× 8 ft.	...	7 ft. 0 ins.	...	9 ft. 8 ins.	...	6 ft. 9 ins.
12 ft.	× 8 ft.	...	7 ft. 0 ins.	...	9 ft. 8 ins.	...	6 ft. 9 ins.
15 ft.	× 10 ft.	...	7 ft. 0 ins.	...	10 ft. 4 ins.	...	6 ft. 9 ins.
18 ft.	× 10 ft.	...	8 ft. 0 ins.	...	11 ft. 4 ins.	...	8 ft. 0 ins.
20 ft.	× 10 ft.	...	8 ft. 0 ins.	...	11 ft. 4 ins.	...	8 ft. 0 ins.
18 ft.	× 12 ft.	...	8 ft. 0 ins.	...	12 ft. 0 ins.	...	8 ft. 0 ins.
20 ft.	× 12 ft.	...	8 ft. 0 ins.	...	12 ft. 0 ins.	...	8 ft. 0 ins.

With Two Pairs of Doors in Front and Two Windows.

18 ft.	× 16 ft.	...	8 ft. 0 ins.	...	13 ft. 4 ins.	...	8 ft. 0 ins.
20 ft.	× 16 ft.	...	8 ft. 0 ins.	...	13 ft. 4 ins.	...	8 ft. 0 ins.
24 ft.	× 16 ft.	...	8 ft. 0 ins.	...	13 ft. 4 ins.	...	8 ft. 0 ins.

Walls made in sections to bolt together, roof prepared and sent bundled, for easy erection. We supply key drawings to facilitate erection. Carriage paid to most Stations in England and Wales.

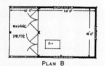

Boulton & Paul Ltd

Page Seven

Wood and Thatch Motor House
No. B207

A PRACTICAL House constructed of strong red deal framing, mortised and tenoned, walls covered outside, partly with rustic jointed weather-boarding stained with our preparation, partly with match-boarding painted white. Stained inside with oil stain, the doors 8-ft. high, framed and match-boarded, painted three coats and fitted with strong hinges, good locks and bolts. The windows glazed with 21-oz. sheet glass, part of each window made to open for ventilation and fitted with butts and set-opes. Roof of principal and common rafters and purlins, with match-boarding for lining, covered with Norfolk reed thatch or Brosely tiles. Eaves-gutters and down-pipes.

For Prices see Special List at End of Booklet

PLAN A   PLAN B

Erection by Boulton & Paul's own men on purchaser's concrete foundation floor. Carriage paid to most Stations in England and Wales.

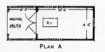

Boulton & Paul Ltd

Page Twelve

97   Pages from a Boulton & Paul catalogue of 1925 depicting one of their most popular designs, available in a wide range of sizes to suit different types of car, and a more elaborate thatched motor house with washing shelter, displaying ornate features more associated with the pre-1914 period.

required.[42] By 1928 integral garages were much more common, provided with many speculatively built estate houses. It still tended to be the larger properties that had them, but they were now being included in four-bedroom semi-detached houses selling at £1,275, where the fourth bedroom was over a garage placed at the side of the house.[43] The following year a writer in *Ideal Home* noted that 'where a goodly number of new homes are built, or in course of erection, at least 60 per cent, are equipped with garages', although this figure seems unduly high.[44]

Provision for car washing was still important until the arrival of cellulose paint in the mid-1920s. A washing shelter was a rarely achieved luxury, most people being content to wash cars in the open air in public. In the early 1920s, however, some degree of privacy was considered essential. Where there was room, a second pair of doors or gates could be placed in front of the garage to provide a screen.[45] An alternative recommended option was to have doors at both ends of the garage, so that washing or tinkering with the car could be done in privacy in the back garden.[46]

Some of the established portable building manufacturers, such as Boulton & Paul and Browne & Lilley, continued to manufacture elaborate domestic garages into the early 1920s. Indeed, it is clear from the illustrations in Boulton & Paul's catalogue of 1925 that they were still using many of their pre-1914 designs; surprisingly, the Edwardian motor cars depicted had not been retouched (pl. 97). Even a design with a glazed washing shelter was still available.[47] Iron and asbestos motor-car houses were offered, as was a 'Cheap Motor House'. A cyclecar shed of the plainest appearance was available for between £19 and £21 15s. Other firms offered them for £12 to £15.

In 1920 *The Motor* published a review of ready-made garages, listing some fourteen manufacturers (pl. 98). Prices averaged around £50 for a single garage, the lowest being £35, while Boulton & Paul's cost £66. The garages were generally quite plain, decoration being limited to half-timbered gables and shaped finials; Nissen were offering a corrugated iron garage in their familiar rounded shape. The article stressed the necessity of lining the garage with asbestos cement sheets, flat galvanised sheets or matchboarding. It recommended a concrete rather than a wooden floor, but pointed out that locally sourced materials such as hard-rolled cinders and broken paving stones might be equally suitable.[48] A further review in 1925 listed nineteen manufacturers, using a variety of materials that included corrugated iron, fluted iron panels, breeze partition slabs, asbestos sheets, weatherboarding and tongue-and-groove matchboarding.[49]

Some local authorities insisted on fireproof garages. This accounts for the boom in asbestos garages, most manufacturers offering one as part of their range. Morris introduced timber, later steel-framed (supplied by Rubery Owen, who made their chassis frames) asbestos garages in 1925 with two inexpensive designs, the Cowley and the Oxford, designed to fit the respective car models (see pl. 81). They were covered against fire by the insurance policy that accompanied new Morris cars.[50] An alternative to asbestos was a garage of corrugated iron sheet bolted on to an angle iron frame: Astley Brooke & Co. made one in which the doors were of flat iron sheets that folded up and ran inwards to the side walls.[51] Some local authorities were particularly strict, insisting on all-steel garages alongside houses.

Technical innovation was rare, but not unknown. As early as 1924 there was a description of how garage doors or garden gates could be opened electrically, triggered by the sound of a car's horn or by its lights.[52] By 1935 such a device was commercially available with the 'Parlee' automatic opener. This operated by means of a contact plate in the drive depressed by the wheel of the car entering it, which completed a circuit to an electrically operated lock above the doors.[53] An up-and-over door, which slid upwards and backwards into the roof space and was composed of leaves about 2 feet deep, was introduced in 1928 by the Educational Supply Association, but it was to be many years before it replaced the traditional arrangement of doors opening outwards: folding doors or sliding ones of timber, which glided inwards on small wheels, initially enjoyed greater success.[54]

The era of popular motoring brought about by the introduction of such cars as the bullnose Morris and the Austin 7 led to a widespread demand for domestic garages. It was some time before builders took note of rising car ownership. In 1923 it was stated that, 'of the tens of thousands of new houses that have been erected since the war, very few are provided with facilities for keeping even a small car or a motorcycle'.[55] Alan A. Jackson, historian of London's suburbia, however, notes that in the early 1930s so remote was the likelihood of car ownership among many house purchasers that estate agents found that a slightly higher-priced house with a garage sold much more slowly than a cheaper one without.[56] Numerous articles on how to construct one's own garage appeared, directed at the less-affluent motorist. Some were of an ingenious nature, such as the one that incorporated part of the roof frame from a Bessoneau aircraft hanger, purchased from a war-surplus dump.[57]

The utilitarian nature of many of the garages that were put up in the 1920s – designs that failed to match in any way the houses they served – led to numerous articles that pointed out that the garage was not intrinsically ugly; by good design, it was possible to build something that would be an ornament rather than an eyesore. An enthusiastic writer in this vein was P. A. Barron, author of *The House Desirable* (1929), who was a leading advocate of Neo-Tudor architecture.[58] He was amazed by the way in which garages were built as far away from the house as possible, screened by trees, when it would be much more convenient for them to be built attached to, or close to, the house. He pointed to the garages that had recently been erected as part of a development of Neo-Tudor weekend cottages at West Chiltington Common and elsewhere in Sussex. These were built of reclaimed materials; some were clad in wavy-edged boarding with the bark remaining, and others were thatched in Norfolk reed.[59] In another article, he suggested that drives could be softened by replacing ugly concrete with two narrow paths for the wheels, with a strip of grass between and a pergola above.[60] But these were exceptions: many garages were simply objects of derision, such as the 'The 20th Century Motor House' covered with 'Brick Pattern Metal Building Sheets to Walls and Metal Scalloped Tile Pattern Sheets to Roofs, all heavily galvanised', an advertisement for which was featured by the *Architects' Journal* in its 'This Arshetecture' column in 1937.[61] Garages illustrated in a review of 1938 showed little advance on those shown in the reviews of 1920 and 1925; if anything, they were even plainer in appearance.[62] If its appearance was too offensive to the eye, the garage could always be hidden behind climbing plants attached to a trellis.[63]

From Council Houses to Country Houses

By the 1930s the provision of a garage – or space for one – had become an important consideration in designing new housing estates. In assessing the evidence provided by 1930s suburban development around London, however, Alan A. Jackson suggests that few house purchasers in the £550 to £900 bracket were expected to be car owners, since developers kept a close eye on the market and provided what that market wanted. In the range £300 to £650, which covered the four- and six-block terraces,

Hawthorn

Hobson.

Brown & Lilley.

National.

South Western Appliances Cº

Percy White.

F. Praffen & Cº

Goddard

T. Bath & Cº

Sutcliffe.

98 (above and facing page)   A selection of prefabricated garages available from the principal manufacturers in 1920. From *The Motor*, 15 December 1920, pp. 1022–4.

only the end-of-terrace houses had any car space. In 1937 there was only one car owner on a lower-middle-class estate of such terrace blocks in Tolworth, Surrey, on a road almost a quarter of a mile long.[64] There is evidence, however, to suggest that by the 1930s some skilled working men were acquiring cars, which could be obtained for a few pounds second-hand. In 1937 Liverpool Corporation drafted conditions for the erection of garages on council estates, specifying that the tenant had to pay an extra 2s. per week in rent and to build the garage to an approved specification if the application was approved by the Housing Committee.[65]

The space provided by the developer, with strips by the side of the house no more than 7 feet wide, was often insufficient to house a car properly. The type of garages used by tenants and owners of the average semi-detached house had interior dimensions of 15 feet by 7 feet 6 inches. Only the smallest cars could be housed in them, and there was barely enough room to open the door to get out. By the mid-1930s cars were getting larger in relation to their horsepower. A Morris 10 of 1933 was 12 feet 3 inches long; the equivalent model of 1936 was 13 feet 9 inches in length. It was argued that the minimum convenient size for a garage was 18 by 9 feet, and for those who intended to service their own cars, 20 feet by 10 feet 6 inches. *Motor Commerce* thought that motor agents should bring pressure to bear on developers to build larger garages or to make more space available.[66] Some volume house builders now integrated garages into relatively small three-bedroom semi-detached houses, often by extending the roof of the house to form a catslide over the garage at the side. On more expensive houses, efforts were made to harmonise the design of the garage and the house by the use of the same materials, such as repeating the half-timbering of the house on the gable end, or by linking the garage to the house with an archway to the garden. Although the side of the house was probably the most common site for the garage, lack of space led to two other solutions in the 1920s and 1930s. One

was a driveway shared with an adjacent house with a pair of garages located a short distance behind the houses – in many cases too close to them, making it difficult to reverse out of the garage.[67] The other was a garage at the bottom of the garden, approached by an unmade back lane, also used for refuse collection (pl. 99).

Even greater difficulties were faced by those who lived in areas of Victorian or Edwardian houses where there was insufficient land between the buildings to accommodate a car. One solution that was eventually quite widely employed was to use the basement below the principal ground-floor room for a garage. The first recorded instance of this was in 1922 at Cannon Place, Hampstead, where the basement floor was level with the pavement.[68] The idea was further developed with the excavating of space below the ground floor of a house, but much of the front garden was then lost and the resulting ramp to the road was very steep. The concept was evidently still novel in 1932, when a photograph of a conversion of this type at Carshalton, Surrey, was published.[69] Two examples exist side by side in Chantry Road, Moseley, and, in the neighbouring Park Lane, a double-fronted Victorian house has had the left-hand ground-floor room replaced by a garage, probably in the 1930s: another popular, if inelegant solution to the garage problem.

At the upper end of the market, integral garages had become much more common by the 1930s (pl. 100). As *The Autocar* put it, 'why not drive right into the hall?', or make the garage into a reception hall into which guests could drive, leave their coats and make their way to the drawing room? Or, to put it another way, 'You do not keep the billiard table in an outhouse and then have to don waterproof and sou'-wester before you can begin to play. Why treat the car so differently?'[70] A guide for potential house buyers in Surrey and Hampshire, published in 1937, included some 134 views depicting new houses of all price brackets, although most were detached; of these, 82 had garages visible (the total figure is likely to be much higher, since many

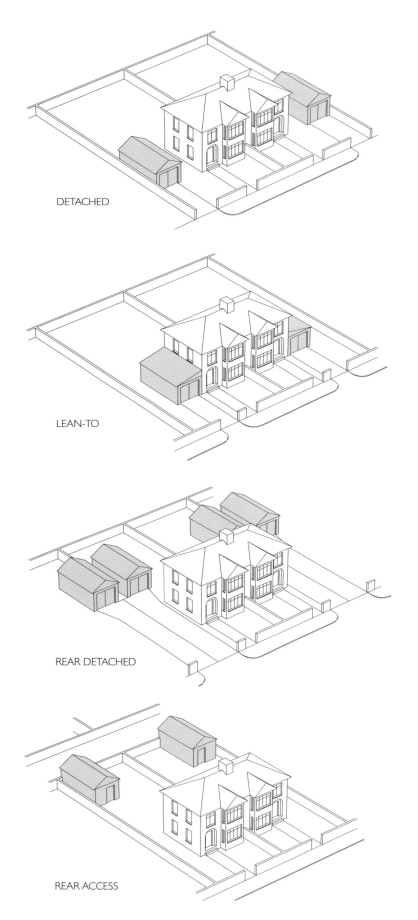

DETACHED

LEAN-TO

REAR DETACHED

REAR ACCESS

must have been out of shot or located behind the houses), of which 25 were integral.[71] A popular approach was to have the garage at one end of the house with a catslide roof running down to it, in a manner similar to that for smaller semi-detached houses. But, on the whole, garages became much more part of the house, and sometimes began to provide accommodation for two cars. Some examples of designs from the *Ideal Home* books of house plans illustrate a number of approaches, which include an L-shaped house where the double garage is almost the dominant feature, occupying half the front elevation; a Neo-Tudor house with the garage within the body of the house alongside the front door with bedrooms above (a very common arrangement); a moderne house with a garage on the rounded corner; and a Neo-Georgian house where the garage at the side is balanced by a gate to the garden with a matching parapet.[72] An exhibit at the *Ideal Home* exhibition of 1934, Wells Coates's Sunspan house for E. & L. Berg, had a small garage, which, although attached to the side of the house, was integrated effectively into the design: it was adjacent to a door on the rounded corner of the house, linked visually by a canopy that also protected passengers as they got out of the car. No door between garage and hall was provided, because car fumes could be detected in houses with such interconnecting doors in hot weather. Car exhaust emissions were far higher than today, and this may explain why, despite *The Autocar*'s invitation, so few garages had interconnecting doors.[73]

Perhaps the ultimate examples of integral garages were those of mews houses in central London, notably in Mayfair and Belgravia. As has been seen, immediately prior to the First World War stables were converted quickly to garages, but in the 1920s, increasingly, what was built as grooms' accommodation was converted into bijou residences for the relatively well-to-do, who were being squeezed out of the West End by rising housing costs. The conversions were often distinguished externally by brightly painted brickwork, although the accommodation remained cramped. In some cases, where a wider site was available, more extensive rebuilding could take place, as at a mews house in Farm Street in Mayfair, given a new façade by Clough Williams-Ellis.[74] As an alternative, existing mews buildings could be demolished and replaced by three-storey houses, such as Wren House, Mount Row (1927; T. P. Bennett).[75] As its name suggests, this was 'Wrenaissance' in style with swags and circular windows, looking slightly odd above a ground-floor elevation consisting mainly of plain garage doors. Throughout the inter-war years, many London mews were transformed in this way, the houses making no secret of the motor car's presence.

99   Four common locations for domestic garages, serving semi-detached houses.

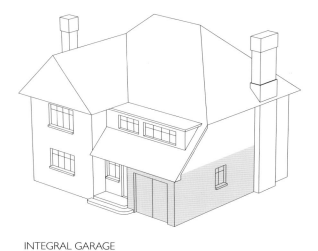

INTEGRAL GARAGE

100   The garage fully integrated with the house, a popular arrangement since the 1920s.

Adapting to the stringent financial circumstances of the post-war era, the well-to-do in the countryside began to make more modest provision for the car. In many cases, redundant estate buildings could be converted into garages at considerably less expense than building anew. Because cars needed less in the way of maintenance, there was no need for the workshops found pre-1914; the car would now be taken to a local garage for repairs. Provision of space for several cars and accommodation for chauffeurs were still to be found, but nothing else was required.

101   Coleton Fishacre, Devon, an Arts and Crafts style garage and chauffeur's accommodation (1923–6; Oswald P Milne).

The motor house at Coleton Fishacre on the south Devon coast, built between 1923 and 1926, typifies this trend towards simpler design (pl. 101). Designed by Oswald Milne, the garage block included a chauffeur's flat and staff cottages. The house it accompanied was the type of family holiday home or weekend retreat feasible only in the age of the motor car. The house was designed in an Arts and Crafts style, and the garage block complemented it with white render, sweeping roofs and simple casement windows. It had a central garage section and a projecting flat-roofed canopy.

A much greater contrast in styles between a garage and a country house can be seen at Thanet Place on the outskirts of Broadstairs in Kent. Both were built to the designs of Edgar Ranger in 1929. The house was classical, whilst the garage was designed in an English vernacular style with tile hanging, broad hipped roofs and tall brick stacks. The garage block was topped with a cupola and clock, reminiscent of a traditional stable building. It had chauffeurs' accommodation on the first floor, with the garaging accessed via a glazed canopy.[76] Something similar was to be seen at Eltham Palace in south-east London, where the garage, designed by Seely & Paget in 1933, was in a style that again took its inspiration from the vernacular, in contrast to the former royal palace converted into a spectacular modern house.[77] Seely & Paget's long, low range had a tall hipped roof and prominent chimney stacks, and was equipped with double garages with domestic accommodation above and at either end. Both at Thanet Place and at Eltham, the garages were at some distance from the house, out of its direct view, indicating that, as in the Edwardian period, the car was still not something to be shown off, although considerable care was taken in both designs to enhance the setting of the house. But such buildings were increasingly rare and, from here, the story of housing cars at country houses loses its distinct character and merges with that of the domestic garage.

The Modern Movement and the Car

Modernism embraced the motor car with enthusiasm. Le Corbusier in *Vers une architecture* (1923) viewed it as an ideal product of the machine age: 'Well, it remains to use the motor car as a challenge to our houses and our great buildings';[78] in other words, architecture had failed to keep up with the progress of the machine as represented by the car. Inevitably, he saw car provision as essential in house design, and included integral garages in his villas from the earliest days. In doing so, he was also perhaps responding to a French tradition that had been established before 1914, as has been seen. In the Villa Cook, Boulogne-sur-Seine (1926), Le Corbusier included a garage with an interconnecting door into the hall; it was recessed from the

102   Chauffeur's cottage and garage, Miramonte, Coombe, Kingston upon Thames (1936–7; Maxwell Fry). Photographed by Dell & Wainwright in 1937.

façade of the four-storey house, which was supported on pilotis. The turning circle of a car determined the proportions of the Villa Savoye (1928–31), which was intended to be experienced first by car: one had to drive around the house to the garage, tucked neatly amongst the pilotis.[79]

In England, garages following the lead not only of Le Corbusier, but also of architects such as Mallet-Stevens, were often integral to the houses of the Modern Movement. A glance through F. R. S. Yorke's *The Modern House in England* (1944) reveals that, almost without exception, garaging was provided for at least one and, often, two or more cars.[80] Such provision was only to be expected, given the type of people who would commission an architect-designed house. But what is more significant is the way that garages were integrated into the houses that Yorke described and illustrated. Here emerges a building type

that became popular in the 1960s: the town house on three or more storeys where the garage occupies most of the ground floor. Denys Lasdun's house in Newton Road, Paddington (1939), and Tayler & Green's house at Highgate Hill (1940) are substantial detached examples of the genre that owed much to the layout of Le Corbusier's Villa Cook. But particularly significant was the terraced group of four at Plumstead, Kent (1934), by Lubetkin, which established a plan that became the prototype for vast numbers of houses: three bedrooms with a first-floor living room and only an entrance hall and garage on the ground floor. Both Connell, Ward & Lucas at Ruislip, Middlesex (1935), and G. Alan Fortescue at Maidenhead, Berkshire (1932), produced designs for semi-detached houses with garages brought forward from the façades.[81] The formalist qualities of Modern Movement houses enabled garages to be integrated seamlessly into a balanced façade design, as at Maxwell Fry's Sun House, Hampstead (1936), and Le Château at Silver End, Essex (1927; Thomas Tait of Sir John Burnet & Partners), where the cantilevered canopy over the garage doors echoed the form of the balcony.[82] Tait also used the garage as a fundamental part of the symmetrical composition of The Haven, Newbury, Berkshire (1929): brought slightly forward of the main body of the house, and with a corresponding walled service yard on the other side, it fulfilled the role of a single-storey pavilion.[83]

Although associated with the pre-1914 era of motoring, the chauffeur's cottage was by no means extinct. In 1936–7 Maxwell Fry built a Modern Movement version at Miramonte, Coombe, Surrey, which accommodated several cars in an integral garage on the ground floor and housing for a chauffeur above, complete with prominent corner balcony (pl. 102).

The growth in blocks of luxury flats in the 1930s posed new challenges, since they were designed to appeal to relatively well-off tenants who would expect parking provision. Berkeley Court, Baker Street, in London (1930; W. E. Masters) had a covered semicircular drive within the building that enabled res-

idents to be set down under cover at the front hall. But it did not have any parking: a roadway for trade vehicles occupied the basement.[84] By the mid-1930s basement car parks had become the norm for those living in the centre of London, often combined with a corner filling station, such as that run by Moon's at Russell Court, Woburn Place (1937; G. Val Myer & F. J. Watson-Hart).[85] Here, the accommodation for cars was unencumbered by intermediate supports, the twelve floors of flats above being carried on reinforced concrete beams of almost 40-foot span. Four turntables eased manoeuvring within the basement. Similar accommodation was designed by the same architects at Fountain House, Park Lane, Mayfair (1938).[86] One of the largest underground garages was probably Dolphin Square in Pimlico (1935–7; Gordon Jeeves), which had a centrally heated car park accommodating 400 cars.[87] Further out, Richmond Hill Court, Richmond (pl. 103; see Chapter 5), had parking underneath a hard tennis court at the front of the development, while at Pullman Court, Streatham (1934–5; Frederick Gibberd), parking was in banks of lock-ups on the periphery of the site – this was the favoured suburban answer.[88] An impressive variant

103   A communal garage at Richmond Hill Court, Richmond, Surrey, that had the roof laid out as a tennis court. Outwardly it has changed little, although extensive rebuilding was carried out in 1950 following wartime bomb damage, with concrete beams replacing steel girders in the roof. Photographed on 15 May 1934.

104   A view, taken by Dell & Wainwright in 1938, from Highpoint 2, Highgate, London, of the accompanying garage block by Lubetkin & Tecton incorporating a rooftop garden.

on this theme was to be seen at Highpoint 2, Highgate (1938; Lubetkin & Tecton; pl. 104), where staggered blocks of concrete lock-ups (seven blocks, each containing four garages) were integrated by a rooftop garden running their entire length. A spiral staircase gave access at one end, and, because the garages were built on a slope, there was a short flight of steps between each block of four. A prestigious development in Chelsea, 'The Gateways' (1935; Wills & Kaula), of fifty houses and fourteen flats, had a garage court with twenty-two garages below the flats.[89]

•

Garaging Away from Home, 1900–1930

In the early twentieth century the need to provide a car with a conveniently placed shelter – a motor house, or domestic garage – may have deterred many would-be motorists from buying one. The chauffeur also needed to live close to the car, not just to be on hand to drive when required, but also because he was expected to undertake the repair and maintenance of the car, and to wash and polish it regularly.

As car ownership cascaded downward from the upper classes, more middle-class town dwellers confronted the problem of accommodating and looking after their new vehicle. For those with space around their house – and sufficient funds – there was a simple solution: build a motor house or convert an old stable or coach house, if necessary with associated chauffeur's accommodation. But not all car owners had the space; many lived in city-centre flats or small houses that had been erected cheek-by-jowl with no thought for the motor car. These owners were obliged to seek garaging further afield, perhaps in a disused stable or mews, or in a commercial garage.

By the early 1900s most commercial garages offered to house cars for private owners, whether they lived locally or not. But if cars were kept in an open parking area – as they often were – they would be vulnerable to damage, or even theft. And so, before the First World War, it became common for cars to be kept in individual metal cages, or lock-ups. This was as much the case in provincial towns as in central London: no examples of cage lock-ups from this era are known to survive, but they can be seen in old photographs (see Wolseley's Niagara Garage in Westminster, pl. 204). Some commercial garages, such as those of the London Motor Car Co. on Page Street and Wardour Street, specialised in this kind of 'garaging', which they undertook on a subscription basis. The Alveston Motor Garage in south-west London not only garaged and maintained cars, but also provided a driver, paid his wages and supplied livery.[90] Annual charges were calculated according to horsepower, up to a mileage limit of 6,000. An owner would simply telephone the garage and wait for his car to be delivered.

Since it was very inconvenient for chauffeurs to live far from a car, a few commercial garages provided driver accommodation, as well as lock-ups, for local car owners. At the Earls Court Motor Garage, the premises of a livery stable keeper were adapted to provide two rows of private lock-ups under rooms for chauffeurs and their families.[91] Occasionally, alternatives were proposed. In 1909, for example, an interesting experiment – ultimately a one-off – took place in Hampstead Garden Suburb. This was a three-storey, L-shaped block surrounding two sides of a square at the end of Corringway, at the southern end of the new suburb. It incorporated integral lock-up accommodation (in cubicles 10 by 18ft) for cars on the ground floor, with rental flats for chauffeurs on the upper floors. The building was replaced in 1996.

By the 1920s motorists were growing wary of keeping their cars in commercial garages. According to the *Light Car and Cyclecar*:

> Motorists themselves are tired of the average open garage. They like to feel that their car has its own particular niche, where it may be stored under lock and key and where it is not likely to be interfered with in any way. The picture of a number of cars being manhandled in an open garage so that a vehicle in a remote corner can be extricated from the general jumble is all too familiar.[92]

Many garages responded by providing solid lock-ups, now erected in a row outside rather than under the main roof, to keep cars out of sight of would-be thieves. An early example served the first inhabitants of Welwyn Garden City, Hertfordshire, where the 'public garage' on Bridge Street (demolished) was built with eight private lock-ups, and space for a further five if necessary. This was soon a woefully inadequate provision for the growing town. In cities, large parking garages sometimes set an entire floor aside for lock-ups, usually in the basement, with separate ramp access. The basement of the Blue Bird Garage,

105   A suggestion for a community lock-up by Max Millar, published in *The Autocar*, 30 March 1928, p. 651.

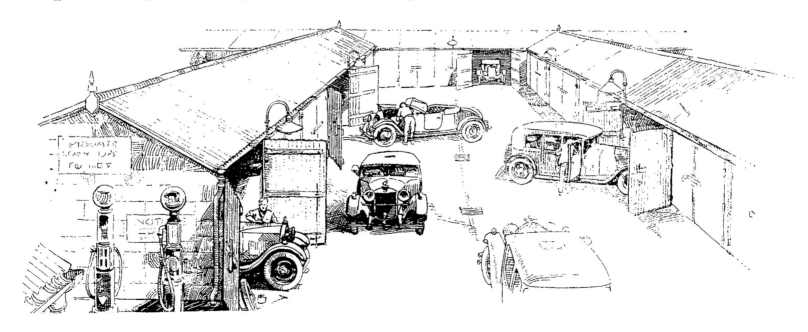

Chelsea, held thirty lock-ups, as well as some open parking space.[93] The Reservoir Garage in Kensington was created in 1925 from a former reservoir, with fifteen sections covered by arc roofs. On the lower level, forty-eight private lock-ups were reached by 'a slow incline', that is, a long ramp. At the Lex Garage in Soho, eighty metal mesh lock-ups on the basement floor, reserved for a permanent clientele, were accessed by ramp from Ingestre Place. Withers & Co.'s new garage of 1929 at 35 Edgware Road was for a private clientele in the neighbourhood: two floors were connected by ramps, with both open garaging and lock-ups.[94] The logical extension of this idea was to build a multi-storey car park, with lock-ups instead of parking bays. In 1927 W. R. Field proposed a multi-storey garage with eighty-five lock-up cubicles set at an angle on each floor;[95] it is not clear where the idea came from, but his scheme was never realised, and no multi-storey lock-up garages were built in Britain until the 1960s (see below), though one was erected in Berlin in 1925, and earlier examples seem to have existed in the U.S.A.

The idea of independent banks of lock-ups, not associated with a commercial garage, and without housing for chauffeurs, had a greater future than other approaches to the problem. In 1912 a scheme for a neighbourhood communal garage was proposed, modelled on existing garages for London cabs but also influenced by the Hampstead Garden Suburb experiment:[96] It was thought that communal garages might be developed by existing garage businesses, or set up by groups of owners. For a fixed annual sum, secure, accessible, heated accommodation would be provided for cars (twelve was the ideal number), and there would be some repair and maintenance facilities, including skilled labour, on site. Several schemes of this nature appeared after the end of the First World War, but none is known before 1914.

Sets of lock-ups (or 'communal garages') came into being after 1918, especially in the London suburbs, charging up to 15s. a week. They were usually erected by developers, by existing garages, or even by groups of enthusiasts formed into clubs or co-operatives (such as the Car Owners Club, which opened a garage in Finsbury Park in 1920).[97] In 1920 a number of lock-ups of different sizes for tenants to rent at 7s. 6d. per week were provided at Ilford Garden City.[98] Another early venture was Mr Loadsby's Cubicle Garage on Springbank Road, Hither Green, near Lewisham, with ten cubicles, 10 feet 1 inch wide and 20 feet long, for single cars; four bays 11 foot 6 inches wide and 24 feet long for commercial cars and charabancs; three open garages of varying sizes for two or three cars apiece; and a workshop, office, petrol store and, in the middle of the yard, a washing space.[99]

Sufficiently few sets of lock-ups existed by 1925 for them still to be categorised as a luxury. Typically, they were cheaply con-structed, with either steel roller shutters or stout wooden doors, brick walls and slightly sloping, corrugated asbestos roofs. A communal washing bay with good drainage was considered essential. One of the first – regarded as a pioneer – was J. & K. Garages, Hayes Crescent, Golders Green, built around 1921. These were taller than later lock-ups, with windows over the doorways. Few lock-ups had architectural pretensions, one exception being the building with three lock-ups erected by a local developer, Richard Ellwood, on Mountfield Road, Finchley, around 1925. With its mock-timber gable and hipped tile roof, this closely resembled Edwardian coach houses. Both this and the Hayes Crescent lock-ups are still extant. One entrepreneur who built several 'nests' of lock-ups was George Scratchley, a building contractor and ironmonger of Thornton Heath, south London.[100] His lock-ups were large, of brick with corrugated asbestos roofs and cement floors; they were fitted with hanging electric lights, a heavy working bench, a plug for the bench, shelves and storage space; there was a gravelled yard, a cemented wash-down fitted with an oil-proof drain, and a pit, but no attendant.

More economical approaches also existed. In 1925 fifty-six lock-ups were created under the new railway arches adjacent to Golders Green Station, where – because of the width of the arches – each garage could accommodate two cars; here, there was an associated service depot. The Autocar noted in 1928 that nests of lock-ups to let were being erected on any spare land available,[101] and, following a proposal for community lock-ups in the same issue (pl. 105), proprietors of the Exhibition Garage, Olympia, built two rows of lock-ups on a narrow strip of land beside the railway, entered from Addison Bridge Place (demolished). The lock-ups varied in size, the largest being 8 feet by 18 feet, and they were divided by roller shutters. Each was lighted, and had hot water heating pipes; a central gutter or drain and standpipes or hoses provided for washing. The rent, inclusive of rates, heating, lighting and free air for tyres, was from 12s. 6d. to £1 per week. In 1930 the Motor Exchange, Lavender Hill, Battersea, had two rows of lock-ups flanking the drive to a large converted house.[102] The garages were on sloping ground and were built by the proprietor.

Lock-ups continued to be provided in parking garages. At Lex, St John's Wood, in 1929, cars were garaged by make: 'thus one finds in these bays a group of Morris cars, then an Austin group or a Singer group'.[103] In 1938–41 the Regent Garage was built at 21–41 Wellington Road, across the road from the Lex.[104] The owner was L. G. Leanse. The complex included three parallel rows of lock-up garages on a rectangular site, with an office block in the centre of the front row. There were ninety-four garages, their fronts enclosed by roller shutters. Small garages outside central London tended to be multi-function establishments: few were solely or even mainly for parking. Lock-ups were added to existing repair and maintenance garages wherever there was space. Bowman's Garage, Stamford Hill (1926), had forty lock-ups at 12s. 6d. per week. Drew's Motor Mart, Manor Park, provided twenty-eight steel-frame lock-up garages to the side of a petrol station in 1929. In each case, these were outside lock-ups, rather than being contained within a larger workshop building. They had significant advantages for the garage owner, since he was responsible for any damage to a car kept in his garage, but liability lay with the car owner when a lock-up was let. The car owner was also required to keep the lock-up in good repair.

After the Second World War

Technically, there was little change in the domestic garage after 1945, with one exception. Timber, asbestos and corrugated iron designs continued as before, their half-timbered gables and finials looking increasingly anachronistic when set against the sleeker car designs of the late 1950s. The one big change was the arrival of the concrete garage. This was a relative latecomer, although isolated examples had appeared as early as 1910. In 1933 the Standard Steel Co. (1929) Ltd introduced the Stanseco reinforced concrete garage. It was of conventional appearance with a pitched roof 'moulded to resemble the old-English roofing tiles' – fakery always seemed to be an intrinsic part of concrete garage design – and supported on a steel framework. The concrete slabs could be dismantled if required, and the cost for a concrete garage measuring 16 feet by 8 feet 9 inches was £39 10s. This was more than a wooden garage but less than a brick-built one. But there were few takers. After 1945 three firms, Batley (who began production in 1948), Marley (from 1949–50) and Banbury (from 1952), dominated the rapidly growing market, but most manufacturers produced concrete designs.[105] A number had roofs sloping towards the rear rather than the pitched roofs found in other types of construction. They varied considerably in appearance: some had panels cast to resemble clapboarding; others had rectangular panels or panels with a masonry effect imitating the appearance and colour of Cotswold limestone. For those unhappy with raw concrete, Kencast offered colouring kits complete with brushes. As an alternative, Batley's 'Leofric' model was faced with ¾-inch brickwork.[106]

Nineteen garage manufacturers were found in a survey by *The Autocar* in 1959, and forty-nine in one by *The Motor* in 1962 (pl. 106).[107] Asbestos garages were the cheapest, with metal and timber costing about the same; concrete, the most expensive material, cost approximately £20 more. Despite this, concrete garages gained ground, since they were more durable and easier to maintain. Another feature that was increasing in popularity was the up-and-over door. By the early 1960s another form of

106 A number of manufacturers of prefabricated garages advertised themselves by the use of cast combined nameplates and finials, as seen in this example in Ferndale Road, Swindon, Wiltshire.

car shelter had made its appearance: the car port, built on to the side of a house. Open at the front and back, it was less intrusive than an ordinary garage and did not obscure the side windows of the house; it cost less in rates too. Its main drawback was that it could not store all the tools and general clutter that people tended to put in their garages; and, since the structure was made of light timber and was more exposed to the weather, it did not last long.

A new phenomenon in the late 1950s was the need to provide garages in large quantities on council estates. Although official guidance recommended banks of lock-up garages, rather than individual ones within people's gardens, lock-ups were frequently omitted from the initial phases of housing schemes. In addition, many older estates were built in an age when it was inconceivable that a substantial proportion of working men would be able to afford to run a car, and there was insufficient spare land to provide garages of any type.[108] But by 1960 local authorities were facing increasing pressure to make adequate provision, with car ownership constantly outstripping even the most optimistic forecasts of growth. Car ownership on public housing estates in Sheffield rose from 5 per cent in 1950 to more than 20 per cent by 1960.[109] The City Architect, J. L. Womersley, explored a number of solutions, including attached garages at the front of three-bedroom terraced houses at Middlewood, integral double garages in the base of maisonettes and wide-fronted houses at Gleadless Valley, and a ramped garage on five floors at Park Hill. Batteries of concrete lock-up garages of utilitarian flat-roofed appearance were built across England. The minimum size requirement was 9 feet 2 inches in width and 19 feet in length, with, ideally, heating and lighting at the bonnet end to enable maintenance to take place. There was rarely any architectural pretension compared with examples overseas, such as some 1950s German lock-ups, which had tapering concrete pilasters, canopies and tile roofs. Integral lock-ups became a feature of the ground level of many apartment blocks, especially those with deck access. By the 1970s a parking to dwelling ratio of 1:1 became the norm, leading to extensive provision of garages and parking areas at basement level in such innovative developments as the Brunswick Centre and the Alexandra Road estate, both in the London Borough of Camden. As with banks of lock-ups, however, garaging under blocks of housing was often perceived as a threatening environment and owners became reluctant to leave their cars there. An example is the now-demolished Hyson Green estate, Nottingham. Where there was a shortage of available land, local authorities occasionally incorporated lock-ups into general open car parks, one extant example being on the east side of The Campus at Welwyn Garden City, built in 1963–4 (pl. 107).[110]

New ways of accommodating the car were explored in the private sector as well. A multi-storey lock-up garage (demol-ished) was built in Barking, Essex,[111] designed and patented by Parking Systems Ltd. Steel-cased fire-protected columns supported a concrete deck and carried wire mesh panels dividing the garages, which were equipped with up-and-over doors. The rediscovery of the urban terrace in the early 1960s was more significant: three-storey houses, broadly similar in plan to the Lubetkin houses in Plumstead, began to appear on infill sites in the leafier London suburbs such as Dulwich, and then spread throughout much of the country. The Lubetkin model was ideally suited to development in relatively high densities, necessitated by the cost of land. It represented a significant change in house design, for very few three-storey houses had been built since 1914. The early developments were in the Scandinavian-influenced modernism of the time with large windows, simple detailing and pitched roofs, and the steel up-and-over doors to the integral garages that took up much of the ground floor harmonised well with it. While such houses were being put up by developers such as Wates, who had the architectural skills on hand to design effectively, all was well, but when Neo-Georgian

107   Municipal car park at The Campus, Welwyn Garden City, Hertfordshire (built 1963–4), incorporating lock-ups for residents.

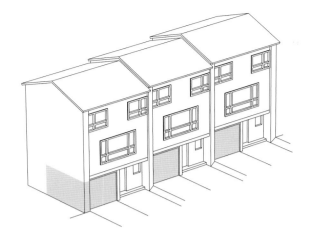

TERRACE INTERNAL GARAGE

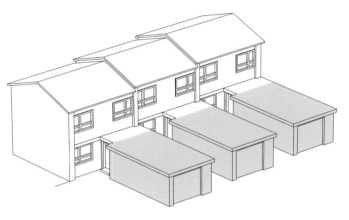

TERRACE EXTERNAL GARAGE

108 New approaches to integrated garages: the town house with the garage on the ground floor (1960s onwards) and the garage attached to the front of the house, which enjoyed a vogue in the 1960s and 1970s.

or Neo-Victorian styles were adopted for the three-storey house with integral garage – as they were increasingly – the results were often strange to behold. The town house (as developers and estate agents soon named it) became one of the most common designs, enduring to the present day (pl. 108).

The New Towns: The Case of Harlow

In the new towns set up under the New Towns Act of 1946, many attempts were made to address the increasing numbers of cars. Harlow is a case in point. The flaw of the Harlow master-plan was that, like Unwin and the planners of the garden cities (see Chapter 12), it failed to envisage the enormous growth in

car ownership and use. Its author, Frederick Gibberd, Architect-Planner to the Harlow Development Corporation (HDC), wanted to provide 20 per cent of homes with garages, but was prevented by Ministry of Health guidelines of 10 per cent. As a consequence, parked cars dominate residential areas throughout Harlow, impeding negotiation of the relatively narrow roads.

Harlow has seen almost the full gamut of attempts to solve the problem of what to do with the car, including a number of schemes that may be described as experimental. It also demonstrates how provision for the car has influenced both individual house design and the spatial relationship of neighbourhoods.

At the first part of the new town to be completed, The Lawn (1950–54; F. Gibberd & Partners) and The Chantry (1950–53; Fry, Drew & Partners), only 10 per cent of homes were provided with garaging, with a further 10 per cent of land kept in reserve. In comparison, Crawley, the new town in Sussex, had only 5 per cent. Only one garage court was provided for many of the early developments at Harlow, such as the Mark Hall North neighbourhood, the Chantry and Broomfield, Tanys Dell and Glebelands developments. Subsequently, garage courts were added to all the early neighbourhoods. Garages could be added between the semi-detached houses of the early schemes, laid out on generous plots, but the occupants of terraced houses had to make use of garage courts or park on the road. In more recent years, car parking spaces have been inserted in open spaces such as greens, but increasingly front gardens are being paved over.

At Great Brays, Mark Hall South (1955–7; Ralph Tubbs), the houses were located around greens. A garage court lies inside one of the blocks; another block of garages (with brick facing matching that of the houses) is slotted into a corner, while further parking spaces have been cut out of the greens. At Orchard Croft, two terraces by HDC Design Group of three storeys with integral garages were built in 1951–4. Gibberd, who was himself responsible for the design, stated that it was inspired by Fortfield Terrace, Sidmouth, Devon, but adapted for the car with the insertion of integral garages. It was almost unknown in public housing at the time it was built, but, like the Lubetkin houses, it formed a prototype of the town-house design popular with private developers in the 1960s.

Radburn layouts became fashionable in the early 1950s (pl. 109). Named after a pioneering attempt to separate cars and people at Radburn, New Jersey, in 1928, they consisted of a spine road off which pedestrian paths gave access to terraces of houses, a group of which formed a block. Car parking was arranged in garage courts within each block of houses. Harlow had two Radburn schemes. A Radburn layout with garage blocks at the rear was employed at Ladyshot (1951–4; F. R. S. Yorke), but according to Frederick Gibberd: 'We have no evidence that tenants prefer it or that it is safer than more conventional layouts.'[112] A further application of the Radburn theory was

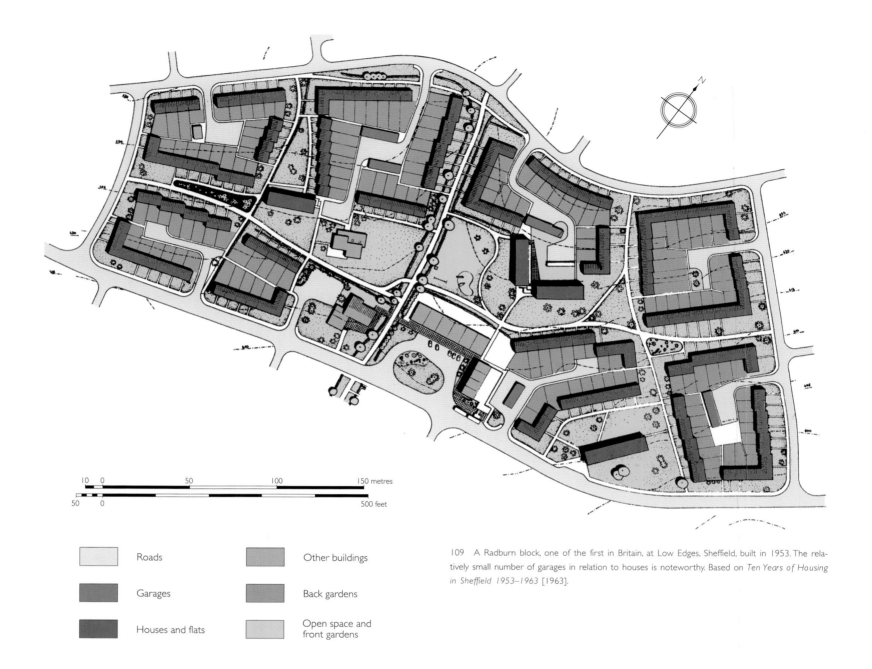

10 0   50   100   150 metres

50 0   500 feet

	Roads		Other buildings
	Garages		Back gardens
	Houses and flats		Open space and front gardens

109 A Radburn block, one of the first in Britain, at Low Edges, Sheffield, built in 1953. The relatively small number of garages in relation to houses is noteworthy. Based on *Ten Years of Housing in Sheffield 1953–1963* [1963].

made at the appropriately named Radburn Close scheme (1960–2; HDC Design Group). The garage courts display a potential weakness of Radburn schemes: a depressing environment of roughly concreted ground surfaces and garage blocks all too clearly visible from the first-floor rear windows of the houses surrounding them. An attempt to avoid these rear access yards was made at the private Old Orchard development by Clifford Culpin & Partners, the winner of a competition sponsored by *Ideal Home* and the RIBA in 1961 (pl. 110). Some houses had integral garages, but most were served by two-storey garage courts and a communal car port. These enabled private gardens to back on to a community open space, shared by the adjacent

houses, akin to the private gardens found at the rear of Ladbroke Grove in west London.

As the development of Harlow continued, population densities increased from forty to seventy persons per acre, aggravating the parking problem. One imaginative scheme was that at Shawbridge (1962–4) by Eric Lyons & Partners. A circular garage court in black brick, matching the neighbouring flats and maisonettes, was adjacent to the distributor road at the entrance to the development. Similar courts were widely used in Cumbernauld New Town. Another was Bishopsfield (1963–6; Michael Neylan & Ungless; pl. 111). Here, the area was entered by car at the top of a hill. The road was carried below a raised concourse

110 A communal car port at Old Orchard, Harlow (1961; Clifford Culpin & Partners).

that has become known as the 'Casbah', with two groups of lock-up garages below. Some of the garages were in what was, in effect, a tunnel, while others faced the open. The concourse or piazza provided access to flats and maisonettes, and single-storey patio houses radiated from it, served by pedestrian lanes. Ramps and flights of steps led down from the concourse to ground level across the service road. There was otherwise a total absence of conventional roads. But this development, with its garages submerged in the gloom of a tunnel, demonstrates the problems that have bedevilled garage provision in public housing – they are located in what is perceived as a threatening environment. There are further parking spaces in front of the complex, which are used in preference to those under the concourse.

In 1967 HDC adopted a standard of 100 per cent garage provision in new developments, 50 per cent of which had to be built at the time, with an additional car parking space for each dwelling. At Moorfield (1966–9; Clifford Culpin & Partners), the provision of car parking dominated the neighbourhood, leading to a rather grim environment of dark alleys, blank walls and drab surfaces. Two massively constructed two-storey garage blocks were separated by a pedestrian walkway. The blocks were of considerable length with two rows of garages facing each other at both lower and upper levels. A ramp gave access to the upper level. The blocks presented a vast and unrelieved wall of yellow

brick to the backs of the surrounding houses. Complete separation of pedestrians and cars was achieved, with pedestrian walkways and an underpass under the distributor road.

111 Garages located under the piazza at Bishopsfield, Harlow, Essex (1963-4; Michael Neylan & Ungless).

Since the 1960s

Harlow illustrates some of the differing solutions to the vastly increased numbers of cars in post-war housing estates. Many led to often threatening, ill-defined areas of public space. But the biggest change has been to the design of the road layouts themselves. Pre-1939 estates generally consisted of through roads, although there was already an increasing number of culs-de-sac, on both private and council estates. From the 1960s onwards, following the recommendation in Buchanan's *Traffic in Towns* (see p. 348) of environmental areas where traffic did not dominate, most estates were planned around a distributor road, with most houses located on short culs-de-sac. It was argued that this layout, with its absence of through traffic, would provide a much safer environment for children. But such developments caused a sense of isolation: the lack of direct roads discouraged people from walking, so they drove everywhere, seldom meeting their neighbours. Journey times increased, since drivers had to negotiate spine roads. The impermeable nature of some neighbourhoods provided opportunities for crime, especially where pedestrian separation created long paths that were not overlooked.

Much more successful were the Span estates designed by Eric Lyons in some of the more affluent outer London suburbs, which put the car in a separate court of garages, screened by vegetation, as part of the overall landscaping of the site (e.g., the Corner Green development, Blackheath, south-east London, 1959).[113] Access to the court was provided by a cul-de-sac running along the edge of the site or behind the houses. The houses were approached by footpaths, and, while the arrangement was similar in some respects to Radburn layouts in public housing, the quality of the landscaping and the regular mainte-

nance made them far more attractive. Since the developments tended to be small in well-established neighbourhoods, they also avoided the problem of isolation.

At the end of the 1990s housing development layouts began to be modified to produce permeable, logical arrangements designed to integrate rather than fragment. Unlike traditional cul-de-sac layouts, streets were again designed to connect with each other so that pedestrians could pass through a development easily and directly. Another noticeable change was that more cars were being left outside. Government policy has been one factor in this, since from the 1990s the aim has been to reduce car usage by restricting the number of garages in new housing developments. The increasing use of sealed units and complex computer-controlled electronics also deterred people from carrying out their own servicing. Many families, now with two or three cars, paved over their front gardens to compensate for inadequate garage space. But cars were now also bigger. The greatly increased popularity of 4×4 vehicles was matched by size increases across all categories of car. In many cases, they were simply too wide or too long to fit garages built before the 1970s. Even some more recent integral garages were too small.

Other broad trends in garage design continued. There was a greater tendency to disguise concrete with brick-effect surfaces, and by the end of the twentieth century roughcast panels had largely taken over from the smooth and clapboard panels of the 1960s. Roofs tended to be flat, while the up-and-over door was almost universal, often with a panelled effect pressed in to it, perhaps to evoke the appearance of a Georgian stable door. Some of the 'New Urban' developments such as Accordia, Cambridge (2003–8), favoured secure car ports of brick to get away from the suburban look.

Timber garages continued to be available for those who wanted them, perhaps to fit in with a rustic setting. But the most significant change was at the top end of the market where, from the early 1980s, there was a move to semi-bespoke garages based on traditional farm buildings. Weatherboarded buildings with oak frameworks, assembled with pegged mortise and tenon joints, became popular, especially with owners of ever more valuable sports and classic cars. The larger ones were modelled on barns, while the most popular was the two-bay open cart shed (pl. 112). Such buildings, tiled with half-hipped roofs, were seductively attractive and a world away in appearance and price from the rock-faced concrete and brick-effect designs of the prefabricated mass-market garages of the later twentieth century. So, in a sense, we have come full circle, from the bespoke garages of the wealthy motoring pioneers to their present-day equivalents, which match the lifestyles and surroundings of their privileged owners.

The building of town houses on three storeys, with the ground floor occupied by an integral garage, a hallway and a

112   A garage of the cart shed type at Barrington, Cambridgeshire.

113 Car parking on pavements and verges due to narrow roads on the King's Reach development (2008–10) in King's Lynn, Norfolk.

room to the rear, has greatly increased with the higher building densities required by central Government in the twenty-first century. At the same time, the trend evident in the 1960s to provide integral garages in other types of low-cost housing, in both the private and public sectors, has lessened. In particular, a garage location that had gained ground in the 1960s – in front of the building line of houses, occupying part of the front garden and flanked by a path leading to the front door – fell from favour. The integral garage, generally located under a couple of spare bedrooms, remained popular in larger houses. Otherwise, substantial brick-built double garages, often with a hipped, tiled roof, became essential adjuncts to the executive homes prevalent from the 1980s, especially in south-east England.

Elsewhere, in public housing and on the cheaper private estates, there was a move away from blocks of lock-up garages to the provision of a driveway and garage beside each house. Partly, this was a result of heightened public consciousness of car theft and vandalism. Garage courts seemed threatening places, and in any case people often wanted simply to display their cars outside their homes. They were often forced to: the diminishing size of houses coincided with growing affluence, so that the garage, always a repository for clutter, now became an extension of a house's storage space. In that sense, the garage was at last truly integrated with the house, and the car was, quite literally, left out in the cold.

Since 2000 several small automated parking units have provided private parking for new apartment and office blocks. One example is the Wohr Parksafe 583 (2006; Brock Carmichael, for eighty-four cars), a ten-storey metal-clad structure serving apart-ments in The Albany, a redeveloped office complex on Old Hall Street, Liverpool. It stands behind the retained façade of Windsor Buildings on George Street, which incorporates the exit. Another is the Wohr Multiparker 740 at Beetham Tower, Holloway Circus, Birmingham (2006; Ian Simpson Architects, for fifty-five cars), an underground installation on five levels. Car stackers are also becoming more popular, whether for a number of vehicles (e.g., the Wohr Auto Parksysteme, serving apartments in a converted Dye Works in Luton, Bedfordshire) or two-car units for private residences (e.g., the Cardok).

At the time of writing (2011), as part of the Coalition Government's localism agenda, the guidelines issued in 2001, which restricted the number of parking spaces on new housing developments, leading many to become choked by parked cars, are being replaced by a willingness to leave such decisions to local authorities. Essex County Council had already challenged the previous policy in 2009 by issuing new guidelines to developers requiring larger driveways and garages (these could now be 7 by 3 metres instead of the existing minimum of 5 by 2.5 metres); it approved the provision of at least two parking spaces for any home with two or more bedrooms, and twenty-five extra spaces for visitors for every 100 homes. The local authority argued that under-provision of garages does not stop people buying cars; it simply ensures that they park them where they cause obstruction and visual clutter (pl. 113).[114]

Other methods of controlling residential car parking have proved of limited success. One was the building of new apartment blocks in city centres without parking spaces, such as the Design House in Smithfield, Manchester, where it was reported that owners simply kept their cars elsewhere.[115] Other schemes have tried to make tenants sign away the right to own a car. Another tactic that has backfired has been the provision of parking bays at the rear of properties that face onto very narrow roads. Since people prefer to leave their cars in front of the house, these narrow roads are filled with cars with two wheels on the pavement, effectively blocking it and forcing pedestrians to walk in the road. So great is the demand for parking space in the centre of major cities that attempts to limit provision have simply increased its value, to the point where spaces in Chelsea can fetch £90,000.[116] A more sustainable solution may lie in car clubs, first introduced into Britain about 2002, where motorists, in return for an annual subscription and mileage payments, have the use of a car when they require it.[117]

Street Parking

As has been discussed, before the late 1930s cars were rarely parked on the street outside one's home. They were not designed to be left outside; the police and local authorities did not approve of streets being used for garaging; and it was generally not considered to be the done thing to own a car without a garage to put it in.

By the 1950s this approach had changed. Growing numbers of skilled working men owned cars, many of them living in terraced housing or on council estates with no garage room. At first, street parking was looked down on, and associated with running 'old bangers', the many pre-war cars that survived prior to the introduction of the ten-year test in 1961. The sight of a car resting on a pile of bricks on the pavement while undergoing running repairs became commonplace, as did the large numbers of old cars apparently abandoned by the roadside. While there were relatively few car owners this form of parking did not pose too many problems, other than aesthetic ones. In many traditional working-class areas of northern England and the Midlands, the numbers of parked cars remained small well into the 1970s. By the 1990s these streets were choked with cars with very few empty kerbside spaces. By this time, it had become the norm to park new and often prestigious cars at the roadside, improved anti-corrosion measures introduced from the 1980s ensuring that vehicles did not deteriorate as much as their rust-prone forebears.

Residents' parking zones first appeared in 1966, when Kensington and Chelsea Council brought in communal residents' bays served by a ticket-vending machine, and Westminster City Council introduced residents-only parking meters in Belgravia. Both schemes required a permit to be displayed in addition to the parking ticket. The following year, the first unmetered parking spaces for residents, controlled by parking cards and tokens, were introduced in Belgravia and Knightsbridge.[118] By the mid-1970s residents' parking was common in the inner suburbs of London and was then taken up in provincial towns and cities. As controlled parking zones expanded, commuters took to parking in the adjacent residential areas, which in turn led to the extension of residents' parking to avoid the perceived nuisance. The introduction of such schemes often led to conflict among residents, councillors and officers, something anticipated as early as 1966 in Westminster: the chairman of the council's car parking committee caused uproar in his response to residents' criticisms: 'Get your priorities right. Residents do not come first . . . The first priority is traffic flow.'[119] Eventually, the areas covered by these controlled zones expanded ever outwards so that they extended, in some cases, 2 or 3 miles from a city centre; they were also often centred around other features of the infrastructure, such as railway stations, universities, hospitals and neighbourhood shopping centres.

While inconvenient to residents and visitors, such parking restrictions have another, more serious effect: the paving over of front gardens to provide off-road parking space, something that has been happening for a long time but received new impetus in the 1980s (pl. 114). Combined with other changes, such as the fitting of replacement windows and the introduction of wheelie bins, it has led to a great deterioration in the appearance of suburbs across the country. The removal of front walls and vegetation can destroy completely the effect of *rus in urbe* that is the essence of suburbia. A soft border between house and road is replaced by a dull, flat, hard expanse of paving. The lush greenery that is the hallmark of the best inter-war suburbs gives way to drab greys and browns. The damage is not just visual. Paving over front gardens causes severe problems with water run-off and

114 Paving the front gardens for car parking in Runley Road, Luton, Bedfordshire, has changed its appearance radically, transforming it from a leafy suburban road into something much more urban in feel.

contributes to the increasing risk of flooding. In addition, the removal of trees and plants reduces the numbers of insects and birds. Regulations were introduced in October 2008 that required home owners to obtain planning permission before installing impermeable paving in front gardens exceeding 5 square metres. The Royal Horticultural Society and other bodies have issued guidelines on ways to accommodate cars without sacrificing an entire front garden.[120]

The aesthetic consequences of almost universal car parking in residential areas go beyond grubbing up front gardens. Controlled zones bring with them yet more obtrusive signage. There are signs to announce the edges of zones, and signs to indicate length of stay, often attached to free-standing poles, while ugly coloured lines invade suburban roads. Architecture is obscured. Georgian areas, with their taller buildings and wider streets, seem able to absorb cars, while in well-to-do Victorian suburbs they are masked by kerbside trees and extensive planting, but other areas fare less well. Victorian terraced housing is particularly badly affected, as are garden suburbs with their narrow roads, while low cottages in villages can be almost completely hidden behind some of the larger modern cars. Indeed, the picturesque scenes that have helped shape our view of what a traditional English village ought to look like – depicted in inter-war motoring journals and in the many topographical series of the same period, such as those published by Batsford – are impossible to photograph today. The view can look more like a car park with a range of low-built, half-hidden buildings in the background.

115 Laurel Garage, Ramsbury, Wiltshire, a corrugated-iron garage of a type once widely found in rural areas, with its fine range of 1950s pumps, still in use when photographed in October 2009, but subsequently removed.

4: MAINTAINING THE CAR

THE WORD 'GARAGE' IS NOTABLY imprecise (see Chapter 6). The repair and maintenance garage is a term chosen here to distinguish premises used for servicing and repairing cars, as opposed to garages where cars are parked, either *en masse* or individually at home, or those primarily in the business of selling petrol.

Repair and maintenance garages have their origins in the many different trades that catered for motorists in the earliest days. Among these were light engineering firms and agricultural engineers. Almost any market town of any size had at least one firm of this type, and many started to carry out work on cars as a natural extension to their business. They had the mechanical skills, the types of basic tools and the machinery required to work on the early cars. As motoring became more than a hobby for the wealthy, some decided to concentrate on the motor business, abandoning their traditional activities. In addition, there were bicycle shops. Many of the early motor cars were produced by firms such as Rover, Humber and Swift, which were established bicycle manufacturers, and selling and repairing cars was seen by cycle retailers as a natural ancillary to their existing business. Again, mechanical skills, tools and machinery were already present to some degree, and in any case some early motor cars were little more than motorised bicycles. A third category to be found in the larger towns comprised the firms that built and repaired horse-drawn vehicles – they may not have had the mechanical skills of some of their rivals, but they had the customer base, and a man who ran a carriage might expect the firm who kept it in repair to do the same for his car. Finally, at village level, there was the local blacksmith, who was a resourceful man used to dealing with a wide variety of machinery, although it is

likely that the technical complexities of many cars would have been beyond his capability.

In addition to these trades that pre-dated the motor car, specialist repairers were established, at first predominantly in the major cities, that were linked to the firms selling new and used cars, and to the large parking garages that were set up in London from 1902, which aimed at offering a complete range of services to the motorist.

Before 1914

Early motor cars were relatively small, and their accommodation posed few problems for existing businesses, both in terms of storage and removing components for repair. For some years, few changes were made to premises of pre-existing firms other than, perhaps, the provision of a pit to enable the underside of the car to be inspected and some sort of hoist for lifting out the engine. As cars became larger and more complicated, premises started to be extended, sometimes in a fairly rudimentary way in corrugated iron or by taking in former stables and outbuildings. The crucial element in the new workshop buildings that began to spring up from around 1905 was the light steel truss roof, used both for purpose-built garages and extensions to existing premises.

Although there were examples of garages that carried out only repairs and maintenance – and many of the largest dealers separated the service and sales functions physically, with service depots in some cases located in an entirely different part of the city from the showroom – most smaller provincial garages tended

116 The former W. Atkinson & Sons premises in North Road, Lancaster, an early (1903) garage of considerable architectural ambition by the noted local practice of Austin & Paley.

to comprise a showroom at the front of the premises with the workshops behind. In one common arrangement, a central opening led to the workshops, with showrooms on either side; in another, access to the workshop was from the side or back of the building. Occasionally, the workshops were located in a separate building at the rear of the site. Such garages would almost invariably sell petrol in 2-gallon cans, which would be stored in a pit, but from 1914 a few supplied it via a pump from an underground tank.

Many early garages in large towns and suburbs were substantial buildings, designed by major firms of provincial architects, in styles that echoed the Baroque favoured for much Edwardian commercial architecture. These buildings were located on prime sites in important streets and served a wealthy clientele. It was only to be expected that their architecture would complement the luxury goods that were sold and maintained within their walls (pl. 116).

A surviving example is Caffyn's, Church Street, Eastbourne, East Sussex (pl. 118). Here, the handsome showroom block in an accomplished Edwardian Baroque style (1911; H. Woolnough) drew the *Motor Trader* to comment that 'it is seldom that such a combination of elegance and usefulness is found in connection with motor garages'.[1] The asymmetrical façade had twin gables with open pediments to the left and a recessed first floor on the right with (originally) circular windows and stumpy columns. Segmental-headed showroom windows and pilasters of alternating bands of brick and stone gave a cheerful appearance. The workshops to the rear – destroyed by bombing in the Second

World War and replaced in 1946 by the present building – were in a similarly ornate style with a cupola and a large half-round window, surmounted by a pediment, over the vehicle entrance. The upper floor was used as function rooms for hire, a use

117 Sheffield Motor Co., West Street, Sheffield (1907, as extended in 1910 and 1919; Hemsoll & Chapman), now used as shops and a bar.

118 Caffyn's, Church Street, Eastbourne, built in 1911, the rear part rebuilt in 1946 after being destroyed by bombing.

echoed in another substantial survival, the garage of the Sheffield Motor Co., West Street, Sheffield, where the upper floors were used as billiard saloons (pl. 117). Designed by the prominent local architects Hemsoll & Chapman in 1907, it was extended twice in 1910 and 1919 in matching style.[2] Flamboyant in appearance with mullioned and transomed windows, much use of faience in its facing, and three enormous broken pediments, it filled an entire block and is today a bar and shops. The service areas to the rear were far less impressive.

Albeit on a much smaller scale, Edwards' Garage, Alma Vale Road, Clifton, Bristol, shares this exuberance. It, too, has a Neo-Baroque façade of brick with bands of stone, a rounded pediment and a highly elaborate cartouche containing an oculus above the central doorway. Workshops (lit from above) are to one side of the doorway; the showroom is on the other. The garage is built into the front garden of a large Victorian house. At Hitchin, Hertfordshire, the former Ralph E. Sanders & Sons

garage (1906), now a branch of Kwik-Fit, is an impressive structure, purpose-built as a motor works and coachbuilders, in pebbledash and red brick, and vaguely Arts and Crafts in style. The motor engineering was carried out on the ground floor, where a central entrance gave access to the large open workshop with its light steel truss roof, while coachbuilding was undertaken in the loft above the showrooms.[3] Another early survivor is Watson's Motor Works, Etnam Street, Leominster, Herefordshire, which remains in its original ownership. Here the frontage building, which was in existence by about 1910, was a simple rendered structure with vestigial rusticated pilasters, while behind was a variegated collection of workshops.

In an article in the *Motor Trader* on a suitable design for a small trader's premises in 1911, it was argued that the ideal lay between the two extremes of an old barn and the fine buildings put up in the previous decade that absorbed so much capital. While a main-road location was the most essential factor, a satisfactory

119 A garage built in 1913 for John Lee & Sons, Townfoot, Rothbury, Northumberland, is an early example of the most common type of repair and maintenance garage with a large shed-like building, its gable facing the road and the façade given some architectural treatment

121 Another example of the shed-type garage at Haywards Heath, West Sussex, on a smaller scale than that at Rothbury, with a lunette over the entrance to light the workshops.

plan was also important. Taking a typical site with a narrow frontage but 80-foot depth to the rear, it proposed a showroom separated by a small office and stores from the workshop to the rear, with a garage and yard (covered for washing down) behind them. A petrol store stood in the furthest corner of the yard, a safe distance from the workshop. The building was entirely functional: brick walls strong enough to carry a second storey, concrete flooring and an 'inexpensive "weaving shed" roof'.[4] Such

120 The service depot and garage of Charles Jarrott & Letts, Page Street, Westminster, shortly after construction in 1913.

buildings were erected in large numbers, to judge from the many illustrations in the trade press and surviving examples, such as the former premises of W. H. Johnson & Sons Ltd in King's Lynn, Norfolk.

Service depots tended to comprise large open workshops, often with the gable end facing the street, and any decoration was limited to some ornamentation in the gable (pl. 119). Crucial considerations were plenty of space to manoeuvre cars, so stanchions or piers inside were unwelcome, and good ventilation to avoid a build-up of toxic exhaust fumes. Good lighting was also essential and glazed roof lights were almost universal, while there was often a lunette in the gable over the front entrance (pl. 121). Early ideal plans suggest that most room was taken up with garaging cars, with a small repair shop and machine room at the rear of the building.[5] A substantially intact survivor of a pre-1914 service depot is that of Charles Jarrott & Letts, Page Street, Westminster, which still bears traces of the original owners' names on its façade (pl. 120).[6] These were the premises of one of the most famous early motor dealers, whose showrooms were in Great Marlborough Street. Jarrott was one of the first and most successful British racing drivers; Sir William Letts was the chairman of the major motor manufacturers Crossley Motors of Manchester. Behind the parking shed (see Chapter 6) was a workshop, 86 by 70 feet, with a largely glazed roof supported on light steel trusses and a floor space unimpeded by columns.

Garages at this time were usually located in the centre of towns and cities or on the main roads out of them, generally no more than a mile from the centre. Manufacturers, particularly

122   The Vinot Cars Ltd service depot, Redhill Street, London NW1 (1912; P. Pilditch).

those based overseas, established service depots around London. One significant survivor is the depot of Vinot Cars Ltd (a subsidiary of the French manufacturer Vinot et Deguingand), Redhill Street, Camden Town (1912; P. Pilditch), a handsome Neo-Georgian building with rear wings and a central courtyard (pl. 122). Access to the courtyard was through a central gateway in the principal façade, surmounted by a bay window. The premises, which were also Vinot's British headquarters, were used by them for only a few years: in 1919 they moved, like much of the retail motor trade, to Great Portland Street (see Chapter 2). Others from this period include Humber, Canterbury Road, Kilburn, west London, where a lengthy single-storey workshop block with the usual light steel truss roof was added in 1910–11, adjacent to an 1860s building formerly forming part of the Patent Railway Signal Works of Saxby & Farmer.[7] Another was Rolls-Royce, which had large, well-equipped premises built for them on Cricklewood Lane in 1914.[8]

Major players in the new motor industry, and often of equal significance to the car makers themselves, were the tyre manufacturers. The largest firms commissioned buildings that reflected this status. Michelin in the years 1909–11 built their London depot at 81 Fulham Road (pl. 123). It is one of the most exciting of all early motoring buildings, an advertisement for their products with glass corner domes resembling a set of tyres, tyre motifs used throughout the decoration of the façade and a representation of Bibendum, the firm's mascot, in a stained-glass window above the entrance. Designed by François Espinasse of Clermont-Ferrand, whose only other known building was

Michelin's Paris headquarters, it has a frame of reinforced concrete on the Hennebique system hidden under white Burmantofts 'Marmo' facing with additional banding in blue, yellow and green. Most striking of all are the thirty-four tiled panels, depicting racing cars achieving success on Michelin tyres, by Ernest Montaut, whose coloured lithographs of such scenes were widely popular at the time. The building – which was extended in 1911–12 and 1922 and remained in use as a Michelin tyre depot until 1985 – is now offices, with a restaurant and shop on the ground floor that pay homage to its past use.[9]

Even larger, if much more conventional, is the nearby Continental tyre depot of 1910–16 at 230–244 Brompton Road, designed by Paul Hoffman, who carried out much work in the area.[10] The depot had an impressive entrance hall with waiting rooms off it and a bachelor flat intended for the use of the company's customers in an emergency. Tyres are again used in the building's decoration, with reliefs of tyres surmounted by wings referencing traditional laurel-wreath motifs repeated at intervals along the lengthy fascia of the building and also on upper floors. The sheer scale of the building, occupying a prominent corner site between Brompton Road and Thurloe Place, indicates the wealth accumulated by some of the companies associated with motoring within a few years of the industry's inception.

•

123   The Michelin building, Fulham Road (1909–11; François Espinasse).

The 1920s

By the 1920s repair and maintenance garages had become a common feature of almost every town in the country. Those that had their origins in cycle shops were located in town centres; many, finding that opportunities for expansion were severely limited, moved to larger premises or attempted to purchase adjoining buildings. They also put in petrol pumps from 1920 onwards, often in locations that were totally unsuited to them. This might entail installing pumps on the pavement or behind it on the garage's frontage, with overhead swinging arms to convey the petrol to the car. Potentially, there was considerable

danger in some of the arrangements where petrol was supplied from shop premises built straight on to the street: Arthur Archer recalled how in his family firm's garage in Dunmow, Essex, two uncovered petrol tanks were installed in the cellars, which were also used for the storage of new car tyres. The family lived above.[11]

In other cases, existing garages carried out more sophisticated modifications to their premises. The Sheffield Motor Co. opened up part of their frontage in 1932 to incorporate an internal filling station.[12] The former engineering firms tended to have larger sites, located outside the immediate centre. In the country, many forges became garages, since blacksmiths spent more of their time working with cars than horses, while houses in villages were often converted to garages by the simple expedient of turning stables into workshops, putting some petrol pumps in the road outside and covering the front of the building with advertisements (pls 124 and 125).

The site of a garage was important. Garage proprietors could be divided into two groups, those catering for a residential trade, who could operate in a secondary location, and those who served the passing motorist, who needed to be on a main through road. Because of high site values, the latter would often be restricted to a narrow frontage. Proprietors would have to

deal with unforeseen and scheduled work simultaneously, since cars were much more prone to break down in this period. As motoring became more and more popular, a new phenomenon came into being with important implications in its impact on the landscape: the small repair business, where the work was executed by the proprietor himself and possibly a lone mechanic. In towns and cities, these were located almost anywhere where property values were low.

On any piece of wasteland, a group of often home-made sheds or garages might spring up, with a small sign announcing that car repairs were undertaken (pl. 126), or a group of squalid outbuildings might be pressed into service. In the country, garages consisting of tin shacks spread along major roads, announcing their presence with a mass of enamelled advertisements. Like its close relative, the filling station, these 'roadside eyesores' attracted much hostility, not least from the established motor trade, which regarded these new garage proprietors as unqualified and incompetent tinkerers who gave the trade a bad name. Steps were taken to try and deal with the worst of these garages (see Chapter 10).

By contrast, by the mid-1920s many urban firms were rebuilding their premises. The favoured style was a rather weak, often stripped-down, classical, which was popular for commercial buildings in the period. Typical is J. W. Walley, Bishop's Stortford (1926), where workshops were fronted by a Neo-Georgian showroom block. Petrol pumps were located down the side of the workshops and lock-ups for fifty cars were available.[13] Another example is Batchelor, Bowles & Co. of London Road, Leicester (*circa* 1926), where a Neo-Georgian showroom block was adjacent to an extensive workshop built of blockwork. There

124   Dane End garage, Hertfordshire, a conversion from a village forge.

125   A typical village garage at Husbands Bosworth, Leicestershire, *circa* 1929, photographed by the CPRE as part of a series intended to highlight the desecration of the countryside by garish signage. The reuse of existing buildings as garages was common practice.

126   Newland Garage, Newland, Cumberland. An example of one of the many rural garages that sprang up in the 1920s. This is more substantial and tidier than many, but its light timber construction is of the sort that many people regarded as an eyesore. Photographed on 5 May 1950, it still retains its original hand-operated pumps alongside a later electrical model.

was an entirely separate Service Department of similar date a mile up the London Road, which had its decorative emphasis placed, as often occurred, on the gable. It, too, was built of block-work behind the brick façade.[14] A large garage that survives with very little alteration is T. Shipside, Collin Street, Nottingham (1927; pl. 128). This, too, is of the characteristic layout with central entrance, showrooms on either side and workshops behind, all within the overall brick envelope. Again, the façade

127 (below) A workshop that is typical of many during the 1920s and 1930s. F. G. Smith (Motors) Ltd of High Road, Goodmayes, Essex, had a central depot, seen here, together with three branches at Romford, Ilford and Wanstead. This view shows the main repair shop *circa* 1925. It is a purpose-built steel-framed structure with brick infill and equipped with the usual light steel truss roof. Service bays on the left have pits under, mostly covered in boarding, with a hoist suitable for removing engines and other major components. Work is being carried out on rudimentary wooden benches at the far end with power supplied by line shafting and belts. The glazed portion of the roof provides plenty of natural light, but the electric lighting appears to be sparse. Cars visible include, on the right, an Austin 7 and two bullnose Morrises.

128 The former T. Shipside garage, Collin Street, Nottingham (1927), a large and little-altered example of the shed-type garage with its pitched roof hidden behind a parapet.

129   Hamilton Motors, Edgware Road, London (1928; O'Donoghue & Halfhide). Built in a somewhat utilitarian version of commercial Neo-Georgian, the former Hamilton Motors is a rare surviving example of a large garage still used as such in a main-road location close to central London.

had the simplest of classical treatments with a pediment and dentilled cornice. Two petrol pumps were originally installed, one to either side of the entrance. This form of garage, a building with gable end facing the street and a large open area unobstructed by columns, with a light steel trussed roof – sometimes with the gable exposed, or sometimes hidden behind a parapet – is by far the most common arrangement to be found in England. Other characteristic features include glazing near the ridge of the roof and a lunette or other glazed opening above the front entrance in the centre of the main façade. It is termed here the 'shed' type. It had its origins around 1904 and continued to be built throughout the country in large numbers during the 1920s and 1930s (pl. 127). Many examples, particularly from the inter-war years, survive in backstreet locations, since they are suited either for continued motor trade use or for other purposes, such as warehousing and retailing, where a large uninterrupted floor area is required.

Altogether more imposing, as befits its prominent site on Edgware Road, one of the principal exits from central London,

is Hamilton Motors (1928; O'Donoghue & Halfhide; pl. 129), a three-storey building with garaging and showrooms on the ground floor. It has a somewhat pinched look with closely spaced, small, steel-framed windows and the ends emphasised by the use of concrete blocks, contrasting with the red brick of the remainder.[15] It is one of the few 1920s garages in a prominent main road location that is still in motor-trade use.

In the 1920s garages had to cater for a variety of uses. For many, the garaging or parking of private cars was still an important part of their activities and much space at the rear was occupied for this purpose, either with the cars parked together or in lock-ups (see Chapter 3). These were always to some extent at odds with the repair function, since congestion could result when everyone wanted to leave at the same time, obstructing the service area. Banks of lock-ups occupying any spare corner of the site were becoming increasingly common in the 1920s. A showroom would always be at the front, sometimes to either side of the main entrance, while the office was usually adjacent to the entrance to enable the manager to see what vehicles were

130   Wells's Garage, Hitchin, Hertfordshire, *circa* 1930. The right-hand pump is still *in situ* today.

131   The interior of Wells's Garage showing some of the machinery found in a garage of the 1920s, including a pillar drill.

going in or out of the premises. The workshop area would usually have a separate smiths' shop and machine shop. There were several schools of thought as to how the workshops should be arranged. One held that the positions of the benches and machine tools should be close together in an almost cramped layout, to reduce the amount of labour and time in moving parts from one area of the workshop to another. A second sought to achieve the greatest amount of uninterrupted working space.[16] The stores were housed in a separate room near the workshop.

A design for a broad frontage corner site published in the *Motor Trader* in 1921 followed these lines, with the building divided into a front and a rear portion. At the front was the showroom, the general and private offices, the repair shop and the machine shop. At the rear, accessed by a separate entrance with its own supervisory office, was the parking garage, with individual lock-ups. An alternative design covering sites with access only from the front had two-storey premises with a wide off-centre entrance between an office and a showroom, the workshop and garaging behind, with paint shop, upholstery and

stores on the first floor, accessed by a vehicular lift.[17] An ideal layout in *The Modern Motor Engineer* suggested that there should be separate areas for stores, a paint shop and a coachwork shop at the front of the building, a showroom and office adjoining the front entrance, the major part of the building occupied by a parking garage, with the repair shop, tyre repair and forge all at the rear.[18] It was important for the various functions to take place in separate rooms, to enable the mechanics to perform their work effectively.

The minimum plant required in a small garage during the 1920s would include a lathe (the most essential machine tool), a drilling machine, a milling machine, a grinding machine, a power hacksaw, a planing machine (for shaping sheet metal), a forge and a vulcaniser. A 5hp gas engine to drive the machinery through line shafting was recommended.[19] Other than the milling machine, the forge and the vulcaniser, all these tools are still to be found *in situ* at Wells's Garage, Hitchin, Hertfordshire, perhaps the most complete surviving 1920s garage interior (pls 130 and 131). Wells's Garage was built by Bert Wells in the years

132   Wellingore Garage, Wellingore, Lincolnshire (1933; F. Glanville Goodin).

133 International Motors, Brook Green, Hammersmith, the principal Ford service depot in London (*circa* 1916; C. H. Heathcote & Sons).

1925–7, he himself designing the building and constructing it of steel stanchions with walls clad in corrugated iron with nearly continuous high-level glazing. The roof was largely of glass. He combined motor repairs with a small engineering business, building prototypes and one-off pieces of machinery. The lower workshop, used as a machine shop, was the first to be built and still contains two pillar drills, a shaper, a power hacksaw and workbenches. Steps led down to a cellar containing a lathe and a Petter oil engine that ran a generator providing electricity to power the machinery and light the garage. A ladder stair led up to a mezzanine office under the eaves. The upper workshop was left largely free of machinery and was where the cars were worked on, having a pit. In its use of corrugated iron with high-level glazing, Wells's garage was typical of many built in the 1920s: entirely functional without a hint of decorative treatment.

In the same way that some attractive rural filling stations emerged in the 1920s and 1930s, garages benefited from rather more attention to their appearance. When the village of Wellingore, Lincolnshire, was bypassed in 1933, a new garage by F. Glanville Goodin was constructed (pl. 132). The walls were built of local stone and the overall effect was that of a great barn with half-hipped pantiled roofs, gabled entrances on either side and a covered way at one end to enable filling to be done in the dry. Large rounded arches marked the covered way, and the building was completed with a weathervane. The interior had an agricultural machinery showroom at the front, a garage in the centre and a workshop at the rear.[20]

By the end of the 1920s some dealers had expanded to the point where they owned numerous branches, either within a single locality or on a national basis. Some of these businesses grew organically by opening new branches in different towns, while others took over existing garage businesses. The trend towards larger, multi-branch establishments gathered pace in this period, and large regional chains such as Henly's and Kenning's vied with local firms such as Watson's of Liverpool.

Such concerns built large centralised repair and service departments. Watson's had a three-storey works of more than 30,000 square feet built on Oldham Street, Liverpool (1929; D. A. Beveridge). It was steel-framed with concrete floors and brick curtain walls. The glazing was especially generous, and pilasters and a cornice gave it a veneer of classical style. Located on sloping land, internal ramps allowed cars to be driven to each floor, although a hoist was also installed. The building was subsequently almost doubled in size to the east and is today, with its roof removed, a car park.[21] Stewart & Ardern, the large London-based Morris distributors, had their central service department at The Vale, Acton, which stood behind a showroom facing the main road. The complex dated from *circa* 1929. Two long ranges of two-storey, north-lit buildings (that to the west still survives in part, reclad) ran to either side of a side turning that was closed by a further long building at right angles. As well as service, these included stockrooms containing some 600 cars occupying 2 acres. The stockrooms had cars lined up in long rows: the public were admitted to view potential purchases, as they were to view similar rooms of second-hand stock.[22] Henly's London service depot was at Hawley Crescent, Camden Town, opened in 1927. It had a floor area of more than an acre, a gallery occupying one side and one end of the building which was accessed by a ramp. There was accommodation for more than 500 cars.[23]

While motor manufacturers were happy to leave large firms to cater for the service needs of their customers in the provinces, many of them, including AC, Rover, Singer and Renault, continued the trend that has already been observed with firms such as Humber, Panhard and Rolls-Royce, in building large service stations in London; unlike the earliest service stations, these were mostly located around the inner suburbs, rather than centrally. Renault and Rover were in Seagrave Road, Fulham; Singer at Brewery Road, Lower Holloway; AC at North Road, Lower Holloway; and Daimler at Edgware Road, Hendon.[24] That for Daimler had waiting rooms for customers and chauffeurs, and could carry out virtually any type of work required on its 5-acre site. Wolseley commissioned W. Curtis Green, who was responsible for their prestigious showrooms in Piccadilly, to design some imposing Neo-Georgian repair shops in Manor Street, Chelsea, immediately behind the town hall, in 1923.[25] One of the first on such a scale was that of International Motors (a subsidiary of Ford), Brook Green, Hammersmith, built *circa* 1916 (C. H. Heathcote & Sons; pl. 133).[26] It was claimed to be the largest service station in the world, acting as the principal sales and service headquarters for Ford in England. Of three storeys (it was designed to have five), it had a reinforced concrete frame (exposed to the rear elevation, clad in brick to the front and sides), with a lengthy and well-detailed façade. In the motoring press it was compared to Albert Kahn's buildings at Ford's Detroit plant. The lightness of the inside was praised – only a few corners required artificial light. Access to the upper floors was by large (still operational) vehicle lifts, one of which opened onto the flat roof. The building, which was taken over by Citroën in 1923, remains largely intact, including an imposing staircase with Greek-key detailing, a tiled floor and panelled wainscot.[27]

The 1930s

There was a growing awareness in the motor trade that the premises in which its business was carried out were not keeping pace with developments to the product itself. In August 1933 Sir Herbert Austin said to his dealers: 'the appearance of many of the buildings of motor traders is not likely to attract sales or service business, or to enhance the reputation of the agents themselves . . . Some of them need a little window dressing, others a charge of dynamite.'[28]

The greatest changes in terms of the layout of garages in the 1930s were the widespread introduction of ramps, running up the sides of buildings, along the rear or internally, and the use of flat concrete roofs for parking cars awaiting repair and new stock. Changes in technology are significant in two respects: concrete framing became much more common for garages, and, as already noted, there were important changes in car design. With the advent of all-steel closed saloon car bodies and cellulose paint in the late 1920s, it became possible to leave cars outside for longer periods.

Another change that occurred in the early 1930s was the increasing standardisation of cars. The vast number of different makes and models that had existed in the early 1920s meant that garages had to be prepared to deal with almost any type of component. By the 1930s it had become economic for garages to purchase much more sophisticated machinery and equipment, some of which was specific to a particular make or model of car. Servicing thus became more of an industrial process and could be organised in an efficient manner along flow-line principles. The layout of large workshops changed to reflect these new organisational principles. Maintenance facilities were growing in size and becoming more specialised. Increasingly, service (washing and lubrication) tended to be split off from repairs. In at least one example, it was displayed in a showroom in a similar way to cars. In striking new premises on the Southend Arterial Road at Woodford that rivalled those of Stewart & Ardern (see Chapter 2), Lamb's built a 70-foot-long service building, open-fronted and with a back wall glazed from dado level. The passing motorist could therefore see the work being carried out, and was intended to be suitably impressed by the Wakefield lubrication battery, described as being of the 'soda fountain' type, that is, sparkling and immaculate.[29] Car washing, too, became increasingly automated. In February 1938 Kennings opened what they described as a 'car laundry' in Edgware Road, Paddington, claiming that it was only the second of its kind in the world; it was capable of handling 500 cars a day. Two Tecalemit conveyors, each taking six cars at a time, moved forward past thirty people to each conveyor, women carrying out the cleaning and men, the lubrication at the end of the process. The cars then left the premises through an imposing exit, shining and advertising the service. Meanwhile, the water was recycled through filters and used again.[30] That year Tecalemit exhibited what was the precursor of the modern car wash at the annual Motor Show. The tunnel wash, through which a single car passed, was a futuristic structure, erected within the garage, with gently rounded contours and a strip of glazing on each side. The car was subjected to high-pressure washing before being finished off by hand. The first tunnel wash to be installed was at Dickinson & Adams, Luton, in February 1939.[31]

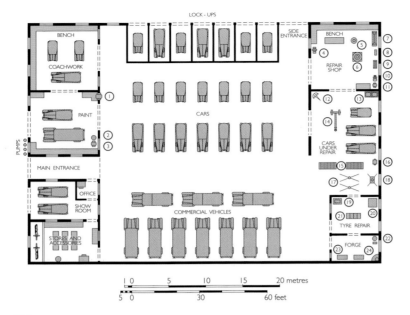

LOCK - UPS

BENCH

COACHWORK

PAINT

MAIN ENTRANCE

OFFICE

SHOW ROOM

STORES AND ACCESSORIES

SIDE ENTRANCE

BENCH

REPAIR SHOP

CARS

CARS UNDER REPAIR

COMMERCIAL VEHICLES

TYRE REPAIR

FORGE

| 0   5   10   15   20 metres

5   0   30   60 feet

KEY

1	Ventilating Electric Motor	13	Component Cleaning Bath
2	Air Reservoir for Paint Spraying	14	Car Lifting and Towing Ambulance
3	Electric Motor	15	Inspection Pits
4	Grindstone - 18 inch	16	Air Compressor
5	Sensitive Drill - half inch	17	Wash - Down Area
6	Radial Drill - one inch	18	Car Hosing Plant
7	Lathe - 7 inch SS	19	Tyre Vulcaniser
8	Small Lathe - 3.5 inch SS	20	Tube Vulcaniser
9	Milling Machine	21	Tyre Changing and Fitting Machines
10	Emery Wheel	22	Oxygen & Acetylene Bottles for Welding
11	Electric Motor	23	Welding Plant
12	Portable Garage Crane	24	Brazing Hearth

The trend towards ever larger uninterrupted floor spaces in garages continued. The Meteor Garage, St Mary's Row, Moseley, Birmingham (1931–2; Baron C. S. Underhill), claimed that its Lamella-construction roof, which had a clear span of 135 feet 6 inches, was the widest of its type in the world.[32] One trend was for garages that were concerned principally with repair and maintenance to favour broad, open frontages, with showroom space subordinated to wide entrances leading to the rear workshops, the whole façade being very simple with perhaps no more than a clock for decoration. The opening was akin to that of a letterbox, being far broader than it was high, examples being Harrison's, Warwick Road, Carlisle (1936), and Rowland C. Bellamy, Cromwell Road, Grimsby (1937).[33]

Stylistically, although Neo-Georgian or 'commercial classical' garages continued to be built into the mid-1930s, there was a noticeable move towards the moderne style. Cars were symbols

136 (*facing page*) The Tower (now Maranello) Garage, Egham, Surrey (1935; Rix & Rix), is an appropriately spectacular backdrop to exotic motor cars.

134 (*left*) The interior plan of an ideal repair and maintenance garage. Work on the cars is carried out around the edges, while the central area is taken up with car parking, commonplace when such buildings had to serve a dual function as both repair and parking garages. The lock-ups within the building are accessed externally, an unusual arrangement, the norm being steel cages with internal access. Redrawn from Arthur W. Judge, *The Modern Motor Engineer*, vol. 1, London, n. d. [*circa* 1930].

135 (*below*) The White Garage, Askern, South Yorkshire. Faience façades tend to be associated with large car showrooms in city centres, and their use to embellish a small wayside garage is unusual. This garage, built around the early 1930s, retains an adjoining owner's house and original lettering.

of modernity and it was important that premises associated with them conveyed the right note. Modernity also had practical aspects: the flat roofs lent themselves to car parking; the uninterrupted spaces associated with steel- or concrete-framed buildings provided necessary space for modern workshop methods; and the large windows greatly aided the mechanics. Above all, though, it was important because in most provincial and suburban garages the sales function was inextricably linked to servicing – moderne complemented the increasingly streamlined cars of the late 1930s (see Chapter 1). These buildings were intended to be visually striking. Crucial features to achieve this were towers and concave façades; the two were combined in the Airport Garage (later Henly's), West Hounslow (1937; Roper, Son & Chapman), which played on its location close to Heston aerodrome with a blue-and-silver colour scheme, both colours associated with aviation.[34]

Many of the most spectacular examples of the moderne garage have been demolished, but there are a small number of impressive survivals. They include the Tower Garage on the Egham Bypass, Surrey, built for the Egham Motor Co. in 1935 (pl. 136).

The architects, Rix & Rix of Burnham, carried out a number of other garages in similar style and, at Egham, used the rounded corners, white render and vertical feature, in this case a stream-lined tower, that are the hallmark of the style. The garage was acquired in 1967 by Maranello Concessionaires, the Ferrari importers, who have greatly extended the building in matching style.

Rootes, Britain's largest motor retailer, replaced their existing buildings at Maidstone, Kent, in 1938–9 with a large new works and showroom by Howard & Souster (pl. 137).[35] Intended as a showpiece for the concern, it included a tower as a central feature, its lower stage rising out of the principal façade in the form of a fin. The building was of steel-framed and reinforced concrete construction, clad in reconstituted stone blocks. What was most striking about it was that the large workshop block, which faced the mill pond of the River Len and was clearly visible from the road, was given the same architectural treatment as the showrooms on Mill Street. Another garage on a prominent site is the Clock Garage, Woodville, Derbyshire (circa 1936). A large workshop building with a pitched roof, gabled towards

137   The former Rootes's garage, Maidstone, Kent (1938–9; Howard & Souster).

the road, is disguised by the device of having two bull-nosed wings flanking it at an angle and a blank rendered façade, incorporating the clock that gives it its name, linking them and hiding the roof pitch. The broad entrance to the workshops takes up almost the entire lower part of this façade.[36]

Moderne was used for an example of an ideal garage designed by G. Alan Fortescue, whose practice specialised in this work. The design was published in the *Motor Trader* and a model was exhibited on the magazine's stand at the Motor Show of 1933.[37] Concrete, flat-roofed with a low clock tower, it summed up much 1930s work with a large workshop at the rear, accessed through a central entrance under a concrete canopy beneath the tower. A road at the rear gave alternative access to the workshop. Ideal garage layouts were regularly featured in the motor trade press in the 1930s, *Motor Commerce* printing many plans taken from actual examples (pl. 140). These showed a variety of sites and it is noteworthy that, in most cases, as late as 1933 significant space within the main part of the building was given over to garaging cars and rows of lock-ups.[38]

As the 1930s drew on, there was a move away from extreme modernism to a more restrained version that employed brick facing to principal façades, often using rustic or other good-quality bricks. This showed the influence of Charles Holden's Underground stations and the new generation of town halls such as Norwich, and was following a trend discernible in other forms of architecture. An example was Oscroft's, Castle Boulevard, Nottingham (1937; Reginald Cooper), where the workshops were concealed by a lengthy façade in red brick with stone dressings that combined a classical cornice with a concave central section containing the vehicular entrance and acting as a backdrop to the pump island (pl. 138). Even more ambitious was H. A. Saunders Ltd, Castle Street, Worcester, designed in 1939 by John C. S. Soutar, who had carried out much work at Hampstead Garden Suburb (pl. 139). There were two long staggered wings, one housing workshops, the other showrooms; the wings flanked a central clock tower, surmounted by an open lantern with a copper roof. The effect was very much in the contemporary town-hall mode, but behind the façade the building was strictly

138 Oscroft's, Castle Boulevard, Nottingham (1937; Reginald Cooper), an example of restrained modernism.

139 The former garage of H. A. Saunders Ltd, Castle Street, Worcester (1939; John Soutar), with a tower that references contemporary stripped classical town halls.

utilitarian, with exposed light steel trusses to the roofs of both workshops and showroom.[39]

The advent of the ramp made multi-storey garages more popular, sometimes extending over four floors. A notable example was the Morris Garage, Oxford (1932; Harry W. Smith; see pl. 226), where, behind the showroom building, a three-storey structure housed the service and repair department on the ground floor, a public garage on the first floor and, on the top floor, a used-car showroom with space for fifty to sixty cars.[40] An apparently unique feature of the garage was the provision of petrol on each floor, which avoided congestion around pumps that would normally be located around the entrance and exit on the ground floor, a common problem with large garages. Motor Sales Ltd, Colin Campbell Court, Plymouth (1938; Barron & Rooke; pl. 141), was built in a clean moderne style with the lengthy frontage broken up by three projecting bays, each with rounded corners. Again, the building was multi-functional, with showrooms on the ground floor, workshops on the third and parking on the intervening two. All the upper floors were accessed by a ramp running along the rear of the building.[41]

The large Kenning premises (1937–8; F. W. Tempest; pl. 142) in Sheffield, now a cinema, were served by the traditional lift, although two of the three floors were directly accessible for cars, since the garage was built on falling ground. The style was again

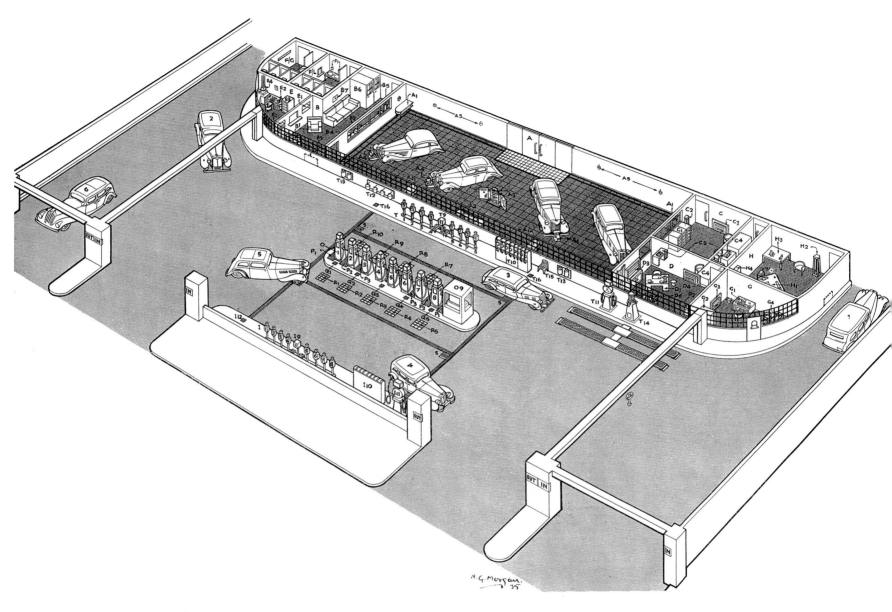

140 An ideal layout for a garage, from *Motor Commerce*, November 1935. The part shown is the forecourt, with the petrol station, and the showrooms and general offices behind. There are separate entrances and exits to the repair and maintenance garage that is located to the rear. See key on facing page.

moderne, with some almost jazzy touches in the use of black and yellow faience for all the exterior cladding. Broad, uninterrupted window bands gave the building a pronounced horizontal emphasis, while the pumps were located in a recessed part of the ground floor.[42] In 1935 Tempest had designed another large garage for Kennings, in Hatherton Road, Walsall, which, although more traditional in its use of brick facings, also employed coloured faience to enliven the façades.[43]

One of the most striking of all the garages to use a ramp was the Tower Garage, Finchley Road, Fortune Green (1933), not least on account of its prominent site at the start of the Hendon Way, one of the principal exits from London. The ramp curved

around the side of the building to give access to the first floor, used solely for garaging, at the rear. Servicing and repairs were on the ground floor with a range of pumps under a canopy. But the stark white of the building, which was of concrete, and its horizontal bands of glazing and clock tower were equally noteworthy in conveying modernity.[44]

From the 1930s some tyre depots began to ape the moderne lines of contemporary car showrooms and garages. The Marsham Tyre Company had a number of depots in this style, while a particularly well-preserved late example is the Southfields Tyre and Battery Service, Merton Road, Wimbledon (pl. 146). Dating from 1949, this has a stylish office and showroom building with

141 The former premises of Motor Sales Ltd in Colin Campbell Court (1938; Barron & Rooke) is one of only a handful of pre-war buildings to survive in the rebuilt city centre of Plymouth.

143 Glyn Hopkin, Bishop's Stortford, Hertfordshire, was built *circa* 1934 for H. R. Moore Ltd. It epitomises the most advanced thinking in garage design of the period with a service department on the first floor and roof-top car parking approached by a ramp

142 The large and imposing Kenning's garage, Sheffield (1937–8; F. W. Tempest), now converted to a cinema.

144 Communication tubes still in place at the former Furlong's garage, Woolwich.

a rounded corner fronting the main road and the tyre-fitting shop itself on a side road. Both buildings are rendered and retain extensive neon signage.[45]

Since 1945

Garage building ceased during the Second World War and few new buildings appeared until the relaxation of building controls in 1954. Post-war garages tended towards the utilitarian, with few of the moderne flourishes seen in the 1930s. Curved windows, towers and fins all largely disappeared and the characteristic garage of the 1950s was brick-faced and sober. There were few

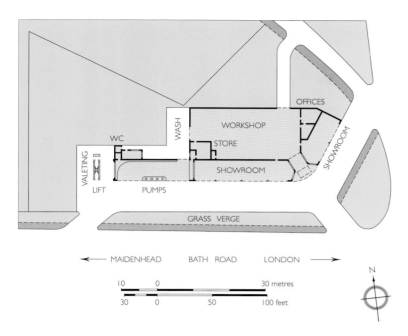

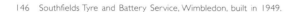

145 Mead's garage, on the Bath Road, designed by Rix & Rix. An example of late 1930s garage planning with the workshop entered on the skew between two ranges of showrooms. Redrawn from *The Service Station Manual*, 6th edition, n.d. [*circa* 1954].

attempts to build in any modern style. It was not until structural engineers started to look at interesting new ways of employing reinforced concrete that garage design began to emerge from the doldrums.

Increasing use was made of prefabricated industrial-building systems – such as that produced by Atcost Ltd, with its concrete arched roof trusses – and the services of firms that specialised in designing, building and equipping garages. This process had begun in the 1930s, when specialist firms such as Pye Quick Service Contractors had offered to design and build garages, and schemes where a company carries out all aspects of the design and build work have been a prominent feature of garage construction to the present.[46]

One significant change made during the 1950s was in the branding of garages, which increased greatly. Hitherto, garages had been prepared to sell any make of car that a customer might specify, and the slogan 'any make of car supplied' was common within the trade. By the 1950s manufacturers were more prone to sign up garages as authorised dealerships, and allegiance to a particular marque at an individual site became obvious, publicised with signage and colour schemes. While garage architec-

146 Southfields Tyre and Battery Service, Wimbledon, built in 1949.

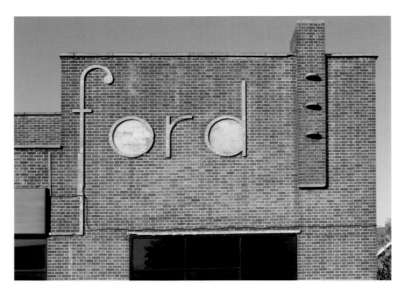

ture showed little influence of the Festival of Britain, some garages adopted new fonts for their signage, which helped to give them at least a veneer of modernity (pl. 147). From 1958 onwards this was often combined with the new colour schemes introduced by oil companies (see Chapter 5) to give a much brighter look (pls 150 and 183).

Although there was little technical innovation in garage buildings of the 1950s (pl. 148) – at least until the end of the decade – there was greater interest in providing better standards of natural light in workshop areas. Increasing use was made of roof

147   The former garage of William H. King Ltd, Southgates, King's Lynn, Norfolk, a Ford dealership with a rare survival of lettering incorporated into the building's design.

148 (*below*)   The Peterborough depot of Kenning's *circa* 1954 shows that although the basic form of workshops changed little, with the familiar light steel truss roof still present, workshops themselves were much more orderly than they had been in the 1920s, with ramps replacing pits as a means of gaining access to the vehicle. Tecalemit lubrication equipment did much to tidy up the heterogeneous collection of oil dispensers that were a feature of many garages. The vehicles include Standard Vanguards and Triumph Renowns and a Mayflower, together with a Bedford van on the ramp.

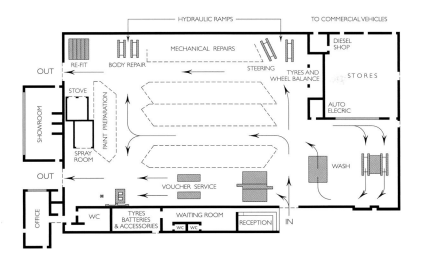

149 A 1960s garage showing how vehicle servicing was carried out on a flowline. The interior is now devoted to repair and maintenance with space no longer used for parking. Hydraulic ramps have taken the place of inspection pits for carrying out work on the underside of vehicles. Redrawn from *Motor Trader*, 14 February 1968.

151 Revesby Garage, Revesby, Lincolnshire, with its monopitch roofs, built in 1961–2, is an example of modern treatment of a small garage.

150 Typifying the arrival of brighter façades in a modern style for garage frontages in the early 1960s is Leyton Garage, Leyton (1961; Challen & Floyd). A showroom block on the left is brought forward and attention drawn to it by the use of exposed concrete framing, while the remainder of the frontage has offices on the first floor, above showrooms, lubrication bays and the entrance to the workshops. The gable ends of these are visible above the frontage.

lights, sometimes with circular lights punched through a concrete roof. Artificial lighting, too, was improved, with fluorescent lighting becoming almost universal.

A major change in garage planning and equipment occurred in the late 1950s and early 1960s as a result of improvements to the motor car. Cars were able to cover much greater mileages between services and the need to carry out greasing virtually died out. With the removal of many old cars from the road following the introduction of the ten-year test in 1961, processes

such as de-carbonisation were no longer in such demand. The emphasis in workshop servicing turned to alerting drivers to potential defects, such as worn brakes, steering and tyres. With servicing less frequent, there was an incentive to turn the process into a much more efficient flowline of the type first seen in larger garages during the late 1930s (pl. 149).

Major manufacturers such as the British Motor Corporation (see Chapter 1) had planning departments that would assist their main dealers to design service areas for maximum efficiency. The

152   Newly built workshops of W. W. Webber Ltd, Basingstoke, Hampshire, on 19 June 1975. The workshop is typical of many constructed since the 1960s, using H-section steel joists, a form of construction that became as ubiquitous as the light steel truss roof on masonry walls was in the earlier part of the twentieth century. Fluorescent lighting and roof lights in corrugated transparent plastic, providing natural light, result in a much brighter interior than the Kenning's workshop of some twenty years earlier. British Leyland cars of the period are much in evidence: a Mini, an MGB, an Austin Maxi, a Morris Marina and a Princess. Webber's sold cars in Basingstoke from 1900 and are still trading.

areas tended to fall into two categories: lift schemes and servo-dock schemes. Diagnostic systems first appeared in the mid-1960s, the predecessors of today's computerised workshops. Laycock Engineering first marketed a complete 'diagnostic track' in 1965, which covered lights, engine tune-up, brake testing, wheel alignment and balancing and, in effect, mimicked the assembly track in a car factory.[47] Such changes did not in themselves affect the external appearance of garages, but they required an interior with a large uninterrupted volume, which led to many workshops being rebuilt. It was in this decade that garages became consciously modern in appearance, adopting the glass-and-steel-panelled cladding associated with offices and public buildings of the decade. Flat roofs became almost *de rigueur*.

Some impressive designs appeared. The Lincolnshire Motor Co., Lincoln (1959; Denis Clarke Hall, Sam Scorer and Roy Bright), employed a hyperbolic paraboloid roof of concrete, only the fourth to be built in England (see pl. 71). The roof covered the workshops, providing a clear floor area, and also a recessed lay-by for petrol pumps. This was one of three linked elements, including a showroom and offices, on the site. The building has

now been converted into restaurants.[48] Another landmark garage of the late 1960s was the K Garage (date unknown) on Watford Way, Mill Hill, north London (pl. 153). Designed to catch the eye of motorists leaving the capital, this was one of the rare examples of a Brutalist design for a combined garage and car showroom. The functions were stacked above each other in a vast, box-like structure. The ground floor was occupied by a showroom, and a mezzanine by offices, with two further storeys used as workshops. These were accessed by a ramp that extended across the rear of the building and was then expressed at the north end, cantilevered from the main structure. The upper parts of the building were largely faced with concrete panels, interspersed with bands of opaque glazing to light the workshops. The most noticeable feature was an asymmetrically placed, projecting, fully glazed bay, which formed a showcase for a single car.

The footprints of the sites of major garages became larger; they had to accommodate more on-site surface car parking and dealt in greater numbers of used cars. Sites could contain a whole complex of buildings serving different functions. Work-

153   K Garage, Watford Way, Mill Hill, a Brutalist 1960s landmark on the A1 for motorists leaving London for the north.

154   At Bradshaw's Garage, Preston, the façade of an existing garage, dating from 1931, was partially demolished and replaced with new cladding of aluminium and weatherboarding in 1963–4 (F. K. Lord & C. J. R. Ratcliff of Building Design Partnership). Garage façades have been subject to constant rebuilding to keep the appearance of the buildings up to date, and recladding was particularly common in the 1960s. Today, complete rebuilding is much more prevalent. The gull-wing canopy above the pumps is a typical addition of the period.

155 A135 Yarm Road and Concorde Way, south of Stockton-on-Tees, near its interchange with the A66, a view graphically showing how from the 1980s large car dealerships became increasingly concentrated in edge-of-town locations. The dealerships seen here represent Ford, Volkswagen Audi Group, BMW/Mini, Volvo and Mercedes-Benz. Each garage is set well back from the road to allow an extensive forecourt for the display of cars, while the layout, which is not constrained by existing buildings, permits ample car parking. Large shed-like buildings contain the repair and maintenance workshops with little attempt to disguise them.

shops still tended to be situated immediately behind showrooms, but during the 1960s architectural expression became less obvious, with the individual buildings subordinated to an overall corporate theme, achieved by larger and bolder signage and flags, and almost overwhelmed by ranks of parked cars on the forecourt. The use of metal extrusions multiplied from the early 1960s, often being used to hide older parts of premises in an attempt to unify a disparate group of buildings into a coherent modern complex (pl. 154).

Petrol sales were still regarded as an essential component of service garages, and the canopies increasingly being used to cover pump islands became a further element that obscured the architecture, although in some cases, as at Dereham Motors, Dereham, Norfolk, in 1965, they were deliberately omitted so as not to obscure new showroom premises.[49] This process continued throughout the 1970s and much of the 1980s, to the extent that the individual parts of garages were reduced to large steel-framed boxes, frequently clad in corrugated metal. All the impact was now in signage; buildings were quite secondary. Large dealerships stopped selling fuel and the resultant vacant space on the forecourt was used for displaying used cars. Today, workshops are externally anonymous buildings that are much more brightly lit, cleaner places than their predecessors, and often physically quite separate from showrooms. Service reception is often located in the showroom, giving vehicle owners opportunities for looking at new cars and accessories.

More significant, perhaps, than any changes in the external appearance of repair and maintenance garages in more recent years has been their removal, along with car showrooms, to new sites on purpose-built automotive retail parks. Here, in some cases they are concentrated with more than a dozen different firms. These automotive parks tend to be located, like other retail parks, on the outskirts of towns, often near ring roads. An example is that on the A135 Yarm Road, south of Stockton-on-Tees, near its interchange with the A66 (pl. 155). This is located near the Preston Farms industrial estate and consists of eight businesses, many of which have large sheds for servicing and repairs behind the showroom buildings. Another at Southend-on-Sea, Essex, has led to several dealers closing their premises on London Road, until recently the principal location for car dealers and repairers in the town; this had fulfilled a role akin to that of the 'Gasoline Alleys' once found in many American cities where dealerships were heavily concentrated in one location. 'Gasoline Alley' is now, like much other retail development, a major component of exurbia.

5: FILLING UP

To drive a car, one had to obtain fuel: usually, but not exclusively, petrol, for the steam car enjoyed a brief vogue, while electric broughams were fashionable in central London. Steam cars required water, easily obtainable domestically, but also needed petrol as part of the process of turning water into steam. Electric cars, which were used only for local journeys of a few miles, required charging at frequent intervals. They were generally hired, rather than owned, and charging was usually carried out at the hire garage.

Carless, Capel & Leonard were the first British company to market petrol on a national basis, from 1891. They were joined in 1898 by Rockefeller's Standard Oil Company, which sold its petrol in Britain under the trade name Pratt's.[1] Initially a waste product from crude oil, this light liquid was used as a cleaning agent until it was found to be an effective fuel for motor launch engines. Frederick Simms, who imported Daimler engines almost two years before the motor car was introduced to England in 1895 (see Chapter 1), falsely claimed to have given it the name 'petrol', but the use of the word goes back at least to the 1880s, and Carless, Capel & Leonard employed it for the motor spirit they sold.[2] Local authorities regulated the safe storage of petrol under the Petroleum Acts of 1871 and 1881, and also issued licences for its sale. The difficulty of obtaining fuel was a constant bugbear for the early motorist, who faced the very real possibility of running out, especially at weekends. A list of petrol stockists in England, published in 1898, gave a total of just 131 outlets, while a list of 1899 included 232 suppliers.[3] The 2-gallon can, introduced by Pratt's, made its appearance in 1900; legislation later that year made its retail sale in this form mandatory.[4] For the ensuing two decades, petrol was sold in cans by a variety of outlets, including repair garages, parking garages, hotels, ironmongers, chemists, light engineering companies and cycle shops (pl. 157). Carless, Capel & Leonard's list of authorised suppliers, dated 1906, gives some idea of how this operated in practice. Although many of those included did not indicate the nature of their business, the list specified sixteen

157 What might be described as a proto filling station at Manchester during the 1,000 Mile Trial of 1900. The petrol is stored in wooden barrels, the way in which it was transported in bulk in the earliest days of motoring. Also visible are the circular 2- and 4-gallon petrol cans used at this period, later to be superseded by the familiar rectangular designs bearing the petrol company's name on the side.

156 (facing page)   Henly's showpiece service station on the Great West Road, Brentford (1937; Wallis Gilbert & Partners), had a battery of twenty-two pumps covered by a sweeping concrete awning. The building was dominated by its illuminated, 150ft-high clock tower, a replica of which stands on the site today; the rest of the building was demolished in the 1960s.

motor garages, thirteen motor companies, two motor works and seventeen cycle companies in London. In the provinces, there were sixty ironmongers, forty-two cycle works, twenty-eight cycle agents, seventeen cycle companies, twenty-eight inns and hotels, and only twelve garages.[5]

The Arrival of the Filling Station

The first moves to supply fuel by pump occurred in the U.S.A. The term 'service station' was reputedly invented by a Bowser salesman in 1908, and the firm developed a pump that would draw petrol by suction from an underground tank. Initially, pumps were located by the kerb. There is some debate over the identity of the first drive-in filling station, solely devoted to that purpose, as opposed to a garage selling petrol and oil. One claimant was R. L. Francis in Detroit, whose filling station opened in May 1911, using a Wayne pump.[6] In June 1913 the Standard Oil Company established a filling station in Columbus, Ohio. In the same year Gulf Oil opened a station in Pittsburgh: this was architect-designed, with a well-laid-out forecourt and canopied office, anticipating in all respects the modern filling station.[7] By this time, what were termed 'sidewalk fillers' were

becoming common throughout the U.S.A.[8] In England, the first pavement pump is generally considered to be an American-made Bowser, installed outside the premises of Legge & Chamier in Shrewsbury in 1915.[9] This, however, did not mark a general transition to more modern methods of supply in England, in contrast to the U.S.A., where, in 1914, Standard Oil of California had thirty-four filling stations of standardised design in operation.[10] In England, pumps were often placed in alcoves in the façade of the garage to avoid paying a licence fee to the local authority, necessary if they were to remain on the pavement.

The introduction of the first filling station in England in 1919 was not actually motivated by a desire to instigate more efficient means of distributing petrol. Rather, it was a response to the difficulties motorists were experiencing in obtaining British-made benzole, which was being actively promoted on patriotic grounds, particularly in the light of what was seen as the Bolshevik threat. Russian petrol, sold under the ROP (Russian Oil Products) brand, was being marketed widely in England, but in the aftermath of the Russian Revolution, with its reports of atrocities, and the recent support of the British Government for the White Russians, many regarded the sale of this Russian petrol as an outrage. Benzole, derived from coal and hitherto used for

158   AA filling station at Stump Cross, near Great Chesterford, Essex, erected in 1920.

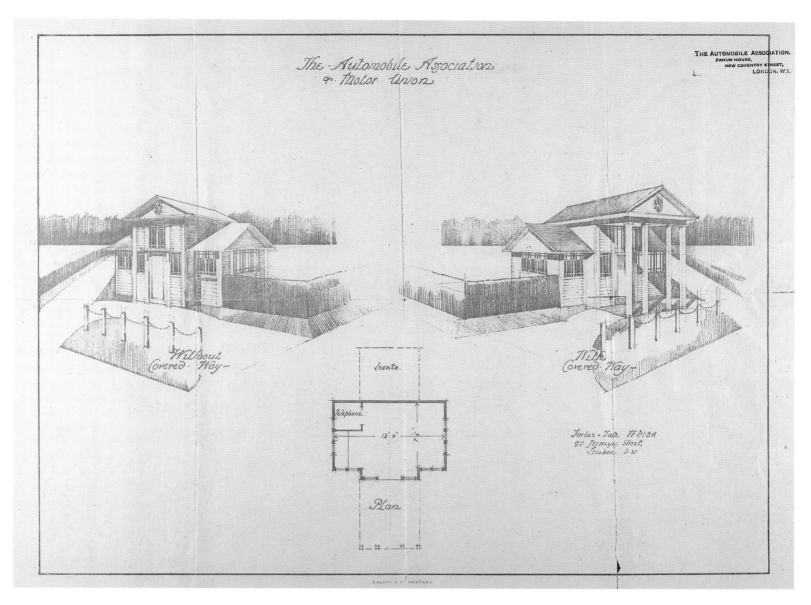

The Automobile Association & Motor Union

THE AUTOMOBILE ASSOCIATION,
FANUM HOUSE,
NEW COVENTRY STREET,
LONDON, W.1.

Without Covered Way–

Isanto.

Telephone

12'0"

Plan

With Covered Way–

Forbes & Tate FFRIBA
9r Jermyn Street
London S.W.

C. ALLOM & Co PRINTERS

159   Perspectives and plan of proposed AA filling stations by Forbes & Tate. The design, with the canopy resembling a pediment, inspired by American examples, was not built in this form.

dyeing and dry-cleaning, was developed as one of a number of substitutes for petrol.

The Automobile Association (AA) took the lead in this campaign by setting up a Motor Fuel Department in 1919. This attacked the high cost of imported petrol and argued for the use of British-made benzole, which had the advantage of being duty-free. The Department made a film to show how benzole was made and issued motorists with lists of suppliers of 50-gallon drums, which it suggested they store at the bottom of their gardens.[11] The disadvantages of this were obvious, and to promote further the use of benzole, the AA opened its first filling station in November 1919. Located at Aldermaston, between Maidenhead and Newbury on the Bath road, this was

officially opened on 2 March 1920, by which time there were approximately 15,000 filling stations in the U.S.A. There was one hand-operated pump supplying benzole obtained from local suppliers – the AA was at pains to point out that it was not in the business of selling fuel, but was setting an example and providing a service to its members, who were served by AA patrol men in full uniform. This was followed by other 'replenishment pits': at Coombe Hill, where the Cheltenham road joined that from Tewkesbury to Gloucester; at Blue Boar Corner on the Coventry–Dunchurch road; at Yarcombe, near Honiton; at Stump Cross, north of Great Chesterford in Essex (pl. 158); at Mere Corner, Cheshire; at Bolney, Sussex, and Bramham Moor, 10 miles north of Leeds.[12] The AA continued to operate

160 One of the earliest filling stations to open in London was that of the Anglo-American Oil Co. (Pratt's) in Euston Road in 1922. It was built to a high standard and the contractors, F. D. Huntington, were evidently sufficiently proud of it to commission Bedford Lemere to photograph it. The curved pump island is stylish, while the kiosk is the forerunner of many that were to follow over the years.

these filling stations for a number of years, the first to be sold off being Bolney and Bramham Moor in 1926, and the last, Mere Corner, given up in 1932.[13]

All these early filling stations were of the simplest timber construction with felted roofs and horizontal unpainted clapboarding, with vertical boarding in the gables; the central part was raised, its gable facing the road (pl. 159). They were, however, designed by architects – Forbes & Tate – and were constructed by Messrs Percy White of Staines, a manufacturer of prefabricated timber garages, which was also responsible for constructing AA sentry boxes.[14] The Aldermaston station differed from those that followed since the central gable extended to form a

canopy over the roadway and pump. The other stations originally had the pump inside the building, the delivery hose being taken through the door to the car. They were very small, approximately 10 by 9 feet, and, inside, contained the pump, a table and a chair to the front, and a generator, batteries and an air tank to the rear. Behind this was a primitive water closet of the bucket type.[15] Some attempt was made to enhance the front of each station with a grass plot and flower-beds in which the letters 'AA' were picked out in grey stones. Despite the provision of these filling stations, benzole was still difficult to obtain. In July 1920, Owen John of *The Autocar* complained that 'nowhere else, except in the North of England, London, and in South Wales, can we ordinary folk get decent benzole today'; on his return journey, the Coombe Hill station had run out of fuel.[16] The Royal Automobile Club (RAC), too, provided benzole stations, one being near Wrotham on the London–Maidstone road. This consisted of a single pump by the roadside with a prefabricated wooden hut located some distance away.[17] Motorists appreciated the opportunity to fill up with such ease by the roadside, and the principle of delivery by pump was applied to the supply of petrol as well as benzole. Benzole, mixed with petrol from 1922, formed a steadily diminishing proportion of the mixture and finally disappeared in the early 1960s, due to reduced production of coke, of which it was a by-product, and health concerns.

Bulk storage of petrol in underground tanks served by petrol pumps rapidly increased when local authorities recognised that the system was safe. Within three years of the first AA filling station, commercial stations, supplied by tanker, were widespread. There was a fundamental distinction between filling stations in the U.S.A. and in Britain. In the U.S.A., filling stations were built predominantly by major oil companies, which took considerable trouble to produce standardised designs of some architectural quality. In Britain until the 1950s, on the other hand, they were nearly always the work of individual businesses and were often run as an adjunct of a repair and maintenance garage. Consequently, design quality was in general far lower than in the U.S.A., where the influence of the 'City Beautiful' movement was often evident.[18] The earliest designs were largely *ad hoc*, with little attempt made to group the pumps in a logical way. The pumps were all operated by hand and were located either on the pavement – with a swinging arm providing clearance to satisfy local authorities, who objected to the presence of pavement pumps – or off the road altogether. Some motorists were wary of the new pumps, because, with the earliest designs, it was possible to receive short measure at the hands of an unscrupulous garage owner; many continued to prefer the old petrol cans, which were sealed by the petrol companies with a lead seal on a wire through the cap, to ensure that the contents could not be tampered with. Indeed, Shell was initially opposed to petrol pumps because their provision removed the guarantee that the branded spirit was genuine; it also doubted the accuracy of pumps.[19]

The new system, however, soon swept all before it. By January 1920 the Wimbledon Motor Works had installed a pump on the pavement, and the specialised filling station began to appear in urban centres. In March that year the market leader, the Anglo-American Oil Co., started to install pumps on a nationwide basis, which led other companies to follow suit. The Anglo-Persian Oil Company (British Petroleum) made arrangements with Bowser to supply pumps and, by May 1921, sixty-nine had been installed. To illustrate the speed with which pump delivery spread, 7,000 pumps had been installed by the oil companies by

September 1923 and this figure had doubled by mid-1925.[20] An early design that took its stylistic cues from the AA stations was the Kingston Vale station of the Pioneer Filling Station Co., erected in 1922. This had a small chalet-type building with a hipped tiled roof, deliberately rustic boarding left unpainted, and a canopy sufficient to cover a car. It gave out information on routes via a specially illuminated map.[21] Filling stations in towns tended to very rudimentary at first, with just the pumps and a small kiosk, although this was often given a modicum of architectural trim to liven it up (pl. 160). One of the first filling stations in central London, opening in 1921, was the Auto Chalet on Marylebone Road, which had a pantiled hut with overhanging eaves in a vaguely Swiss style and sold petrol until midnight.[22] The practice of adding some embellishment to what was little more than a hut continued well into the later 1920s in stations such as the Lighthouse Filling Station, Catford, which had crenellations on the kiosk.[23] The ephemeral nature of these early filling stations ensured the early demise of most of them, but there are still some significant survivals in rural areas.

West End Garage, Turnastone, Herefordshire, which was granted the second licence to sell petrol in the county in 1922, is probably the oldest surviving filling station, still selling petrol, in England (pl. 161).[24] It is of a type once common in villages where cottages were adapted for the purpose. Here, an early nineteenth-century cottage has had two petrol pumps installed in the front garden. They are separated from the road by a low brick garden wall, over which the filling takes place. The exist-

161 At the West End Garage, Turnastone, Herefordshire, the pumps situated in the front garden of a cottage, on either side of the garden gate, are still in use. The garage bears period enamelled signage on its walls.

ing pumps date from the 1930s and 1950s: customers are served by the grandson of the founder of the business and sales take place in one of the front rooms of the cottage. Such buildings were usually adorned by a multiplicity of enamelled advertisements for tyres, oil and other motoring requisites, and West End Garage retains two on its façade. Now listed, it is probably the most complete example of its type.

Another early filling station, dating from 1926, is the former Colvin Brothers garage on the main Hastings Road at Flimwell, East Sussex.[25] This reflects the local vernacular in its use of clapboarding, in the half-timbering on its half-hipped gable and in the rustic supports to the gable, which is brought forward from the building to form a canopy (pl. 162). It originally had a range of five pumps and a lounge where teas could be purchased. The gable extending in front of the building is a common feature in rural filling stations. It is to be found at Drayton's Garage, High Street, Barley, Hertfordshire, where an existing timber building, possibly a stable, was extended *circa* 1922 over the forecourt and fitted with diamond-pattern tiles.

162   The former Colvin Brothers garage of 1926 on the main road to Hastings at Flimwell, East Sussex, now used by a coach firm, retains much of its original appearance.

The Filling Station under Attack

The elements of the filling station as it evolved in the 1920s were a forecourt, which could vary greatly in size, and a hut or kiosk for the attendant and pumps, together with oil and water points. In addition, there might be a building for repairing cars and a café at the rear of the site. At this stage, there was no clear view on how pumps should be arranged. The most common layout was a straight row of up to twelve individual pumps. Filling stations generally sold a number of brands of petrol, since the competing oil companies tried to get their pumps onto every site, with a different pump for each, so that there would often be six pumps when two or three would have been adequate. The advent of the Wayne multi-pump, which could supply up to six different brands from a single pump, reduced numbers to some extent. There were always at least two pumps, so that more than one customer could be served at a time. Another popular layout was for the pumps to be set in a broad arc. Less popular at this time, another alternative was for the pumps to be grouped into parallel islands, either running parallel to the road, or at right angles to it, or at a 45-degree angle.

The examples at Flimwell and Barley were perhaps atypical of the many early filling stations that were little more than corrugated iron shacks. The intense competition between the oil companies for the custom of motorists resulted in large numbers of enamelled signs on and around the building and on its approaches. Pumps carried distinctive illuminated glass globes to draw attention to the brand supplied at each one and extra globes were sometimes mounted on top of the filling-station building or at the entrance to the premises. The total effect could be extremely garish, while the sites were often roughly finished, with the forecourt left unsurfaced. The multiplication of these filling stations in the mid-1920s, as popular motoring gained ground, caused an outcry against 'roadside eyesores' across a broad spectrum of society. Opposition to them was led by the newly formed Council for the Preservation of Rural England (CPRE), which documented many instances of what it saw as the ruination of the English countryside (pl. 163). This was part of a wider concern about the impact of the car on England that is explored in more detail in Chapter 10. As argued there, the motoring magazines had a conservationist's view of the countryside and gave much support to the movement to improve the appearance of filling stations. As early as 1923, *The Autocar* was attacking the wayside garage: 'Every accessory connected with motoring is trumpeted forth on tin-plate placards of the crudest hues imaginable. Singly these things are deplorable; *en bloc* they are insufferable.'[26] Filling stations were singled out for especial excoriation: 'The scarlet and gamboge Aunt Sallies of the petrol filling-in stations . . . are a national disgrace', thundered Margot, Countess of Oxford and Asquith, in 1928.[27]

In 1928–9 the appearance of petrol stations became a subject of major public concern. The situation was considered so serious that legislation was required. The Petroleum (Consolidation) Act of 1928 gave local authorities powers to prevent filling stations from damaging the amenities of rural scenery and places of beauty and historic interest (pl. 164). By 1933 fifty-four county and borough councils had made bylaws under the Act for the control of filling stations. These gave local authorities the powers, when permitting the building of new filling stations, to prescribe the type of building, its colour and that of the pumps, signage,

163 Wolvey Filling Station, Warwickshire, *circa* 1929 after it had been tidied up, an example of the unsightly roadside filling station deplored by campaigners against wayside eyesores.

and the marks on pumps indicating the brand of fuel supplied. Excessive advertising and the use of corrugated or galvanised iron were also prohibited. In some districts, filling stations could be prohibited altogether. The laws also applied to existing filling stations in specified areas of natural beauty. In particular, all pumps and other 'visible apparatus' had to be painted the same colour throughout, and the only permitted sign was a standard one illustrated in the regulations.[28] This was based on the winning entry in a competition organised by the RIBA in 1928, for which a prize of £100 was awarded.[29]

Local authorities started laying down very specific requirements for colour schemes: Devon insisted that pumps and other 'visible apparatus' be painted cinnamon-brown, while Leeds required them to be painted dark green.[30] The trade press, while on the whole welcoming the legislation, since it might well wipe out the *bête noire* of the traditional motor trader, the 'tin shed merchant', also considered that the motor trade was being unfairly singled out and put to great expense.[31] A number of traders had been arguing for some time that the Ministry of Transport should be doing more to provide better roads rather than 'footling about the beauty of petrol pumps', and suggested that it might end up 'debating whether the pump should not be disguised as a tree, a cow, a rustic gateway, a giant mushroom, or a sunflower'.[32] The first case under the Act was brought to court in 1933 when a Worcestershire garage owner was fined for having some of his pumps and oil containers in a mixture of colours, including green, cream, black and white, rather than the single colour required under the county by-laws.[33]

Other positive steps were taken to encourage better filling-station design. In 1928 the Royal Society of Arts competition for industrial design included a category for an unobtrusive filling station. The winner, Thomas Mitchell, proposed a circular forecourt on a corner site with the pump islands hidden behind a screen.[34] Another competition was held in 1930 by the Incorporated Association of Architects and Surveyors. The winning design was a simple moderne structure with three filling bays under a concrete canopy, the runner-up a Beaux-Arts-inspired layout with a building with a curved colonnaded façade.[35] The National Gardens Guild in 1929 organised a brighter petrol stations contest in which 500 entries were received, the *Daily Express* awarding a gold trophy to the winner, the Coombe Bridge Service Station on the Kingston Bypass by H. Paul (pl. 166).[36]

There was also some discussion in the architectural press. The *Architect and Building News* held that the essential features in filling-station design were 'quickness of service, avoidance of danger from fire, elimination of danger to passing traffic or to users of the station, distant visibility for the approaching motorist, service conveniences for the customers and staff, and, in general, a pleasant lay-out'.[37] There was no reason why good design with clean approaches and an orderly layout 'should not confer upon the filling station an honourable place in town planning'. The highest echelons of the architectural profession became involved. In 1932 Sir Reginald Blomfield designed an elegant neo-classical pavilion with a domed copper roof for Appleyard's filling station at the end of Eastgate, Leeds, as part

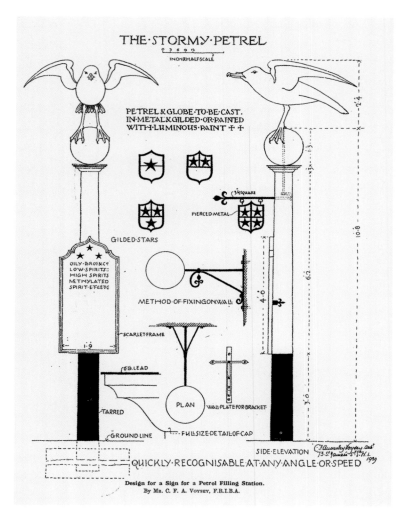

164 Brimfield Filling Station near Kidderminster, Worcestershire, displays the approved signage under bylaws made under the Petroleum (Consolidation) Act of 1928 in a photograph taken *circa* 1932.

165 C. F. A. Voysey's design of 1928 for a filling-station sign. From *The Builder*, 28 June 1928, p. 1165.

of his work on the elevations of the new street. Hexagonal in plan and intended to resemble a market cross, it was located in the centre of a triangular site marked by elegant curved railings (pl. 168).[38] The seven Bowser electric pumps were in archways on three sides of the structure. One of the last architectural designs by C. F. Annesley Voysey was a sign for a filling station in 1928 (pl. 165).[39]

An English Style?

But what were the principal available options for less exalted practitioners? There was the exotic, the quaint or the downright quirky, or there was the design intended to harmonise with its surroundings. Examples of the last, usually with hipped, tiled roofs, which were held to exemplify good taste, were legion, especially in the more attractive parts of south and west England

(pls 170 and 171). One such was the Wych Cross Filling Station, built in 1932 at one of the highest points in Ashdown Forest on the Eastbourne road. The filling station was surrounded by beech and fir trees; no advertising was displayed, and the pumps were covered. It was built in an Arts and Crafts style with timber piers on stone bases and a half-hipped tiled roof, the rafter ends exposed and shaped.[40] The open areas have subsequently been glazed and the building is currently used as a car showroom. The same fate has befallen another early example in a sensitive location, the former Anchor Hotel Filling Station of 1931 in the centre of Shepperton village, Surrey (pl. 167). This was a highly sophisticated design with a tiered roof supported on massive banded red brick piers.[41]

Petrol pumps were often seen as inherently ugly. The ideal was to cover them up to some extent, as at the Coombe Bridge Service Station of 1928 (see pl. 166), which was much acclaimed at the time for the way in which it harmonised with its

166   The Coombe Bridge Service Station by H. Paul, opened in 1928 on the Kingston Bypass, won several awards for what was considered to be its tasteful design.

168   Reginald Blomfield's classical filling station acted as an eye-catcher at the end of the widened Eastgate, Leeds. It was photographed shortly after completion in 1932.

167   The Anchor Hotel Filling Station, Shepperton, Surrey, of 1931, has been enclosed to form a car showroom, but the layout of the original open structure through which people drove to fill up is still evident.

169   The Colyford Filling Station (1928), now England's only filling station museum, with its array of 1950s petrol pumps.

surroundings. A rustic shelter, which also incorporated a kiosk whose walls were formed of brick nogging, with many timber posts supporting the roof, was accompanied by a self-consciously rustic sign advertising the station, which was set in landscaped gardens. The shelter had something in common with a lych gate, while the garage building itself was well-detailed Neo-Tudor, similar in style to the high-quality detached houses being erected in the Coombe area at the time.[42] The lych-gate approach to covering petrol pumps was generally praised, receiving support in the *Architectural Review* and in the CPRE's publications.[43] Another much-praised design was that of the Countess Weir filling station near Exeter by E. H. and A. C. Harbottle, where Old Delabole slates were used for roofing the simple timber structure enclosing the pumps.[44]

From the late 1920s and throughout much of the 1930s many filling stations in small towns or rural areas were designed in a simple yet attractive style, again employing a hipped roof. The Colyford Filling Station in Devon (1928; pl. 169) took its inspiration from Countess Weir, but was given a half-timbered gable. It survives as a petrol-station museum and retains a bank of 1950s pumps *in situ*. The Clovelly Cross Filling Station (1930; Orphoot & Whiting) had roughcast walls and a slated roof. It is a good

surviving example of the better type of inter-war filling station, as is the broadly similar Newbury Electric Filling Station (1934), designed by R. A. Wickens, a local builder, which had broad segmental arches in the central section and green glazed pantiles on the roof (pl. 172). Many rural filling stations had a house or bungalow in similar style for the owner. Bond's Garage, Barkway, Hertfordshire, is a largely intact example of 1938 that retained its two original pumps until well into the twenty-first century; it has matching brickwork on the house and filling station (pl. 173).

The quaint or quirky tended to be in the west of England, near the principal tourist routes. Typical was the Thatched Filling Station at Kennford, Devon. Two kiosks covered in shiplapped rustic boarding stood to either side of a bank of pumps, and the whole, including the area over the pumps, was thatched, the resulting canopy screening the pumps.[45] At Blashford, Hamp-

170 (*facing page top*)   Typifying the tasteful filling station of the early 1930s, Waresley Filling Station, Hartlebury, Worcestershire, has an owner's bungalow adjacent in matching style.

171 (*facing page bottom*)   The Waresley Filling Station is little altered today.

144

172   The Electric Filling Station, Newbury, Berkshire (1934; R. A. Wickens).

173   Bond's Garage, Barkway, Hertfordshire, was virtually unchanged from when it was built in 1938 until it was photographed in 2009. The two Beckmeter electric pumps (since removed) are visible under the canopy, while on the right is the owner's house matching the filling station itself.

174 (above)   The KCB Filling Station with the café (described at the time as a roadhouse) at Benson, Oxfordshire. The car is a Daimler Double Six.

shire, the owner went one better by grouping the pumps in pairs and thatching them, surmounting them with globes on the ridge. Two pairs of pumps flanked a kiosk (also thatched) with diamond-paned windows. A third example was the Evergreen Service Station, Stanway, Essex, where a thatched pump island was accompanied by a thatched kiosk and owner's house.[46] Perhaps the most spectacular of all was the KCB Roadhouse and Filling Station at Benson on the London–Oxford road, designed by Mrs Carlton Oakey (pl. 174). The initials KCB stood for 'Keep the Country Beautiful', and when Sir Lawrence Chubb, Chairman of SCAPA (Society for Checking the Abuses of Public Advertising), opened it in 1931, he hailed it as the most beautiful filling station in the country. It was awarded first prize in a local CPRE competition for beautifying filling stations. Two circular stone pavilions with conical thatched roofs had pumps mounted in niches and were linked by what resembled a lych gate housing more pumps. Two cafés behind provided snacks and a most elaborate thatched signpost advertised the premises. The enlargement of the neighbouring RAF station during the Second World War brought about its demise.[47] The rustic look, however, was not confined to the country: the Berkeley Filling Station (1934) on the Bath road at Cranford had a small round office building with a conical thatched roof and an interior boasting old oak beams and a big open fireplace. A sign resembling that of a village inn, and four kiosks, whose roofs aped in miniature that of the office building, completed the ensemble.[48]

One significant factor is the influence of filling stations in the U.S.A. on those in England. A great variety of designs had appeared there, ranging from old English cottages to Neo-Colonial, Neo-Classical and Spanish Mission, as well as the downright odd and eccentric. American influence may have been present in the prime example of the exotic in England, the Chinese Garage at Park Langley, Beckenham, Kent (pl. 175). Despite its name, it was based on Japanese pagoda architecture. It resembled the numerous filling stations built in a Neo-Japanese style by the Wadhams Oil Co. in the Milwaukee area from 1917 onwards.[49] Erected in 1929 by the proprietors, Taylor Brothers, who were also responsible for the adjacent Park

175   The Chinese Garage, Beckenham, seen from across its Japanese garden.

176   East Sheen Service Station, East Sheen, Richmond upon Thames, a filling station of *circa* 1926 in the American idiom, built for Cory Brothers. This is one of very few filling stations of this vintage still in use for its intended purpose, and perhaps the best surviving example of an early purpose-built filling station.

Langley estate, the Chinese Garage had ridges rising to goat's-horn finials and a central small pagoda. A gable broke forward to form a lengthy canopy across the forecourt. Six Wayne visible pumps (so named because the customer could see the fuel passing through a glass container as it was pumped from the storage tank) were painted black and gold, representing the rays of the rising sun. Both the offices and the showroom were decorated in Japanese style. In front of the filling station was a semicircular Japanese garden with a stream and ponds, filled with lilies and goldfish. Dwarf shrubs were surrounded by a fence of oriental design and eight stone Japanese lanterns, which at night set up shimmering reflections in the pond. The garden survives, but the garage is now used purely for car sales with no pumps.[50]

A number of filling stations showed direct American influence. One was the giant Sphinx in Islington of 1931 (inspired by the vogue for all things Egyptian in the wake of the discovery of Tutankhamun's tomb in 1922), from whose mouth a filler hose projected, a rare English equivalent to the outsized hats, windmills, dinosaurs and other whimsical edifices associated with roadside American architecture.[51] The Sphinx station, which was really only a publicity stunt using a theatrical prop, did not last long, falling foul of the London County Council inspectors, and English garage proprietors tended to eschew the wilder flights of fancy. In this, they were encouraged by local authorities and the new amenity societies. More conventional was the still extant East Sheen Service Station, Upper Richmond Road, East Sheen (*circa* 1926), which closely resembled many U.S. stations of the mid-1920s, notably in its use of a projecting canopy (pl. 176). It was in a simple and dignified classical style, clearly related to that employed by several U.S. oil companies, such as Standard Oil of Indiana, with shaped eaves brackets, a tiled roof and elegant, slightly curving lintels above the forecourt.

The arrival of exotic designs provoked *The Autocar* to express concern that they were inappropriate in an English context:

. . . we would like to interject one word of appeal to designers and builders of wayside filling stations. This is to remember they are building structures which when erected are part and parcel of Britain, and should thus be essentially British in character, form and substance. There is observable a tendency, doubtless due largely to the desire to be rather 'different', to design these stations in a foreign and often rococo style. The architecture of the East even is invoked, and, worse still, is sometimes blended with purely English styles. However temporarily attractive these buildings may appear, they are not English in style and conception, and cannot, therefore, harmonise with the English nature of the countryside or with the purity of the architecture in so many of the villages . . . [52]

It went on to say that the answer was to be found in the tried and tested period styles much beloved of the speculative builder:

The Tudors gave us the most intimate, English and satisfying form of architecture we have ever had, and Queen Anne's period possessed a peculiar dignity. These are safe styles to follow, but let them be followed faithfully, and let any temptation to 'improve' their innate simplicity be sternly repressed.

Let us, in a word, have English architecture for English soil.

Such traditionalist views were not universal. The *Architectural Review* considered that what was needed was a new type of building to fulfil a new need. There was little to be gained simply by copying Tudor or other past styles. It singled out for praise the Esher Filling Station (Imrie & Angell) on the Kingston Bypass, where a plain rendered wall provided a backdrop to a three-arched canopy, under which the pumps were hidden.[53]

These views were echoed by the Design and Industries Association (DIA) in their booklet *The Village Pump: A Guide to Better Garages* (1930), which they sent to 1,500 garages and filling stations. The RAC effectively funded the project by purchasing 2,500 copies, distributing them to their authorised repairers and provincial offices.[54] The DIA devoted its attack to the smaller filling stations:

Let us make it clear that we do not want petrol stations to be made 'picturesque', or disguised as rustic arbours as is sometimes done in America. That is not intelligent designing. The petrol station need not be ashamed of itself if it is properly fit for purpose . . . A standardised petrol station is not wanted. What would be happy in one village would be a horror in another.[55]

To judge from the examples illustrated, the DIA favoured the lych-gate approach to pump canopies and simple hipped roof structures (pl. 177). The Chinese Garage was criticised because 'the romantic East' had 'no right place in Western motoring', and the Esher Filling Station was again singled out for praise as 'perhaps the best-designed filling station in the country, hinting at great possibilities'.

The Modern Movement did not impact greatly on English filling stations. Even the moderne, as seen in so many U.S. stations, with their rounded corners and porcelain tile exteriors, did not catch on to the same extent. The principal reason must be that the situation in Britain differed from that in America: filling stations were not owned by the major oil companies with their standardised designs; consequently, the provision of buildings was left to individual garage proprietors.

Nevertheless, a small number of stations aspired to be different. R. H. Collier had a dramatic scheme at its filling station at Sheldon, Birmingham, where a circular building had a cantilevered canopy running round it and neon lighting was used to great effect. Campbell Symonds & Co. had something similar at their Empire Garage at Wembley, where pumps were tightly set either side of the stanchions for the canopy. Wessex Motors employed an impressive rounded concrete canopy covering almost the entire forecourt of their filling station of 1934–5 in Salisbury.[56] A particularly elegant filling station was built in 1939 by Appleyards on one of the arterial roads leading out of Leeds, perhaps the only English example to equal the many minimalist designs being built at the time in mainland Europe. It had a circular tower-like building at one end fully integrated into a concrete canopy over the pumps, its rounded ends echoing the form of the tower. Door facings and window frames were in stainless steel.[57] But these were the exceptions. It is hard now to gain an impression of what represented the norm in the 1930s since so few filling stations from the era survive. Leeds City Council photographed many examples, probably in the course of granting petrol licences, and these photographs give a broad view for a single city. What is evident is that many of the filling stations were ramshackle and unsightly agglomerations of unrelated structures and signage, fully justifying the criticism levelled at them. There were notable exceptions, but these were very much in a minority.[58]

The layout of the filling station had evolved by the late 1930s (pl. 179). The pumps were more likely to be grouped in islands, often with four pumps on a single island with a kiosk between, creating two filling bays. The island would be equipped with water and air points. Oil pumps would be placed in front of the

The Autocar

FOUNDED 1895

4D

The New "BP"

Puts New Life into Your Car

178 (*above*) An illustration from a Nuffield brochure of *circa* 1952 gives an idea of the level of service expected by motorists in the pre-self-service era. White-coated pump attendants stand ready to deliver petrol as a Morris Oxford approaches.

179 (*right*) Loach's Service Station, Kennford Bypass, Exeter. A design that anticipated the move towards more comprehensive facilities after the Second World War with the inclusion of a café and a small repair shop. The pumps are neatly grouped on a single island. Gardens and a camping ground indicate that the service station was there to serve the needs of holidaymakers on the way to the pleasure grounds of Devon and Cornwall. Based on a drawing in *The Service Station Manual*, 6th edition, n.d. (*circa* 1954).

177 (*facing page*) A BP advertisement of 1929, based on a filling station at Muswell Hill in north London that won a competition organised by the National Gardens Guild. It was illustrated in the DIA pamphlet *The Village Pump: A Guide to Better Garages*.

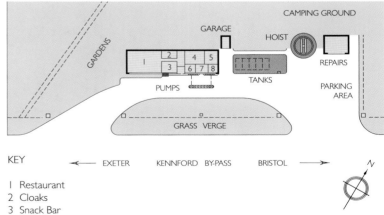

KEY

1 Restaurant
2 Cloaks
3 Snack Bar
4 Kitchen
5 Stores
6 Sitting Room
7 Sales
8 Office

180 The glamorous ambience may suggest Hollywood, but the location is Effingham Street in the heart of Sheffield's steelmaking east end. The Coronet Filling Station was claimed, when built *circa* 1956, as the longest filling station in the country, with its groups of Beckmeter model M3 pumps. The rear wall and raised platform for the kiosk survive today.

office building, which by this time accommodated lavatories for both men and women. In general, newly opened filling stations would be less rudimentary than their 1920s predecessors, although the overall standard, as suggested above, was not high. Technical changes included the introduction of electric pumps, with Wayne putting in the first individual electric pump at the Caterham Motor Co., Purley, Surrey, in 1930, and Bowser installing their first electric pump station at Blackfriars Road, Salford, in August 1931.[59]

The Second World War and its Aftermath

Petrol rationing was introduced on the outbreak of war in 1939 and motoring, other than for essential purposes, soon became impossible. The individual brands of petrol ceased to be available, to be replaced with a single low-grade 70–72 octane fuel, known as 'Pool' petrol. Although rationing ended in May 1950, 'Pool' remained the only grade on sale. Following complaints by car manufacturers that its poor quality was inhibiting the devel-

opment of higher performance cars for the export market, the familiar branded varieties of petrol were reintroduced in February 1953.[60] At the same time, an initiative that was to have momentous consequences for the future of petrol retailing took place. This was the introduction of 'solus' agreements by the oil companies. Up to this point, filling stations were free to sell any brand of petrol that they wished and many sold a number of different brands. The solus agreement tied a filling-station proprietor to a particular brand for the period specified in the contract with the supplier. The oil companies put pressure on retailers to enter into agreements and, although there was much opposition, freely expressed in the pages of the trade press, eventually most sales were governed by such agreements. By 1951 more than 50 per cent of all garages had some sort of agreement with an oil company; by 1953 it was 80 per cent, and by 1964, 95 per cent.[61]

In the immediate post-war era, building licences generally were hard to come by and very little advance in filling-station design was to be seen for some time. The Government, however, was sufficiently concerned to set up the Waleran Committee to investigate the problem posed by unsightly filling stations. Its report in 1949 recommended minimum standards for different grades of station and control of the number and grading of stations in rural and urban areas.[62] Although its findings were not implemented, the oil companies began to take more interest in the appearance of the stations. The solus agreement gave them a much greater incentive to promote their brand, and several began to seek the advice of design consultants to devise comprehensive corporate logos and colour-scheme applications. In addition, some of the oil companies started to run petrol stations themselves for the first time, a trend that would grow to the extent that, by the 1970s, most prime sites on the principal trunk roads were in their ownership. This resulted in a major change in the appearance of filling stations, which began to follow the American model established as early as 1914, of standardised designs erected by oil companies.

The need to establish a strong brand identity was made more urgent by the arrival in 1952 of a newcomer, Mobil, which had previously sold only lubricants, to the ranks of the major oil companies operating in Great Britain. The existing 'big four' were Esso, Regent, Fina and Shell-Mex/BP. The last, while remaining separate companies, had set up Shell-Mex & BP Ltd as a joint marketing operation for their products in the United Kingdom in 1932. Their subsidiaries were Power and Dominion, and they were closely associated with National Benzole (acquired by BP in 1956).

As the most design-conscious of the major oil companies, Shell-Mex & BP, which had set up an architectural section in 1951 under D. A. Birchett, instigated a competition in 1952 with the RIBA for a modular design of filling station appropriate to a period when prefabrication was seen as the answer to many building needs.[63] There were three sections: one for a service station in the country, one for a suburban neighbourhood and one for a motorway, some eight years before the opening of the Preston Bypass, England's first motorway. The winner of the suburban category was an Australian architect, Maxwell Gregory, but it was not until 1957 that he had an opportunity to build a service station, at The Stow, Harlow, Essex, for Kennings Ltd (pl. 181). By this time he had returned home, and the work was supervised by Ramsey, Murray, White & Ward with D. A. Birchett as consultant. The final design was quite different from Gregory's winning entry. It was built on a 40-inch grid using the constructional system by Hills & Co. that was used in Hertfordshire County Council schools. This employed exposed light steel truss roofs, continuously glazed clerestory windows and exposed steel columns. The external cladding was of brickwork panels and Western red cedar. Three disparate buildings – a showroom, washing bay and workshops – were linked together by the use of modular components. The overall effect was clean and sophisticated, and had much in common with the celebrated Hert-

fordshire schools. Today, only the workshop block survives, currently derelict and mutilated by the addition of sheet metal over two of its façades.[64]

By the time the Harlow filling station was opened, the first of the modular petrol stations designed by D. A. Birkett had already been opened on the Oxford Road near Reading in 1955 (significantly opened by C. H. Aslin, the Hertfordshire County Council Architect and President of the RIBA; pl. 182), with a second at Aylesbury in 1957.[65] The stations were built around a 4-inch module and 8-foot-high steel curtain walling panels by Hills & Co. The smallest structure that could be created was a kiosk, the most basic was a small office 26 by 16 feet, which could then have an addition of a lubricating bay, washing bay and oil store. A particularly svelte example was that at Trumpington, Cambridge (demolished), by H. C. Hughes and Peter Bicknell, which incorporated a small group of shops on adjoining land.

But, despite these examples, the move towards standardised filling-station buildings was slow to take off, in contrast to the U.S.A. and Europe, where there had been more than thirty years' development of such designs. By the late 1930s the super service station with covered washing and lubrication bays had become ubiquitous in the U.S.A., and these were frequently the work of leading industrial designers, such as those produced by Walter Dorwin Teague for Texaco.[66] The two additional bays enabled filling stations to compete on minor servicing work with repair and maintenance garages. The concept spread to England in the 1950s, many examples appearing from that time. This had much to do with several of the oil companies using the same designs of filling station on an international basis, so that what might be seen in Birmingham was identical in all respects to a filling station in America or Japan. Esso were in the forefront of this move towards standardised designs with the introduction in the early 1950s of one with a splayed corner containing the sales office adjacent to two bays for washing and lubrication, all under a flat roof that extended some distance beyond the eaves. Mobil had a similar design that substituted cement render for the porcelain panels favoured in the U.S.A. The boxy Shell Type A design, used throughout Europe, Asia, Africa and South America and introduced into England in 1956–7, had its sales office projecting forward from the washing and lubrication bays.

In 1956 a New Look was introduced for Shell-Mex filling stations; the following year a similar exercise was applied to BP stations, following research that indicated its image seemed dated and stodgy. Its New Look was the work of Harold Barnett of the design consultancy Compagnie de l'Esthetique Industrielle of Paris, founded by Raymond Loewy.[67] This made much more use of colour, very much in tune with the 1950s liking for colour, seen both in homes and in the two-tone schemes used on cars of the period. The colours used were white, green and

181 The Shell Service Station at The Stow, Harlow (1957; Maxwell Gregory and D. A. Birchett).

182 The first of D. A. Birchett's modular filling stations for Shell Mex & BP opened in 1955 on Oxford Road, Reading.

183   Artwork from an undated (*circa* 1958) National Benzole brochure to introduce the company's new branding to filling-station owners.

yellow, and the BP shield was simplified so that it was 'less pointed, less heraldic in a medieval way'.[68] It was argued that the new colour schemes would be far more visible to the passing motorist. National Benzole, which was linked to Shell-Mex & BP, devised its own new look based on white, blue and yellow, shortened its name to 'National' and introduced striking new graphics (pl. 183).

Into the 1960s

Perhaps the most striking changes of the 1960s were brought about by the continued growth of oil-company-owned sites and solus agreements. These led to a far more homogenous look. By 1964 Shell-Mex & BP owned 2,330 sites, Esso 1,281, Regent 718, Mobil 467 and Petrofina 262.[69] In addition, competition grew with the arrival on the British market of many smaller British-based firms and existing foreign oil companies. These included Jet, Total, Gulf, Burmah, AGIP, Murco, Continental, Amoco and APEX. While up to 1960 Shell-Mex & BP and Esso continued to dominate the market as they had done in the 1930s, with 50 and 30 per cent of market share respectively, by 1970

Jet and the other new entrants had 22 per cent.[70] Competition was initially generated largely through trading stamps, but later through price.

The Shell-BP marketing organisation led the way with a further development of their mid-1950s New Look. A new range of standard prefabricated filling-station designs was introduced in 1959 and appeared in almost every part of the country (pl. 184).[71] Along with the Scott telephone box, the Neo-Georgian post office and the 'prefab', they were perhaps some of the most replicated buildings in Britain. In many areas, they were among the first undeniably modern structures to be built, their white finish standing out amongst the dingiest surroundings. The design was so distinctive that it was even reproduced as a plastic kit by Corgi Toys to accompany their miniature cars.

Construction was modular, so examples varied greatly in length, while the components could be combined with local stone to harmonise with rural surroundings. Common to all was a timber frame, a flat roof, an enclosed compound with horizontal painted boarding and a panel on which the Shell or BP logo was displayed (pl. 185). Pump islands had canopies with rounded ends supported on a single tubular steel upright, and the overall look of the site was unified by modern signage.

184   London Road Service Station, Thetford, Norfolk, a large example with lubrication and washing bays of the Shell-Mex & BP standard design introduced in 1959.

185   The BP New Look as applied to one of the standard filling stations. Illustration from *Shell-BP News*, April 1963.

A modern BP service station in a country setting. Care is taken in the design of service stations to ensure that they fit well into their backgrounds

186 Esso's 1973 branding applied to one of its standard service stations from the 1950s, with the twin lubrication bays externally distinguished by their raised roofs. The use of paint to create rounded corners to the salesroom doors and windows is typical of the era, as are the posters for Green Shield Stamps and offers of free tumblers

Although once ubiquitous, not a single surviving example of the design has been traced in England, testimony to the changes that self-service brought about in filling-station layout, and also probably to the use of low-quality softwood in their construction. The dilution of the New Look began with BP in 1967. An existing site, the Greenford Park Filling Station in Greenford, Middlesex, was revamped with a V-shaped canopy over the pumps, new illuminated signs and a raked awning on the main building.[72] In 1968 Shell also devised new decor for its stations, making greater use of yellow in the colour scheme. A larger canopy was provided and the pumps lost their familiar globes.[73]

The other oil companies also continued to develop standardised designs. One of the most distinctive changes was that rooflines became stepped so that the roof of the sales areas was lower than that of the service bays, which made the buildings less overwhelming. Esso brought out such a design (pl. 186), while Mobil introduced a 'New Mobil Look' in 1960, with a standardised design based around a shop with a gull-wing roof with deep eaves, which stood proud of twin flat-roofed lubrication and service bays. The prototype was built at Shepperton, Surrey. Total introduced a prefabricated design, the Standard Series II, an extensively glazed structure with clerestory lighting

for the lubrication bay, in 1963.[74] Gulf entered the British market with a distinctive design, built in brick with a curved roof, an idea that was to proliferate in car showroom designs from the 1990s. The first station to be built to its standard design, used throughout the world, was opened at Leigh-on-Sea, Essex, in 1962, and still survives.[75] In 1968 Gulf introduced a new standard design, much more boxy, in white glazed brick with blue surround and orange trim. A heavy canopy, which was visually an extension of the eaves cladding, was a prominent feature.[76] From 1965 the Italian giant AGIP opened a number of filling stations using distinctive and very stylish Italian prefabricated components. These stood out against the staid design of many of their competitors, but AGIP's British operations had been absorbed by Esso by 1967.

For a brief period during the late 1950s and '60s experimentation with concrete canopies resulted in some highly individual and visually exciting designs. The most spectacular was the hyperbolic paraboloid roof at the National station on the A1 at Markham Moor, designed by Sam Scorer in 1960–61, converted in later years to a roadside restaurant. (pls 187 and 188) The station was operated by the Lincolnshire Motor Co., for which Scorer had earlier designed an equally impressive garage in

187 The hyperbolic paraboloid canopy at Markham Moor, Nottinghamshire, on the A1, designed by Sam Scorer and a German refugee engineer, Dr Haynal-Kónyi. The restaurant is a later insertion.

Lincoln (see pl. 71). An impressive series of umbrella units, each consisting of four hyperbolic paraboloid shells, was used to create the buildings and canopy at Five Ways, Wolverhampton (*circa* 1961; Charles E. Mason & Richards).[77] A cantilevered concrete canopy at Hythe, Kent (1958; Wallis, Gilbert & Partners), which raked upwards, had a 22-foot overhang.[78] Equally exciting results were achieved in 1959–60 by Erdi & Rabson in Henly's filling station at Dover, which had an aluminium canopy in the form of a truncated cone with concave sides cantilevered out from a circular kiosk.[79] Canopies were becoming increasingly common in all types of filling station from the early 1960s, with a flat-topped example of chipboard and concrete, 110 by 40 feet, claiming to be the largest in England in 1963.[80] Victor Christ-Janer

created an impressive internally lit steel canopy for Mobil in the early 1960s.[81] Among the most popular designs was a lightweight metal gull-wing design by Conder International Ltd, which started producing them in 1959. The Conder canopies were of corrugated aluminium on tapered steel rafters with steel fascias and were supported on steel-box stanchions that carried rain-water in concealed pipes. Others came from a variety of suppliers, including some elegantly minimal Continental designs imported by Petrol Station Canopies Ltd. Auto Kraft Shells, who produced kit cars, offered a glass fibre canopy in 1962. This material became increasingly used in the 1960s, with National Benzole adopting it for a combined forecourt kiosk and lighting unit that exploited the ability of the material to produce

188 Markham Moor Filling Station, while still in use with its petrol pumps, in May 1970.

The Development of Self-Service Petrol Retailing

The most significant change to the design of filling stations occurred with the introduction of self-service. Earlier changes such as the 'tidying-up' campaigns of the major oil companies affected the appearance of petrol stations but not their form, which had remained largely unchanged since the first examples opened in the 1920s. Service was still considered to be a crucial factor in petrol sales, with the checking of oil and tyres and the cleaning of windscreens an essential part of filling up.

The concept of self-service was almost as old as the filling station itself. In 1927 a coin-operated pump, equipped with a

189 The Galgate Service Station, Barnard Castle, Co. Durham, with petrol-dispensing hoses suspended from the glass-roofed canopy.

striking curved surfaces.[82] BP built an experimental filling station at Baldock, Hertfordshire, entirely out of plastics in 1968, as did Esso.[83]

As new designs were appearing, one traditional element in petrol retailing began to come under threat. Street Urban District Council in Somerset decided in 1964 not to renew petrol licences to filling stations that dispensed petrol across the pavement. It was the first local authority to introduce such a ban. Gradually, following such initiatives by local authorities, the impact of self-service and the closure of small rural filling stations, the numbers of stations dispensing petrol across the pavement declined to the extent that now (2011) there are only a handful of stations still selling petrol in this way. The Galgate Service Station in Barnard Castle, Co. Durham, has two pumps outside its premises (pl. 189). Petrol is dispensed through hoses suspended from the canopy that has been added to their early nineteenth-century building. At Moors Garage, South Street, South Molton, Devon, two pumps are located in recesses and arms swing out from the façade of the building across the pavement to dispense fuel.

•

190 Turnbull's Self-Service Filling Station, Plymouth, the first of its kind to be opened in England. A Standard 8 of pre-war design adds a somewhat incongruous note. Photographed on 3 September 1963.

'Brecknell' automatic petrol-selling device, was installed at Mortimer's Service Depot near Bristol and advertised under the slogan 'insert your shilling and do your filling'.[84] But although this was publicised in the motoring press, the idea does not appear to have taken off and it was not until the 1960s that self-service was revived in England. It was already well established in other parts of Europe: there were more than 300 self-service filling stations in Sweden by 1963.[85]

The first self-service filling station in England was opened in April 1963 by Turnbull's Garage Ltd at the Charles roundabout on the edge of Plymouth city centre. G. H. Turnbull, the managing director of the garage, had visited Sweden, and Swedish Ljungman pumps were employed. Its form was radically different both from the traditional filling station and from what was to emerge as the accepted layout for self-service: a group of nine pumps spaced out at intervals around a circular forecourt area. Each driver filling up could move away without obstructing others. Payment was made after filling up. In the centre of the forecourt was a control kiosk staffed by an operator and an assistant. This kiosk was the hub of a concrete roof structure that was supported on a central core of struts. The building had a circular perimeter wall, partly open for access, with a broad band of continuous glazing below the eaves (pl. 190).[86] Turnbull's enclosed forecourt and dispersed pumps were not followed by any of the subsequent self-service stations.

Self-service was relatively slow to take off. The next example, claimed to be the first with all-British equipment, and of conventional filling-station layout, opened in August 1963 at Manor Garage, Bitterne Road, Southampton.[87] The petrol supplier, Mobil, saw it as an opportunity to assess self-service, and became the first of the major oil companies to develop the concept. The system of operation was generally similar to that employed today, except that the customer first spoke to the cashier via a two-way microphone next to the pump to get a go-ahead to use it.

191 Perhaps the sole surviving examples in England of the Eliot Noyes-designed Mobil Pegasus canopies on the A6 at Leicester. They display Esso branding following its takeover of Mobil.

The Wayne pumps were covered by a substantial canopy, which was to become the hallmark of self-service. The first self-service station in south-east England was Nazeing Service Station, Essex, opened in January 1964, using Ljungman's equipment,[88] followed in June by the first in the North at Mottram, Cheshire,[89] and the first in London in January 1965 at University Motors Premier Garage, Chase Side, Southgate.[90] Over the next few years, each major city gained its first self-service station. Initially, self-service was promoted by independent retailers who sold petrol at cut prices, such as Alan Pond, APEX and Heron.

The relatively slow take-up of self-service may have had something to do with the conservatism of local authorities, which had to approve the change (in the U.S., the states of New Jersey and Oregon have still not legalised self-service), and the concern that women would not be able to operate self-service pumps. It was pointed out that the radial arm of a pump in a new station in Tottenham could be 'moved easily with one finger', which 'should make things easier for the ladies'.[91] From 1965 conversion to self-service gained strength to the extent that, by the late 1960s, almost all new stations were of this type. A major factor was the increasing cost of labour and, especially, the introduction of Selective Employment Tax in September 1966. A self-service station could be operated by female cashiers who, before the advent of equal pay, could be paid less than men. By the end of 1969 it was estimated that there were 515 self-service stations in Britain.[92] They were seen as modern – ordinary filling stations were 'about as out-moded as milk float, churn and pint dipper', according to the managing director of Gem Petroleum, which had twenty-seven APEX stations, each with 'an attractive white-gloved and neatly uniformed young "electronic cashier", reminiscent of an air hostess'.[93]

Approaches to self-service methods varied. For a while, some oil companies regarded self-service as a back-up facility, as an additional service to customers that enabled them to obtain

192 The Kingston Autoway Centre, Kingston upon Thames, an early 1970s example of a large canopy covering much of the filling-station site, which became ubiquitous with the advent of self-service. The sales building is located at one end of it.

petrol when the station was closed. One self-service pump would be provided that took coins or notes as pre-payment. The question of whether petrol should be paid for before or after delivery of fuel remained unresolved for some time. Some oil companies, such as National, had pumps that took two half-crown coins (2s. 6d.), then, from 1971, the 50p piece. From June 1967 at Everton's Garage, Long Lane, Blackheath, Birmingham, motorists could buy up to 14s. worth of three grades of BP petrol by inserting coins into a 'computer' located on a wall away from the pumps, which were the first Wayne coin-operated self-service pumps in the U.K.[94]

The layout of self-service stations was still not finalised in the late 1960s, and most resembled their manned predecessors, with the addition of a larger canopy. BP built a self-service station in Stalybridge, Cheshire, in 1968 that was intended as a prototype for their stations across Europe. The pumps were set towards the rear of the site at an angle to the road and were covered by a 112-foot-long gull-wing canopy with a kiosk of timber and glass, built to a metre module, all of which was set at 45 degrees to the road. The overall appearance was crisp, but the design, the work of Evan E. Morgan, Bentley & Associates, Harrogate, was not adopted as a European standard.[95] Also stillborn was Raymond Loewy's radical MAYA (Most Advanced, Yet Acceptable) design for Shell in 1970–71, intended as a new worldwide design but which failed to get beyond the prototype stage.

Other experiments were made. In 1968 Shell brought in a 'no pumps' filling station at Acocks Green, Birmingham, where motorists filled up from electrically operated overhead hoses that were lowered automatically to shoulder level from a canopy covering the forecourt. A similar arrangement was tried by Mobil at the Cassio Garage, Watford, but the idea did not gain favour.[96]

Two major changes occurred following the introduction of self-service. First, because customers had to stand in the open to fill up their cars, protection from the weather became of paramount importance, and a canopy over the pumps became ubiquitous. Initially, canopies were enlarged versions of those commonly found since the beginning of the 1960s. As in the earlier years of the decade, some striking designs emerged. In 1968 the Mercury Self-Service Garage, Harborne, Birmingham, had three linked hyperbolic paraboloid canopies (demolished), each supported on a single round column, with lighting hidden in a collar that shone upwards onto the concrete membrane, illuminating the forecourt with soft bounced light.[97]

But by 1969 the high, flat canopy (pl. 192), covering a large part of the forecourt, had appeared and soon swept all before it, becoming a standard component of filling stations, a position it still retains. Each of the oil companies adopted the big canopy, although Mobil initially did things a little differently, using highly distinctive circular canopies designed by Eliot Noyes as part of its comprehensive Pegasus redesign in 1966 (pl. 191). These canopies, which were supported on a single circular stanchion, were perhaps the most elegant ever used in filling stations and may have been inspired by one designed by Arne Jacobsen at Skovshoved, Denmark, in 1937.[98] The Pegasus scheme was intended to employ design to identify the brand to such an extent that a Mobil station would be recognisable without seeing the name. This was achieved by the canopies and by the equally distinctive cylindrical pumps, which sadly did not survive the move to self-service. The inspiration for the concept came from AGIP stations, of which a few had been built in England (see above).[99] The first example in England went up at Bilston, Staffordshire, in 1970, and by 1971 many others were built or under construction, including two at motorway service areas. They also incorporated a crisp building with a deep white fascia and brick flanking walls.[100] Shell had their 'Canopus Concept'. The first, Bearwood Service Station, Smethwick (now West Midlands), was opened in May 1971. Shell compared it to a department store, likening the facilities to counters, with a roof to protect the customer, and, 'as in a department store, the counters may be changed to provide new merchandise and service'.[101] This latter point is significant, since the canopy remains the one constant: filling-station buildings are frequently rebuilt and the pumps replaced, but the canopy is usually retained.

Secondly, with post-payment, customers now had to get out of their cars and pay in the shop, instead of handing the money to a pump attendant. This created a whole new series of marketing opportunities. Initially, the emphasis was on selling tyres, batteries and accessories (known as TBA in the motor trade). BP opened its first self-service Autoshop at West Molesey, Surrey, in March 1966, selling motoring accessories as well as items for travellers, such as sweets.[102] Vending machines with hot drinks and snacks followed in some of the outlets. From here, it was only a matter of time before the garage shop was expanded to cover other non-motoring items. By 1969 Gerald Ronson of Heron was saying: 'It's amazing the things you can sell to motorists', as he explained that his firm was selling items such as records and paperbacks in its fifty autoshops.[103] Retailing thus became a far more significant part of the filling-station operation, a change that in turn would be reflected in its architecture.

Since the 1970s

By 1973 the number of self-service sites had grown to 2,900, more than 8.8 per cent of the total, which stood at 32,974.[104] A Monopolies Commission report in 1965 had recommended a reduction in the duration of solus agreements to five years. This led to an increasing trend for oil companies to own their sites, and by the end of 1973 they had 7,754 sites in direct ownership, some 23.5 per cent of outlets.

Major changes to filling-station design were made in the 1970s, since the vast majority of sites became self-service. When the site was large enough, the cashier's office was moved from the rear to the right end (looking from the road), where it faced the pumps. This enabled cashiers to see what was happening on the forecourt and to note the registration numbers of vehicles entering. This change occurred gradually, with early examples noted in 1971.[105] In addition, pumps, which for many years had been arranged on islands parallel to the road, were now often placed at an angle to it. Some pumps were fitted to canopy stanchions, which permitted a more open forecourt layout. The service bays were the principal victims of the move to self-service, since forecourt areas needed to be much larger, and most were demolished. The move of the building to one end enabled not only more effective supervision but also a larger retail area: in the 1990s filling stations started to become convenience stores, often acting as a substitute for local shops, a change pioneered by the independent sector and taken up by the major oil companies. This trend reached its logical conclusion in the mid-1990s when supermarket groups began to acquire sites or make agreements with oil companies for the establishment of small shops, linked to filling stations. Entrants to this field include Tesco (linked to Esso), Sainsbury and Marks & Spencer (linked to BP; pl. 193). The inclusion of shops and fast-food outlets has since gained pace, as margins from petrol sales decline.

193 Today's filling stations often incorporate a small supermarket such as this Marks & Spencer outlet on the A21 at Pembury, near Tunbridge Wells, Kent.

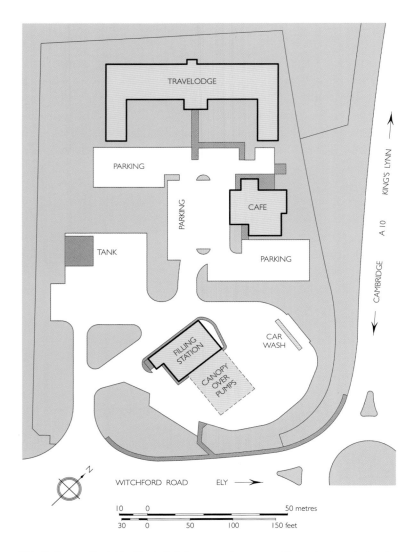

TRAVELODGE

PARKING

PARKING

CAFE

PARKING

TANK

FILLING STATION

CANOPY OVER PUMPS

CAR WASH

KING'S LYNN

A 10

CAMBRIDGE

N

WITCHFORD ROAD   ELY →

10   0   50 metres

30   0   50   100   150 feet

194 Ely Services, Cambridgeshire, typical of many service areas provided on trunk roads since the 1980s with a large shop, restaurant and budget hotel, together with ample parking. The shop is more usually sited facing the pumps than behind them, but local conditions often produce variations on the basic plan.

Since the 1970s the design of filling-station buildings has become less and less distinctive. Corporate treatments are now more pervasive, since oil companies have sought increasingly to allay the environmental concerns of local authorities and of those living nearby. In 1973 Esso announced a £2 million programme to refurbish its 1,400 directly owned sites within twelve months, to be followed by its remaining 4,500 outlets. The specific aims were to clear clutter by grouping promotional material and to improve safety by floodlighting entrances and exits, outlining the extent of a filling station with an illuminated front boundary fence. Significantly, the service-station name was reduced to small lettering over the door of the building, reflecting the subservience of the individual outlet to the brand. Visually, the hallmark of the new style was the use of rounded corners to the

salesroom windows and doors to impart what was described as a 'boutique' effect.[106]

In the following decade the most obvious development was the replacement of the plain brick boxes of the 1970s with hipped roof structures, while brick construction in turn showed signs of going out of favour. Groups such as BP were favouring steel construction by 2000. Steel-framed structures with metal cladding enabled more frequent revamping to take place. But the dominant feature remained the canopy covering the forecourt and its attendant signage. Design almost atrophied, with stations criticised for their uniformity and lack of site specificity. It was the supermarkets (whose entry into petrol retailing, begun by Asda in the 1980s and greatly expanded in the early 1990s, had such a major impact on the industry) that led the way with some imaginative designs at their superstores. Sainsbury's commissioned designs by Lifschutz Davidson at Canley, Coventry (*circa* 1993), and the Dome Roundabout, North Watford, that moved beyond the usual boxy canopy.[107] Canley had canopies that, in profile, resembled aircraft wings and which employed PVC-coated polyester fabric, the lightness of which permitted the thinnest of steel supports. At North Watford there was a return to the gull's-wing concept popular in the 1960s, but here joined by glazing. To illustrate just how short the life of this building type can be today, the Canley filling station has already been demolished and rebuilt.[108] Currently, the cost of a filling station can be written off in ten years, and this is a further factor in their constant remodelling. Innovation is chiefly to be seen in rebranding, such as the redesign of BP's logo and signage in 2001.

According to the UK Petroleum Industry Association, the number of filling stations fell from approximately 18,000 in 1992 to just over 8,900 in 2009. The supermarkets' share of the market rose from 19 per cent in 1997 to around 40 per cent in 2009.[109] Approximately 2,000 to 2,500 filling stations are owned by the major oil companies, and the remainder by independents. Site sales by oil companies have increased greatly since *circa* 2000: Gulf, Jet and Texaco have now sold virtually all their holdings. Despite this, the oil company sites still account for most sales, excluding supermarkets, because they are in the best locations. The influence of oil companies remains visually strong through the loans available to independents to rebuild stations in corporate styles.

Competition from supermarkets is not the only reason for the decline in the number of filling stations: another is stricter environmental legislation. Many sites could not justify the investment that would keep them up to an acceptable standard. All this, together with the reduction in the number of oil companies supplying the British market, means that, at present, the move towards further standardisation seems set to continue. There is unlikely to be a return to the days when thatched pumps could coexist with tasteful Neo-Georgian or extreme modernism, despite the best efforts of the late Giles Worsley, who, in 1990, commissioned a group of artists, architects and landscape designers, including Glynn Boyd Harte, Roderick Gradidge and Alan Powers, to design filling stations of character for *Country Life*.[110] While some of the results were undeniably whimsical, others offered striking and imaginative alternatives to the accepted approach.

Perhaps in the future the emphasis may be on finding new uses for the increasing numbers of redundant filling-station sites.

In 2010 Ideas Tap, a collective of young architects and artists, turned a former filling station in Clerkenwell Road, London, into a cinema, the Cineroleum, by enclosing it in a membrane usually used for insulating buildings. The installation, which was open for three weeks, was intended to highlight the potential of filling-station sites for imaginative reuse.[111] As with many brownfield sites, however, the cost of removing underground tanks and cleaning up or replacing the soil under the former stations is high.

195   The stylish Daimler Hire Garage (1931–3; Wallis Gilbert and Partners) – shown here in a contemporary photograph by H. Felton – was one of the first garages to be listed. Daimler was among the most successful upmarket car-hire outfits in London. It offered an air service to France in the early 1920s, and took over Harrods' car-hire business in 1930.

6: PARKING, 1896-1939

THE NEED TO PARK CARS AWAY FROM the home base has transformed English towns and cities since the 1890s, just as much as the need to get around on four wheels. The bulky multi-storey car park is generally regarded as a fairly modern phenomenon, yet the history of the parking garage goes back to the earliest days of motoring. Prior to the Second World War a great deal of parking provision was made in central London, in seaside towns, by railway stations, and near places of popular entertainment. This included multi-storey car parks as well as simpler parking sheds, surface car parks, and even a few pioneering underground car parks.

Parking Garages, 1896-1914

In the earliest years of motoring, garaging and parking were just two of the myriad services offered to motorists by multi-functional commercial garages, although at first neither 'garaging' nor 'parking' was common terminology, both usually being referred to as 'storage', or even 'stabling'. Once a distinction was drawn, 'garaging' came to mean the secure long-term storage of vehicles for owners who did not possess their own motor house, while 'parking', whether on an hourly or a daily basis, was a more transient arrangement. Despite this, in certain contexts these two words have always been used interchangeably.

Perhaps the first occasion that a car park was required in England was when participants in the Emancipation Day Run gathered in London on 13 November 1896, in readiness for a 10.30am start from Northumberland Avenue the following morning (see pl. 6). Their cars were 'stored' overnight in Central Hall, High Holborn,[1] and when they arrived in Brighton, storage was provided at Nye's Stables behind the Hotel Metropole.[2] Just a month earlier, in October 1896, the Indestructible Ignition Tube Syndicate had opened at 100c Queen Victoria Street, London, advertising 'arrangements for repairing and storing autocars'.[3] As yet, there cannot have been any reasonable call on these services. The Syndicate probably expected the Locomotives on Highways Act to stimulate demand, but three years later only nine London establishments undertook the 'storage of moto-vehicles'.[4] Most of these were long-established businesses, such as Coulson's Livery Stables on Endell Street near Long Acre,[5] which were either diversifying or making use of surplus space. Despite this paucity of 'storage', demand was growing in the metropolis, generated largely by visitors who hired cars – with or without chauffeurs – and by theatre-goers. Open-air parking was limited and undesirable. Strictly speaking, it was illegal to leave a car unattended on the 'Queen's highway', since this could be regarded as obstruction. Moreover, vehicles were open or soft-topped and could not be locked; they were vulnerable to weather or accidental damage, and also to theft or vandalism. Under these circumstances the 'garage' was invented.

The word 'garage' (derived from the French *gare*, a place for the storage or shelter of boats or locomotives) had entered the English language by November 1900, when it was announced that a 'garage . . . where vehicles may be left' was being erected for visitors to the Crystal Palace.[6] This was, potentially, the first purpose-built public parking garage in the U.K. By May 1901 the General Automobile Agency at 100–104 Long Acre was advertising 'petrol, repairs, garage'.[7] Photographs of its spacious interior show cars parked in an unsystematic manner on an unmarked floor. Owner-drivers and their passengers would not have entered the garage proper: this was the preserve of atten- dants, mechanics (generally called engineers) and chauffeurs. Despite quibbles by those who disdained the adoption of a French word,[8] by 1902 'garage' – initially italicised to indicate its foreign origin and pronunciation – had been adopted as the stan- dard term for any business offering a wide range of services to the motorist, though the *Car Illustrated* defined it more narrowly as 'a motor-car store-house'.[9] Certainly, for most early garages, it was parking that took up most space and defined the layout of the premises.

Charles Harrington Moore, secretary of the Motor Car Club (founded 1896) and later of the Automobile Club (founded 1897), reputedly set up the first garage for motor cars in central London, 'in a big hall near the old Royal Aquarium'.[10] This was the Automobile Club Garage at 19 Prince's Street, Westminster, now demolished. Later, in January 1902, Moore opened the City Garage, a public establishment at 34 Queen Street. Photographs show that this had a steel-frame structure and a fireproof jack- arch roof, and was thus eminently suited to its new purpose.[11] The stanchions were widely spaced, allowing vehicles to manoeuvre into position without too much trouble. As well as providing 'storage', Moore's City Garage held auctions and offered to wash, repair and hire out cars. In 1903 the Automo- bile Club quit 19 Prince's Street for a converted stable and coach house on Down Street and Brick Street, behind the clubhouse on Piccadilly.[12] The conversion was undertaken by the club's honorary architect, Edward Keynes Purchase, who was one of the first members of his profession to specialise in buildings for cars. The L-shaped garage was arranged around a narrow, glass- roofed gallery that originated as a mews. Each of the three lower floors could accommodate approximately twenty cars, which were transported by hydraulic lift, while the top floors contained dressing rooms and offices. Daily garage charges were 2s. 6d. for a large car and 2s. for a small one. Another remarkable garage conversion of around 1903 was Shaftesbury Buildings, 6 Denham Street, near Piccadilly Circus, for the City & Suburban Electric Carriage Co., which had a vehicle lift that served seven floors.[13]

Parallels were drawn between garages and stables. In 1903 it was observed that '"Motor-Garages" . . . stand in the same rela- tion to the automobile as do livery and bait stables to horses and carriages'.[14] In practice, the garage attendant met every require- ment of the car, just as the liveryman had cared for the horse. But, 'to the uninitiated the interiors of these garages present a curious appearance. They boast no stalls, no loose boxes, no mangers.'[15] Having said this, the layout of some Edwardian garages was clearly rooted in stable design. As late as 1911 Edmund Wimperis designed the Pembroke Garage (demolished) in Belgravia with two parking floors lined by 'motor boxes', looking for all the world like stalls (pl. 196). The first floor was reached by a long ramp with a 1:7 gradient: perhaps the very

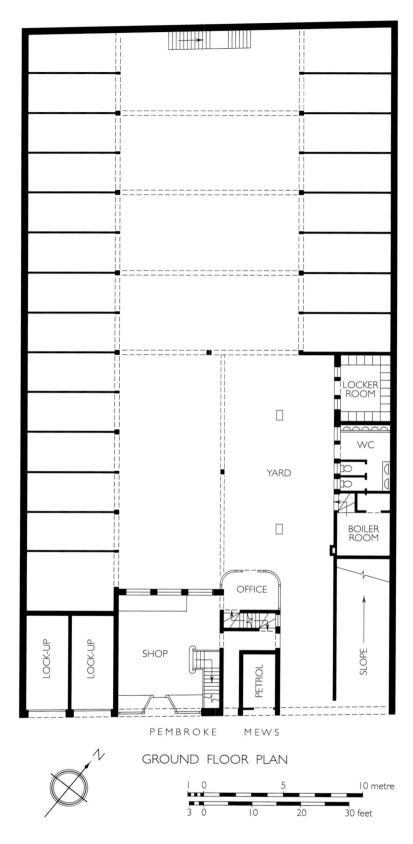

196 Ground-floor plan of the Pembroke Garage, Belgravia, London, designed by E. Wimperis and built in 1911, showing the stall-like motor boxes and 'slope'. Based on London Metropolitan Archives plan GLC/AR/BA/37011.

197 This advertisement for the London Motor Garage on Wardour Street was published in the *Motor-Car Journal* in June 1903.

198 The London Motor Garage Co.'s premises at 33–37 Wardour Street in Soho (1902–3) can be regarded as the earliest multi-storey garage to be built in England. Although the interior has been remodelled, the glazed brick façade is largely unchanged.

first that was purpose-built to enable cars to be driven to an upper floor. But this elicited no comment at the time, presumably because such structures were familiar from the multi-storeyed commercial stables and carriage repositories that existed in Victorian London.

The first purpose-built garage that might be recognised today as a multi-storey car park was erected on Wardour Street in 1903 by the London Motor Garage Co. This company had opened its first 'subscription' garage in 1902, at 81 Page Street, 'to assist those who have no convenience for keeping their motor cars'.[16] When the company opened a new garage at 33–37 Wardour Street in 1903, this was proclaimed as the first building 'constructed from foundation to roof for the purpose of garage' (pls 197 and 198).[17] The rear of the garage spread laterally behind five plots, and rose through a basement and two storeys, to provide accommodation for 200 cars. Behind the original façade, the interior has been

thoroughly remodelled: it became a club in the 1920s, was reinvented as the Whiskey-a-Go-Go in the 1950s, and now houses a public house and a betting shop. The fittings have long gone, but in 1909 the electric car lift incorporated special safety features – nowadays taken for granted, but then considered worthy of note:

199 The courtyard and vehicle lift at Mitchell Brothers' Motors on Wardour Street, London, photographed in 1907.

cars to be parked so close together that the doors would not open; vehicles were simply pushed into place, then pulled out when needed. In 1907 unified turntable-lifts were installed in several London premises, such as the Hills-Martini Garage on Great Windmill Street.[21] This innovation failed to catch on widely, though variants were still being produced in the 1920s.[22] Name plates identify the engineering companies that manufactured garage turntables, such as Francis Theakston of Crewe and H. & C. Davis of Birmingham. Lifts (whether hydraulic or electric) and turntables remained the normal method of transporting cars to the upper floors of garages until the 1920s, and were still considered a viable option in the early 1960s.

In 1906 Mitchell Brothers' Motors opened at 114 Wardour Street, and was trumpeted as 'the largest motor garage in the world'.[23] Built on the site of a brewery, to the rear of the Royalty Theatre in Dean Street, this marked a huge leap forward in the scale of garages, holding 500 cars, which remained the optimum size for the next twenty years. An oblong central courtyard was surrounded by fireproof buildings of reinforced concrete with jack-arched floors, a brick skin and large metal-framed windows. An electric car lift occupied a recess at the south end of the courtyard (pl. 199).

A more cautiously phrased claim to be 'the world's greatest garage' was made in 1907 for the Electromobile Co. Garage, Carrington Street, Mayfair.[24] Still standing, this can be recognised much more clearly as an ancestor of the modern multi-storey car park, but it had some very specific requirements since it dealt in electric vehicles, which were popular for hiring, as well as with cabbies and private owners.[25] Two storeys high, with a basement and a flat asphalt roof used – like the flat roofs of other garages – for washing cars,[26] this garage was built of reinforced concrete within a brick shell, to Electromobile's own designs. It occupied a long rectangular site, 350 by 80 feet, surrounded by other buildings and with no street frontage other than a cul-de-sac entrance on Carrington Street (pl. 200). The structural supports permitted a layout of three aisles on each floor, with parking bays (300 spaces) flanking a central roadway, something that would become a classic arrangement (pl. 201). As well as being a car park, this was a recharging station. When a car arrived, its battery was removed and lowered to the basement (where there was space to charge 300 to 400 sets of batteries); then the carriage was placed on a turntable, either to pick up a fully charged battery from the hydraulic lift, or to be transported to storage on a platform that ran on a traverse or trolleyway.[27] By 1914 the garage was accepting petrol as well as electric cars, and when it was taken over by University Motors around 1927 a 'runway' was built, enabling cars to be driven up to the first floor.[28]

Electromobile was just one of many garages with a fleet of cars available for hire in London. For some, this was their

At each floor the full height of the lift opening is covered by a pair of collapsible gates that are locked together by a spring latch. Until this latch is pulled over and the gates closed the lift cannot be worked, and whilst the lift is moving, or not opposite each floor, the gates cannot be opened, the control level being on the lift.[18]

This makes one realise how dangerous some early garage lifts must have been, since many were simply rudimentary hoists of the type that had served carriage repositories and manufactories since the late nineteenth century.[19] Before long, it was normal for car lifts to be accompanied by turntables. Turntables, which revolved on ball bearings, were uncommon in English garages before 1904, when it was reported that several American garages used them to manoeuvre motors.[20] They measured around 14 feet in diameter and were usually aligned with a lift on each floor. Like car lifts, turntables are often an indicator of attendant parking, as neither owner-drivers nor their chauffeurs would have been expected to operate them. To save space, they enabled

200 The Electromobile Garage opened in London's Mayfair in November 1907 and survives today as a NCP car park, although the three hydraulic lifts have been superseded by long, straight ramps. Despite its urban context, this is an invisible structure, entombed within the centre of a city block, with no major street elevations.

primary, or sole, business activity. At their busiest during the summer months, these companies relied heavily on contracts with hotels: the Harrington Garage on Gloucester Road, for example, hired cars for weekend trips in conjunction with Empire Hotels.[29] The chief requirement of hire premises was a large space for garaging vehicles, with adjoining offices and rooms for chauffeurs (pl. 202). One of the largest businesses of this type was Daimler Hire (founded 1907), which occupied a succession of spacious premises.[30] Another important company belonged to Thomas Wolfe, who began in 1889 as a jobmaster – hiring out horses and carriages – and entered the motor- business in 1907. His business was dispersed between several mews (in and around Woburn Square), a carriage repository (Ridgmount Street) and a carriage factory (Eden Street). A more modest hire business was carried out by the Pembroke Garage of 1911, which provided ample accommodation for chauffeurs: a kitchen, dining rooms, card rooms, billiard rooms and twelve bedrooms (pls 196 and 203). This reflects the fact that many cars were hired with a chauffeur, whose travelling expenses were paid by the customer. In residential areas, some garages housed pri-

vately employed chauffeurs, occasionally with their families, and always with the car under their charge. At seaside resorts, large garages – such as Motor Mac's in Bournemouth – began to provide boarding houses for chauffeurs.[31] Thus the car and its

201 The interior of the Electromobile Garage helped to establish the standard aisled parking layout that has endured to the present day in covered car parks. From *Car Illustrated*, 4 December 1907, p. 146.

202 The Chauffeurs' Room at Mitchell Brothers Motors in 1907. The Hiring Department opened in 1906, offering 'any kind of car from a Landaulette to an Open Touring car, or powerful Limousine'. In such establishments, the car came with a chauffeur.

203 Accommodation for chauffeurs on the second floor of the Pembroke Garage, Belgravia, London, of 1911. Based on Westminster Archives plan WPD2/770/9.

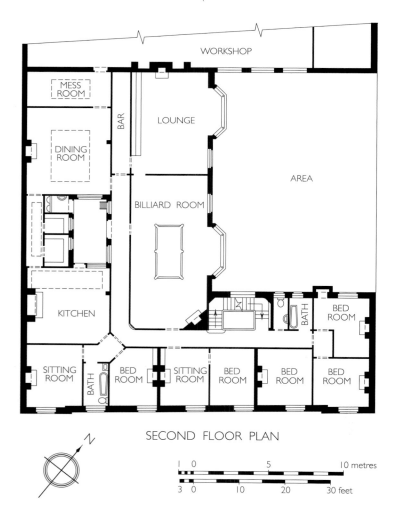

SECOND FLOOR PLAN

chauffeur could be appropriately separated from the holidaying vehicle owner or hirer, who would be lodged in greater luxury at a nearby seafront hotel.

By 1910 more than 40,000 motor cars were registered in London alone. Of 176 public garages that had come into existence in the capital, only 10 were thought to be purpose-built.[32] Most still occupied old buildings, such as stables, coach houses and workshops, and *The Motor* bemoaned their unprepossessing appearance and hidden locations, fearing that they might dismay or elude foreign visitors. Some conversions were ingenious, such as the Westminster Motor Car Garage's adaptation of a former bakery on Greycoat Street in 1912.[33] But the most splendid of all conversions was a garage on York Street (later known as Petty France), Westminster. It occupied Niagara Hall, the former premises of the Westminster Panorama Co., which had been built with iron galleries and a glass roof *circa* 1888.[34] A skating rink was created in the circular hall in 1895, but the business closed in 1902. It was quickly resurrected as 'The New Niagara', the premises of the City & Suburban Electric Carriage Co., which claimed to house 800 carriages, and thus to be 'the largest "garage" in London' – obviously there was fierce competition for this accolade.[35] The circular form of 'The New Niagara' had American precedents: in 1897 'the first recorded parking garage in the United States' had come into existence when a skating rink at 1684 Broadway, New York, was taken over by the Electric Vehicle Co., and amongst the first parking structures in Boston and Washington, D.C., were converted cycloramas.[36] In 1906 the Wolseley Tool & Motor Car Co. took over 'The New Niagara' (pl. 204). It garaged sixty cars on the former rink, fifty on the gallery, twenty-two in lock-ups and twenty in the

204   The Wolseley Tool & Motor Car Co. Garage ('The New Niagara'), York Street, Westminster, photographed in 1913. Hot-water heating pipes snaked around the gallery of the former skating rink. The mesh lock-up compartments on this gallery were for 'private owners who do not keep servants'.

basement.[37] The garage boasted a wide range of facilities for chauffeurs, who were strictly forbidden to smoke. There was a small repair shop, solely for the use of chauffeurs, a reading and recreation room, and a clothes-drying room. From 1911 RAC members parked in this garage, with RAC staff to look after their cars, and with a private telephone connection to the club 'so that a Member can get quickly into communication with his motor servant at all times'.[38] In the same year a competitor, the Mansions Motor Garage Co., at 76 York Street, was praised for its large entrance, which enabled cars to move in and

out with ease.[39] Before long, the Wolseley trumped its rival with separate gates marked 'In' and 'Out', which had to be raised to allow ingress or egress, thus closely controlling access alongside a timekeepers' lodge (pl. 205).[40] Barriers of this kind were widely introduced in large garages at this time, chiefly to prevent people stealing cars. Indeed, garages were often judged on the stringency of their security. In Friswell's garage on Albany Street (see pl. 52), cars were housed on several floors accessed by an electric lift, and in 1909 the following security measures were in place:

205 Stringent security at 'The New Niagara', with controlled entrance and exit gates.

206 The parking garage added to Warne's Hotel, Worthing, Sussex, in 1902 had an ornate gable depicting a motor car.

. . . where cars are intended to be stored for more than a few hours, all the tools, spare tyres, lamps and other loose fittings are removed from the vehicle and placed in a numbered box. The box is taken into a specially-arranged room in the basement . . . and placed in proper numerical order in a series of racks, those on the upper tiers being reached by step ladders made to slide along rails near the ceiling. Only duly authorised persons can obtain possession of a box, and must be accompanied into the storeroom by the custodian.[41]

207 The Green Dragon Hotel in Hertford erected motor stables, with a pit, in 1903. It was boldly advertised in this terracotta panel on the gable end. The building, designed by James Farley, is listed.

Single-storey garages were uncommon in central London, where there was pressure to maximise prime sites. One remarkable survival is Charles Jarrott & Letts, built in 1913 on Page Street, Westminster, featuring a parking shed spanning 62 feet, with a glazed roof (see pl. 120).[42] Such garages were more usual in outlying areas, where they offered garaging for local residents as well as parking for visitors. One example was the Cadogan Garage (demolished) in Chelsea, which was extended around 1909.[43] Inside, the proprietors erected wooden galleried structures with a stable-like character, to either side of a central aisle. One side provided ten private lock-ups, while the other had open space to park about thirty cars. Above this, one gallery was fitted with chauffeurs' lockers, while the other had a recreation room complete with billiard table.

Multi-functional provincial garages offered secure covered parking for casual visitors as well as garaging – often in mesh-fronted lock-up cages within the main garage space – for local motorists. Seaside resorts, spa towns and historic centres attracted motoring tourists and provided rather more casual parking than other towns. Caffyn Brothers' three-storey garage opened on Marine Parade, Eastbourne, in 1906 and could accommodate around 100 cars.

Hotels made a particular effort to attract the touring automobilist, either by converting their existing stabling into garages or building anew. If stables were to be converted, fittings had to be removed, solid floors laid, a pit dug, and entrances widened and repositioned. New garages involved a larger outlay, but were generally more convenient. From 1899 *The Autocar* published lists of approved hotels with garages for guests' cars; *The Automobile*

Handbook (later the *RAC Year Book*) fulfilled this requirement from 1904, as did the AA handbooks from 1909. The Empire Hotel in Buxton is known to have built a motor garage by 1902,[44] but the single-storey garage attached to the rear of Warne's Hotel, Marine Parade, Worthing, was hailed in 1925 as 'the oldest hotel garage in England' (pl. 206).[45] Also built in 1902,[46] this could accommodate thirty to forty cars, and had a separate repair shop. George Hilbery Warne had a particular interest in motor racing events, and the garage at his hotel may have been provided specially for motorists taking part in a trial he arranged from Crystal Palace to Worthing in 1902. The gable over the entrance was adorned with a relief depicting a car and the words 'Headquarters ACGB&I' (i.e., Automobile Club of Great Britain and Ireland). A year later, in 1903, the Automobile Club invited Edward Keynes Purchase to publish an article on garage layout for the benefit of hotel proprietors.[47] This included Purchase's own plan for a garage recently erected at the Felix Hotel, Felixstowe. Built of red brick with Dutch gables, this well-equipped 'motor garage' had lockers for rugs, an engineer's shop, a glass-roofed washing space and lavatories. A similar garage was built for the Pulteney Hotel in Bath (pl. 208) in 1907: in the 1920s this red brick building was still being advertised as 'the finest equipped garage in the West'.[48] It survives intact, with the glass-roofed parking and repair shed, the resident engineer's house and a glazed washing bay. Another fine survival, on two

storeys, is the two-storey garage of the Savoy Hotel in Blackpool, which opened at Easter 1915. Some establishments, such as the Queen Hotel in Harrogate,[49] offered lock-ups rather than open-plan garaging; the provision of an inspection pit (pl. 207) was normal, and most had a mechanic on hand, or even a fully staffed repairs facility.

The Spread of the Parking Garage, 1918–1939

In central London, the need for parking space grew enormously after 1918, and new parking problems emerged elsewhere, notably on the promenades of seaside towns, around places of entertainment such as cinemas and theatres, and at major transport termini, especially suburban railway and Tube stations. It was in these places – and not, as yet, in the shopping and commercial districts of the largest and most prosperous provincial cities, which still had excellent public transport systems – that the most innovative parking solutions were introduced between 1918 and 1939.

As car ownership expanded in the aftermath of the First World War, so commercial garages proliferated. The most commonly adopted form of building for such garages was the single-storey shed: its wide span unencumbered by obstructive supports; its spacious interior lit by strips of glazing in its pitched roof. This

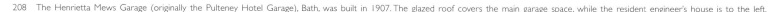

208   The Henrietta Mews Garage (originally the Pulteney Hotel Garage), Bath, was built in 1907. The glazed roof covers the main garage space, while the resident engineer's house is to the left.

209 Inside the Morden Station Garage in June 1927, with the Underground station in the background.

210 This whole-page colour advertisement for Salmons & Sons Garage in central London comes from the *Motor-Owner*, July 1919, lii. The site was redeveloped in 2009.

type of garage (see Chapter 4) continued to serve the parking – and, more especially, the garaging, repair and maintenance – needs of towns and suburbs throughout England for generations to come. However, it did not always suffice.

In the 1920s cinemas and theatres realised that the provision of parking attracted custom. One of the first to take this step was the Chiswick Empire Theatre of Varieties, which built a garage in 1923.[50] The County Garage (demolished) built next to the Opera House in Scarborough had space for 200 cars in 1928, and plans were already afoot to insert a floor that would increase capacity to 300.[51] Meanwhile, hotels added garages on an unprecedented scale. In 1926–7 the architect Henry Tanner designed the Park Lane Hotel in London together with a garage, positioned to the rear on Brick Street, beneath four floors of bedrooms.[52] This survives, as do a number of provincial hotel garages of the same vintage, for example, at the Adelphi Hotel in Liverpool.

Parking became a lucrative sideline for garages close to railway termini, since it was still unwise to leave a car in the open all day. In the 1920s, however, railway companies began to build parking sheds on their own sites, sometimes with repair and maintenance facilities. In 1924–5, for example, a garage with mesh cages was created over the platforms of St John's Wood Station, on the Metropolitan Line,[53] and in 1926 the London & North Eastern Railway (LNER) opened a parking garage at Parkeston Quay, Harwich, an important terminal for Continental sailings, popular with American tourists. Ferry companies took similar steps: in 1933 a 200-space parking shed formed part of general improvements to the ferry terminal at Seacombe, serving daily commuters to Liverpool.[54] This may have been

preparation for competition from the soon-to-be-opened Mersey Tunnel. Although such moves were welcomed by drivers,[55] motor traders regarded them as an intrusion into their own province. In 1927 the City & South London Railway Co. opened a garage for 200 cars opposite Morden Station, the end of the Northern Line in south London (pl. 209). This was erected by the Underground's own building department, but, in a thin disguise, belonged to an affiliated company, the Morden Station Garage Ltd.[56] Its defenders argued that it was not competing with private traders since there was, as yet, no commercial garage in the vicinity. Within a few years, however, it was dropping its prices, from 1s. 6d. to 1s. per day, to match other rates in the area. Another interesting, but brief, experiment took place in 1933, when the LNER decided to provide portable garages (essentially domestic motor houses) for commuters at stations such as Welwyn North.[57] Theoretically, when not in use these could be packed up and dispatched elsewhere by train.

In central London, where parking problems were of a different magnitude, multi-storey garages continued to be built on the format established prior to 1914. The three-storey Salmons Garage on Castle St/Mercer Street, near Long Acre, is said to have been begun before the war (pl. 210). It opened in 1919 for 200 cars, and with the completion of the Mercer Street block in 1924 it had more than 400 spaces. The Mercer Street block was by the architect Walter W. Gibbings, who had designed the first garage on the site for the motor-car agent Harvey Du Cros in 1911, and had subsequently become something of a garage specialist.[58] Although Salmons depended on electric lifts and turntables,[59] the ground-floor connection between Castle Street and Mercer Street was gently ramped. The flat garage roof – apparently destined for further parking floors – became a practice golf course, enclosed in netting, and equipped with a golfers' lounge and partitioned tee boxes.[60] Golfing and motoring were often pursued by the same enthusiasts, hence the logic of the *Car Illustrated* magazine being reinvented as *Car and Golf* in 1922, and the inclusion of golf courses at car parks, and vice versa.

While Salmons attracted a theatre-going West End clientele, the businessmen of the City were drawn to the Barbican Garage at 43 Beech Street (1920),[61] or to the City of London Garage on Worship Street (1924),[62] which both had hydraulic lifts.[63] Improvements continued to be made in the capacity of car lifts, for example, in the new garage built at 75 Dean Street in Soho (1925; Sir Henry Tanner) for Shaw & Kilburn, which had taken over Mitchell's on Wardour Street in 1919.[64] This claimed to have the largest car lift in London, capable of carrying four light cars at once.[65] From contemporary accounts it is evident that owner-drivers could accompany their vehicle from ground floor to roof: 'the experience is as thrilling as any that can be enjoyed at the Amusement Park at Wembley'.[66] As at Salmons, the roof was not for parking. Instead, mechanics worked here on cars on dry summer days.

The Advent of the Ramp Garage

Before long, ramps presented a serious alternative to the tried-and-tested lift-and-turntable combination. As with all things motor-related, the U.S.A. was now ahead of the game. The first recorded ramp garage had been built for the New York Taxicab Company in 1909,[67] but until the mid-1920s ramps were generally used in combination with elevators, which served levels above the first floor. Ramps in England were not entirely novel: for example, one had been in use at the Pembroke Garage since 1911 and, more recently, 'a concrete roadway, up and down which cars can be driven under their own power', had been built at Heard Bros. coachworks at Bideford, Devon.[68]

Throughout the early 1920s, on both sides of the Atlantic, architects and garage proprietors weighed up the pros and cons of lift and ramp systems. Lifts occupied less space, but experience quickly demonstrated that they were slower than ramps in dealing with rush-hour demand. The installation costs of lifts and ramps were on a par, but lifts were more expensive to maintain and attend. Furthermore, ramps literally paved the way to self-parking, allowing garages to employ fewer attendants, and enabling drivers to enjoy an extension of the exhilarating sense of freedom and control they derived from car ownership. By 1925 ramps had won the argument in the U.S.A., and in 1929 *Motor Commerce* declared lifts to be 'hopelessly outclassed'.[69] Nevertheless, it was only in the early 1930s that ramps became the preferred method of vertical movement in British garages.

In England, as in America, the first ramps connected full-height floors, and were long and straight. They were contained within separate walled compartments to comply with fire safety regulations, and occupied marginal floor positions. This was the case at the first ramp garage known to have been built after 1918, the West Central Garage (later Mount Pleasant Garage, demolished) on Margery Street in Clerkenwell, London, designed by Boreham & Gladding.[70] Another very early ramp garage was the three-storey Blue Bird Garage on King's Road, Chelsea (1923–4; Robert Sharp; pl. 211). Although an electric lift served every floor, this was supplemented by a 'roadway of easy gradient (1 in 10)' leading from Vale Avenue (now The Vale) down to the basement, which held lock-ups plus parking space for seventy-five cars.[71] A second roadway 'of similar gradient' led up to the

211 A general view of the Blue Bird Garage, King's Road, London (1923–4; Robert Sharp), photographed by Bedford Lemere in July 1927. This was one of the first garages to incorporate a petrol-filling forecourt into the design. The building was converted into a restaurant by Terence Conran in 1997.

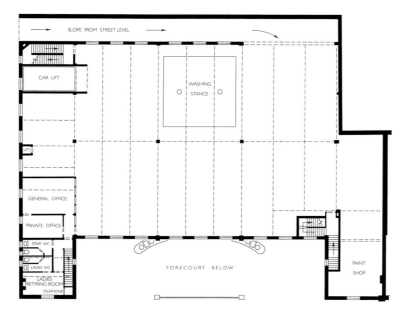

FIRST FLOOR

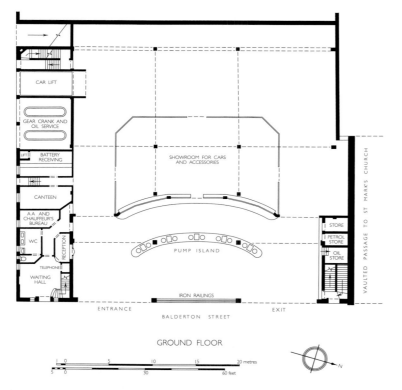

GROUND FLOOR

212 Ground-floor and first-floor plans of Macy's Garage, Balderton Street, London. Built in 1925–6, this was later used, in succession, by the Car Mart, Dagenham Motors and Avis. In its early years it provided parking for Selfridge's customers. Based on Westminster Archives plan WPD2/309/26.

'gallery' floor. This was suspended from the roof, to prevent stanchions cluttering the floor below.

Initially, in multi-storey garages, ramps did not rise above the first floor, while lifts continued to serve higher levels. The most

ambitious garage of this transitional type to be built in London was Macy's Garage (1925–6; Wimperis, Simpson and Guthrie; pls 212–214) on Balderton Street, south of Oxford Street.[72] As one of the first garages to cater principally for shoppers, Macy's offered free parking to the customers of Selfridge's nearby department store. A long, straight ramp ran along the back of the building to first-floor level (pl. 213), while a lift provided access to all four floors.[73] As at the Blue Bird, the centre of Macy's façade was recessed to accommodate a filling station between projecting pavilions, in accordance with London petrol regulations, a feature that became standard for metropolitan inter-war car parks. More importantly, Macy's represents an attempt to discover an appropriate architectural treatment for this bulky new building type. Instead of the generic warehouse idiom adopted by most earlier London parking garages, Macy's resembled a grand residential or civic building. Its Neo-Classical stuccoed façade was fitted with windows of almost domestic scale. Despite its architectural presence, Macy's business may not have thrived, since it was taken over by the Car Mart in 1927.

Ultimately, the most successful system, which did away with the need for car lifts, was the staggered-floor or split-level garage: essentially two abutting structures with levels 'staggered' at half-floor intervals, connected by short ramps. The original design was known as the d'Humy Motoramp, because it had been invented by the American Fernand Emile d'Humy in 1919. In the d'Humy system (pl. 215), the staggered floors were connected by two ramps, each having two lanes, one up and the other down; only as garages grew larger in later years did sets of four, or even six, one-way ramps develop. In early

213 The first floor of Macy's Garage, looking down the ramp to Providence Court. Note how the ramp is set within a separate fireproof compartment at the back of the building.

214   The Neo-Classical façade of Macy's Garage – recessed, like the Blue Bird Garage, for a petrol filling station – retains its original metal-framed glazing.

examples the ends of the ramps were slightly curved, and so cars were driven up or down in an elliptical or helical formation. Significantly, the floors could be separated by fire shutters without compartmentalising the ramps themselves, which thus became a prominent feature of garage interiors for the first time. By 1922 a six-level garage (effectively just two storeys high) on the d'Humy system was being erected on Poland Street, just off Oxford Street, on the edge of Soho (pl. 217).[74] Designed by Walter W. Gibbings and built by Sir Leslie Parkinson & Co.,[75] the Poland Street Garage opened in March 1925 with 500 parking spaces, chauffeurs' rooms, reading rooms, owner-driver dressing rooms and lockers. It occupied the site of the St James's Workhouse and – like the Electromobile Garage of 1907 – had little architectural presence, since it was buried behind other

buildings. Despite its novel circulatory system, this rather in-visible garage did not receive much press coverage, and may not have been an instant success; it certainly did not inspire an immediate following. Only after 1930 was the staggered-floor system taken up widely for English garages. Though popular in America in the 1920s, perhaps it proved problematic at a time when many cars still had wide turning circles. The main objec-tion, however, was the difficulty of converting a staggered-floor garage to an alternative function, should it fail commercially as a car park.

Parking had become big business, and in spring 1928 Lex Garages Ltd was formed to establish a chain of parking garages throughout London. This was to be achieved by acquiring some existing establishments and developing new ones. Garages taken

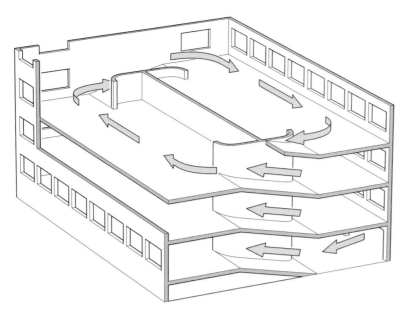

215 This diagram illustrates the form of the staggered-floor garage, invented by Fernand d'Humy after the First World War. Eventually, this became the most common type of multi-storey car park in Britain.

217 The Poland Street Garage (1922–5) in central London was the first staggered-floor car park to be built in Britain, and is still in use, though the upper floors have been remodelled. This shows one of the original short ramps, which has a ridged surface to ensure a good grip, and retains its fire shutters.

over by the company included the Reservoir Garage in Kensington, an extraordinary conversion of a disused reservoir dating from 1925.[76] Lex also acquired two garages in St John's Wood, on Wellington Road and St John's Wood Road: these were remodelled for the company by Robert Sharp, who had previously designed the Blue Bird Garage. Sharp developed a distinctive house style for Lex – embracing its buildings as well as its signage and petrol pumps – crowning each of the St John's Wood garages with an eye-catching octagonal turret topped by a dome.[77] This became a leitmotif for Lex. A prominent corner tower with a cupola proclaimed the presence of the huge new garage built by the company on Lexington Street and Little Pulteney Street (later renamed Brewer Street) in Soho (pl. 218). With approximately 1,000 spaces – twice as many as the largest exist-

216 This section through the Lex Garage shows the succession of long, straight ramps leading from floor to floor, and the lock-up garages in the basement. From *Building*, July 1929, p. 312.

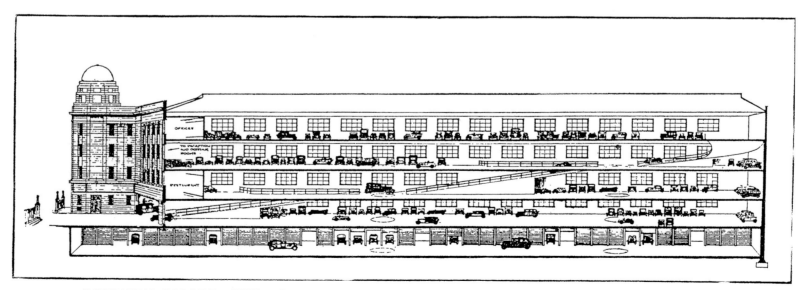

BRITAIN'S BIGGEST YET.—Sketch plan of the new Lex 1,000-car garage close to Piccadilly Circus.

218 The Lex Garage on Brewer Street, London, was built in 1928 to serve 'Theatreland'. It was given a cream-coloured faience frontage, recessed behind a filling station, with the corner tower boldly displaying the name LEX GARAGE, and its copper dome shining at night like a beacon. The architect was Robert Sharp, with J. J. Joass.

ing London garages – this was announced as 'the most luxurious, the most up-to-date and the most efficient [garage] on this side of the Atlantic'.[78] It was opened by the Duke of York, the future George VI: a publicity coup that contrasted starkly with the quiet arrival of the nearby Poland Street Garage.

When the Lex Garage was being designed in 1928, staggered floors were considered and rejected. In the event, the elongated site invited an unusual solution: three long, straight ramps were aligned with one another on the west side of the four parking floors, so that drivers could ascend or descend in one fell swoop (pl. 216). These were two-way ramps (width 32 ft, length 275 ft) with a gradient of 1:8, and drivers were warned by signage to stay in a low gear. *The Times* speculated that 'jaded motorists may be thrilled by the novelty of seeing cars being

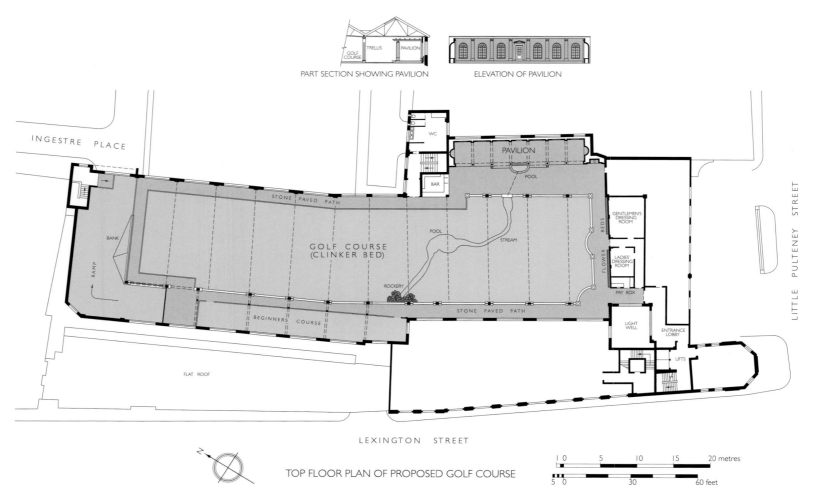

PART SECTION SHOWING PAVILION

ELEVATION OF PAVILION

INGESTRE PLACE

LITTLE PULTENEY STREET

WC

PAVILION

BAR

POOL

STONE PAVED PATH

GENTLEMEN'S DRESSING ROOM

BANK

POOL

STREAM

FLOWER BEDS

LADIES' DRESSING ROOM

GOLF COURSE (CLINKER BED)

RAMP

ROCKERY

PAY BOX

STONE PAVED PATH

BEGINNERS COURSE

LIGHT WELL

ENTRANCE LOBBY

FLAT ROOF

LIFTS

LEXINGTON STREET

TOP FLOOR PLAN OF PROPOSED GOLF COURSE

1 0   5   10   15   20 metres

5 0   30   60 feet

219   It is unlikely that this golf course, designed in 1930 to occupy the top floor of the Lex Garage, was ever installed. It illustrates how closely motoring was allied with golf through the 1920s, as the popularity of both greatly increased. Based on Westminster Archives plan WPD2/841/13.

driven into the top storey of a high building'.[79] This building was intended – at least in busy times – for attendant parking,[80] though its 31-foot column spaces made it suitable for adaptation to self-parking. With the aid of two turntables on each floor, attendants could park cars close together, with their handbrakes off and the driving seats inaccessible, sometimes in light contact with adjacent vehicles. When cars were required by their owners, they were pulled out by their bumpers or grilles. During rush hour, cars were directed to each floor in turn, so that no single floor was faced with a steady stream of arrivals. Because the Lex Garage was convenient for West End theatres and restaurants, it was at its busiest in the evenings between 7.30pm and 11.30pm. Perhaps the upper levels were under-used, since in 1930 a golf course – complete with 'velarium' (probably a canvas painted to look like sky, attached to the underside of the steel roof trusses), stream, pool, rockery, flower boxes, trellises and orangery – was designed for the top floor by the architects Barker & Walford (pl. 219).[81] This, rather sadly, does not appear to have been installed.

The Lex had a 'café' for owner-drivers and a 'canteen' for chauffeurs. Garages in Westminster seem to have catered for chauffeurs to a greater degree – and for longer – than those elsewhere, perhaps because many wealthy residents lived in mansion flats, but also because of a need to accommodate chauffeurs for hire cars. After the takeover of Wolseley (see Chapter 1), its old garage on York Street was remodelled by E. H. Major in 1928 as the Westminster Garage, providing chauffeurs with first-floor bedrooms, mess rooms and recreation rooms; its kitchen served meals from 8am until midnight.[82] There were plans to provide an additional sixty bedrooms on the roof. Such facilities were not exclusive to London. In 1924 Howarth's Garage in Manchester opened with a rest room – with wireless, telephone, canteen and billiard room – for chauffeurs. There was also a ladies' waiting room 'so that wives can await their husbands, and should those husbands be temporarily deprived of a driving licence, or for any other reason not wish to drive their cars home, there will be a skilled driver available at all hours and capable of handling any make of car'.[83] Even in a smaller town,

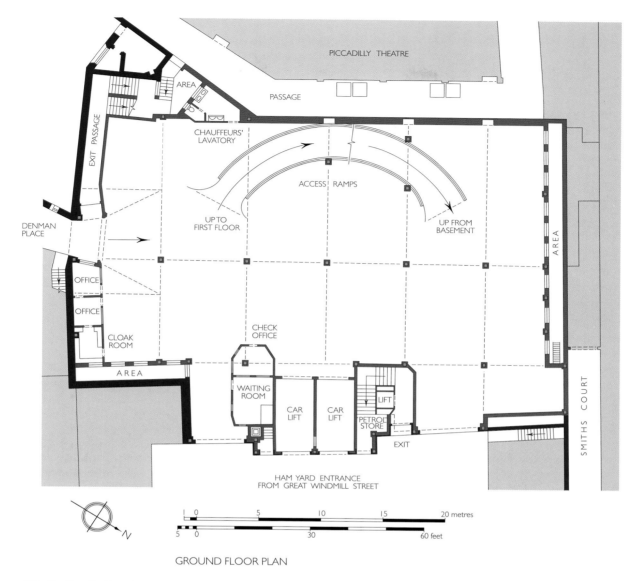

PICCADILLY THEATRE

PASSAGE

AREA

EXIT PASSAGE

CHAUFFEURS' LAVATORY

ACCESS RAMPS

DENMAN PLACE

UP TO FIRST FLOOR

UP FROM BASEMENT

AREA

OFFICE

OFFICE

CLOAK ROOM

AREA

CHECK OFFICE

WAITING ROOM

CAR LIFT

CAR LIFT

LIFT

PETROL STORE

EXIT

SMITHS COURT

HAM YARD ENTRANCE
FROM GREAT WINDMILL STREET

| 0 5 10 15 20 metres |
| 5 0 30 60 feet |

N

GROUND FLOOR PLAN

220   The Piccadilly Circus Garage, London (1928–9), had curved internal ramps. The shell of this site was still standing in 2011, with the line of the ramps visible in the ground. Based on Westminster Archives plan WPD2/741/01.

William Vincent's premises on Station Approach, Reading (1926–8; W. Roland Howell), provided dressing and waiting rooms for owners and chauffeurs. A vehicle entrance to the side of a galleried showroom led into a three-storey garage where 500 cars could be parked in the herringbone fashion that was the latest innovation. Cars were driven from floor to floor on straight ramps.[84]

The commencement of the Lex Garage inspired the RIBA to announce a competition for August 1928 to design a 1,000-space parking garage for a (hypothetical) theatre site in London.[85] None of the top four adjudged designs depended on lifts: two had staggered floors and two had curved ramps. Their elevations demonstrated the current stylistic tensions between pronounced verticality and horizontality. The winner of the £350 prize, Thomas Spencer,[86] opted for a pared-down classical façade with a strong vertical emphasis, like the Lex, while the second premium went to a horizontal moderne design,[87] with ribbon-strip glazing that better expressed the functionality of the building type and pointed the way to its future architectural expression.

The 1920s was a highly experimental decade as far as parking garages were concerned, and the Piccadilly Circus Garage (1928–9; Edward A. Stone; pl. 220) on Denman Street was probably the first in England to connect full-height floors by curved ramps.[88] Curved or elliptical ramps had connected the six parking floors of the Hotel La Salle Garage in Chicago, built in 1918.[89] This idea was certainly current in England by 1927, when paired one-way elliptical ramps formed part of an unexecuted proposal by W. R. Field for a multi-storey lock-up garage,[90] and the concept resurfaced in the RIBA competition of 1928. At the Piccadilly Circus Garage, curved two-way ramps (actually segments of a circle with a 30 ft radius, rising with a 1:7 gradient) connected the basement, ground and first floors, while two electric car lifts served the upper floors. The only turntable was located in the basement. As this suggests, the Piccadilly Circus, unlike the Lex, did not offer attendant parking: tickets registering the date and time of arrival were issued from an automatic machine; strings of coloured lights directed cars to different floors; and traffic signals obviated the possibility of cars meeting in the middle of the single-carriageway ramps. Nevertheless, a large staff undertook diverse services for motorists. In the absence of a filling station, for example, petrol was dispensed rather laboriously from a three-wheeled trolley. As well as changing rooms and bathrooms for theatre-goers, the garage had a dog crèche that charged 1s. a day (food for large dogs being extra), and had a staff of vets on hand. Since the Piccadilly Circus Garage has been demolished, the earliest extant example of curved ramps in England is probably the strikingly modern Daimler Hire Garage on Herbrand Street near Russell Square in London (1931–3; Wallis Gilbert & Partners; see pl. 195).[91] While the ramps of the Piccadilly Circus Garage were buried within the building, those of the Daimler Hire Garage protruded boldly from the façade, becoming a feature of its design.

In the early 1930s fully helical ramps appeared. Distant precursors may be identified in the spiral ramps built for horses and carriages in Renaissance Europe, for example, at the Château d'Amboise in the Loire valley. Confusingly, the terms 'spiral' and 'helical' were sometimes applied to slightly curved short ramps within staggered-floor car parks. These were quite different from continuous helical ramps, which could be arranged singly or doubly, and could be either concentric/'nested' (e.g., Eliot Street Garage, Boston, 1927) or corkscrewed/doubled (e.g., Richmond Garage, Richmond, Virginia, 1928). Helical ramps could project externally from the side of a garage; alternatively, they could be recessed or fully embedded. Often such ramps were provided solely for rapid descent from the upper floor: these were known as express ramps, and were banked to maximise speed and control. One of the first in England was attached to a car park erected at Clapton Greyhound Stadium, north London, in 1930 (demolished).[92] Perversely, some helical ramps were given a vertical architectural treatment. That at Sir Owen Williams's Daily News Garage at Commercial Wharf on the south side of the River Thames (1938–9, demolished) was divided into bays by close-set piers, alternating with tall, narrow windows and disrupted by stepped panels masking the curving ramp.[93] This may have been an effort to suppress, or at least minimise, the helical form.

Private enterprise was slow to meet parking needs outside London and local authorities often threatened to step in, to the consternation of those in the motor trade. In the U.S.A., municipal public parking had been provided for the first time in Cleveland in 1916.[94] Some English authorities were operating free open-air car parks by 1918; this was bad enough in the eyes of garage proprietors, but running commercial garages was an altogether more controversial matter. That municipalities might have to provide 'self-supporting' garages was intimated – or threatened – by the Ministry of Transport in 1925,[95] and the principle that local authorities could provide garaging seemed set in 1930, when Belfast obtained special powers to establish and operate garages in the city.[96] There were suggestions of similar powers being legislated in Sheffield and Glasgow. Around the same time, Hastings became the first English authority to provide covered parking, by creating a series of underground car parks (see below), and in 1933 rumours circulated of 'a northern town' providing a covered parking area, in competition with a private trader. This may have been a reference to Blackpool, which suffered from great traffic congestion. By 1930 the town, with a population of 100,000, was receiving 7 million visitors each year, many of them car-borne.[97]

In Blackpool, the possibility of building a municipal garage had been raised in the early 1920s,[98] but it looked as if private enterprise might fill the need and a fuss was averted. In March 1928 a new 'super garage' with lifts and turntables was proposed for a central site.[99] Nothing transpired, and in July 1928 a different scheme was published for a site on Church Street.[100] This was to be on the d'Humy system, and would be built by the same firm as the garage on Poland Street, London. Again, nothing happened. Then, around 1931–2 a garage hailed as 'Blackpool's New Super-Garage', and officially called the Winter Gardens Garage, was designed by J. C. Derham and built on Church Street/Leopold Grove.[101] Compared with the earlier proposals, this was rather basic: a long dog-legged external ramp of reinforced concrete ascended to the first floor of a steel-frame parking shed. Remarkably, this survives today. Another privately run garage in Blackpool housed 400 cars in what was essentially a reinforced concrete hall beneath the railway arches at Harrowside.[102] The proprietors of these garages must have been unhappy in 1932–3 when the Corporation built the town's first underground car park (see below) and announced plans for another.

The closest thing to a West End garage outside London was the Dex Garage in Newcastle upon Tyne (1930–31; L. J. Couves & Partners), surely named in homage to the metropolitan Lex Garage and similarly situated close to a cinema and theatre.[103] In fact, it was marketed as 'The "Paramount" Garage in Newcastle!'. The reinforced concrete design comprised seven staggered floors connected by straight ramps, and supplemented by lifts and turntables (pl. 221). Externally, the building presented a simple rendered Art Deco front with towers flanking a

221   The Dex Garage (1930–31) in Newcastle upon Tyne was one of the most impressive provincial car parks built in the 1930s. The central canted bay gave a clear view of the garage entrance, though it rather compromised the modernity of the design.

222   Another splendid provincial car park of the early 1930s, with staggered floors, Motor Mac's (1932) was located in the centre of Bournemouth, Dorset, with access from two streets. It could hold 900 cars. Only the northern half of the building, on Hinton Road, is still in operation as a car park, the rest having been converted for hotel use.

223 A dramatically lit view of the interior of the Cumberland Garage in 1934. Situated near Marble Arch in London, this is still used as a car park today.

central projecting bay. One of the towers (decorated with the name of the garage in bold *sans serif* lettering, again imitating Lex) contained the car lift; the other held the pedestrian lift and stairs.

Another large ramp garage to be built outside London was Motor Mac's on Westover Road/Hinton Road, Bournemouth (1932; Seal & Hardy).[104] Of steel-framed construction, this appeared to stand six storeys high, but because it had staggered floors it included thirteen parking levels. For possibly the first time, it was contemplated that the flat roof (later roofed over) could be used for parking, but only 'for emergency purposes'. This garage had attractive faience frontages to two streets; only that to the rear survives intact (pl. 222). In 1936–7 a similar garage was built in Blackpool, which, despite so many earlier initiatives, still suffered from congestion at the height of the holiday season. This 800-space garage by G. W. Stead, built on Talbot Road for the Corporation, was significant for two reasons: it was the first municipal multi-storey garage in England, and the first to be integrated with the public transport infrastructure, with a bus station occupying its unusually tall ground floor.[105] Like Motor Mac's, it was on the staggered-floor system and had a

faience façade, with rows of square glazed windows. Though it was reclad in the 1960s (pl. 224), a fragment of green tiling survives around the pedestrian entrance. It is worth noting that in 1937 yet another car park was proposed for beleaguered Blackpool. Designed by Erich Mendelsohn, this was a hotel and garage complex on the tower-and-podium principle, including a fifteen-storey garage. Like Talbot Road, this anticipated the integration of parking with other building types that became such a feature of new developments after 1945.

In the early 1930s a horizontal emphasis was adopted with increasing confidence for the façades of car parks, encouraged by international exemplars such as the vast Autorimessa Comunale (1931–4; Eugenio Miozzi), built to serve the car-free city of Venice.[106] In the Italian climate it was possible to provide uncovered rooftop parking, and the flat-roofed building was characterised by unbroken bands of white concrete alternating with strips of glazing, interrupted only by the gentle bulge of the helical ramp embedded at either end. In London, the Daimler Hire Garage (see above) was designed in a similar aesthetic spirit, although on a very different scale and on a less prominent site. Before long, larger parking garages in England began to embrace this horizontal moderne style, but generally displayed a preference for brick finishes. This can be seen in the side elevations of the Dex, with their ribbon-strip windows, but not in its main façade. It was embraced more fully at Moon's Garage in Kensington (1932; Robert Sharp; demolished), a seven-storey steel and concrete structure, clad in brickwork, with the horizontality of its metal-framed glazing exaggerated by white bands of artificial stone forming sills and lintels, while black stone was used to make vertical mullions almost invisible. Sharp had become the pre-eminent car park architect of his age, and the *Architect and Building News* declared this 'easily the best-looking garage in London', making a point of praising its signage, something that was usually panned by architectural journalists.[107] This, however, was an old-fashioned garage, with car lifts and turntables rather than ramps, a factor that might have contributed, ultimately, to its demise.

At last, with successful staggered-floor garages operating in Newcastle and Bournemouth, London was ready to embrace this form of car park.[108] The first to be built in the capital since 1925 was the Cumberland Garage on Bryanston Street, near Marble Arch (1933–4; Sir Owen Williams),[109] another brick-clad moderne garage. To prevent noise pollution, the garage was insulated from the adjoining Mount Royal Flats by a layer of cork. It offered the full range of facilities expected in pre-war West End garages, and was self-parking (pl. 223). Drivers negotiated one-way ramps (all with left-hand turns) under the guidance of attendants; they parked on colour-coded floors and were issued with corresponding colour-coded tickets. The floors were warmed by hot-water pipes in winter to keep them dry and ice-free. A similar aesthetic approach and circulation system was adopted for the very large, flat-roofed, curvaceous Olympia Garage in Kensington for 1,200 cars (1936–7; Joseph Emberton; pl. 225),[110] but a third example of a 1930s staggered-floor garage in London received a very different architectural treatment. This was the Eton Garage by Chalk Farm Station in north London (1938; Toms & Partners), which was designed to harmonise with three adjacent blocks of flats ('The Etons') and had a domestic appearance, with rows of small, square windows on each floor.[111] All these pre-war garages were glazed. Surprisingly, although the harmful effects of carbon monoxide were well known, ventilation does not seem to have been a major concern. Certainly, garages were equipped with extract fans, and ventilators were located in chambers on roofs (which were usually pitched, of light steel construction). Interiors were heated by hot-water pipes and radiators. Fire safety was a great preoccupation: all large garages were fitted with automatic sprinkler systems, escape stairs and fire doors.

'Multi-storey garages' with ramps were not always built primarily for public parking. Repair and maintenance garages on restricted sites could rise to several floors. Examples include Tate's

224 This bus station and car park on Talbot Road in Blackpool (1936–7) lost much of its character when it was reclad after the Second World War. Nevertheless, it was the most ambitious venture in municipal parking prior to the 1950s.

on New York Road, Leeds (1933; Victor Bain & Allan Johnson),[112] Barton's in Plymouth (branches of 1930 and 1938) and Furlong's Garage in Woolwich (1938–9; Corney Newman & J. A. Emes).[113] Some of these garages incorporated at least one

225 When it opened in 1937, this long, narrow garage at Olympia, London – designed by Joseph Emberton – claimed to be the largest in Europe, with 1,200 spaces. It was built of reinforced concrete with a facing of white bricks, and was glazed with Crittall casements.

226   It was quite common for large city repair garages to allocate space for parking. For example, one entire floor of the multi-functional Morris Garage (1932; H. W. Smith & Son) in Oxford – now the Crown Court – was a public car park.

public parking floor. At the Morris Garage, St Aldates, Oxford (1932; Harry W. Smith; pl. 226) – now the Crown Court – the public garage was on the first floor, accessed from the rear by an external ramp. Architecturally, this building seems to have been inspired by Macy's (see above), with its concave centre flanked by pavilions and its bold Neo-Classical styling.

In 1935 two extra floors were added to the Poland Street Garage. This almost doubled its size, although some areas on the third floor were reserved for Charles Kurpstein's gown manufactory, which was based in an adjoining property. The most unusual feature of the addition was the uncovered rooftop parking.[114] Until now, only a few repair garages had flat roofs suitable for parking, and this was often a temporary or emergency arrangement. Tate's of Leeds, for example, had been built in 1933 with a roof where 150 cars could be parked, but it was always intended to heighten the building, which was completed as planned, with a mansard roof, in 1937. On the roof of the new extension at Poland Street, 100 cars could be parked by motorists 'who do not mind exposing their cars to the elements', at a charge of only 1s. per day. Just two years later, however, the larger part of this area was covered to create a clothing factory for Kurpstein; it was reclaimed as a parking floor only after the war.[115] This reflects the uncertain commercial value of exposed parking roofs in the 1930s.

The incorporation of parking into the basements or ground floors of new buildings – especially apartment blocks, hotels and offices – became common in the mid-1930s, though this was not entirely novel. As long ago as 1905 a twenty-five-car garage for

visitors had opened beneath the Hotel Cecil in London, and in 1912 Austin's premises on Oxford Street had included basement parking. The publication of more recent examples in Paris whetted interest.[116] The layouts of basement and ground-floor garages were complicated by the need for supports for the superstructure, and they required powerful artificial ventilation, lighting and heating. Ventilation was of especial importance, since open windows would cause a nuisance (in terms of smell and noise) to the occupants of upper floors. Despite these complications, such garages received a spur in the mid-1930s, when the London County Council began to refuse permission for substantial new developments that did not include garage accommodation, and a spate of examples reached completion from 1936. These included office blocks such as the Adelphi Building on the Strand (1936–8; Stanley Hamp), which let its basement garage to the nearby Savoy Hotel. At 57,000 square feet, the Savoy Adelphi Garage claimed to be the largest on one floor in London: it could hold 400 cars, and had five access points.[117] Most integral garages built in the late 1930s, however, belonged to central London apartment blocks, such as Rossmore Court at the top of Gloucester Road (1936).[118] While most of these catered mainly, or exclusively, for residents (see Chapter 3), Charles Rickard's 150-car basement garage at Arthur Court in Bayswater, near Whiteley's department store, offered parking for shoppers. It featured an hydraulic turntable lift, and one of the first petrol filling stations to be installed within a building.

In the late 1930s several blocks of flats were built with air-raid shelters, and the idea of constructing car parks that could double as shelters was hotly debated. Several shelter schemes took the form of underground car parks (see below), but at least one convertible reinforced concrete multi-storey garage was devised, to be erected in 'an important provincial town'.[119] It is unlikely that this – or anything like it – was ever built.

Outdoor Parking before 1939

Formal roadside parking restrictions took time to evolve. It was not sensible to leave an early motor car parked in the street for any length of time, yet photographs from the early 1900s do show cars parallel-parked by the kerbside in the centres of English towns and cities. In many cases, these cars would have been parked with the full knowledge of the occupants of adjacent buildings, and they would have been left in the care of chauffeurs. The possibility that a parked car might be deemed an obstruction was an excellent reason to employ a chauffeur – who not only stayed with the car, but also moved it every hour or two if necessary – even if the owner was, himself or herself, an enthusiastic motorist. In practice, cars were often left unattended, and drivers were sometimes prosecuted or fined by the police. Since occupants of buildings had the right to object to any parking outside their premises, metropolitan motorists traded information about streets where objections were never raised: in the early 1920s this included side streets off the Strand.[120] Cars still had many easily removed components, and were vulnerable to joy riders – who, in those days, tended to 'borrow' cars rather than trash them[121] – but by 1921 several locations had been demarcated where cars could be parked in the open under supervision. In London, the RAC had two car parks in the charge of RAC guides, one in St James's Square and another in Waterloo Place. Members of the AA and Engineers' Club were assigned twenty-five spaces on Whitcomb Street. Less formally, the Kingsway Motor Co. offered to keep an eye on cars parked outside its premises in Catherine Street. A crucial factor that inhibited the creation of more public parking places on back streets and squares was the need for cars to be guarded, and the question of how to fund this service.

Slowly, local authorities began to provide official street parking. In 1922 Birmingham allotted twenty-two parking spaces,[122] and in 1924 Liverpool Corporation provided places, principally for shoppers and visitors, though in the event they were taken up by commuters.[123] The Public Health Act of 1925 (Section 68) clarified such actions by giving councils power to provide parking places for motor cars to relieve congestion, but not to impose charges. In September 1925 the Minister of Transport, under Section 10 of the London Traffic Act of 1924,[124] licensed regulated parking spaces on specific streets and squares, with waiting limits; in some places an experimental system was

in operation whereby 'messengers' administered a ticketing system. These unpaid attendants, often ex-servicemen, wore badges and relied on tips. Amongst the largest concentrations of regulated parking were Lincoln's Inn Fields (pl. 227) and St James's Square, where cars were parked at right angles to the kerb, facing the road for an easy exit. It was only in 1927 that signs bearing the word 'Car Park' were recommended, to help people identify such parking places.[125] Other towns followed London's lead: Blackpool, for instance, introduced 'free parking' on certain streets, with an attendant who wore a badge, issued tickets and collected a gratuity. In these licensed car parks, motorists often had a legal obligation to leave their cars unlocked, so that they could be moved if necessary. This encouraged theft by 'motor bandits', leading, in 1932, to a successful campaign by the RAC and the *Light Car* to have this rule rescinded.[126] Though cars were parked around London squares, they were never parked within the squares themselves, which were invariably given over to gardens. In 1939 the architect and planner James Burford, writing in *The Builder*, made the 'shocking suggestion' ('opposition will at once be rampant') that these squares be paved over and used as car parks, citing French squares where cars were parked under trees – as, indeed, they still are to this day.

Regulations controlling parking places on London streets were set down and monitored by the police. In the absence of clear notices, confusion reigned. Lists of streets where short-term parking was allowed were published in newspapers, and the police rather vaguely advised that while a short stop for a shopping expedition was permissible, a longer stay to attend the theatre or transact business was not. They had no power to apply specific time limits, yet could cancel an authorised parking space at any moment. As a result, many drivers unwittingly broke the

227 Parking in Lincoln's Inn Fields, London, in January 1933, marked by a blue 'P' sign.

228 Debenham's motor park. Opening in 1925, this was one of London's first official open-air car parks, and certainly the first provided by a department store.

rules. The risks involved in parking on London streets aroused great disquiet.

In reaction, London department stores began to provide customer parking. In May 1925 Marshall & Snelgrove and Debenham & Freebody advertised their sixty-space 'private motor park', which was free to customers (pl. 228).[127] This open-air car park occupied the site of Debenham's former stable yard, and it was noted that the space to be occupied by each car was marked out on the ground in white paint, with many spaces set diagonally. It operated a ticket system with an electronic indicator board and gong to alert chauffeurs when their cars were wanted. This initiative prompted other department stores to provide customer parking: in 1926 Harrods bought the nearby Beaufort Garage for this purpose,[128] while Selfridges acquired space in the new Macy's Garage.

In 1925 the idea of the open-air car park was still new. The identity of the first is disputed: it may have been in Pennsylvania in 1914, or Detroit in 1917.[129] A parking lot in Union Square, New York – created during a railway strike – had been illustrated in a British journal in 1920.[130] By 1921 Blackpool – which, as has been seen, saw a great influx of tourists after the First World War – was providing a large open car park, the 'Corporation Park', on the corner of Rigby Road and Central Road, on the site of the Corporation Stables.[131] This was full at holiday time, and was free; another outdoor car park 'at the Coloseum Garage' was filled mostly with charabancs. Other resorts took similar measures, sometimes banning or restricting parking on promenades so that vehicles would not mar the seaside experience. So-called parking grounds at seaside resorts counted amongst the first municipal car parks in Britain; the largest included the Western Esplanade car park at Southend, which, in 1932, could

hold 507 cars (free), while the nearby Marine Parade car park could hold 1,000 cars (1s. per day).[132] In 1933 the Southend Garage Proprietors' Union contested a local election on the parking issue, maintaining – in what had become a common refrain up and down the country – that the local authority was trading against private enterprise. Other seaside towns with a parking problem included St Ives in Cornwall, which, in 1931, considered erecting a concrete parking raft on pillars on the seafront, such was the demand for parking places.[133] Instead, in 1936 fishermen's cottages were levelled to provide a new car park.

From the late 1920s the urban surface car park became more common. In 1927–8, as part of a slum clearance scheme, Windsor's Borough Engineer, E. A. Stickland, created a 139-space 'motor parking ground' on River Street, close to the Theatre Royal, at a cost of £9,399. This survives (pls 229 and 230), together with the original kiosk, with a bay window that let the attendant supervise the park from a single vantage point. The car park was also equipped with a two-storey Neo-Georgian building containing public conveniences and a large cloakroom. Other surface car parks of the 1920s were closely associated with entertainments and exhibition halls: at Wembley and Olympia in London, for example. On a smaller scale, in 1928 a seventy-five-space surface car park formed part of the scheme when the Lido Cinema was built at Golders Green in north London;[134] it was free, and the attendant relied on tips. By 1930 railway companies had begun (officially) to provide parking in open yards, charging daily commuters around 1s. a day, and in 1933 the London Midland & Scottish Railway inaugurated season tickets for parking at more than 300 stations, followed by the Great Western Railway at 115 stations.[135] Grumbling garage proprietors were appeased with the argument that the parking problem might place 'a very serious brake upon the natural development of motoring' unless more parking was provided.[136] But traders were particularly alarmed when the Road Traffic Act of 1930 gave local authorities power to restrict parking on streets by introducing waiting periods, and to charge for municipal parking spaces off a thoroughfare.

In November 1934 the Minister of Transport, Mr Hore-Belisha, criticised unauthorised parking on roadways, acknowledging that the availability of free street parking deterred the provision of parking garages. The position regarding street parking had become clearer, and colour-coded maps of central London were published, showing official parking places. These were concentrated around large squares. Parking on main thoroughfares was discouraged beyond limited periods for loading and unloading: the only major route with parking spaces was Piccadilly, alongside Green Park, where it would not interfere with frontages. Small stretches of kerbside parking were provided on some secondary streets, where parked cars caused less of an

229   The River Street Car Park in Windsor, photographed in 1930. Note the Neo-Georgian attendant's kiosk and cloakroom block by the entrance on the right. The external steps led up to the huge cloakroom.

230   The River Street Car Park, Windsor, photographed from the same vantage point as pl. 229 (i. e., the terrace of Windsor Castle) in 2010. All that has changed is the herringbone pattern of the parking spaces and the style of the lamp standards.

obstruction, but were sometimes restricted to evenings and night.

The proliferation of street parking and surface car parks after 1930 reflects the fact that cars were more difficult to break into and better able to withstand the elements. Concerns remained, however, and waterproof car covers were available for those who parked in the open. According to the manufacturer Coverall, 'of particular interest to the woman motorist is the variety of colours from which to choose in the better qualities (they include pale green, three gradations of brown and mottled shades blue, red and green)'.[137]

Mechanical Parking Schemes before 1939

Parking was partially mechanised from the earliest days of motoring, since car lifts were used extensively. Lifts had their drawbacks: not only was there expensive machinery to install and maintain, but also attendants had to be employed to park and collect cars – something that was optional in ramp garages. Their proponents pointed out that lifts occupied less space than ramps, thus allowing more parking spaces to be provided in garages. Roadways and areas for manoeuvring could take up to 50 per cent of floor area in a ramp garage: a serious deterrent for garage owners trying to maximise profits in areas of high land values. Thus entrepreneurs in Britain and overseas were encouraged to develop and market many ingenious, space-saving, mechanical parking systems. None of these actually entered production in Britain prior to 1939, but they were, nevertheless, influential. By the outbreak of war, the Government had become convinced that the adoption of these mechanised systems was necessary to combat growing congestion in British cities.

Internationally, the first automated garage seems to have been A. & G. Perret's reinforced concrete Garage Ponthieu, built in Paris in 1905. Behind an astonishingly modern façade, the garage stood three storeys high and was lit by a glazed roof. Cars were parked on the first floor by a lift that rose vertically, then slid horizontally on tracks through a well in the middle of the garage, before depositing vehicles in parking bays, perpendicular to the axis of the building. This had no immediate impact in England.

One of the earliest systems to be advertised in Britain was developed in 1924 by the established engineering company Mitchell Brothers, and was demonstrated by a working model.[138] In this 'rotary garage system', three rings of cars were parked in the central garage area, which was traversed by a gangway, with ancillary services in the four corners (pl. 231a). The middle or rotary ring ('or in the case of large sites each alternate ring') revolved on ball bearings – it was, essentially, an enormous doughnut-shaped turntable. To park or retrieve a car, the vehicle

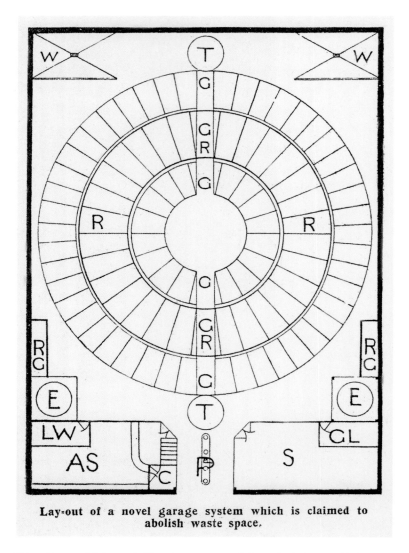

Lay-out of a novel garage system which is claimed to abolish waste space.

231a–c (*above and facing page*) Three inter-war proposals for mechanical garages: (a) the rotary garage system (*Motor Trader*, 9 January 1924, 48); (b) the Chaudoir garage system (*The Autocar*, 18 July 1930, 149); and (c) a double unit of the Simon Patent Vertical Garage, marketed in Great Britain by Henry Simon Ltd of Cheadle Heath, in 1932 (*The Autocar*, 16 November 1934, p. 961).

was loaded onto this ring, which was then turned to face a parking bay or the exit gangway, respectively. Conventional turntables at either end of the gangway facilitated access to the corner services.

Also in 1924, William Whitehead Richardson devised a multi-storey garage with floors fitted with rollers.[139] A fixed central lift or platform rose through nine open-plan floors. The car was driven onto the platform, raised to the parking floor, then the platform was rolled into a parking space. In 1929 designs for a moving – or 'auto-actuated' – floor system were published. Cars were parked in groups of eight on platforms or transporters, which were moved by cables operated by underground electric motors.[140] This was developed and offered for manufacture by

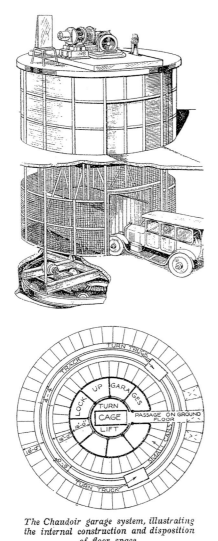

The Chaudoir garage system, illustrating
the internal construction and disposition
of floor space

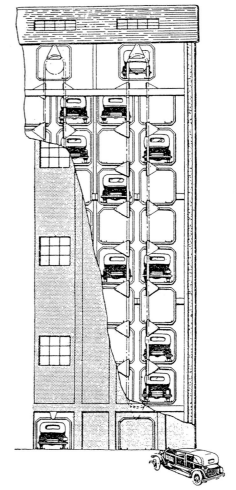

Cars are lifted and parked in cages
suspended from endless chains.

the ironworkers Ransomes & Rapier of Ipswich and London, who prepared a model. Various systems based on auto-actuated floors were adapted for underground garages in the 1930s, but were never put into practice in Britain (see below).

Meanwhile, in the mid-1920s a number of semi-mechanical 'skyscraper' garages were being built in the U.S.A. Based on a system patented in 1923, the thirteen-storey Hill Garage, Los Angeles (1928), had three lifts with open sides and turntables, allowing vehicles to move off in different directions. The first to transport cars in three dimensions were the towering Kent Automatic Garages (1928–30; Jardine, Hill & Murdock) on 9th Avenue, New York (the prototype), on Quincy Street, Chicago, and in Cincinnati, which could each hold around 1,000 cars.[141] Nothing this ambitious was dreamt of in England, where the Building Acts limited the height of new buildings, but in 1928 a fully rotating electric lift was designed by Eugène Chaudoir for manufacture by William Wadsworth & Sons of Bolton (pl.

231b).[142] This central 'turn-lift', capable of both vertical movement and rotation, would occupy the core of a cylindrical multi-storey garage,[143] 'the garage of the future', which was conceived for both garaging and parking. On each floor, the lift would be surrounded by concentric rings of fireproof lock-ups and parking 'compartments', separated by a track fitted with 'turn trucks' with turntables. Thus cars could be manoeuvred in and out of parking spaces with ease.

The Simon Patent Vertical Garage (pl. 231c), published in 1932,[144] was based on yet another American design, the 'Westinghouse Vertical Parking Machine' that had been invented by H. D. James, with examples built in 1929 in East Pittsburgh, followed by another two in Chicago in 1932.[145] Units consisted of a series of cradles (one for each car) suspended from endless vertical chains, on the paternoster lift principle. These were revolved by an electric motor in the basement. In the Simon system, each unit held eighteen cars, and occupied the ground space of two.

It could be operated by an attendant or a coin-in-the-slot system, and cars could be retrieved in thirty seconds. There was, however, a glitch: only one car could be delivered at a time from each unit. A similar system was devised by Mr S. W. Moss-Blundell of Harrogate under the name of the 'Rev'.[146] It was suggested that the basic idea embodied in these designs could be adapted horizontally for underground parking, for small three-car domestic garages, and even for car showrooms. Eventually, a few English car parks were created on the paternoster principle, but not before the 1960s (see Chapter 7).

Underground Car Parks

In the fifteen years before the outbreak of the Second World War, debates about parking beneath open spaces were as lively as those on mechanical systems. Discussions concentrated on London, but in the event Hastings and Blackpool were the only English towns to provide underground car parks before the late 1950s. Elsewhere, they proved prohibitively expensive due to the cost of excavation, drainage and heavy roof construction. Adding to their initial cost, they required permanent artificial lighting and ventilation. Furthermore, because potential locations were open-air amenities such as squares, parks and promenades, they usually had to be constructed by local authorities rather than private enterprise. An exception to this was Manchester's 'underground' car park: built for Thomas Maiden and positioned beneath a ground-level car park surrounded by a garden border, this was known as the St James's Car Park and Filling Station, but it does not seem to have enjoyed much longevity.[147]

The idea of building car parks beneath parks had been current in the U.S.A. since 1913 and a two-level ramp garage was built under a garden in Philadelphia in 1926.[148] England was slow to follow, but in 1925 the Automobile Association prepared a model of a single-level underground car park for Leicester Square.[149] It would hold 170 cars: there would be two ramped entrances and exits; stairs would be provided for drivers; and attendants would control traffic and signal when spaces were full. The gardens would remain, though large trees would be lost. It was realised that the local authority would have to obtain a large loan to build the garage, and this was a major stumbling block. Meanwhile, European cities pressed ahead. Paris embarked upon a chain of eight underground car parks in 1932–3, including the Garage Gouvion St Cyr.[150] All eight were built by motor agents, rather than local authorities, seven by a single consortium known as the Société des Grands Garages Souterrains.

The clutter of parked cars on promenades was a major issue for seaside resorts, and in 1930–31 Hastings Town Council erected a new sea wall in front of Carlisle Parade, creating a promenade and road over an underground car park on land

232 The first underground car park in Britain, on the promenade at Hastings, Sussex, was shown on the cover of the *Light Car and Cyclecar* on 10 March 1933. This was probably England's first purpose-built municipal car park, as well as its first underground one.

reclaimed from the sea (pls 232 and 233).[151] One wall of the car park was formed from the old sea wall, and the roof was raised slightly above this, admitting some natural light and ventilation, though fumes had to be extracted by electric fans via reinforced concrete shafts disguised as seaside shelters. On Carlisle Parade, wide, gently sloping entrance and exit ramps, flanked by rusticated wall faces, led down to the centre of the car park. The interior was divided into three aisles by rows of reinforced concrete piers, at 20-foot spacings, and was served by two centrally placed lifts. This work was a crucial part of the modernisation of Hastings masterminded by the Borough Engineer, Sidney Little, who designed the car park himself.

This was followed in 1934–6 by two additional underground car parks, one close to Hastings Pier, and the other between

Warrior Square and Undercliff, which were opened on the same day by Mr Hore-Belisha, Minister of Transport.[152] The small car park at the pier was accessed by single ramps at either end and comprised a simple roadway with parking spaces along one side. The larger car park at Warrior Square rose several feet above the ground to create a clerestory on both sides, providing daylight illumination. On the external, sea side of this clerestory were glass-screened wind-proof shelters. In summer 1936, with a total of approximately 800 underground parking spaces, Hastings was already planning a fourth underground car park, at St Leonards, which would bring the total to 1,200.

Hastings was followed by Blackpool, where the sea wall was extended north from Arundel Avenue at Little Bispham in 1932–4. The single-level underground car park that formed part of this development was entered by a long entrance ramp from the south, enabling visitors to park close to the beach. Its segmental reinforced concrete roof supported the promenade and permitted a pillar-less interior.[153] After this had opened, in autumn 1934, a 1,000-space underground car park was proposed under the promenade by the North Pier,[154] with a third 'near the Cleveleys boundary'. In the event the Corporation abandoned these schemes and provided the multi-storey car park on Talbot Road (see above). Another town seemingly inspired by Hastings was Brighton, where plans were prepared in 1936 for a new sea front between West Pier and Palace Pier, with an open promenade and gardens overlying an underground car park and covered promenade. This was never built. Plans for a car park under the Hall of Memory Gardens in Birmingham, developed in 1936–7, were similarly aborted.[155]

It may have been the success of the Hastings scheme, or the example presented by Paris, that prompted the City of London Corporation in 1932 to appoint a committee to investigate the possibility of building its own underground garages. It was proposed that these could be excavated under Finsbury Square, Finsbury Circus, Trinity Square, West Smithfield and Charterhouse Square.[156] In 1930 the architect Thomas Spencer – who had won the RIBA car park competition (see above) in 1928 – came up with the idea of a ring of approximately thirteen underground car parks distributed around the periphery of London.[157] Motorists would leave their vehicles and continue their journey by public transport: conceptually, this was a precursor of modern park-and-ride schemes. At the west end of the ring was Marble Arch, and Spencer worked up a detailed scheme for this site. It would have a two-level garage accessed by ramps, requiring a

233   The long, aisled interior of the underground car park on Hastings promenade.

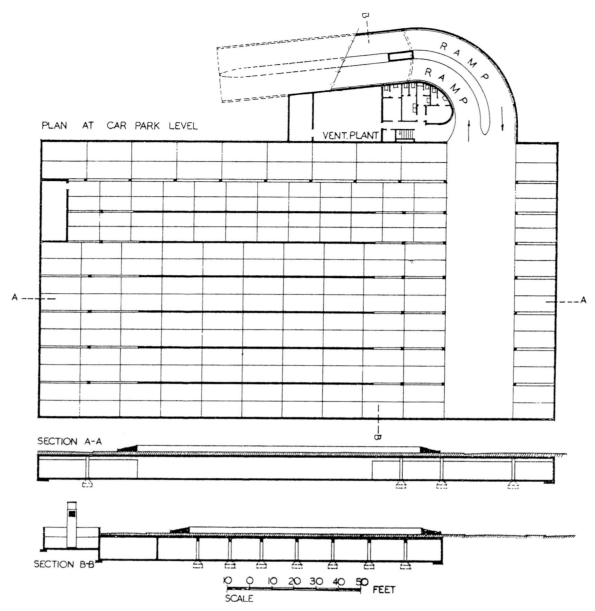

PLAN AT CAR PARK LEVEL

RAMP
RAMP

VENT. PLANT

A --- ---A

SECTION A-A

SECTION B-B

10 0 10 20 30 40 50
SCALE FEET

SCHEME FOR CAR PARK AND AIR RAID SHELTER,
KINGSTON-ON-THAMES.
MR. SYDNEY CLOUGH, F.R.I.B.A., ARCHITECT
Only the Air Raid Shelter, whose position is indicated by the spine walls in the
centre of the above plan, is at present being built. Further details and a plan of
the Shelter are on the next page.

234 A scheme for a combined car park and air-raid shelter, designed for Kingston upon Thames in 1940 by Sydney Clough, published in *The Builder*,
12 April 1940, p. 449.

complex ventilation system with extraction vents appearing above ground.

The closest London actually came to an underground car park in the 1930s may have been the semi-subterranean garage created beneath a tennis court and ornamental garden within the court-yard of a U-shaped block of flats, Richmond Hill Court, at Richmond Hill (see pl. 103).[158] Like some of the Hastings car parks, it was lit naturally, with windows concealed in the sides of the garden. In the year that this was built, 1934, Westminster followed the City by considering the potential of its squares.[159]

In November 1935 it revisited the idea of a garage under Leicester Square, but could not finance the project without further statutory powers.[160] It was suggested that underground car parks should be excavated, not beneath squares, but under London's Royal Parks, which were in Government, rather than local authority, control, and were laid with fewer pipes than the squares. One propagandist for this notion was quoted as saying in February 1935: 'think what splendid shelter for the Government and thousands of other people these subterranean car-park-funk-holes would provide during air raids in the next war!'[161]

In fact, this was already being considered seriously by those on high. In March 1935 it was reported that the Ministry of Transport had come up with a design for a circular underground car park that would also serve as a bomb-proof shelter from air attack (for 2,500 to 3,000 people), to be located under a London square: two units, it was suggested, could fit beneath St James's Square.[162] Cars descended to a single parking floor in a central lift. They transferred to an electronically controlled rotary table that could accommodate seventeen cars, with one space always left vacant. The table would stop opposite one of the parking bays arranged in a concentric ring, outside the rotary table. To leave, cars reversed onto the table, which then delivered them to a peripheral exit ramp. Related to the rotary systems previously proposed by Mitchell Brothers and Eugène Chaudoir, this closely resembled the 'Pact' system, developed in summer 1935 by Sydney Clough for Hanover Square.[163] In this, two superimposed floors each comprised a number of concentric rotating annular platforms, but ingress and egress was by ramps.[164]

By the beginning of 1939 several local authorities were considering schemes for underground car parks that could double as air-raid shelters. With little guidance provided by the Home Office, these schemes varied in character. Birmingham, for example, proposed a simple basement car park/shelter beneath a market hall.[165] The Borough Engineer for Holborn, J. E. Parr, prepared more sophisticated plans for Russell Square.[166] This car park/shelter would be 35 feet deep (with a 5 ft concrete roof and steel-frame construction); it would accommodate 44,869 people (rising, in an emergency, to 76,918), or 850 cars, with ramp access. Air conditioning plant would have to deal with both sets of conditions; there would be electric lighting with a back-up system in case the utility companies were put out of operation by bombing. The possibility of flooding was also anticipated, and so pumping apparatus would have to be installed, as well as a first-aid post and lavatories, which might be converted into decontaminating centres. Since this would take three years to complete, the proposal was shelved. Another scheme that came to nothing was Tecton's proposal for Finsbury Square, drafted in winter 1938–9.[167] In this case, a continuous parking ramp – burrowing into the ground like a corkscrew – would wind around a central lift shaft, creating space to shelter 7,300 people. The idea of the ramped floor may have been inspired by stunning designs for an underground double-helix parking ramp designed by the architect Louis Ploussey and the engineer L. Rank, for the Place Saint Augustin, Paris, first published in France in 1929,[168] and republished in Britain in 1937. In the event, the Government did not approve of Tecton's design and ten straightforward air-raid shelters were constructed within Finsbury Square.

In a lecture presented in April 1940, Sydney Clough – rapidly becoming an expert in the field of parking garages – continued to maintain that mechanical systems were necessary to make underground garages viable. By this time, however, he had abandoned the 'Pact' system of rotary rings in favour of the Baldwin-Augur (or puzzle-parking) system. This comprised a unit two cars wide and up to ten cars long, with two parallel rows of platforms (forming a flush floor of concrete slabs with gratings) mounted on rollers and operated by electric motors. These platforms could move longitudinally, and the end bays could also move sideways. One space always remained empty to enable the platforms to shuffle around to deliver a car when required. The customer simply dialled the number of the bay for his car to be delivered automatically. The shells of two such car parks/shelters were built: one was reportedly erected in Cardiff to Clough's designs in October 1939,[169] while one on Wood Street, Kingston upon Thames, was completed in spring 1940. As built, the car park/shelter in Kingston was a heavily modified version of Clough's design (pl. 234). To serve effectively as an air-raid shelter by localising the impact of bombs, the structure had to be subdivided into cells. It would have been possible to do this by erecting spine walls to create long spaces, 15 feet wide, which could later hold nineteen-car units on the Baldwin-Auger system (171 cars in total).[170] It was thought that during the war these long bays would be further subdivided by traverses or sandbags, and their ends would contain lavatories. In the event, however, just the central area of the proposed car park was built, with bays only 13 feet wide. Neither the Cardiff nor the Kingston upon Thames shelters ever contained a Baldwin-Auger mechanism. By the time that the construction of car parks resumed in the late 1950s, as the post-war economy began to recover, very different designs of car park were preferred, including open decks, continuous parking ramps and mechanical 'pigeon-hole' systems. This is the story of the next chapter.

235   The Unicorn Hotel and Car Park in Bristol (now The Bristol Hotel and Princes Street Car Park) was developed by Parcar in 1963–6, with a drive-in reception bay. An aborted Parcar project in Gibraltar (1964), involving a car park beneath – rather than alongside – a hotel, was to have been clad in the same manner.

7: PARKING SINCE 1945

SINCE 1945 THE BUILT ENVIRONMENT HAS been re-engineered to accommodate the car, to such an extent that modern life would quickly crumble if we could no longer park, whether as part of the daily commute, for shopping trips, for evenings out, or for weekend and holiday jaunts. By the mid-1960s most English towns had acquired at least one multi-storey car park (MSCP). Such structures were welcomed at first, but disenchantment followed. As the pre-war emphasis on customer service was abandoned, car park interiors became gloomy and malodorous. Without a large supervisory staff, they attracted a wide spectrum of anti-social behaviour. Eventually, the unpleasantness and expense of town-centre parking helped to push new developments out of town, to retail, leisure and business 'parks': their name carrying the two-fold expectation of landscaped grounds and, more realistically, ample free parking. Regeneration schemes have subsequently attempted to restore the lifeblood to urban centres, an approach that has spawned a new generation of brightly lit, neo-modern MSCPs, including some award-winning 'landmark' buildings. In many cities – perhaps paradoxically – these coexist with park-and-ride schemes and other measures designed to deter cars from entering the urban realm.

Controlling Urban Parking

Restrictions on building materials and labour put a brake on the development of parking garages for more than a decade after the Second World War. But this did not stop national and local government analysing the parking problem and investigating potential solutions. By 1945 the number of cars in England had dropped below its pre-war level (see Appendix), yet congestion in London's West End seemed as bad as ever; street parking impeded traffic flow, inconvenienced businesses, and was deemed unsightly. Predictions of growth in car usage caused alarm. When the County of London Plan (1943) indicated that 7,000 parking spaces were required in 'Theatreland', the Minister of Town and Country Planning, Lewis Silkin, realised that existing approaches could not meet demand. He advocated mechanical parking, especially for underground and basement car parks, and believed that the provision of adequate parking space should be a condition of planning consents for new buildings.[1]

Tackling the immediate problem, in 1946 the Ministry of Transport requisitioned twenty-seven London bombsites for use as surface car parks: by March 1948 forty-two sites with space for 2,240 cars were in use (pl. 236).[2] This was regarded as a temporary palliative, since it was recognised that buildings would eventually be erected on such valuable sites. Bombsites were also bought by private companies, such as National Car Parks (NCP), which had been founded by Colonel Freddie Lucas in 1931 and had operated parking for major events in the 1940s. A new player in the game was Central Car Parks, formed in 1948 when Donald Gosling, a trainee surveyor with Westminster City Council, teamed up with Ronald Hobson, a demobbed serviceman: together they bought a site in Red Lion Square for £200 and converted it into a car park. In 1958 they acquired NCP from Lucas's widow, and from there expanded to become the principal provider of public parking in the U.K. The bombsite car park was not an exclusively London phenomenon. Many endured into the 1990s, and it is quite possible that some are still in use today. It was another decade before surface car parks within the urban environment were habitually screened by trees, shrubs or hedges, and planted with additional trees to break up

236   A 1950s bombsite car park, close to St Paul's Cathedral in London.

the mass of parked cars. Through the 1950s and 1960s the approach remained essentially utilitarian.

The idea of building floating or fixed parking decks over the River Thames was rejected by the Working Party on Car Parking in the Inner Area of London in 1953, but returned in 1958 when Bernard L. Clark & Partners proposed that decking be erected over the foreshore of the north and south embankments.[3] Striving towards a more realistic long-term solution for London's parking problems, the London and Home Counties Traffic Advisory Committee Report of 1951 suggested that experiments be made with parking meters. However, since this involved charging for parking on the 'King's Highway', it would require legislation. The Comprehensive Parking Plan produced for London in March 1953 proposed that meters should form part of a broad policy, whereby the provision of underground and multi-storey car parks would be accompanied by the implementation of 'no waiting' in major thoroughfares, and the introduction of meters for short-stay parking (two hours maximum) in minor streets near new garages. The revenue from the meters (6d. an hour) would subsidise the cost of the new garages. Anticipating great demand, Venner Ltd took up an American licence to manufacture parking meters in England. A year later, tired of awaiting legislation, the company began to export its meters to the Commonwealth. Although a Road Traffic Bill to legalise meters on London streets was published in December 1954, it encountered opposition from motorists' groups, and Parliament was dissolved before it could be enacted.

In 1955, in the first experiment of its kind, NCP installed twelve meters on the razed site of Queen's Hall on Portland Place, London. Later that year, when the Road Traffic Bill was reintroduced, inspiration for a workable meter scheme was sought from further afield. Coin-fed meters had been used in the U.S.A. and Switzerland for many years. Indeed, the first U.S. meters ('Park-O-Meters'), invented by Carlton C. Magee, had been installed as long ago as 1935, in Oklahoma City,[4] and a MSCP was currently being built in Rochester, New York (1956), with metered stalls – an idea that would never be tried out in England. An intriguing alternative to meters was presented by the new Swedish system of 'pay and display', but the prospect of motorists having to carry a punch to validate pre-purchased tickets caused a quandary.[5] The disc scheme being introduced in 'blue zones' in Paris (1957) was studied,[6] and a group travelled to Canada to examine the parking systems there. Eventually, on 1 January 1957 the Road Traffic Act legalised the installation of parking meters on public roads.

Westminster City Council became the first local authority to take advantage of the Act, inaugurating a pilot scheme on fourteen streets in Mayfair in July 1958.[7] In this area, where 1,500 vehicles street-parked each day, only 647 metered spaces were provided.[8] Attendants (soon to become traffic wardens, who superseded the police as parking monitors) were authorised to issue fixed penalties.[9] St Marylebone followed in 1959, and by the end of 1960 Venner's had installed 4,600 Park-O-Meters in London (pl. 237). In March 1961 Bristol became the first provincial city to introduce meters,[10] whilst in May 1961 Woolwich became the first London suburb to follow suit.[11] The popularity of meters did not preclude other initiatives, and in 1965 Cheltenham became the first English town to introduce a disc scheme.[12] Since this did not require the installation of intrusive street furniture, it was favoured in other historic centres, such as Harrogate.[13] Pay and display, with coin-fed ticket-dispensing machines, became a popular alternative in the mid-1960s, on streets as well as in car parks. In tandem with these systems, 'no waiting' was signalled by yellow lines, painted parallel to the kerb, following a successful experiment undertaken in Slough in 1955–7.[14] The wheel clamping of offending vehicles – introduced in the U.S.A., where clamps became known as 'Denver boots', in the 1950s – was initiated in London in 1983. More controversially, in later years private firms were authorised to impound illegally parked vehicles, which were released only upon the payment of a hefty fine.

Once post-war building restrictions had been lifted and street parking was under some semblance of control,[15] construction work began in earnest on a new generation of parking garages. Local authorities assumed the lead role: although motor traders had objected strenuously when the first municipal car parks opened in the 1930s, the Minister of Transport stated somewhat

237 This Park-O-Meter on Fore Street in the City of London, with modern office blocks in the background, was photographed around 1963 by John Gay.

Though the notion had been mooted as early as 1913, the first 'wall-less' garage was built in Boston in 1933.[17] A much-published Miami car park (1948; Robert Law Weed), however, is often cited as a radical departure: the point at which the layered parking structure ceased to imitate other building types and came into its own. By 1960 the skeletal open-sided car park with exposed rooftop parking was standard in America. The adoption of this design, coupled with self-parking, cut installation and maintenance costs dramatically. Such garages required minimal artificial lighting, and no mechanical heating or ventilation systems. Furthermore, there was no large staff of attendants to pay; liability for damage or theft was minimized; and car owners enjoyed being in control. Initially, there was some resistance to this approach in the U.K. Although some self-park garages had existed since the 1920s, proprietors preferred attendant parking because cars could be more densely packed. Moreover, before 1960 London planners fretted that open-deck car parks might pose a fire risk.

In this context, it is not surprising to find that the first MSCP to be built in London since the 1930s was something of a throwback. This was the 800-space Lex Selfridge Garage (1958–60) on Duke Street: a partnership between Selfridge's and Lex Garages.[18] London department stores had provided parking for customers before the war, but the scale of this new venture may have been influenced by more modern American garage-and-store combinations, such as ZCMI, which had built a car park beside its store in Salt Lake City in 1954. The architects of the Lex Selfridge Garage were Sydney Clough, Son & Partners, but its curtain walling, fitted with blue and grey opaque glass, was designed by Duke & Simpson (pl. 238). Inside, above a basement marshalling yard and ground-floor service station, were seven parking floors, with points of access to the store. This was a traditional garage, with long two-way ramps and attendant parking assisted by turntables, rather like the thirty-year-old Lex Garage on Brewer Street (see pl. 218). Differently sized spaces were created, with a new electrical device to determine the dimensions of a car, to calculate the appropriate charge. Like its pre-war predecessors, this garage had glazed sides, with a heated, ventilated interior. Rather than being available for parking, the flat roof carried the extractor fans.

A tentative step forward was taken by the Audley Square Garage in Mayfair (1961; Shingler & Risdon; pl. 240), which could be adapted to either customer parking (270 spaces) or attendant parking (350 spaces). The lower floors were accessed by ramps, the upper floors by lifts.[19] The elevations were semi-glazed, with bands of louvred glass ventilators alternating with centrally pivoting windows, and so the interior still required mechanical ventilation. A year later the Great Eastern Street Car Park (1962–3; Oscar Garry & Partners; pl. 241) was built on a triangular site in Shoreditch.[20] Although open-sided, this was one

baldly in 1946 that 'private enterprise unaided has not found it possible to provide car parking on the required scale on an economic basis'.[16]

Parking garages of the 1960s and 1970s included underground car parks, mechanical car parks, rooftop car parks, basement car parks and American-style open-deck MSCPs, which could opt for level floors, staggered floors, warped floors or continuously ramped floors (see below, for a description and discussion of each type). Stand-alone car parks were still being built, but, to a much greater extent than before the war, many achieved commercial viability through physical integration with other categories of development, such as shopping centres, hotels and transport hubs. In these multifarious guises, car parks were to play a prominent role in the post-war transformation of urban centres.

The Arrival of the Open-deck MSCP

When Britain was ready to resume the construction of MSCPs, architects and planners looked abroad for ideas. Great changes had taken place since 1939. The U.S.A. now preferred self-parking to attendant-parking systems, and had developed the open-deck car park. This was made possible by improvements in the design of cars, making exposure to the elements feasible.

238 In 1958–60, Selfridge's, the London department store, provided one of the first – and in many ways one of the most old-fashioned – multi-storey car parks to be built in England after the Second World War. Like pre-war car parks, it had glazed elevations.

of the last MSCPs in the country to be built with a traditional car lift, albeit one operated by the driver rather than an attendant. Contemporary with this was the car park of Keddie's department store in Southend, Essex, by Yorke, Rosenberg & Mardall, which occupied two levels of a podium, sandwiched between the store and an eight-storey office slab.[21] This, too, was

239 This functional Coventry car park, on the right, built in 1959–60, was one of the very first open-deck examples in Britain. It was linked with the car park on the roof of the circular Market Hall, shown on the left. Around 2008 it was replaced by a warped-slab car park, visible in pl. 270.

served by conventional car lifts, but these were operated rather laboriously by attendants, who drew the cars out of the lifts onto trolleys on rails, and thence into parking spaces, arranged two bays deep to either side of the tracks. The future, however, lay with ramps.

The first open-deck car parks in London included the 'Fram-park' on Aldersgate Street (1961; Oscar Garry & Partners),[22] with balustrading prefabricated by the Fram Reinforced Concrete Co., and a car park on Upper Thames Street (1962, by the City Engineer Francis J. Forty), both now demolished.[23] Outside London a handful of new car parks – including a scheme for Moor Street, Birmingham (1955), and a building erected on Princesshay in Exeter (*circa* 1959) – were designed with glazing.[24] On the whole, open decks and exposed rooftop parking were embraced earlier, and more wholeheartedly, than in the capital. The first car park of this type to be completed in England appears to have been that serving the Lower Precinct in Coventry (1959–60, demolished; pl. 239). It was uniquely adapted to a backland site, with a service road running through its centre and a first-floor link to another car park, on the roof of the adjacent Market Hall (1958; see pl. 270). This was all part of City Architect Arthur Ling's plan for the new, heavily integrated, city centre. That it was not wholly successful is indicated by an observation made of the Coventry car park a decade later: 'cars have the better deal . . . people have to make their way across a tarmac wilderness, windswept and graceless. The car–pedestrian interface is still largely unexplored.'[25] The structure of this car park had a daringly simple concrete portal frame, with level floors, a straight ramp and free-standing staircases.[26] Within a few years, this had become the norm and such bleak structures no longer appeared alien.

At first, large town-centre MSCPs were objects of local pride. Thus 'the commencement of the construction of the first multi-storey car park in the city of Leeds', at the Merrion Centre (Gillinson, Barnett & Partners), was commemorated by a plaque, laid by the Lord Mayor on 4 April 1963. One particular reason for the populace of Leeds to celebrate was the fact that, with 1,100 spaces, this was the largest public car park in the U.K. The record was, of course, soon broken, as British cities embraced the MSCP with competitive zeal.

•

240 This car park by Shingler & Risdon was built on Audley Square, Mayfair, in 1961. Strips of louvred glass ventilators alternated with windows to light and ventilate the parking areas.

241 The open-deck Great Eastern Street Car Park (1962–3) in Shoreditch, London, adopted the 'Meyers Brothers Parking System' (note the lettering), with a car lift rather than ramps.

The Open-deck MSCP:
Construction Materials and Style

The preferred material for post-war car parks was concrete, either precast or poured *in situ*, which deals better than steel with heavy and differential loadings, and reduces the risk of fire. Available and affordable precast systems included 'Bison', 'Unipark' and 'Truspan'. Holst's 'Ribspan', developed primarily for car parks, was a fast way of erecting long spans *in situ* with a semi-automatic shuttering system. The 'lift-slab' system, introduced by British Lift Slab Ltd in Birmingham, had been developed in 1947 in Texas for speed and economy: floor slabs were cast on the ground floor and then raised by hydraulic jacks.[27] Whichever

system was adopted, the design of the concrete frame was contrived to reduce, as far as possible, the occurrence of structural supports between cars. At Nelson Street in Bristol (1962; see pl. 252), the outer parking rows were column-free since the supports were positioned on the elevations.[28] At Allhallows in Bedford (1961; F. W. Dawkes; pl. 242),[29] mushroom columns at 17-foot spacings carried shuttered concrete *in situ* floor slabs: this technology was not new, but in car parks it dispensed with the need for downstand beams, which could be such an oppressive feature of interior spaces, for example, at the Merrion Centre in Leeds. For many years, the use of structural steel was largely restricted to mechanical car parks and temporary parking structures, such as the Braithwaite 'Tempark' erected on Canal Street,

242   Allhallows Car Park, Bedford, was built in 1961. Typically, the interior was utterly functional. This view shows the mushroom construction and shuttered concrete floors.

243   The long façade of the Mount Pleasant Car Park, Liverpool, built in 1972–4, is arranged en echelon, but still dominates the streetscape.

Nottingham (1965; F. M. Little), and the 'Wheelwright Arch' on Summer Row, Birmingham (1964; designed by John Smith and built by John Lysaght of Bristol), both regarded as demountable, and both now demolished.[30] Naturally, steel car parks had concrete decks, with exposed slopes being electrically heated to prevent ice forming.

While engineers developed cheap, quick ways to erect parking structures, the principal challenge for planners and architects was to integrate car parks with the built environment, both functionally and aesthetically. The environment in question was not always historic, since many town centres were in the throes of 'comprehensive redevelopment'. Under such circumstances, the modernist ethos – eschewing artifice and demanding that form follow function – was seldom challenged. New car parks ignored older neighbours, though a keen awareness of skylines often led to restrictions on their heights. Some, however, did display some sensitivity to their surroundings. In 1964, for example, the Borough Architects in Guildford were required to screen the side of a car park facing Holy Trinity Church in solid brickwork, with lattice-pattern openings.[31] In general, materials were deployed to draw an appropriate distinction between spaces used exclusively by people and those occupied by cars. The contrast, usually between brick and concrete, signalled the layout of a car park to users at a glance (see pl. 253).

Aesthetically, the most distinctive features of the MSCPs of the 1960s and '70s were their horizontal balustrades, which were attached to the edges of the concrete floor slabs (pl. 245). Inter-

nally, for safety, these were supplemented by fenders. Balustrades could be of steel, brick or wired glass, but were usually of concrete, a material that inevitably streaked grey and spalled over the years, with the result that many have subsequently been patched, painted or clad. Concrete balustrades could be treated decoratively, not just to add visual interest, but also to disguise discolouration and reduce the perceived scale of a structure. Some were simply angled or chamfered, but the surface could be cast with a texture. In the early to mid-1960s aggregate panels (with granite or cobbles) enjoyed a widespread fashion, but by the mid-1970s dark red or brown brick facings in stretcher bond had become ubiquitous.

Some parking decks were fully screened (pl. 246). Vertical aluminium fins were first used for wind resistance on mechanical car parks (see below, pl. 265), but before long precast concrete or metal fins, or box louvres, were being applied to the elevations of conventional car parks in perfectly sheltered situations, simply to subdue their extreme horizontality, or disguise sloping floors. Patterned concrete blocks often concealed parking floors in composite developments. The most striking screens had diamond-shaped units, as at the Unicorn Hotel in Bristol (1963–6, see below) and the Yield Hall in Reading (1967).[32] Another way to relieve the tedium of long elevations was to arrange façades en echelon, or in sawtooth formation (pl. 243).

Stylistically, the most robustly Modern, or Brutalist, car parks were those designed by Owen Luder and his partner Rodney Gordon as part of monolithic shopping complexes: the Tricorn

Centre in Portsmouth (1962–6) and Trinity Square in Gateshead (1962–9; pl. 244), both demolished. In designing the 'heavily chamfered parking trays' of these towering structures, Luder and his team may have been influenced by the Temple Street Car Park in New Haven, Connecticut (1962; Paul Rudolph), although this feature was anticipated in their own work, in the canopy of Eros House (1962) at Catford in south London. Such flair and international influence recurred only occasionally, notably in the car park over Preston Bus Station (see below).

Most post-war MSCPs adhered somewhat more tamely to the tenets of modernism. By the mid-1970s, however, the age of comprehensive redevelopment was over; the conservation movement was gaining momentum; and some effort was being made, generally through the adoption of brick cladding and the application of superficial stylistic touches, to integrate new car parks with their surroundings. With the advent of postmodernism around 1980, this often assumed the form of generic giant arcad-

ing, as at the Moorfields Car Park in Liverpool (pl. 247). Some historic referencing, however, was more site-specific. Increasingly, car park architects plucked motifs from local vernacular building stock, incorporating gables (pl. 248), turrets, pitched roofs and mock framing into their designs, tricks that would have been abhorred by their modernist predecessors. An early example of this is the car park serving the Coppergate Centre in York (1984; Chapman Taylor & Partners). Set alongside warehousing on the banks of the River Fosse, this was an exercise in industrial vernacular. Very different versions of historical allusion include Birds Portchmouth Russum's Avenue de Chartres Car Park in Chichester (1991; pl. 249), representing a fictional extension of the ancient city walls, and the retro Ocean Village Car Park in Southampton (2006–7; Tiger Stripe Architects). This indulges in nostalgia for England's seaside heyday, with moderne curves to its spiral ramps and pedestrian staircase, reminiscent of the 1930s Daimler Hire Garage.

244   Owen Luder's Trinity Square Car Park towered over central Gateshead from its completion in 1969 until its demolition in 2010. It featured famously in the film *Get Carter* (1971), starring Michael Caine, and was crowned by a café that never opened to the public.

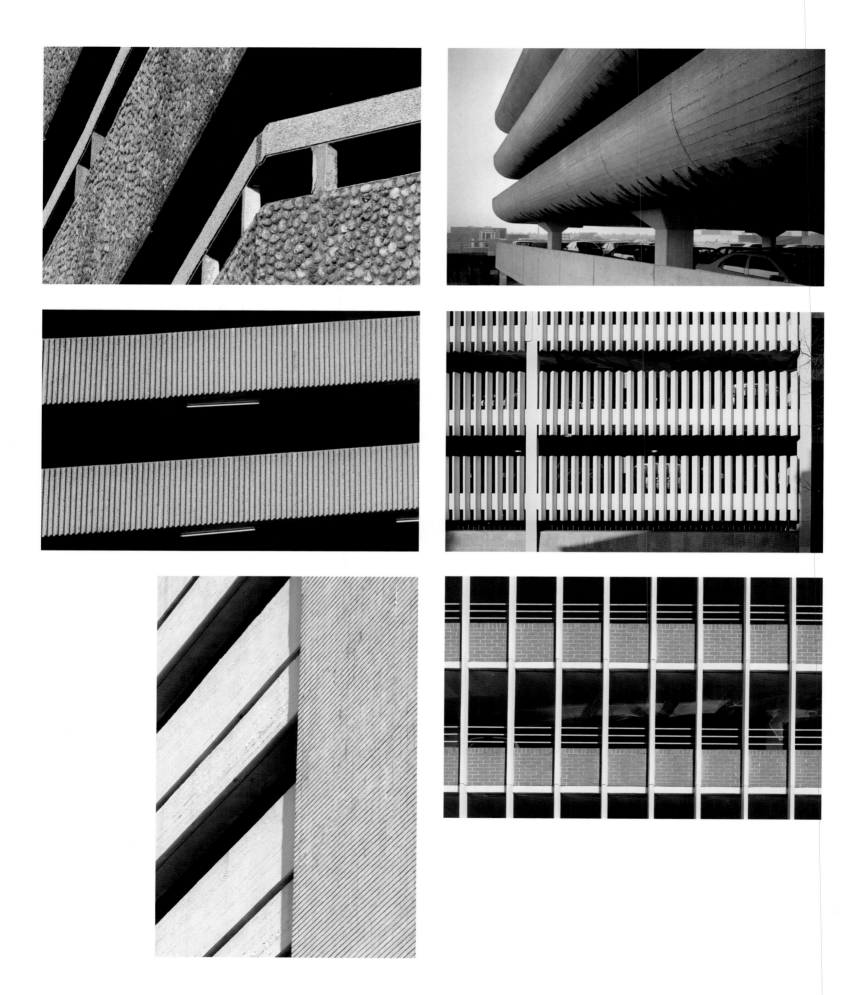

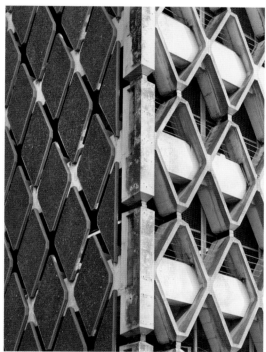

245 (*facing page*) A selection of car park balustrades from the 1960s and 1970s:

a (*top left*) Matilda Way/Eyre Street, Sheffield (*circa* 1965), with a cobbled aggregate

b (*centre left*) Maid Marian Way/Friar Street, Nottingham (1967–8), with a ribbed texture

c (*bottom left*) Cole Brothers, Sheffield (1963), with shuttered concrete

d (*top right*) Tricorn Centre, Portsmouth (1962–6, demolished), concrete with an upward sweep

e (*centre right*) Park Street, Cambridge (1962–4), with concrete fins

f (*bottom right*) Bridge Street, Welwyn Garden City (1970–73), with brick facings

246 (*above*) Car park screen façades of the 1960s and 1970s:

a (*top left*) Grosvenor Hotel Car Park, Sheffield (1967), with patterned concrete blocks

b (*top right*) Grafton Car Park, Marine Parade, Worthing (*circa* 1970), with precast openings

c (*bottom left*) Unicorn Hotel Car Park, Bristol (1963–6), with diamond units

d (*bottom centre*) Welbeck Street, London (1968–70), with triangular units

e (*bottom right*) Young Street, London (1968–70), with asbestos louvres

247 Giant arcading was commonly applied to car parks in the 1980s and 1990s: this example is Moorfields Car Park in Liverpool. Visible in the background is the art installation *Turning the Place Over* (2007) by Richard Wilson.

248 The neo-vernacular Whitefriars Car Park, Watling Street, Canterbury (2004), located close to Canterbury Cathedral, replaced an uncompromising and controversial 1960s car park.

249   The Avenue de Chartres Car Park in Chichester (1991) was conceived as a new city wall, carrying a tree-lined walkway and punctuated by colourfully lit towers.

The urban, neo-modern MSCP of the new millennium usually conceals the horizontality of its parking floors with a textured screen, and is colourfully lit at night. Historical referencing is less persistent than it once was, and there is a strong fashion for sleek metal cladding, often with steel-mesh screening (an early example serving The Oracle, Reading, 1999) or fragmented frontages (for example, the Charles Street Car Park, Sheffield, 2008; pl. 250). A slightly softer effect is created by framing metal screens with warm materials such as brickwork, reconstituted stone, or red terracotta tiles laid in stack bond, as at the St James's Car Park in King's Lynn (2005). Another contemporary option is timber – often cedar – cladding (as at St Paul's Place, Liverpool, 2009).

Despite their dominance of public space, few post-war car parks incorporated artworks. Indeed, colour was generally lacking from these buildings, except for functional signage. Occasionally, bold lettering was cast into concrete ('Lift' at Temple Gate, Bristol; 'Car Park' on Pydar Street, Truro).[33] One of the best examples of decoration cast into the structural elements of

a car park is Abbey Walk, Grimsby (1969; pl. 251). Here, the local sculptor Harold Gosney made glass fibre shutters from plaster moulds, in which the reliefs were cast, while the contractor cast the edge beams with a weatherboarded effect.[34] A different approach to decoration can be seen on the side of the three-level Hillfield Road Car Park (1961; Fuller Hall & Fousham), erected over shops in Hemel Hempstead. This displayed a mosaic map, showing local attractions, by Rowland Emett.[35] Although many car parks possessed at least one blind façade, few were exploited artistically in this manner. Similarly, opportunities for landscaping were neglected, with a handful of exceptions. The simple row of plane trees planted as saplings along the frontage of Allhallows in Bedford in 1961 have grown so large that the car park is now all but concealed from sight. Perhaps this was the original intention.

•

250   The façades of Allies & Morrison's Charles Street Car Park in Sheffield (2008) are manufactured from folded aluminium panels hung in four different orientations, with the inside faces painted green. This metallic origami glows green at night.

251 Cast concrete reliefs decorate this car park on Abbey Walk, Grimsby (1969).

Self-park Floor Systems

Since the 1960s, when it came to choosing the form of a new car park, there have been two principal options: the staggered floor or the continuous parking ramp. An alternative, available since 1970, is the warped slab. Each of these systems is discussed below, but they coexisted with many atypical designs involving level floors. Dictated by its long, thin site, the car park on Gascoyne Way, Hertford (1969; W. A. Weeks), comprised four level parking floors, served by a helical access ramp at one end and a helical exit ramp at the other.[36] An example on a more generously proportioned site is Havana Road, Romford (1967; D. M. Rickard), where access and exit were via a two-way spiral ramp with a circular roof.[37] Larger still was Frederick Gibberd's car park at London Airport, Heathrow (1963, now Terminal 1a), which had long, straight ramps.

Although several staggered-floor car parks had been built in the 1920s and '30s (see Chapter 6), developers had harboured reservations about them, since they could not be converted to

new uses when they were no longer required for parking. Motorists, however, found them easy to use, and a great many were built in the 1960s. One of the earliest to be completed after the war was the Hughes Garage on Princesshay, Exeter (*circa* 1959; Redfern & Gilpin; demolished). By 1963 several others had opened, for example, in Bedford, Bristol, Cambridge, Croydon, Leeds, Liverpool, London and Shrewsbury.

As at Allhallows in Bedford, many staggered-floor car parks were perfectly regular boxes, with identical rows of parking spaces flanking a single aisle on each level, and one, two or three sets of ramps, depending on their length, permitting separate up and down circulation systems. The existing urban street layout was often regimented, or even obliterated, to accommodate these structures. Car parks, however, could follow the contour of an existing road, as demonstrated by a MSCP that curved along the east side of Dingwall Road in Croydon (1969; H. M. Collins).[38] Similarly, the two sides (or 'bins') of a staggered-floor car park could adopt different footprints to fit awkwardly shaped sites, as at Nelson Street, Bristol (pl. 252). The asymmetrical staggered-floor car park quickly became the most common type of MSCP in England.

It was now usual, following pre-war precedents, for the ground floors of car parks to be devoted to shops, showrooms, a bus station or some other secondary function. In such car parks, instead of driving directly into a parking level from the street, drivers had to leapfrog ground-floor facilities by negotiating an access ramp, positioned either internally or externally. At the Unicorn Hotel, Bristol (1963–6; Kenneth Wakeford, Jerram & Harris; pl. 235), the parking levels over the hotel's reception rooms were reached by a curved internal ramp, whilst on the rear of Allhallows in Bedford, a more gentle external

252 The Nelson Street Car Park, which opened in June 1962, was one of several early MSCPs to be erected in Bristol.

211

253   The external access ramp of the Allhallows Car Park, Bedford (1961), is positioned on the rear elevation. The solid end wall of the building, with its per-functory decoration, disguises the staggered-floor system.

254   This aerial view shows the 1,000-space, triple-pile car park over the market in Chelmsford, Essex (1970). A similar combination of car park and market hall can be found in many other English towns, such as Birmingham, Luton and Stevenage.

255 The Multidek on Rupert Street in Bristol (1960), with its distinctive cantilevered parking floors, was one of the first open-deck MSCPs to be completed after 1945, and may be the earliest of this type that is still in use.

256 The Auto-Magic Shopping Park (1960–61) in Leicester has been re-named Lee Circle Car Park. This aerial photograph of 2009 shows the double, or superimposed, ramp system and the internal stair towers. It also shows how the parking spaces on the upper level were roofed. At top left is the drive-in post office discussed in Chapter 13.

257 The structure above the Abbey Street Car Park, Leicester (1963–7), was the Abbey Motor Hotel, run by Thistle Hotels Ltd. The juxtaposition was somewhat ungainly.

ramp spanned the height of ground-floor storerooms, positioned behind shops (pl. 253). Internal access ramps could be daunting: that of the Merrion Centre Car Park in Leeds was heavily criticised when it first opened in 1963. A small payment kiosk and barrier at the top of such ramps generally marked the entrance to the car park proper. Entry was often quicker than exit, especially when staggered-floor car parks assumed a gigantic size (pl. 254), and since the mid-1960s car parks with more than 800 spaces have usually been provided with an 'express' (or 'clearway') ramp for rapid descent. At Woodhouse Lane, Leeds (1970; see pl. 273), for example, this took the form of a long, straight, external ramp.

While most post-war car parks adopted the staggered-floor system, many had a continuous parking ramp: something not seen before in England, although the concept had been published in pre-war journals.[39] In these ramped-floor garages, cars were parked on a gradient, flanking a central roadway. Like the staggered floor, the ramped floor met some initial resistance

because such garages were not easily adapted to alternative functions. It found favour, however, because it incorporated little unproductive space and was relatively inexpensive to build. The concrete surface of the ramp needed an inward camber, or crossfall, and its surface was always textured to ensure a good grip. Internationally, the first example had been designed by Albert Kahn for a garage in Detroit in 1922, and the form evidently fired the imagination of Frank Lloyd Wright when he was designing the Guggenheim Museum in New York (1956–9).[40]

The first continuous parking ramp in England, by the Multidek Development Group, was designed for a site on Rupert Street/Lewin Mead, Bristol, by the architect R. Jelinek-Karl and the engineers G. C. Mander & Partners (1960).[41] This elliptical structure of reinforced concrete, cast *in situ*, comprised a single ramp that rose steadily at a gentle gradient of 1:32 to make six circuits around an open well, with 540 parking spaces flanking the central two-way roadway (24 ft wide), which ran continuously for half a mile before stopping, as if in mid-air (pl. 255). Jelinek-Karl produced a similar design for a site on Walcot Street in Bath: this was reportedly 'under construction' in March 1960, but – as with a proposal published in 1962 for a circular parking ramp in Hemel Hempstead[42] – may never have got off the ground. Whilst the Bristol 'Multidek' had a corrugated asbestos roof (later removed), the Bath car park was planned to have an open top deck from the outset.[43] A much later circular car park of this type was built in the 1970s in Newcastle.

Multidek went on to erect two elliptical car parks in Leicester, each with a dual function. The first was the Auto-Magic Shopping Park (now Lee Circle Car Park; 1960–61; Fitzroy Robinson & Partners; pl. 256), which owed its name to a car wash and a Tesco supermarket on the ground floor. This was similar to the Bristol Multidek, but on a double (or superimposed) ramp system, with each ramp giving access to different levels and curving round the ends of the building. Multidek's car park on Abbey Street (1963–7; pls 257 and 258) took longer to complete, possibly because, as well as being built over a garage and shops, there was a two-storey 'panorama' hotel and restaurant on the roof. Here, the lift and stair towers were positioned on the exterior, rather than within the central well. Multidek went on to develop another continuous ramp car park, in Kingston upon Hull (1966; Gelder & Kitchen). This was elliptical at one end, but had a long rectangular tail at the other, fitting the shape of the site.[44] Vertical fins were fixed to the end elevations, presumably to disguise the sloping floors. Similar car parks can be seen on Maid Marian Way, Nottingham, and on Glen Fern Road, Bournemouth.

Towns developed preferences for particular car park types, and Bournemouth clearly favoured continuous ramps. The striking Roundhouse Hotel at Lansdowne Cross (1967–9; see pl. 348) may have been inspired by the Abbey Motor Hotel in Leicester.

258   This interior view of the Abbey Street Car Park, Leicester, shows the continuous parking ramp with its ridged surface.

259   A 1960s advertisement for Lift Slab Construction featuring Austin's car park at Longbridge (demolished), which could hold 3,300 cars.

260 The 500-space Crowell Road Car Park (now known as Castle Car Park) was the second built to serve the new Cowley Centre in south Oxford It. was designed with superimposed parking ramps, with cross-overs, by the City Architect, D. Murray, and built in 1963–5. Note the bridge to the shops.

261 A helical exit ramp serving the Church Street Car Park (1966) in Watford, Hertfordshire.

This cylindrical building, designed by Jelinek-Karl for Dekotel Ltd, included parking on the first and second floors, sandwiched between the restaurant (ground floor) and function rooms (third floor). Another Dekotel development was The Thistle Hotel (now Strathallan Hotel, 1970–71; Duke, Simpson & MacDonald), Hagley Road, Edgbaston. Again cylindrical, this had honeycomb-screened parking on the first to third floors, beneath four storeys of hotel rooms.[45] The concept of these parking hotels (though neither their scale nor execution) evokes American 'skyscraper' hotels, or even Marina City Towers ('The Corncobs') in Chicago (1962; Bertrand Goldberg Associates). The parking ramps in this pair of cylindrical apartment blocks rose through seventeen of their sixty-five storeys. Marina City Towers have been described as 'simply the most extreme piece of parking engineering'.[46] Their English equivalents are undeniably (and, perhaps, thankfully) meek in comparison.

The rectangular parking ramp had greater longevity than its helical or elliptical counterparts, remaining popular throughout the 1960s and 1970s. One of the first and, it was claimed, the world's largest, was built at the south end of CAB1 at Longbridge (1961; Harry Weedon & Partners; demolished) for the storage of 3,300 new cars (pl. 259).[47] It was constructed quickly, using lift-slab technology. Many considerations affecting public car parks did not apply at Longbridge, where the building could rise higher than normal without testing the patience of paying customers or invoking planning restrictions.

One of the first rectilinear continuous-ramp car parks to be built by a local authority was the Hockmore Street Car Park (1960–62), serving the Cowley Centre, a new shopping precinct in south Oxford. This had a single two-way ramp, cast *in situ*. By the mid-1960s this type of car park had become quite common, with examples in operation in Bristol, Guildford, Nottingham and elsewhere. Various strategies were developed to disguise sloping floors on prominent elevations: fins were the default solution, but at the Cole Bros. (now John Lewis) Car Park in Sheffield (1963; Yorke, Rosenberg & Mardall), the elevations were camouflaged by white ceramic tile panels. Planners sought to reduce the long and tedious descent faced by drivers in such car parks. The Crowell Road Car Park at Cowley was built in the years 1963–5 with double (or superimposed) ramps, providing a one-way system, with odd floors providing the ramp up and even floors the ramp down, and with connecting floors running through a square well in the centre of the building, enabling drivers to switch easily from one parking ramp to the other (pl. 260). Another improvement to this type of car park was the express exit ramp. On Broadway, Maidenhead (1968–9),[48] a spiral exit ramp was recessed within the footprint of the building and treated boldly with a smooth concrete finish. At King William Street, Exeter (1969; John Brierley, with Vinton Hall), this was positioned on a corner and screened by vertical fins.

The Shrubbery Car Park in Watford (1965; F. Sage) had an exit ramp projecting from the centre of one side. Here, rather than maintaining a consistent gradient from ground level to roof, two-thirds of each level was flat, and the remainder ramped.[49] Three other car parks of the same type were built in Watford, with ramped floors and helical ramps, illustrating how the preferences of local authority engineers and architects, and their relationship with a particular contractor (in this case Holst), could create a local style of MSCP (pl. 261).[50]

The warped-slab car park was first proposed by the American engineer E. M. Khoury around 1960.[51] To create a warped slab, a level parking floor was split along its axis (pl. 263): whilst its periphery remained level, to one side of the central split the floor was depressed (giving access to the floor below), and on the other side it was elevated (giving access to the floor above). Only short ramps were required. Furthermore, because the periphery was level, these car parks had regular elevations: this was their chief appeal. In terms of construction, the warped slab is erected by the lift slab process, with floors and roofs being cast at ground level around the columns and then jacked up. The first warped-slab car park in the U.K. was built on Birmingham Road, Lichfield (1969–70; D. E. Lawrence), soon followed by the Bridge Street Car Park in Welwyn Garden City (1970–73; pl. 262).[52] A more recent example is the Luton Airport Parkway Car Park (1999; Devereux Architects) and Coventry Corporation Street (2008; Michael Aukett Architects; see pl. 270).

Mechanical Parking

In 1945 the Minister for Town and Country Planning, Lewis Silkin, began to investigate mechanical parking systems that would reduce unproductive floor area in garages. While attempting not to express bias in favour of any particular patent,[53] Silkin was evidently swayed by the Baldwin-Auger System, with its auto-actuated floors.[54] The paternoster or ferris-wheel system was still available, with a recent variant being the 'Storinair' garage available from the Weldall & Assembly Co.[55] Another option was the 'Rotapark', a cylindrical car park with a central bank of four lifts associated with turntables: in 1956 a garage of this type, by Shingler & Risden, was proposed for a site on Upper Thames Street in London, but never built.[56]

Models of these various systems continued to draw attention throughout the 1950s and early 1960s. Despite meeting Silkin's approval, only one garage with an auto-actuated floor seems to have been installed in England: the Carpack, a British system manufactured by Fuller Electric Ltd, erected at Bow Bells House on Bread Street in the City of London.[57] Similarly, the paternoster principle was rarely adopted, with the exception of the Butterley Wulpa Liftpark, manufactured at Ripley in Derby-

262   This view of the upper levels of the warped-slab car park on Bridge Street in Welwyn Garden City, Hertfordshire (1970–73), shows the buckled form of the concrete floors.

263   This diagram shows how the so-called warped-slab car park worked. Each floor was warped towards the centre of the building, either dipping down or banking up to meet other floors. The chief appeal lay in its regular elevations.

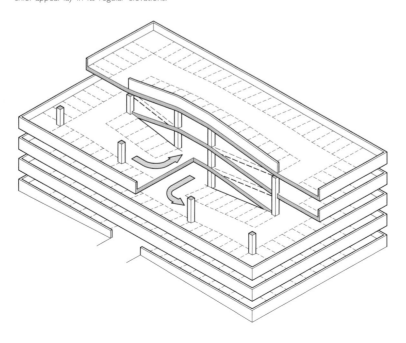

shire.[58] This was a rectangular steel tower containing twenty cabins suspended between two heavy chains that were driven by an electric motor. Each cabin could hold a single car, which was driven in at ground level. A handful of these were erected in the 1960s, including one serving a new office development at 36–41 South Norwood High Street in south London (1963). Others appear to have been installed at a couple of service stations, and there was a demonstration model at Ripley itself. The Chamberlain Keypark at Ashby de la Zouch, Leicestershire, advertised in 1965, also assumed the form of a vertical tower, but used lifts rather than the paternoster system.[59] Another unusual option was the simple car stacker, with hydraulically controlled platforms that enabled one car to park on top of another. This developed from an invention dating from 1925, and featured in a Mechanical Handling Exhibition held in London in 1956. Variations produced in the 1950s and 1960s included Sky-Park, Astrolift and Dubl Park. Although auto-stackers were rarely used for public parking in England, Harrods is known to have installed two units of the Space-O-Matic in its car park on Brompton Place.[60]

In the event, most of the mechanical public parking garages built in England before 1970 were variants on the 'pigeon-hole' type, in which cars were transported to vertically stacked storage bays by lifts. This was the most popular type in the U.S.A., too, where the commonest systems were the Pigeon Hole (first example built in the late 1940s in Spokane, Washington; fifty existed by 1957) and the Bowser (first example built in 1951 in Des Moines, Iowa; fourteen existed by 1956). By the late 1950s America was awash with smartly named mechanical systems, such as the Park-O-Mat, Park-A-Loft, MinitPark, File-A-Way, LektroPark, Electromatic Autopark and Vert-A-Park.[61]

The first mechanical – or, rather, semi-mechanical – garage to be built in England was the Pearce Autopark at 11–19 Cornwall Street, Birmingham (1955–7; T. M. Ashford; demolished).[62] This backed onto the Great Charles Street service station of its builder, R. S. Pearce, who firmly believed that the provision of parking garages should be left to the private sector. The Autopark was a very basic rectangular structure: little more than a concrete box with aluminium cladding. It was traversed in one direction by a trolley runway, and in the other by car lifts in fixed cages. Each quadrant contained two parking bays, each capable of holding six cars. Vehicles were manhandled from an entrance bay to the lift, from the lift to a trolley, and from the trolley into a stall, hence the soubriquet 'semi-mechanical'. Like Keddie's car park, mentioned above, this was a heavily staffed operation. It was only in 1961, however, that the first fully mechanical garage, with all operations carried out from a push-button control point, opened in the U.S.A.: this was the Speed-Park at Columbia University, New York.

A model of a Zidpark – a more automated version of 'pigeon-hole' parking than the Pearce Autopark – was demonstrated in London in 1956. Invented by André Thaon de Saint-André, this had operated successfully at Karlsruhe since 1955.[63] It involved a fixed-lift cage: by push-button control, cars were raised parallel to parking stalls and were moved sideways (for parking or collection) on roller conveyors. In February 1957 it was announced that a prototype was to be erected at Southall by Taylor Woodrow Ltd for staff vehicles.[64] The outcome was presumably positive, and before long 'Britain's first automatic car park' was being planned on the Zidpark principle (though it was sometimes erroneously referred to as an 'Autosilo', which parked forwards rather than sideways) for a site on Upper Thames Street, by Southwark Bridge in London: the very site that had previously been earmarked for a Rotapark.[65] This seven-storey box, with fins of plastic-coated steel ('Stelvetite') bolted to the frame, was designed by the architects C. Edmund Wilford & Son, and erected in 1960–61 by Taylor Woodrow's subsidiary Myton Ltd.[66] The structure was traversed by four entrance passages, each with four lifts along one side (pl. 264). It could hold 464 cars: a number that would have been greater had a higher building been permitted, but the view of St Paul's Cathedral was protected by the planning authorities.

264   Operating a lift in the Zidpark, a mechanical car park built on Upper Thames Street, London, in 1961. This experienced teething troubles in its early days. Like most mechanical car parks of the 1960s, it has been demolished.

In 1958 Woolwich Council's engineer, W. H. Gimson, began to prepare alternative schemes for a 500-car parking garage. The Council, taking its cue from Westminster, planned to introduce parking meters as soon as this garage opened. Gimson is known to have visited a 'semi-mechanised' facility in Birmingham, presumably the Pearce Autopark. Subsequently, the Parking Research Co., with T. & P. Braddock as architects, worked up a scheme to patent designs by Auto-Stackers Ltd. The Stirling Auto-Stacker, built on Beresford Street in 1960–61, claimed (as, indeed, did the Zidpark) to be the first mechanised car park in the country, and the first municipal car park in the country to boot, though this was clearly mistaken (see Chapter 6). The mechanism, however, did not function properly at the opening, by Princess Margaret, on 11 May 1961: the demonstration vehicle got stuck and had to be manhandled. This was not a mere teething trouble, and the Autostacker soon proved its unreliability. It was reportedly never used by the public; the Council refused to certify payments to the contractor, and the structure was demolished circa 1965–6. This was not an isolated experience. The Bull Ring Car Park in Birmingham, designed by Sydney Greenwood, opened on 4 November 1963 but never worked properly. It languished, disused, for many years before its demolition circa 2003. These fiascos may explain why mechanical schemes proposed for some other provincial centres, including Bristol and Liverpool, were eventually abandoned.[67] London, however, persevered for several years.

Parcar – a subsidiary of Mitchell Engineering Ltd and the Unit Construction Company Ltd – specialised in car parks of all control cabin flanked by cradles for cars. The machine platform for each lift travelled on guide rails at the top of the shaft. Originally, cars were transported on and off the lifts by dollies (like pallets), but these were discontinued, reportedly following an accident. Lobb's designs for the Parcar on Houndsditch were superseded by a fifteen-storey structure by R. Seifert Partners (1964–6; demolished).[70] The system resembled Shoe Lane: a central well held three lifts manufactured by Mitchell's, each capable of vertical and horizontal travel and able to transport two cars at one time.

Another option was the Autosilo (later known as the Auto-Silo Park). This had been designed by a Swiss engineer, Edouardo G. Bianca, in 1949, with the first example being built in Stuttgart in 1955. In the 1960s three Auto-Silo Parks were erected in England: in London on Old Burlington Street (1962–5) and Rochester Row (1965–8), both by Howard V. Lobb & Partners, and in Leeds on Greek Street (1968–70; Maurice Sanders Associates).[71] The operation at Rochester Row was slightly different from the other two, since it had a moving elevator rather than a stationary lift with traversing cross-carriages. Only the Greek Street car park survives, and is still (in 2012) fully operational.

The Greek Street car park was erected at a cost of £200,000 by Leeds Corporation (pl. 265).[72] It opened to contract parkers, mostly workers in nearby office blocks, on 1 April 1970.[73] The ground floor is taken up by four entrance bays (on Russell Street) and four exit bays (on Greek Street), to either side of the lift shaft, which occupies the centre of the building for its full length and height. Upon arrival, customers are given a unique number, which is used as a reference for retrieval. Cars are driven into one of four entrance bays: A and B being wider than C and D. Signage instructs drivers to 'come forward slowly'. Once the driver has left a vehicle, it is straightened by a centring device, with rollers under the front wheels. Next, a dolly is automatically propelled from the cross (or traversing) carriage on the hoist, underneath the car, which is lifted and whisked onto the hoist, ready to be raised and parked. There are two hoists, each with an operator's cab with push-button control in the centre, and a cross-carriage to either side, enabling two cars to be parked at once. Once a car is on a hoist, the entire platform is raised to a parking level (pl. 266). As it rises, the cross-carriages shuttle left or right, to align with potential spaces on the designated floor. The dolly shoots into the parking bay with the car, deposits it on wooden wedges that prevent it rocking in the wind, and returns to the hoist (pl. 267). Metal fenders were added to each parking bay following an accident in 1988, when an operator tried to park two cars in one bay, shunting one through the aluminium fins on the Russell Street façade, leaving it dangling in mid-air, to the mirth of the national media.

Although mechanical solutions for public parking were abandoned in England in the last quarter of the twentieth century,

265   The side elevation of the Greek Street Car Park, Leeds (1968–70), shows the rooftop plant room positioned over the central lifts. The main façades are clad in slender hollow aluminium fins (attached to the edges of the concrete floors at 2ft centres), which act as a windbreak.

types, whether mechanical or ramped. In the late 1950s, working with the architects Howard V. Lobb & Partners and Mitchell's, Parcar developed two mechanical car parks for sites in London: one on Houndsditch,[68] near Aldgate Station, and the other on Shoe Lane, near Holborn Circus. In the event, only the Parcar on Shoe Lane (1960–63; demolished) was built to Lobb's design. This was twelve storeys high, with twelve parking stalls to either side of a central lift shaft on each of its long elevations.[69] The headroom inside the parking bays was only 5 feet 8 inches, compared with 8 feet in a self-park facility. The central shaft contained two lifts that moved horizontally as well as vertically (known as traversing and hoisting), and each comprised a central

266 A car being moved onto a hoist at the Greek Street Car Park, Leeds. This is the earliest and largest mechanical parking facility still operational in England.

they continued to be popular abroad, especially in the crowded cities of eastern Asia. More recently, there has been a renewal of interest in Great Britain. In 2001 the Autosafe Sky Park opened

on Morrison Street, Edinburgh, but it closed two years later when the operator went into receivership. This experience has probably discouraged other ventures. Since then, however, several small automated parking units have successfully provided private parking for new apartment and office blocks (see p. 103), and similar systems are being adapted for display towers at dealerships (see p. 71).

Underground Car Parks

The expensive underground (as distinguished from 'basement', with which it is often treated as synonymous) car park formed a cornerstone of the Comprehensive Parking Plan for London of March 1953.[74] By the late 1950s many examples existed abroad, especially in the U.S.A. In engineering terms, these were much more sophisticated than the rudimentary cut-and-cover examples created in Hastings and Blackpool in the 1930s (see Chapter 6). The Union Square Garage, San Francisco, had been constructed beneath a public park in 1942, with four levels connected by spiral ramps. Even bigger was the car park under Pershing Square, Los Angeles, which opened in 1953 with 2,150

267 A vertiginous view of the parking bays inside the Greek Street Car Park, Leeds.

spaces on three levels. By the 1960s underground parking could be found 'almost everywhere' in the U.S.A.[75]

In the early 1950s it was recommended that single-level garages for long-stay parking (i.e., three hours or more) in London be built under Grosvenor Square, Berkeley Square, Cavendish Square and St James's Square, to be followed by Soho Square, Leicester Square, Lincoln's Inn Fields, Finsbury Square and Portman Square, at a total estimated cost of £3,030,000.[76] Essentially, large holes would be dug, exit and entry ramps built, and the roofs would be planted with trees and grass. Attendants at the foot of the access ramps would park the cars. The first four garages, with a total capacity of 1,820 cars, would be built by the Ministry of Transport – partly funded by the Civil Defence Fund, since they could be transformed into shelters in the event of another war – then leased to the local authority, or a private concern.

In 1953 Grey Wornum & Partners designed an underground car park for St James's Square,[77] and in 1954 Sir Owen Williams & Partners, Messrs Bylander & Waddell and Sir William Halcrow & Partners produced plans and estimates for Grosvenor Square, Finsbury Square and Cavendish Square.[78] This was followed by inaction: the great cost had rendered these schemes impossible. When the project resurfaced a few years later, the economic model had changed: local authorities were taking the lead, sometimes in partnership with private enterprise. Of the nine London squares earmarked in the early 1950s, only two would ever receive an underground car park.

Throughout the 1960s and early 1970s the construction of underground car parks remained, primarily, a metropolitan phenomenon, though a handful went up (or, rather, down) elsewhere. As with the above-ground MSCP, various floor and ramp systems were adopted. The first was a simple car park beneath a new road (London Wall) in the City of London, begun in 1957 and opened in 1959 by the Duchess of Kent.[79] It was followed by the first underground car park to be created, after so much debate, beneath a London square. This project, in Finsbury Square, could not begin before the site was purchased from the Church Commissioners (for £50), and an Act of Parliament (the Finsbury Square Act, 1957) had been passed.[80] The scheme, developed by Lex Garages and Finsbury Borough Council with the architects Shingler & Risdon, opened in December 1961.[81] The single-level garage was accessed by ramps on the northern corners of the square, while separate exit ramps, protected by canopies, emerged beside filling stations on the east and west sides. The roof carried a cafeteria and playing fields. Interestingly, the air-raid shelters built in 1939 as a prelude to a car park (see p. 197) could not be incorporated into the design and had to be demolished.[82]

As Finsbury Square opened, work began on Westminster's Park Lane Garage, a much larger single-level car park lying beneath the north-east corner of Hyde Park. It was built in 1961–2 at the cost of £1 million, to designs by the City Engineer.[83] The vast interior was reached by access tunnels from north and east, and the roof was pierced by ninety shafts that could be opened by the fire brigade from above ground in the event of fire. Every tree over the garage had to be felled, but, since the structure lay well within Hyde Park, a row of mature trees could be preserved along the edge of Park Lane. A pedestrian subway, a daunting 400 yards long, led to Marble Arch and Oxford Street.

Occasional opportunities arose to create an underground car park relatively cheaply, by covering an existing void below ground level: an old gravel pit was treated in this way to form a car park under Fairfield Gardens in Croydon in 1963. Emulating London, car parks were excavated under squares in some provincial towns: that beneath Regency Square in Brighton (1968–9; F. N. B. Patterson) had three levels and a pedestrian subway to the beach. Even more ambitious, the first underground helical parking ramp in Britain was created on a cleared site, destined for a new Civic Centre, in Ipswich (1964–7; Vine & Vine; pl. 268).[84] This may have been inspired by a pre-war

268   The Spiral Underground Car Park at Ipswich Civic Centre is landscaped with a pool and a fountain, a 40-foot ventilation shaft clad in black granite, and a pedestrian terrace with precast concrete paving, flower containers and seats. A foundation plaque commemorates the opening of the car park by the mayor in 1967.

269 Plans had been afoot to provide a car park under Cavendish Square in central London since 1950. The Oxford Street Car Park (1968–70) has three annular levels and holds 510 cars.

proposal for a helical car park for Finsbury Square (see p. 197), or by the first Continental example, in Geneva. The interior had a clear span, with radial parking to either side of a two-way central aisle. The core contained a spiral pedestrian ramp and stairs. Just as work was beginning on the Ipswich car park, a double-helix parking ramp was being planned for Bloomsbury Square in London.[85] This was designed by Sydney Cook, Borough Architect of Holborn, together with the patent holders, Helical Car Parks Ltd, in consultation with the car park specialist Sydney Clough, but it was not actually built until 1972. The choice of this design for a London square meant that mature trees could be preserved around the periphery. The double parking ramp provided a one-way system with crossover points, winding around a central core containing stairs and a lift, while the outer 'diaphragm' walls were surrounded by six ventilation shafts.

London's underground car parks adopted varied designs. The Abingdon Street Garage close to the Houses of Parliament (1963–4) comprised two levels connected by a curved ramp. The Oxford Street Car Park (1968–70) in Cavendish Square had three levels connected by ramps. The doughnut-shaped parking floors encircled a solid core, with pedestrian stairs placed at three points on the periphery (pl. 269). The underground car park at New Palace Yard, outside the House of Commons, provided 500 spaces for MPs' cars on a combination of level and ramped parking floors. At the time, in 1972–3, the enormous cost sparked controversy, and some alarm was expressed about the impact of the excavations on the foundations of Westminster Hall and Big Ben.

As with mechanical car parks, appetite for underground car parks had faded by the mid-1970s. Perhaps this was due to their huge cost (£1,850 per space at Cavendish Square); perhaps because of the wearying length of time needed to steer a development from conception to completion; or perhaps because of public protest at the loss of trees and amenities. More recently, with developments such as Millennium Square in Bristol, there has been a renewed interest in underground car parks, possibly inspired by successful foreign examples, such as the Parc des Célestins in Lyons.[86]

Rooftop Parking

One particularly interesting innovation, seized upon by municipal planners, was rooftop parking, meaning uncovered parking on top of shops, market halls and other types of building. This had been implemented in North America for decades: the Seattle Public Market offered rooftop parking in 1930.[87] More recent European examples included a store in Hamburg.[88] In England, however, this remained uncommon until the late 1950s. While it was relatively easy to access car park roofs by driving up from level to level, roofs over other buildings required either very long straight ramps or helical ramps, depending on the size and configuration of the individual site.

Truscon is said to have constructed a building in Wolverhampton with an open roof for parking by 1957, but it was in Coventry that rooftop parking was adopted most extensively.[89] In the mid-1950s Arthur Ling, the City Architect, and Granville Berry, the City Engineer and Surveyor, designed a combination of multi-storey and rooftop car parks to serve Coventry's new city centre. Much of this had been completed by 1960. The roof of the circular Market Hall (1957; Douglas Beaton, Ralph Iredale

270 Coventry explored the possibilities of rooftop parking like no other British city. This shows the car park on the roof of the circular Market Hall (275ft diameter), which is linked (top) to parking on the interconnected roofs of shops in the adjacent pedestrian precinct, and (bottom) to a new multi-storey car park (2008) of warped-slab construction. This replaced the car park in pl. 239.

and Ian Crawford; pl. 270) was reached by a curved ramp, and was connected to car parks on the roofs of other retail buildings by aerial roads that spanned the pedestrian precinct. This was described in 1965 as 'virtually a secondary road system'.[90] The exposed ramps, as was now normal, were fitted with electrically heated panels that would come into automatic operation if ice formed.

Rooftop parking over shops was adopted in new towns, in centres that were rebuilt following bomb damage, and in those affected by comprehensive development, notably in Blackburn. Aerial roadways connecting rooftop car parks – or even car park rooftops – also made an appearance, for example in Luton, where a roadway joined the roofs of the Arndale Centre and Library car parks. Today, Basingstoke provides one of the most extensive areas of rooftop parking in the country (see pl. 419).

●

Urban Integration

A persistent theme throughout this chapter has been the considerable effort made in post-war rebuilding programmes to integrate parking with town centre amenities, especially department stores, precincts, malls and market halls, on the park-and-shop principle. Parking, however, was built into many other types of complex, including offices, apartment blocks, hotels, leisure facilities, transport hubs and even churches. One of the more surprising examples is the car park beneath Frederick Gibberd's Liverpool Metropolitan Cathedral (1962–7), forming an extension of Lutyens's pre-war crypt. Equally unusual, however, was the open-air car park created on the roof of the Roman Catholic church in Brixham, Devon, in 1967. Integrated parking was not entirely novel, but it became a very prominent aspect of many developments in the 1960s, resulting in architectural solutions that looked like nothing built previously in English towns and cities.

In urban retail complexes, a MSCP was often situated alongside shops, clearly defined and instantly recognisable. The Merrion Centre Car Park in Leeds (1963–4) offered direct access, at ground level, to the adjoining shopping precinct and, via a glazed bridge, to a hotel. Such developments often included evening entertainments, which kept the car park in business outside retail hours: in the case of the Merrion Centre, a bowling alley, cinema and dance hall. But the pressure exerted on the Merrion Centre Car Park at peak times (especially when shops shut simultaneously at the end of the day) was not anticipated, and drivers often faced a long, tedious exodus.

Many hotels, office blocks and flats had been built with basement car parks in the 1930s, especially in central London. This trend became more widespread in the 1960s, when the developments in question often assumed the form of stand-alone towers (with basement car parks, sometimes spreading beyond the footprint of the building) or towers with podiums. The tower-and-podium was undoubtedly one of the most distinctive and prevalent new forms of structure to emerge after the war, typically combining shops (podium) with offices or flats (tower), in an attempt to inject a hint of American metropolitan glamour to British city centres. Whatever the mix of functions, some parking provision was essential to these developments, and the most visually satisfying solution was to conceal parking floors below ground. Thus, at Grosvenor Hill Court, an apartment block in Mayfair (1964–5; B. & N. Westwood, Piet & Partners), a continuous parking ramp was installed in the basement.[91] Similarly, the Hilton Hotel on Park Lane (1961–3; Lewis Solomon, Kaye & Partners) was built with a two-storey basement car park. Elsewhere, the podium itself could incorporate parking floors (pl. 271). On Whitcomb Street, near Leicester Square, eight levels of a staggered-floor car park (1964–6; Oscar, Garry & Partners) rose into a podium, while the remaining eight lay below ground.[92] Locating all parking floors in a podium obviated the need for expensive excavation and engineering, but such arrangements were inhibited by the need to reserve commercial frontages for shops. One solution, seen at Stonebow House in York (circa 1970), was to create an open-air car park on the podium roof, wrapped around the base of the tower. Very occasionally, an entire tower was devoted to parking, whilst the podium contained other functions. The most notable examples of this were the parking towers devised by Owen Luder, which dominated shopping precincts in Portsmouth and Gateshead (see above). A similar approach was adopted in Southend, where the Victoria Centre (1968) was overshadowed by a car park.

Following the precedent of Blackpool (see p. 186), MSCPs could be associated with local transport infrastructure. They were built over bus stations in Bath, High Wycombe, Preston and

271 Lowerwood Court, Ladbroke Grove, London: a typical example of a residential tower with a parking podium of *circa* 1970.

other towns.[93] The building at Preston (1969; Keith Ingham of BDP; pl. 272) is exceptionally long and dramatic, the upwardly sweeping ends of the cantilevered parking decks visually reminiscent of the Temple Street Car Park in New Haven (1962). The ground floor, designed to accommodate double-decker buses, is exceptionally high. For a British car park of the 1960s, this building has a rare and bold elegance, but until recently it was earmarked for replacement by an open-air shopping development, the Tithebarn, designed by its original architect, BDP. A more recent car park/ bus station combination is the steel-framed John Lewis Car Park at Liverpool One (2006; Wilkinson Eyre). At suburban railway stations, parking usually occupied long, narrow stretches of railway land alongside the tracks. At its simplest, this was resurfaced and marked out with parking spaces. Some, however, were built with multiple levels. At Gunnersbury, on the District Line in south-west London, the railway line was flanked by long, thin, triple-deck car parks (*circa* 1964–7), having, on one side, a sawtooth frontage to facilitate parking on such a narrow site. At Mutley Plain, Plymouth, a car park of similarly long, thin proportions straddled the line.

Car parks were integrated with roads as well as with buildings. The idea of the commuters' car park was not new: in 1930 the architect Thomas Spencer had proposed a ring of thirteen underground commuter car parks, each with a capacity of 2,000, around London (see p. 195).[94] By the 1960s ambitious cities were building stand-alone car parks linked to urban motorways, serving – and ultimately encouraging – the daily commute into urban centres. Having observed the peak-time congestion at the

272   Preston Bus Station and Car Park was built in 1969 and is well known for its sweeping balustrades. Although its vast scale was not commensurate with the ultimate requirements of Preston, from an architectural point of view it is probably the most admired car park in the country.

Merrion Centre (see above), the Leeds City Engineer, C. G. Thirwall, added a straight, rapid-exit ramp to the huge car park at Woodhouse Lane (1970; pl. 273). This ran diagonally across the elevation, taking drivers directly from the eighth level onto the ring road. Four large multi-storey car parks had been planned as part of the Leeds Inner Ring Road development, which was proposed in 1955 and opened in 1964, but only Woodhouse Lane was ever built. It is a reminder of Leeds' one-time ambition to become 'the Motorway City of the Seventies'.[95] In the same vein, Liverpool planned four massive car parks, each with a capacity of 5,000, with direct access from the inner motorway.[96] Other expanding cities and towns, such as Croydon and Newcastle (see pl. 407), took similar steps, thus avoiding the need for costly distributor routes between urban motorways and central areas. In Bristol the Parkway Car Park (1968; J. B. Bennett) was erected close to the route of the proposed M32, with external helical entry and exit ramps to speed up the morning and evening rush hours.

The integration of parking with the urban environment is not always the result of careful municipal planning. In many towns one comes across streets that retain an assortment of buildings and plots, of various dates and types, which have been adapted over the years to provide public parking. An example of this organic integration is Piccadilly in York. Towards the north end of the street, the large Piccadilly MSCP backs onto the Coppergate development, but south of this are a number of much less visible sites that accommodate varying amounts of public parking, generally on cleared industrial land accessed through buildings on the street frontage, including former warehouses and iron works, and bounded by the River Foss. Since 1989 parking has also been available at the south end of the street, in a building originally erected by Unwin's, a Ford dealership, in 1957, with a barrel-vaulted concrete roof.[97]

•

273   The huge commuters' car park of 1970 on Woodhouse Lane in Leeds straddles the access roads to a busy junction on the 1960s ring road, north of the city centre. It was built with 1,320 spaces, and has an express exit ramp.

'Tarmacing the Countryside'

Even before the Second World War, motorists congregated at events held beyond the boundaries of towns and cities, such as Epsom and Ascot, where parking could be provided with ease, usually on a temporary, *ad hoc* basis. Since 1945, however, the various requirements and demands of modern life have been increasingly catered for in out-of-town locations, for example, at airports, shopping centres, retail and leisure parks, business parks, hospitals and heritage sites. The amount of parking provided in such locations is staggering. Furthermore, unconstrained by a regulated urban environment, this often takes the form of expansive surface car parks, leading to accusations that the countryside is being tarmaced over.

Airports expanded greatly in the 1950s, and so did their parking requirements. While huge MSCPs were erected at Heathrow, Gatwick and Manchester, most airports acquired vast surface car parks, designated for short-, mid- or long-stay, located

some distance from terminals and serviced by shuttle buses that visit numerous bus stops within each park. These sprawling car parks are so large that they are generally divided (sometimes by green strips) into zones that open in rotation. They exist on the periphery of most English airports, including Birmingham (pl. 274), Stansted and Luton.

In the 1980s and early 1990s central government encouraged the creation of new retail and leisure facilities on brownfield sites in marginal locations, where capacious surface car parks could be created. This can be seen as a logical response to the problems besetting parking in urban centres: consumers were complicit with developers, being all too willing to forego the fraught experience of urban parking. Like their much-earlier American equivalents, the first English out-of-town malls, such as the MetroCentre at Gateshead (1986), were marooned in a sea of visitors' cars, usually parked in colour-coded or themed zones so that they could be retrieved with ease. Some malls made more economical use of land by erecting tiered car parks (e.g., Blue-

227

water in Kent, 1999; pl. 275), or even the sort of MSCP one would expect to encounter in a town centre (e.g., Lakeside in Essex, 1990). Since retail parks and superstores sold heavier categories of goods, and relied on customers being able to park near the door, they have seldom deviated from the surface car park, though individual units (e.g., B&Q, Stevenage, 2007) may have tiered car parks with direct access to different selling floors, and internal travellators. Out-of-town leisure parks and attractions also provide ample parking: the NEC, Birmingham (pl. 274), is surrounded by surface car parks, while Dickens World at Chatham, Kent (2007; Kemp Muir Wealleans), has its own MSCP, clad in stainless-steel mesh. Even the heritage industry has spawned large surface car parks, especially at major sites such as Chatsworth and Stonehenge.

Certain categories of hospital have always been located in the countryside: sanatoria, isolation hospitals and asylums. More recently, new general hospitals have been built on the edges of towns, where large sites are readily available at low cost. Unlike their Victorian predecessors, these require ample parking for patients, visitors and staff. Until the late 1990s most hospitals were served by free surface car parks. As these became overcrowded, and as hospitals began to charge for their use, they became the target of much criticism. It was thought that they could trigger anxiety when a patient or visitor was already in a state of distress, or hurried. Since the turn of the century, in an effort to solve this problem, MSCPs have been erected at many hospital sites. It is often claimed – though not always evident – that safety and security are peculiar hallmarks of these projects, reflected in their design and especially in their bright lighting. Q-Park's Cedars Car Park at Musgrove Park Hospital, Taunton (2006; Potter & Holmes Architects), owes its name to its red cedar louvred cladding, but is notable chiefly for the display of multi-coloured fluorescent strip lighting on its façade.

In a pay-off between rural and urban amenities, some of England's largest car parks are rural or semi-rural park-and-ride facilities, which sacrifice fields in an effort to reduce traffic – primarily commuter traffic – in towns. Futuristic visions of park-and-ride were expounded in the 1960s, with the Ministry of Transport suggesting that cars would be automatically parked and drivers transported by travellator to a monorail, guided bus or automatic taxi for the last stage of the journey to their workplace.[98] A 'park and ride by bus' scheme was announced for Leeds in 1964, and introduced in April 1965.[99] But since only ten motorists used this service on the first two mornings, it was

274 The National Exhibition Centre and Birmingham International Airport were built on fields west of the city, just off Junction 6 of the M42. Out-of-town sites such as these owe their success to near-universal car ownership, and are ringed by vast surface car parks, rather than the MSCPs more typical of urban environments.

275   This aerial view of the Bluewater shopping centre (looking north) illustrates its proximity to the M25 (note the Queen Elizabeth II Bridge, completed 1991, top left) – which greatly enlarges its catchment area. The photograph also shows the extensive parking provision and the road system encircling the mall.

swiftly abandoned. By the early 1970s several cities, such as Leicester,[100] were experimenting with park-and-ride (or 'Park 'n' Ride') schemes on a small scale, but the defining experiments were carried out in Oxford and Nottingham. In Oxford, the first of four park-and-ride schemes opened on Abingdon Road in December 1973. An operational study carried out in July 1974 suggested that the scheme, which was served by an express bus between 7am and 7pm, from Monday to Saturday, was well used.[101] By this time Nottingham had abandoned its 'primary highways programme' and was planning an alternative traffic management system for the city. In November 1972 a limited park-and-ride system had been introduced for Saturday shoppers. In August 1975 this was taken much further in a one-year trial known as the 'zone and collar experiment'. Four park-and-ride car parks were opened from Monday to Friday and, at the same time, buses were given priority on roads running in and out of the centre, whilst other traffic was strictly regulated by a

'collar', with carefully phased traffic signals, just inside the ring road. This aimed to 'Strike a balance between the environment, the pedestrian, public transport, the commercial vehicle and the private car, so as to obtain the maximum freedom of movement that is compatible with a civilised way of life.'[102] The four appointed park-and-ride sites (giving a total of 1,300 spaces) were located 2 miles from the city centre, on its western side.[103] A fleet of eighteen 'semi-luxury' buses, dubbed the 'Lilac Leopards', ferried drivers in and out of the centre. In the first months only fifty cars a day used the parks, and the reaction of the public was hostile. The scheme was abandoned in July 1976, and fourteen of the 'Lilac Leopards' were sold to Maidstone Council.[104] Studies revealed that in the course of the experiment it was still quicker to travel into Nottingham by car rather than public transport, and suggested that it might have been more effective had it been accompanied by complementary parking controls. Only 'refugees from high cost central area parking' used the

230

park-and-ride.[105] Other towns learned valuable lessons from this experiment: bus priority schemes became more popular, and eventually park-and-ride became a common weapon in the battle against urban congestion (see pl. 349).

A related phenomenon was the 'park-and-ride' railway station, allowing commuters to travel from far-flung places to London, as an alternative to taking the motorway.[106] The first was probably Bristol Parkway (1972; not to be confused with the earlier 'Parkway' car park in Bristol), while later examples include Luton Airport Parkway (1999), for those commuting between Luton and other cities, or those driving to Luton to use the airport.

In contrast to the expanses of tarmac described above, surface parking at heritage sites and beauty spots is more carefully sited and landscaped. Hollow blocks have been preferred to tarmac or even gravel in such places since the 1960s, as this produces a permanent, hard green surface that blends into the environment.

Car-park Heritage

Disapproval of the post-war MSCP found a voice in the mid-1960s. These vast storage units dominated urban space through their sheer bulk, obliterating historic routes and plots, and clashing with more traditional neighbours. Reception of MSCPs, at first tinged with pride, became muted: they came to be regarded pragmatically, as necessary by-products of the motor age. But by the mid-1960s opposition was brewing. It was realised that comprehensive redevelopment could erode communities, heritage and identity to an unacceptable degree. The least bearable – or least evidently humane – element of such schemes was often a car park.

In 1967 the populace of Canterbury was confronted by an artistic depiction of a proposed seven-storey car park to be built inside the medieval city walls.[107] Alarm bells had not rung when this was first announced in 1966, as part of the Whitefriars Shopping Centre, which would occupy a bomb-damaged site only 400 yards from the cathedral. It was a pictorial presentation of the scheme that prompted the Royal Fine Art Commission to interfere and inspired local people to organise protest groups. As a result, the height of the car park was reduced by one storey, but concerns about its character were rebuffed. It was built much as planned, and stood for thirty years in bleak contrast to the old city on its doorstep, daring to challenge the towers of nearby Canterbury Cathedral.

Throughout the 1970s it became increasingly common for car park proposals to be resisted, especially in historic towns such as Oxford and Cambridge. Underground schemes that threatened trees were especially contested. For example, in 1965 the people of Welwyn Garden City opposed the construction of an underground car park that would have entailed excavating the Campus, an area of green land in the town centre. Because of such protests, many plans had to be scrapped or modified, and this had an impact on car park design, as well as driving developments out of town.

Perhaps dislike of modern car parks encouraged nostalgia and appreciation for their pre-war counterparts. The first to be listed, in 1982, was the Daimler Hire Garage, followed by the Blue Bird Garage (1987), and then, after a long pause, the Lex Garage on Brewer Street (2002) and Macy's on Balderton Street (2009), all in London. Post-war MSCPs are a more challenging proposition. After twenty years of constant usage many became ill kempt, and the response has been either to remodel or reclad these structures, or to demolish them altogether. Occasional attempts to designate post-war car parks have, to date, proved unsuccessful. Owen Luder's Tricorn Centre illustrates how the perception of buildings can swing dramatically with the passage of time. Although it was hailed by critics such as Ian Nairn, and won a commendation from the Civic Trust, it was voted one of Britain's ugliest buildings in a series of vox pop polls, notably by the listeners of Radio 4's *Today* programme in 2001.[108] On the eve of its demise, fans of Brutalism emerged, declaring it 'iconic', but they failed to prevent its demolition in 2004. The story of Trinity Square (pl. 244) is very similar.

In 2010 uncompromising concrete decking is a thing of the past and, although there is a return to a modernist ethos, it is far from the version pedalled by municipal engineers in the 1960s. Parking floors are usually screened, often with materials that create a texture or move in a waving or rippling motion. Interiors are lighter, brighter and cleaner than the generation of car parks that went before, though the essential form is unchanged. They are also sometimes bigger – with the largest MSCPs in the country having more than 2,000 spaces. A potential future direction for this building type is suggested by proposals for the Lister Hospital Car Park on the edge of Stevenage. It is proposed that this will have small wind turbines, charging points for electric cars, and a 'living green wall' facing the hospital, designed to use recycled rainwater to maintain a façade of greenery.[109] Some may doubt, however, that a car park can ever be environmentally friendly.

276   The yard of Charles Trent, the 'scrap car king' at Poole, Dorset, in the 1930s. Cars were simply parked in a field and dismantled over a period of time. The vehicles seen here nearly all date from the 1920s.

8: SCRAPPING THE CAR

MOTORING JOURNALS MADE NO MENTION of the scrapping of old cars until the mid-1920s.[1] Before then, it is likely that cars were quietly dismantled by garages. With the advent of motoring on a much larger scale, however, increasing numbers of old cars were being discarded. In the mid-1920s in the U.S.A., Ford inaugurated a precursor of present-day recycling schemes by buying in obsolete Model Ts and systematically stripping them of useful parts on what amounted to a production line, before disposing of the remainder. Recycling in England followed a less organised path. Car dumps began to spring up in rural areas, where large numbers of old cars were left in fields. Useful parts were sometimes removed immediately or left on, awaiting a buyer to call, and the cars were left to sink into the soil. Many remained so long that weeds and even trees began to grow through them. Others, once stripped of parts, were burnt to destroy all but the metal components, which were then sent away for melting down. No attempt was made to prevent petrol, oil or battery acid from leeching into the ground, nor was there any concern about the fumes produced by burning.

Details of the number and location of early scrapyards are notably sketchy, perhaps not surprisingly, since, by the late 1920s, they were regarded as a major problem, although more for their aesthetic effect than pollution. Perhaps the largest was that of C. Trent & Sons at Newtown, Parkstone, near Poole, Dorset, which opened in 1926 and where some 3,000 cars were sprawled across fields behind newly built houses (pl. 276).[2] In 1938 the Council for the Preservation of Rural England arranged for the AA to have their patrolmen report on scrapyards visible from classified roads. A total of seventy-nine were reported and, although not comprehensive, this is probably the best indication

available as to their extent.[3] Comments were made against each entry, such as, 'old car bodies strewn everywhere' and 'very unsightly'. The main concern was that the cars be screened from view by trees. Some of the yards, such as Goodey's yard at Twyford, Berkshire, Voakes' at Adversane, West Sussex, and Parsons' at Crewkerne, Somerset, lasted for decades. The appearance of scrapyards changed little over the years, the most notable change in post-war years being a tendency to stack cars two or three deep. Accommodation was often a shack, sometimes a cottage or farmhouse, or even an old bus or tram body.

Change began to occur in the 1960s when crushers were introduced that could reduce a car to a small cube of metal in minutes. The first crusher in England was installed at Bird's scrapyard at Long Marston, near Stratford-upon-Avon in August 1965 (pl. 277). Built by Sheppard & Son of Bridgend, it was mobile, so that it could be hired out to yards that had more than 300 vehicles to crush.[4] It could handle eighteen cars per day, reducing them to bales 24 by 12 by 22 inches. Technology to destroy cars on a much greater scale arrived in 1967 with the Proler-Cohen shredding plant at Willesden in north-west London. Based, like the Scrapmaster crusher used at Bird's, on an American installation, it was able to process up to 1,500 cars per day, shredding them into pieces about the size of a man's hand.[5] At first, such equipment was confined to the largest yards; the smaller rural ones carried on unchanged.

The Environmental Protection Act of 1990, however, changed the face of scrapyards completely. They now had to be registered recycling depots and had to comply with very strict environmental requirements, which included paving the yards and having facilities for the safe disposal of waste products. These recycling businesses are organised on a quite different basis from

277 The first car crusher to be installed in England at Bird's scrapyard, near Stratford-upon-Avon, being demonstrated to the press in August 1965. Unfortunately, the car chosen for the exercise, a 1936 Buick, a make known for its robust construction, proved too strong for the crusher and, after several attempts, the crushing had to be abandoned for the day.

the old yards, with end-of-life vehicles (ELV), as they are now called, neatly stacked on metal frames as they are dismantled before being crushed. Many of the older yards closed in the face of the costs involved, and gone completely are fields full of decaying cars. What was once almost a cottage industry is now a regulated industrial process involving approximately 2 million vehicles a year.

The requirements for the disposal of cars were further strengthened by the imposition of the EU End of Life Vehicle Directive of 2000, which was put into effect in England and Wales by regulations issued in 2003 and 2005. ELVs can be broken up only at one of the 1,616 Authorised Treatment Facil-

ities, which meet the depollution requirements for tyres, fuels, oils, batteries, antifreeze and air bags, and only they are authorised to issue Certificates of Destruction with which the vehicle's existence is formally ended. In a typical destruction, an ELV is brought into a compound where its details are recorded and the Certificate of Destruction issued. The processing of the vehicle takes place under cover in a large shed. The battery is removed, as are wheels, glass and large items such as bumpers. Parts for reuse are then taken off and the car is raised to allow fluids to be drained off. The car is then taken to a shredder, which may be at another location. Within the shredder, the car is first flattened to prepare it for size reduction. It is then smashed by rotating large hammers to break it into small pieces so that the different component materials can be separated. Light materials such as foam are drawn away by strong wind turbines. The remaining heavy materials pass through magnets to separate ferrous metals. The non-ferrous metals and other materials go through an eddy current separator to split off the metals from the remainder. The non-ferrous metals are then dispatched, some to U.K. foundries but most for export.[6]

The life cycle of the car is now complete: it is ended as formally as it began with documentary proof of its destruction being sent to the licensing authority. In the same way that most cars today arrive in England by ship from their manufacturers, so at the end of its life some 80 per cent of its raw materials leave the country by sea to be recycled.

278   Sculpture from scrapped car parts at a garage in Kettlewell, North Yorkshire.

2: DRIVING AROUND

279   A view east along Piccadilly in the late 1950s, with a Ford Popular in the foreground.
One of the signs at Piccadilly Circus had changed from 'MORRIS CARS' to 'AUSTIN VEHICLES' in the course of the exposure by the photographer, John Gay.

280   Motoring just outside Ludlow in Shropshire in the mid-1930s. The car is an Austin 7, or 'baby' Austin, with the addition of polished wheel disks.

9: ON THE ROAD

THE ENGLISH ROAD SYSTEM WAS TRANSFORMED to accommodate motor vehicles in the course of the twentieth century, speeding up connections between far-flung towns and cities, and leaving an indelible mark on the contours of the land-scape. The most radical aspect was the creation of motorways. With their snaking dual carriageways and concrete overpass bridges, these have become intrinsic features of many views, as well as themselves providing the passing motorist with new vistas of England's countryside. As the roadscape has evolved, it has increasingly become encumbered with the untidy paraphernalia that is considered necessary to secure safe driving conditions in the modern world.

English Roads before 1918

The first motorists venturing into the countryside in the 1890s discovered that England's roads were quite unsuited to the new means of locomotion. The turnpike roads had been sorely neg-lected since the mid-nineteenth century. They were frequently too narrow, winding or steep for cars to negotiate without a struggle and, while their surfaces turned to mud in winter, in summer they generated dust (pl. 281). This was deposited in thick layers over roadside properties and bedevilled motorists themselves, forcing them to don goggles and substantial outer clothing.

By 1900 the increasing reliability of cars was encouraging motorists to delve deeper into the countryside, regardless of the poor roads. But it was easy to get lost. Signposts were set incon-veniently high for drivers; sometimes they were decayed, or half-hidden in hedgerows, their small lettering scarcely legible at speed. Many displayed just the names of nearby villages, and not the ultimate destinations of motorists. London's exit routes were particularly confusing, prompting the *Car Illustrated*, in 1902, to publish a series of articles on 'the best ways out of London'.[1] Travellers became heavily dependent on such advice, and invested in road atlases and maps (pl. 282). These showed con-tours: a crucial factor in determining a route, since the hill-climbing ability of some early cars was limited. Some warning signs had been erected at the behest of cyclists in the late nine-teenth century, and these now helped motorists to anticipate sharp bends and steep inclines. Although additional warning signs were recommended by the Local Government Board in 1904 (see Chapter 12), these were introduced haphazardly by highway authorities. Motoring organisations such as the RAC and the AA took it upon themselves to erect warning signs, as well as place-name signs and direction signs, in their own livery.

In 1900 the future prime minister Arthur Balfour mused: 'I sometimes dream, perhaps it is only a dream, that in addition to railways and tramways, we may see great highways constructed for rapid motor traffic, and confined to motor traffic'.[2] Indeed, struggling along England's unsatisfactory country roads, with their low speed limits – 12mph in most areas from 1896 to 1904, then 20mph (though often ignored) from 1904 until 1930 – many motorists dreamed of the idyllic motor roads of the future. Some contemporary writers managed to forecast, with unnerv-ing accuracy, the impact that motor roads would have on the English landscape. In *Anticipations of the Reaction of Mechanical and Scientific Progress upon Human Life and Thought* (1902), H. G. Wells predicted: 'through the varied country the new wide roads will run, here cutting through a crest and there running like some colossal aqueduct across a valley, swarming always with a multi-

281 'A Quiet Sunday in our Village'. This *Punch* cartoon by H. R. Millar, published on 6 June 1906, illustrates the nuisance caused by weekend motorists, and especially the clouds of dust raised by their pneumatic tyres

tudinous traffic of bright, swift (and not necessarily ugly) mechanisms'.[3]

Serious proposals for motor roads were quick to emerge. As early as 1896 the engineer and inventor Morland M. Dessau obtained a patent for a special elevated track for cycles and self-propelled vehicles, which he thought could be built from London to either Birmingham or Brighton.[4] This was a metal structure with an asphalt road surface and rest areas, carried on columns over existing roadways and accessed by inclines at toll-gates. *The Autocar* suggested that most people would prefer 'the greater freedom of movement and variety given by the Queen's highway'.[5] Nevertheless, the idea of dedicated motor roads had wide appeal. It was assumed, almost universally, that these would be built by private companies and funded by charges levied on users, in much the same way as the railways. An 'automobile road to the south coast' was suggested by George Lowthian in 1901,[6] and a motor road from London to Carlisle, and thence to Scotland, was proposed by the engineer B. H. Thwaite in 1902.[7] Thwaite's road – with separate tracks for motor cars and cycles – was to have a concrete foundation with a wood-block surface, and would be equipped with passing places, resting pavilions, 'motor car accessory air-charging, lubricants, and petrol stores', and even storage stations for electric cars.

John Scott Montagu, MP (1866–1929), the proprietor of the *Car Illustrated* and soon (in 1906) to become 2nd Baron Montagu of Beaulieu, strongly promoted the idea of a London to Brighton 'motor way', believing that this had greater commercial potential than a road to the North. He sought the power to create this through a Private Bill, which was deposited on 30 Decem-

ber 1905, but had to be withdrawn in February 1906 in the face of considerable opposition from the railway lobby.[8] This 'motor way', designed by the engineer Sir Douglas Fox, with Hassard & Tyrrell and J. H. Harley Mason, would have been restricted to mechanically propelled vehicles and free from speed limits (pl. 283). It was conceived, somewhat precociously, as a dual carriageway, with super-elevation (i.e., banking) and manageable

282 British holidaymakers, many of them now touring by car, were amongst W. H. Smith's core customers in the early twentieth century. These tiles, advertising road maps, decorate the firm's branch at Belle Vue Terrace, Malvern, Worcestershire.

ROAD MAPS

THE PROPOSED TRACK CARRIED OVER AN EXISTING ROAD.

283 The London to Brighton Motor Way was promoted by The Hon. John Scott Montagu MP, who formed the London, Brighton & South Coast Motor Road Syndicate. The Motor Way was envisaged as a dual carriageway, with fifty-three bridges, running 40 miles from Croydon to Patcham. From *Car Illustrated*, 25 October 1905, p. 302.

gradients. The carriageways were to be separated by a low wall incorporating plinths for electric lamp standards, and would be carried over existing roads by bridges to allow for the continuous flow of traffic. Slip roads (though not yet identified by this name) would feed traffic on and off the secondary roads that passed beneath the motor road. The inclusion of grade separation in such an early road scheme is not so very surprising. Roads that bridged other roads already existed, though they were few and far between. The best-known examples were in London: The Archway (1813), created by accident when a projected tunnel collapsed and had to be replaced by a bridge over a cutting, and Holborn Viaduct (1863–7). More to the point, grade separation was common on the railways, and familiarity with its viaducts and cuttings must have inspired those now toying with the design of motor roads.

A new 'royal' road running straight from Hammersmith in west London to Windsor in Berkshire was proposed in 1901: this was to supersede the notoriously congested Bath and Oxford roads, and would comprise three tracks, including one for automobiles and cycles.[9] Frontage development, allowing London's expanding population to spread along this road, was an integral part of the concept. Motor roads on similar routes were the subject of two unsuccessful Private Bills in 1908.[10] One, a boulevard from Shepherd's Bush to Langley, near Slough, was proposed in the London Motor Roadways Approach Bill.[11] It was to be planted with three avenues of trees, defining a central motor track, 70 feet wide, flanked by public roads for horse-drawn traffic. The other, involving a motor road between Hammersmith and Windsor, was outlined in the London and Windsor Motor Roads, Tram Roads and Tramways Bill.[12] This road would be lined by tramways and carried over secondary roads on bridges. Some very different proposals for motor roads were published around the same time, showing that there was no agreement on their ideal form. Following in the footsteps of Dessau, the motor road proposed by P. E. Kemp bestrode an all-purpose country road like a roller coaster.[13] In 1909 Captain George Swinton – primarily motivated by a desire to increase national prosperity and disperse population rather than the need to improve roads for cars – published his plan for a 'garden road' that would run the length of England.[14] To either side of an all-purpose road, land would be leased for smallholdings, allotments and parks. Swinton may have been inspired by the American parkway. The 45-mile Long Island Motor Parkway, built in 1907–8, was the world's first toll road solely for motor cars. Its originator was the motor racing enthusiast William K. Vanderbilt, and the road was free from speed restrictions.[15] Its use of overpasses at intersections prefigured American's freeway system and, indeed, Britain's post-war motorways.

In England, suitable motor roads materialised at a much slower pace than motorists wished. Road improvement and construction remained a matter for local highway authorities, which held limited funds and seldom coordinated their efforts fruitfully. The secretary of the Roads Improvement Association (founded 1889), W. Rees Jeffreys (1871–1954) – who had proposed the 'royal' road to Windsor in 1901 – lobbied for highway reform, advocating the creation of a central government department that would fund an adequate trunk road system. Eventually, in 1909, the Chancellor of the Exchequer, David Lloyd George, established the Road Board under the Development and Road Improvement Funds Act. The Board, with Rees Jeffreys as its secretary, was to administer a Road Improvement Fund, distributing the sum – to begin with – of approximately £600,000 per annum. Since this derived from motor-car licence fees and fuel taxes, motorists would bear the brunt of the costs: much to the delight of those angered by the visible expenditure of public money on resurfacing roads for motor cars. The principal aim of the Road Board was to create fast roads, explicitly for motor traffic (pl. 284).[16] In practice, however, these roads never came about. The Board was thwarted by the multiplicity of highway agencies, by disagreements with the London County Council (LCC), and by the high cost of projects.

Although the Road Board made slow progress, crucially, it was at this time that plans were laid down for a system of new and

284 'An artist's dream of what the Road Board may accomplish': a far-sighted visualisation of a two-level junction with two-way slip roads and bold signage. Nothing quite like this would be created until after the Second World War. From *Car Illustrated*, 13 December 1911, p. 149.

improved arterial roads to serve London. These roads were presented in the third annual report of the London Traffic Branch of the Board of Trade in 1910 – partly based on the results of traffic censuses – and were debated at the London Arterial Roads Conferences between 1913 and 1916. The most significant schemes included the Great West Road (including the Brentford Bypass), Western Avenue, Eastern Avenue, the Great Chertsey Road and New Cambridge Road. Beyond Greater London, bypasses were proposed to deal with bottlenecks such as Kingston upon Thames and Croydon. Proposals also included the North and South Circular Roads, although the Arterial Conferences preferred the idea of an outer orbital. With these diverse projects to consider, the Road Board gave priority to the Great West Road.[17] A draft scheme for an 80-foot carriageway was prepared in 1914 by Henry T. Wakelam, the Middlesex County Engineer, and the cost was estimated at £500,000 (including a contribution of £300,000 from the Road Board). This was put on hold, however, by the First World War, as was the more modest Croydon Bypass (estimated cost £76,000, including a contribution of £49,000 from the Road Board), for which the Board also succeeded in securing planning and financing before 1914.

Beyond London, one of the most significant proposals concerned an 11-mile road – 6 miles of which would be brand new – to run between Birmingham and Wolverhampton, with 28-foot-wide grass margins and 10-foot footpaths to either side of a single carriageway. This was influenced by the boulevards being created on the outskirts of Liverpool around this time (see p. 329). It was approved by the Association of Midland Local Authorities in 1909, but not funded.[18] Despite the fact that no new long-distance roads were built prior to 1914, the Road Board did help to improve existing roads by widening, straightening, and allaying the dreaded dust. This generally involved resurfacing with tar, tarmacadam or asphalt, and included some of the first English road bridges to be constructed of reinforced concrete.[19] These improvements certainly aided the passage of the motor car, though not to the desired extent.

The outbreak of war stopped all schemes, and the income of the Road Board was diverted to war work. In 1915 the duty on motor spirits was raised and the proceeds (now approximately £1 million per annum) retained by the Exchequer. Shortly afterwards, all existing taxation was diverted from the Road Board, leaving it with an accumulated fund of £3 million to last the duration. With little to spend on maintenance, and shortages of

285 An artist's impression of the Northern and Western Motorway, *circa* 1923. Note the fences.

labour and materials, the condition of English roads deteriorated quickly. Nevertheless, some small schemes progressed: in 1916, for example, it was reported that Dorset County Council was to set German prisoners of war to work building a new coast road, with the aid of a small Road Board grant.[20] Otherwise, activity focused sharply on the wartime requirements of the military.

New and Improved Roads, 1918–1939

The powers held by the Road Board passed, in 1919, to a new Ministry of Transport, which embarked on a major programme of road building but did nothing to advance the construction of dedicated motor roads. These still interested the private sector, especially Lord Montagu of Beaulieu, who – at a time when Italy was constructing its first *autostrade* – became involved in a company that obtained Parliamentary powers to build a toll road (not a motorway, but 'a high-class motor road') and ferry between Bournemouth and Swanage in 1923. Encouraged by this success, Lord Montagu headed a syndicate to promote something more ambitious: a Northern and Western Motorway,

designed by the engineers Whitley and Carkeet-James (pl. 285).[21] This was the first road to be described as a 'motorway' (unhyphenated): it would have a 50-foot carriageway and, on completion, would run for 216 miles, from Uxbridge to Liverpool. In the course of 1923–4 at least three attempts were made to acquire the necessary powers, including a general Motorways Bill that would facilitate a preliminary section between Coventry and Salford.[22] The local authorities through whose areas this motorway would pass were unanimous in their support, but the Government refused to back the project, insisting that its financial basis was unsound. Undaunted, in 1925 a company was formed to promote a London and South Coast Motorway. Engineered by Carkeet-James and Douglas Cooper, this was conceived as a 40-foot-wide motorway running between Kingston upon Thames and Brighton (or, rather, Pyecombe), a distance of 57 miles.[23] On joining the motorway, motorists would pay 3 farthings per mile and receive a ticket, which they would relinquish upon leaving. Needless to say, the Government failed to support the Southern Motor Road Bill of 1928, and attempts by the Roads Improvement Association to revive the Northern and Western Motorway project in 1929, after Lord Montagu's death, were strongly discouraged.

All these motorway schemes met fierce opposition from diverse interest groups: primarily the railway companies (who were anxious about competition), commercial road users (who were unwilling to pay tolls) and preservationists (who were concerned about the despoliation of the countryside and the loss of footpaths). The railway companies were particularly chary of Lord Montagu who, in 1913, was one of the first to suggest that railway lines be converted into toll roads.[24] Anyway, it was argued that motorways were unnecessary, since adequate all-purpose roads were currently being constructed under the auspices of the Ministry of Transport.[25] Aesthetic arguments also held sway, with the Royal Commission on Transport of 1930 objecting to 'the unsightly features which these roads would produce – for they would have to be carried over existing highways by means of viaducts'.[26] But what really thwarted Lord Montagu and other entrepreneurs was an abhorrence of tolls, based on a memory of the turnpikes, and a growing realisation, in central government, that motorways should be built by the state rather than private enterprise. The Government, however, had no intention of pressing ahead immediately with motorways, despite the regular publication of ingenious schemes by the motoring lobby.[27]

The greatest impetus towards the creation of a national motorway network came in September 1937, when Dr Fritz Todt, the General Inspector of German Highways, invited a British delegation to view the progress of the *Autobahnen*, the first high-speed road network in the world. This programme had begun under the Weimar Republic, but accelerated under Hitler from 1933, perhaps partially for military reasons. By 1937 more than 1,000 miles had been completed. Unlike the Italian *autostrade*, the *Autobahnen* were built as dual carriageways, with gleaming concrete surfaces, grassed central reservations and carefully regulated roadsides, free from the *ad hoc* advertisements or ramshackle garages that characterised the English roadside. The British delegation marvelled at these roads and, on its return, recommended that 'a plan be prepared forthwith for a national scheme of motorways', advice reinforced by its Report of January 1938.[28] In fact, such a plan already existed: a map showing 2,826 miles of motorway drawn up by the Institution of Highway Engineers in 1936. This, however, had been undermined by the Minister of Transport and the AA, since both bodies had declared a preference for improving existing roads.[29] Much more influential was a coordinated scheme drafted by the County Surveyors' Society in 1938, with 1,165 miles of motorway that would cost around £60 million to build (see pl. 303a).[30] By the outbreak of war, Lancashire had worked up a motorway plan that won approval from the Minister of Transport, though no funding was forthcoming.[31] This gave the county a head start when work began on English motorways in the 1950s.

England may not have acquired any motorways between the wars, but in 1919 the Ministry of Transport initiated the largest programme of road building undertaken since the days of the turnpikes. It offered generous grants from the Road Fund, which was augmented by high motor taxes imposed by the Finance Act of 1920. In the first full financial year of operation, 1921–2, £10 million was dispensed in grants and loans.[32] For the first time, following the French *route nationale* system, principal roads – totalling 36,000 miles – were classified and numbered. Classification affected grants, with Class I roads being eligible for 50 per cent grants and Class II roads for 25 per cent. It was stipulated that 50 per cent of the cost of any scheme was to be spent on wages for unskilled men.[33] This reflects the fact that projects were designed not just to meet the growing demands of motor transport but also – under the Unemployment [Relief Works] Act of 1920 – to provide much-needed work for the unemployed, prioritising demobilised soldiers.[34] Not surprisingly, given the London-centric nature of the motor car (see Chapter 12), most major schemes were directed at getting people in and out of the capital speedily. Indeed, many of London's 'pleasure-exits' – such as the Croydon Bypass (on the way to Brighton) and the Southend Road (to Southend-on-Sea) – improved routes that connected the metropolis with seaside resorts. Road building continued apace throughout the 1920s, with occasional hiccups, such as the Chancellor's controversial raids on the Road Fund in 1927 and 1928. The financial crisis of 1931 brought a reduction in the expenditure of the Road Fund and caused the postponement of many schemes. Nevertheless, by this date many of the roads begun in the early 1920s had reached completion. Some, in fact, already required enhancement.

The new roads of the 1920s can be divided into three broad categories: bypasses (otherwise known as 'loop' or 'switch' roads), ring roads and arterial routes, although these definitions were far from clear-cut, since bypasses might be regarded as improvements to existing arterial routes, and sometimes represented the first step towards the creation of a ring road that was, in a sense, a glorified bypass. By the mid-1920s the Croydon Bypass (Purley Way, opened 1924) and the Brentford Bypass (Great West Road [A4], opened 1925) – both conceived and planned prior to the First World War – had been completed, and many others (including those around Watford, Kingston upon Thames and Sutton) were well advanced. Bypasses were often criticised as ugly motor roads that ruined virgin fields, but it was also realised that they restored tranquillity to the villages and towns they circumnavigated.

Standards for new roads varied. Some were built entirely of concrete, usually reinforced concrete, but many had a black crust. Most new routes ran through undeveloped areas to minimise disruption to existing infrastructure, as well as minimising compulsory purchase. Laid out with footpaths, verges and fences, they incorporated gradual curves and easy gradients. Typically, roads were built as single 30-foot carriageways with two one-way tracks that, until the 1930s, had no central dividing line or reservation. Some carriageways, however, accommodated three or four undifferentiated tracks, each 10 to 12 feet in width.[35] The Barnet Bypass (opened 1929), for example, comprised three 10-foot tracks, with the central track used for overtaking in each direction. In the absence of lane markings, traffic often straddled the tracks, leading to accidents. Similarly, the 50-foot carriageway of the Great West Road – at £143,000 per mile probably the most expensive new road yet built in England – was denounced as 'an unregulated wilderness of space'.[36]

Clearly, dual carriageways were the safest option, but these took time to materialise. Early examples, such as Queen's Drive and Broad Green Road in Liverpool (see p. 329), were suburban avenues or boulevards rather than long-distance routes. Some arterial roads planned in the early 1920s, such as the Southend Road (opened 1925) and the Kingston Bypass (opened 1927), were intended to have two two-track carriageways, though only one was built initially. By 1928 the Southend Road (pl. 286) was being called a 'Via Dolorosa' due to its appalling accident rate, but work on the northern carriageway commenced only in 1937.[37] Meanwhile, the first arterial road to be planned and built as a dual carriageway was a stretch of Western Avenue between Ruislip and Hillingdon, which was completed with a 14-foot central reservation separating two 27-foot carriageways in 1934 (see pl. 293c).[38] This was combined with restrictions on side roads and frontages, in an effort to curb ribbon development, which was now recognised as a menace. The Western Avenue scheme proved immediately influential: plans for the Coventry Bypass (stalled by the financial crisis of 1931) were revised along similar lines, and the Ministry of Transport began to make certain grants conditional on the adoption of dual carriageways.[39] One common feature of the new dual carriageways of the late 1930s, such as the Winchester Bypass (see pl. 293d), was an anti-dazzle screen in the form of a hedge or shrubbery, grown on the central reservation.

Road signs multiplied between the wars. From 1921 roads were classed as 'A' or 'B' and assigned a number that thenceforth appeared on signposts (pl. 287) and maps. The six main trunk roads radiating from London were numbered clockwise, beginning with the Great North Road, which became the A1. Rather than replace existing fingerpost signs *en masse*, it was suggested that the new number be bolted to the arms of existing signposts, with black on white for A roads and white on black for B roads. While the Ministry stipulated that posts should be white, the AA advocated black and white stripes, which were adopted widely.[40] It was recommended that the name of the highway authority be included, and that lettering should be in upper case, in black on a white ground, and with a height of 2½ to 3 inches.

286   The new Southend Road, which opened in 1925, proved very dangerous until it was widened as a dual carriageway in 1937. This photograph was taken in 1936.

Warning signs were the same as those introduced in towns (see Chapter 12), but some peculiar arrangements were devised for junctions and bends on arterial roads. A remarkable concrete lighthouse with illuminated notices and a flashing light was erected on a bend outside Congleton, Staffordshire, in February 1924.[41] Then, in 1925, when George V opened the Great West Road, 'it was noticed that at the cross-roads "lighthouses" have been erected for guidance of the traffic at night-time'.[42] In the same year Kent County Council erected automatic gas beacons that flashed red in all directions along the London–Folkestone road (A20), which had recently been improved with widening and bypasses.[43] In 1933 new flat direction signs (pls 288 and 289) were introduced, and it was now obligatory for posts to be painted with black and white stripes. On country lanes, some warning signs of this vintage may still be found, often rusting in hedgerows. Over and above official signs, a plethora of notices and other gimmicks advertised businesses along major routes. Amongst the most helpful to the motorist in the 1930s were the Leyland Clocks, roadside towers erected by Leyland Motors at around ten sites throughout England. Clearly visible to the passing motorist, the clock faces were studded by reflectors and surmounted by the legend 'Leyland Motors For All Time'. One formerly on the A1 at Alconbury is now on display in the National Motor Museum, Beaulieu.

White lines – marked on the highway to guide motorists around bends and at junctions – came into widespread use in the 1920s. One of the first instances occurred in 1916, when the proprietor of the Old Toll House Garage on the main road from Bradford to Morecombe used chalk to mark the carriageways following an accident.[44] In 1921 he was given paint by the local authority to continue the practice. White lines were first used

287a–d Surviving examples of mid-twentieth-century fingerpost signs:

a (*top left*) Middleton Tyas, North Yorkshire;

b (*above left*) Woolsthorpe-by-Belvoir, Lincolnshire ('KCC' in the annulus stands for Kesteven County Council; the blank fields at the ends were provided for road numbers);

c (*top right*) A7, Cumberland (with 'Cumberland County Council' on the post; 'Arthuret', the parish, on the annulus);

d (*right*) Ashwell, Oakham, Rutland (a concrete post with slots for wooden arms that display applied lettering).

officially in 1923, as an experiment on a blind bend at Jockey Hill in the Birmingham suburb of Sutton Coldfield, where a 3-inch strip of concrete was embedded in the tarmac.[45] Lines began to appear at road junctions in towns, with white glazed fireclay pins let into the wood blocks that still paved the junction of the Strand with Wellington Street in London in 1925.[46] In 1926 the Ministry of Transport issued a circular to encourage uniformity in the positioning and appearance of white lines, though it was not prescriptive about what materials to use, whether paint (which wore off and was costly to maintain), concrete, or plates and studs of metal or rubber.[47] Lines were not used to divide carriageways into traffic lanes until 1931, but thereafter became commonplace.[48] Another safety measure involved painting black and white stripes on potentially hazardous structures. On blind corners, where buildings stood flush with the footpath, motorists were assisted by traffic mirrors: the first is thought to have been erected around 1909 by Sir George Sutton at Park Langley, Beckenham.[49] Reflective studs improved the night visibility of bollards and traffic signs, and in 1934 Percy Shaw (1890–1976) patented the 'Catseye' reflective road marker, which was manufactured by his company, Reflecting Roadstuds Ltd.[50] Catseyes were made from glass beads, set in pairs within an elasticated rubber moulding, on a cast-iron base. They came into their own when a blackout was imposed during the Second World War, and have been used extensively since the late 1940s.

In general, the most complicated and expensively engineered elements of inter-war roads were not yet their intersections, but the bridges, viaducts and tunnels that were erected to negotiate the railways, rivers and canals that lay in their paths. One of the most ambitious road structures of this period was the Lea Valley Viaduct (1925–7; Simpson & Ayrton, with the engineer Sir Owen Williams), which bore London's North Circular Road over several stretches of water between Edmonton and Walthamstow.[51] Maxwell Ayrton and Sir Owen Williams had recently collaborated on the British Empire Exhibition at Wembley (1924), and went on to design many bridges and viaducts together. The massive concrete pylons at either end of the Lea Valley Viaduct were probably Ayrton's work. These served as markers in the flat, desolate surroundings of the valley, and possessed a powerful sculptural quality. The carriageway was lit by elaborate gas lamps on concrete posts, with vertical fluting echoing the form of the pylons. Though the Lea Valley Viaduct has been demolished, many notable road bridges of reinforced concrete survive from the 1920s and 1930s, for example Ayrton's and Williams's bridge over the River Nene at Wansford on the Great North Road (the northbound carriageway of the present A1), built in the years 1925–9 (pl. 290).[52] Also on the A1 was the Royal Tweed Bridge at Berwick-upon-Tweed (1928; L. G. Mouchel & Partners): one of its four arches had the then-unequalled span of 361 feet 6 inches. The viaduct crossing the River Chelm on the Chelms-

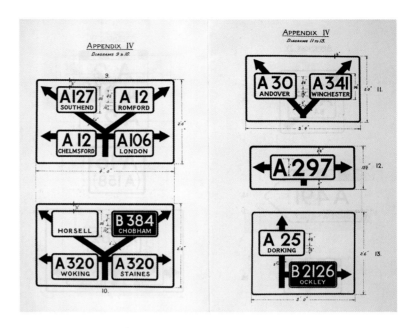

288 From 1933, map-style direction signs displayed black lettering (in Llewellyn-Smith font) on a white ground for 'A' roads, and white on black for 'B' roads. Specifications were laid down in the circular 'Traffic Signs (Size, Colour and Type) Regulations'.

289 An RAC approach sign for a bend on the A7, near Donaldsons Lodge, Northumberland, complying with the official regulations issued in 1933. Direction signs dating from 1933 to 1965 can occasionally be spotted in the countryside, but survive mainly in towns, especially when they were affixed to buildings and proved difficult to remove.

290   From the 1920s the engineer-architect Sir Owen Williams created many daring concrete structures, including, in collaboration with the architect Maxwell Ayrton (with whom Williams had worked on the Wembley Exhibition of 1924), this bridge (1925–9), which carries the A1 over the River Nene on the Wansford Bypass. Note the lettering and the expansion joints over the spandrel arches.

291   The viaduct over the River Chelm on the Chelmsford Bypass, the old A12 (now A138), opened in 1932. The original fluted lighting standards survive, together with some of their metal light fittings. There are currently (2012) proposals to replace this structure.

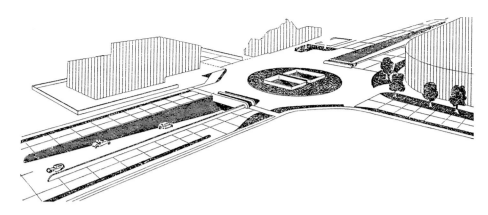

THE HOOK FLY-OVER
—An impression by one of our artists of how the proposed fly-over on the Kingston By-pass will look. It is at the Hook-Leatherhead road crossing and the by-pass will have a direct through route below the roundabout.

292   The proposed Hook Road flyover, or 'fly under', Kingston Bypass (1938). If executed, this would have been the first roundabout flyover in England, but owing to the outbreak of war, work did not begin until 1958, and the junction opened only in February 1960 (*The Times*, 8 August 1958, 5; 13 February 1960, 4). This image was published in *The Motor*, 6 September 1938, p. 225.

ford Bypass (1929–32; pl. 291) was also impressive: remarkably, its reinforced concrete lamp standards and metal gas fittings survive to this day, although demolition is in the offing.

Gyratory systems originated in city centres (see Chapter 12), but by 1930 conventional crossroads on arterial roads were being replaced by roundabouts. One of the first was constructed at the Hook Road junction of the Kingston Bypass, by the Ace of Spades garage, in 1929.[53] Others quickly followed, for example on the Liverpool–East Lancashire Road, built between 1929 and 1933, which was one of the most important new routes to be created outside the South-East. Only 2½ of its 28-mile length incorporated old roads, but all of its twenty-four junctions were – as one would expect at this date – at grade, that is, on one level. Belatedly, it included circles and roundabouts, with the first, on the A49 at Haydock, opening in July 1933.[54] By 1934 some roundabout islands were being formed as grassy mounds, to reduce glare from oncoming headlamps.

It took some time for two-level junctions, with or without roundabouts, to appear. One of the first, contemporary with the Silvertown Viaduct in London (see Chapter 12), was created on the Guildford Bypass (A3) of 1929–34 (pl. 293b). As it joined the Hog's Back, the Farnham Road (A31) bridged the new bypass – which was buried in a cutting at this point – and was linked to it by slip roads.[55] Remarkably, the essential features of this arrangement survive to the present day. In the late 1930s the fascination of British engineers with free-flowing American intersections resulted in a spate of proposals for more complex 'fly-over junctions'. Plans were laid in 1937 for 'fly-over junctions' at the east end of the Farnham Bypass and by the Ace of Spades garage (pl. 292),[56] and it was decided to build Britain's first clover-leaf junction on the Maidstone Bypass.[57] In the event, none of these flyovers was built. The Winchester Bypass (1935–40; pl. 293d), however, flew over the Petersfield Road (A272), to which it was connected by a looping slip road. This,

and the overpass bridge carrying the Alresford Road (B3404), with their parabolic arches and upright spandrel walls, foreshadowed many structures built on post-war motorways. The cutting and bridges were actually constructed in 1933–4, ahead of road building.

In the realm of road transportation, the greatest engineering feat of the 1930s was the 2-mile-long Mersey Tunnel ('Queensway'; 1925–33, by Sir Basil Mott and J. A. Brodie), which was opened by King George V and Queen Mary in July 1934. It connected Liverpool with Birkenhead, and formed part of the Liverpool–East Lancashire Road. Queensway was the longest sub-aqueous tunnel in the world, built at a cost of £7,500,000, and was a highly glamorous expression of the golden age of motoring. Originally, it accommodated two lanes of traffic in each direction, the lanes being demarcated by blocks of yellow rubber with ridges set into a pavement of cast-iron setts, and the walls lined by a dark purple Vitrolite dado framed in stainless steel (pl. 294). This was without doubt the most ambitious road tunnel of the time. Work on the much shorter Dartford Tunnel, which was to form a crucial link in London's Orbital Road, began in 1936, but ceased on the outbreak of war, and was not completed until 1963.

Liverpool's ring road (Queen's Drive, pl. 295; see Chapter 12) was completed in the 1920s, and many others were initiated, for example, around Birmingham, Leeds, London, Sheffield and Sunderland, but these generally took many years to complete, often stalling due to lack of finance, or being delayed by bridge or tunnel construction. They seldom formed a complete circle; indeed, they rarely comprised an entirely new road, instead combining stretches of old and new carriageways. The North Circular Road in London, lying an average of 7 miles from the city centre, was typical in this regard: of 15 miles created by 1934, only 9 miles were new.[58] Since the complementary South Circular Road – formed, to a much greater extent, by improv-

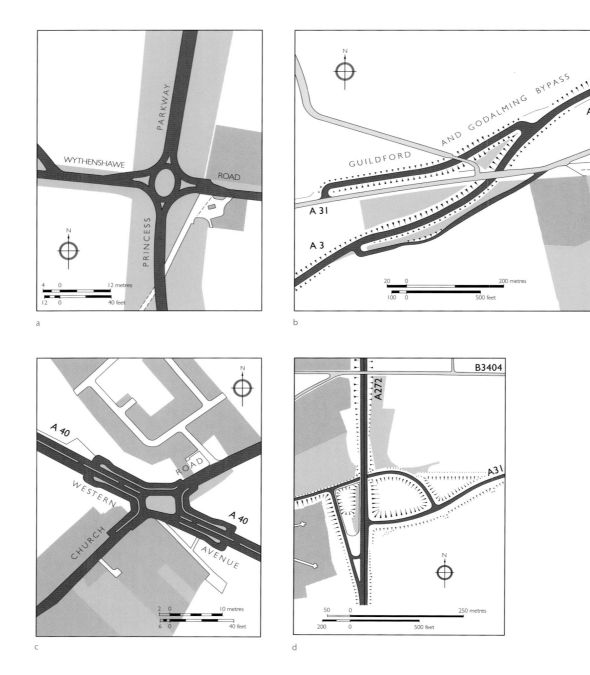

293a–d Four advanced 1930s road junctions: (a) Princess Parkway, Wythenshawe, 1929–32; (b) Guildford Bypass, 1929–34; (c) Western Avenue, Northolt, 1935; (d) Winchester Bypass, 1935–40.

ing existing roads – failed to keep pace, the North Circular Road remained, to all intents and purposes, a semi-circular. London's outer ring road, the North Orbital, was to lie 17 to 20 miles from the city centre: 12 miles existed by 1934, 8 of them new, including the St Albans Bypass (A414). One of the most publicised and admired of all ring roads was that of Leeds, half of which had been completed by the mid-1930s.[59] Like London's North Orbital, this appeared to plan for the distant future by adopting a position well beyond the urban fringe and incorporating space for widening to either side. Those lying closer to

city centres, such as the Norwich ring road, built in the early 1930s, quickly attracted ribbon development.

The failure to foresee the repercussions of developing land that fronted new arterial roads on the outskirts of towns was disastrous in terms of traffic management. Initially, such development was positively encouraged, since it opened up new districts for commercial and residential development. Furthermore – as the Assistant Commissioner of Scotland Yard (turned traffic planner), Herbert Alker Tripp, later explained – there was 'a natural disinclination in a free country to interfere with or

294　The interior of the Mersey Tunnel, which was opened by George v in 1934. This postcard, made before the tunnel opened, is an artistic impression.

295　Ribbon development on Queen's Drive, Larkhill, Liverpool, photographed on 7 September 1927. Note the policeman on traffic duty, chatting with a pedestrian.

shackle private enterprise'.[60] Lord Montagu declared that frontagers should welcome new roads, because they could 'sell their land for much enhanced prices'.[61] But the extent to which houses, shops, factories, side roads and parked cars would interrupt the flow of through traffic was simply not imagined until it became a reality. When this trend became evident, in the mid-1920s, the authorities responded by building parallel service roads, rather than stopping development altogether.[62] Tripp dismissed this as the kind of layout that 'gives rise to those pitiful cases where children, given by their parents a penny for sweets, rush joyfully out to spend it, and never return'.[63] It is unclear who coined the term 'ribbon development', but a leading contender must be the town planner Patrick Abercrombie (1879–1957), who pointed out in 1925 that 'ribbon' development was being 'unconsciously adopted throughout the whole of England' (see Chapter 10).[64]

In 1929, under the heading 'Save the New Roads!', *The Autocar* argued that parked cars rendered arterial roads 'a colossal waste of time and money'.[65] The County Councils of Surrey and Essex obtained powers through Private Acts to purchase land flanking specific roads in order to control lateral development. The Town and Country Planning Act of 1932 failed, somewhat controversially, to extend such powers to all local authorities, but, somewhat belatedly, the Restriction of Ribbon Development Act of 1935 made it illegal to build within 220 feet from the centre of any classified road without obtaining permission from the highway authority. By this time, however, many of the new arterial roads, especially around London, were thoroughly congested.

As traffic grew, in the mid-1930s the idea of segregating cyclists, pedestrians and motor traffic spread from town centres (see Chapter 12) to outlying areas. In 1934 the stretch of Western Avenue between Hanger Lane and Greenford Road became the first arterial route to incorporate cycle paths.[66] This prompted vociferous complaints from cyclists' associations, who fought to preserve their right to use main carriageways. Pedestrians, in turn, were outraged when some of the arterial roads and bypasses built in the 1920s were doubled in width to carry more traffic. Although built for speedy motoring, these roads had attracted residential developments to either side, and now became very dangerous to cross. For the first time, modern roads were becoming barriers. As a result, what was perhaps the first public road protest in England took place on Western Avenue in Acton in July 1938. The demonstrators mocked a temporary footbridge that had been erected to help pedestrians cross the road:

A procession led by Mr T. C. Foley, Secretary of the Pedestrians' Association, marched up to the bridge and unfolded a 15ft poster bearing the words 'Pons Asinorum', while Mr Foley performed the mock [naming] ceremony with a christening cup. Some of those taking part carried a miniature

coffin bearing the words 'Burgin's Folly Bridge', while others carried a perambulator containing a baby up the steps of the footbridge to demonstrate the difficulty which will be experienced by mothers.[67]

In fact, pedestrians had no option but to use these bridges, since guardrails prevented them crossing elsewhere.[68] Further protests took place on the Kingston Bypass, which had been 'dualled' in 1937 (pl. 296).[69] Disgusted with the six temporary footbridges that had been provided, women and children marched across the carriageways, demanding the imposition of lower speed limits.[70]

296 The Kingston Bypass, following its widening to become a dual carriageway, in 1937. Note the lateral service roads and the ribbon development.

The action of these protestors in obstructing traffic on major roads was attacked by the belligerent motoring journals, which pointed out that, 'if we are not very careful, these demonstrations will be but the beginning of a war between non-motoring citizens and progress as represented by the logical development of road transport'.[71]

By the end of the 1930s it was evident that Britain lagged behind some other motorised countries, notably Germany. While Britain had no more than 200 miles of dual carriageway, Germany's national motorway system was far advanced. Many of Britain's principal roads remained inadequate and problematic. Most notoriously, the A1 still wove through the centres of large towns such as Stamford, Grantham, Newark and Doncaster; it was impeded by several level crossings, and in many places provided barely enough width for two large vehicles to pass. On the entire route, there was not a single stretch of dual carriageway.[72]

On the eve of war, the British Road Federation (BRF) – a powerful pro-roads lobby group – vigorously promoted a new approach with an exhibition, *Road Architecture*.[73] Held in 1939 at the RIBA headquarters in Portland Place, London, this illustrated German and American roads and showed what could be done if a proper plan was implemented. Fundamentally, this was a recognition of how Britain had failed to keep pace with its rivals, rather than a realistic blueprint for the immediate future.

The Beautification of Roads, 1918-1939

In 1925 journalists pondered why the newly completed but 'somewhat dreary' Croydon Bypass was deserted by motorists: 'the police are frequently "trapping" them along it, so that may be a reason. Or is it too uninteresting?'[74] Three years later the writer H. J. Massingham condemned the new arterial roads: 'The motor road, inhuman, unnatural, and altogether relentless, drives like a ram through the countryside with as much regard for its forms and design as a hot poker drawn over a carpet.'[75] As this suggests, many of the new bypasses and arterial routes were inexpressibly dull, and took little account of the landscape through which they passed. Several groups were formed in the course of the 1920s to ameliorate this situation.

One of the first was the Roads of Remembrance Association (RRA), which was formed in 1919 to promote the embellishment of roads as war memorials.[76] The Association was concerned principally with enhancing roads by planting trees – ideally by schoolchildren on Armistice Day – in memory of the fallen. With its backing, roadside planting ceremonies took place in ordinary towns all over the country. Typically, commemorative tablets were displayed on iron guards around new trees, but these features were lost as trees expanded in girth. The RRA also suggested that roads might be widened or bridges rebuilt as memorials. Another idea was the creation of new highways 'of exceptional dignity and beauty, with open spaces at intervals, to serve as special memorials of the Great War'.[77] As ever, Rees Jeffreys – who had retired from the Road Board on the eve of its demise in 1919 – was ready with advice. He proposed the formation of a square opposite Sutton railway station,[78] and also suggested creating boulevards along the Croydon Bypass, which was then under construction. Others came forward with more ambitious projects: a memorial road running from the south of England to the north of Scotland, or even a Channel Tunnel ('a compliment to our French allies').[79] Despite its ambitions, the RRA achieved little beyond tree planting.

Although some argued that, given time, nature would heal the scars left by road building, the widespread recognition that landscaping should form an integral part of road design influenced the Road Improvement Act of 1925. This enabled local authorities to plant trees and shrubs along roads, and permitted the Road Fund to disperse grants to assist them. Expert advice, however, was not readily available and much municipal planting was unimaginative. From 1928 guidance was supplied by a new organisation, the Roads Beautifying Association (RBA), which was set up to advise public bodies on 'the adornment of highways by the skilful planting of well-selected trees and shrubs'.[80] It was the brainchild of Dr Wilfrid Fox (1875–1962), a noted amateur botanist and founder of Winkworth Arboretum.

The Kingston Bypass, where a hawthorn was ceremonially planted in October 1928,[81] was the first experimental 'beautifying' scheme to be undertaken by the RBA. This was rather suburban in character, with a rock garden at the London end of the route, tall single poplars to mark crossroads, and clumps of flowers and trees elsewhere.[82] A year later, the Guildford–Godalming Bypass was designed to be at its most beguiling during autumn, with copper beech hedges separating the footpaths from the road.[83] As well as advising local authorities, the RBA undertook projects of its own. In 1930 it acquired a 5-acre plot of woodland on the North Orbital Road near Denham in Buckinghamshire to save it from ribbon development. This was described at the time as 'the first attempt in this country to form one of the roadside reserves which are so attractive and essential a feature of the Motor Parkway scheme successfully carried out in the neighbourhood of New York'.[84] The Association also did much to engage public co-operation. In 1930, for example, it set up a Children's Branch, which distributed a leaflet, with a poem by A. A. Milne, encouraging mothers to buy trees at a cost of 2 guineas each to commemorate the births of their children. These trees formed Children's Cherry Avenues, and the new patroness of the Association, the Duchess of York, allowed two of the cherry trees to be dedicated to her daughters, Princesses Elizabeth and Margaret.[85] The RBA absorbed the RRA in 1928, and continued for some years to encourage avenues of remembrance, in memory of distinguished citizens, as well as fallen servicemen (pl. 297).

The RBA was beset by problems and criticisms. Vandals damaged 103 of the trees planted on the Kingston Bypass in the first year, and a bronze statuette of a child by the Merton spur – perhaps one of the first pieces of public art on an arterial road – was removed from its plinth.[86] Moreover, despite their efforts, much roadside planting remained monotonous, with trees planted exactly the same distance apart.[87] The RBA complained that aesthetic and horticultural issues were not taken into proper consideration at a sufficiently early stage in the planning process, and so verges were often too narrow to accommodate group

297 Avenue of Remembrance, Cymbeline Way (Colchester Bypass), 1933. The trees were planted under the auspices of the Roads Beautifying Association (RBA) and the Borough of Colchester, and were divided into sections devoted to servicemen, citizens, children and Girl Guides. In 1930 one of the first urban rescue digs was undertaken by archaeologists on a section of this bypass, corresponding to the modern Colne Bank Avenue, where many Roman remains were discovered.

ment and limited side roads, the parkway was more than just a fast artery: it was designed to enhance the pleasure of the driving experience.[93] Parker went on to create two would-be parkways in England: Princess Parkway, on the approach to the new municipal garden suburb of Wythenshawe, on the southern outskirts of Manchester (1929–32; pl. 293a), and Letchworth Gate, forging a link between Letchworth Garden City and the A1 (1929–32; pl. 298). Neither scheme was a parkway in the true American sense, since these were all-purpose roads, but each had a sinuous carriageway flanked by broad verges with irregular clumps of planting, winding footpaths and cycle paths. Princess Parkway was perhaps closer to the American ideal than Letchworth Gate.[94] Since it was to be crossed by another parkway, running east–west, it was considered that this 'might provide an excellent opportunity for trying, for the first time in England, the American device known as a "fly-over" bridge'.[95] The main junctions, however, took the form of roundabouts – in fact, some of the earliest purpose-built examples in the country – described at the time by Barry Parker as 'traffic circuses', and later replaced by flyovers when the parkway was transformed into the M65 in the 1960s. Parker's schemes may not have been true parkways, but they were noble attempts to provide an alternative to the dreary trunk roads that led in and out of England's towns and cities. Furthermore, they anticipated the parkway-style primary roads, flanked by greensward and devoid of building frontages, that later came to characterise Britain's post-war new towns.

Of all the road schemes of the 1930s, it was the Mickleham Bypass (1935–8; pl. 299) in Surrey that received the greatest praise for its landscaping. It ran through the Mole valley, near the base of Box Hill. Sometimes described as a 'parkway', this was a dual carriageway from the start, planned with 20-foot carriageways, 12-foot reservations and 9-foot cycle tracks. The sinuous carriageways followed the lie of the land, separating and then converging, with mature trees retained in the central reservation. The influential landscape architect Sylvia Crowe criticised the hard line at the top of the cuttings and the planting of non-local species such as *lonicera* and *buxus*, yet the Mickleham Bypass was often illustrated to show how new roads could look if they were carefully landscaped.[96] It retains much of its original character to this day.

planting.[88] But the RBA was, itself, criticised for favouring non-native species, and for its 'incorrigible addiction for little exotic timidities', more suited to the suburbs than to the open road.[89] Leading landscape architects and the Council for the Protection of Rural England (CPRE) expressed antipathy to the horticultural prettification of fast roads, believing instead that they should merge seamlessly into the landscape.[90] Despite this, when the Trunk Roads Act of 1937 brought 4,500 miles of arterial road under central control, the RBA was appointed the Government's official adviser on roadside planting.

By this time, the American parkway was influencing the landscaping of roads in England, thanks to the architect and planner Barry Parker, who had visited the U.S.A. in 1925 and subsequently advocated parkways as a means of preventing ribbon development. This idea was reinforced by the architect and conservationist Clough Williams-Ellis in his savage attack on ribbon development, *England and the Octopus*, published in 1928.[91] Often used as a synonym for 'boulevard', the 'parkway' (exemplified by the 'unfenced friendliness' of the Bronx River Parkway in New York,[92] completed in 1923) may be more properly defined as a corridor of land laid out with a road for fast through traffic, restricted to cars – indeed, sometimes with deliberately low overpass bridges that deterred commercial vehicles – and flanked to either side by a permanent green belt that respected natural topography. The main drawback was that the cost of the parkway could not be recovered by developing the frontages alongside it, since these did not exist. But despite its ban on lateral develop-

The Motoring Experience, 1918–1945

So what was it like to motor through the English countryside in the inter-war years? An expatriate Englishman, A. M. C. Scott, set down some brief impressions on taking home leave in 1930, after ten years in Rhodesia.[97] From reading English motoring journals, he anticipated congestion, accidents and appalling roads.

298 Letchworth Gate, one of the first parkways in the U.K., connected the town with the Great North Road (A1). It was primarily for the benefit of lorries serving Letchworth Garden City's industrial area.

299 The snaking white carriageways of the much-admired Mickleham Bypass, photographed from the top of Box Hill, Surrey, in 1939.

300 The AA Box No. 372, at Mere in Wiltshire, is of timber, with black and yellow paintwork. Probably dating from the 1950s, this rare survivor has been listed. A handful of others survive *in situ*, sometimes surrounded by a garden kept by the patrolman.

the road, with smooth blacktop replacing the rough – albeit more picturesque – surfaces found at the turn of the century. Scott was touring just months before the speed limit was abolished, effective from 1 January 1931. A subsequent spate of accidents led to the imposition of a 30mph limit in towns from 1934 (see Chapter 12), but rural roads remained free from speed restrictions until the mid-1960s.

Many would have challenged Scott's enthusiastic account, and the notion that roads were unpleasantly congested was already prevalent. It can be detected, for example, in an advertisement placed in *The Motor* in 1930 by the De Havilland Aircraft Company. Headed 'Buy a Moth – and fly there instead!', this combined an image of a Gipsy Moth aircraft flying over a suburb with a text that must have resonated with some of the magazine's readers:

> Motoring to-day means nothing more than a bonnet-to-luggage-grid procession . . . gone forever are the joys of the old open road . . . the traffic congestion has reached such a pitch that to escape it successfully one must now travel in another dimension. The air offers you pleasant relief from the crowded and dangerous roads . . .[98]

Congestion may have been rife in certain places, but modern eyes are struck by the absence of clutter in contemporary views of inter-war arterial roads. One common item of roadside furniture, however, was the AA or RAC telephone box, provided for members of these organisations who required assistance. Since its formation in 1905, the AA had employed scouts – a total of 950 men by 1913 – to warn motorists of police speed traps by failing to salute. The first shelters for patrolmen, erected in 1912, were black boxes with a simple gable facing the road, displaying the yellow AA sign. Before long telephones were installed in the boxes, and in 1920 members were issued with keys. Subsequent developments included a 'Super box', with a 20-foot-high illuminated signpost rising from its roof, which was put up at major junctions from 1925.[99] In 1927 the standard box was redesigned, with a gable on every face (pl. 300). RAC boxes were distinguishable from those of the AA by their blue colour. As redesigned in 1930 by Sir Edwin Lutyens, they displayed the letters 'RAC' in a shaped panel beneath an opening hatch.[100] The AA had 71 boxes in 1922, followed by rapid increases, reaching a peak of around 787 in 1967;[101] the RAC had 550 boxes in 1948. The need for so many roadside telephone boxes reflected the unreliability of cars, which were strained to the limit when heavily laden with passengers and luggage. Breakdowns were frequent and roadside repairs were a common sight, since inter-war cars were much easier to work on than modern cars, having none of their electronic complexity. On narrow main roads, a broken-down car could cause a major obstruction whilst awaiting the arrival of a 'motor ambulance' (i.e., a breakdown truck).

But his expectations were confounded. On a journey from Totnes in Devon to Folkestone in Kent, he discovered – provided arterial roads were avoided at weekends – that traffic 'appeared to be negligible'. Exeter's 'excellent and splendidly efficient' traffic lights were singled out for praise. The roads themselves he found 'simply wonderful': he 'never ceased to marvel at their superbly hard, punctureless, and almost vibrationless surface . . . countless miles of what I knew as rutty and stony lanes had invariably this beautiful hard, black surface'. Such accounts lend credence to the view that, away from the main coastal routes on summer weekends, this was a golden age for the motorist – a time when the almost mythical 'open road' became reality, at least for a privileged few (pl. 280). It also highlights the visual changes that had come about, transforming the topography of

301 'The first authorised parking place beside a highway': on the North Orbital Road between Rickmansworth and Denham in Buckinghamshire. The bends have been ironed out, and no traces remain of this car park. From *The Motor*, 24 March 1931, p. 314.

It was many years before designated stopping places were provided for motorists along main roads. Until 1930 motorists could park more or less at will in the countryside, but, following protests about parked cars desecrating landscapes of great beauty, such as the South Downs, the Road Traffic Act limited them to within 15 yards of a roadway. The first authorised parking place beside a highway in the open country was provided in 1930 at the roadside reserve mentioned above, on the North Orbital Road north of Denham.[102] This comprised a car park, provided by Buckinghamshire County Council, and a tract of woodland equipped with green-painted litter bins (pl. 301). There were qualms about behaviour in roadside reserves, and a 'watcher' was stationed in the wood 'to see fair play'.[103] While such initiatives were few and far between, it was suggested that loops of roadway rendered obsolete by straightening should be retained as lay-bys (a borrowed term, previously applied to railway sidings, and to river frontages where barges were moored). By 1934 several lay-bys had been created in this manner in north Wales, but not in England.[104] The new Liverpool–East Lancashire Road, however, opened in 1933 with a number of purpose-built lay-bys equipped with water points for steam wagons.[105] Meanwhile, unauthorised stopping places proliferated, especially on the wide verges of the new arterial roads. At weekends and on holidays these were often used by motorists, who parked their cars facing the road, set up deckchairs and enjoyed picnics whilst watching the traffic go by – a peculiar British pastime that endured into the 1960s (see pl. 335).

When war broke out in 1939, the experience of driving in urban areas, especially at night, was transformed by regulations enforcing the blackout (see Chapter 13). In rural areas, too, driving became more difficult, and not just because of shortages of petrol and components. In May 1940 thousands of signposts were either painted over or removed, since it was thought that these might assist the enemy in the event of an invasion (pl. 302). By 1942 Abercrombie could claim that road signs were 'now lamentably non-existent', but later that same year they began to be re-erected.[106] Another trial for wartime drivers was the condition of road crusts, which were poorly maintained. Civil engineers concentrated on airfield construction, work that taught them valuable skills that they were able to apply to road building after 1945.

302 Signage being removed during the Second World War, in case it assisted an invading German army.

England's Motorways

The scheme for a 1,000-mile network of motorways – as recommended in 1938 – garnered support in the course of the war. In 1942 Frederick Cook, Chief Highways Engineer in the Ministry of War Transport, drafted a paper encouraging the Government to support motorways.[107] Meanwhile, various organisations

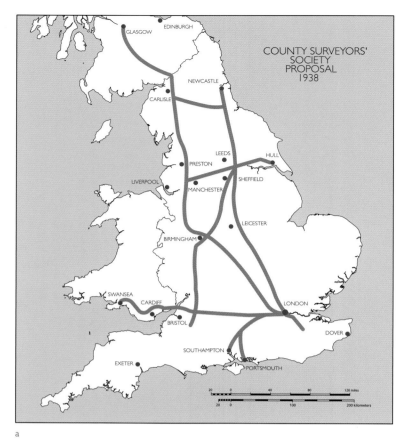

a

COUNTY SURVEYORS'
SOCIETY
PROPOSAL
1938

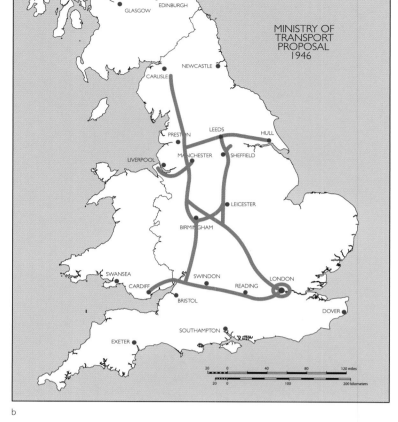

b

MINISTRY OF
TRANSPORT
PROPOSAL
1946

KEY

Proposed
Motorways

303a–d (*above and facing page*) Maps of English motorways: (a) the County Surveyors' Plan, 1938; (b) the Ministry of Transport Plan, 1946; (c) the motorway system as built, *circa* 1969; and (d) the motorway system as built, 2010. Three English cities, London, Birmingham and Manchester, are now completely ringed by motorways. These form hubs from which the national network, comprising 2,200 miles, radiates.

stirred enthusiasm for the idea. In January 1943 the Institute of Municipal and County Engineers published *The Post-War Development of Highways*, advocating motorways, and in December 1943 Sir William Rootes opened a British Road Federation (BRF exhibition, *Motorways for Britain*, designed by the landscape architect and town planner Geoffrey A. Jellicoe. A series of 'faked views', showing motorways superimposed on different types of landscape, illustrated the BRF's vision of 'Britain's post-war roads programme – 1,000 miles of motorways and their connecting roads designed to harmonise with typical British scenery'.[108] A year later, the BRF publication *New Roads for Britain: A Plan for the Immediate Future* argued that the construction of motorways should be given even greater priority after the war than urban reconstruction. It claimed that motorways would enable travellers to enjoy 'new vistas of scenery unimpaired by ribbon building'.[109] Furthermore, motorways would assist 'in the preservation of the beauties of Old England by making road-widening in picturesque towns and villages unnecessary'.

In May 1946 Alfred Barnes, the Minister of Transport, announced an ambitious ten-year plan for British roads: part of a master plan to disperse populations and industry away from the crowded and affluent South-East.[110] As yet, motorways were not the top priority: it was more important to deal with the deficit of road maintenance, to resume schemes interrupted by the war, to improve accident black spots, and to undertake projects that would contribute directly to growth in less prosperous 'development areas', such as building the Severn Bridge and the Tyne Tunnel, to boost industry in south Wales and the North-East, respectively. In the last years of the plan, however, attention would turn to new motor roads (pl. 303b), the most important routes being London–Birmingham–Penrith, London–Reading–Bristol–Cardiff, Hull–Doncaster–Birmingham–Bristol and Liverpool–Manchester–Leeds–Hull. The statutory powers required to build motorways were granted in 1949 by the Special Roads Act.[111] This stipulated that, once a scheme had been confirmed by the Ministry of Transport, the relevant highway authority

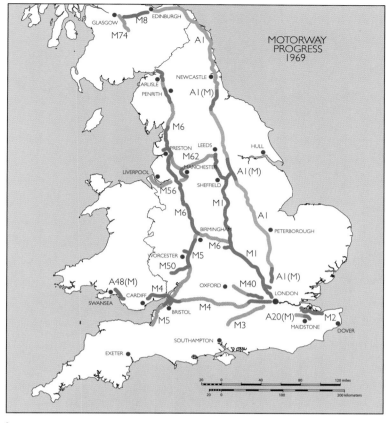

MOTORWAY
PROGRESS
1969

c

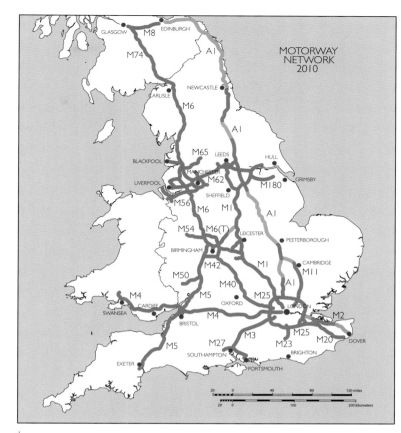

MOTORWAY
NETWORK
2010

d

KEY

Motorways

Motorways
under construction

Improved A roads

could take steps to acquire the necessary land, including sites for service stations.

The building of motorways was now a Government commitment, but the dire economic situation meant that for years only preparatory work – surveying routes, preparing contracts and purchasing land – could be carried out. Even the Severn Bridge and the Tyne Tunnel projects were postponed. It was the middle of the 1950s before construction actually began on England's first motorways: the M6, the M1/M45 and the M50. Aspects of these were pioneering in nature, with economy to the fore, and so it is unsurprising that problems emerged soon after carriageways opened, especially relating to road crusts and hard shoulders. In the longer term – by the late 1970s in many cases – it was found that extra lanes had to be added, something that could often be achieved only by rebuilding overpass bridges, for example, along the M5 in Worcestershire in the 1980s. Consequently, few early motorways retain their original character for lengthy stretches: the most evocative today are probably the under-used M45

and M50, and sections of the M1 in Buckinghamshire and Northamptonshire.

England's first completed motorway was the 8¼-mile Preston Bypass, ultimately part of the M6, which was opened on 5 December 1958 by the Prime Minister, Harold Macmillan. The M6 had been conceived in the late 1930s, and the Lancashire County Surveyor, James Drake, began to design the road in 1949.[112] In the mid-1950s, however, only the Preston and Lancaster bypasses could be financed. The process of creating the Preston Bypass was initiated in 1953, and construction – by Tarmac Ltd – began in 1956. Despite arguments for a three-lane national motorway standard, economy dictated that the road be built with two-lane carriageways. Nevertheless, the width of the central reservation and the spanning of the bridges allowed for future widening.[113] The twenty-two bridges adopted varying designs and technologies: concrete was preferred, although the 420-foot-long Samlesbury Bridge and the 474-foot-long Higher Walton Bridge – each built under separate contracts – had steel

PRESTON BY-PASS

OFFICIAL OPENING

BY THE

PRIME MINISTER

THE Rt. Hon. HAROLD MACMILLAN, M.P.

5th DECEMBER 1958

MINISTRY OF TRANSPORT AND CIVIL AVIATION
AGENT AUTHORITY—LANCASHIRE COUNTY COUNCIL

304 Samlesbury Interchange, illustrated on the cover of the Preston Bypass opening brochure. Lighting standards were erected by Tarmac, but removed by order of the Ministry of Transport, on the grounds of cost.

superstructures.[114] The motorway dipped beneath or soared over secondary roads, but terminated at ground-level roundabouts. It included just one intermediary junction, the tulip-shaped Samlesbury Interchange, where curved slip roads descended to roundabouts on the A59, just where the carriageways rose to bridge the River Ribble (pl. 304). This was, quite possibly, the English motorists' first experience of a two-level junction incorporating roundabouts.

The experimental Preston Bypass, thoroughly rebuilt and widened to four lanes in the mid-1990s, began its existence as a disjointed fragment of a motorway that took sixteen years to complete. The Lancaster Bypass – including the graceful Lune Bridge – opened in April 1960 (pl. 305).[115] Bridges were usually erected before roads, and the M6 to the south of Preston began in 1959 with the Thelwall and Gathurst viaducts. When the route between Birmingham and Preston opened in 1963, the architect W. G. Howell commented: 'unless you are a connoisseur of bridges, you could be anywhere from Watford to Preston'.[116] Already, the idea of the motorway as some characterless non-place was taking root. The M6 linked up to the Lancaster Bypass

in 1965, and reached Carlisle in 1970. Its southern end (the 'Midland Links') eventually connected with the M1, near Rugby, in 1972. Since motorways were invariably constructed under numerous separate contracts, this rate of progress proved fairly typical.

Meanwhile, priority was given to the 55-mile London to Birmingham (ultimately, the 150-mile London to Yorkshire) motorway, the M1.[117] Sir Owen Williams & Partners were commissioned in 1951 to study the proposed route between St Albans and Doncaster, and then, in 1955, to design the stretch from Junction 10 (Slip End/Pepperstock) to Junction 18 (Crick), as well as the M45 spur to Dunchurch, south of Rugby. The southern section, which began at the present-day Junction 5 (Berrygrove) and included a new St Albans Bypass (M10), was designed by Hertfordshire's County Surveyor, Lt. Col. C. H. ffolliott. The contractors, John Laing & Sons, began in March 1958, close to Slip End, and the motorway was opened in November 1959 by the new Minister of Transport, Ernest Marples, who was a vigorous promoter of roads over rail. The M1 comprised two-lane carriageways as far as Junction 7 (Beechtrees), then three-lane

305 The Lune Bridge on the Lancaster Bypass. This reinforced concrete, open-spandrel, fixed-arch bridge actually comprised two separate arches. It opened in April 1960.

survive – followed a uniform design, enabling shuttering to be recycled (pl. 306).[118] These bulky structures appeared to belong to another age, and were widely criticised at the time:[119] Williams's later bridges on the northern stretch of the M1 – with their raked columns, precast side units, aluminium railings and (often) single spans – were more contemporary in style. The M1 was extended south to Junction 4 (Elstree) in 1966, to Junction 2 (Fiveways) in 1967, and to Junction 1 (Staples Corner) in 1977, while the link from Crick to Doncaster was built between 1962 and 1967, with a connection reaching the outskirts of Leeds (Junction 44) by 1968. Finally, the M1–A1 Link in Yorkshire opened in 1999.

The practical experience of using the first motorways was salutary. In January 1959 the still-new Preston Bypass was damaged by frost and had to close for repairs. Then, soon after opening, asphalt surfacing on the M1 in Northamptonshire began to craze.[120] Much was yet to be learned about road crusts and drainage under motorway conditions. Hard shoulders, with 'soft' grassed surfaces and widths of just 8 feet, were unable to support the weight of jacks or to contain broken-down trucks with safety. Another problem was the speed adopted by some drivers, something that so shocked Ernest Marples at the opening of the M1 that he began immediately to contemplate

carriageways to Crick, while the M45 had two-lane carriageways for its full length. It was well understood that long, straight motorways lulled motorists to sleep, and the rhetoric surrounding the M1 lauded its gentle curves, but the reality was a rigidly straight motorway that imposed its own discipline on the landscape. Its massive, reinforced concrete bridges – many of which

306 Sir Owen Williams's reinforced concrete M1 bridges provoked controversy in 1959. Technologically and aesthetically, with their bulky form and faintly Neo-Egyptian styling, they appeared old-fashioned. The cultural critic Reyner Banham described them as 'the ugliest set of standardised structures in Britain' (Merriman 2003, 117), but for many they have strong period charm. Most are altered and patched with repairs: this well-preserved footbridge is near Milton Malsor in Northamptonshire, between Junction 15 and Junction 15a.

the imposition of speed limits.[121] This resulted, in 1965, in the introduction of a national speed limit of 70mph, reduced to 60mph on single carriageways in 1977. Motorway speeds pushed cars to their limit, contributing to breakdowns. On the M1, motorists had recourse to telephones, positioned on the hard shoulder at 1-mile intervals, sheltered within blue open-fronted cabinets marked 'SOS'.[122] These were connected to the local police station, which transferred calls to the appropriate motoring organisation or local garage. Despite breakdowns, the M1 coped well with heavy snowfall in the winter of 1959–60 due to the foresight with which depots of snow-clearing vehicles and gritters were dotted along its length, every 12 miles. The standard metal salt hoppers or bunkers of the 1960s have been superseded in more recent years by gigantic salt barns that often adopt a domical form, suggestive of a more pious purpose than simple salt storage. As at Newport Pagnell and Watford Gap on the M1, these maintenance depots were often co-located with service stations (see Chapter 11). Police posts were also based at service stations whenever possible, but were sometimes sited separately. An early example survives on the Stevenage Bypass, on the roundabout at Junction 7 of the A1(M), complete with its original building and lettering.

Special signs were designed for motorways by Jock Kinneir and Margaret Calvert, under the auspices of a committee chaired by Sir Colin Anderson. Provisional signs – influenced by European examples and tested at Hendon Airfield – were installed on the Preston Bypass in 1958.[123] These appeared, at first, ludicrously large, since they were designed to be read from a distance of up to 600 feet and at a speed of 70mph. On a bright blue ground – copying practice in Belgium, the Netherlands and West Germany – they displayed white mixed-case lettering in sans serif fonts known as 'Transport' and, for route numbers, 'Motorway'. An alternative font called 'MOT-serif' was produced by the typeface designer David Kindersley, but this unsolicited and rather dated offering was shelved following inconclusive tests. Kinneir's signs were slightly modified in the light of experience: in particular, a pictorial symbol depicting two motorway lanes as parallel lines within a circle was dropped. Otherwise, the simplicity and elegance of the blue signs ensured their retention, though they have been augmented by additional signage over the years. For example, a series of dramatic crashes in fog led to the installation of flashing amber warning lights (switched on by radar guns fired from passing police cars) in 1965, followed a year later by electronically controlled dot matrix signs, set on the central reservation, which advised specific speed limits in the event of fog, ice or accidents.[124] The first computer-controlled warning signs came into use on the M6 and M62 in 1972, with a computer centre established at Westhoughton, Lancashire, soon followed by others at Perry Barr (M6), Scratchwood (M1), Hook (M3) and Almondsbury (M4/M5).[125] One form of motorway

sign that never materialised, despite investigations by the Road Research Laboratory in 1969, was the 'talking road sign', with site-specific messages delivered to drivers through their radios.[126]

The cost of building the motorway network was huge: Ministers considered imposing tolls from time to time, but road pricing never proved politically expedient. Nevertheless, progress was rapid. No less than 150 miles of motorway were in use by 1961, 400 by 1966, and 1,000 by 1972. Then it could be claimed that England possessed a basic motorway network (see pl. 303c).[127] This included the M1 from Fiveways to Doncaster (completed in 1972), the M2 from London to Faversham (completed in 1965), the M3 from Lightwater to Popham (completed in 1971), the M4 from London to Newport (completed in 1971), the M5 from Avonmouth to Birmingham (completed in 1971), the M50 (Ross Spur, embarked upon as a cheap alternative to a Severn Bridge and completed in 1960) and the M6 from Rugby to Carlisle (completed in 1972), plus small sections of the M20, M40, M60 (originally M62) and other shorter motorways. The M62, built across the mountainous terrain of the Pennines in severe weather conditions, tested the skills and endurance of engineers and construction workers more than any other motorway. This project also tested the extent to which motorways can respect England's most beautiful and untamed landscapes.

In 1958 Professor Colin Buchanan stated:

> It is ludicrous, in the author's view, to pretend that a road 100ft wide can *enhance* any traditional British landscape; such a gash cannot possibly be anything but a destroyer of the countryside, a devastator of trees, woods, hedgerows, wild life, quietude, topography and natural drainage.[128]

He may well have been recalling Jellicoe's 'faked views' (see above). Motorways could not simply be rolled out, like a carpet, over the existing countryside; instead, the landscape had to be sculpted to receive them, with embankments that raised them over flat plains, and cuttings that reduced gradients on hilltops, chiefly for the benefit of HGVs. The landscaping of such colossal earthworks required a sensitive approach. Generally, the landscape architects assigned to motorway projects were assisted by the independent Landscape Advisory Committee, which had been established as the Standing Advisory Committee on Landscape Treatment of Trunk Roads in 1947.[129] This addressed issues such as earth mounding and contouring, as well as planting. Treatments particularly responsive to landscape could be seen in the split carriageways of the M6 north of Tebay in Cumbria. On the M62, the carriageways were famously diverted to either side of the eighteenth-century Stott Hall Farm, the road being built while the house was still occupied.

Motorway earthworks (pl. 307) will probably endure for centuries, but to the uninformed eye they are less conspicuous than bridges, which accounted for 25 to 30 per cent of motorway

307 Scammonden Bridge on the M62 was the largest single-span fixed-arch bridge in the country when it was built in 1971. The arch had a span of 410 feet, and carried a 66-foot deck on eight spandrel and four abutment walls. In the foreground is the motorway embankment built alongside the Scammonden dam.

spending.[130] In 1964 the Ministry of Transport collaborated with the Royal Fine Art Commission to produce design guidance for bridges, illustrating the Lune Bridge on the cover.[131] The text advocated occasional departures from the principle that function should be the sole basis of design.[132] Despite this, standardisation was often imposed on motorway projects. Motorway bridges were usually designed by the county engineer and his staff, with the aid of consultants (occasionally architects, more usually engineers), and with only high-profile designs being referred to the Royal Fine Art Commission.

Notwithstanding Sir Owen Williams's preference for reinforced concrete bridges on the M1, pre-stressed concrete, with its improved tensile strength, was rapidly taken up for motorway bridges, except those – for example, spanning railway lines and waterways – that were so large that they had to be built of steel.

Pre-stressed concrete had been used for road and rail bridges since the 1940s,[133] an early example being the Northam Bridge, Southampton (1954). The relatively shallow beams of such bridges, for example the Medway Bridge on the M2 – designed by Oleg Kerensky of Freeman, Fox & Partners, and thought to be the longest bridge of its kind in Europe when it opened in 1962 – produced economical and elegant designs. Gilbert Roberts of Freeman, Fox & Partners was responsible for seminal bridges, such as the Maidenhead Bridge (M4, 1959–61), the Severn Bridge (M4, later M48, 1961–6) – the first motorway bridge to be listed – and the Humber Bridge (A15, 1981). Freeman, Fox & Partners also designed the two-level steel box-girder Tinsley Viaduct (1965–8) over the River Don, with the M1 on the upper deck and a local road (A631) below. Internationally, a number of steel box-girder bridges collapsed during

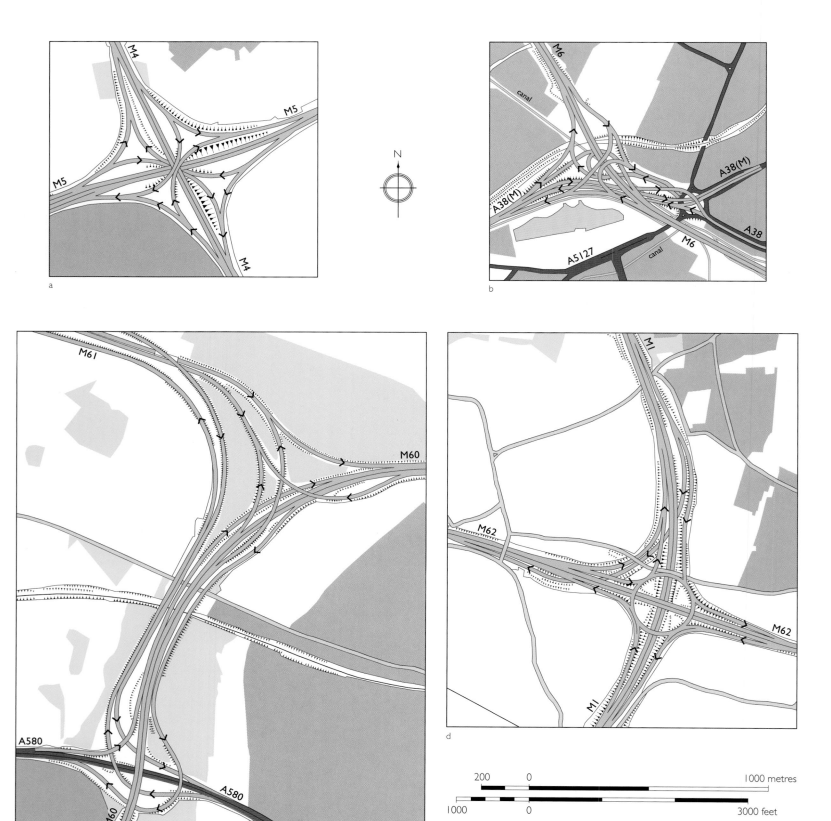

308 Diagrams of English motorway junctions drawn to scale: (a) Almondsbury Interchange (M4/M5; 1964–6); (b) Worsley Braided Interchange (M61/M62; 1967–70); (c) Gravelly Hill (Spaghetti Junction; M6/A38(M); 1969–72); and (d) Lofthouse Interchange (M1/M62; 1969).

construction in the late 1960s and early 1970s, including two by Freeman, Fox & Partners, and so the safety of such structures became a matter of grave concern. Around forty-six had been built on the motorway network. Following an Inquiry by the Merrison Committee in 1973, these were tested and, where necessary – as in the case of the Tinsley Viaduct – strengthened. By this time, in the pursuit of elegance, most motorway bridges were simple trabeated (slab and beam) structures, often with raking struts or columnar stanchions. Open parapets and cantilevered decks with narrow edges emphasised the slenderness of slabs. Solid abutments and wing walls were often textured, to disguise the inevitable staining of the concrete, and were softened by dense planting. Open abutments, however, were recommended for rural settings, and some of the most successful designs were arcuated, with open spandrels (pls 305 and 307). Unlike bridges of the pre-war period, decorative detail was absent.

Initially, motorway interchanges were relatively simple: slip roads led to roundabouts, and junctions (unnumbered until 1966) were restricted to two levels. In the mid-1960s, coinciding with the advent of computer-aided design, more complex junctions came into being to engineer free-flowing connections between major routes, without intervening roundabouts (pl. 308). Depending on the sensitivity of the site and the availability of land, slip roads could lie low, sprawling over a large area (something impossible in the urban environment), or they could be tightly stacked, creating tall sculptural forms in the landscape. One of the first free-flow junctions, at Brentford on the M4 (1964), was particularly economical in terms of land use, because straightforward parallel slip roads linked the superimposed carriageways of the M4 and A4 (see Chapter 13).[134] Several three-tier junctions opened in 1965. The first, the Brent Cross Flyover carrying Hendon Way (A41) over the North Circular (A406) in London, was not actually on a motorway, but it adopted what would become a classic, even ubiquitous, arrangement – used later, for example, at Sandiacre (1966) and at the Lofthouse Interchange (1969), both on the M1[135] – with a roundabout sandwiched between, or positioned above, major routes flowing north–south and east–west. In contrast, the Broughton Interchange (i.e., a remodelling of the north end of the Preston Bypass, opened in 1965) connected the M6 and M55 seamlessly, with long, interlacing slip roads and no roundabouts.[136] The four-tier Almondsbury Interchange (1964–6; Freeman, Fox & Partners) on the M4/M5 was the most remarkable junction in the country when it opened: unusually symmetrical, it occupied 100 acres and rose 65 feet in height. Very different, but equally notable, were the long and densely entwined slip roads of the Worsley Braided Interchange (1967–70) – really two interchanges plus a link – which connected the M61, M62 (now M60) and A580.[137] In places, this was seventeen lanes wide. Most famous

of all, however, was Spaghetti Junction (1969–72; Sir Owen Williams; pl. 309), more properly known as Gravelly Hill, at the junction of the M6 and A38(M) Aston Expressway: a seemingly undisciplined tangle of roads on eight levels, rising to 80 feet in height and occupying a 30-acre site, representing great economy in land use. This single junction cost £8 million to build. The architectural historian and critic Reyner Banham, who admired American roadside culture, dismissed it as an 'agreeable little suburban megastructure'.[138]

Through the 1970s and 1980s the developmental stage of motorway projects was increasingly protracted by public inquiries. Nevertheless, in these years many of the motorways begun in the 1950s and 1960s, such as the M40 to Oxford (1967–74) and the M62 (1966–76), were completed, and new motorways were built, including the M11 (1972–80), M42 (1974–6), M69 (1975–7) and M54 (1981–3). On 29 October 1986 the final section of the 117-mile M25, London's outer ring road, was opened by Margaret Thatcher.[139] This road had a particularly long gestation period, involving significant revisions. Its roots lay in the North Orbital, started in the 1920s, but Sir Patrick Abercrombie's Greater London Plan of 1944 had postulated an 'express arterial' ring, lying 12 miles from central London, rather than the North Orbital's 17.[140] These routes evolved, in convoluted fashion, into the M25, set between 13 and 22 miles from the centre, and equipped with thirty-two junctions. The northern loop of the motorway included two particularly sensitive stretches lying close to housing. Cuttings were proposed, but the ultimate – more expensive – solution was cut-and-cover tunnels, with their flat tops grassed over. The landscaping of the M25, with 2.1 million trees and shrubs planted by 1986, was a major undertaking. This has been undermined in more recent years, since the addition of a fourth (or, in places, fifth) lane has involved truncating the original embankments and shoring them up with vertical retaining walls constructed of steel sheet piles. Together with the addition of closely spaced metal gantries, this has lent the M25 an industrial aesthetic, closer in character to a railway line than any other British road.

Orange cones came to symbolise the state of English motorways in the 1980s, as ageing carriageways were upgraded to suit modern traffic conditions. Many aspects of motorway design had changed over the years. They were now being built with three rather than two lanes (i.e., 36-foot rather than 24-foot carriageways), and had thicker surfaces, to cope with the growth in HGV traffic. Embedded detection pads and CCTV had been introduced to monitor traffic from the mid-1960s. Various safety features had developed, such as edging hard shoulders with noisy rumble strips and installing safety barriers. Although an anti-dazzle fence had been erected on a curve of the M1 in 1960, the early motorways had no crash barriers. These remained controversial throughout the 1960s: it was argued that they would

309 An aerial view of the complex Gravelly Hill Intersection, otherwise known as Spaghetti Junction (1969–72).

310 In the early 1990s the RAC built five Supercentres (Rescue Control Centres), including this prominent building overlooking the M6 at Walsall, designed by BDP (1990). Still a landmark for drivers, it is often compared to a patrolman's cap.

be expensive and might increase the chances of serious accidents. Besides, in the opinion of a Ministry of Transport engineer, 'it would ruin the appearance of the motorway [M1] to have a great fence down the middle'.[141] But as traffic grew, the potential life-saving benefits of safety barriers became apparent. Erected from the late 1960s onwards, they were initially of either wire rope or metal beams, with those on central reservations embedded in gravel to slow vehicles down.[142] It was only in 1970, however, that the Minister of Transport decided that barriers should be erected on all busy motorways. The arrival of lighting standards was equally tardy: these had been removed from the new Samlesbury Interchange on the orders of the economically minded Ministry in 1958, and it was 1973 before they became an accepted feature of motorway junctions.[143] Adding to the now-cluttered appearance of motorways, fixed speed cameras arrived in 1992, and average speed cameras ten years later. Since the 1990s traditional and computerised signs have been displayed on gantries rather than posts. These steel structures must fail safely if hit by a vehicle, so they are very robust. The Highways Agency bridge design guidance of 1996 admitted that 'contemporary technology still needs to be integrated into the landscape', illustrating heavy gantries, laden with signs, 'generally out of character with the surroundings'.[144] The paraphernalia of today's motorways can be contrasted with the clean lines of the M1 at its opening in 1959: safety comes at a high aesthetic price.

The 1980s ended on a high note for road building, with a White Paper, *Roads for Prosperity* (May 1989), which proposed 2,700 miles of new or widened roads to be built at a cost of more than £12.4 billion.[145] The archaeological recording required to deal with this programme would have cost £70 million.[146] This was out of kilter with the times, however, and

was quickly scaled down. The 1990s were coloured by road protest on a hitherto unimagined scale. Heightened environmental awareness was promoting a massive surge in anti-road sentiment and numerous schemes were scrapped in 1994–5, including a new link between the M1 and the M62, and the M12 to Chelmsford. The Labour Government issued *A New Deal for Transport* in 1998, cancelling many other road schemes, including the remainder of the M65. Meanwhile, several projects reached completion, such as the M40 from Oxford to Birmingham (1987–91), the M65 from Preston to Colne (1997), the M60 Manchester Orbital (2000) and the M6 Toll Road (2003; pl. 312). The M6 Toll Road originated as a public sector project, the Birmingham Northern Relief Road, but was offered to the private sector in 1989 and built by Midland Expressway Ltd in the years 1997–2003. Another scheme, the M1–A1 Link, which opened in 1999, was built under a similar DBFO (design, build, finance, operate) private sector arrangement, but in this case the company, Yorkshire Link, will receive 'shadow tolls' from the Highways Agency until its thirty-year concession expires in 2026. Other private sector toll schemes include estuarial crossings, such as the Second Severn Crossing (1997). By 1996, 2,000 miles of motorway existed, then carrying 17 per cent of all road traffic.[147] It might appear that no new motorways are currently being built, but existing motorways are being upgraded with extra lanes, and lengths of the A1 (see below) continue to be remodelled in piecemeal fashion to motorway standard.

As the motorway network reached completion at the end of the twentieth century, its transformative influence on society became apparent. As well as encouraging longer commutes and weekend breaks, motorways have facilitated the growth of out-of-town shopping. They have greatly expanded the potential

311 Distribution warehouses are an increasingly familiar aspect of the modern English roadscape. Typical of the genre is this River Island Distribution Centre at Magna Park near Milton Keynes in Buckinghamshire, built in 2008–10.

312 A bird's-eye view of a toll plaza on the M6 Toll Road. Planned in 1980, this 27-mile motorway bypasses the old M6 between Junction 4 and Junction 11a, north of Birmingham. Midland Expressway won the contract to build and operate the road. It is claimed that 2½ million Mills & Boon novels were recycled for the blacktop (Moran 2009, 256).

catchment areas of huge malls, such as Bluewater in Kent (see pl. 275). To an even greater extent, motorways have driven the growth of the logistics industry, which is served by enormous steel-framed warehouses at the major junctions of motorways and 'A' roads, especially throughout the Midlands (pl. 311). These bulky structures are conspicuous features of the modern road-scape, despite the application of graduated bands of cornflower-blue paintwork, designed to make them blend seamlessly into the pale English sky. Magna Park at Milton Keynes, next to the M1, incorporates wind turbines and grey water recycling. The environmental implications of such developments, however, unthinkable without a modern road system, have fed the back-lash against motorways.

•

Motorway Protest

Opposition to motorways mounted in potency over many years: the language of protestors grew in vigour and their methods became increasingly disruptive, ranging from clever manipulation of the Public Inquiry process to plain sabotage. Neither the M1 nor the Preston Bypass had drawn concerted protest concerning damage to the landscape or the environment, though cyclists did grumble about their exclusion from the new roads. In general, people were enthusiastic about motorways, and supported the endeavour.

One of the first real controversies in the 1950s was the route of the M1 through Charnwood Forest in Leicestershire: the Ministry tried to defuse opposition by promising to hide the motorway in cuttings as it ran through the forest, something that was carried out to a limited extent.[148] Similar dismay was expressed in 1962, by John Betjeman and others,[149] when it was suggested that the M4 might take a route north of Reading, threatening the Berkshire Downs. As well as pointing out that noise from the motorway would destroy the tranquillity of the area, objectors cited the damage that would be inflicted on the natural contours of the landscape. Emotive language was deployed. In a report for the Berkshire Downs Villages' Association, Geoffrey Jellicoe – the landscape architect who had conjured up 'faked views' in support of motorways in the 1940s – wrote: 'the proposed motorway would itself not just be contrary to the natural process, but it would infest the area with all the urban diseases of which motorways are both heirs and carriers'.[150]

By the 1970s protestors had become adept at marshalling their arguments, but still found it hard to sway officialdom. The route of the M40 prompted several wrangles over two decades. In 1970 a controversial route through the Chilterns at Lewknor was reaffirmed by the Minister following a Public Inquiry, an alternative, known as the Arup–Jellicoe line, being rejected.[151] Protestors were left with a bitter sense of injustice, and the CPRE maintained that the outcome was predetermined. The extension of the M40 from Oxford to Birmingham was also fiercely opposed, especially where it was destined to pass through marshy land at Otmoor in Oxfordshire, described by James Lees-Milne in 1973 as 'an oasis of medieval England', and also through the nearby Bernwood Forest butterfly reserve.[152] Various new tactics were tried: for example, on the eve of a Public Inquiry in 1983 – giving the Ministry no time to refute the allegation – it was claimed that the area was littered with unexploded bombs. This Public Inquiry was held, as usual, before an independent inspector, who strongly advised that the route should avoid Otmoor. When the Ministry adhered doggedly to its original plan, protestors devised a cunning strategy. A field on the route, known as Alice's Meadow, was purchased by the Friends of the Earth and divided into 3,500 tiny plots, which were sold to its supporters, each of whom intended to oppose the compulsory purchase process. Eventually, victory was theirs: the route veered to the east, away from Otmoor and Bernwood Forest.

By 1969 it was clear that motorway construction was having a devastating effect on buried archaeology, and committees were formed for the first time to coordinate rescue digs along proposed routes. The first of these were created to work on the M5 (1969), the M40 (1970) and the M11 (1971). Instead of just targeting known sites, archaeologists now began to develop new techniques of prospection and monitoring, and to look at sites in a whole landscape context. In 1972 it was resolved that the M3 Archaeological Rescue Committee be formed to plan excavations on selected sites along the new motorway. Only eight sites had been excavated on the 37-mile London to Popham stretch, begun in 1968. In contrast, on the 10½-mile stretch between Popham and Winchester (Bar End), which opened in 1985, forty-five excavations were carried out, including an Iron Age site on Winnall Down.[153] This was indicative both of changing attitudes and of enhanced funding for rescue archaeology between the 1960s and 1980s. But it also reflected the longer period of time granted to archaeologists to dig in advance of roadworks on the controversial southern section of this motorway, due to protracted opposition. Between 1990 and 1993 Wessex Archaeology, funded by the Department for Transport, undertook important excavations between Bar End and Compton, through Twyford Down, to the east of Winchester.[154] It was here, where the motorway was to occupy a 400-yard chalk cutting, that road protest famously exploded into direct action.

Twyford Down was designated as a Site of Special Scientific Interest (SSSI) and an Area of Outstanding Natural Beauty (AONB), as well as including several Scheduled Ancient Monuments (SAMs). Despite the recognised status of the land, this route had been adopted for the M3 in 1990, following several public inquiries.[155] Campaigners preferring a tunnel, instead of a cutting, took their case to the High Court, which found against them, then to the European Community Commissioner for the Environment, who did not support their case. With legal avenues exhausted, in 1992 the so-called Dongas tribe – self-styled after ancient local trackways – arrived on the scene, setting up Britain's first road protest camp, which was perhaps inspired by the earlier CND protest camp at Greenham Common. The Dongas – who quickly formed a strange alliance with more conventional local protestors – were travellers, steeped in mysticism and proclaiming a spiritual connection with the land. A tribal member recalled: 'we were simply 15-odd (very, very odd) people on a hill, with a goat, running out to stop two old bulldozers and a few site officials and cops who'd come up to try and catch us unawares'.[156] The violent eviction of the Dongas' camp served to swell the numbers of protestors in the course of 1993. By this time, however, the cutting was well advanced and in 1994 the road opened, two scheduled monuments having been destroyed. The protestors – many of whom went on to occupy tree houses on the Newbury Bypass (1994–6), build tunnels under the A30 at Fairmile in Devon (1996–7), or declare 'independent republics' along the route of the M11 extension in London (see Chapter 13) – had lost the battle, but they were winning the war. Policing Twyford Down proved costly – £2 million by July 1993 – and was a public relations disaster, focusing environmental protest on the roads issue. By mid-1993 more than 200 (mostly middle-class) anti-road groups, all strongly opposed to the Department of Transport's policies, had been established, and the Government was 'running scared'.[157] New motorways were almost certainly dropped in the mid- to late 1990s as a consequence of events at Twyford Down. Significantly, the protestors left their own permanent mark on the landscape by erecting an inscribed

313 The Twyford Down monument in Hampshire, a chalk monolith erected by road protestors, is inscribed 'this land was ravaged by . . . ', followed by a list of names that includes J. Major and M. Thatcher. This was excluded when the scheduled area was redefined in 2000.

country's brief flirtation with modernist design, or compare the regimented, white-line landscape of the road with the classical regularity of Georgian terraces. Industrial archaeologists will purr over the motorway maintenance depots and the rock salt barns used for gritting. . . . If the roads are unused and overgrown, then maybe we will simply experience what Rose Macaulay calls that 'morbid pleasure of decay' that the Romantic poets and painters felt among the ruins of Gothic abbeys and Greek temples.[159]

All-purpose Roads since 1945

Most arterial road schemes were abandoned at the outbreak of the Second World War in 1939. Little maintenance was carried out for six years, but after 1945 many roads were resurfaced using machinery that had been introduced to build airfields during the war. The idea of planting roads of remembrance was revived, very briefly, with the A20 being designated an avenue of remembrance of the Battle of Britain.[160] Cherry avenues were planted by several Women's Institutes, for example, in Cherry Hinton, Cambridge, with each tree representing thirty-four fallen servicemen.[161] In 1947 the Ministry of Transport set up its own Landscape Advisory Committee, and the Town & Country Planning Act gave local authorities the power to control outdoor advertising and tidy up the roadscape. Subsequently, many 'wayside eyesores' surviving from the 1930s were either spruced up or swept away.

The Government's ten-year road plan, announced in May 1946, prioritised the completion of existing road schemes above the creation of motorways. But economic circumstances meant that progress was frustratingly slow. The Roads Campaign Council, with representatives from various motoring organisations, launched a crusade in 1955 to press for 'more and better roads'. In May 1956, for example, it published advertisements in the national press, exposing how the promises of the ten-year plan had failed to materialise.[162] It also organised trips, so that British MPs could witness modern European roads at first hand. This, it hoped, might shame them into action.

The dualling of major trunk roads, including many arterial routes created in the 1920s and 1930s, resumed in the late 1950s and gathered momentum in the 1960s. The top priority, announced in 1957, was the 270-mile Great North Road, the A1, from London to Newcastle. As well as being transformed into a dual carriageway (57 per cent of the route by 1963, 76 per cent by 1966), many bypasses and roundabouts were built along its length, and its first stretch of motorway, the Stevenage Bypass, opened in 1962. This mixture of single carriageway, all-purpose dual carriageway and motorway, attended by sudden changes in driving conditions, was regarded by some interest

monolith to the east of the cutting in 1992 (pl. 313).[158] Once the new motorway was open, the 1930s Winchester Bypass, to the west of St Catherine's Hill, was returned to nature, and one of the earliest 'flyover junctions' in England was consigned to history.

The motorways of the twentieth century may, themselves, some day be superseded by a new transport system. In 2009 Joe Moran imagined how heritage enthusiasts of the future might perceive their remains:

Perhaps the motorway heritage society of the next century will campaign to save the precious Jock Kinneir signs, our

314   Anthony Gormley's *Angel of the North* (1998) is Britain's best-known example of roadside art, providing a landmark for travellers.

groups, such as the County Surveyors, as highly dangerous.[163] The completion of the Tyne Tunnel in 1967 formed a crucial link in the north–south route (now the A19) until the Newcastle Western Bypass opened in 1990. This was adorned in 1998 with one of the best-known pieces of road art in the country: Anthony Gormley's monumental steel sculpture, the *Angel of the North* (pl. 314). John Major's commitment to turn the A1 into a motorway for its entire length between London and Newcastle was overturned by Tony Blair in 1997. Currently (2011), work is under way to upgrade a stretch through County Durham and North Yorkshire, but it is unclear just when the full length of the A1 might become an uninterrupted motorway.

Many post-war 'A' roads included bridges and viaducts of comparable ambition to those on motorways. Devon and Cornwall were linked by the Tamar Bridge at Saltash (1959–61; Mott, Hay & Anderson), a suspension bridge with a three-lane carriageway, built alongside Brunel's railway bridge. The same consultant engineers came up with a very different design for the Widnes–Runcorn Bridge (1957–61), which superseded a transporter bridge over the Mersey. On this steel bow-arch bridge, the transverse girders carrying the deck were hung from a gigantic arch. Many of England's post-war road bridges made claims to international pre-eminence: in this case, with a span of 1,082 feet, as the largest arch bridge in Europe. One of the earliest post-war viaducts worthy of note was the pre-stressed concrete Wentbridge Viaduct on the A1, which opened in 1961. Once again, claims were made: this time as 'the largest viaduct of its

kind in Europe'.[164] Intersections on 'A' roads rarely occupy as much land as those on motorways, nor do they rise to the same heights. Generally, they are simple roundabouts, or two-level junctions with a roundabout either dropped beneath or raised above the main carriageway. An early instance of this type of intersection had been designed for the Hook Road junction of the Kingston Bypass in the late 1930s (see above, pl. 292), but was not completed until 1960.[165]

In 1965 new traffic signs were introduced nationally, following the recommendations of the Worboys Committee (see Chapter 13). Direction signs for primary routes changed too, following a trial on the A34 at Hall Green. These used white lettering and yellow route numbers on a green background, the exact hue of the background ('Slough Green') sparking much debate amongst landscape architects. Signs on minor roads were to deploy black lettering on a white ground. This spelled destruction for many fingerpost signs: several counties had discarded these wholesale by 1975, when they were given a reprieve.[166] The replacement signs were of sheet aluminium with a reflective coating. Posts, rather than being striped black and white, were now painted gunmetal grey, as were the backs of signs. The new signage had a transformative effect on the national roadscape, but even today it has not fully superseded earlier signs, which can occasionally be spotted in both rural and urban environments.

While roads such as the A1 were being improved piecemeal, some completely new routes were created. One of the principal

315   A village scene on the A1. The dual carriageway drives a barrier through Beeston, located south of Sandy in Bedford-shire. This is mitigated, in part, by a footbridge of industrial character, high enough to give clearance for HGVs and doubling up as a gantry to display traffic signs. Note the speed camera and associated road markings.

new 'A' roads was the 127-mile A14, connecting the Midlands with Felixstowe. The route from Huntingdon to the M6 was one of the first non-motorway routes to be subjected to public consultation (1974) and public inquiries (1984–5) as part of its preliminary stages. Like motorways, such roads could threaten historic sites or beautiful landscapes. In the case of the A14, the route crossed the Civil War battlefield of Naseby, prompting the formation of a special protest group (the Society for the Preservation of Naseby Field) led by eminent historians such as John Plumb, which took the Department to the High Court.[167] The section east of Huntingdon was completed – or rather upgraded – first, between 1973 and 1982, while the section west of Huntingdon, linking the A1 with the M1, was built from 1989 to 1994. The A14 was a dual carriageway with grade separation, with only the Cambridge and Newmarket bypasses built to motorway standard, complete with hard shoulders. Over the years, quite a number of trunk roads have been built as motorways, only to be downgraded to receive all types of traffic, one example being the Tring Bypass of 1973–7, the former A41(M).[168]

One project that had stalled due to the war was the Stilton–Alconbury Bypass on the A1. When completed in 1958, this was used to test different road pavements under operational conditions.[169] The construction of dual carriageway bypasses, as the chief means of improving trunk roads, had resumed apace

by 1960, though it was now recognised – for example, in the short film *The Village Sleeps Again* (1962) – that delivering peace to village streets also meant loss of custom for local businesses.[170] As the landlady at The Bell in Stilton quipped, 'they call us still town now'.[171] According to *The Times*: 'the [Stilton] by-pass cast an air of desolation over the village; all the licensees of public houses on the main road left, two cafés, a filling station and an hotel closed down'. Here and elsewhere, village services were signposted from the bypass, but to little effect. Meanwhile, the prevalence of piecemeal bypasses, as Tripp had highlighted in 1942, was transforming some main roads into series of loops, strung together by roundabouts.[172]

The logical alternative to a bypass was brutal severance: slicing a village in half with a dual carriageway. The effects of this may be seen, for example, in Beeston in Bedfordshire, where traffic on the A1 ploughs along the High Road at a speed of 50mph, controlled by signage and speed cameras, which add their own clutter to the environs (pl. 315). An industrial-style footbridge, quite out of scale with its surroundings, links the two sides of the settlement, and residents have to put up with dirt, thrown up by traffic and caking the façades of their houses. The impact is quite different when the single carriageway of a more minor road wends its way through an English village. These roads are decorated with a plethora of signs to welcome and thank the careful motorist, combined with threats of speed cameras, chi-

316   This aerial view of Ely in Cambridgeshire shows how new housing extends to the curved bypass, which forms a rigid boundary on the west side of the town. This development pattern has been repeated throughout the country.

canes and speed humps for the careless. As Bell has astutely observed, the resulting visual cacophony 'makes every village look like an *It's a Knockout* assault course'.[173]

Since the 1980s bypasses have encouraged a peculiar pattern of suburban development (pl. 316). Because the land encompassed by the arc of a bypass was not protected as a green buffer zone, it was targeted by developers, who bought up the fields to build vast housing estates. In the past, the outskirts of towns had straggled along main roads, merging imperceptibly into the countryside, but now the bypass created a hard boundary. Aesthetically, the ubiquitous bypass housing estate might be regarded as the modern-day equivalent of inter-war ribbon development. Bypass housing, however, is less of a nuisance: it is accessed indirectly and does not disrupt traffic flow on main roads. Jams are

more likely to be caused by traffic using the various businesses that are attracted to major junctions.

Road fatalities have dwindled from a high point of 7,985 per annum in 1965 to around 1,857 today (2010), partly due to the efficacy of drink-drive laws (1967), the compulsory wearing of seat belts (1983) and improvements in car design (*passim*), but the rise of the temporary roadside memorial, commemorating those killed in accidents, has been striking. The idea originated in Catholic countries where such shrines were created as permanent structures. The first roadside shrine in England is unrecorded, but was probably made in the early 1990s. Typically comprising cut flowers wrapped in cellophane, teddy bears or football shirts, English shrines are essentially informal and ephemeral (pl. 317). Nevertheless, they have become a commonplace addition to the roadscape and – together with road kill, pitch-black skid marks, dented barriers, shreds of tyre, shattered lights, fragments of bodywork and temporary police signs appealing for witnesses to fatal accidents – are ever-present reminders of the devastation that can be wreaked by the motor car. From their invention in the 1890s until around 2000, motor cars were responsible for a staggering 18 million deaths worldwide.[174]

317 A typical roadside shrine commemorating a fatal accident in Cambridgeshire in 2010, with bunches of flowers wrapped in cellophane and attached to a road sign.

318   This 1930 Shell advertisement by Rowland Hilder captures all the appeal of motoring in the country in the inter-war years. The car is seen with no others in sight against a background of Wealden countryside, with the Downs outlined in the hazy distance.

10: THE CAR AND THE COUNTRYSIDE

FROM THE EARLIEST YEARS, the car and the countryside have enjoyed an uneasy relationship. One of the prime reasons for acquiring a motor car, certainly in the period pre-1939, was to enable the owner to go out and explore the countryside. This amounted to a significant change in lifestyle – the arrival of what was described at the time as a 'weekend habit'. That this was perhaps the most significant factor in car ownership is borne out by the nature of articles in the motoring press and by the way in which cars were advertised:

> Every weekend a holiday. Where shall it be this week? Through highways to old world towns and villages or byways to the woods and fields; a quick straight run to the silvery sea or a dawdle amid hills and dales? Each weekend a new scene – a new delight.[1]

In its earliest years, the car was primarily an object of pleasure, in the way that a horseman valued a fine hunter, but it enabled people to travel that much further than was possible with a horse. A writer in 1912 argued that the horse-drawn vehicle 'had reached the limits of its possible development and could never, in any circumstances, approach the level of efficiency that the motorcar can attain'.[2] In the period between the end of the First World War and the early 1930s, when road surfaces had improved and cars had reached a high degree of mechanical sophistication, but before car use became universal, motoring was a very pleasurable activity. When asked, many people would include motoring among their pastimes or hobbies. Something of the excitement and pleasure – an almost visceral sensation – to be derived from motoring is captured in this extract from an article published in 1933, which encouraged motorists to drive their open cars in winter: 'What sound is sweeter than on a frosty morning to hear the engine fire at the first flick of the starter? How satisfying to settle down with a good thick rug – still warm from the radiator – around one.'[3]

That there were many other uses for the car – to go shopping, to make excursions to the seaside, to visit friends, as a brake to meet visitors at the railway station or to get to work – soon became apparent, but, if there is one use that stands out, it was the desire to see the countryside and commune in some semi-mystical way with nature. Much of what people came to view as their heritage was defined by what they were now able to see through the agency of the motor car. But at the same time, the act of carrying out this exploration had the effect of damaging the very things that attracted the motorist in the first place: beautiful untouched villages and remote open countryside. By opening up the countryside to the masses, followed by developers moving in to cater for those who wished to live there, the motor car was viewed by many as its destroyer. This chapter will look at how people were encouraged to use their cars to discover 'the real England', at the consequent impact of the car on the countryside, and at attempts to resolve this apparent contradiction.

The question of the role of the car in the countryside falls within a much broader debate about the effect of rural culture on the English psyche. Among historians, there has been much discussion as to how the identification of England with a nostalgic, rural past influenced its history in the twentieth century. It has been argued that many people held a deep-seated belief in a 'mythical England', an England of thatched cottages and rolling hills, a pastoral idyll that was largely the creation of the twentieth century and which was, in part, a reaction to the horrors of the 1914–18 war. In turn, this provoked a counter-argument that such beliefs were in fact those of a small, if vocal, minority, and discussion continues over the extent to which those associated with the preservationist cause were backward-looking or modernisers.[4] Such debates are not unique to England: similar questions of landscape and national identity have been explored in the U.S.A., Germany and France.

While the debate goes beyond the scope of the present study, the interest in the countryside and in heritage shown by motorists and by the journals that they read provides evidence that 'the rural myth' was by no means the creation of a few alienated individuals. From the start, the motor car had its role to play, in making the rural dream so much easier to achieve for so many more people. Apart from some use by doctors, prior to 1900 the car was essentially a hobby. By 1900 the availability of second-hand cars, which depreciated quickly, ensured that motoring was available to a much broader range of people, although still only the relatively affluent (i.e., the upper and middle classes) could afford it, at least until the advent of cycle-cars around 1910. Many viewed it as a form of sport – it was no accident that a volume on *Motors and Motor Driving* appeared in the Badminton Library of Sports alongside books on fishing and hunting.

Touring

The pleasure of motoring at first lay in the sheer novelty of speed. But the use of the car for touring followed very shortly after, as soon as cars were sufficiently reliable to be taken on longer journeys with a fair chance of reaching their destination. By the early 1900s articles began to appear on places worth visiting, and the *Car Illustrated*, a motoring equivalent of *Country Life* and aimed at the same market, featured lengthy articles on touring. What was emphasised was the old and quaint, with articles relating mostly to places in the south of England, not least because that was where most car owners lived.

Guidebooks and volumes of itineraries for motor tours soon appeared. The RAC issued a series of guides produced by the Cheltenham guidebook publisher Edward J. Burrow. Motorists broadened the scope of travel literature with titles such as *Through East Anglia in a Motor Car*. The all-important question of gradients was addressed in a series of Contour Road Books.

Tours could take the form of short or full-day excursions or weekends in the country, reviving the fortunes of many country hotels (pls 319 and 320; see Chapter 11). Picnics became especially popular, and firms such as Dunhill's Motorities produced a vast range of appropriate accessories for the motorist who wished to dine alfresco. More ambitious travellers could plan longer trips, and once it was sufficiently reliable (by about 1906), the motor car became an invaluable part of the social round, for visiting country houses and attending society events such as Henley, the Derby and Ascot. By the 1920s the use of cars for these activities, in preference to the train, was much more widespread among the moneyed classes, although well into the 1950s there was still sufficient business for the railways to run first-class Pullman race specials. The car also facilitated new forms of entertainment, such as the opera at Glyndebourne, which would have struggled without it.

With the growth of popular motoring in the mid-1920s, the number of articles on touring increased, and here the role of motoring journalists is significant. In a sense, their stance was somewhat ambivalent, in that they naturally sought to promote the increased use of motor cars, both to boost their own sales and those of their advertisers, on whom they were reliant for much of their revenue. Almost every issue of the principal weekly magazines, *The Autocar*, *The Motor* and *The Light Car*, from the 1920s until the 1950s and beyond, contained at least one article on touring.[5] Special Summer Touring issues were produced in the spring to suggest destinations for the motorist and to guide his preparations. The best paper in the journals, sepia with photogravure reproduction, was often reserved for beguiling photographs of country cottages (usually in the Home Counties), always with a car visible somewhere in the picture. A freelance photographer, W. J. Brunell, made a speciality of such views, which were widely published.[6] These articles were supplemented by others on picnicking, caravanning and motor camping. This emphasis on what the motorist could do with a car was in strong contrast to motor magazines today, which are almost entirely about the cars themselves.

Touring articles could vary from giving specific guidance on what to see in a particular part of the country to much more lyrical pieces reminiscent of the 'Nature Notes' column in a newspaper:

> Mother Nature is always preparing surprises for those who love her ways . . . For there is this about the use of a car – that the road never becomes boring but always more fascinating as one grows to know it like an old friend.[7]

Typical is H. Massac Buist's suggestion that the motorist awakes an hour and a half before dawn and drives to a high place to watch the sun rise, when

> . . . Nature reminds us more memorably than at any other time that man's moving picture artistry is merely in its crude beginnings, for you will view the very spirit of the coming day leaning farther and farther across sky and land, clad in colours the most delicate, as palest salmon and Star of India blue.[8]

Sometimes the approach was almost mystical, as when A. B. Heckstall-Smith imagined the Roman legions, Cavaliers and

319 Touring and trips into the country formed one of the earliest uses for the motor car. Enterprising hoteliers soon realised that the well-to-do motorists who took part in such activities were a useful source of income and began to cater for them. One of the most popular destinations for short trips out of London in the earliest days of motoring was the Wisley Hut Hotel on the Portsmouth Road to the north-east of Guildford. The hotel is seen here in 1911 with a mixture of open touring cars and limousines with chauffeurs in attendance.

320 At weekends, by the mid-1920s, motorists were flocking to recognised beauty spots not far from major cities. Box Hill, near Dorking, Surrey, was one such, and the Burford Bridge Hotel at its foot drew much of its custom from motorists. It is seen here in 1925.

Roundheads, and highwaymen that had preceded him on a particular stretch of road – 'the romance, the history, the legendary that lie hidden beneath the surface of the open road . . . an English road . . . posing Kipling's question "What should they know of England?" to the Whitsuntide motorists passing by'.[9]

The car also enabled people to find out far more for themselves about the past, so that they could travel in time as well as space (pl. 321).[10] The *Light Car and Cyclecar* thought it

> . . . only natural that motorists are often filled with a desire to know more about some delightful and picturesque spot than can be gathered from a hasty survey as the car glides along the wide streets under the shadow of the grey stone church that has stood, sentinel-like, on guard over the village for hundreds of years.[11]

Journals were anxious to ensure that motorists understood the significance of the places they passed through. Under the heading of one such article of 1927, the *Light Car and Cyclecar* asked: 'How much will you really know of the places through which you pass at Whitsun?'[12] Owen John felt that the car was the key to getting to know one's own country:

> The automobile is teaching us history as nothing before ever managed so to do; especially local history. How many of us knew anything at all about even our own county before its arrival? I myself was always a diligent searcher for knowledge of antiquity, but how little I knew of it even in my own particular neighbourhood no one ever guessed until the car came along to show us how big was our field of exploration.[13]

321 Motoring magazines urged their readers to go out and get to know the heritage of England. Such articles were usually illustrated with photographs or line drawings, such as this one from the *Light Car and Cyclecar* of 15 April 1927, p. 577, showing a car in a suitably attractive setting.

" The first thing to see in an old-world village is the church, for the whole history of the place is often written on its grey old stones ; stories of bygone days may be read upon the walls, and the ancient church is rich indeed in historical associations "

The atmosphere of a place was just as important as the antiquarian details of the parish church, argued one contributor, attacking traditional guidebooks well in advance of John Betjeman's notable spoof of one in 'Antiquarian Prejudice'.[14] The tone of the articles was cultivated and assumed a familiarity with English literature and history, appealing to an educated middle-class readership. There was an expectation that this heritage was an intrinsic part of everyone's background, and that all motorists would have a desire to participate in it. A deep conservatism runs throughout all this writing about England. Arthur Mee's *The King's England* series showed a preference for sentimentality over factual accounts. Many motorists, following H. V. Morton in his search for that 'deep England', visited old English inns. Owen John, in one of his more purple passages, declared:

> The inns I am thinking of are all alike and yet all different . . . And they are English. Nay, more than English, they are England itself, and the sentiments of those people who dwell in them and resort to them are invariably of the most sound, reasonable, solid, good old conservative type – nothing new or revolutionary about them or theirs – they are what they were and they will be what they are.[15]

Yet again, this illustrates the tension between modernity and tradition evident so often in motoring journals. Whether conservatism of the type expressed by Owen John was instilled by the aristocratic origins of the motor car or whether it was inherent in the middle classes of the early 1920s is debatable. By the 1930s things had changed. The Singer house journal, *Popular Motoring*, suggested a new form of sightseeing in which readers 'tired of mouldering castle keeps and the graves of marauding barons' went out and looked at new things – 'not at the glory that was England, but at the glory that *is* England'.[16] It suggested Croydon Airport, a modern concrete factory, steel girder bridges and Broadcasting House. Heading the piece with a photograph of pylons beside a widened road, it calls to mind the advocacy of Stephen Spender in *The Pylons* and the Quennells' attempt to proselytise children in the cause of modernity, *The Good New Days* (Batsford, 1935).[17] There was a keen interest in the visual impact of the car on the landscape and an evident desire on the part of those promoting motoring that its expansion would not mean the destruction of all that was appealing about England. It was even suggested that 'Motoring has given us a new type of beauty' in its bridges and new roads striking straight across the country, at the same time as enabling many more people to enjoy it.[18]

Journals also promoted an image of motoring that was mature and responsible. Hence, they campaigned against bad behaviour by motorists, unsightly shacks and filling stations, unattractive new roads and any way in which the car appeared to despoil the countryside. Yet their support for rural England went further

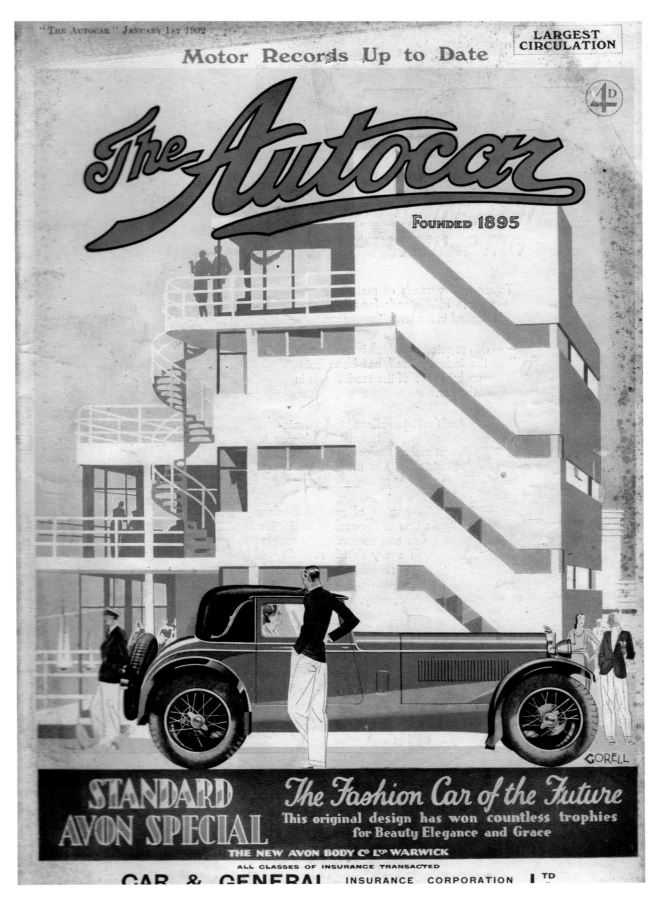

322 Modernism finally makes some headway in motor advertising against an overwhelming tide of 'ye olde England'. This 1932 advertisement for the Avon Special, an upmarket special-bodied Standard, has Joseph Emberton's newly completed Royal Corinthian Yacht Club at Burnham-on-Crouch in Essex as its background.

than this – there were articles on cottages and church architecture; articles encouraging motorists to stop and explore the places through which they passed; and support for the founding of the Council for the Preservation of Rural England (CPRE), the body specifically set up to respond to many of the ills the car brought to the countryside. They were in the vanguard of the movement to preserve rural England, while, at the same time, promoting the very activity that was putting it in the greatest danger.

Manufacturers, too, used tradition and heritage to sell their cars. The major motor companies followed the lead of the weekly motoring journals in assuming that the principal reason for buying one of their cars was to visit historic places. House journals such as the *Morris Owner* carried similar touring articles. Just as his namesake William Morris had conducted a fervent campaign to stir people to buy British, so Morris encouraged motorists to explore England's heritage, urging them at least to buy a British car, even if they chose not to buy one of his own. Austin's book *Travels with an Austin* (*circa* 1930) suggested a whole range of locations both at home and abroad, and contained line drawings illustrating an Austin at many of them. In its press advertising the firm also used historic buildings as a backdrop for its products – in one, an Austin 7 with Fountains Abbey in the background was accompanied by the words: 'What roaming will then be yours; what joy to visit those places your mind has travelled; to discover your England.'[19] Morris depicted its Oxford model with an old half-timbered inn and the ghostly form of a stagecoach in the background. It is interesting to consider why a product that epitomised modernity – as it certainly did for Le Corbusier, and for the Futurists before him – should be advertised in this way. Perhaps it was the natural conservatism of the self-made men of the Midlands, still in charge of the business empires they had created; or, to be more conspiratorial, perhaps it was the idea that a revolutionary product would become more readily accepted if it were disguised in traditional garb, as had happened with railway architecture earlier. By the early 1930s, however, modern buildings were beginning to creep into car advertising – one of 1932 for the Standard Avon Special has Joseph Emberton's Burnham-on-Crouch Yacht Club in poster-like rendering – so perhaps the conservatism was not quite so deep-seated as it appeared (pl. 322).[20]

Country-house Visiting

In the period before the First World War, the numerous county-based motor clubs that had sprung up within a few years of the introduction of the car organised many of their gatherings in the grounds of country houses. The owners of these houses were often motor owners themselves, and many of the local elite were members of the club, with committees often made up of the landed and titled. But while this meant that the privileged early car owners were able to make country house visits, it was to be some years before access was available to a wider public.

The National Gardens Scheme, in aid of the Queen's Institute of District Nursing, whereby people paid a small admission fee (usually 6d. or 1s.) to visit gardens not normally open to the public, started in 1927, just after mass motoring took off, and it would not have worked on such a significant scale without the car. Motoring journals gave it extensive publicity, publishing details of opening times.[21] By the 1930s more than 1,000 gardens were being visited by 250,000 people each year.[22]

The position with country houses was quite different. Many had always been open to some degree – to gentlemen of the appropriate class who could produce an introduction or by application to the butler or housekeeper – while their grounds were often accessible on a few specified days to the general public for charity. Most, still in family ownership in the interwar years, were open only for one or two days a week if at all, while many, previously open to the public, actually closed their doors to visitors in the 1920s and 1930s.[23] An article in *The Motor* in 1936 publicised a number within the reach of a day trip from London, including Knebworth, Hatfield, Ashridge, Ightham Mote, Knole, Penshurst Place, Broughton Castle, Chastleton and Goodwood.[24] But, on the whole, country-house owners took no advantage of these potential new visitors. By contrast, increasing numbers of visitors came to castles and ruins in the hands of the Ministry of Works, as well as the open spaces and houses owned by the National Trust.[25] The increases were in some cases dramatic: for Stonehenge, there were fewer than 4,000 visitors in 1901, then 60,000 in 1924–5, and 100,000 in 1929–30 (pl. 323).[26]

It was not until after 1945 that a new era of country-house visiting got into its stride. Faced with an increasingly hostile financial climate, a number of country-house owners began to open their homes on a far more frequent and systematic basis, developing their estates to cater for tourists with shops and restaurants.[27] Simultaneously, the National Trust, with the persuasive powers of James Lees-Milne much in evidence, began to acquire large numbers of country houses from those families who were unable to go it alone. With membership growing rapidly, country-house visiting became an activity in itself, although some participants were more interested in a day out than in traditional antiquarian concerns. Some of the more commercially minded private owners turned part of their estates into theme parks, such as the drive-in zoo – in other words the wildlife park, where motorists could drive around to see animals in the open air rather than cages (pl. 324). A 'drive-in tiger reserve' was proposed for Chilham, Kent, in 1968. Several wildlife safari parks existed by the 1970s, including Woburn Safari Park. There was no need to step out of the car.

323 Stonehenge on 31 July 1958, showing the provision for car parking, close to the monument and with little attempt to screen it.

Despite the fact that some visitors were more interested in lions and cream teas than houses and gardens, many, if not most, did visit them for what they were, unique cultural assets. While it may be argued that the car has been responsible for much damage, it is also true that it has made an important part of the built and natural heritage available to more people than ever

324 A postcard view of Knowsley Safari Park at Lord Derby's seat of Knowsley Park, near Liverpool, probably taken soon after it opened in 1971.

before. This, in turn, has influenced public opinion – as reflected in legislation – to the extent that, today, it is impossible to demolish a significant historic country house except in the case of accident, such as fire. The car has surely played a major role in bringing this about.

The increase in visitor numbers had an important impact on the setting of country houses. Parking was initially often arranged on parkland near the house, but, as numbers rose, car parks were constructed, sometimes at a considerable distance from the house, so as not to damage its setting, and usually screened by trees. This, in turn, entailed complicated arrangements for access. Sometimes existing estate roads were used, but often new roads were built so that a one-way system could be constructed, to avoid overloading the often-narrow roads around the perimeter of the estate. Visitors might find themselves leaving the estate several miles away from where they had entered it, on a different road. There might be a third and completely separate private entrance for the occupants of the house and for estate staff. Opening to the motoring public might therefore affect not only the layout of the estate to a considerable degree, but it also had an impact on the use of estate buildings. Stable blocks and garages were often converted to cafés and shops. Garages, with their open interiors and perceived lack of historical content, were especially favoured for conversion.

The car also made other heritage-related activities easier. The urban collector of antiques could now go out to look for 'finds' himself, rather than having to rely on the London salerooms. Farmhouse sales, local auctions and purchases from cottages could all yield real bargains.[28] The attractions of this were so obvious that antique dealers sprang up in many small towns around London, such as Amersham, catering for the car-borne trade. The boom in antiques, as well as growing interest in historic houses, reflected the situation in the U.S.A., where the number of historic house museums increased from 20 in 1895 to 400 in 1930.[29]

With the aid of motoring journals, the new motoring public discovered alternatives to the overcrowded roads to resorts, exploring the lesser-known parts of inland England. A whole new generation of guidebooks emerged to cater for them. Traditional guidebook series, such as the Black's Guides and the Little Guides, had been based around the railway network. Motorists had the celebrated Shell Guides and other books,[30] but the greater ease of access vastly enlarged the market for titles on 'heritage' subjects such as castles, inns, abbeys, villages and churches. Batsford series, such as 'The Face of Britain' and 'British Heritage', were produced from 1933 in editions of unprecedented size. They, and works such as H. V. Morton's *In Search of England*, demonstrated that the car had opened up England to a far greater extent than the railway, with its infrequent weekend rural services and limited network.

325 Motorists in the inter-war years began to take their cars abroad for holidays. This was expensive and time-consuming, since cars had to be winched aboard the cross-channel ferries by crane. A car ferry terminal at Dover, enabling motorists to drive directly on to the ships, was opened on 1 July 1953. It is seen here on 29 June 1961.

Wayside Eyesores

Almost as soon as they appeared on the roads, concern was expressed that cars posed the greatest threat that the English countryside had ever faced. Initially, motorists were often viewed as arrogant, ill-mannered louts, obsessed with speed ('scorching' in contemporary parlance), who raised vast clouds of dust and drove recklessly, frightening horses and killing livestock and domestic animals that got in their way – indeed, a character epitomised in Kenneth Grahame's immortal creation 'Mr Toad'. But, as more of the population began to own cars, the focus moved away from the lunatic fringe to different concerns, to the effect of large numbers of cars descending on popular locations within easy reach of major cities (pl. 327). In particular, considerable anger was directed at those who, seeing the motorist as a potential customer, erected large numbers of signs outside or affixed to their premises, advertising motoring products such as tyres and petrol, or teas and refreshments.

Motoring journals and organisations recognised the problem themselves very early. The invasion of the country by town dwellers on wheels was not a new phenomenon: since the advent of the bicycle, large numbers of people rode out each weekend, either individually or as members of groups such as the Cyclist's Touring Club and the Clarion cycling clubs. But the car enabled people to roam much further afield. As early as 1910, *The Motor* published a cartoon depicting the same village in 1896 and in 1910, after the landscape had been disfigured by a plethora of signs enticing motorists to stop for teas or to purchase motoring products, as well as a mass of road signs (pl. 326).[31] To reiterate the point, it repeated the cartoon in 1913, along with two others, under the heading 'Scenery Desecration'.[32] Another cartoon of 1912 suggested that the multiplicity of signs was such that 'motorists are almost cautioned out of existence'.[33]

Such views were entirely consistent with the preservationist tone adopted even more forcefully by journals in the 1920s. If it was to be a contest between the car and 'olde England', they generally came down on the side of the preservationist cause. An example was Buckland, Surrey, where the demolition of some attractive houses was proposed because of road improvements between Reigate and Dorking:

326 As early as 1910 the impact of the car on the countryside was giving cause for concern. Motoring journals were in the lead in drawing attention to it, as seen in this cartoon, published that year. From *The Motor*, 20 July 1910, p. 947.

ROAD BOARDS FOR WHICH THE ROAD BOARD IS NOT RESPONSIBLE.
Sweet Auburn, loveliest village long ago,
Now in appearance like the sketch below.

327 The A2, Watling Street, just to the west of Rochester on 30 July 1938 with a lengthy line of traffic, mostly cars, heading for the Kent coast. Such traffic congestion had become common on arterial roads leading to seaside resorts. The photograph also shows how houses sprawled along arterial roads, with another development growing up behind them.

There is scarcely a village in England which cannot be con- demned if the view be taken that the ways through them are not altogether suitable to modern motor traffic, but if they are to be sacrificed without consideration being given to alter- native diversions, nothing can compensate for their loss.[34]

Cartoons often provided the most telling means to make the point that the car was devastating the appearance of the English landscape. 'The English Village as it might be and as it is likely to be' gave two contrasting visions of the future, the one a village

with half-timbered houses and a Neo-Tudor garage, complete with a knot garden in front of the petrol pumps, and the other depicting a hellish place with much unpleasant new develop- ment and all the buildings covered in signs (pl. 328). The tech- nique of juxtaposition accurately anticipated that of Osbert Lancaster in works such as *Progress at Pelvis Bay* and *Drayneflete Revealed*.[35]

Time and again, Owen John in his 'On the Road' column in *The Autocar* castigated 'countryside horrors' and urged readers to boycott those firms that were responsible for 'the plague of ugli-

285

THE ENGLISH VILLAGE AS IT MIGHT BE——

328 A glimpse of the future as it might be if development in the countryside went unchecked and how it could look if it were strictly controlled. From *The Motor*, 24 July 1923, pp. 1080–81.

ness that is descending so quickly on the villages of this country'.[36] *The Motor*, in an editorial quoting the President of the Royal Institute of British Architects (RIBA), Guy Dawber, argued that 'within a measurable period . . . the whole aspect of the countryside will be changed', that 'the planning and construction of new roads usually results in the wiping out of existence of wayside features of charm and interest and the laying out of bleak, barren stretches of highway' and that 'in administering to the needs of motorists too, traders are laying a trail of ugliness and blatant colour throughout the countryside'.[37] One 'wayside feature' deemed to be under threat was the hedgerow. In an article entitled 'The Doom of the Hedgerows', Allan Phillip highlighted how hedges were being swept away for road safety purposes to give motorists greater visibility and also to

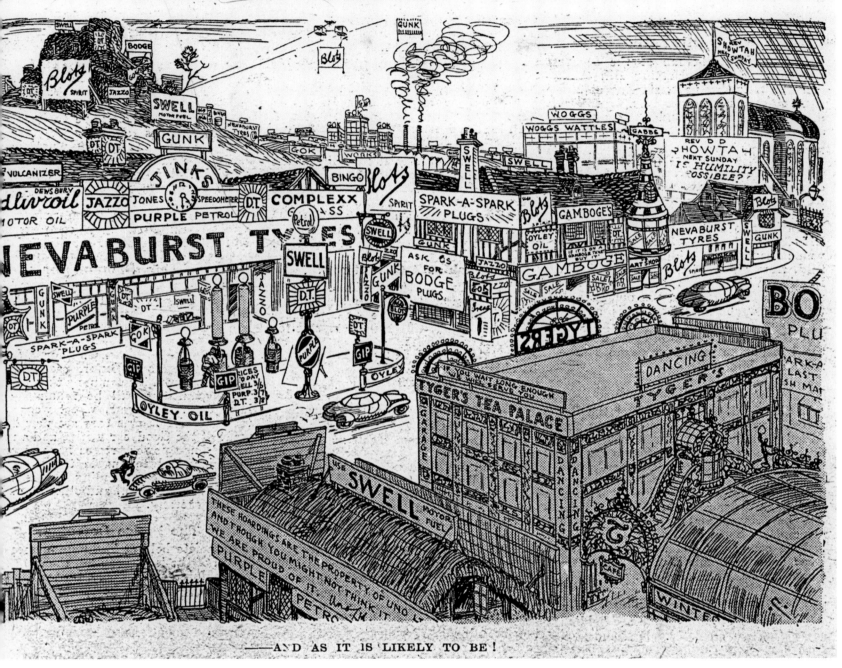

—AND AS IT IS LIKELY TO BE!

enable farmers to enlarge fields so that they were better adapted to tractors.[38] That motoring journals were drawing attention to the grubbing up of hedgerows as early as 1922 puts them very much in the vanguard of conservationist pressure.

Motoring journals actively supported the work of societies that aimed to prevent the countryside being ruined by advertising and 'roadside eyesores'; in turn, the societies praised them for what amounted to a campaign. SCAPA (the Society for Check-

ing the Abuses of Public Advertising), founded in 1893, was given an article to itself in *The Autocar*, which also publicised, in an editorial headed 'Our Disfigured Countryside', an attack by the Archbishop of Canterbury. He complained that 'at every point where he expected to see a piece of the glorious Garden of England his eye met a petrol pump, a tea kiosk, or one of those bungalows for which, he confessed, it was impossible to find a suitable adjective'.[39] SCAPA was also given prominence in *The*

Motor, which published a statement by its chairman, Richardson Evans: the society had obtained the consent of firms that were putting up signs in the country advertising petrol and motor accessories to abandon the practice, but because one firm was obdurate, all the rest were carrying on.[40] The National Trust, too, agreed with the line taken by the journal, with letters of support written by Lord Crewe and E. C. Ouvrey, elected members of Council.[41] The establishment of the Council for the Preservation of Rural England (CPRE) in 1926 again received much coverage against a background of almost apocalyptic headlines, such as 'Is the Countryside Doomed?'[42]

The CPRE was a direct response to the impact of the car on the historic environment. Its statement of purpose specifically mentioned the motor car as a prime agent of change:

> The CPRE was founded to link up and act as a clearing-house for all the associations working for the preservation of the countryside, and to help to direct the almost revolutionary changes that the motor car and modern conditions are bringing in.[43]

It embarked on a major lobbying campaign aimed at raising the profile of the conservation movement. Parliament, too, took an interest in the question. The Rural Amenities Bill, introduced by Sir Hilton Young, a Conservative, as a Private Member's Bill in 1930 and supported across the political spectrum, including, among others, Clement Attlee, sought to preserve the ancient and historical features of the English countryside, to control disfigurement by advertising, to preserve open spaces and village greens, and to prevent the export of ancient buildings. The Bill was supported by almost all the amenity groups then active, including the National Trust, the CPRE and the Society for the Protection of Ancient Buildings (SPAB), together with other bodies such as RIBA and the Town Planning Institute. In introducing the bill, Sir Hilton argued that 'the invention of the motor, I suppose, has been largely responsible for the tremendous acceleration of the spoiling of the countryside' and had 'brought the town into the country'. Another speaker in the debate, the novelist John Buchan, felt that change had to come – 'Rural England is not an antiquarian museum' – and that some disfigurement was essential, but change should be made as inoffensive as possible; while 'our countrymen are at last awake to their heritage and desire to preserve it; but they have awakened only just in time'.[44] The Bill failed to get beyond a unanimous second reading, but it helped to pave the way for the Town and Country Planning Act of 1932, although this was much watered down from the 1930 proposals, and the Restriction of Ribbon Development Act of 1935.

Individuals were also concerned about the effect of the car on the countryside, perhaps the most influential of whom was Clough Williams-Ellis. In two books, *England and the Octopus*

(1928) and *Britain and the Beast* (1938), the latter under his editorship, he and his contributors warned of the damage inflicted by the car. Sheila Kaye-Smith pointed out how 'the car, unlike the train, does not clot its horrors at the journey's end but smears them along the way'.[45] Sir William Beach Thomas deplored the impact of motorists on the commons of the Home Counties, where motorists left 'litter that is more offensive than the relics of a gipsy caravan or even a tramps' meeting place'.[46] The philosopher C.E.M. Joad was the most vociferous critic, and, as well as an essay in *Britain and the Beast*, in which he delivered a celebrated and oft-quoted rant against 'fat girls in shorts, youths in gaudy ties and plus-fours, and a roadhouse round every corner . . . for their accommodation',[47] had already made his own contribution in 1931 with *The Horrors of the Countryside*. Joad was exceptional in his desire to provoke, but litter, ribbon development, bungalows, cafés and filling stations were the recurrent concerns of individual writers just as they were of the CPRE, planners and motoring journalists. Throughout all these attacks, however, there could be discerned the voices of middle-class critics unhappy at the way in which working people in the country had recognised business opportunities in the great increase in car-borne visitors (pl. 329).

The development of garages, filling stations and cafés, and attempts to control their appearance, are dealt with in Chapters 4 and 5, but some further comment on the aesthetic implications of their multiplication in the mid-1920s may be made here. For many, the petrol pump was intrinsically ugly and Owen John was not alone in singling it out:

> Nothing could be more ugly – except Olympia – and as they at present exist they lack even the gaunt boldness of the tank or the tapering gracefulness of the belching factory chimney. They are likely to be with us for ever, the silly Cubist and perverted type of so-called Art that was twin with them in the beginning is played out; surely it is about time that these monstrosities – the only permanent memorials of the era of Dadaism – should be made to fit themselves into their surroundings and in some way contrive to melt themselves more into the usual order of things. Automobilism need not imply ugliness. Why should its accessories insist upon it?[48]

A series of cartoons humorously suggested ways in which pumps could be disguised or made fashionable, but the most popular suggestion was to paint them all the same colour.

Some of the most stinging criticism was levelled at the enamelled iron advertisements that were used to cover every available surface of many garages. It was argued that the practice was pointless, since the sheer number of signs so displayed defeated their own object – they simply cancelled each other out. *The Autocar* in 1928 was so incensed that it was prepared to name names and described the BP sign based on a background of the

329 Many people living in the country soon realised the potential for making money out of the large numbers of touring motorists. They put up shacks and stalls selling produce, much to the dismay of those who saw these ramshackle erections as ruining their vision of a pastoral idyll. Mrs Harlow is serving the owner of a 10hp Swift at Chilham, Kent, from her stall, which offers apples, oranges, eggs and poultry, as well as cups of tea.

Union Jack as 'beastly' and the Vacuum Mobiloil sign as 'hideous'; it held that the petrol companies, Pratt's, Shell, Redline, Power and BP, were all equally to blame. Those responsible had created 'a National Disgrace'.[49]

Ribbon Development

The phenomenon of ribbon development in the 1920s and 1930s was perhaps the most significant impact of the car on the landscape (pl. 330). While the growth of the railways had encouraged similar forms of development to some extent, the nature of the two differed. Railway-led development faced natural constraints: it was focused around stations, because houses had to be within easy walking distance. By contrast, development based around

the car tended to be linear, following the line of a road and in many places literally lining the sides of it. With little building behind, it wasted space and blurred the distinction between town and country.

Such development was reviled, although there was no shortage of buyers. Critics ranged from town planners and architects to novelists and poets. All held the car responsible. Thomas Sharp employed an extensive vocabulary of emotive terms to express his anger, among them 'ruin', 'disease', 'infection' and 'corruption', and argued that, 'over great areas, there is no longer any country bordering the main roads: there is only a negative semi-suburbia'.[50] This type of development was at least reasonably substantial, if monotonous. The expression 'ribbon development' was also used to deplore collections of tatty shacks, small cafés, rubbish dumps, scrapyards and other horrors that lined main

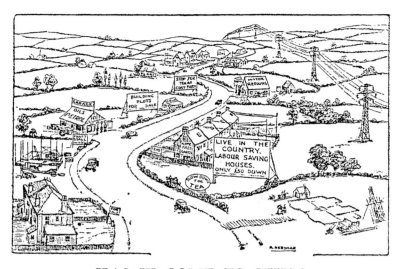

HAS IT COME TO THIS?

Scene: Any main road between any two towns.
Extract from guide book prior to 1932: "On reaching the summit of the hill one sees the road winding like a ribbon amidst our lovely peaceful farm lands."

330 Despair at how the countryside was being gobbled up by ribbon development expressed in a cartoon published in the *Light Car and Cyclecar* on 9 December 1932, p. 83.

roads. Ribbon development was the focus of the major town-planning legislation of the inter-war years, the Restriction of Ribbon Development Act of 1935, which gave powers to highway authorities to block future development of this type.

The Threat to the Coastline

With the advent of popular motoring in the mid-1920s, the most popular destination was the seaside. Much road congestion resulted from day trips to resorts such as Margate, Brighton and Southend-on-Sea in southern England and Morecambe and Blackpool in the north, and a high proportion of the earliest major road-building schemes were intended to alleviate the problem (see Chapter 9).

Social historians often argue that, although motoring became available to a much wider range of people in the mid-1920s, it was still out of reach of the vast majority of working-class people. The fact that the cheapest new car in the early 1930s, a very basic version of the Morris Minor, cost £100 is used as evidence to support this view.[51] But this ignores the fact that cars depreciated very much faster at that time, so that a five-year-old car was often practically worthless. Cars were advertised by dealers in the national motoring press for as little as £25 and could be obtained for far less locally or through private sales: a running Morris Cowley or Austin could be bought from 30s. in

the early 1930s.[52] In addition, many people shared ownership of a car, either within a family or with friends. Such factors meant that their ownership was not confined to the middle classes.

Many working-class people were now able to expand their horizons and contemplate trips to the seaside, and to acquire small parcels of land on which they could erect shacks or old bus, tram or railway carriage bodies as holiday homes. The declining value of agricultural land enabled marginal plots a long way from any rail links, and with no services, to sell for only £3.[53] Plotlands developments, as they became known, were common at locations within two hours' drive of London (pl. 331). In addition, new resorts served by the car, located a considerable distance from the railway, grew up all over England, especially along the south coast. Perhaps the best known was the

331 The arrival of the car stimulated the growth of new settlements in out-of-the way places, in the country and by the sea. Such settlements, often known as plotlands developments, were frequently made up of old railway carriages, buses or trams. Bungalow Town, Shoreham-by-Sea, West Sussex, the earliest of these communities, really owed its existence more to the railway, with a halt of the same name being opened in 1910, but it was soon being used by motorists, as seen in this 1920s photograph. In the background are typical bungalows, made up of 1880s ex-London, Brighton & South Coast Railway carriage bodies raised off the ground on brick piers and with timber balconies added to the carriage sides.

notorious Peacehaven, to most planners the epitome of all that was going wrong in England, but there were others, from Rye in the east to Hayling Island in the west. On the east coast, Jaywick Sands, near Clacton, was specifically aimed at the motorist, with the London *Star* headlining its story on the resort 'A Motorists' Mecca by the sea, with Brooklands the main thoroughfare'.[54] The promoters were so anxious to appeal to motorists that they named roads after car marques (pl. 332). At the same time, the car opened up beaches in smaller, more out-of-the-way places; here, one could drive the car on the sands

and use it as an *ad hoc* beach hut (pl. 333). Some examples of this type of resort were Angmering, Camber, Cliff End, near Hastings, Oddicombe, Braunton Sands and Bracklesham.[55] Existing resorts, already served by poor rail services, such as Minster-on-Sea and Leysdown-on-Sea on the Isle of Sheppey, expanded considerably. The car thus encouraged the growth of whole new patterns of settlement on unpromising coastal or estuary land.

There are two ways of looking at these changes. At the time of their construction, there was almost universal hostility to the new developments from architects, planners and 'the educated classes'. That they covered large areas of formerly open landscape with sprawling developments of often unsightly structures with little in the way of facilities is unarguable, but they also gave an opportunity to many people who would have been unable to afford a house of their own the chance to join the property-owning classes. It also has to be said that, over time, many of these developments have acquired a charm of their own; indeed, in many cases they are now considered worth preserving.

The Beauty Spot

Although (or because) so much was published on places to visit in the 1920s and 1930s, it is evident that by the end of the 1930s many attractive country places had lost much of their charm at weekends. The beauty spot had always been there: it was the subject of cyclists' excursions, of rail and hiking trips; nineteenth-century guidebooks talked about the 'Lions' of a district; and, by the early 1920s, villages in the Home Counties were being overrun by visitors arriving, mainly by charabanc, a market catering primarily for working-class day trippers, the numbers of whom had grown exponentially in the hands of ex-servicemen purchasing ex-War Department vehicles, but increasingly by car. This had reached the point that, in 1923, after the August Bank Holiday, under the heading 'Mob Motoring', *The Motor* attacked the behaviour of what it called a holiday rabble who had descended on an unnamed village with vehicles parked all over the village green, booths selling food and litter everywhere.[56] The litter question reached a stage where the RAC instructed its road guides to tell motorists how best to dispose of their litter.[57]

The advent of mass motoring, however, in the form of reliable and relatively cheap cars, such as the bullnose Morris and the Austin 7, meant that by their sheer physical presence cars made much more of an impact than the charabanc or the cyclist. In 1937, under the sub-heading 'Places to avoid at the Week-end or on Public Holidays', *The Motor* painted a graphic picture of the effect of mass tourism on Dovedale, the crowds making so much noise that 'it was almost impossible on some occasions to hear yourself talk', people waiting in queues to cross by the Stepping Stones or patronising the five makeshift refreshment stalls that had sprung up there.[58] More than 150 cars had parked in a nearby field at 6d. each. Nor was the problem confined to Dovedale. *The Motor* gave a list of places that swarmed with people – in the Cotswolds, Broadway, Bourton-on-the-Water and Chipping Campden were choked with parked cars, while in Devon, at Clovelly, aggressively strolling sightseers rendered the place 'hideous'. A list of places to avoid followed, here cited in full to give a clear picture of the favoured destinations of motorists in the 1930s: Hindhead, Box Hill, Waggoner's Wells, near Liphook, British Camp in Malvern, Winter's Hill Marlow, Leith Hill, Ivinghoe Beacon, Friday Street, Guy's Cliffe Mill in Warwick, Cheddar Gorge, Stonehenge, Runnymede, Tintern. All these, it was argued, gave no more pleasure on a Sunday than Hampstead Heath: motorists did not know England sufficiently well to avoid 'the herding instinct'. By the late 1930s the encour-

agement given by motoring journals for people to go out and discover 'their England' was coming home to roost in its effect on the historic landscape (pl. 334).

•

334   The arrival of the motor car and the motor coach fundamentally changed the nature of many rural places that were regarded as 'beauty spots'. This is Dartmeet in Devon, where the east and west branches of the River Dart meet in a beautiful steep-sided and heavily wooded valley, with large numbers of cars parked by the roadside. The photograph, taken soon after 1951 when Morris Minors (one is visible beyond the coach) acquired wing-mounted headlights, is a late example of work by W. J. Brunell, who specialised in photographing cars in rural settings for the travel articles of the motoring weeklies.

Motor Caravanning, Motor Camping and Motor Picnicking

Outdoor activities have become synonymous with the inter-war years. While many of their adherents made their way by bus, train or bicycle, camping, caravanning and picnicking, in particular, were greatly stimulated by the car. A distinction was drawn between caravanning and camping with a car: 'Motor camping is merely camping, with all the added facilities and enlarged accommodation that motor transport provides.'[59] In contrast to staying in a fixed camp with a car, a caravan enabled the 'home on wheels' to move on from day to day, with the occupants enjoying relative luxury. Camping reached new levels of organisation during the 1920s. Many sites, described perhaps somewhat optimistically as 'villages under canvas', had pitches where tents could be left up for the whole summer, where tradesmen called to deliver supplies and where evening entertainments were arranged. In 1933 the AA issued a list of 1,500 sites where people could camp or park caravans.[60] The camper was viewed as a person who appreciated the simple life; accordingly, it was suggested that items taken should be kept to a minimum. Despite this, reflecting the type of people who, in 1925, were still most likely to be enjoying such a holiday, it was advised that 'Where a party is more than three or four, a man-servant of the handyman or Army batman type is well worth the extra expense. The right kind of man will save endless trouble and inconvenience.'[61] At this time, motor caravanning was still in its infancy and organised campsites were almost unknown. A writer in 1921 advised against travelling with any exact itinerary in mind: 'it is much better to travel as the spirit rules – any old how, any old where, at any old time'.[62]

The production of caravans to be towed behind cars got under way in 1919. Early vans, certainly until the beginning of the 1930s, rather resembled mobile Neo-Tudor cottages in that they were half-timbered, had leaded windows and, often, a small bay window – quite literally a home from home and again displaying that conservative 'Olde-England' approach found in so much domestic architecture of the time. Interiors tended towards the chintzy. A streamlined style was favoured from about 1930, again matching developments in car styling.[63]

The Caravan Club of Great Britain was formed in 1907, but it initially catered for those touring with horse-drawn vans. A dedicated journal, the *Caravan and Trailer*, appeared in 1933 with an initial print run of 6,000 copies, giving an idea of the growth of the activity.[64] Caravan Club membership rose from 1,300 in 1937 to 360,000 households in 2009. In the early years caravans were often hired – one trade source stating that not more than 25 per cent of caravanners owned their own vans. A selection of caravans for hire was parked on open ground alongside the

335   A family picnic by the roadside in Devon in 1960. The car is a Fiat 1100, a relatively rare car in Britain at that time when the products of British car manufacturers predominated.

Kingston Bypass in the case of the Nomad company, and the Barnet Bypass for the London Caravan Co., each with sales offices having suitably rustic-looking timbered gables.[65] But what is less clear is where the caravan could be parked overnight. The organised caravan site was a post-1945 invention: previously, caravaners would simply ask permission from a farmer or use one of the informal sites, shared with campers, listed by the Caravan Club. The attacks on caravan sites on aesthetic grounds relate less to sites for touring caravans than to those for permanent caravans or mobile homes. These have largely taken the place of the pre-war collections of old bus and tram bodies, some of which were used as holiday homes, but many, inland, were used by the homeless as cheap accommodation.

Picnicking could be a most involved affair with a number of accessory makers such as Smith's providing a whole range of equipment including luncheon and tea cases. Dunhill's even produced a portable washing outfit. In terms of the impact on the landscape, unlike in the U.S.A., formal picnic sites were not provided, and picnics were simply taken by the side of the road (pl. 335), with the car running board often used as an *ad hoc* table in the 1920s and 1930s.

Living in the Country

The building of country houses in the more beautiful parts of south-east England that were easily accessible from London by train, such as the hills around Godalming or Hindhead, and the High Weald around Tunbridge Wells, had been going ahead since the 1870s. Many of the country houses built by Shaw, Lutyens and others owed their existence to the railway. The arrival of the car opened up a whole new range of lifestyle choices for those on a reasonable income. Weekend cottages became much more popular in the 1920s. Someone working in London, who might occupy a flat there, could drive down to either a renovated or a newly built cottage. The availability of the car meant that a location within striking distance of a railway station was no longer essential. The necessary supplies could easily be brought down in the car, or shops were merely a drive away. Already in the 1930s there were complaints that motorists were pushing up the cost of housing, because they were prepared to rent weekend cottages for far more than local people were able to pay, a phenomenon that was to become much more noticeable in the 1960s and 1970s.

P. A. Barron, author of *The House Desirable* (1929), published a number of articles encouraging motorists to consider living in the country. He gave much publicity to the settlement at West Chiltington, Sussex, built by Tiles & Potteries Ltd, established by Reginald Fairfax Wells (1877–1951).[66] Wells, who was a man of many parts – property developer and aircraft designer, but best known as a studio potter – developed an area (which became known as Roundabout) to the south of West Chiltington Common in the 1920s and 1930s, with small cottages in large gardens. The cottages, thatched and employing much timber framing, were designed to look suitably aged by the use of green timber and uneven whitewashed brickwork. Nearly all had garages in a matching style. The joinery was produced by Wells in his factory using local materials.[67] The smallest were described as 'nutshell cottages' and were advertised as 'designed for the convenience of golfers, yachtsmen, motorists and others who want a small getaway place in the country'. These, without bathroom, cost £400, exclusive of land.[68]

As well as homes for weekenders, Barron also drew attention to the 'colonies of motorists' that were making permanent homes along the south coast.[69] The difference here was that a man might travel to his office in London by train, but use his car to drive to the station, as well as for runs in the evening and at weekends for touring the countryside. Among the places that had expanded in this way were Angmering on Sea – where 'practically every house' had a garage – Lancing, Worthing and Rottingdean. Such a lifestyle enabled one to live far from the overcrowding of the city, yet avoid the ills of creeping suburbia and ribbon development. The long-distance commuting undertaken by well-to-do City men from towns such as Brighton since the nineteenth century thus spread to other areas and to those on lower incomes, a process hastened by railway electrification in the 1930s. Station forecourts were usually sufficient to deal with the numbers of parked cars, but some provision of covered accommodation was made (see Chapter 6).

The Car and the Post-war Countryside

Many of the worst excesses of uncontrolled development in the countryside were done away with by the Town & Country Planning Act of 1947. New development was strictly controlled, as were outdoor advertisements, and the legislation achieved many of the goals set out by bodies such as the CPRE and SCAPA in the 1920s. Yet the ingenuity of advertisers ensures that, whatever controls are in place, someone will seek to subvert them. For example, there was a short-lived phenomenon around 2005 for placing old lorry semi-trailers bearing advertisements in fields adjoining motorways in order to attract passing drivers.

At first, change in the countryside was gradual. Many more acres of land were brought into cultivation during the Second World War, and in the quest to obtain higher yields of produce extensive use was made of tractors on farms to replace horse-power. As the 1950s progressed, increasing mechanisation led to a great reduction in the need for agricultural workers. The low wages earned by farm labourers had precluded car ownership, but earnings from other sources of employment in local industries and in neighbouring towns were higher. By the late 1960s car ownership in the country, once the prerogative of the squire, the doctor and the farmer, was becoming universal. It was also becoming essential as rural railway lines were closed and bus services withdrawn.[70]

The availability of the car enabled those living in the country to work in towns, where they earned higher wages; it also gave them far greater access to sporting and cultural activities and enabled them to visit a much wider range of shops. But, at the same time, village shops began to close, unable to compete with supermarkets on price (especially since the ending of resale price maintenance in 1963) and the variety of goods on sale.

Many country dwellers moved away altogether to live in cities and towns, but their departure was balanced by those escaping from urban or suburban life. Much wider car ownership from the 1960s enabled people to live in an attractive rural setting and still work in a town. Country cottages that had been ill regarded by their previous occupants became desirable properties when renovated. Rural property prices rose dramatically as the countryside became more accessible, so that indigenous families became priced out of the communities in which their ancestors had lived for generations. The nature of many villages, especially those near urban centres, changed entirely, since they became little more than rural dormitory suburbs. The process was magnified when new estates of expensive houses (so-called executive homes) were built in many villages, giving an increasingly suburban look to what was once a small rural community. None of these fundamental changes in the rural landscape could have taken place without the car, since the incomers were totally dependent on cars to work, shop and enjoy themselves. Because rural bus services had been withdrawn in so many places (and they had never been frequent, often running only on market days), all family members needed a car. While previous generations might have been content listening to the wireless, digging the garden or visiting the local pub, people's expectations of life had risen – and the car was the only means of satisfying them.

Today, the car is more firmly ensconced in the countryside than ever before. Communications technology has made working from home an attractive possibility for many who need no longer live near their place of employment. These new opportunities increase still further the numbers of those choosing to live in a rural setting who are totally dependent on a car.

336   The interior of a Happy Eater restaurant on the A21 Hastings road, photographed in the 1970s.

11: HOSPITALITY FOR THE MOTORIST

DURING THE EARLY YEARS OF MOTORING, there was a great revival in the fortunes of coaching inns in market towns and larger public houses by the side of highways. Ever since the advent of the railway, they had fallen out of favour with the traveller. Now their proprietors had new opportunities in which to prosper. In 1903 the *Car Illustrated* highlighted an inn in an unnamed country town in the Midlands where 'hardly a day goes by but what some motorist sails in with his friends and demands to be fed'.[1] Although cyclists had for some years been boosting trade at country inns, motorists were in a different league altogether: 'If he can afford £600 or £700 for his Panhard or Daimler, he can afford superior accommodation, at a hostelry of his choice, and enjoying a good dinner does not mind paying for it.'[2]

Although some hotels and inns were keen to attract motorists, many were less cooperative, and the pages of motoring journals are full of complaints, well into the 1920s, about poor service and high prices. A particular complaint was the reluctance of many hotels to provide any form of refreshment to travellers outside set meal times. Central heating and running water in bedrooms, if not en-suite bathrooms, together with some relief from roast meat, greens and potatoes, followed by tinned fruit and custard, was another deeply held desire.[3] The Trust Houses were singled out as an exception, providing economical stays that were directed towards the needs of motorists.[4]

The provision of hospitality reflects, as usual, the class of people who were motorists. So until the beginnings of popular motoring on a grand scale in the 1920s, much of it revolved around the hotel and dining room. The more modest individuals who ran cyclecars and light cars before 1914 would probably have patronised the establishments that catered for cyclists and

motor cyclists – the cottage selling teas, the tea garden and the village pub.

Many of the wayside filling stations and garages that sprang up along trunk roads in the 1920s with the advent of mass motoring had a café attached to them. These were generally rudimentary affairs and were condemned by the press as roadside eyesores, along with other shacks. At the end of the decade, there was a great boom in tea rooms. This was attributed to the cost of hotels and their dowdy nature:

> . . . a light meal at a reasonable charge being nearly always preferable, and especially in summer, to the set table d'hôte of doubtful worth with which one is often confronted. How much better than the stuffy dining-room of the old-fashioned hotel, hung with musty pictures and faded wallpaper, is the spacious lounge of the modern tea-house, with its comfy chairs and restful, clean, distempered walls.[5]

In 1928, on the London to Margate arterial road, there were twenty-five tea houses in 80 miles. They varied much in size and appearance, and many were simply new uses for existing buildings, timber-framed structures such as the Ye Olde Bolney tea rooms and garden on the Brighton road being popular on account of their quaint appearance. A selection illustrated in 1928 included a thatched *cottage orné* at Cuplow, Warwickshire; a bungalow with a broad veranda at Kenilworth; the Manor House, Kingsdown, Kent; and a purpose-built garage and café near the Brooklands motor racing circuit.[6] While new construction might adhere to a simple approach, such as using former Army huts, some more ambitious structures were built. The Maison Lewis (built *circa* 1926) was a rendered twin-gabled building on the Great North Road just north of Welwyn with a veranda at the

A restaurant of 1950, with the ground floor occupied entirely by garage space.

337 A forecast in Leonard Henslowe's *Motoring for the Million* (1922) of what a restaurant might look like in 1950. The ground and basement floors were taken up with car parking, with the entire frontage open to the street for easy access by car. With the aid of turntables, 400 cars could be parked.

front and a large car park to the side with chairs and tables alongside it.[7] The Tudor Tea House at Bearsted, near Maidstone, was, as its name implies, in the Tudor style of oak construction and was of considerable size with a central courtyard. Built by Eustace Short in 1927, its design and construction were carried out by employees of Short Brothers, seaplane manufacturers of Rochester.[8] One tea house that still exists, incorporated into a hotel, is the Bridge House, high up on Reigate Hill (*circa* 1935). A single-storey brick building, it had a handsome open-raftered roof and deep French windows giving access to a terrace with spectacular views. The emphasis was on quaintness – blackened oak beams, wrought-iron lamps and stuffed birds.[9]

Although tea houses are not well documented, they appear to have been mainly a Home Counties phenomenon, with some in the West of England on the tourist routes to Devon and Cornwall. A crucial element was a garden with rustic fencing and arbours and, by 1930, a number – such as the Clock House Restaurant on the Welwyn Bypass and the Pantiles Tea Barn, Bagshot – had swimming pools to appeal to the new craze for lidos.[10]

Roadhouses

Within two or three years after 1930, perhaps arising from the popularity of tea houses (significantly, both the Pantiles and the Clock House were later described as roadhouses), the roadhouse arrived, almost out of the blue. The roadhouse is ill defined; to some extent, it was self-selecting in that an establishment would proclaim itself to be a roadhouse. Roadhouses were like mini resorts to which people would drive out in the evening. They

were cheaper than hotels and more genteel than pubs, and so filled a gap for those desiring a night out. There was always more to do in a roadhouse than just drink; all had ancillary activities such as dancing, live music, a restaurant, accommodation and, in many cases, a swimming pool and other sports facilities. Indeed, many were not licensed, relying on food and entertainment to attract visitors. They tended to be located outside – but not too far from – major centres of population and, because everybody had to drive to them, had large car parks. Sometimes, in appearance, they can be hard to distinguish from suburban pubs, many of which had concert rooms or restaurants, particularly in the form that became known as the Improved Public House. The critical factor is who used them. If the building was surrounded by suburban housing and was used primarily by locals, it was really a pub. If it was on its own, had a large car park and was used mainly by passing motorists, then it was a roadhouse.[11]

The term acquired its present meaning in the early 1930s. Contemporaries thought that the concept originated from the U.S.A., but they were careful to draw a distinction between 'the more lurid types of American roadhouses, under the roof of which anything and everything may be expected to happen' and the more sedate and rather gentrified English version.[12] Nevertheless, there is evidence that not all were quite as respectable. The *Morris Owner*, under the heading 'Rowdy Road Houses', expressed concern: 'It is disquieting that in some few – very few – instances these road houses are developing an unpleasant character and attracting a rowdy class of person, for whom they were never intended, so that one hesitates to take a lady passenger, or, say, the village parson.'[13] W. G. McMinnies in *Signpost*, an 'Independent Guide to Pleasant Ports of Call', had gained the impression that, to some, 'the very words "road house" meant something rather naughty' and was at pains to point out that the roadhouses he described were 'not only attractive in appearance and surroundings, but also perfectly respectable and pleasant places'.[14] Despite these concerns, as a rule motorists were seen as superior beings in the highly hierarchical layout of the pre-war pub. An account of an unspecified main-road pub in the Birmingham area in 1928 had 'the private motorist and better-class customer' in the smoke room, the lounge for charabanc visitors and the public bar 'chiefly used by the agricultural population'.[15]

The expression 'road house' was used in an article in *The Autocar* in 1928, but in a different context, relating to the way in which touring by car had outstripped the capacity of country hostelries to provide overnight accommodation.[16] By April 1932 it was being used to describe the Ace of Spades at Tolworth on the Kingston Bypass when it was noted that there were one or two other roadhouses run on similar lines, the Ace of Spades being the only one south of the Thames.[17] The Ace of Spades was really the prototype roadhouse (opened in 1928) and became so well known that it gave its name to the adjacent roundabout.

338 The Neo-Tudor Spider's Web on the Watford Bypass exemplifies one model available to the architects of roadhouses. Roadhouses hoped that the sort of customers they aimed to attract would drive just the type of sporty car seen here in front of the building, a Riley 9 Monaco.

It was located on the edge of a built-up area, had a filling station, a small repair workshop, a circular swimming pool with changing rooms and a Neo-Tudor building with four gables for the roadhouse itself. It was open all night, offered dancing and, with it, a level of sophistication: 'it is so clearly an outpost of a city instead of a product of the countryside'.[18] The exterior had herringbone brick nogging between the timbers and a large projecting sign like that of a coaching inn. The interior of the building was in the same Neo-Tudor as the exterior, with exposed beams and rustic chairs. E. B. Musman enlarged the building to the east in 1933, accompanying a greatly enlarged swimming pool, and designed a club room. This was much more sophisticated, in Art Deco style with black cellulose on laminated wood walls and red columns. The ace of spades motif was repeated on the doors, the floor and the walls.[19] Modernity was embraced to the extent of having a nearby field laid out as a landing ground for light aircraft.[20] The Englishness of the concept was emphasised, one of the directors of the Ace of Spades claiming that he had not studied American examples. An article in *Popular Motoring*, the house magazine of the motor manufacturer Standard, proclaimed:

Road-houses as we have them in this country now are entirely British by birth and growth. First mere petrol stations, then grandiose coffee stalls and now – something that seems to belong more to the films than to real life, something exceedingly exciting.

Twentieth-century England in truth! A score of crowded tables in a flood-lit garden: cars driving up and cars driving away. And behind the robot line of petrol pumps, a dance band with an excellent floor. It's great fun to sit behind the plate glass windows swallowing up eggs and bacon – or French delicacies if you wish, for there are five chefs – and watch the continual movement of cars and headlights on the darkened road beyond reach of the neon signs. It is still thrilling to get out of your car and plunge into artificially warmed water, and then, after dressing, to dance away the night.[21]

This excerpt captures the sheer exhilaration engendered by automobilism – the sense of the exotic and the modern – now easily achievable. The Ace of Spades roadhouse building partially survives, much altered, in retail use. Part of the site continues to be used for a filling station, but the swimming pool is long gone, swallowed up when the Hook underpass was opened in 1960.

Briefly, the roadhouse enjoyed a boom – the Pantiles roadhouse, Bagshot, enlarged in 1931 with two reused ancient barns, had 47,000 visitors in the 1933 season.[22] Next to the Ace of Spades, perhaps the best-known roadhouses were the Thatched Barn and the Spider's Web, situated respectively on the Barnet and Watford bypasses. The Thatched Barn had been built in 1927 (although not turned into a roadhouse until 1932) and was reputed to have cost £80,000. It was built in an L-shape around a 150-foot swimming pool, had parking for 1,000 cars and a restaurant seating 500. A thatched and half-timbered water tower was a prominent feature of the building, which, with its vast roof of Norfolk reed and numerous gables, was demolished in the 1980s. The Spider's Web (1932; pl. 338), too, was half-timbered, although in a much more half-hearted way. It boasted a French restaurant and a grill room, a ballroom, a golf course and tennis courts, along with the inevitable swimming pool.[23]

Despite the appeal of modernity, roadhouses built in modern styles were decidedly in the minority, to judge from both contemporary accounts and present survivals. Neo-Tudor, following the example of the Ace of Spades, predominated, although this approach met with some opposition. The *Standard Car Review* poured scorn on a recent rebuilding of an inn in Neo-Tudor style: 'have they designed it so that the modern man and his car will feel at home? Not in the least. To be in keeping with its architecture, you'd have to drive up through ruts a foot deep, in a wooden-wheeled wagon drawn by heavy cart horses.'[24] Many of the best surviving examples of Neo-Tudor are in the West Midlands, where the style was widely adopted for the 'Improved Public Houses' that were built in large numbers in the Birmingham suburbs. The Clock on the Coventry–Birmingham road is a substantial building whose half-timbering makes much more of an effort than the Ace of Spades to capture an authentically Tudor look. While it had some Tudor mullions, the Berkeley Arms (E. B. Musman) on the Great West Road at Cranford, Middlesex, took its inspiration from France, with two circular towers with conical roofs flanking the entrance and a courtyard garden with loggia, archways and pergolas, reminiscent of the Loire valley rather than the heathlands of west London (pl. 339). It had a small room off the public bar where chauffeurs' meals could be served.[25]

Genuine timber-framed barns were often turned into roadhouses. Examples of conversions are The Wagon Shed, Horley, Surrey; The Moat Farm, Wrotham, Kent; and the Burford Bridge Hotel, Boxhill, Surrey, the last a re-erected barn from Abinger Manor, where the central space was used for dancing and the aisles for serving meals. The architect was Harry Redfern, who was responsible for many of the pubs in Carlisle in the interwar years under the State Management scheme.

340   The Showboat, Maidenhead, Berkshire (1933; D. C. Wadhwa and E. Norman Bailey), showing its wealth of Art Deco forms, intended to give the appearance of an ocean liner. This impression, in its present use as a factory, is heavily disguised.

Although widely employed in the 'Improved Public Houses', indeed to a greater extent than any other style, Neo-Georgian was less popular for roadhouses, perhaps because of the association of the open road with the traditional English inn, which was seen as timber-framed and Tudor, despite the fact that many such inns were Georgian or at least had eighteenth-century façades. They were not unknown, though, examples being The Winning Post, Twickenham, on the Great Chertsey Road, the main road to the South-West out of London (1938; F. J. Fisher & Son), and The Myllet Arms by the ever-versatile E. B. Musman on Western Avenue.

339   The Berkeley Arms (1932), E. B. Musman's homage to a French château in the unlikely setting of Cranford, Middlesex, was refurbished in 2010 as part of a hotel development.

341   The Nautical William, Fenn Green, Worcestershire (1937), extensively altered with pitched roofs and now used as a care home.

342   The Chez Laurie (1938; W. Michael Bishop), near Herne Bay, Kent, a roadhouse *par excellence*, displaying all the visual cues to attract the passing motorist.

Modernity *par excellence* was to be seen at The Showboat at Maidenhead, which was intended to resemble an ocean liner (pl. 340). Designed by D. C. Wadhwa (its owner) and E. Norman Bailey and built in 1933, it had a large swimming pool, a restaurant and ballroom, tea and sun-bathing terraces and a clubroom and bar. A large car park stood between the road and the entrance, which was approached via steps. The pool was to the right, the other facilities to the left with three terraces, stacked up like the decks of a ship, facing the water. The top terrace, or deck for sun lounging, extended right across the top of the ballroom. A low corner stair tower helped the massing, while some voluptuously curved ends to the decks relieved the overall angular look of the building and added to the effect of a beached ship. At night, extensive neon lighting made The Showboat look like a glamorous harbinger of a future that owed more to Hollywood than to the Olde England of the Ace of Spades.[26] The building still exists, incorporated into a factory. Maidenhead was an important location for roadhouses, just the right distance from central London to be an easy run in the evening and enjoying a louche reputation, epitomised by John Betjeman discussing young clerks in his poem *Slough* (1937):

> It's not their fault they often go
> To Maidenhead
>
> And talk of sports and makes of cars
> In various bogus Tudor bars[27]

Another moderne roadhouse on ocean-liner lines was The Nautical William, Fenn Green, Worcestershire (1937; F. Webb; pl. 341). This, in addition to the almost obligatory swimming pool, had a captain's bridge, a quarterdeck from which lifebuoys were suspended, and port and starboard anchors. The nautical theme was emphasised by the bar staff dressed as yachtswomen, the car park attendant as an old-fashioned sailor with striped trousers and a pigtail, and the bandsmen as pirates. The client, Derick Burcher, was the Morris distributor for the area, and the accommodation comprised two bars, a large ballroom and a grill room.[28] The building survives, heavily disguised under pitched roofs, as a care home, with some coloured glass of nautical themes by the entrance as a reminder of its original use.

In generally similar vein was Oliver Hill's Prospect Inn, Minster, Kent, on the main London–Ramsgate road. This was not as comprehensive in its facilities as some roadhouses, offering only dining but in the most modish of surroundings. The building was oval in shape with bull-nosed protuberances at the rear housing toilets. The flat roof was extended to form a loggia at the sides, and a concrete pylon on the roof, floodlit and surmounted by a neon star, attracted motorists' attention at night. A large car park stood in front of the building bounded from the road by a crinkle-crankle wall. After years of neglect, the inn has been restored as part of a hotel development. Less fortunate was the Chez Laurie (1938; W. Michael Bishop) on the main coast road near Herne Bay, Kent, demolished in the 1990s.[29] With

THE IDEAL RENDEZVOUS FOR THAT SPECIAL OCCASION

343   The Hinckley Knight, one of the Knights on the Road, seen here in largely original condition as depicted in a postcard of *circa* 1964. The garages, which were allocated to guests staying overnight, are on the right.

rounded corners and a semicircular central tower to the front elevation, all in white render, it was the epitome of the road-house and had two large rooms, one for dining and one for dancing (pl. 342). Also employing rounded forms, The Comet at Hatfield, Hertfordshire, was designed by E. B. Musman, the architect of numerous pubs for Benskin's Brewery, in 1933. The plan was intended to resemble an aeroplane to mark an associ-ation with the nearby De Havilland factory, where the Comet aircraft was manufactured, but the resemblance is slight. Like the Prospect Inn, The Comet was built of brick around a central plan, with the kitchen at its heart surrounded by a restaurant and a cocktail lounge. An illuminated lantern and a model of the Comet aircraft, fulfilling the function of an inn sign, attracted the passing motorist, whose eyes were then drawn to the moder-nity of the building, expressed in such details as the pastel blue metal casements.[30]

A chain of roadhouses, the Knights on the Road, was set up by C. Knight. His inspiration may have been the Haute-Relais hotel designed by Marcel Bernard for the National School of Decorative Arts old students' association and exhibited at the Paris Exhibition of 1926. This was to be the prototype of a string of hotels along the main French highways, each having identi-cal prices, meals and accommodation.[31] The moderne style, the large number of bathrooms and the dining terrace for alfresco meals were all to be found in Knight's chain.

Knight's architects were E. L. W. Davies and Knight, who produced a standard design that was repeated with minor variations at Coventry (the first to open in 1932), Wansford, Nottingham, Hinckley and Leicester (the last in 1933).[32] Each of them was on a major road just outside the settlement after which it was named. It was intended to extend the chain across England with one every 50 miles on the principal roads, but only the five Midlands Knights were opened. Each Knight was flat-roofed and rendered, painted green and white and had a covered balcony over the entrance (pl. 343). A prominent stair tower with a full-height window was placed asymmetrically on the façade and metal-framed windows were given a pro-nounced horizontal emphasis by green and white banding linking them on the ground floor. The interiors had built-in furniture and fabrics by Gordon Russell. Although not licensed, the Knights could provide a meal or snack at any time in the dining room and lounge, and they had four bedrooms, each centrally heated with its own bathroom and a corresponding garage. Clough Williams-Ellis described his visit to the Hinck-ley Knight, finding it 'serenely flood-lit and looking like a visitant from some other and better world'.[33] The Knights differed from other roadhouses in that they were there prima-rily to provide accommodation for the motorist, and, as such, were the true ancestors of the motel and the present-day chains of motorists' hotels.[34]

344 Looking more like the temple of some sinister owl cult than a roadhouse, this is the building that might have startled passing motorists on the Barnet Bypass had the Blinking Owl come to fruition in 1933. From *The Motor*, 2 May 1933, p. 524.

The Coventry Knight has been demolished save for one wall incorporated into the Marriott Hotel that occupies its site, but the other four remain, all considerably modified. The most original is that at Wansford, used for many years as a Little Chef restaurant, although its windows have all been replaced. That at Hinckley has had a pitched roof added, and some out-of-character windows do much to disguise its appearance.

Most roadhouses adhered to prevailing notions of good taste, be it moderne or traditional, but one that definitely did not was the proposal for the Blinking Owl on the Barnet Bypass, which boasted a tower 70 feet high in the form of a decidedly sinister-looking Art Deco owl in full evening dress, whose eyes were powerful searchlights that blinked intermittently (pl. 344).[35] Sadly, this monstrosity, which *The Motor* described as 'a new road eyesore', and which would have been one of the few English buildings that could compete with American roadside vernacular architecture, was never built in this form.

Country Clubs

Another new form of recreation that was totally dependent on the growth of popular motoring was the country club. In certain respects, it was allied to the roadhouse, for the facilities of the former tended to merge into those of the country club; indeed, it was noted in a survey of roadhouses that at certain of them one had to be a member in order to enjoy all the facilities. One such was the Pantiles at Bagshot, which took over an adjoining house for the Pantiles Social Club (£1 1s. 0d. annual subscription, £1 11s. 6d. for two people).[36] This offered a badminton hall, two smoke rooms, two bridge rooms, a lounge, a cocktail bar and a garden roof lounge with three hard tennis courts outside, in addition to the putting green and swimming pool of the Pantiles roadhouse. Perhaps the greatest distinction between the two was that the roadhouse, by its nature, was located close to a main road, while the country club was usually set back in extensive grounds. The other major difference was that many roadhouses were purpose-built, while country clubs were usually conversions of existing country houses.

The country club as a phenomenon appears to have had its origins in the Country Road Club, established in 1921, with its committee and vice-presidents (Lord Montagu was a vice-president) 'well known in society and automobilism', and which was to elect its members 'on the same principles that rule in ordinary London clubs'.[37] It acquired Ham Manor, Newbury, near the Bath Road and offered ten bedrooms, a dining café and tennis and croquet in the 5 acres of gardens. Newbury was to be the first of many club houses, with Tewkesbury and Bath due to be the next, but, in the event, only the Newbury premises opened and the Club went into receivership in 1924.[38] The idea resurfaced in the late 1920s, *The Autocar* asking in 1931: 'Are we about to witness the American system of roadside club houses over here? Perhaps not yet awhile, but things are taking shape that way.'[39] The country club finally received the full glare of publicity at about the same time as the emergence of the roadhouse in 1932. In 1936 *Signpost* listed fifteen establishments calling themselves country clubs.

Country clubs blur into country hotels: many began as golf clubs that realised that day membership would be popular with the increasing numbers of people motoring in the country, and then started to add other facilities. Golf clubs had benefited greatly from the introduction of the car, since both appealed to the same clientele, who were able to play at new courses far from public transport. Like roadhouses, country clubs were to be found predominantly in the Home Counties. Some examples were Effingham Country Club, Surrey, with accommodation, a restaurant and tennis courts; Heatherden Hall, Iver, Buckinghamshire, which could offer Turkish baths, trap shooting, hunting, riding, canoeing, water polo, bowls, croquet, garden parties, tennis tournaments and fancy-dress balls; while Poulsen's Club, Datchet, Buckinghamshire, had an aerodrome attached and a ballroom with an opening roof. All this was available at low cost, although to a 'select' clientele. The ambience was different from that of the roadhouses, which catered for a younger, albeit still quite affluent, crowd who wanted to dance until midnight – it was 'the gracious gleam of oak, the coolness of chintz and the warmth of welcome'.[40]

Developments since 1945

Little in the way of new provision for motorists was made in the immediate post-war period. Building licences ensured that there were no new roadhouses for several years, and, perhaps, what had seemed avant-garde in the 1930s seemed somehow a little passé in the 1950s. The two major innovations had their origins in the U.S.A., but neither achieved either the ubiquity or the glamour of their American prototypes. One was the motel and the other the chain diner.

THE MOTEL

The motel was well established in the U.S.A. by the time the first English examples arrived in the 1950s. The concept had developed from motor camps, which were literally just that, to more organised municipal campsites to private camps made up of small wooden cabins, which were established around the mid-1920s.[41] Although these started off in the camp idiom with shared toilets and showers, they rapidly became more sophisticated and started to have private bathrooms. The word 'motel' is believed to date from 1925, when Arthur Heineman used it to describe his Spanish-style premises (in fact, more a hotel for motorists) in San Luis Obispo, California. In the earlier years, they were often known as motor courts and the cabins, cottages.[42]

In a true motel, the doors of rooms open to the outside, rather than into a corridor as in a hotel, and there is parking. The American motels, which adopted their classic form by the late 1930s, were built in a great variety of styles – some wild, such as Indian tepees – and were accompanied by large neon signs, all with the intention of attracting the passing motorist. They soon became an institution that took over much of the leisure-travel market from hotels: an American Automobile Association survey of 1939 found that only 32 per cent of its members stayed in hotels, as compared to 75 per cent in 1929.[43] Motels started out as cheap, no-frills accommodation for the traveller who could either not afford a city-centre hotel or who wanted to avoid the difficulty of parking near one, although the arrival of national chains started to move them somewhat higher up the scale. The first major chain, Holiday Inn, was founded in 1952. Others soon arose to rival it.

In Britain, by contrast, motels were initially seen as upmarket alternatives to hotels, offering facilities that went beyond those of many provincial hotels in the 1950s. A precursor, and what might be considered a 'proto-motel', was the Hotel Cottages, Boroughbridge, in the West Riding of Yorkshire, opened in 1934 by Lady Lawson-Tancred, but these differed significantly from the American model in having the garages as separate lock-ups, situated some distance from the cottages. A restaurant was flanked by ten small hipped-roof, red-tiled bungalows,[44] which could accommodate up to five guests, at a cost (in 1934) of 10s. 6d. to £1 per cottage per day.[45] Something along the same lines was the Beau Regard Auto Camp beside the Thames at Wallingford, Berkshire, where a 12-acre site had a licensed restaurant, dance hall, swimming pool and Swiss chalets for motorists for either a night or a weekend. They were evidently not a great success, since, by April 1939, they were being advertised for £20 per annum as a 'splendid ARP retreat'.[46] Scotland had the Oakwood Rustic Motel, opened in the 1930s and constructed in an extraordinary Canadian rustic style.

The first English motel on American lines was the Rouncil Towers Auto Villas, Kenilworth, Warwickshire, which opened in 1952 (pl. 345).[47] It comprised quadrangles of single-storey chalets or 'villas', brick-built and flat-roofed, twenty to each quadrangle. Each had what was described by the proprietor as its own garage attached at the side, although strictly these were car ports, not having doors. Inside, the chalets had a private bathroom and lavatory, together with a fold-down bed. The chalets were within the grounds of a large Victorian house, converted to provide restaurant facilities. They had lawns and flower-beds in front of them, either side of the driveways to the garages, making them look more like a housing development than temporary accom-

345   The Rouncil Towers Auto Villas, Kenilworth, Warwickshire (1952), formed a harmonious composition with car ports well integrated into the design of the chalets.

modation. Charges were one guinea a night, including breakfast. Significantly, the motel was located near the Shakespeare country, in the hope of attracting American tourists who would be familiar with the concept. The proprietor, John Collins, made much of the fact that, like American motels, it was open day and night.[48]

346   Graham Lyon motels attracted much publicity. The rustic edged boarding was very much a motif of the company, as seen in this brochure of *circa* 1955.

The next English motel was that at Newingreen, Kent, which received much publicity on its opening in 1953. It was built for Graham Lyon, a Dover hotelier, who had made several visits to the U.S.A. to study motel operation and who claimed to have introduced the motel to England.[49] He intended it to be used for motorists on their way to and from the Continent. Again, this indicates the type of clientele expected, for those motorists able to afford to take their car to continental Europe in 1953 would have had high expectations as regards their accommodation. Lyon appointed Louis Erdi as his architect. Erdi was later to design the Dover Stage Hotel (1956–7; demolished) for Lyon, one of the best hotels of its period. At Newingreen, an existing inn, the Royal Oak, provided a restaurant and offices and was linked to the motel blocks by a covered way. The three blocks were arranged in a splayed 'U' shape, with the end units of each outer block two-storey, the others single. Ten garages and twelve sets of rooms were provided, and each unit had a bathroom, except for two single bedrooms. The garages were on the ground floor of the two-storey units and alongside the accommodation in the single-storey ones. The exterior was modern in style with wavy-edged elm boarding to suit the rural location. Newingreen

served to reinforce the pattern established at the Auto Villas: that a prerequisite of the English motel was that it had individual garages and private bathrooms, when both were seldom found elsewhere.[50] Indeed, of the six purpose-built hotels opened in Britain between 1945 and 1960, one had no en-suite bathrooms and two others a proportion only.[51]

Graham Lyon then built a number of further motels in association with Watneys, the brewers (pl. 346). The Watney Lyon Motels were all on main roads that led to tourist destinations. They included the New Forest Motel, Ower, Hampshire (1954), the Devon Motel, at Alphington on the Exeter Bypass (1955), and the Mendip Hotel, Frome, Somerset. Like Newingreen, they were linked to existing pubs and, while in a modern idiom, considerable efforts were made for the motels to suit the particular site. At Ower, a pitched roof, brick facings and cedar shingles were employed; at Alphington, the units, which used falling ground to locate a corridor between the bedroom on the top floor and the garage below, were faced in a local stone. In 1965 these motels cost between 37s. 6d. and 42s. 6d. per night for bed and Continental breakfast, roughly comparable to a conventional hotel and considerably more than bed-and-breakfast rates.[52] By 1963 Watney Lyon was proposing to provide a chain of motels about 100 miles apart on major routes. The problem with English motels was that they were small by comparison with their American counterparts, with just twenty bedrooms as opposed to more than a hundred in many U.S. motels. Unable therefore to achieve the economies in staffing that U.S. motels achieved, where staff numbered one third of those in conventional hotels, they were thus relatively expensive.[53]

The next motels, by Erdi & Rabson, in Chichester and Oxford (1965), were considerably larger, with thirty-four and fifty-four bedrooms respectively. Both were located at major road junctions on the bypasses of the cities they served. The one at Chichester was built around a grassed courtyard with a pair of two-storey bedroom wings at right angles. The third side joined the reception wing and the fourth was open with a covered way running across it. Garages and car ports, together with open car parking, were on the outside of the bedroom wings. The Oxford motel was built around a courtyard whose entrance passed beneath the public wing. In contrast to Chichester, the individual garages and car ports, separated from the rooms by a passageway, were inside the courtyard, with additional parking in its centre. Both motels were prefabricated using the Taylor Woodrow 'Swiftplan' system, the first time Watney Lyon did so, and marking a step towards the way in which budget hotels are built today.[54]

The number of motels grew in the early 1960s: there were fifteen in 1961, twenty-eight by 1963 and an estimated seventy-five by 1965, with a total of 3,500 beds – and they had their own section entitled 'Motels A La Mode' in W. G. McMinnies's *Signpost* guide.[55] Motels began to be located in urban settings: the Watney Lyon Epping Forest Motel was at the back of the existing Cock public house in the centre of Epping, while old coaching inns such as the Angel, Chippenham, Wiltshire, turned parts of their extensive yards into motels.[56] The Epping motel was, like the earlier Watney Lyon buildings, the work of Erdi & Rabson: a visiting journalist was impressed by the 'Scandinavian atmosphere of polished wood and spaciousness'.[57] Louis Erdi confirmed that the design was influenced both by Scandinavia and Switzerland, adding: 'But I am not a dogmatist about styles – with a motel one expresses a function and tries to make it as interesting and pleasant as possible.' The Epping Forest Motel had a two-storey bedroom block raised off the ground on V-shaped reinforced concrete supports with car parking beneath. It marked a transition from the traditional motel towards its successor, the motor hotel: all its bedroom doors faced inwards into a central corridor. In west London, the Master Robert Motel on the Great West Road, Hounslow, offered what was described in 1962 as London's first luxury motel, with seventeen bedrooms and electric car heaters, concealed in flower boxes, which meant that

drivers did not have to coax cold engines into life in the morning, a common problem with cars of the time.[58]

What was common to all the English motels was their style. Because they were intended to offer a new and exciting alternative to hotels, they were invariably in a modern style, with flat or monopitch roofs and large windows that would appeal to motorists, who, in the 1960s, were less inclined to be seduced by 'Olde Worlde' charm than earlier or later generations. It was perhaps the one period where the unashamedly modern was a selling point for the mass market. In contrast, in the U.S.A., while architecture was used as a form of advertising for motels, it followed an explicitly anti-modernist agenda. As Warren Belasco, historian of motels, noted, Ramada Inns echoed styles seen in Williamsburg, the preserved colonial capital of Virginia, while there was a long tradition of Neo-Colonial being used for all types of roadside architecture in the eastern U.S.A.[59] Log cabins and mission style remained popular in the West, while Elizabethan-style English pubs were popular generally in the 1960s and Neo-Victorian in the 1970s.

By the 1970s the motel in its original form had begun to go out of favour. Increasingly, conventional hotels had en-suite bathrooms, while the walk, often in the open, to the restaurant for breakfast lost its attraction. Motel units, with their large windows, were difficult to heat and failed to meet the higher standards of insulation then demanded. The concept of each unit having its own garage was regarded as too costly, and in any case unnecessary, since people were increasingly leaving their cars in the open. They were supplanted by the motor hotel, an idea that had developed out of motels in the 1960s, where cars were left in a car park and all the rooms were within the main body of the hotel, a much more effective use of space, more economical to heat and maintain, and more able to cater for the greatly increased numbers needing an overnight stay.

Very few motels of the traditional type survive: with such good locations beside main roads, their sites were most attractive to those building the new budget hotels, and the logic of replacing a run-down, low-density motel with a hotel that could accommodate four times as many guests was inescapable. Some that still exist include the Norman Cross Motel (now Premier Inn), south of Peterborough on the A1, a drum-shaped, two-storey building with a hollow centre (1962–5; Charrington's Architects' department); the bungalow-like Cambridge Motel at Shepreth, Cambridgeshire; the Anglia Motel on the A17 at Holbeach (inspired by a trip the owner made to Florida; pl. 347); and the already mentioned Epping Forest and Master Robert motels. The basic concept with individual units and a separate restaurant building (but without the garages and certainly not aimed at the luxury end of the market) can also be seen at a number of Ibis hotels, such as those at Marsh Mills, Plymouth, and at Birmingham.

347   The Anglia Motel on the A17 at Holbeach, Lincolnshire, built on American lines with individual units.

THE MOTOR HOTEL

Motor hotels set a conventional hotel building within a large plot with plenty of parking. Trust House Hotels Ltd was a pioneer, with three Motor Hotels at Alveston, Gloucestershire, and Stevenage and Hemel Hempstead, Hertfordshire, by 1965. Trust Houses announced that it would put £35 million into a major development of fifty to sixty motor hotels with some 7,000 rooms in 1969.[60] An early example of an independently owned motor hotel was the Saxon Motor Hotel, Harlow (now the Park Inn), which had a U-shaped layout with two two-storey bedroom wings and the public rooms in a third wing. Selby Fork Motor Hotel (1966–8; H.V. Lobb & Associates) on the A1 exemplified the new approach, although it was still low density by comparison with later developments. It had a two-storey bedroom block linked at right angles to an elevated single-storey block, under which there was car parking. Both bedroom blocks were in load-bearing brick, while the reception and restaurant building, attached to the two-storey block, was steel-framed. To either side of the raised bedroom block was extensive open car parking.[61]

The motor-hotel idea was taken up by large companies in the entertainment and hospitality trade, such as the Rank Organisation, which took over the Brampton Hut Hotel on the A1 and converted it to a Top Rank Motor Inn and filling station in 1963.[62] Oil companies, too, began to become hoteliers, with Esso opening a string of motor hotels from the late 1960s, as part of its pan-European expansion into the holiday and leisure market. The Esso Motor Hotel at Maidenhead (1968; Derek Lovejoy & Associates), the second to be built for the company, had a three-storey bedroom block linked by a lounge to a two-storey reception wing with a porte cochère. Car parking surrounded the buildings on three sides of a large landscaped site.[63] Both the Maidenhead and Selby Fork hotels had service stations on the site and were flat-roofed, simple, modern structures, that at Maidenhead having modish arched concrete fascia slabs. Holiday Inn opened its first hotel in England in Leicester in 1971: a concrete-framed slab block by William Bond of Memphis, Tennessee, it was designed specifically for motorists and was located in the centre of a large gyratory scheme, St Nicholas Circle, adjacent to the city's inner ring road (see pl. 408). The only pedestrian access to the hotel was via footbridges and it adjoined a four-storey car park. Many other Holiday Inns followed, although less obviously oriented to the car.[64] These examples show how the hotel building was no longer related so directly to the car; owners were restricted to parking away from the buildings, rather than the parking being directly integrated into them, as with the early motels.

Some less conventional designs appeared, however, that continued to integrate car parking with the building. The Dekotel was described at the time of construction as a 'vertical motel'. It was a circular concrete building combining hotel accommodation and parking on a small site. Two were constructed, one in Bournemouth and the other in Edgbaston, Birmingham. The Bournemouth hotel (1967–9, a patented design by R. Jelinek-Karl; pl. 348) had restaurants and bars on the basement and ground floors; a spiral-ramp car park, masked by concrete screens, on the first, second and third floors; and a staff and a breakfast room with the bedrooms on the three upper floors, where, it was claimed, guests would be away from noise. They reached their rooms direct by lift from the car park.[65] The Thistle (now Strathallan), Edgbaston, which followed in 1970–71, was

broadly similar, although the upper storeys were clad in brick rather than concrete panels.

From the 1980s a wide range of major chains developed the concept further, with almost identical buildings throughout the country, in contrast to the site-specific designs of the early motels. Little Chef introduced accommodation alongside many of its restaurants, initially called Little Chef hotels, which later were absorbed by Travelodge, the first budget hotel chain to operate in England. The first Travelodge was opened in 1985 at Barton-under-Needwood on the A38, north of Lichfield, to be followed by another six roadside hotels the same year.[66] By the end of the 1980s more than 100 Travelodges, prefabricated by the Potton group, hitherto better known for their timber-framed houses, had been opened. Granada, too, had its own brand of Lodges for motorists. Travelodge was followed by such operators as Ibis, Formule 1 (both part of the French-owned Accor Hotels group) and Premier Inn. Many of their buildings are straight-forward brick-clad, hipped-roof, structures produced under

348   The Bournemouth Dekotel (1967–9; R. Jelinek-Karl). This shows the access ramp to the car park occupying the lower floors.

349   Peartree services on the Oxford Bypass with a Holiday Inn Express (left), a Travelodge (centre) and a Little Chef restaurant (right), with associated car parking. At top right is car parking for one of Oxford's park-and-rides.

design and build schemes, devoid of any frills, and hard to distinguish from the many office developments that are so often their neighbours on the business parks at the edge of cities. But their influence should not be underestimated. In terms of numbers alone, they form a significant element in the visual appearance of most towns and cities in England, whether at the roadside, in the leisure park or the office park. Occasionally, there is an exception to the generally somewhat bland designs employed, especially where an existing building has been reused, such as the office block of the former Swift car factory in Coventry, now an Ibis hotel, and a Premier Inn that has retained the façade of a former car showroom in York.

What started as a relatively exclusive operation, catering in small numbers for the affluent motorist, has, through a process of evolution, become the budget hotel, the mainstay of the modern hospitality industry, offering everyone the same facilities that were once available only to the few (pl. 349).

THE CHAIN RESTAURANT AND DRIVE-IN

Although there were many individual roadside restaurants and cafés, until the late 1950s there was no attempt to create any national or regional chains. This is perhaps surprising in view of the existence of numerous chains of cafés such as J. Lyons, Wimpy, Fuller's and Kardomah, and mass caterers such as Forte.

The first U.S. style drive-in restaurant in England was the Ox in Flames on the Farnborough Bypass in Kent (pl. 350).[67] This was opened in September 1960 by a Minnesota entrepreneur, Marshall Reinig, who intended it to be the first of forty. The building was a flat-roofed structure with large windows and a deep fascia, typical of its American ancestry. Like its U.S. equivalents, it had a prominent sign announcing that it was a drive-in. There was parking for thirty-five cars; meals were ordered at the counter; and the food was served on disposable plates. Food was fried, grilled or cooked by 'magic rays', that is, microwaved. The Ox in Flames was about twenty years ahead of its time and the concept was not multiplied, with the Farnborough establishment closing by the end of the decade. It was converted to a Little Chef and survived for many years in this form.

Rather half-hearted attempts were made in the 1960s to induce filling-station owners to install snack kiosks on their forecourts. Wimpy was promoting the Wimpy Kiosk, a 10 foot by 10 foot affair selling hamburgers, and which could be bought outright or run by a concessionaire.[68] At Ashford, Middlesex, a Car Bar, the first of what was intended to be 'a nationwide chain of meal-a-minute drive-in restaurants for motorists', opened in 1965. It was a bizarre glass fibre octagonal pod, windowless with a hatch, making use of new microwave technology to offer a wide range of meals, although even the usually anodyne *Motor Trader* admitted that 'some were considerably better than others

350   The Ox in Flames in Kent, England's first drive-in restaurant, photographed by Sam Lambert at the time of opening in 1960. The glamorous waitress posing by a Volkswagen Karmann-Ghia is there only for the publicity photos – customers ordered at the counter.

but, without exception, all were extremely hot and 100% hygienic'.[69] Although several more Car Bars were opened, neither they nor the Wimpy Kiosks made much of an impression: the Car Bars were of some significance as among the first to describe themselves as drive-in restaurants. Some of the petrol companies, including new entrants such as AGIP, introduced restaurants at their filling stations in the 1960s. Gulf opened a drive-in restaurant run by a Wimpy concession as part of a new filling station at Seacroft, Leeds, in 1965. The building was a flat-roofed structure matching the filling station and separated from it by the pumps.[70]

In 1958 the first, eleven-stool Little Chef restaurant opened in Oxford Road, Reading, as an experiment by a catering equipment manufacturer.[71] It was based on an American diner of the same name, using the same red and white colour scheme and a symbol of a smiling, behatted chef.[72] The early outlets were prefabricated, based on the technology used in caravan construction by Sprite, to which Little Chef was initially linked, and remained small well into the 1960s, each accommodating between eleven and fifteen people served by a single attendant as late as 1962.[73] They were placed at filling stations and had outside tables. From 1960 owned by Trust Houses Ltd, Little Chef aimed at a middle-class clientele: 'Meals are of high quality,

351   Little Chef on the A1 at Roxton, Cambridgeshire (the Black Cat roundabout), with its distinctive 'chimney'. Note the proximity of the petrol filling station and the Travelodge.

and prices, though reasonable, are not cheap . . . Lack of music keeps the Mods and Rockers away.'[74] Expansion continued slowly throughout the 1960s, with more substantial brick-built outlets seating around forty introduced from the late 1960s. By 1969 there were 27 units, rising to 136 by the end of 1973, following a merger of the parent company with the Forte organisation, which brought about significant internal pressure to enlarge the business. Many sites were converted from existing buildings, but there was a substantial number of purpose-built outlets. These were flat-roofed, boxy structures with prominent red and white painted fascias, to which distinctive striped window blinds in matching colours were added in the early 1980s.

Trust House Forte (THF), as the operators had become in 1970, launched a franchise scheme in 1975, and the rapid expansion seen in the early 1970s resumed in the 1980s, with the total number of outlets rising to 270 in 1987. They grew, too, in size, with the standard Little Chef in 1986 having seating for sixty-four to eighty customers and parking for thirty to thirty-five cars.[75] A new design, of red brick with a hipped or gabled roof, emerged for both new outlets and rebuilds (pl. 351). Various permutations of this quasi-bungalow form were devised, to accommodate the requirements of particular locations and expected customer flows. Decoration was minimal and the restaurants relied on signage for their impact. There was further expansion during subsequent years, with the number of outlets peaking at approximately 435 around 2000, all on A roads, other than thirty-two at Granada motorway service areas. Successive changes of ownership, increasing competition from other chains such as McDonald's and the public's changing tastes, however, led to

mass closures of outlets. Eventually, in 2007, Little Chef went into administration. The subsequent revival of the brand is on a smaller scale with 90 restaurants. Today, the essential elements of the Little Chef are still clearly recognisable with the signage and colour scheme little changed from the original concept, even though the outlets themselves are far more sophisticated, with the involvement of the chef Heston Blumenthal, who devised a new menu. The interior of the branch at Popham, Hampshire, was redesigned by Ab Rogers in 2008 to complement the new image.[76] Many of the outlets closed by the company are now run as restaurants by individuals, and two on the A1 near Grantham and Sandy have found a new use as sex shops, part of a trend that has seen such establishments, aimed at motorists, move to isolated locations on major roads, due in part to the difficulty of obtaining planning permission in towns.

Little Chef was joined by other chains such as Happy Eater and AJ's Family Restaurants (see pl. 336). Happy Eater was founded in 1973 by a team who had broken away from Trust House Forte, and its outlets numbered sixty-four by 1986, when it was acquired by Trust House Forte. THF also purchased AJ's, developed by the same team as Happy Eater, and both brands' restaurants were fully converted to Little Chefs by 1996. The ending of Little Chef dominance in this sector has led to many more independent roadside restaurants and the growth of new small chains. The most striking are the OK Diners (eight in 2010), which consciously emulate the appearance of American diners with stainless steel façades and neon lighting (pl. 352).

The next phase was the advent of the drive-through (or drive-thru, in American usage) restaurant in the 1980s.[77] A drive-thru is where it is possible to obtain meals from a hatch and eat

352 An OK Diner on the A1, just north of Newark, Lincolnshire, an attempt to create a distinctive identity for a roadside restaurant chain.

without sitting in a restaurant or leaving the car at all. They were opened by chains that were already familiar names on the High Street, rather than brands targeted specifically at motorists. McDonald's opened its first on Wilmslow Road, Fallowfield, Manchester, in 1986,[78] and now has 735 drive-thru restaurants. Other operators such as Burger King and KFC followed its lead and drive-thrus are now found in most retail and leisure parks (pl. 353). Some of the buildings, such as those of Pizza Hut, with distinctive high ridge roofs and bold lettering, are based closely on American counterparts.

353 The 'drive-thru' fast-food restaurant, such as this KFC outlet at King's Lynn, Norfolk, is now ubiquitous at retail and leisure parks.

The Motorway Service Area

When the new motorways were planned, service areas at regular intervals were an essential part of the overall scheme. For their design, it was necessary to look abroad to the structures built on the new interstate highways in the U.S.A. and on the *autostrade* in Italy. Both had substantial buildings spanning the roads, providing a comprehensive range of facilities for travellers.[79] While the Ministry of Transport chose the sites, the detailed design and operation were left to private operators, who submitted tenders for fifty-year leases. A variety of operators took on leases during the 1960s and 1970s, among them Blue Boar, Top Rank, Ross, Mecca, Forte, Granada, Mobil, Shell-Mex and BP, and Esso. Today, Moto (formerly Granada), RoadChef and Welcome Break (formed from parts of Trust House Forte and Granada) are the only national operators, together with a recent entrant, Extra.[80]

A Motorway Service Area (MSA) site incorporates a number of different functions supporting motorists. Besides the principal facilities of restaurant, café, shops, lavatories (usually incorporated into a single structure or linked group of structures) and filling station, there is often a storage unit for grit, a police post, provision for breakdown vehicles and, in an increasing number of cases, hotel accommodation. In looking at the structures housing the principal facilities, from the earliest in 1959 to the latest in 2010, a clear pattern of development emerges, interwoven with changes in consumer expectations and Government regulation. In his thesis on the MSA,[81] David Lawrence established a typology for these structures. He argued convincingly that they fall into five distinct categories: the 'railway station', the 'restaurant on bridge', the 'pavilion', the 'barn' and the 'shed'. This form of classification has been adopted here in analysing the development of the MSA.

The 'railway station' type constitutes a layout of two blocks on either side of a motorway, linked by a footbridge, in the same way that a railway station has two platforms, one on either side of the tracks. The 'restaurant on bridge' is a highly distinctive form that has facilities, other than fuel supply, for both directions of travel concentrated in a single large building placed over the motorway on a bridge. The 'pavilion' is a form that is centred less on the motorway itself and set back well away from it, with the buildings looking outwards towards the surrounding countryside. The 'barn' is a development of the pavilion type that followed the 1980s fashion for disguising large buildings, such as supermarkets, with tiled roofs to resemble barns. This in turn gave way to the 'shed', a large open building, typically with metal cladding and large areas of glass, flexible enough to allow for frequent internal rearrangement. The 'shed' is the type universally employed today.

The earliest designs such as Watford Gap and Newport Pagnell, both opened in 1959, had almost identical buildings on each side of the motorway, although Newport Pagnell had a covered footbridge over the carriageway, integrated with the service buildings. While this arrangement was both functional and cost-effective, it lacked distinctiveness, at least in its earliest form. With the encouragement of the Minister of Transport, Ernest Marples,[82] the restaurant-on-bridge type seen at Keele (1963), Charnock Richard (1963; pl. 354), Knutsford (1963), Farthing Corner (1963) and Leicester Forest East (1966), amongst others, made headway in the early 1960s. These were much more adventurous and striking buildings, intended to catch the eye of passing motorists, enticing them to pull in, and drawing their inspiration from American and European highway restaurant designs.

Leicester Forest East (Howard V. Lobb & Partners) was the final and most fully developed of the restaurant-on-bridge type.[83] Built for the Ross Group, it had cafés situated at each end of the bridge with a grill room and a silver-service restaurant, 'The Captain's Table', designed by Terence Conran, in the centre. These were served by two kitchens. Balconies at each end gave customers the opportunity to sit outside. Located on the ground floor to each side of the motorway were duplicated facilities, shops, lavatories and staff accommodation. Access from this ground floor to the bridge was via fully glazed staircases cantilevered out at each end. The dominant motif of the building was the great span of the bridge restaurant, some 300 feet long, which was balanced by a tower that acted as a landmark while having a practical use as a chimney flue. Transport cafés were provided in separate buildings, one on each side. Leicester Forest East survives largely intact, although the impact of the staircase towers has been diminished by subsequent additions and the building of a hotel hard up against that on the northbound side. 'The Captain's Table' is long gone, as are the balconies.

A variant on the theme of the restaurant on bridge is the Farthing Corner (now Medway) MSA, opened in 1963 for the benefit of those travelling on the M2, the newly constructed artery linking London and Dover. Consisting of two rectangular pavilions joined by a wide bridge spanning the carriageway, the 'Motorport' was erected for Top Rank Motor Inns.[84] Today, the services are operated by Moto. Medway was constructed to the designs of the London-based architects Sydney Clough & Partners, who had also been commissioned to design the Newport Pagnell MSA for Forte in 1959. The bridge across the motorway was originally intended to function as an open terrace, replete with tables and sun umbrellas, sheltered from the motorway by glazed screens: those seated on the 'bridge restaurant', as it was described, could enjoy a view of speeding vehicles, all part of the new motorway experience.[85]

At either end, the two principal buildings of the MSA were rectangular in plan with distinctive folded plate roofs. Elevated forecourts were laid out to the side of the buildings, and, as

354 Charnock Richard services (Terence Verity Associates) on the M6, seen soon after opening in 1963, is an example of the 'restaurant-on-bridge' type of motorway service area.

in the case of the open bridge, the services were designed around the use of these exterior spaces. At Medway South, for instance, the forecourt gave direct access to the longitudinal cafeteria, running east–west beside the motorway, to a takeaway Wimpy booth, opening from the east elevation of the building, and to a free-standing shop, housed in a glazed hexagonal kiosk, and providing the only access to the lavatories, situated parallel to the cafeteria. Such an arrangement was in direct contrast to a present-day MSA, where all the facilities are accessed through a single entry point.

The slightly larger of the two buildings, meanwhile, was situated at Medway North. The public area appears to have been identical in layout to that across the motorway, albeit with the addition of a transport café on the north side of the lavatories. It was capable of being used independently at times of low demand. The elevations were clad with wood curtain walling interspersed with glazing and infill panels of asbestos cement beneath the gables. While both buildings remain in use today, as with many early MSAs most of the cladding has been replaced in sheet metal, and glazed corridors were added to the entrance

355   Forton services on the M6, the tower and the restaurant, seen soon after opening and before the original buildings became overlaid with subsequent additions.

elevations in the 1970s by Conran Associates to give covered access to all the previously separated facilities.

The anticipated advantages of the 'restaurant-on-bridge' type were that construction and administration costs would be lowered through the use of a single shared facility, but they actually proved to be more expensive to run and difficult to expand. Consequently, the 'railway station' type continued to be the most favoured pattern employed, but with increasing use of more flamboyant designs, culminating in Hilton Park and the tower restaurant at Forton, both for Top Rank, who were perhaps the most adventurous of the early MSA operators. Again, the intention was that such striking features would attract motorists who were keen to experience all that the new motorways had to offer, including fine dining in stylish restaurants, as well as snacks

in utilitarian cafés. Forton, designed by T. P. Bennett & Partners, opened in 1965 on the M6 in Lancashire (pl. 355).[86] Its most obvious feature, the 65-foot restaurant tower, hexagonal in shape and resting on a hexagonal stalk, is one of the most exciting car-related buildings of the post-war period. It captures, perhaps subliminally, all the optimism of the motorway age before motorways became synonymous with tailbacks and the stress engendered by ever increasing traffic. The tower was well balanced by polygonal restaurant blocks on each side of the motorway, linked by the usual bridge. The complex survives today, with some recladding, added glazed lobbies and extensions, although the tower restaurant was converted to offices in 1988–9.

The interiors of these 1960s MSAs were as modern as the exteriors, although their plans were compartmentalised, reflecting the varied clientele that was expected to patronise them. Varnished natural wood, aluminium and Formica surfaces were especially favoured, while seating was often in the form of banquettes in primary colours, making much use of vinyls. A more upmarket approach was evident where there was an attempt to encourage motorists to dine out in silver-service restaurant surroundings. Areas used by truck drivers and by motorists were distinguished by different levels of finish, perhaps the most extreme being a mural by Trevor Pattison in the transport café at Aust Services (now Severn View, 1966), Gloucestershire, which featured a mix of trucks, construction equipment and scantily clad girls.[87]

The novelty of the MSA meant that, for a few years, it became somewhere to visit as part of a day out, to experience the sensation of sitting in a restaurant watching fast-moving traffic pass below. It became a fashionable destination, particularly for younger people and bikers, Watford Gap and Newport Pagnell being an easy journey from London. Older visitors were initially happy with the food, although less so with the prices.

The Ministry of Transport commissioned a detailed architectural study of service areas in 1965. The report, which was delivered in 1967, aimed to increase understanding of factors affecting the quality and profitability of service areas in Britain compared to international examples.[88] Based on this information, the Government introduced new recommendations and a set of simple designs that were more easily adapted to changing needs, the 'pavilion' type. These designs were mainly single-storey in height, those built between 1969 and 1974 favouring the use of exposed brick or concrete block – these being maintenance-free, quick to lay and relatively cheap. Woolley Edge on the M1 reflects many of the elements suggested by the 1967 report, as do sites such as Scratchwood (now London Gateway, M1, 1969), Washington Birtley (A1(M), 1970) and Leigh Delamere (M4, 1972). With their open-plan interiors, these designs made full use of the space available and anticipated the 'shopping mall' spaces seen in later designs. Some of the 'pavilion' designs were architecturally spectacular, such as Membury on the M4 (1972; H. V. Lobb & Partners),[89] with its massive, wave-form roofs, and Patrick Gwynne's Burtonwood services on the M62 (1974), where steeple-like projections housing chimneys rose from the roofs (the building on the westbound side has been demolished).

One of the most striking of the 'pavilions' was Woolley Edge service area, located between Junctions 38 and 39 of the M1 on a double-sided site. The services were designed by Frederick F. Steyn for Challen Floyd Slaski Todd on behalf of Esso Motor Hotels in 1972.[90] The brief was to provide two self-service restaurants with associated transport cafés and petrol stations, orientated so as to provide the best vistas. Accordingly, the buildings were unusually far apart from one another, and set within a broad landscape of earthworks and trees. The south-

bound (or west) services were the most comprehensive, with a transport café, workshop and police post in addition to the main catering building, car parks and filling stations. Set far above the motorway, with its unusual design and wood-panelled interior, Woolley Edge is a good example of how the focus of the motorist was moved away in the 'pavilion' type from the road to the countryside surrounding the MSA.

As originally built, the catering buildings were rectangular in plan, with white-painted red brick enclosure walls and dark grey concrete roof tiles. The most striking design feature was the boldly sweeping roofs, which extended beyond the outer wall of the building on the entrance front. The projecting trusses, faced with dark weatherboarding, were carried down to the ground as aluminium-lined rainwater gutters emptying into cast concrete hoppers (pl. 356). The overall impression, so the *Architectural Review* believed, was of 'an alpine hut, suitably enlarged and exaggerated *a l'Americaine* . . . all ready, so it seems, to receive 50 tons of alpine snow'.[91] A clerestory rose above the lower pitched roof at the rear of each building, lighting the restaurant areas.

356 Woolley Edge on the M1 – the distinctive projecting roof trusses that doubled up as rainwater gutters throwing the water into the concrete hoppers that formed their bases.

Both buildings have been considerably extended, but the original form is still clearly recognisable.

As the 1970s wore on many MSA interiors were looking distinctly well worn, and the first of many refurbishments began. The process of watering down the distinctively modern 1960s interiors was a protracted one. The 1970s saw the widespread introduction of restaurant furniture designed with more regard for durability than style and a general descent into a look that can be charitably described as downmarket. The decline in the appearance of many MSAs was matched by that of their reputation. Their place in popular culture was by now enshrined: as a place where football hooligans fought, where touring bands met up in the middle of the night, and where food was almost

357 Tebay East services. The buildings, constructed of local materials in a landscaped setting, seem far removed from the much more urban feel of the first generation of motorway service areas. Those designing more recent motorway service areas have enthusiastically taken up the idea of lakes and ponds to soften the surroundings and divert customers' attention away from the motorway itself.

universally awful and appalling value. The critic Egon Ronay led the many attacks on MSA catering in the press, and their reputation reached a nadir around 1978, when guides to places to eat just off the motorway began to prove popular. By the 1980s many MSAs were espousing an Olde Worlde country kitchen look with much natural timber and the use of various shades of brown. Planters and trolleys designed to look like market barrows were employed to give a village feel. Others went for a cheap and cheerful look with bright colours, especially red and yellow, and extensive use of plastics. Moves towards more sophisticated MSA interiors had to wait until the introduction of franchising and much stronger branding later in the decade.

One MSA that stood out at this low point was the locally owned Tebay West, opened in 1972, in the spectacular Lune valley on the M6. Stables & Gilchrist, again a local firm, based in Windermere, designed a low, unassuming building of stone and timber with a slated roof that looked forward to the Neo-Vernacular styles popular in the 1980s. Subsequently altered and enlarged, it was joined in 1993 by Tebay East (Unwin Jones Partnership), again unassuming and, like its predecessor, located some distance from the motorway. It won a Civic Trust Award with its simple, uncontrived design, alongside a water garden (pl. 357). These two MSAs had a completely different character from those of the major operators and this, combined with the provision of locally sourced food, offered an attractive alternative to many motorists.[92]

During the 1970s the number of new MSAs was reduced, due in part to the oil crisis of 1974 and cuts in Government expenditure, and, when work resumed around 1978, there was a move towards the 'barn' schemes that prevailed from the mid-1980s to the mid-1990s. The structure of these buildings was hidden behind brick walls and tiled roofs, while the interiors adopted a 'street' or 'mall' approach where all the facilities were visible from the entrance, with a food court with a seating area shared by the various restaurant outlets, deriving its inspiration from contemporary developments in retail practice rather than traditional transport catering.

Built by Granada at the height of the fashion for barn-like structures, Chieveley (1986; EPR Partnership) is located off the M4 at Junction 13 for the A34 to Newbury, and was originally known as Newbury services. Chieveley was a single-sided site with a single-storey, square, red brick building with a hipped roof. The apex of the roof was formed by a large glass skylight, and this was set back slightly from the line of the tiled roof below. Surprisingly, this did not light the main seating area, which was situated further to the west. The interior made use of exposed brickwork to add further to the Neo-Vernacular 'barn' theme hinted at outside. The filling station had distinctive hipped canopies in the shape of elongated octagons, tiled to match the main amenity building. Both this and the filling station remain largely as built.

Deregulation of MSAs, which had started in 1980 when restrictions on retailing were removed, gained pace in 1992, giving the operators much more freedom in how they ran their sites, although Government retained some powers intended among other things to ensure that MSAs did not become shopping destinations. The freeholds of the sites were sold off four years later. From the mid-1990s the 'shed' style, where structural and technological features are on display, or even emphasised, has become ubiquitous. The interiors are industrial in feel, with wide-span roofs free from internal structural columns, permitting open-plan spaces where the central seating area is ringed by catering and retail units. These buildings generally have distinctive curved or wave-form metal roofs, often paired with prominent entrance canopies, whilst the exterior walls are generally formed from structural glass on the entrance front, with simple block walls to the service areas at the rear or sides. Crucially, there is far more natural light in these designs, and in comparison to their predecessors the much higher roofs give an airy feel to the buildings, helping them to avoid the sometimes claustrophobic atmosphere prevalent in many MSAs when in heavy use.

There is more of a willingness to use forms that go beyond the somewhat bland approach of the 1980s. One of the earliest examples was the Thurrock MSA of 1992, between Junctions 30 and 31 of the M25, where hotel and catering functions were unusually combined within the same building, instead of the normal arrangement where a budget hotel block, unrelated in appearance, is located some distance from the catering building.

358 Norton Canes on the M6 toll exemplifies the 'shed' approach to motorway service area design. A spectacular exterior, largely of glass, taking motifs from high-tech architecture, encloses a highly flexible and largely open interior.

At Thurrock, entry to the building was gained via free-standing raised walkways supported on splayed concrete piers above landscaped areas running up to the edges of the trapezoidal glass lobby. Such an expression of style was more reminiscent of the era of Forton and Leicester Forest East.

At Donington Park, the main amenity building displayed the exposed structural elements that were typical of the 'shed' type. It was a single-sided development at Junction 23A of the M1, opened in 1998. The building was symmetrical with triple-height glass walls to the north and south, allowing a view from the main car park through the building and out to the landscape beyond, whilst the central atrium was flanked by three-storey rendered blocks to the east and west. In front of these, to the north, stood a single-storey block that ran right across the building, acting as a lobby area as well as housing further retail space. Inside the triple-height atrium, a south-facing clerestory roof was carried on exposed trusses above the central seating area. The atrium was flanked by retail and restaurant units to the east and west, above which a Travelodge hotel was incorporated within the main structure. The building was given a 'piazza' theme with a number of umbrellas over tables, patio-style heaters and a central suspended clock.

The area to the south of the main building was carefully landscaped with outdoor seating, picnic benches and a small lake well away from the traffic. Built immediately to the south of East Midlands Airport, the location of the service area played a crucial role in its design. The proximity of the airport meant that a large number of rooms were required, and this in turn was a major factor in bringing together the catering and hotel functions. The use of the food court and shopping-mall concept, with a number of publicly recognised branded retail outlets, was also in line with contemporary airport practice.

Thurrock and Donington Park, with their integral hotels, are relatively complex designs; many 'sheds', such as South Mimms on the M25 (1999; J. Ward Associates) and Norton Canes on the M6 toll (2002–4; Wilson Mason & Partners, operated by Roadchef),[93] are straightforward but none the less dramatic designs. At Norton Canes, the curved front and one side wall are all glass, enclosing a vast open interior and topped by a sweeping wave-like canopy supported on steel tubes outside the building, ensuring a column-free space inside (pl. 358).

In one sense MSAs have come full circle, in that their designers today use style prominently to attract the motorist in the way that the 1960s examples did, but they operate in a totally different market. Deregulated, relying on the introduction of well-known brands for retail and catering, they are used by generations accustomed to fast food who would never contemplate the type of formal dining anticipated by many operators in the early 1960s. At the same time, with innovations such as coffee shop franchises, they provide a range of facilities, offering drinks and food of considerably higher quality than that of the 1970s. They also cater for numbers of users then unimaginable, with clear implications for their design: hence the move towards big airy structures with internal layouts sufficiently flexible to allow for further change. Few MSAs have been totally rebuilt: the great majority of the 1960s and 1970s buildings soldier on, albeit well disguised behind metal cladding and wave-form entrance canopies.

359　A two-decker street drawn by Nickless in 1938. From *The Motor*, 22 March 1938, p. 324.

12: TRAFFIC IN TOWNS, 1896–1939

IN 1934, MARVELLING AT THE PROLIFERATION of cars, the motoring pioneer Selwyn F. Edge wrote:

Sometimes when I am walking through London, I cannot help stopping and asking myself whether it really has come to this – a never-ceasing stream of motor traffic everywhere; practically every clerk and butcher-boy owning some form of motor vehicle; the horse almost extinct in everyday life.[1]

For many of Edge's generation and class, this transformation must have seemed astonishing and, on the whole, beneficial. But burgeoning traffic introduced fresh problems to towns and cities. Annual statistics enumerating injuries and fatalities caused by motor vehicles were shockingly high. In response, the movements of pedestrians and cyclists became subjected to unprecedented restrictions. In the rhetoric of the day – which effectively silenced opposition – this was for their own safety. But by these very measures, motorists and their cars obtained the upper hand. They came to govern urban space, their smooth passage aided by a wide range of controls and directions that had a radical effect on the visual appearance of the English street.

The Horse World of Late Victorian England

The towns and cities negotiated by the first motor cars in the mid- to late 1890s had evolved over centuries to be served and traversed by horse-drawn vehicles and foot traffic. Queen Victoria's long reign (1837–1901), however, had already witnessed revolutionary advances in transportation, affecting the physical fabric of towns and the lives of town dwellers. The greatest agents of change had been the railways, which thrust close to urban centres, encouraging the movement of goods and people as never before. By the 1890s regular train services had already promoted a commuter lifestyle and encouraged the development of seaside resorts.

Within urban centres, however, for public, commercial and private transportation, the horse reigned supreme (pl. 360). Horse-drawn omnibuses had first appeared on the streets in the late 1820s.[2] From the 1860s they coexisted with horse-drawn

360   High Holborn in London, thronged with traffic around 1900.

361 The Road Car Depot, Fulham, depicted here in 1893, was a storage place for both horses and trams. Today it is a garage.

trams, and from the 1880s with electrified trams.[3] These vehicles shared the streets with the multitudinous carts and vans of carriers and delivery men, with cabs, private carriages and bicycles. They also shared their space with pedestrians, who could dodge and weave through the slow traffic without restraint. This was not wholly satisfactory, and the spatial separation of pedestrians and vehicles was proposed from time to time, for example, by spanning Ludgate Circus with iron walkways, or by building a 30-foot-high 'Crystal Way' between Oxford Street and Cheapside.[4] Although these schemes came to nothing, control was not entirely absent. Bollards protected pavements from vehicles, and policemen on point duty offered assistance to pedestrians who struggled to cross busy roads.

The urban environment reflected society's long-standing dependence on the horse, both in the layout of its streets and in the design of its buildings. Provision for horses – which existed in their tens of thousands in every city – included retail outlets where horses and accessories could be bought (such as sale yards, saddleries and harness shops); stables where horses could be kept or hired (such as jobmasters' depots); smiths' and farriers' shops, to keep horses well shod; accommodation for the army of grooms, liverymen and stable boys that cared for horses; infirmaries where sick or injured horses could be treated by veterinarians; granaries for feed and bedding;[5] pits and depots where manure could be collected; slaughterhouses for the dispatch of old and infirm beasts, and places to process carcasses (such as the infamous glue factory or 'cats'-meat man'). It is shocking to modern sensibilities to learn that just one company, Harrison Barber Ltd, killed 26,000 horses a year at its London depots in the early 1890s.[6]

Unhitched omnibuses, trams, carts and carriages – and cycles too – made their demands on urban space, since each vehicle had

to be manufactured, bought, stored and maintained, as well as run on the streets. Specialist factories existed for the manufacture of trams and omnibuses. In the 1890s, for example, the coach factory and repair shop of London's second largest omnibus company, the Road Car Co., stood next door to its depot on Farm Lane, Fulham.[7] New carriages were generally made to order by carriage builders, but second-hand vehicles could be purchased from carriage repositories, auction houses and bazaars. Of course, numerous domestic coach houses and cart sheds were scattered throughout cities for private use, from the mews of Buckingham Palace to the shacks provided behind humble terraces. As for cycles, these were produced at factories in west Midland towns and sold through the hundreds of cycle shops that had sprung up in recent decades.

From the 1870s some of the largest buildings provided for city horses were multi-storey depots that belonged to railway companies, major carriers (for example, Pickford's), livery stables, omnibus and tram companies, and consumer co-operative societies. Some examples still stand in provincial towns,[8] but these buildings survive mainly in London, where one of the most complete complexes, associated with the former London and North Western Railway Camden Goods Station in north London, includes several two- to three-storey blocks with external horse ramps, built between the 1850s and 1890s.[9] Others of note include the Road Car Co.'s depot in Fulham (1890, now a garage; pl. 361); the Great Western Railway stables on South Wharf Street, Paddington (1876, now part of a hospital); and Whitbread's Stables, Garrett Street, Finsbury (1897, now offices).[10] To give some idea of the scale of these buildings – the Victorian equivalents of today's multi-storey car parks – in the 1890s the London General Omnibus Co.'s depot on Chelverton Road in Putney could accommodate 375 horses.[11] By this time, London General owned half of the capital's omnibuses. It maintained 10,000 horses, which operated in 'studs' of ten or eleven to draw its 1,000 vehicles. The horses – always mares – were bought aged five, and had a short working life of about five years;[12] it was reckoned that two out of every three would die in service.[13] When the horses of the Road Car Co. were worn out, they were sold for 30s. as carcasses.[14] The harsh lives of city horses afforded ready propaganda for those promoting the motor car: it was a common – and deeply distressing – sight to witness a horse collapse in agony on the streets, through exhaustion or injury. Motor cars seemed to promise a kinder future.

The diverse buildings associated with horses and carriages occupied appropriate locations within towns. Horse bazaars, carriage repositories and carriage builders, which were patronised by well-to-do customers, held prominent positions on main thoroughfares. Cab stands, cab shelters and horse troughs, too, were a common sight in city centres. In outlying areas – for example, at the ends of omnibus routes – commercial depots

362 In cities, mews were converted into bijou houses and garages in the course of the twentieth century. This photograph by John Gay dates from 1960–65.

were often engulfed by terraced housing. Manure yards were usually placed alongside railway lines, and must have blighted the lives of those lodging nearby. Naturally, such places always stood at a safe remove from genteel residential districts. In all areas, however, the everyday stable and coach house was generally hidden behind street frontages. The impact of this concealment on the layout and appearance of streets can still be seen in small towns such as Baldock on the Great North Road in Hertfordshire, where many of the buildings – including former inns and maltings – lining Whitehorse Street and Hitchin Street still incorporate a carriage arch. This was very different from the approach adopted in well-heeled parts of, for example, Bath or London's West End, which had been laid out, usually on behalf of aristocratic landlords, from the early Georgian period.[15] In Mayfair and Belgravia, for example, the neat stables and coach houses of wealthy residents lined paved courts, back lanes or culs-de-sac (pl. 362). Generally, these mews had no pavements and the buildings lining them seldom rose above two storeys – though there were notable exceptions, such as Kensington Court Mews (1886) and De Vere Mews (1877) in Kensington, each of which had upper levels for horses, reached by ramps. The existence of mews generally allowed polite dwellings to maintain a decorous and continuous frontage, uninterrupted by carriage arches, whilst ensuring that horses and carriages stood conveniently to hand. Neither the traditional approach exemplified by Baldock nor the improved approach of Belgravia allowed town dwellers, whatever their social status, to escape the pervasive smell and noise of the horses that shared their world.

The principal rule of the road in the 1890s, followed by urban and rural traffic alike, was to adhere to the left, especially when passing a vehicle that was approaching from the opposite direction. This custom went back centuries, and had been enshrined in law by the Highway Act of 1835. Courtesies, however, could not always be maintained. Most English towns had a complex, irregular street pattern, with bottlenecks where vehicles were unable to pass side by side. By the 1890s many urban thoroughfares had been straightened and/or widened to provide sufficient width for two vehicles. From the late 1890s some of this widening was undertaken specifically for trams, though central tram lines – especially if electrified, with a line of posts – often created an obstacle for carts and carriages and, in time, for motor cars too. At night, however, on poorly lit and unmarked roads, the shining tracks provided a welcome guideline for drivers.

In cities – but not always in the smallest towns – streets were lined by raised, kerbed footpaths for pedestrians, who, in wet weather, risked being splashed with muck by passing traffic, or in dry weather being choked by clouds of dust raised by wheels. Town dust was none other than dried dung, as clarified for its more delicate readers by *The Times*:

> It would shock many beautifully dressed ladies who are fond of allowing their gowns to sweep the pavement to be told that what was clinging to the hem of their expensive garments, and being brought into their outwardly clean houses and thence distributed through the living and bed rooms, was nothing less than dried horse manure . . .[16]

By the 1890s at least four different materials were used for paving urban streets: stone setts (or 'cobbles'), macadam, wood and asphalt.[17] In London, where the parish vestries were responsible for their own streets, drivers encountered a great variety in the quality and condition of roads as they passed through the city, making abrupt transitions from one surface to another. The most established option comprised hard stone setts – usually granite setts from Aberdeen – cut to a regular wedge shape and embedded in mortar, with a convex face uppermost.[18] Setts were durable and hygienic, but uneven and noisy. In some fashionable towns, or in entries running through houses, bands of flat stones ('wheelers') were embedded in setts or cobbles to provide a smooth, quiet surface for carriage wheels. Macadamised streets comprised layers of granite and chipped stone, cemented simply by the pulverising action of wheels or (from the 1870s) steamrollers, rather than any binding agent. Many of the wide streets that ran through London's newer suburbs were paved with a central band of granite setts, flanked by strips of less durable macadam. One of the first experiments with wood paviors set in pitch took place on Oxford Street in 1838, and by the 1890s wood block covered many busy London thoroughfares, such as Piccadilly and Fleet Street, as well as streets in Manchester and other cities. Wood muffled the clatter of horses' iron shoes and the grinding sound of iron wheels, but this type of paving invented by Joseph Whitworth and used in Manchester in 1834, and the 'Hercules', invented by Herr Hentschel in Germany, which was capable of both washing and sweeping. After collection, dung was taken to local authority depots or dustyards, where it was sorted (i.e., mixed with stable manure) and prepared to be sent to the countryside. One of the largest depots was established around 1873 by Newington Vestry, close to a railway viaduct and surrounded by dense terraced housing in Walworth in south London, whence 'Newington Mixture' was transported by rail to enrich the hop fields and orchards of Kent. Much of it was unloaded in the goods yard at Swanley Junction, where the residents of surrounding houses complained of various ailments, including 'dumb ague', blamed on the proximity of so much manure and its attendant flies.[21]

It has been pointed out that 'Victorian London may have been smelly, dusty and muddy, but it had no parking problem'.[22] Vehicles used the streets principally as conduits, to get from A to B, but kerbside stops of short duration appear to have been widely tolerated. Kerbs, however, were treated as the property of 'frontagers', those living alongside them, and anyone allowing a cart or carriage to stand for any length of time without permission risked prosecution. Even outside one's own property there was no question of leaving a horse hitched to a cart or carriage all night or, indeed, for long stretches during the day. Because of frontagers' rights, special places had to be set aside for waiting Hansom cabs, often in the middle of particularly wide streets, such as Queen Victoria Street in London (pl. 363), or where streets were not fronted by private buildings, alongside parks or blank walls. Whilst moving around, drivers encountered little in the way of signs, whether for guidance or direction; no lines were painted on the road surface, and no attempts were made to regiment vehicles into lanes, although policemen did direct heavy traffic at crossings. The few signs that existed were set at a height convenient for coachmen.

One of the first documented traffic signals – obviously influenced by railway signals – was a 'street signal post' designed by the railway manager John Peake Knight. This was installed 'to allow the passage of persons on foot' outside the Houses of Parliament in December 1868.[23] A column with semaphore arms was topped by red (stop) and green (caution) gas lamps for night use: the light was turned to face the appropriate traffic by a lever, operated by a policeman. Gas leaks were common, however, and on several occasions the signal exploded, injuring the policeman on duty. Having failed to win compliance from either vehicles or pedestrians, the signal was superseded by a subway, and went out of use in 1872.[24] Generally, since horse-drawn transport moved so slowly – at a maximum of 8mph – little need was expressed for fixed pedestrian crossings. At principal junctions, strips of granite setts sometimes made the going good underfoot, while crossing sweepers regularly brushed manure and mud

363   A cab stand in the middle of Queen Victoria Street, London, with St Mary Aldermary on the left, *circa* 1900.

appears to have been unhygienic and, when wet, emitted a 'fetid and ammoniacal stench from decaying animal matter'.[19] Additionally, heavy rain sometimes caused the surface to break up. Asphalt – at this time usually an amalgam of tar with finely ground limestone – was the most controversial surface, arousing strong emotions amongst carriage folk. It had been laid experimentally in Threadneedle Street in 1870, and by 1890 was used extensively, especially by the Corporation of the City of London. Many Englishmen considered its hard, slippery surface to be dangerous to horses, and it required very frequent washing.

Regardless of surface materials, all streets had to be cleansed (i.e., watered and swept) daily to prevent dirt accumulating and flies breeding.[20] The time-honoured way of dealing with this was for parishes to employ scavengers to collect and remove horse dung, which was then sold to farmers as manure. In the second half of the nineteenth century several horse-drawn street-cleaning machines were introduced, including a street sweeper to one side, and policemen were on hand to provide assistance. One of the most common safety measures, on wide streets, was the island refuge.[25] Despite such provisions, road accidents were already a feature of everyday life.

The Car and the Town, 1896–1914

Pioneer motorists drove with some bravery – or, perhaps, bravura – into this world of dusty, muddy, slippery streets, of clanking trams, timorous horses, reckless pedestrians and scant signage. Breakdowns and punctures were common but there was, as yet, a complete absence of garages and petrol stations, let alone breakdown services. There was, essentially, no support system: motorists – unless, sensibly, travelling with chauffeurs or mechanics – had to fend for themselves.

At first, while still a novelty, cars drew curious crowds. When Frederick Simms and Evelyn Ellis (for whom, see Chapter 1) undertook a pioneering drive from Micheldever in Hampshire to Datchet in Berkshire in July 1895, 'whole villages turned out to behold, open-mouthed, the new marvel of locomotion'.[26] However, the growing toll of people and animals injured or killed in motor accidents soon stirred a backlash (pl. 364). The high-handed attitude of some motorists, who displayed offensive arrogance towards other road users, exacerbated this. Furthermore, drivers of horse-drawn omnibuses, carts and cabs saw their livelihoods threatened as increasing numbers of motor vehicles populated the streets. All this generated disapproval, resentment and fear. According to Selwyn F. Edge, 'in driving through London . . . one was bombarded by jeers and insults from practically every bus-driver and cab-driver one met'.[27] Indeed, at times it seemed that the motor car might precipitate serious social unrest. Once alert to this danger, motorists' champions did

364 An early motoring accident, in Worthing in 1908. The horse, apparently, survived.

what they could to counter negative propaganda, and to encourage courteous behaviour. But it was some time before antagonism eased.

It also took time for an infrastructure to develop in support of motoring, and horses remained a ubiquitous part of the street scene until the First World War. For the first few years of cars, the urban environment – its streets as well as its buildings – underwent little physical change to accommodate them. Experience was needed before the precise requirements of cars could be gauged and, furthermore, the future dominance of the car was simply unimaginable to a generation habituated to the horse. Thus, as has been seen, cars were bought from showrooms that differed little from other high street shops. Most automobilists already possessed outbuildings that could readily be adapted as motor houses. In mews, stables could easily be converted to garage large touring cars; coach houses could store 'run-abouts'; harness rooms were used as repair shops, whilst the quarters assigned to coachmen became chauffeurs' flats.

As noted in previous chapters, investment in new purpose-built facilities for motorists picked up noticeably around 1905, as it became clear that the automobile was here to stay and that a policy of adaptation would no longer suffice. The existing geography of urban areas was not yet threatened, but particular towns, or particular neighbourhoods, became increasingly associated with the car. Motor cars enabled people to explore and enjoy English towns, just as much as the glories of the countryside, and motorists were particularly attracted to seaside resorts, spa towns and the great cathedral cities. The appearance of such places changed as they began to provide purpose-built and well-signposted facilities where the motorist could find shelter, fuel and repairs. Meanwhile, Coventry emerged as the centre of the motor industry, and its suburbs expanded greatly as ever-larger car factories were set up in and around the city. In Birmingham, the motor retail trade coalesced around John Bright Street and Broad Street, while in London Great Portland Street took pride of place (see Chapter 2). Before long, London's coachbuilders, car factories and repair depots had gravitated away from Long Acre and other central London sites, to the northern and western suburbs. West London, in particular, was ripe for development at this time: it offered large tracts of land, ideal for colonisation by a new industry, accessible by public transport, and with developers erecting housing that could accommodate a large workforce.

Privileged motorists cut a swagger in metropolitan centres, their perceived hauteur highlighted by the exclusive showrooms and clubs set up for their convenience and pleasure. Despite the growth of Great Portland Street, elite marques maintained a presence in London's West End, especially in Bond Street and Regent Street. One of the first clubs, the Motor Car Club, was set up in January 1896, but its unfashionable location at 40

365 The success of motoring was reflected in the grandeur of the new RAC building on Pall Mall, seen here in a view by the architectural photographer Bedford Lemere from June 1911. It is decked out for the Coronation of George V.

Holborn Viaduct, its lack of on-site facilities for members, not to mention its association with Harry J. Lawson (see Chapter 1), all meant that it enjoyed little long-term cachet. In August 1897 Frederick Simms founded the Automobile Club of Great Britain and Ireland (ACGBI). This rapidly acquired a superior status, and – after winning approval from Edward VII – became the Royal Automobile Club (RAC) in 1907.[28] Since female motorists were not admitted to the ACGBI, in 1903 they set up the Ladies' Automobile Club at Claridge's in Brook Street. Then, in 1905, a rift in the ACGBI led to the formation of the more militant Automobile Association (AA), which was originally based in Fleet Street but moved, in 1909, to Whitcomb Street near Leicester Square. Of these organisations, the RAC was the first to erect a new clubhouse. In fact, no expense was spared for its headquarters on Pall Mall, a classical building designed by Mewès & Davis, along with the club's own honorary architect, E. Keynes

Purchase, and built in 1908–10 (pl. 365).[29] With its imposing portico and pediment – with sculpture depicting *Science* as the inspiration of the motor industry – its grandeur rivalled that of any existing gentleman's club. Motorists could unwind on the terrace overlooking Carlton Gardens, in the card room, billiard room, silent room or library; they could expend their energy in the racquet courts, rifle range or fencing room, and take their choice of baths, whether Turkish, plunge or swimming, with Caldarium, Frigidarium and Laconicum. In addition to this, the building contained offices for staff and bedrooms for members. It was some years before the AA undertook a major building project, erecting new headquarters, Fanum House, on Leicester Square in 1926.[30] The RAC and AA both opened provincial headquarters, but motorists' clubs outside London tended to meet in local hotels, rather than fund permanent premises. The Bedfordshire Automobile Club, for example, provided a garage

324

I.

For 10 mile or lower limit of speed, a white ring, 18 inches in diameter, with plate below, giving the limit in figures.

II.

For prohibition, a solid red disc, 18 inches in diameter.

III.

For caution (dangerous corners, cross roads, or precipitous places), a hollow red equilateral triangle, with 18-inch sides.

IV.

All other notices under the Act to be on diamond-shaped boards.

366 The four principal types of traffic sign recommended to highway authorities in 1904.

367 This rare cast-iron prohibition sign, of a type current from 1904, still stands on a street at Overstrand, Norfolk. The black and white banding on the post would have been added in the early 1930s. A plate, now missing, probably stated the nature of the prohibition.

and workshop for members but held its gatherings at the Swan Hotel in the centre of town,[31] while the Eastern Counties Automobile Club met at the Great White Horse in Ipswich.[32]

One subject that exercised the ACGBI/RAC and the AA was existing road surfaces, which were far from ideal for cars, whether in town or country. The blinding clouds of dust thrown up by pneumatic tyres revolving at speed on macadamised roads – forcing the occupants to swathe themselves in greatcoats, hats, scarves, masks and goggles – irritated pedestrians, was potentially damaging to engines, and was a clear sign that the road surface itself was being destroyed. The ACGBI undertook a series of experiments, and various proposals and inventions were put forward, including brushes or vacuum cleaners fitted beneath cars. But rather than adapt cars, it was evident that road surfaces themselves must be sealed. Unsatisfactory trials were conducted with water, oil and calcium, but local authorities eventually settled on pitch or tar. At first, macadamised roads were simply sprayed with tar,[33] but the ultimate solution was tarmacadam, more commonly known as tarmac.[34] This involved mixing hot tar with stones, producing a rougher surface that gave a better grip for tyres. A trial length of tarmac was laid on Madeira Drive in Brighton in 1905, and over subsequent decades this material underwent continual refinement to improve its non-skid properties. Concrete soon presented an alternative material for road building. By 1914 many urban streets had been laid with a concrete base and a tarmac top, its black colour distinguishing it from its dusty forebears and arousing much comment. One of the first streets to have a pale concrete surface, without a black top, appears to have been Roberts Lane, a suburban road on the outskirts of Chester, built in 1912–14. Bare concrete surfaces did not become widespread before the 1920s, and never overtook tarmac: especially after the introduction of white lines, which showed with greater clarity on a black crust.[35] Concrete, however, retained the advantage that it gave better illumination at night.

Signage specific to cars was introduced belatedly and without much consistency. In 1904, following the passage of the Motor Car Act, the County Councils Association and the Association of Municipal Corporations submitted a series of proposals for road signs, which were approved by the Local Government Board.[36] These were then recommended to local authorities, but uniformity was not enforced. The signs (pls 366 and 367) were categorised as follows: a hollow red equilateral triangle with 18-inch sides (signifying caution before bends, level crossings, etc), an 18-inch-diameter white ring (signifying speed limits, with the figure displayed on a plate below the ring) and an 18-inch-diameter solid red disc (signifying prohibition).[37] All other notices were to be displayed on a diamond-shaped board, of a type that was already in use, mainly on railways and canals. Within a few years these were joined along the roadside by

CONFUSION WORSE CONFOUNDED.

BEWILDERED MOTORIST: "WHAT'S THE GOOD OF ALL THIS TO ME?"

The multiplicity of road signs is becoming a serious nuisance to motorists and a disfigurement of the landscape.

368 Before long, the multiplication of traffic signs in some places was causing confusion. This cartoon, showing a 'Bewildered Motorist', appeared in *Car Illustrated*, 5 February 1913, p. 457.

various warning and direction signs erected by the RAC (in blue) and the AA (in yellow), often designed to defuse criticism of the motoring community by demonstrating its eagerness to adhere to low speeds and apply caution, but also serving to advertise the clubs themselves. Before long the Local Government Board felt obliged to contact local authorities to complain that some of them had erected too many signs, others too few, and that their inconsistent approaches were causing bewilderment (pl. 368).[38] The message was clear: either follow the official recommendations more closely, or face the prospect of statutory enforcement. Meanwhile, Britain opted not to comply with European standards for signs, set at the first International

Road Congress, convened on the initiative of the French Minister of Public Works and held at the Jeu de Paume in Paris in 1908.[39] Though this independence – based on the argument that conditions on British roads were quite different from those on their European counterparts – was maintained in later years, the influence of Continental signs, with their emphasis on symbols rather than words, strengthened as time went by.

Other users of urban streets gradually became accustomed to cars, which were much faster than any horse-drawn transport and thus more dangerous to unwary pedestrians, who were frequently – in fact, almost invariably – labelled 'careless' by motorists. The pedestrian, however, was 'undoubtedly by law king of the road':

> . . . every good driver upon the road, whether of horses or of motor-cars, should thoroughly grasp the fundamental fact that the pedestrian is master of the highway – that he can pass and repass at his own sweet will; that he can take up any position on the busiest road so long as he does not deliberately obstruct traffic . . .[40]

As early as 1903 the electrical engineer R.E.B. Crompton pointed out the need for dedicated pedestrian crossings superintended by a crossing-keeper or, in very busy thoroughfares, pedestrian subways or bridges.[41] In *The World Set Free* (1914), H. G. Wells also envisaged the need for pedestrian bridges, describing mid-twentieth-century London as a version of Chester's medieval Rows, adapted to the motor age. These Rows would run along the fronts of buildings at first-floor and upper levels, connected by bridges. Below, the road would be devoted to cars, while the pedestrian was 'forbidden at the risk of a fine, if he survived, to cross the roadway'.[42]

In fact, little was done to help the Edwardian pedestrian cross the street safely. Similarly, little was done to keep traffic flowing at junctions. Although semaphore signals were suggested from time to time, none was installed, and traffic control at busy crossroads remained in the hands of the police.[43] Crompton suggested enlarging busy circuses and ensuring that there were long gaps between vehicles, 'through which the crossing traffic can pass without interruption'.[44] This would have been very difficult to enforce, let alone choreograph. More realistic was the notion of one-way gyratory flow around traffic circles – that is, the concept of the roundabout – which was first proposed by the engineer Holroyd Smith in 1897, then in France by the architect Eugène Hénard in 1903. This principle was applied in New York (notably with Columbus Circle, designed by the traffic management specialist William Phelps Eno in 1905) and Paris (at the Place de l'Etoile in 1907), but not in the U.K., although W. Noble Twelvetrees, President of the Civil and Mechanical Engineers' Society, did advocate gyratory control at Piccadilly Circus and other London locations in 1907.[45]

369 Sollershott Circus in Letchworth Garden City, Hertfordshire, photographed from the south-east around 1912. This shows the original island, or pedestrian refuge, with its surrounding footpath, prior to its reduction in 1923.

Since 2005 Sollershott Circus, a roundabout in Letchworth Garden City, Hertfordshire, has borne a sign reading 'UK's First Roundabout Built circa 1909' (pls 369 and 370). This cautious dating reflects the fact that – while the completion of the circus seems to have passed without record – it was planned in 1908 and existed by 1910.[46] Its claim to be the 'UK's first roundabout' requires close scrutiny.

Sollershott Circus forms the intersection of six leafy residential roads, including Broadway, the main avenue approaching Letchworth town centre from the south. The island at its centre was conceived as a pedestrian refuge encircled by a footpath. The primary motivation for the arrangement was clearly aesthetic, to create long vistas on the approach to the garden city, a planning device that can be traced back, in the U.K., to Sir Christopher Wren's unexecuted post-fire designs for the City of London. By 1909 small circuses were a familiar aspect of metropolitan planning, usually with some central feature: for example, a drinking fountain at Oxford Circus, a urinal at Seven Dials, and an obelisk at St George's Circus. Outside London, examples could be seen in Hull, where the junctions of avenues on the Westbourne Park

370 The island in the centre of Sollershott Circus has been enlarged, and displays a sign reading 'UK's First Roundabout Built circa 1909', although a gyratory system was not enforced until the early 1930s.

371 One of the first one-way street systems was implemented on St James's Street, London, in 1912.

Estate were laid out in the 1870s with ornamental fountains, with circular basins protected by railings. In all these cases – as at much large circuses with central gardens, like The Circus in Bath and the Inner Circle in Regent's Park in London – traffic could simply press on, rather than having to rotate in a one-way direction. This appears to have been the case, too, at Sollershott Circus. Letchworth's designers, Barry Parker and Raymond Unwin, were aware of the gyratory principle, but were not wholly won over by it. In 1909, writing about Hénard's 'chaussée annulaire', Unwin considered: 'one would regard it as an undesirable form of *place* except in cases where traffic considerations must be the all-important ones'.[47] Traffic considerations were certainly not to the fore at Sollershott Circus. And even if Parker and Unwin had expected the small central island refuge to encourage rotary circulation from the outset, in the absence of signs, motorists – quite unfamiliar with the concept – did not instinctively select this course. That this was the designers' intention, however, is implied in a letter written in 1923 by Parker to the Secretary of the First Garden City Ltd, expressing his concern at a proposed reduction in the size of the island, and complaining about 'drivers of vehicles not circulating round it

in the way they were intended to do but coming onto their wrong side of the road in order to pass it'.[48] 'Keep left' signs, however, were erected only in 1932,[49] by which time roundabouts were entering general use throughout England (see below). The vagueness concerning the direction of traffic flow at Sollershott Circus was mirrored in 1912 by a proposal, or rather a supposition, that 'in squares and open spaces, without introducing any hard and fast gyratory system, traffic might with advantage keep to the left'.[50] One must conclude that Sollershott Circus represents an intermediate stage between the traditional circus-with-central-feature, designed as an aesthetic device or pedestrian refuge, and the modern roundabout, which is a tool of traffic management. Perhaps it should be described, more properly, as a proto-roundabout.

A closely related feature of traffic control, which made a fleeting appearance before the First World War, was the one-way street. There are some claims that a one-way traffic system was introduced on Albemarle Street, London, in the nineteenth century, but this appears to have been a temporary arrangement, to ease access for those attending Sir Humphry Davy's lectures at the Royal Institution.[51] Certainly, one-way systems had been introduced in New York in 1907 and had spread to other cities, including Paris. In 1912 the London Traffic Board suggested that such schemes could be implemented most effectively on parallel streets, each of which would convey traffic in a different direction.[52] Three experiments were made towards the end of 1912 by Westminster City Council, with the approval of the police, in Deanery Street, Jermyn Street and Arlington Street, off Piccadilly.[53] At the St James's Street (i.e., western) entrance to Jermyn Street a sign was set up, displaying an uplifted white hand and the wordy and emphatic notice: 'Drivers should *not* enter Jermyn Street *from this end unless calling* in the street' (pl. 371).[54]

Between 1895 and 1914 cars were rarely prioritised in urban improvement schemes. This was certainly the case in London. A Royal Commission on the Means of Locomotion and Transport in London (or, in short, 'on London Traffic') was appointed in 1903 and reported in 1905, having considered the requirements of all types of traffic. Drawing on earlier proposals by the railway engineer Sir John Wolfe Barry,[55] it recommended the creation of two new roads that would cross London from north to south and from east to west (with bridges or sunken roads at their intersection), each with trams on the road and railways in shallow tunnels underneath. This scheme literally sidelined the motor car. William Rees Jeffreys of the Road Improvement Association had put forward something very different in his evidence to the Commission: a ring road (or 'boulevard round London'), approximately on the route of the present North and South Circulars, roughly 7 miles from central London, with separate lanes for slow traffic (such as carts and traction engines), trams, motor cars and pedestrians.[56] Another witness, R. W. Perks MP, chairman of the Metropolitan District Railway, also suggested a ring road, but one lying further from the centre of the city, with a radius of about 12 miles.[57] Thus the issue of a London ring road – which was to command so much attention over the next eighty years – was first placed before the authorities.[58] It was disregarded by the Royal Commission on London Traffic, but already the concept had been adopted in Liverpool – significantly, a port city where large quantities of heavy goods, for export and import, were transported by road – and it was receiving consideration from several industrial towns.

Liverpool's 'circumferential boulevard', Queen's Drive, was the most important new road scheme undertaken for cars prior to the First World War in England. It was not just the first British ring road, but also one of the earliest dual carriageways, and a precursor of ribbon development.[59] The road was designed by

the City Engineer, John Alexander Brodie. A keen motorist, Brodie served as Vice-President of the Liverpool Self-Propelled Traffic Association (he also, incidentally, invented the goal net used in football matches). The notion of a road bounding the landward side of Liverpool had been proposed in the 1850s by the Borough Engineer of the time, John Newlands. This was revived by Brodie, who adopted a different alignment, passing through farmland at a greater distance from the centre of the city, which had expanded greatly over the intervening fifty years. Work began in 1903, and although the 6½-mile length of Queen's Drive was not completed until the mid-1920s, several sections had opened before the First World War. While a single carriageway was adopted for initial sections in Walton, to the north, later sections – for example, Queen's Drive, Wavertree (pl. 372) – were constructed as dual carriageways with a grassed central reservation, broad verges and footpaths. Conceived as a

372   This view of Queen's Drive, Wavertree, Liverpool, was taken on 24 May 1915. It shows a section of dual carriageway, with Gladstone's Mission Room on the right, and a circular island (not a roundabout) in the foreground. A flyover now springs from this point on Queen's Drive, forging a connection with the M62.

'linear park', this ring road resembled the broad single carriageways being laid out by Parker and Unwin at the same time in Letchworth, such as Sollershott West and Broadway. It was partly financed by a 'frontage charge', levied on developers for the chance to build new houses along the road, and quickly attracted lateral development. Brodie designed a number of other Liverpool boulevards – mostly radial routes spreading from the suburbs into the countryside – as dual carriageways with central reservations that were devoted to grassed tramways. These boulevards, such as Broad Green Road, which opened in 1914, were widely imitated in the 1920s (see below). Meanwhile, Queen's Drive inspired cities such as Birmingham, Sheffield and Manchester to contemplate ring roads. Prior to 1914, however, the only scheme that progressed to any degree was Birmingham's: this was assigned funds in 1913, but was inevitably postponed by the outbreak of war.[60]

In London, disjointed improvements such as the widening of Piccadilly (begun 1902), the construction of Kingsway and Aldwych (opened 1905), the rebuilding of Vauxhall Bridge (1904–6) and the construction of the Rotherhithe Tunnel (opened 1908) were undertaken for general, rather than specifically motor, traffic. Even Kingsway – planned primarily for electric trams, before the arrival of the motor car – was dwarfed by some of the 'Utopian' schemes published at this time including the 'thoroughfare of the future' pictured by the artist Guy Lipscombe in 1908, showing a ten-lane urban highway with subway access to two central tramways, flanked by lanes for fast and slow traffic: this streamed in each direction, separated just by lines of bollards (see pl. 427).[61] Similarly, in 1913 F. Fissi published a vision of London as it might be in 1933, with a street devoted exclusively to motor vehicles: pedestrians were banished to moving platforms that ran along the frontages of buildings at first- and second-floor levels, while cable cars ran at a higher level still, and footbridges spanned the road.[62] Most of the visionary road proposals of the Edwardian period, however, were designed to enhance connections between London and towns popular with motorists (see pp. 240–41), rather than to improve communications and reduce congestion within the city. Similarly, the recommendations of the London Traffic Branch of the Board of Trade (1909–10) and the London Arterial Roads Conferences (1913–16) (see p. 242) focused intently on new and improved arterial routes leading in and out of the metropolis, and not on the city centre itself.

Cars did not receive much more consideration within new urban developments on greenfield sites, whether these happened to be traditional suburban extensions or garden cities. The planners of new Edwardian settlements, such as Letchworth Garden City (from 1904) and Hampstead Garden Suburb (from 1907), failed to anticipate the extent to which inhabitants would adopt cars. Thus, space for drives and motor houses was not incorporated into plots – it was fortuitous, in later years, if this existed – and land was not set aside for parking or garaging in the town centres. Moreover, many of the carriageways on the tree-lined residential streets were unusually narrow, even if they were flanked by wide verges and the opposing houses were set far apart. Apart from the aesthetics, this saved money on road construction. In Hampstead Garden Suburb, a special building on the southern edge of the development, close to dwellings assigned to Garden Suburb staff, was provided for cars and chauffeurs, with lock-up garages on the ground floor and rental flats for chauffeurs above. According to *The Motor*, 'the primary idea has been to discourage the erection of motor-houses alongside dwelling-houses on the estate by providing this substitute'.[63] Evidently, despite the presence of a quasi-roundabout in Letchworth, cars were not compatible with the garden city ethos of *rus in urbe*.

For all the problems they dragged in their wake, motor cars were indisputably more hygienic than horses. In June 1914 the *Car Illustrated* commented on 'the remarkable absence of flies from the London Streets . . . due to the diminishing numbers of horses to be found in the metropolis and the fact that mews are everywhere giving way to up-to-date garages'.[64] Conspicuously less forage was being transported through the streets, and market gardeners were paying a higher price for manure, which was becoming increasingly difficult to source. The First World War accelerated the process whereby the car replaced the horse within England's towns and cities. Not only did its demand for drivers of ambulances and military vehicles familiarise many people with motor vehicles, but also, by shipping hundreds of thousands of horses to a horrific fate on the Western Front, it forced many commercial companies to switch to motor transportation.[65]

Controlling Traffic and Pedestrians, 1918–1939

As cars superseded horses, the atmosphere of urban streets was transformed. Not only was there less manure and dust to worry about, but the smells and sounds of the city had also changed. In 1927 Owen John considered that London was quieter these days, due to its smoother roads and the adoption of pneumatic tyres. He wrote: 'before the coming of cars the streets of London were so noisy that, like the skylark's song at Lodre, any one particular noise was absorbed into the city's universal hum and so passed unnoticed and unidentified'.[66] Now, any abnormally loud sound, such as the blaring of a horn, was startling. Even if they were truly quieter, the streets were busier than ever, and the potential speed of motor cars made congestion more frustrating and dangerous than before.

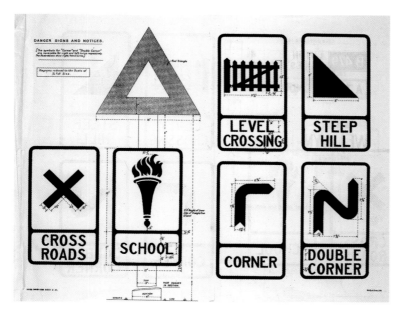

373 Designs for the 'danger' sign, issued in 1921. Cast iron, with details raised in relief, was recommended for traffic signs. Flat enamelled sheet iron was deemed unsuitable, because it was easily damaged.

Urban traffic congestion was tackled in a number of different ways, usually with the new Ministry of Transport, created in 1919, seizing the initiative. Over the next two decades the urban landscape was affected by additional signage, by lines and instructions on road surfaces, by pedestrian crossings, by guardrails, by roundabouts and, in suburban areas, by bypasses, footbridges and subways. These innovations greatly assisted the motorist, by encouraging the free flow of traffic. At the same time they attempted to secure the safety of pedestrians, but only by eroding their freedom to walk as they wished through towns and cities. Furthermore, these controls had a strong visual impact on streetscapes throughout the country. Surprisingly, though many contemporary observers complained about motoring paraphernalia ruining the pristine beauty of the English countryside (see Chapter 10), very few commented adversely on the plethora of signs and painted lines that now cluttered the urban environment, except to denounce it as confusing for motorists.

A major frustration for drivers wishing to move speedily around towns and cities was the obstruction of highways, leading to traffic jams. Amongst the chief offenders were horse-drawn vehicles, but these were now in the minority, and decreasing in number with each passing year. While extreme calls to ban horse-drawn transport altogether were generally disregarded, some realistic efforts were made to address the problem, including an experiment undertaken in 1920 in east London whereby signs invited slow drivers to keep to the left.[67] A second cause of obstruction was parked cars. The Ministry of Transport actively discouraged the erection of 'no parking' signs on streets,

believing that any parking on the highway should be prohibited and that signs should be erected only where parking was positively allowed. Nevertheless, steps were taken – usually in the form of fines or summonses – to persuade drivers to park their cars off major thoroughfares, in commercial garages or authorised parking spaces (see Chapter 6). A third cause of obstruction was public transport. Until the early 1920s passengers could ask a bus driver to drop them off anywhere; now there was an insistence on official bus stops.[68] Trams were regarded as a worse obstacle than omnibuses, and motoring journals constantly called for them to be scrapped. This cause was taken up by the Royal Commission on Transport, whose report of 1930 recommended that no additional tramways be built and that existing ones should gradually disappear. No fewer than eighty-one tramway systems were abandoned in the 1930s, and if it had not been for the Second World War this trend would have continued unabated.[69] A fourth type of obstruction – perhaps the one that elicited most complaints from motorists – was road works. These were a perpetual irritant, only partly soothed by the introduction of 'stop' and 'go' signs, red and green respectively, to institute one-way systems through road works from 1933.

Road signs now proliferated. In 1921 the Ministry of Transport issued a Circular recommending standard warning signs.[70] The principal categories of sign proposed in 1904 were retained, but the hollow triangle (always painted 'signal' or 'post office' red) now signified 'danger', rather than 'caution'. This 'danger' sign was augmented by a rectangular plate depicting the source of the danger as a pictorial symbol (for instance, a torch for a school or a gate for a level crossing), as well as lettering (pl. 373).[71] The symbols were based on European standards, though not slavishly followed. Significantly, although a 'crossroads' symbol could be displayed on a 'danger' sign, there was still no compulsion to erect warnings at junctions. The need for this was expressed repeatedly throughout the decade. An important step forward was the adoption of the 'dead slow' sign, following a conference convened by the Ministry of Transport in 1928.[72] On a rectangular plate beneath a red disc containing a triangle, the 'crossroads' symbol was modified to indicate which road had priority at a junction. This quickly entered widespread use.

Uniformity in road signs still proved elusive. One elegant variant was the so-called Gilbert Scott sign of 1930, named after the architect who designed it. This sign, incorporated into a decorative Neo-Classical post, was created for sensitive areas where 'the installation of unattractive, utilitarian signs might detract from the amenities'.[73] All the 'no entry' signs in Trafalgar Square, for example, were of this type. Although a Memorandum of April 1930 reinforced and augmented the recommendations made in 1921,[74] it was not until 1933 that uniform traffic signs became a statutory requirement. This was achieved under Section 48 of the Road Traffic Act of 1930 – an Act that also, famously,

374 The concrete and metal 'Pillar of Salt' signpost on Angel Hill in Bury St Edmunds, Suffolk, was designed for the Borough Council by the local Arts and Crafts architect Basil Oliver and erected in 1935. Because it did not conform to the national standard, approval had to be obtained from the Ministry of Transport.

A 'halt' sign could be used with a special dispensation from the Ministry; this was superseded in 1935 by the 'halt at major road ahead' sign, the predecessor of the modern 'stop' sign.[78] White lines (see p. 245) had been used to control the positions of vehicles at junctions since the mid-1920s, and in 1935 a Ministerial Circular explained how to place these lines to best effect in conjunction with the new 'halt at major road ahead' sign. The Road Traffic Act of 1934 modified the 1930 Act by introducing a speed limit of 30mph in built-up areas (i.e., areas with 'a public lighting system'), as well as bringing in driving tests and cycle lanes.[79] The signs introduced for the new speed limit displayed the number '30' within a red ring, studded with reflectors, and those marking the end of the speed limit comprised a white disc bisected by a diagonal black band.[80] Standardisation had been imposed, but it remained possible for local authorities to seek special permission to erect different signs (pl. 374). The placement and clarity of signage remained a matter of much complaint.[81] Although the various traffic signs introduced in the 1930s were superseded in the 1960s (see Chapter 13), a small number can still be found on British streets today (pl. 375).[82]

Enormous numbers of policemen were engaged in traffic control throughout the 1920s. As late as 1931 a German commentator noted that 'the traveller familiar with other big cities of the world is immediately struck by the exorbitant number of police used on traffic-control in London'.[83] Already, however, policemen on point duty were being replaced by automatic controls. Modern traffic lights (or traffic 'robots' as they were occasionally called, using a term coined by the Czech author Karel Čapek in 1920) arrived only after several experimental systems had been tested and discarded. These were influenced by various American systems, ultimately inspired by signals on railroads. One of the first, with manually operated red and green lamps, had been introduced in Salt Lake City in 1912, whilst the first three-colour signal (red, green and white) was erected in Detroit in 1918.[84] By 1920 many American city streets were controlled by semaphores with coloured discs or lamps, usually manually operated and accompanied by gongs, whistles or bells. Lights could be attached to poles, to policemen's clothing, or even set in towers. The first experiment with a traffic tower had taken place in Paris in 1912, but was short-lived. It was reprised around 1920 on Fifth Avenue in New York, where high towers down the centre of the street were manned by attendants and fitted with coloured lights. Although traffic towers were not favoured in English towns, busy crossings in Brighton were controlled by semaphore signals, accompanied by bells and red globe lights. This unique system was originally operated by levers, but electric controls were fitted in 1934 (pl. 376).

Another early experiment involved electric lights set on island refuges in The Mall in London. These showed a white light to

removed the speed limit, introduced the Highway Code (based on the French *Code de la route*) and made third-party insurance compulsory. In the wake of the Act, a committee was appointed under Sir Henry Maybury to examine traffic signs.[75] This reported in 1933 and, soon afterwards, 'Traffic Signs (Size, Colour and Type) Regulations' was issued by the Minister.[76] Most significantly, signs were brought to the eye level of the motorist;[77] posts had to be painted with black and white stripes – something that had already been in widespread use for a number of years – and the 'dead slow' sign was renamed the 'major road ahead' sign. It was stipulated that signs should be of cast metal, and should be illuminated at night, if only with reflective lenses.

a

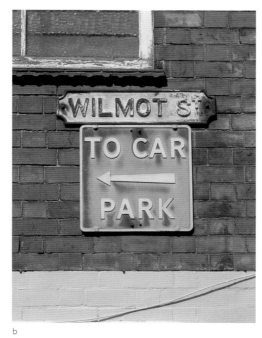

b

c

d

e

f

g

375a–g   A selection of mid-twentieth-century road signs, of types that may still be found in English towns, though often rather worse for wear: (top, left to right) (a) Bath Street, Ilkeston, Derbyshire (finger-type direction signs attached to a building, with modern CCTV cameras in the foreground); (b) Wilmot Street, Ilkeston (blue car park sign, introduced in 1933); (c) Catmos Street, Oakham, Rutland (direction sign with chequers [introduced in 1933 to indicate a main through route] and a yellow background [introduced in 1957]); (bottom, left to right) (d) Upton Bishop, Herefordshire (this 'school' sign superseded the torch sign in 1957); (e) and (f) Church Road, Kersey, Suffolk (note that the pre-1957 torch sign reads 'children' rather than 'school'); (g) Stamford, Lincolnshire, 'no through road' sign. Note the reflectors on d, e, f, and g.

pedestrians and a red light to traffic. In March 1924 a different experiment was made on The Mall, derived from marine navigation lighting, with automatic gas lights that showed a green pulsating light.[85] More significantly, in 1926 eight electric light signals coloured red ('stop'), green ('proceed') and yellow ('a change in signal') were set up on the pavements of Piccadilly, at major junctions.[86] This installation was heavily manned: a policeman stationed in a cabin on the central refuge at the juncture with St James's Street operated the lights by levers, while constables stationed by the light standards could press buttons to convey the state of the traffic to the central control point (pl. 377). These were, effectively, the first true traffic lights in England, though the first fully automatic system was installed in Princess Square, Wolverhampton, in November 1927. This was followed, in 1928 and 1929, by installations in Leeds, Coventry, Nottingham, Manchester (where, for the first time, pedestrians

376 Brighton's traffic-control system was probably unique in England. From 1927 the busiest crossings in the town were controlled by semaphore signals. Before a signal was given, a warning bell rang. As the semaphore arm was raised into the 'stop' position, a red globe came alight. This photograph shows one of the crossings just after electrical controls (background) had been introduced in 1934.

could control the traffic by pushing a button), Derby and else-where.[87] As usual, the main problem was the absence of stan-dardisation from town to town. A memo issued by the Minister of Transport in September 1929 stressed the desirability of uni-formity, recommending three colours (red, green and amber) on each signal, which would show in succession.[88]

One of the most sophisticated traffic-light systems was in Trafalgar Square in London, where, from 1933, the lights were triggered by the passage of vehicles over 'electromatic' strips: a form of vehicle actuation that had been introduced for the first time in Baltimore in 1928.[89] The Trafalgar Square installation also included green filter lights, enabling cars to turn right or left

when the lights were against them, and pedestrian crossings instructing people to 'Cross Now' or 'Don't Cross'. By all accounts, most pedestrians ignored this advice, and so it was decided not to erect such signals elsewhere.[90] By 1933 nearly a hundred crossings were controlled by lights in the capital, leading to the – with hindsight, conservative – observation: 'the time is not far distant when signals on the roads will be almost as numerous as on the railways'.[91]

An alternative method of controlling traffic at crossroads was the roundabout. As outlined above, gyratory control was not enforced at Sollershott Circus in Letchworth. Similarly, the *rond points* shown on Louis de Soissons' original plans for Welwyn

377   Britain's first three-colour traffic-light system was installed on Piccadilly, London, in 1926. This shows the junction with St James's Street, where a small cabin was installed on the central refuge for the policeman on duty. None of this street furniture survives.

Garden City, drawn up in 1920, are unlikely to have been planned as roundabouts.[92] The idea was still novel in 1926, when a number of gyratory systems were introduced at busy junctions in central London. First of all, an experimental system was set up in Parliament Square in January 1926, enforced by policemen on point duty, together with guidance painted on the road surface: the words 'turn left', with arrows at the turnings round the square.[93] This was followed swiftly by an experiment on The Mall, where the roadway around Queen Victoria's monument formed a perfect circle (but, it must be admitted, never suffered from heavy traffic); at Hyde Park Corner, Trafalgar Square and Piccadilly Circus.[94] In April the Minister of Transport adopted

the term 'roundabout', which gradually overtook 'gyratory' in normal usage.

One-way streets became common at the same time as roundabouts, which were, at their simplest, a form of one-way circulation. Following Westminster's experiment in 1912 (see pl. 371), further trials were made in the early 1920s. One of these, implemented in 1923 on Hill Street, Birmingham, was suspended after shopkeepers and motorists complained. Others were undertaken more successfully in London in 1924, in Mare Street, Hackney, and on Long Acre.[95] It was explained that Long Acre – the former centre of London's carriage trade, briefly ceded to motor car agents prior to the First World War – had completely changed

378 An early fixed pedestrian crossing at Parliament Square, London, in 1926. The first gyratory, or roundabout, system in the country was implemented here, making it difficult to cross the road safely.

its character, becoming 'an overflow from Covent Garden Market', with the loading and unloading of lorries stopping the traffic in one direction. Once gyratory systems were introduced in 1926, one-way streets proliferated, for example, in the area

379 One of the new Belisha beacons in Kensington, London, in September 1934. The unlit orange globes were supposed to throw reflected light at night.

around Piccadilly (notably on Haymarket) and at Hammersmith Broadway. Shopkeepers complained, of course, but their gripes were less important to local authorities than the free and fast flow of London traffic. From 1933 the exits from one-way streets were identified by signs displaying a solid red disc signifying prohibition, accompanied by a 'no entry' plate.[96]

High volumes of traffic caused problems for pedestrians, especially in shopping areas. Conversely, pedestrians troubled motorists, and the respective rights (or culpability) of the two groups – as the principal users of public space – were often disputed. In the mid- to late 1920s, as traffic lights and roundabouts came into existence, affecting pedestrians as much as vehicles, organisations sprang up to defend the rights of those on foot, as well as to ensure their safety. The Pedestrians' Protection Association was formed in 1925, and the more long-lived Pedestrians' Association in 1929.[97] At this time, many of the measures adopted ostensibly for the safety of pedestrians also served to speed the motorist on his way. There was a good excuse for this: in 1930 pedestrians accounted for nearly half of all road deaths.

The first fixed pedestrian crossings were probably those set up in Parliament Square in 1926, marked by parallel white lines and signs, with green lettering on a white ground, reading 'PLEASE CROSS HERE' (pl. 378).[98] According to *The Times*: 'it is too early as yet to say whether the Londoner will accommodate himself to the official desires. Unlike his fellows on the Continent, he has been brought up on the legal principle that the right to use the roadway is not restricted to vehicles, which must therefore make allowances for him.'[99] By the early 1930s various crossing types had sprung up in London: some bounded by broken white lines, others marked out with white chevrons or 'ladder lines' and a 'C' sign.[100] In 1933 chequered 'checkon' crossings were introduced in Salford, Manchester and London.[101] These were soon superseded by a new type of crossing marked by Belisha beacons, named after Leslie Hore-Belisha, the Minister of Transport, who was responsible for their introduction.[102] In the course of 1934, 9,000 Belisha beacons were erected in London, and in November of that year the scheme was extended to the provinces.[103] The beacons comprised orange globes on black and white poles, as they do today, but initially the edges of the crossings were defined simply by steel studs, and the globes were not illuminated (pl. 379); alternating black and white stripes – the 'zebra crossing' – did not appear until 'Pedestrian Crossing Week' in March 1949.[104] *The Spectator* complained that Belisha beacons made London look like 'a fifth rate carnival', while an MP quipped that London streets now 'had the appearance of orange groves'.[105] From the outset, if a pedestrian stepped onto a Belisha crossing, cars were required to stop.

Several measures adopted in the mid-1930s can be interpreted as harbingers of the segregation of the diverse users of urban spaces that would shape post-war developments. This was most evident in the erection of safety barriers, which enabled drivers to speed along the road corridor without fearing that pedestrians might stumble into their path. At the same time, these barriers corralled pedestrians. Some of the first experiments of this nature took place in 1934–5 in Wolverhampton, Scarborough and Brighton, all of which erected safety barriers to compel pedestrians to use marked crossings.[106] In 1935, having overseen the erection of beacon crossings, Hore-Belisha inaugurated a series of experiments in London, with fixed guardrails or removable 'safety chains'.[107] One of the first was a small fixed barrier by a Belisha crossing on Nightingale Lane, Clapham Common, erected in February 1935. A far more ambitious scheme was put forward in October 1935, when it was proposed that automatic traffic lights be erected at every junction along a 3-mile stretch of road from Stepney to Poplar – an accident blackspot, with 260 pedestrians killed or injured each year – and that the edges of the pavements be railed off, compelling pedestrians to use the crossings.[108] This was completed in May 1936, and received much publicity. In the late 1930s the long footpaths that lined London's suburban dual carriageways were habitually protected by railings or wire fences (pl. 380). Schemes of this type multiplied, and 'segregation' began to enter the everyday language of the planner. Another manifestation of this was the 'play street', created by closing streets to traffic at certain times, allowing children who had no access to open spaces to play safely out of doors. The first play streets were created in Salford in 1929 (pl. 381), on a voluntary basis, but in 1933 the Corporation obtained legislative powers to close streets for this purpose.[109] Subsequently, the Road Traffic Act enabled all local authorities to adopt this course of action without special sanction, and play streets appeared in Manchester and elsewhere.[110] In 1938 the first special 'play street' traffic sign was devised for London's four experimental play streets.[111] This was a rare example of segregation that was not in the best interests of motorists. The concept remained popular into the 1970s, and some play streets survive today.

Local authority planners eagerly grasped the concept of segregation. The Association of Municipal Corporations, for example, in its evidence to the Alness Committee on the Prevention of Road Accidents in 1938, suggested that it become an offence for a pedestrian 'to walk carelessly', while the resulting report argued that it should be an offence 'for a pedestrian to enter the highway needlessly'.[112] Perceptions had changed greatly since 1908, when the pedestrian was still deemed 'master of the highway'. One of the most influential advocates of segregation was Sir Herbert Alker Tripp (1883–1954), an Assistant Commis-

380 (*above*)   Eastern Avenue, Ilford, London, photographed in 1937, clearly showing the segregation of motor vehicles, cyclists and pedestrians.

381 (*right*)   Around 1929, as it became increasingly dangerous for children to play in the street, some streets were closed to traffic at particular times and declared 'play streets'. This shows a special sign being erected in Salford on 13 September 1937.

382 A temporary footbridge being built over the Kingston Bypass – newly converted into a dual carriageway – in 1938. In time this was to be superseded by a subway; in the meantime, it provoked an outcry because many people were unable to climb the steep steps. Guardrails prevented people from crossing elsewhere.

sioner at Scotland Yard, who spent some years considering the incompatibility of motorists, pedestrians and cyclists. His first book, *Road Traffic and its Control* (1938), became a standard text on the subject. His second, *Town Planning and Road Traffic* – published in 1942, in the middle of the Second World War – tackled the question of post-war reconstruction and advocated the complete segregation of pedestrians from vehicular traffic, not just with railings, but with high-speed urban roads and precincts, something that would involve a radical remodelling of the urban domain (see Chapter 13).

Dual carriageways, which began to appear in London suburbs in the late 1930s, posed a particular problem for pedestrians. Guardrails prevented people from making a dash across roads flowing with automobiles, and footbridges enabled them to cross without stopping the traffic. These structures, often temporary in nature, were not attractive to look at or to use. They were invariably accessed by steep steps, which could not be negotiated easily by the infirm, or by women with prams and young children (pl. 382). Unsurprisingly, they prompted angry protests (see p. 252). But footbridges were quicker and cheaper to build than subways. Pedestrian subways were not new *per se*, but they now became

a feature of the suburban edge for the first time. One of the first to be excavated under an arterial road was built in 1936 under Watford Way in north London.[113] In 1939 a roundabout at Wapses Lodge, Caterham, Surrey, marked a further development (pl. 383). Sloping tunnelled ramps led to an open area ('a bowl around the rim of which vehicles travel'), set below road level and crossed by footpaths, a design that would be replicated countless times in the post-war rebuilding of English towns.

One of the main problems faced by city centres was that some congested streets – such as London's principal shopping thoroughfares – could not be widened, let alone dualled, because they were lined by pavements and immovable building lines. This provoked many ingenious proposals for the vertical segregation of pedestrians and motor traffic, but since most of these schemes would have involved the wholesale re-engineering of the urban environment, they remained – at least for the time being – in the realms of fantasy.

As mentioned above, the idea of vertical segregation was already current in the mid-nineteenth century and was revived in the Edwardian period. In 1923 Leigh Martineau considered that a roundabout could be created at Piccadilly Circus by

383 The Caterham roundabout of 1939. A contemporary press account was struck by its novelty: 'the arena resembles those of ancient Rome without the lions!', while the footpaths 'link like the threads in a spider's web' (*The Autocar*, 17 March 1939, p. 436).

384 Grappling with the incompatibility of pedestrians and vehicles, Major Livingstone Oke came up with this proposal for Regent Street, London, in 1926, drawn by Bryan de Grineau and published in *The Motor*, 17 December 1935, p. 943.

1 SHOW ROOMS.
2 PAVEMENT LEVEL.
3 BRIDGE FOR PEDESTRIANS
4 STAIRWAY TO BUSES.
5 STORES ETC.
6 GARAGE AT GROUND LEVEL.
7 LIFT TO SHOPS.
8 UNDERGROUND GARAGES

directing pedestrians up ramps, onto bridges, and thus removing them from the space required by traffic.[114] In 1926 Major A. Livingstone Oke proposed a system of first-floor footpaths and showrooms in the Quadrant on Regent Street, leaving the entire width of the road free for motor cars (pl. 384).[115] In 1937 the Cement and Concrete Association published a vision of a metropolitan street, with cantilevered walkways (concrete, of course) running along the façades of buildings at first-floor level.[116] These were linked periodically by curved footbridges that spanned the roadway, which was given over almost entirely to traffic, leaving only a residual strip of sidewalk at ground level so that people could still queue at bus stops and hail taxis. More radically, the idea of 'two-decker streets' was advanced by Walter P. W. Elwell in 1938 (see pl. 359).[117] The road at ground level would be fully roofed, carrying pedestrianised civic spaces, planted with grass, shrubs and flowers, and lined by shopfronts. For once, the experience of the motorist might not be so pleasurable: 'in a tunnel, by all means – but who drives about a city for pleasure?'. No showrooms would be permitted at ground level; instead, shops could turn their ground floors into car parks. During the war, several proposals inverted Elwell's notion, suggesting that raised roads be built over shops, whilst others envisaged roundabouts with a lower level for pedestrians and an upper one for traffic (see Chapter 13). Segregation, clearly, could assume an endless variety of physical manifestations, and a number of ideas that originated in the 1930s, often to stimulate debate rather than as practical proposals, would become a reality in the 1950s and 1960s.

•

New and Improved Streets, 1918-1939

Motorists benefited from a great improvement in the quantity and quality of roads, funded by the Road Fund administered by the Ministry of Transport, in the 1920s and 1930s (see Chapter 9). Most new and improved roads served routes in and out of London. Indeed, half of the full sum available from the Road Fund was allocated to the metropolitan area, where the country's worst bottlenecks existed. These schemes affected London's existing suburbs, and encouraged the creation of new suburban districts, but stopped short of the urban core. The same was true of provincial towns and cities, where many new suburban roads were leafy boulevards in the form of single-track dual carriageways with central tramways, influenced by those created by J. A. Brodie in Liverpool (see above, p. 329), such as Aigburth Road, begun before 1914 and completed in 1921. In some cases, a central reservation was simply grassed or planted with trees (for example, Ryhope Road, Sunderland), but may have been provided just in case a tramway was needed in the future. In fact, by the late 1920s it was more likely that existing tramways would be grubbed up, allowing urban and suburban carriageways to be widened for motor traffic. Beverley Road, a new street in Hull, was originally planned with a central tramway, but was completed in 1924 with a 'ballasted area along the centre reserved for fast traffic'.[118]

Although most new roads were rural or suburban, in town centres some important new streets were created, and older streets improved. As ever, urban projects of this nature were often prompted primarily by a competitive sense of civic pride, or a desire to clear overcrowded, insanitary (or simply poorly maintained) 'slums'. By the 1920s, however, the need to relieve traffic congestion imbued some proposals with great urgency. The principal feature of Ferensway (1930-31), a new street in Hull, was a recessed parking area.[119] Between 1928 and 1932 traffic flow through Leeds was greatly improved by the widening of old streets to create New York Road and The Headrow/Eastgate (see pl. 168). Unavoidably, such schemes involved the demolition of existing structures, sometimes buildings of obvious historic and architectural merit. On The Headrow, the entire north side of the street was rebuilt to set back the frontage. But even just removing a blind corner could entail demolition. Thus, in 1934 the former Red Lion at Elstree in Hertfordshire was removed to improve visibility at a crossroads in the centre of the town.[120] A year later, a dispute arose in Amersham, Buckinghamshire, over the proposed demolition of a row of medieval houses identified as the cause of congestion near the market hall, on Broadway. Local protests succeeded in overturning this decision, and in 1937 the local authority opted for a bypass to the north-east of the town. As *The Motor* commented at the time: 'to have demolished the old houses for the sake of road widening would have

been an act of sheer vandalism'.[121] Nevertheless, within a few years the medieval row had vanished from the map.

One town with good reason to create new streets suitable for the motor vehicle was Coventry, the centre of motordom. Many of the city's councillors had a vested interest in the vehicle trade, and wanted to create a car-age city, with roads to match. Moreover, Coventry seems to have had an unusually high level of car ownership, perhaps because the workers in its factories possessed the mechanical skills to maintain second-hand cars at a reasonable cost. Two major new streets were created, with some controversy, in the 1930s. Corporation Street (1931; pl. 385) was driven through industrial backlands, while Trinity Street (1936) superseded the old Bull Ring and Butcher Row (pl. 386), narrow streets lined by ancient buildings on small plots. This involved the demolition of large numbers of buildings of considerable age. In Butcher Row, Little Butcher Row and the Bull Ring, Coventry had one of the most picturesque assemblies of jettied half-timbered buildings in the country. The Society for the Protection of Ancient Buildings (SPAB) had expressed concern about

385 An aerial view of Coventry in 1931, showing the new Corporation Street looking east.

386 The picturesque but run-down Butcher Row in Coventry, shown in a postcard of *circa* 1910–20. This was sacrificed to a road improvement scheme in the 1930s.

Butcher Row since road widening had first been proposed in 1914.[122] Subsequently, the Council assured SPAB that it would not be necessary to demolish Butcher Row,[123] but a letter of 12 April 1935 made its intentions clear:

[I]t is impossible, without spoiling the whole scheme, to keep in being the buildings which at present front to Butcher Row, Bull Ring and Ironmonger Row. As a matter of fact, however, many of these buildings are comparatively modern and are architecturally of no interest at all: as they stand, they do certainly contribute in some degree to the picturesqueness of Butcher Row because the frontages are 'higgledy piggledy', but this is not a condition which in any event could be perpetuated, and with its disappearance a good deal, if not the whole, of the quaintness of Butcher Row will disappear also.[124]

Besides, the Council argued, the public benefit of the road scheme would outweigh the value of the buildings:

[the Councillors] do not consider that simply because a building is old then it must, in any event and at any cost, be preserved: their view is that the whole of the circumstances must be taken into consideration, and it is this principle that has guided them in the formulation of their scheme for Trinity Street.[125]

Public protest concerning the demolitions was widespread, though muted within Coventry itself, perhaps because of the town's investment in motor manufacture.

Bypasses (see Chapter 9) were regarded as the least damaging method of relieving urban congestion. They were generally routed through fields, but their junctions could clip the edges of settlements, necessitating some demolition, as at Egham in

1934.[126] But bypasses were the saviours of some urban buildings. For example, it was undoubtedly the building of the Croydon Bypass in the early 1920s that prevented the Elizabethan Whitgift Hospital falling foul of a street-widening scheme.

Throughout the 1920s and 1930s planners came up with various schemes for fast urban roads, for the benefit of through traffic. Most of these proposals concerned London. Some involved futuristic elevated roads, or 'overways', while others buried roads in tunnels.[127] Such ideas were not wholly new,[128] and one of the most persistent concerned an elevated road that would traverse south London, spanning the roads and railways that lay in its path.[129] As it turned out, the most significant step towards the post-war flyover was taken with the construction of a curved reinforced concrete viaduct of 1,300 yards called Silvertown Way (designed by the civil engineers Rendel, Palmer & Tritton, 1926–30, and built 1930–34; pl. 387), which led to the Royal London Docks.[130] This was primarily for the benefit of road haulage rather than private motor cars, but it provided an important exemplar for post-war planners, as a precursor for the Westway and other urban flyovers. It spanned roads, dock entrances and a railway line. Hundreds of houses lying in its path had to be cleared, and 600 new dwellings were built for displaced people on Prince Regent Lane to the north-east. Hore-Belisha declared this project 'surely as bold an undertaking as the Imperial Road of Rome', a new thoroughfare

387 As well as being an impressively long viaduct, Silvertown Way (1934) in London was a two-tier junction, with parallel slip roads. These slip roads, connecting with streets at ground level, distinguish this structure from contemporary viaducts spanning railways and rivers. The design is very simple, with large-scale Art Deco touches.

388 One of the toll booths still standing at the entrance of the Mersey Tunnel, Liverpool. These were designed by Herbert J. Rowse. The three colourful sculptures in the background are replicas made in 2010 of the mini 'superlambbananas' that decorated the streets of Liverpool when it was the European Capital of Culture in 2008.

created by Benito Mussolini.[131] An even more ambitious project that opened in the same year, 1934, was the Mersey Tunnel (see Chapter 9). While the interior of the tunnel has been altered, much survives of its external architecture, in Liverpool and Birkenhead. The tunnel approaches, its arched entrances, the toll booths, the lighting pylons and the six monumental ventilation towers were designed by the established local architect Herbert J. Rowse (pl. 388). These structures were of good-quality materials, with finely detailed Neo-Egyptian or Art Deco decoration, including *Speed – the Modern Mercury* on the George's Dock Ventilation and Control Station, carved by Edmund C. Thompson and George Capstick.[132]

It was also in 1934 that Hore-Belisha commissioned Sir Charles H. Bressey (since 1928 Chief Engineer of the Roads Department at the Ministry of Transport) and the eminent architect Sir Edwin Lutyens to prepare a traffic plan for London. Published in May 1938,[133] this proposed three concentric ring roads,

something that would remain an objective for London into the 1970s (see Chapter 13). The innermost ring would form a 'loopway' around the City; the central ring comprised the partly extant North and South Circular Roads; while the outer ring involved the (again, partly extant) North and South Orbital Roads, roughly on the line eventually adopted by the M25, 18–20 miles from Charing Cross. Arterial roads, parkways and motorways all received consideration, and the report expressed the need to build viaducts and tunnels for motor vehicles (pl. 389). It adhered to the belief that an overhead road should be built through south London, suggesting that this follow the line of the Southern Railway as far as Camberwell New Road. Lutyens and Bressey went on to refine their ideas whilst working together on the Royal Academy Planning Committee during the war (see Chapter 13).

One other report to appear on the eve of the Second World War was a master plan for Greater London prepared by a committee of the Modern Architectural Research Group (MARS) and published in 1939. This conceptual plan proposed that the backbone of the city be formed by arterial roads, providing numerous lanes for all kinds of public transport (such as fast and slow coaches, buses and trains), with private cars having to use existing roads. As later pointed out by Colin Buchanan, the MARS plan failed to recognise the dominant role that would be assumed by the motor car in the near future, and the extent to which public transport would be sidelined.[134] The MARS plan presumably adopted a contrary stance quite deliberately. By 1939 it was plain that the needs of motor cars within English towns and cities overrode those of other road users. The dominance of the car was ingrained in the thinking of mainstream planners, and underpinned the radical reshaping of urban centres that would be undertaken in the aftermath of the war.

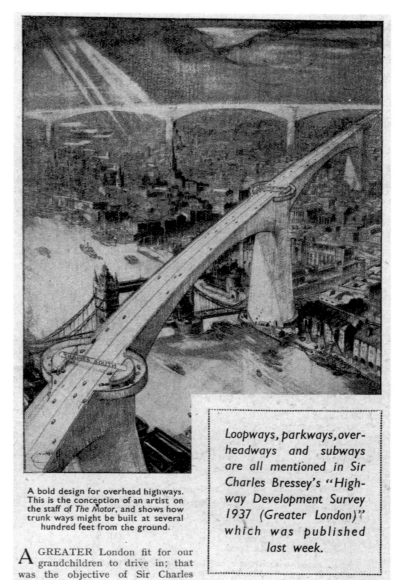

A bold design for overhead highways. This is the conception of an artist on the staff of *The Motor*, and shows how trunk ways might be built at several hundred feet from the ground.

Loopways, parkways, over-headways and subways are all mentioned in Sir Charles Bressey's "Highway Development Survey 1937 (Greater London)" which was published last week.

A GREATER London fit for our grandchildren to drive in; that was the objective of Sir Charles

389 *The Motor*'s interpretation of the new overhead London roads, as suggested in the Bressey-Lutyens Report of 1938. From *The Motor*, 24 May 1938, p. 744.

13: TRAFFIC IN TOWNS SINCE 1945

BRITISH ROADS COPED WITH TWO MILLION motor cars in 1939, five million around 1960, ten million around 1970, twenty million around 1990 and cope with thirty million today (see Appendix). Until the early 1970s planners and engineers maintained an unshakable belief in the superiority and inevitability of the car. They assumed a leading role in reshaping the urban environment to accommodate and speed up ever-growing traffic, creating dual carriageways, flyovers, tunnels, subways and round-abouts. The discomfort and inconvenience foisted upon non-motorists by fast new urban roads was offset, to some degree, by the provision of car-free precincts. But it was the unremitting misery of those living alongside elevated motorways, such as London's Westway, that triggered a reaction and allowed the road protest movement to gain momentum. At the same time, the soaring costs of land and compensation payments, together with other mitigating factors, were making new urban roads prohibitively expensive. From the mid-1970s the mindset of urban planners was transformed, as they shifted away from major infrastructure projects and began to implement a range of increasingly sophisticated traffic management tools. In particular, they began to grapple with alternative ways to restrict and calm traffic within the urban setting, a trend that has culminated in the influential 'Shared Space' schemes of the present day.

Planning for the Future

The re-engineering of the urban environment to speed up the passage of the motor car had begun between the wars, but had concentrated on the suburban fringe. Here, bypasses and ring roads were built, with modern features such as roundabouts and subways, causing the emergence of a new type of marginal urban landscape, populated by the semi-detached houses satirised in 1938 by Osbert Lancaster as 'Bypass Variegated', and imbued with a character disparaged in 1955 by Ian Nairn as 'Subtopia'.[1] The new roads of the 1920s and 1930s seldom encroached on town centres, where novel gyratory and one-way traffic systems were improvised without greatly disturbing the existing infrastructure. A few new thoroughfares were created, but these functioned in much the same way as older ones. Ingenious plans for the complete segregation of pedestrians and vehicular traffic were devised, but no such scheme had yet left the drawing board. To date, the organisation of space within urban centres remained much as it had been a century earlier. Down-town areas continued to provide a forum where people spent much of their lives: shopping, working, meeting friends and having fun. Only a few commercial facilities, such as car showrooms, had begun to decentralise. Aesthetically, however, city-centre streets had been transformed by the advent of the car: they now bristled with traffic signs and signals; their kerbs were bordered by guardrails; their asphalt surfaces were painted with lines; and they were gradually being stripped of their tramlines. The experience of moving through urban space, for vehicular and foot traffic alike, was changing rapidly.

The war of 1939–45 brought a pause. Petrol was rationed and, for several years, motoring was fraught with difficulties. During the black-out headlamps were hooded, traffic lights were reduced to cross slits, and street lamps were switched off or replaced by 'amenity' lighting. To compensate for the darkness, white marks were painted on carriageways, kerbs and posts, and Catseyes were

390 The sweeping underbelly of the Hammersmith Flyover (1960–61), seen from Queen Caroline Street. With its cantilevered carriageways, this was a much more modern structure than the Chiswick Flyover. It shelters a miscellany of parking, public toilets and telephone kiosks.

391   A raised ring road, illustrating the interim report of the Royal Academy Planning Committee in 1942.

used more than ever before, to guide motorists. Although a 20mph speed limit was enforced in the nightly black-out from February 1940, the accident rate was very high. One reason may have been the wartime suspension of driving tests, since people were allowed to drive with provisional licences, without the usual safeguards. After a ban was imposed on fuel for private motoring in 1942, however, fewer accidents occurred. This may have been aided by the widespread introduction of the kerb drill – taught in schools by visiting police officers – which became a mantra for a generation of schoolchildren.[2]

Extensive war damage compelled planners to reconsider, with urgency, the ideal form of the modern British city. By and large, their attention focused on the separation of vehicles and people, though they were also preoccupied with zoning, slum clearance and decentralisation. Within these various, interlacing strands of investigation, the primacy of the car was rarely, if ever, questioned. It was persuasively argued that Hitler's bombing raids had delivered a 'wonderful chance' for the comprehensive redevelopment of established cities that had grown organically – that is, in an unsatisfactory *ad hoc* manner – over centuries.[3] Even if this attitude was adopted, in part, to boost the morale of a bomb-weary populace, it quickly became enshrined in the language and thinking of the period. In 1942, for example, few would have contradicted Sir Herbert Alker Tripp's dismissal of British towns as 'an unplanned muddle'.[4] Furthermore, comprehensive redevelopment itself offered an opportunity to solve long-standing problems by clearing tracts of outdated, insanitary

housing and dispersing the population. It was decreed that people ousted from the slums of London's East End, as well as industrial sinks in Merseyside, Tyneside and Birmingham, should be rehoused in a series of new towns. The idea of new towns had been sidelined after the creation of Welwyn Garden City in the 1920s, but returned to the national agenda with the Barlow Report of 1940. Commissioned by Prime Minister Neville Chamberlain in 1937, this advocated the dispersal of Britain's industrial populations to garden cities or satellite towns.[5]

Politicians gradually assembled the planning machinery that would generate both comprehensive redevelopment and new towns after the war. Shortly after the heavy bombing raids of autumn and winter 1940–41, Lord Reith, then Minister of Works and Buildings, was handed responsibility for physical reconstruction.[6] He began by liaising with the local authorities of three heavily bombed cities – Coventry, Bristol and Birmingham – to initiate planning for post-war redevelopment. Indeed, Coventry's city architect, Donald E. Gibson, prepared a reconstruction plan as early as February 1941. Reith went on to commission a plan for the County of London from the architects and planners Patrick Abercrombie and J. H. Forshaw.[7] Their work would influence many subsequent urban reconstruction plans.

While Abercrombie and Forshaw were formulating their plan, other initiatives were afoot. In 1942 Sir Charles Bressey and Sir Edwin Lutyens (the authors of the 'Bressey-Lutyens Report' of 1938, see p. 342) published *London Replanned*, the interim findings of the Royal Academy Planning Committee.[8] Although

392 A sunken ring road with grassed sides, proposed for London by the Royal Academy Planning Committee in 1944.

their main concern was architectural setting, they suggested that through traffic be separated from local traffic by raising arterial roads over shops (pl. 391).[9] They also advocated an inner ring road connecting London's main railway stations: any station lying within the ring, such as Charing Cross, would be relocated to the periphery. This concept had already been put forward in 1929 by the engineer Mervyn O'Gorman, of the RAC, whose ring road was raised on arches, forming a 'ring wall' around the city.[10] In his influential book *Town Planning and Road Traffic*, published in 1942, Alker Tripp also favoured an elevated ring road, surrounding an inner area divided into 'precincts'.[11] There was nothing new by now in use-zoning, but Tripp stressed that precincts (defined as 'little systems of shopping, business, industrial and residential streets') must not communicate directly with arterial roads, which he repeatedly compared with railway lines.[12] Abercrombie and Forshaw's County of London plan, issued in July 1943, also embraced precincts – alternatively known as neighbourhoods, a term adopted by the American architect and planner Clarence Perry in the 1920s – that would be sequestered from through traffic. Their preferred solution to improve traffic circulation within the city was described as the 'ring-radial-cross' system. This involved three concentric ring roads, labelled 'A', 'B' (the most important ring, conceived as an arterial road) and 'C', plus two arterial cross routes ('X' and 'Y'), which would meet with a flyover at the north end of Waterloo Bridge.[13] These roads would necessitate the construction of six new tunnels under London.

The County of London plan prompted lively debate. The Royal Academy Planning Committee – following Lutyens's death, chaired by Sir Giles Gilbert Scott – responded with *Road, Rail and River in London*, published in 1944.[14] It saw no role for Abercrombie's cross routes and tunnels, and considered that it was the inner ring road ('A') that should be arterial, rather than ring road 'B'. While most planners (including themselves) had hitherto envisaged London's principal ring road as a prominent landscape feature, visually comparable to the fortifications that encircled a medieval town, they now believed that it should be concealed as much as possible. They suggested that it be sunken, flanked by grassy banks, with all junctions raised above the continuously flowing traffic and treated as two-level roundabouts, with a lower level for pedestrians and an upper level for traffic (pl. 392). In later years, Professor Colin Buchanan expressed his belief that the controversy stirred by this counter-proposal ('unfortunately') led to the abandonment of London's inner ring, though its estimated post-war costing – £88 million in 1950 – had much to do with its demise.[15] Abercrombie's Greater London Plan of 1944 added to the number of rings that would potentially encircle the metropolis, by proposing an outer 'D' ring, to arterial standard (see Chapter 9). Another publication providing food for thought was George C. Curnock's *New Roads for Britain: A Plan for the Immediate Future*, published by the British Roads Federation (BRF) in December 1944. This favoured flyovers at junctions on main urban roads. These were flyovers with a difference: pedestrian subways would remain at ground level, rather than being excavated, while the road rose over them; they would be equipped with 'public conveniences having adjacent waiting-rooms (heated when necessary), telephones and drinking water; and all should have continuous and ample lighting'.[16]

Responsibility for post-war planning was invested in a new Ministry of Town and Country Planning in 1943, and the Town and Country Planning Act of the following year enabled local authorities to designate areas ('declaratory areas') for general redevelopment. In 1947 this was superseded by a more comprehensive Town and Country Planning Act that provided the legislative basis for the compulsory purchase of property and the rebuilding of extensive urban areas in the post-war era. The chief planning officer (or, in some cases, the surveyor, engineer or architect) of county councils and county borough councils was required to produce development plans for principal towns, even those that had not suffered significant war damage. These 'town maps' were statutory documents that laid down what new infrastructure projects were anticipated over the next twenty years. The approach adopted by local authorities, their planners and professional consultants, was influenced heavily by the work of Tripp and Abercrombie, whilst proposals for new roads were shaped by a manual issued by the Ministry of War Transport in 1946.[17] This publication, *Design and Layout of Roads in Built-up Areas*, dictated that arterial roads – which had so often been rendered ineffective by ribbon development between the wars – were to be free from pedestrians and standing vehicles, and would have as few junctions as possible, preferably with grade separation.[18] In other words, they would be more like motorways. The manual also did much to propagate the idea of the 'ring and spokes', advising, for example, that a town with a population of 250,000 should be encircled by three concentric ring roads, cutting across the radial routes. The inner ring would be dotted by bus stops and would define a traffic-free central area, ideally not more than 600 yards in diameter. This inner ring road 'theory' was propagated further by the Ministry of Town and Country Planning's handbook, *The Redevelopment of Central Areas*, published in 1947.

Many of the ambitious urban plans drafted in the 1940s were eventually abandoned, or came into being painfully slowly, and in a modified form. They were simply too expensive to put into operation at a time of acute financial constraint and materials shortages. Through the 1950s the Government could do little to promote ring roads and urban motorways. Instead, there was a determination to 'squeeze more out of existing streets'.[19] Nevertheless, the road lobby exerted as much pressure as it could muster: the principle of urban motorways was endorsed at an international conference held by the BRF in 1956; various proposals were published in daily newspapers; and by the early 1960s, with the economy improving, urban motorways were being included in the revised development plans of several large towns and cities.[20] Regardless of the slow genesis of the urban motorway, throughout this period new and improved roads were deemed essential for the future economic and social well-being of the country. It was assumed that the demands of traffic should be fulfilled: there was, as yet, no clear understanding of the phenomenon whereby traffic increases in direct proportion to the capacity of roads provided. At the same time, perhaps fortunately given the prevailing ethos, future traffic growth was severely underestimated. Indeed, it was largely to redress this problem that *Traffic in Towns* (known as the 'Buchanan Report', commissioned by the flamboyant Minister of Transport, Ernest Marples, and written by a team headed by Colin Buchanan) was published in 1963. Although this did not present brand new approaches, it was widely publicised and gave urban redevelopment a fresh impetus, despite emphasising just how expensive it would be to adapt towns for mass car ownership. Another spur was the publication in 1963 of *London 2000*, written by the young town planner Peter Hall, who complained that comprehensive redevelopment was failing – because it was just not comprehensive enough.

Meanwhile, aspects of new town development had been examined by a number of commissions, culminating in the New Towns Act of 1946 and the establishment of the first designated new town, Stevenage in Hertfordshire, in 1947. Most of the first generation of English new towns lay close to London: as well as Stevenage, they included Harlow, Crawley and Hemel Hempstead. Later new towns, designated in the 1960s, were more dispersed. These included Telford, Runcorn, Redditch, Washington and – much larger than any of its predecessors – Milton Keynes. In addition to these, a number of existing settlements were designated, under the provisions of the Town Development Act of 1952, as 'overspill' or 'extended' towns. Thus, London County Council (LCC) entered into agreements with towns such as Ashford in Kent, Basingstoke in Hampshire and Swindon in Wiltshire to absorb some of the city's excess population. Such agreements demanded new infrastructure projects, including roads and central shopping facilities, as well as extensive housing estates.

Speeding round Town

After years of thinking, legislating and putting new planning machinery in place, work began in earnest on post-war reconstruction in the early 1950s. Priority was given to rebuilding badly bombed cities such as Bristol, Coventry, Exeter, Hull, Liverpool, London, Plymouth and Southampton, and to the creation of new towns, but by the early 1960s comprehensive redevelopment was affecting many relatively undamaged cities that were simply viewed as out-of-date, or had been designated

for 'overspill'. Thus, in the 1960s and 1970s many English city centres were refashioned with pedestrian precincts or malls, with servicing, parking and traffic pushed to the periphery. Fast urban roads – inner ring roads – pressed closer to the urban heart than ever before, creating physical barriers between the central civic and shopping areas and the inner suburbs that encircled them. These barriers were not quite impassable, because subways and footbridges were provided for pedestrians. But the dangers lurking in dark, dank subways quickly became apparent, while pedestrians using footbridges were battered by wind and rain. As ever, those travelling on foot were to suffer for the convenience of the motorist (pl. 393), but their reward was the utopian environment they would encounter once they reached the car-less precinct or mall. Outside this oasis, however, the car was king.

One of the first inner ring roads to be created in its entirety, from scratch, was that of Stevenage, begun in the early 1960s. More rectangular than ring-shaped, it ran around the central area in four stretches, linked by roundabouts (pl. 394). Like the

393 'Pedestrians do not have Priority' as they leave the Milton Keynes shopping mall. Although seldom articulated so directly, this message was clearly conveyed by the new road layouts that were created on the peripheries of many English post-war town centres.

394   A ring road in the form of a dual carriageway encircles the largely pedestrianised centre of Stevenage, Britain's first post-war new town.

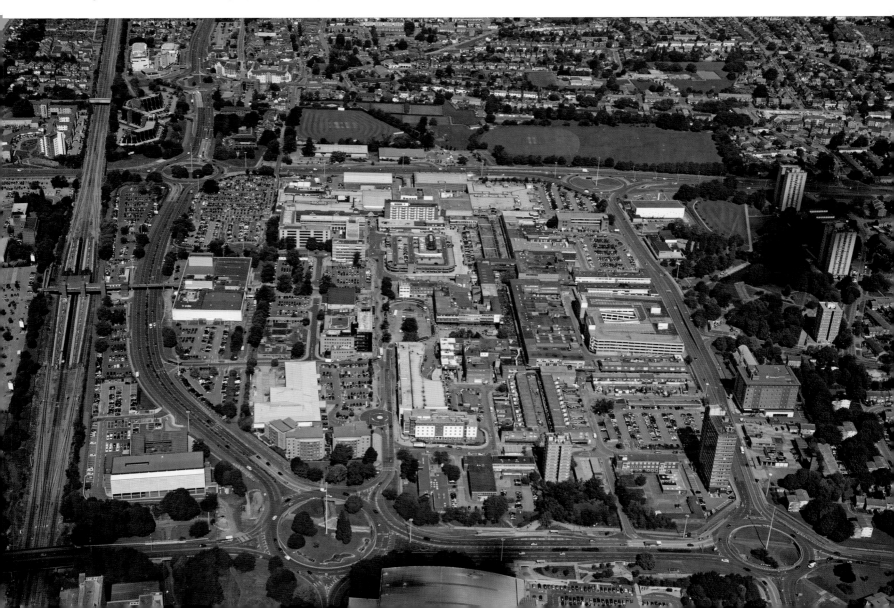

395 A junction on the Coventry ring road: note the pedestrian route running through the centre of the two-level junction.

pre-war Caterham roundabout (see pl. 383), the sunken centres of these were landscaped and crossed by paths, while traffic remained on a single, upper level. As well as connecting to fast roads that sped cars in and out of the centre, the ring road provided access to delivery yards and car parks situated behind the shops and offices of the pedestrianised precinct.

Coventry's slightly later ringway, built in the mid-1960s,[21] was rather more circular, and curved around a large central area, certainly bigger than Stevenage's, but only partially in the form of a pedestrian precinct. In other words, access had to be provided for cars travelling through the encircled area, as well as for cars entering and exiting the radial roads that fed the ring. Following American precedent, junctions were vertically layered, or graded, with most roundabouts lying below or above the dual carriageway, which pressed on through underpasses and flyovers (pl. 395). In contrast to Stevenage, few roundabouts actually interrupted the motorists' progress around the ring road itself.

In both places, however, pedestrians were forced to make long detours to crossing points, frustrated in their progress by the demands of the car. In Coventry, once pedestrians had negotiated the ring road, they encountered a second barrier, since they also needed to cross the conventional roads that formed a less formal 'inner circulatory road' around the pedestrianised shopping precinct. As early as 1963, before the ring road was even built, the Buchanan Report conceded: 'it is difficult not to have misgivings about the circumferential severance of the city centre which will result'.[22]

The most notorious of all post-war ring roads was probably that created in Birmingham, a city that – like nearby Coventry – had been heavily bombed in 1940–42, and embraced comprehensive redevelopment with relish. Roads played an important part in this, partly due to pressure from industry, which was becoming more dependent than ever on road haulage. During the war, the City Engineer and Surveyor, Herbert Manzoni, had

396 A contemporary postcard depicting Smallbrook Ringway (1957–60), in central Birmingham. The scheme was designed by the local architect James A. Roberts.

drawn up plans to accommodate three concentric ring roads, but it was some time before work could begin on his schemes.[23] In the meantime, increasing motor traffic was absorbed – here, as in other cities – largely by abandoning trams in favour of motor buses. The first section of the inner ring road (Queensway) to be built, from 1957 to 1960, was the Smallbrook Ringway, which ran from Holloway Circus along Smallbrook Street to the Bull Ring, and was edged by new buildings with a continuous street frontage that lent it a metropolitan character (pl. 396). Its junction with Digbeth, a major arterial route that had been widened as a dual carriageway in 1953–5, took the form of a ground-level roundabout. In contrast, later sections of the ring road incorporated flyovers and underpasses, which Manzoni and the Public Works Committee had admired during a fact-finding mission to the U.S.A. in 1956. These sections were more like urban motorways. 'Circumferential severance' was an issue here as much as in Coventry, if not more. The complete inner ring road, which was opened by Queen Elizabeth II in 1971, formed an aggressive barrier around the central area. Moreover, Paradise Circus Queensway cut through the Civic Centre, while St Martin's Queensway disconnected the Bull Ring – Birmingham's historic market place, and the site of Britain's first indoor shopping mall – from the High Street, with grim subways offering the sole access for pedestrians.

In the course of the 1960s new ring roads and radial routes became engineered increasingly boldly and expensively, with cuttings, tunnels, overpasses and flyovers. While the inter-war arterial road had attracted ribbon development, the post-war flyover – rather like the narrower railway viaducts of the nineteenth century – sought no rapport with its surroundings, and remained a disjointed and alien presence within the townscape. At the same time, it offered an exhilarating experience, with superb panoramic views of the shifting cityscape, to those travelling in cars. Over decades, some urban landscapes were remodelled to respect flyovers. But instances of successful rapprochements are rare.

Some of the first post-war flyovers were erected in west London, where the slow road connection between the city centre and London (later Heathrow) Airport was considered very problematic. Once the idea of a monorail had been discarded, it was decided to improve the road (the A4 and, later, M4), including a series of dramatic flyovers. The first of these was the Chiswick Flyover, spanning a new roundabout on Chiswick High Road, at the east end of the pre-war Great West Road (pl. 397). This was built in 1958–9, to designs by the engineer Harry Brompton and the architect George Stewart, and was opened in September 1959 by the voluptuous American actress Jayne Mansfield. The carriageway was supported on massive concrete piers:

397   The Chiswick Flyover looking east, towards central London, photographed soon after its completion in 1959. This was the first flyover to be built in London since Silvertown Way in 1934 (see pl. 387).

398   Driving at dusk along the elevated section of the M4 (built 1962–5), towards west London. The tower on the left belongs to the church of St John the Evangelist on Boston Park Road. In the distance can be seen a neon-lit Lucozade advertisement (installed 1954; removed 2004; reinstated 2010), and the brightly lit Audi showroom of 2009 (see pl. 79).

really cross-walls in the form of four-bay arcades. The visual impact of this huge structure was softened by facing the sides of the abutments in hand-finished red brick, laid in Flemish bond. J. E. Dayton, the managing director of the construction company, dismissed this brickwork as 'an architectural whim', clearly wishing to dissociate his firm from what he considered a most retardataire design, whilst signalling his eagerness to create something more progressively modern.[24]

The Hammersmith Flyover (1960–61; pl. 390), linking the Cromwell Road extension of 1959 with the Great West Road, was undoubtedly a more elegant and modern structure. Designed by G. Maunsell & Partners, in association with the LCC's engineers and architects, it was constructed by Marples, Ridgeway & Partners Ltd, a firm founded by the Minister of Transport, Ernest Marples, who now – because of an obvious conflict of interest – was obliged to sell his shares.[25] Dayton's firm, perhaps significantly, was not even invited to tender.[26] The Hammersmith Flyover soared over a railway line and necessitated the demolition of much terraced housing lying in its path. Its flaring, cantilevered carriageways were carried by a massive precast concrete spine beam, supported in turn by a row of tapered piers, joined axially by segmental arches. Even more ambitious than this, in terms of its scale, was the Great West Road (or M4) Viaduct, designed by Sir Alexander Gibb & Partners and built in 1962–5 (pl. 398). This ran for 1½ miles between the Chiswick Flyover and Brentford,[27] but involved much less demolition than its predecessors since the pillars carrying the cantilevered carriageways sprang from the central reservation of the pre-war Great West Road. It was said to have been influenced by a viaduct running across the Place Sainctelette in Brussels.[28] Outside London, one of the longest urban flyovers to be built in the 1960s was the 4,200-foot Mancunian Way, the A57(M), forming the south side of Manchester's ring road (1964–7; pl. 399). G. Maunsell & Partners designed the elevated section with thirty-two spans. The beams, cantilevers and deck slabs were combined as single precast units, marking a technological advance on the firm's Hammersmith Flyover, where the decks had been of *in situ* concrete construction.[29]

A number of steel flyovers were erected in the 1960s. One of the most remarkable was the Camp Hill Flyover in Birmingham, which comprised a single 10-foot carriageway. This off-the-peg structure, called a 'Carbridge' (designed by Major Eric Strologo of the RAC and developed by John Lysaght's Bristol Works), was erected in a single weekend in 1961. Considered semi-permanent, it was dismantled in the 1980s. A similarly flimsy-looking steel flyover, again supposedly temporary, was built over the Hogarth Roundabout on the Great West Road in 1969, and is still in use today (pl. 400). This was erected on the 'Bridgway' system, offered by Marples-Ridgeway Ltd. Marples himself had initiated a competition for a temporary flyover structure in 1964, the winning design being erected at Movers Lane on the East Ham and Barking Bypass (A13) in 1967, but replaced in 2003 by an underpass.[30] The Churchill Way flyovers in Liverpool and Birkenhead, built to relieve traffic congestion at the entrances to the Mersey Tunnel (Queensway) in 1967–9, were of composite concrete and steel (pl. 401). Another significant flyover in Liver-

399   Mancunian Way (1964–7), Manchester's southern ring road, photographed in the 1970s. Because of its urban situation, eighteen subways were provided for pedestrians.

400   This single-carriageway flyover at the Hogarth Roundabout in west London was erected in 1969. It is one of a handful of steel flyovers of this vintage that still serve their original purpose. Most were regarded as temporary structures.

401   Churchill Way was a popular name for new urban roads in the 1960s, in honour of Sir Winston Churchill. In Liverpool, Churchill Way was planned to create 'an entirely new kind of townscape in which the architecture of the motorway and the buildings on either side of it are conceived as a total environment' (Tetlow and Goss 1968, 207).

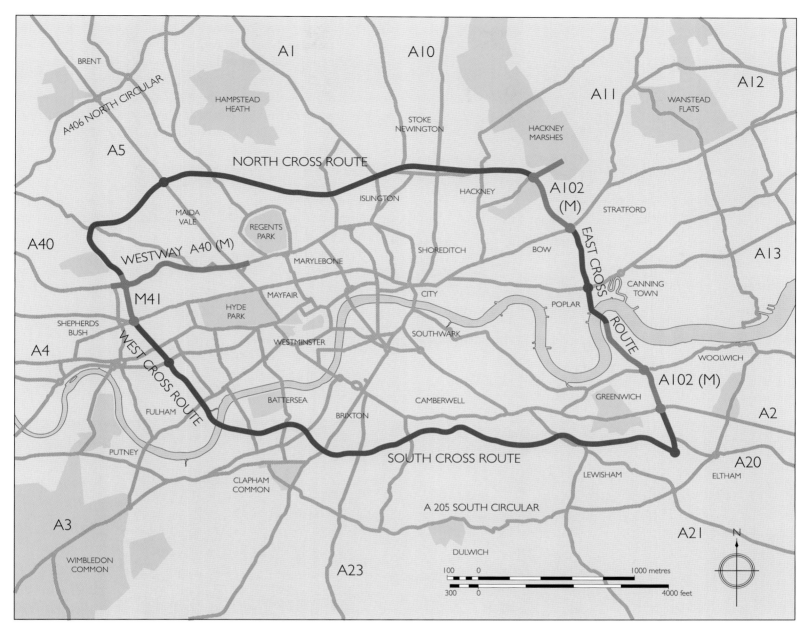

KEY

▬▬▬▬▬▬▬▬▬ Proposed

▬▬▬▬▬▬▬▬▬ Motorways built 1967 - 1973

402   This plan shows the proposed route of London's Motorway Box, approved in 1965 and abandoned in the early 1970s. It was killed off by the gentrification of areas such as Islington and Notting Hill – by the prohibitive cost of compulsory purchase in these areas, as much as by articulate middle-class opposition.

pool was Queen's Drive Viaduct (1972–6), which ran above part of the city's historic ring road and created a link with the M62. The contrast between the tree-lined Edwardian boulevard and the superimposed 1970s viaduct, each representing the most up-to-date urban road design of its particular era, was stark.

In 1965 an ambitious scheme for a 37-mile 'Motorway Box' (successor to Abercrombie's 'B' ring, and known as Ringway 1; pl. 402), lying well inside London's North Circular Road and comprising north, south, east and west 'cross routes', was promoted, sparking years of controversy and planning blight. As the metropolitan equivalent of Birmingham's ringway, this was to be the innermost of London's concentric ring roads. In the event, only one of London's proposed rings would ever be built in its entirety: the outer orbital ring ('D'), a refined version of the pre-war North Orbital Road, which ran through open countryside and was completed in the 1980s as the M25 (see Chapter 9).

Nevertheless, the 'improvement' of radial roads, pressing into the centre of London, has to be considered against this bigger planning backdrop, since these rings and radials were to form the warp and weft of a single unified traffic system. While motorists undoubtedly benefited from these roads, local residents suffered as the traffic carried by flyovers thundered past their front windows. From the mid-1960s until the early 1970s a number of new flyovers reached completion around the capital, including the southern extension of the M1 (pl. 403),[31] the Barnet Bypass flyover (at Watford Way), the Brent Cross Flyover (at Hendon Way) – the first three-level junction in the country – the Harrow Road Flyover and, most notorious of all, the Westway (A40).

The Westway was Europe's longest elevated road: a 2½-mile 'three-minute motorway', representing an extension of Western

403 (*left*) Mrs Eve Pearce contemplates the M1 flyover at Five Ways, Mill Hill, which was only 15 feet from the window of her flat in Gilda Court, in November 1969. Gilda Court still stands today, surrounded on all sides by motorways.

404 The Westway blighted North Kensington by its presence. This is the White City Roundabout, looking north-east. Note the sports centre and riding ring under the roundabout. The stubs to the north represent slip roads for an extension of the West Cross Route (part of London's Motorway Box) that was never built.

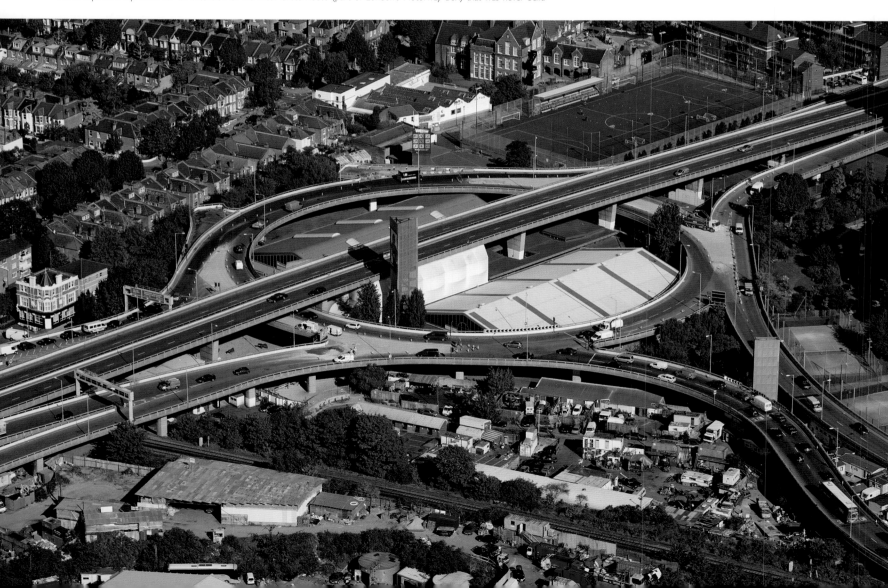

405   Life under the Westway. The landscape of this road inspired the novelist J. G. Ballard to explore the dark side of car culture in disturbing, dystopian stories such as *Crash* (1973) and *Concrete Island* (1974). In the latter, the protagonist is stranded, injured, in a wasteland bounded by several motorways.

Avenue from White City in the west to Paddington Green in the east (pl. 404). Although the new Westway was proposed in 1960, work did not start until 1964. It was opened by Michael Heseltine in July 1970, against a hullabaloo of protestation – 'rehouse us now'; 'don't fly over people's lives' – from those condemned to live in its shadow.[32] The impact on local residents, mostly living in conventional Victorian terraces, was intolerable. Co-habiting with this gigantic alien structure, they had to suffer loss of light during the day, the glare of sodium lamps at night, constant noise, vibrations, the smell of fumes, and emissions that coated their walls and windows in a film of dirt. Within days of the opening ceremony, writs had been issued and disruptive protests organised. Ultimately, the Greater London Council (the GLC, which had succeeded the LCC in 1965) was compelled to re-house a large number of North Kensington residents and demolish their old homes; it also leased the wasteland under the Westway to a play group, and to the North Kensington Amenity Trust (founded 1971), whose first action was the construction of a housing action centre beneath the flyover.[33] Today, in the care of the Westway Development Trust, the underside of the flyover accommodates a travellers' site, a horse-riding track, a sports centre, garages, a shopping centre and diverse social amenities, with buildings – some two storeys high – occupying the full height of the space beneath the carriageways (pl. 405). Jonathan Bell has remarked that 'nowhere else around London so closely

resembles a North American "Edge City"',[34] but this is a unique urban landscape, with its own character and colour, and surprisingly little traffic noise. Nevertheless, around 1970 it was clear that a huge mistake had been made by planning the Westway without anticipating – or, worse still, minding – the impact it would have on its environs. The Land Compensation Act of 1973 ensured that authorities henceforth possessed the power to mitigate the nuisance caused by new urban roads, and to compensate those affected, to a much greater degree.[35] Urban roads suddenly became more expensive propositions, possibly explaining why, in the same year, the Minister of Transport quietly announced that resources would be diverted away from urban roads, in favour of public transport.[36]

The underpass was a more palatable solution to traffic congestion than the flyover, but was rarely implemented – except for short lengths beneath roundabouts – due to the high engineering costs. A prime example was the four-lane underpass running beneath Hyde Park Corner to connect Piccadilly with Knightsbridge, opened by the Duke of Wellington in 1962.[37] The first underpass in a provincial town is thought to have been built in Birmingham, where Birchfield Road dips beneath a roundabout on Aston Lane, on the outer ring road. Proper cut-and-cover underpass tunnels, however, formed part of ring roads in Birmingham (pl. 406), Croydon, Leicester, Leeds and elsewhere. Underpasses and flyovers were amongst the first roads to be

406　An underpass on Suffolk Street Queensway, Birmingham's inner ring road, *circa* 1980, looking west.

embedded with heating cables, to prevent ice forming in winter, a treatment that had been applied to the ramps of multi-storey garages since the 1930s.

In London the flyover had expanded – quite literally in the case of the Chiswick Flyover – to create some of the first urban motorways. Elsewhere, one of the first roads to have the character of an urban motorway was the Stretford–Eccles Bypass, which opened in 1960 and became part of the M62. Around 4¾ miles of its 6-mile length were raised on high embankments, and interchanges were positioned just 1¼ miles apart, much closer than they would be on an inter-city motorway. Leeds soon followed. The city had acquired an outer ring road in the 1930s, and formed one of the principal case studies in the Buchanan Report of 1963. The Leeds inner ring motorway, the A58(M)/A64(M), designed by the City of Leeds Engineers' Department, was really a loop, forming a northern bypass, with the southern section of a notional ring formed by the M1, M62 and other roads. It was proposed as a ring road in 1955, and upgraded to motorway status by 1963.[38] Work began in 1964 – in the same year as the Westway and the Mancunian Way – and the road was completed in 1975 (see pl. 273). To minimise its visual impact and reduce noise levels, it was largely submerged within a cutting, lying approximately 20 feet below ground level and flanked by concrete retaining walls: rather different from the gently sloping grassy banks proposed for London's sunken ring

road by the Royal Academy Planning Committee in 1944. The motorway ran through five tunnels: the longest beneath the University Hospital precinct, the others carrying intersections. In three places, however, the carriageways rose on viaducts to span junctions, and one of these blighted the Quarry Hill Flats – an inter-war council housing development, originally much admired but mired in problems and demolished in 1978.

Leeds was not unique. In Birmingham, the seven-lane Aston Expressway (A38(M); 1968–72) ran from Spaghetti Junction (see pl. 309) to a point close to the city centre, midway between the Queensway and Middleway ring roads, where it met up with Corporation Street.[39] In Newcastle, the A167(M) was created in 1972–5 on the east side of the city centre, linking the Tyne Bridge with the Great North Road (pl. 407). As with the Leeds and Birmingham motorways, this had a long gestation. The preface of the first plan for Newcastle, published by the City Engineer and Planning Officer Percy Parr in 1945, had reiterated the maxim of the time: 'prosperity after the war will depend to a large extent upon roads and road transport, and every effort should be made to improve these vital communications and expedite the flow of traffic'.[40] The plan drafted *circa* 1955 by Derek Bradshaw, City Engineer and Town Surveyor, envisaged two new motorways, 'Central Motorway West' and 'Central Motorway East' (with a spur forming the 'Central Motorway By-pass'): these would flank the central area and be linked by

407 Newcastle's Central Motorway East, with its direct link to the curved Manor Car Park.

an 'East–West Underground Motorway' – perhaps inspired by the tunnelled cross-routes proposed for London by Abercrombie in 1943 – which would form a continuation of yet another dual carriageway, aligned with New Bridge Street. In the event, only the Central Motorway East, the A167(M), was constructed; the Central Motorway West and the East–West link being abandoned. Like similarly affected cities, Newcastle lost many historic buildings, including the Royal Arcade, to this scheme.

Even the most attractive and historic English cities, noted for their cathedrals, castles and market places, lost tracts of historic buildings, streets and lanes to dual carriageways. In the excitement of the motor age, this seemed a sacrifice worth making. In Canterbury, for example, a dual-carriageway ring road was built against the medieval walls to the south-west and south-east of the cathedral city, where numerous old buildings – some of them admittedly bomb-damaged – were cleared.[41] Worcester probably sacrificed more of its historic fabric to new roads than any other cathedral city, though when City Walls Road was built on the line of the ancient walls in the 1970s, the losses were offset to some degree by new archaeological discoveries. Inner ring roads could disrupt established relationships between important historic loci. Maid Marian Way (built 1957–65) bounded the west side of Nottingham town centre, cutting across the medieval street pattern and severing the market place from the castle. In Carlisle, too, the castle was isolated from the town centre by a busy new dual carriageway, Castle Way, part of an aborted ring

408 The Magazine Gateway, Leicester, was tightly encircled by the separated carriageways of the central ring road (Southgates). This photograph was taken in 2008 during remedial works to realign the carriageway on the east side of this Scheduled Ancient Monument, and infill a pedestrian subway.

road. Such roads affected the economy of the streets they bisected: it was a great commercial disadvantage to find oneself on the wrong side of a ring road. Furthermore, such roads altered the character of places profoundly. Writing in 1974, the historian Jack Simmons described what had happened to Leicester, where a ring road had been driven through the west side of the city, entraining massive demolitions:

> In the course of the last fifteen years – no more – the Old Town of Leicester has been almost entirely destroyed. In the late 1950s its medieval street pattern was clearly visible . . . Now nearly all this has gone: not merely the streets but their very names – Applegate Street, Blue Boar Lane, Bakehouse Lane, Red Cross Street . . . In their place we have a huge swathe of concrete, taking the traffic through the city north and south, with windy and desolate stretches, of concrete again, on either side of it. The Old Town in its former state was grimy, and in many respects an inefficient anachronism. Nevertheless it was full of interest, of oddity: it was lovable and contained surprises. Not one of those things is true of its successor. It has become a passage-way, a mere hyphen between larger units. Can anyone feel the interest in such a place?[42]

Simmons accepted the need for Leicester's new road system, yet he presented the impact of the car on the historic urban environment in the bleakest terms. Referring to the town's main historic sites, as identified by Pevsner in 1960, he observed: 'those

buildings are all still there, but they no longer exist now as a group: the new road system has ripped them apart' (pl. 408).[43] He pointed out that these enticing monuments were all but inaccessible to the (perhaps American) visitor staying in the new Holiday Inn (built 1971; see p. 307), stranded in the midst of St Nicholas Circus like 'a prisoner on an island'.[44] With devastating logic he asked: 'what is to be thought of the city, when it takes so much trouble to illuminate and display its monuments, yet renders them inaccessible to just the kind of visitors who might be expected to appreciate them most highly?'

Some historic cities successfully fought off dual carriageways, usually by holding out long enough for schemes to be discredited. Thus, just as Cambridge had resisted plans for a bypass through Grantchester Meadows in 1931,[45] so Oxford, through the 1960s and 1970s, stood firm against persistent proposals for a road that would cross Christ Church Meadows.[46] Bath resisted the idea of a twin tunnel, proposed by Buchanan's consultancy in 1963, that would run beneath the historic core.[47] Other cities had to accept compromises. Salisbury's ring road was built slightly further from the centre than first envisaged by the planner Thomas Sharp. Winchester thwarted an eastern bypass that would complete the M3 by passing through the town's water meadows, but the city had to accept the rerouting of this controversial road through the chalklands of nearby Twyford Down in the early 1990s (see p. 270). In less esteemed provincial towns, such as Southampton, new urban roads did provoke some protest in the late 1960s, but this was usually focused on the demolition of housing, and rarely achieved modifications to road design and layout.[48]

Dual carriageways formed armatures for new settlements. Not all followed the wheel-and-spokes – or ring-and-radials – format, exemplified by the earliest new towns, such as Stevenage (see above). Very different patterns were developed for Washington in Co. Durham (now Tyne & Wear) and Milton Keynes in Buckinghamshire, which, unlike the first generation of new towns, were designed for full car ownership. Washington Highway (A182), which opened in 1971, was essentially a landscaped dual carriageway that soared over a series of roundabouts, giving separate access to the town centre, industrial and residential areas. The urban dual carriageway probably reached its apogee in Milton Keynes, designated in 1967 and largely built in the 1970s (pl. 410). Here, landscaped dual carriageways known as grid roads were connected to one another by conventional roundabouts (without underpasses or flyovers, except on the A5 as it passed through the town) at approximately 0.6-mile intervals. According to its architect and planner, Derek Walker, this decentralised plan was inspired by the contemporary Californian planner Melvin M. Webber, who originated the notion of 'community without propinquity', embracing car-related low-density sprawl as something that should not be derided.[49] As in Washington,

360

the roads of Milton Keynes were designed on the parkway principle, with wide central reservations planted with trees and shrubs. The sides were landscaped as baffles or 'berms': mounds with dense planting that sheltered the occupants of the grid squares from the sights and sounds of heavy traffic. The outlying grid squares included approximately 100 semi-autonomous neighbourhoods. The central squares, devoted to retail, business and leisure, were defined by roads with traffic lights at their intersections, rather than roundabouts, theoretically to keep the traffic moving. This grid plan and low-density sprawl, unsurprisingly, has always invited allusions to Los Angeles, the ultimate car-city. One would not argue with the assessment of Fraser and Kerr, that Milton Keynes represents 'a hitherto unsurpassed peak of U.S.-style, market-orientated planning based on car ownership'.[50]

Many schemes for ring roads and urban motorways were abandoned from the early 1970s, following the Westway debacle, and alternative methods of traffic control were devised (see below). Wilfrid Andrews, Chairman of the RAC from 1945, is said to have once declared: 'I am staggered by the colossal impertinence of those who complain of the aesthetics of urban motorways.'[51] Even in the early 1960s, urban motorways were not welcomed by everyone; indeed, they had their fair share of outspoken critics from the outset. The town planner Ernest H. Doubleday, for example, cautioned that new roads should assume 'a more human scale' after visiting America in 1960.[52] He reported that, whilst American towns had solved their traffic problems, in the process they had 'almost ceased to be towns for living at all'. In particular, he deplored the impact of freeways that ignored the buildings flanking them. The Buchanan Report of 1963 also expressed qualms, while Peter Blake, Lewis Mumford and others pointed out the adverse consequences of American car-based planning. But local authorities paid little heed to these auguries, as they vied with one another to accommodate and speed up the car, as if their economic survival depended upon this strategy. Leeds, desperate for regional supremacy, even proclaimed itself 'the motorway city of the seventies'.[53]

Throughout the 1950s and 1960s the public seldom questioned the need for new urban roads, only quibbling about their exact routes. The experience of the Westway, however, opened eyes to the damage being inflicted on British towns and cities, and on British lives, by new roads. There was, quite suddenly, a heightened awareness of what was being lost, and a corresponding increase in the value assigned to the infrastructure inherited from earlier generations, even the once-vilified Victorians. Individually, civic and amenity groups had amassed experience of road protest, and now they began to pool their expertise, for example, at a conference entitled 'Planning, Participation and Protest' organised by York 2000, an anti-ring-road group, in 1972.

409 A traffic protest in Highgate, photographed *circa* 1970 by John Gay. The growth of road haulage was causing problems in urban areas.

From this time, protestation dogged every project; it was expected, planned for, even built into road-building budgets (pl. 409). Protesters were a motley bunch, driven by different motives: attachment to their homes and communities, appreciation of historic buildings and landmarks, or fondness for trees and landscapes. Some were politically motivated, or had developed a straightforward opposition to the car, especially as studies revealed its damaging impact on the environment and, eventually, linked it to climate change. By the early 1990s road protests and the soaring price of urban land (especially in London) were adding millions of pounds to the cost of new roads. Another new factor was rescue archaeology, which escalated in the mid-1970s thanks to increased Government funding. County archaeological units were born, relying on Government grants to undertake rescue digs. Developers were not yet required to take account of archaeological potential in the planning process, but major construction projects could be held up by excavations, causing conflict with archaeologists. This was just one of several factors that combined to ensure that very few new major roads would encroach on established towns and cities in the foreseeable future.[54]

Some of England's last major urban roads were built in the 1990s. London's ringway system had been modified by the Layfield Inquiry of 1970–72, then abandoned (save for the M25) when the Labour Party took control of the GLC in 1973, yet

410 The grid of roads in
Milton Keynes was linked by
roundabouts, not flyovers.
As with roundabouts all over
the country, the planting and
maintenance are sponsored by
companies exploiting an
advertising opportunity.

411   The M11 Link running through a cutting, with the Victorian terraced housing of Grove Green Road, Leytonstone, perched above it. This view looks north, towards Wanstead.

proposals for the 4-mile A12–M11 Link were kept alive.[55] Between 1993 and 1999 this ploughed its way through the Victorian suburbs of north-east London, from Redbridge, through Wanstead and Leytonstone, to the Hackney Marshes, where it met the completed East Cross Route (A102[M], built 1966–8) of the defunct Motorway Box, aligned with the Blackwall Tunnel (itself doubled by a second bore in 1964–7). The cost was £167.8 million.[56] Although the M11 Link followed a railway line for some distance, this had to be trebled in width, involving the demolition of hundreds of houses and, sometimes, entire streets (pl. 411). This project coincided with the highpoint of the road protest movement, and was impeded by one of the most protracted and widely reported anti-road campaigns ever to take place in London. As terraced housing was compulsorily purchased from resigned locals, it was rented to housing associations, or left empty, in a classic instance of planning blight. The area thus became populated by squatters and by experienced road

protestors. As workmen moved in, these protesters deployed a variety of obstructive techniques: occupying trees (notably an ancient chestnut on George Green, Wanstead), declaring autonomous republics such as 'Wanstonia', 'Leytonstonia', 'Euphoria', 'Munstonia' (a listed house on Fillebrook Road) and 'Greenmania' (a camp on Wanstead Flats), and making a daring stand on doomed Claremont Road.

Elsewhere in the early 1990s dual carriageways were still being built in minor provincial towns without becoming *causes célèbres*: thus Chalons Way, a concrete-lined dual carriageway, was driven through the centre of the Victorian town of Ilkeston in Derbyshire without generating much fuss (pl. 412). This, however, was one of the last of its kind.

·

412 Chalons Way (talked about since the 1950s and opened by the Mayor of Erewash in 1993) was driven through the essentially Victorian town of Ilkeston in Derbyshire, involving much demolition. By 1993 the tide had turned against such inner relief roads, and its northern extension was never constructed. Here we can see that Boar Lane, on the right, now overlooks a broad concrete-lined cutting, with a footbridge superseding the west end of Byron Street. There is a rue d'Ilkeston in the twin town of Châlons-sur-Marne.

The Drive-in

The creation of the modern motorised metropolis did not stop at roads, or even at the gigantic multi-storey car parks they led to. The prospect of the motorist accessing a wide variety of services without stepping out of the car was greeted with enthusiasm for a few years around 1960. This formed part of a general embrace of American popular culture. By 1958 there were around 5,200 'drive-ins' of different types in America, including cinemas, restaurants and even chapels. Despite some attempts to import the concept to England, the drive-in remained a novelty until the 1980s, when drive-thru (*sic*) Americanised fast-food outlets became widely popular (see pl. 353).[57]

In January 1959 – by which time 2,681 drive-in banks existed in the U.S.A. – Martins Bank announced that it was about to open Britain's first drive-in bank on Charles Street, Leicester, 'to ease transport problems for their customers'.[58] This opened on

2 March, with the Minister of Transport presiding, but Martins had been pipped to the post by the Westminster Bank, which opened a drive-in window on Princes Road, Liverpool, on 30 January.[59] Rather than being directed to the appropriate department by a receptionist on roller skates, as sometimes happened in the U.S.A., customers visiting these drive-ins pulled up at a hatch where they were served by a cashier behind an armour-plated window, using a speaker system (pl. 413). Drive-in windows had to overcome the height differential between the teller and the motorist: those at the Westminster were designed by its own architects, whilst Martins' were imported from America. The system had its limitations, since only straightforward deposits or withdrawals could be transacted in this way. Nevertheless, the format enjoyed limited success and additional drive-ins were opened in 1960–61: for example, by the Westminster in Gidea Park, Leeds and Watford, by Lloyds in High Wycombe, and by Drummonds (Royal Bank of Scotland) at

413 The drive-in window of Martins Bank, Charles Street, Leicester, opened on 2 March 1959. It was planned as Britain's first drive-in bank, but was overtaken by the Westminster Bank in Liverpool, which opened a month earlier. The car is an Austin A70 Hereford.

Boots in a former McDonald's in Colchester, Essex, but this was merely a hatch where the motorist could pull up to collect a prescription. Then in August 2010 Tesco launched its 'click and collect' drive-thru service at its branch in Baldock, Hertfordshire: a variant on internet shopping as much as a step in the evolution of drive-in shopping. Apart from fast-food restaurants and wildlife parks, the drive-in concept has never truly caught on in the U.K.

The Car-less Precinct

As observed above, it was neither easy nor pleasant for pedestrians to reach the car-less precincts created in the hearts of new or reconfigured post-war towns such as Stevenage and Coventry, because they had to negotiate footbridges or subways to cross inner ring roads. Once they arrived, however, they could wander safely through the precinct, sheltered from rain (or, occasionally, sunshine) beneath permanent canopies that projected over the shopfronts. There was no traffic to disturb them, and no guardrails or designated crossings to control their movements. Shoppers' cars were diverted to hidden car parks. Like delivery yards, these lay behind or above the shops. In new towns this approach could be planned; elsewhere, it proved hugely problematic.

The open-air pedestrian shopping street was not entirely novel in 1950s England. Amongst earlier examples were The Pantiles (late seventeenth century) in Tunbridge Wells, Kent, and Sicilian Avenue (1906–10) in London, but these were isolated developments – allied to the upper-class fashion for the shopping promenade – with no impact on mainstream town planning.[64] The idea was resurrected *a novo* as the most complete expression of pedestrian and vehicular segregation. In 1942, in the Introduction to Tripp's *Town Planning and Road Traffic*, Abercrombie referred to England's principal shopping streets, such as Lord Street in Liverpool and Oxford Street in London, as 'grotesque survivals of the horse-drawn vehicle age'.[65] The intermingling of through traffic with the essentially pedestrian activity of shopping was deemed dangerous, not to mention uncongenial. The optimum solution in existing towns, for Tripp and others, was vertical segregation, in its various hypothetical permutations – though as a makeshift solution, a system of guardrails and subways could ensure a high degree of horizontal separation. For new towns, however, Tripp proposed a main shopping centre that would be reached via local roads, with two rows of shops on an oval-shaped island site, surrounded by a one-way local road and facing onto a narrow footway (pl. 414).[66] This was, essentially, a pedestrianised shopping precinct in embryo, although Tripp did not apply that terminology; nor did he believe that the concept would prove acceptable to either shopkeepers or shop-

Admiralty Arch, London.[60] Barclays and the Midland decided not to partake in these experiments.

Leicester may have failed – just – to open Britain's first drive-in bank, but, undeterred, laid claim to the country's first drive-in post office in December 1959 (see pl. 256).[61] This was an integral part of the design of a new telephone exchange built on Lee Street to a design by Eric Bedford and John Heard. The cashiers' windows were similar to those in drive-in banks, and cars could queue under the shelter of a covered way, which operated a one-way system. A different experiment was tried a few months later in Luton, where motorists could pull up at post office machines. In this automated drive-in, they could buy a stamp and post a letter without having to be served by a clerk.[62]

In 1968–9 two brewery companies dabbled with the drive-in format. Courage opened a drive-in off-licence in Ashford, Kent, at Christmas 1968 – the first in a series to be called 'The Vineyard'.[63] Watney Mann followed with a branch in Streatham, London, called, more prosaically, 'Liquor Value'. To put this in context, just a year earlier the Minister of Transport, Barbara Castle, had introduced new drink-drive laws and the breathalyser test. Brewery shares had dipped, and the drive-in off-licence was surely part of the fight-back. Nevertheless, it was inevitable that this combination of drinking and driving – even if designed to let the motorist buy alcohol conveniently, then drink it at home – raised a few eyebrows.

It was some time before the next experiments in drive-in – or drive-thru as it is now called – shopping were made. In August 2008 Britain's first drive-thru chemist was opened by

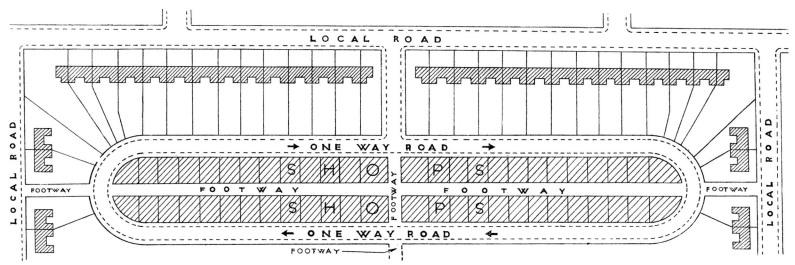

FIG. 15.—A main shopping centre in a new town. This is so designed that no vehicular traffic will have any inducement to enter the area unless it has actual business there. The shops are erected on both sides of a central footway on an island site ; each shop has a frontage upon the central footway and also upon the road. There is a cross footway in the centre ; and access for foot passengers to and from the adjacent roads is provided. On the road surrounding the shops, there are waiting spaces and parking spaces. The houses that are shown as built facing the ordinary roads of the locality have no direct access to the road surrounding the shops.

414 In 1942 Sir Herbert Alker Tripp proposed a design of shopping centre for new towns in which the shops would face a footway, rather than a road. This idea – that of the pedestrian shopping precinct – was used extensively after the war.

pers. Around the same date, Donald Gibson was conceiving Coventry's new city centre with separation of pedestrians and cars.

Tripp's suggestion attracted little interest in 1942, but after the Second World War examples of pedestrian precincts in Continental towns, such as the Lijnbaan in Rotterdam (1951–3; van den Broek & Bakema), had a profound influence on British architects and planners. One of the first to be completed in England was the Lansbury Shopping Precinct in Poplar in east London, a neighbourhood centre designed by Frederick Gibberd and displayed as part of the Festival of Britain in 1951. Soon after this, Coventry's new city centre was built with two pedestrianised shopping precincts, Upper Precinct and Lower Precinct, separated by a cross-route for traffic. In 1955, however, the cross-route was closed and full pedestrianisation was implemented.[67] Writing in 1968, Tetlow and Goss noted: 'it is paradoxical that the hub of the British car industry will probably be the first to give pedestrians freedom of movement in its centre'.[68] Similar schemes were developed for new towns. While the centre of Harlow retained a vehicular road separating the Market Square from Broad Walk, traffic was barred completely from Stevenage town centre from the outset. By the early 1960s precincts were forming part of extensive redevelopment schemes in established towns and cities.

The St John's Centre in Liverpool and the Merrion Centre in Leeds, later roofed over as malls, both originated as open-air shopping precincts. They were located off main thoroughfares, but from the late 1960s – aping Continental examples like Strøget in Copenhagen (1962–3) – many towns began to pedestrianise the street itself. This was not undertaken lightly by local authorities: it was opposed by many shopkeepers, some of whom benefited more than others from the transformation, and it required the re-routing of bus services as well as of local and through traffic. In some centres, pedestrianisation was effective only within certain hours, with access for delivery vehicles permitted from evening until early morning. Others were more radical, clearing backlands to create rear servicing and, with this, twenty-four-hour pedestrianisation.

Proposals for pedestrianisation in historic towns came thick and fast from the late 1960s. Amongst the first schemes to be implemented were the High Street in Southend-on-Sea (1968) and London Street in Norwich (1969). Others were in Sheffield (Fargate, 1969), Leeds (Land's Lane, 1970), Old Harlow (1970) and Yeovil (Middle Street, 1971). In 1971 the Department of the Environment issued a *Circular on Pedestrianization*, including the directive that a pedestrianised street must be paved. The distinction between pavements and roads was eliminated by removing kerbs, and the resulting level surface was usually paved with 18-inch-square precast concrete slabs, which were sometimes varicoloured or interspersed with other materials to form a pattern. In autumn 1973 trendy Carnaby Street, London's first pedestrianised street, took this to extremes, being 'paved overall in gaudy

415 In its 1960s heyday London's Carnaby Street was open to traffic. This photograph, taken in the late 1970s, shows the boldly patterned paving that was laid in 1973, when the street was first pedestrianised. This evidence of official acceptance and control must have detracted from Carnaby Street's hip, off-beat image.

geometric patterns with orange, white, yellow and black nylon tiles. They are slightly elastic, so pedestrians feel like pawns on a vast, spongy chess and ludo board' (pl. 415).[69]

Herringbone blocks, hitherto associated more with garden landscaping than public paving, were introduced on St George's Street in Canterbury in 1975–6. In time, these would become just as ubiquitous as square concrete blocks. Pedestrianised streets were furnished to create outdoor rooms, with seating and planters, semi-mature trees, litter bins, and sometimes a fountain or a piece of sculpture. From the late 1970s until the 1990s these elements were often designed in a quasi-Victorian or Georgian style, reflecting the contemporary reaction against functional modernism, as well as expressing nostalgia for a golden age of shopping – as if realisation was dawning of what had been lost in the course of post-war reconstruction. Attempts to prettify street furniture, however, simply made it all the more conspicuous, and it was often tawdry.

Pedestrianisation in established towns meant that motor traffic had to bypass the main shopping area, creating irregularly shaped inner rings, often incorporating confusing one-way systems. Buildings, or even entire lanes, behind high street shops were cleared to create a mixture of rear servicing and shoppers' car parks. Thus much ancillary historic fabric was swept away, including outbuildings, coach houses, stables, factories, work-

shops and cottages. The aesthetic result of this approach, in towns such as King's Lynn in Norfolk (though, in this case, subsequently improved), could be regrettable, or even disastrous. The rear elevations of high street buildings, which were never designed to be seen, were exposed rather cruelly to view, together with their paraphernalia of fire escapes and downpipes, the scars of demolished wings, utilitarian shop extensions and industrial-scale dustbins. Their former walled yards and gardens, once hidden from sight and accessible only through carriage arches or from back lanes, were now laid with hard standing for parked cars and delivery vans, and were visible to anyone approaching the town on foot or by car. In new towns the backlands surrounding town centres gained some neatness from being planned; in old town centres they were invariably a mess. These dreary exposed landscapes did much to encourage car use, by deterring foot traffic.

By 2000 the hearts of many English cities, such as Derby, had been transformed into extensive pedestrianised areas. In the evening, without the bustle produced by cars and people, these become silent, unsettling places – haunts of skateboarders or lone drinkers, eyed by surveillance cameras. In more recent years, attitudes towards the presentation of pedestrian precincts have undergone subtle changes. It is now recommended that kerb lines – with a distinction between the notional footpath and the

416 This well-known and influential illustration by Kenneth Browne comes from *Traffic in Towns*, published in 1963. Based on American exemplars, it shows the vertical segregation of vehicles and pedestrians in a town centre.

roadway – are retained for 'visual continuity' and, in historic towns, to provide 'a plinth for the adjacent buildings'.[70] Colourful or decorative paving is eschewed in favour of a minimalist approach with natural materials. In addition, local authorities are being encouraged to remove surplus street furnishings (see below), while, at the same time, establishing a sense of place through specially commissioned artworks. This can sometimes be a delicate balancing act.

An alternative method of segregating pedestrians from vehicles involves vertical separation, with people and cars assigned to different levels or decks (pl. 416). This was advocated by the Buchanan Report of 1963, but was not new at that time, having been presented in numerous earlier schemes, going back to the nineteenth century (see pls 359 and 384). It was embedded in early redevelopment plans for cities such as Bristol, Sheffield, London and Leeds, which all intended to provide pedestrian walkways at first-floor level. In Bristol, this system was introduced at Nelson House, on the south side of Rupert Street, in 1966, and expanded as adjacent buildings, such as Trafalgar House, were erected. In 1970 it was extended to Froomsgate House on the north side of the street, with pedestrian bridges spanning both Rupert Street and Lewin's Mead. Eventually, however, the scheme was abandoned, leaving disjointed fragments that survive to this day (pl. 417). A comprehensive network

of aerial walkways had proved almost impossible to implement on a gradual basis, since old buildings – not yet candidates for redevelopment – stood stubbornly in the path of completion.

417 A concrete walkway on Lewin's Mead, Bristol, with the Rupert Street multi-storey car park in the background. This was one of several aborted attempts to raise pedestrian routes above the stream of traffic in British towns, something encouraged by *Traffic in Towns*.

The first British town to layer traffic and pedestrians using decks was Cumbernauld in Scotland (started 1955), the first of a 'second generation' of new towns designed, in the words of Buchanan, 'to master the motor car', with an allocation for 0.7 cars per household.[71] Throughout Cumbernauld, separate circulation systems were provided for pedestrians and vehicles. The town centre was raised on a deck above the approach road, with vehicles passing beneath the shops. In England, a similar scheme was proposed for Hook, a new town in Hampshire. Planned by a team under Oliver Cox and Graeme Shankland of the LCC Architects' Department, Hook was described as 'the first [new town] to be designed wholly and from the beginning to answer the problems posed by the growth of motor traffic',[72] but the project was aborted, largely due to opposition from Hampshire County Council, in 1961. It was superseded by plans for the expansion of the nearby market towns of Basingstoke and Andover for London overspill. Basingstoke was re-planned for growth that would more than triple its population (from 26,000 in 1961 to 75,000 in 1981), with an anticipated 1.5 cars per family. The Ringway (built between 1968 and 1975) included Churchill Way, a cross-route of near-motorway standard (pl. 419). This enabled free-flowing traffic to pass through the town centre, which – with its shopping precinct (covered and extended in 2002) and car parks – was built on a platform suspended over the dual carriageway, making use of the natural topography of the valley site. The conventional roundabouts (with subways) at either end of the cross-route were regarded as temporary measures, to be replaced by dual-level roundabouts in due course – something that is yet to happen.

Although vertical segregation proved unachievable by piecemeal development in established towns, and was rarely implemented on a large scale in new towns due to its expense, unrealised utopian – or, rather, autopian – schemes reveal the extent to which architects and planners toyed with this concept in the early 1960s. In 1961, for example, a £12 million scheme called 'High Oxford Street' was proposed for London's Oxford Street by the architect and planning consultant D. Rigby Childs.[73] A mile-long two-level pedestrian deck would span the street: it would be linked to the shop frontages by bridges and to the old pavement by escalators and stairs. Above this would be a travellator, covered by a glass roof. At ground level, the old pavement would be used for parking and banned to pedestrians, though it was observed that shop windows could be retained at this level for the benefit of passengers in vehicles passing through the street. Childs declared that 'in time the character of the street would rival or surpass new shopping centres elsewhere'. Many practical objections, however, could be levied at schemes of this nature, not least the clearance height that would be required beneath the footbridges and decks.

An alternative vision of vertical segregation – one that would have demanded very expert structural engineering skills – was published in 1961 by the landscape architect and planner Geoffrey Jellicoe as *Motopia*, a scheme for a new town specifically designed for the motor car, initiated by the Glass Age Development Committee of Pilkingtons.[74] Motopia was a city – sited, for the purposes of the exercise, by the Staines Reservoir – with a grid plan delineated by multi-storeyed buildings carrying two tiers of roads (a mews road with parking on their fourth floors and a motorway on their fifth, or top, floors), including roundabouts on the roofs of doughnut-shaped neighbourhood circles, positioned at each intersection (pl. 418). The centres of the grid squares contained woodland, lakes, churches and schools. The town 'centre', counter-intuitively pushed to the periphery (as if anticipating the phenomenon of edge-of-town shopping), had rooftop parking. Nothing this radical was ever built, though the grid plan of the roads in Motopia may have influenced the later plan of Milton Keynes. Motopia may also have inspired David Stephens, a scientist with John Laing Construction Ltd, to propose 'roof roads' in 1969.[75] These, he thought, could be applied to the Westway. And indeed, this is exactly what came

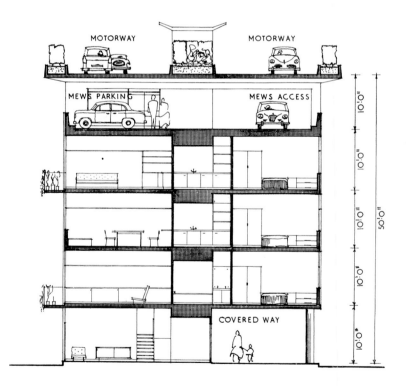

418 (*above*)   The buildings of *Motopia* (1961), devised by Geoffrey A. Jellicoe, placed pedestrians at ground level, local roads and parking at fourth-floor level, and motorways on roofs.

419 (*facing page*)   This aerial photograph shows how Basingstoke's shopping centre spanned a dual carriageway, Churchill Way. It also shows the extensive rooftop parking serving this development.

about (see above), but accidentally, rather than as part of a planned scheme.

Regardless of its exact form, segregation emphasised the alienation of cars from pedestrians and, consequently, attracted its share of adversaries. On several occasions over the years protest groups have intervened, questioning the boundaries separating the realms of cars and people and throwing the ownership of public spaces – including roads – into question. The most active movement, since the early 1990s, has been 'Reclaim the Streets', which portrays streets as 'open sewers of car culture'.[76] In May 1995, on Camden High Street, this group staged a mock car crash and unfurled a banner proclaiming: 'Reclaim the Streets – Free the City – Kill the Car.'[77] The street was carpeted and taken hostage for some hours, becoming a temporary pedestrian precinct. Similarly, in July 1996 Reclaim the Streets organised the occupation of the M41, the West Cross Route of the long-abandoned Motorway Box. Here, the activists held a party, placed a car on trial, and – concealed beneath the wide skirts of stilt-walkers – drilled up the tarmac to plant saplings.[78] Not surprisingly, once the protest disbanded, the motorway had to be closed for resurfacing; the trees were thrown away. In a cruel twist of fate, Reclaim the Streets' website was taken over by 'cyber-squatters' in the course of 2011.[79]

Signage and Street Controls

As seen in Chapter 12, it was between the wars that English streets first became cluttered with signage, as most still are today. Much of this was introduced for good reasons: to direct and warn traffic, to keep it flowing, to regulate behaviour at junctions, to restrict parking and waiting, and to ensure the safety of pedestrians and cyclists. These trappings had a profound effect on the urban environment. Inevitably, they changed the character of streets everywhere. Images from the late nineteenth century show unmarked streets, only an occasional bollard on the pavement, and pedestrians free to roam in the road as they pleased. By the mid-twentieth century streets had lost the stench of horse dung, but they had become visually restless, displaying a chaotic mixture of instructions and warnings, kitted out in a range of colours, materials, styles and fonts. Rather than being allowed to take the direct route from A to B, the 'desired line', pedestrians were increasingly shepherded to official crossings, and so the business of moving through towns on foot became a frustrating experience. Factoring the noise, speed and fumes of motor traffic into the equation, it is clear that urban centres had become more challenging environments in which to live, as well as work. After the war, the pedestrian precinct offered respite in some restricted areas, but elsewhere the visual cacophony

increased, as planners continued to invent new types of crossings, junctions and signage.

Occasional changes were made to the standard traffic signs stipulated in 1933 (see Chapter 12).[80] In 1950, for example, two significant amendments were introduced. One was the introduction of a new 'no entry' sign based on the European standard, with a white horizontal bar, bearing the words 'no entry', on a red disc. The other was the inversion of the triangle within the disc topping the 'slow – major road ahead' and 'halt major road ahead' signs.[81] In 1957 directional curves replaced 'Z' on the 'bend' sign, and the torch symbol for 'school' was superseded by an image of a boy and girl carrying books and a satchel.[82] In the late 1950s and early 1960s a number of influential traffic-management schemes were introduced in London, where congestion was at its worst, prompting a rash of new signage relating to parking restrictions, waiting and unloading bans, one-way streets, tidal-flow schemes and, from 1964, clearways. Such techniques spread throughout England in the 1960s, with the encouragement of the Ministry's Traffic Advisory Unit, not just preventing gridlock but also – perhaps surprisingly – helping speeds to increase.[83]

The new motorway signs (see p. 262) made those on all-purpose roads and streets seem inadequate and outdated, and in 1962 the Traffic Signs Committee was appointed under the chairmanship of Sir Walter Worboys. Its recommendations, presented in July 1963, were accepted and brought into force on 1 January 1965 (pl. 420). This was the biggest revolution in traffic signs since 1933. The new signs, like those for motorways, were designed by Jock Kinneir and his assistant Margaret Calvert, using their 'Transport' typeface and mixed-case lettering. While the time-honoured discs (instructions), triangles (warnings) and rectangles (other) were retained, some sweeping changes were introduced. In general, the new signs marked a further move away from words and letters, in favour of Continental-style symbols. A diagonal line was now superimposed on a symbol to indicate a particular type of prohibition, such as no overtaking or no right turn. Most significantly for the urban environment, 'Halt' and 'Slow' were replaced by 'Stop' and 'Give Way'. The 'Give Way' sign (an inverted triangle) was to be used at all junctions with major roads, the 'Stop' sign (an inverted triangle within a disc) only where poor visibility made a stop necessary on every occasion. Other new signs included 'turn left/right' and 'keep left/right', with white arrows superimposed on a blue disc, which became common on refuges and roundabouts. Lines on road surfaces also received attention: regulations concerning lines at junctions were tightened up, and a uniform system of yellow lines, combined with signs indicating the time limits of restrictions, was introduced on the edges of roads and on kerbs to control waiting vehicles. Yellow lines, in particular, would prove

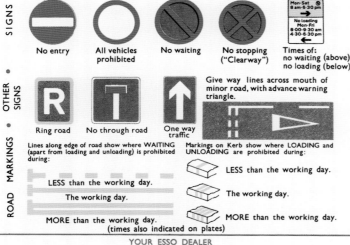

420 A selection of the most common traffic signs introduced on 1 January 1965, shown on the back of an Esso road map, published in the same year.

grid was painted on the road surface at such junctions, and motorists were forbidden from entering the grid unless their exit was clear. Following a series of successful experiments in London in 1965, this was rolled out across the country, and increasingly came to be used to keep roads clear outside fire stations, railway stations, ambulance stations and other places where access was vital at all times. Another method of distinguishing certain road surfaces (for bus routes, cycle lanes, etc.) was coloured asphalt. Available since the mid-1930s,[85] this became increasingly popular after the war, for example, with red asphalt being laid on The Mall in 1949.[86]

In 1943 the Committee on Road Safety in War became, simply, the Committee on Road Safety. This produced an interim report in 1944 and a final report in 1947. Meanwhile, the Government, local authorities, the Pedestrians' Association and the Royal Society for the Prevention of Accidents (which originated as the National Safety First Movement in 1916) launched a concerted road-safety campaign, with books and games for young children: the slogan was 'keep death off the roads'. It was promised that driving tests would be reintroduced,[87] more guardrails erected and blind corners removed. In March 1949, 1,000 zebra crossings, a refinement on Belisha's beacon crossings, were introduced during Pedestrian Awareness Week.[88] This adaptation proved successful – the stripes made the crossings more visible to drivers, and encouraged pedestrians to use them with confidence – and was extended to all Belisha crossings from October 1951. Flashing beacons were introduced in 1953.[89]

Though the zebra crossing remains popular to this day, in the course of the 1960s several new types of push-button crossing were trialled successively as potential alternatives, culminating in the widespread adoption of the pelican crossing. These were not the first controlled crossings to appear on British streets: some had been set up as long ago as the 1920s, in conjunction with traffic lights (see pl. 377), but no single system ever attained universal acceptance. The first important experiment, the panda crossing, was initiated in 1962.[90] Ernest Marples opened the first in York Road, opposite Waterloo Station in London. Panda crossings were then installed at forty-five locations, including Lincoln and Guildford. The new crossings were painted with white triangular markings, and were signalled by modified Belisha beacons with black stripes added to the globes and traffic signals attached to the poles. After pressing a button, pedestrians were shown a 'wait' sign, followed by a 'cross' sign, which began to flash as time ran out. Puzzled drivers were faced with a sequence of pulsating amber, followed by pulsating red, then flashing amber. The subtle difference between pulsating and flashing lights caused particular confusion, and so an alternative was developed.[91] 'Saint' crossings – so-called because pedestrians were shown a matchstick man resembling the logo of The Saint

disfiguring in residential streets in years to come. The changeover to the new signs did not happen all at once, in order to stagger the huge cost, which was estimated at £22 million over five years.[84]

Shortly after the arrival of the new traffic signs, box junctions were introduced in an effort to prevent gridlock at busy city intersections, especially during rush hours. A yellow diagonal

421 The Minister of Transport, Ernest Marples, opening the first 'Saint' pedestrian crossing in Tottenham, London, in September 1963. 'The Saint' was currently being serialised on British television, starring Roger Moore as Simon Templar.

pedestrians: 'two can'), the tiger (for cyclists, with yellow and black stripes) and the Pegasus (for horse riders, with high push buttons and horse pictograms). But the two types of pedestrian crossing most often encountered on British streets in the early twenty-first century are the zebra crossing of 1949 – virtually the last vestige of the black and white striped posts that were once so ubiquitous throughout the built environment – and the pelican crossing of 1969. For several decades these have been used in association with blister or bubble paving, to assist the visually impaired.

Many of the new initiatives introduced after the war, including the zebra crossing, emerged from the Road Research Laboratory. When this organisation was first established in Harmondsworth, Middlesex, in 1933,[94] it was concerned exclusively with road building. In 1946, however, its interests were extended to embrace road safety and traffic flow, with a new division located at Langley Hall, near Slough.[95] Eventually, a new test track (1958–60) – not unlike those developed by motor manufacturers for testing cars (see p. 39) – and laboratory accommodation (1963–7) was built at Crowthorne in Berkshire (pl. 423).[96] Amongst other things, the organisation began to consider how roundabouts might be improved. Since their introduction in the 1920s, roundabouts had been a free for all. Following isolated local experiments in the late 1950s, the offside priority rule (i.e., giving way to traffic already on the roundabout) was tested for

422 The median refuge of a pelican crossing, with guardrails to corral pedestrians, on Kensington High Street, London, around 1970. The staggered pedestrian crossing, or 'cattle pen', is no longer recommended.

(Simon Templar) from the detective novels of Leslie Charteris – appeared in 1963 (pl. 421). The next significant experiment was the 'X-way' crossing, which was introduced in 1967, again on an experimental basis, in west London and eight other towns.[92] It had no road markings, expect for rows of studs and a white line marking the stopping point for traffic. Drivers were faced with a sequence of red, amber and a white cross on a black background, while pedestrians were shown symbols, a red standing man to signify 'wait' and a green walking man for 'cross'. A buzzer sounded to assist the visually impaired. When the green man began to flash, pedestrians retained priority, but if the way was clear, traffic could set off.

As with panda crossings, the light sequence accompanying the X-way confused drivers. It was superseded in 1969 by the pelican (or 'pedestrian light controlled') crossing: the white X was replaced by a steady green light, and the green man would now flash for only a few seconds, towards the end of the crossing time (pl. 422).[93] Later variants in the zoo of British crossings include the puffin (with infrared sensors, and lights mounted on the near side of the crossing), the toucan (for cyclists as well as

423   The Road Research Laboratory at Crowthorne, Berkshire, was opened in 1967 by Barbara Castle and underwent various name changes before becoming the Transport Research Foundation in 1995. This aerial photograph of 2010 shows an experimental junction layout; the laboratories and offices are at top left.

three years, between 1963 and 1966, then introduced as a general advisory rule.[97] The traffic engineer at the Road Research Laboratory who promoted this idea, Frank Blackmore (1916–2008), went on to invent the mini-roundabout. He carried out experiments in Peterborough, Cardiff and Hillingdon in 1968–9,[98] but the first true mini-roundabouts are probably those installed at South Benfleet, Essex, in May 1970, at Upton Cross, Dorset, in June 1970, and at Eastcote, London, in July 1970.[99] With the island whittled down to a painted circle on the road surface, mini-roundabouts could be used at small junctions, where there was simply not sufficient space to erect a full roundabout. They were particularly popular in certain towns, such as Dunstable in Bedfordshire, where they were paired at staggered junctions.

Another of Blackmore's inventions was the ring junction, involving a cluster of mini-roundabouts around a large roundabout.[100] In 1972–3 he carried out a series of trials in Colch-ester (A134), Swindon, Sheffield, Halesowen, Hemel Hempstead and Slough, with existing large roundabouts being converted to the new system overnight. Those at Swindon (the County Islands or Magic Roundabout, 1972; pl. 424) and Hemel Hempstead (Moor End or Plough Roundabout, 1973) have endured, whilst the other experiments were abandoned. Only a few ring junctions were built subsequently, including those at Colchester (A133), High Wycombe (Abbey Way) and Denham (under the M40). In each case, cars were driven anti-clockwise around the main roundabout, then clockwise around the encircling mini-roundabouts. These 'magic roundabouts' encouraged low speeds but baffled those unfamiliar with the format: this is the explanation for their limited appeal.

One of the first intimations that cars no longer enjoyed absolute priority on British streets was the introduction of traffic calming. This generally involved the construction of physical

424 The Magic Roundabout in Swindon, Wiltshire, so confusing for many drivers at ground level, is a model of clarity from the air. Created in 1972, it was the brainchild of the traffic engineer Frank Blackmore.

obstacles such as chicanes, rumble strips, 'sleeping policemen' (raised ridges or mounds running from kerb to kerb) or 'road humps' to slow cars, especially as they passed through residential or shopping areas. The road hump is said to have been introduced by the Dutch road engineer Joost Vahl, the inventor of the *woonerf* ('living yard' or Home Zones), in the late 1960s. One of the first mentions of a 'sleeping policeman' in England occurred in Norwich in 1969, when one was erected to slow down delivery vehicles crossing the pedestrianised London Street.[101] It was some time, however, before the Government gave highway authorities the power to introduce speed humps, perhaps because of concerns that they might damage cars, but also as a result of sustained pressure from the pro-car lobby. Humps were being considered by the Ministry in 1973,[102] and the Transport and Road Research Laboratory (as it was known by this date) subsequently undertook six experiments, including

one on Cuddesdon Way, Oxford, in 1975–6.[103] Speed humps, however, were given the go-ahead only in 1981.[104] From that time – despite protestations from various constituencies, including the emergency services – many variants have been developed, in different shapes and materials. These include 'thumps' made of thermoplastic and 'speed cushions'.

Speed cameras have mushroomed along major routes where traffic calming is impractical ever since they were introduced in Nottingham in 1988. Internationally, one of the first speed cameras, the 'auto speed recorder', was invented in the U.S.A. in 1909, and actually used as evidence in a court case.[105] The ancestor of the modern speed camera, however, was devised much later, in 1959, by the rally driver Maurice Gatsonides, whose Dutch company (Gatsometer BV) continues to manufacture such devices for a global market. The technology was adapted to record road traffic offences in the 1960s, but its adoption in

376

Britain came rather late. Here, the Road Traffic Act of 1991 enabled courts to accept evidence from cameras in prosecutions, whether for speeding or crossing traffic lights at red.[106] The first systematic use of so-called safety cameras was in west London, where twenty-one fixed-speed cameras and twelve red-light cameras were installed in 1992. Take up was initially slow, but numbers grew in the late 1990s, and by 2010 there were an estimated 6,000 safety cameras on British roads. In particular, the bright yellow boxes containing 'Gatso' speed cameras had become a familiar sight on both urban and rural routes. These cameras record the speed of passing cars from the rear using radar technology, with white measurement strips painted on the road surface as a check. Since 1997 many front-facing Truvelo or 'pink eye' cameras, made by a South African company, have also been installed.

Theoretically, cameras act as a deterrent to speeding, thereby reducing the accident rate. They are expensive, however, and the recent economic recession has witnessed a reversal in their popularity. In July 2009 Swindon decided to deactivate all its speed cameras: this caused alarm, but statistics published a year later showed that accidents had fallen, possibly as a result.[107] More significantly, in May 2010 Government funding for speed cameras was removed. Oxfordshire promptly followed Swindon's lead by switching off all its cameras, while other counties deactivated a high proportion of them. In April 2011, however, with statistics indicating that fatal accidents had actually increased, and an alternative source of funding guaranteed from speed awareness courses, Oxfordshire's cameras were switched back on.[108] Thus yellow camera cases, such a conspicuous feature of today's urban and rural environment, are not immediately fated to become a thing of the past.[109] At the same time, average-speed cameras are being introduced on the edges of the urban environment, for example, on the A13 in east London.

Since the 1980s various other traffic-control initiatives have introduced yet more signage and markings to urban streets. In 1982, for example, the Government permitted the Metropolitan Police to use wheel clamps for the first time, to deter unauthorised parking, generating warning signs.[110] In 1991 'red route' clearways were introduced under the Traffic Director for London (now Transport for London, or TfL). To keep traffic flowing on major routes in and out of the city, yellow lines were replaced with red lines, with 'red route' signs controlling stopping and loading. As well as conveying a greater sense of danger than yellow, the red lines had a very different aesthetic effect on streets (see pl. 241). The road markings of the twentieth century have been described as 'a great semiotic code waiting to be unstitched by the archaeologists of the future'.[111]

The most drastic attempt to reduce traffic in central London was the introduction of the Congestion Zone Charge by the Mayor, Ken Livingstone, in 2003; this was extended to west London from 2007.[112] Such schemes had been mooted in earlier years, only to be dismissed out of hand. In 1951, for example, it was considered that 'the difficulties of arranging an equitable scheme to prohibit certain cars from making journeys into inner London are so great as to make the idea impracticable'.[113] The Smeed Report on Road Pricing Policy of 1964, however, recommended just such a scheme: the idea of 'area licensing' was proposed in the early 1970s, and by the Greater London Authority Act of 1999 the power to introduce road charging was conveyed to any future mayor of the city.[114] The boundaries of London's congestion zone are indicated by street markings (a white 'C' on a red disc), very large signs and automatic number-plate recognition cameras. Most cities continue to discourage traffic from entering the central area through a combination of high-priced limited parking facilities and an efficient park-and-ride system. But more subtle moves are afoot.

Re-balancing the Urban Environment

Since the early 1990s many towns and cities have taken positive steps to reduce the dominance of traffic and enhance the freedom of pedestrians on busy shopping streets.[115] In some cases, for example in Leicester and Sheffield, this has extended to inner ring roads, where the subways and footbridges of the 1960s and 1970s have been replaced by ground-level pedestrian crossings. In Birmingham, the topography of the city made it possible to build a continuation of High Street over the ringway, to reintegrate the Bull Ring with the main shopping streets.

Drawing on Continental models, streets – especially in historic towns – have been remodelled to grant a higher priority to people, rather than traffic. On High Street, Shrewsbury, for example, this rebalancing act involved widening the pavements at the expense of the carriageway, which was paved with setts to act as a continuous 'rumble strip', slowing down cars.[116] Other towns, such as Cambridge, have restricted access to certain streets through the use of rising bollards. An important feature of such schemes – including the high-profile refurbishment of Kensington High Street in 2000–03 (pl. 425) – has been the adoption of traditional paving materials and the removal of clutter, including signage, guardrails and painted lines. Nottingham alone removed 2,000 signs between 2003 and 2005.[117] Where traffic signs are still needed, they are often combined, sometimes gauchely, on a single post.

The belief that signage and other furnishings had become confusing and dangerous was not new: this very charge had been levelled at highway authorities before the First World War. It was only around 2000, however, that this complaint caught the public imagination, was married with an argument about urban aesthetics, and was widely acted upon by local authorities, with

425 A high-profile street redesign experiment was carried out on Kensington High Street between 2000 and 2003, creating a calm and unfussy environment. It featured raised crossings, a central strip with cycle parking, and the removal of 640 metres of guardrails. Compare with pl. 422.

subsequent advice and guidance issued by bodies such as English Heritage, Living Streets (the successor to the Pedestrians' Association) and Civic Pride. Local societies have taken up this campaign, for example in Salisbury and Oxford. In autumn 2010 Ministers were reported to have written to council leaders in certain areas urging them to rid streets of signs and obstructions. One of their grievances was: 'our streets are losing their English character'.[118] Yet it must be acknowledged that many features defined as 'clutter' (including Belisha beacons, guardrails and pelican crossings) have contributed, whether positively or negatively, to the distinctiveness of English streets – and even to the distinctive *Englishness* of streets – for several generations. The removal of these elements, and a return to traditional materials such as setts, reverts our streets to their Edwardian, or even pre-car, condition, mercifully without the odour and the 'dust'. But as well as representing nostalgia for a long-lost English streetscape, it is clear that decluttering represents a desire to apply a spare, minimalist aesthetic – equally identifiable in contemporary mainstream architecture and interior design – to townscapes. It also complies with modern beliefs on what comprises a safe environment. For so many reasons, it is spreading throughout England.

All of this is a manifestation of a much bigger initiative, now known as 'Shared Space'. This term describes a number of recent schemes that seek, as their primary motivation, to modify – or even overturn – the rigid segregation that has gripped urban streets since the 1930s, when motorists began to win the battle for public space, waged against the hapless pedestrian and cyclist. Shared Space schemes involve redesigning an urban area, typically a shopping street, to encourage the happy cohabitation of

pedestrians, cyclists and cars. Traffic speed is reduced to 20mph and physical distinctions between areas traditionally assigned to certain categories of street user (for example, pavements, roads and crossings) are blurred, largely by removing controlling signage and guardrails, by modifying kerbs, and by paving the road surface in a manner familiarly associated with pedestrian precincts. Sometimes this includes gentle speed humps or coloured strips that serve as 'courtesy crossings', although these have no legal status. In this way, non-drivers regain some of the freedoms that had been surrendered in the course of the twentieth century, while drivers are forced to display more consideration and courtesy towards pedestrians and cyclists: essentially, Shared Space aims to equalise the status of all road users, in itself an acknowledgement that pedestrians and cyclists had been treated as second-class citizens in the past. It may seem counter-intuitive, but casualty numbers fall in Shared Space schemes. One abiding concern, however, is the safety of the disabled, especially the blind, since the success of Shared Space often depends on negotiation by eye contact or the interpretation of body language.[119] This flaw has sparked considerable opposition to some schemes.

The idea of Shared Space evolved from the Dutch concept of the *woonerf* ('living yard'), which was translated into English planning as 'Home Zones'. This involved redesigning residential streets, not simply to calm traffic, but also to persuade drivers to cede priority to other users, such as playing children, cyclists and pedestrians. This was achieved principally by disrupting the driver's sightlines – by planting or sculpture – to enforce a cautious approach, and by eliminating any differentiation in the levels of roads and pavements. Following a number of pilot schemes set up in 1998, the Government sponsored sixty-one additional schemes through its Home Zone Challenge of 2002. One of the pilot schemes was the Methleys in Leeds, an area of traditional terraced housing where locals had reclaimed Methley Terrace from cars for a full weekend in August 1996 by laying it with turf, some years before they had even heard of Home Zones. While most English Home Zones are 'retrofit', some new build, such as Gun Wharf in Plymouth, has incorporated its essential principles.[120] Significantly, these opt for interconnected streets rather than culs-de-sac.

In urban centres, Shared Space was pioneered by Hans Monderman, a municipal traffic engineer in the Netherlands, who removed the street furniture in the village of Oudehaske in 1985 and in the village of Makkinga in 1991. More significantly, in 2001 he created a 'squareabout', by removing traffic lights from a busy junction, the Laweiplein, in the large town of Drachten.[121] This proved surprisingly successful. Monderman's ideas spread throughout Europe and were championed in Britain by CABE, the architect Ben Hamilton Baillie and the geographer John Adams. They influenced the Department for Transport's guidance document, *Manual for Streets*, published in 2007. A companion document, *Manual for Streets 2: Wider Application of the Principles*, was produced by the Chartered Institute for Highways and Transportation (CIHT) in 2010: this promotes awareness of local context and independent thinking amongst highways practitioners.

One of the most interesting experiments in Shared Space took place in the traditional market town of Ashford in Kent, which was identified in 2003 as a Growth Point, the modern-day equivalent of overspill. In 2007, in anticipation of significant urban expansion, the 2-mile 1970s ring road was converted from a three-to-four-lane one-way system into a series of linked two-way streets, intended to become public places and destinations in their own right, although still open to vehicles (pl. 426). This was designed by the landscape architects Whitelaw Turkington, who worked alongside engineers and public art consultants. The process of decluttering and re-landscaping was completed in 2009 at a cost of £15.3 million. Traffic signals were reduced in number, rather than being completely eliminated, and much of the new street furniture (for example, seating, bollards and lighting columns) was designed by artists. The opening was celebrated by Ashford hosting a stage of the Tour de France and by a temporary art installation programme named 'The Lost O' (i.e., the lost ring), curated by Michael Pinsky. Some of the artworks recycled Ashford's discarded road signs – though several were later moved because they were said to confuse drivers.

Other high-profile schemes have been undertaken in London, where various facelifts were carried out in advance of the 2012 Olympics. These include the remodelling of three major intersections: Oxford Circus, Trafalgar Square and Piccadilly Circus. Oxford Circus was reorganised in 2009. The existing pelican crossings – one across each line of traffic, with central refuges – were replaced by diagonal 'scramble' crossings. The traffic lights were rephased so that all vehicles stood still for 30 seconds while pedestrians crossed the street according to their 'desired lines'. The new design, by Atkins, was reputedly based on Tokyo's Shibuya crossing, but was not entirely novel in Britain: similar crossings had existed in Aberdeen since the 1980s, and in Balham since 2005, to mention just two examples. In spring 2010 a new scheme for Piccadilly got the go-ahead – to revert to two-way traffic for the first time since the 1920s, and to remove railings that were put up in 1963.[122] This opened in October 2011.

Already, the publicity afforded to these schemes has influenced mainstream planning, since some provincial streets are being re-landscaped along Shared Space principles, sometimes with a 'pick-'n'-mix' approach, and without brandishing the 'Shared Space' tag. Traditional shopping streets, East Cheap and Leys Avenue, in Letchworth were remodelled in 2009–10 to become more pedestrian-friendly and encourage shoppers. Evidently,

426 Elwick Road, Ashford, Kent: in this town, taming the dual-carriageway ring road was prioritised in advance of expected urban growth.

Shared Space is not a dogma, and authorities are encouraged to adapt it to local circumstances. If Shared Space principles are disseminated throughout the country, and the misgivings of disabled groups can be assuaged, the relationship between the car and other street users will have undergone a radical power shift. In the near future, we may look back on guardrails and other control systems of the twentieth century with mounting horror and disbelief.

427   Guy Lipscombe's 'Utopian idea of a thoroughfare of the future', published in *The Motor*, 17 March 1908, p. 169.

CONCLUSION: CARSCAPES AND THE FUTURE

Looking Back: Heritage and the Car

Cars have spawned their own material culture and our responses to it are continually evolving. Today, for example, we look at images of the 'wayside eyesores' excoriated by the CPRE in the 1920s – roadside garages and tea shacks covered in advertisements – and we are struck by their charm. Far from wishing to see rare survivors removed, one would hope to preserve them *in situ*. J. B. Priestley may have suspected how attitudes would change when he wrote: 'perhaps the confounded things are pretty, and we are all wrong about them'.[1]

Few 'wayside eyesores' survive intact, however, and the contents of such garages are often treated as portable ephemera. Early petrol pumps and enamelled signs, in particular, sell for large sums to collectors. Indeed, the collecting of such artefacts has acquired its own name, 'petroliana'.[2] Many seemingly old-style village garages are, consequently, modern re-creations, often cleaner and shinier than the genuine article, and treated as period-style settings for one or two splendid vintage cars. Priestley would probably have been astounded to know that museum-quality reconstructions of historic garages have become popular attractions. Notable examples can be seen in the National Motor Museum, Beaulieu (pl. 429). Others are erected on a temporary basis at the annual Goodwood Revival racing meetings, instigated by Lord March in 1998. These include an Art Deco Woad Corner design and a replica of the Tourist Trophy Garage at Farnham, once owned by the famous British racing driver Mike Hawthorn. All this illustrates how responses to the physical environment – fed by a complex amalgam of nostalgia and the objec-

tive curiosity that develops over time – can change dramatically. It took the best part of 100 years for railway infrastructure to be appreciated; now it is the turn of the car.

428 'Beware of Motor Cars': a sign photographed *circa* 1960 by John Gay on a rural road in Cornwall.

429 A garage reconstruction at the National Motor Museum, Beaulieu.

Decades before interest in car culture took root in Britain or other European countries, the U.S.A. had learned to appreciate 'vernacular Americana'. Admittedly, the car played a greater role in American society, at a much earlier date. Furthermore, the buildings and signs related to car culture were bigger, brighter and brassier than their English equivalents. The American road-side strip – with its neon-lit burger bars and gaudy motels – has progressed from its portrayal as 'God's own junkyard'[3] to attain iconic status, constantly referenced in American art and litera-ture, and influencing architects such as Robert Venturi – for example, in his showrooms for Best and Basco. As aspects of strips become threatened, steps are taken to preserve them, and to present them as attractions. Thus, parts of the famous Route 66 have been designated a National Scenic Byway called 'Historic Route 66', and guides to historic motels can be down-loaded from the internet.[4]

Ironically, England was one of the first countries to recognise the importance of historic motor vehicles: one of the world's earliest motor museums was set up by Edmund Dangerfield in 1912; the Veteran Car Club of Great Britain was founded in 1930, and the Vintage Sports Car Club in 1934. Despite this, England lagged behind the U.S.A. in valuing its motoring buildings and roads. While popular and scholarly publications on the roadside, gas stations and car parks multiplied in the U.S., the English carscape was ignored. For years, the motoring journalist and his-torian Michael Worthington-Williams fought a lone campaign on its behalf in his column in *The Automobile*. Perhaps there was a sneaking suspicion that much of this landscape was not quite English, that it had been imported from America and was, con-sequently, debased.[5] Since the late 1990s some redress has been made, for example with David Lawrence publishing on motor-way service stations, David Jeremiah on filling stations and

Simon Henley on car parks. But interest – and appreciation – remains at a lower ebb than in the U.S.A.

The pattern of official designation (i.e., listing or scheduling by the relevant central government department, currently the Department for Culture, Media and Sport) can be regarded as a barometer of attitudes towards the buildings of the past. Listing began after the Second World War and requires buildings to be thirty years old before they can be assessed. The first car-related structures to be listed were, unsurprisingly, those of outstanding architectural quality, in the finest state of preservation, in metropolitan locations. Amongst them were the Michelin Building in South Kensington (listed in 1969; pl. 123) and the Wolseley showroom on Piccadilly (listed in 1972; pl. 62).

Since the 1980s humbler car-related buildings, including provincial examples, have been designated. Several pre-1914 car factories are listed: all representing the pioneering days, rather than the inter-war heyday of the industry. As for domestic motor houses, only one – on Highbury Road, Wimbledon – is listed in its own right. Unsurprisingly, this is an Edwardian building. The situation with showrooms, however, is quite different. While many of the city-centre buildings that once accommodated important early-to-mid-twentieth-century showrooms have been listed, this is rarely on account of the showrooms themselves, since most of these have changed beyond all recognition. The Wolseley is, in fact, an extremely rare survivor. The listing of commercial multi-purpose garages is pleasingly representative: perhaps these are easier to appreciate than other categories of 'carchitecture'.[6] Examples range from small roadside garages and filling stations, such as the Clovelly Cross Garage in north Devon and the distinctive Chinese Garage in Beckenham, to some spectacular 1930s garages in the moderne style, such as the Tower at Egham and Rootes in Maidstone (pls 136 and 137). The first post-war garage to be listed – as recently as 2009, and only after it had been converted into a public library – was the former Lincolnshire Motor Co. in Lincoln, which, with its dramatic hyperbolic paraboloid roof, possesses considerable architectural quality (pl. 71). The Daimler Hire Garage in London was the first multi-storey car park to be listed, in 1982 (pl. 195). While other inter-war car parks have subsequently been listed, post-war Brutalist examples, such as the 'Get Carter' car park in Gateshead (pl. 244), have been turned down. The most highly valued buildings related to cars are still those from the earliest days of motoring.

Significant elements of the motoring roadscape and streetscape have also received official recognition. Some twentieth-century road bridges have been listed, notably examples forming part of the arterial routes created in the 1920s and 1930s (such as the bridge across the River Nene at Wansford (pl. 290)), and a few post-war motorway structures (such as the Severn Bridge). Even traffic signs and crossings have been designated in recent years: for example, some fingerpost signs, and the zebra crossing on Abbey Road, London, famously depicted on the cover of The Beatles' album 'Abbey Road', released in 1969. Other trappings of roads and streets have received local recognition – an example being Letchworth's Sollershott Circus (pls 369 and 70), with its claim to be the U.K.'s first roundabout. As for roads themselves, there is no real equivalent to the American National Scenic Byways. Local authorities have signposted and mapped some as scenic routes to attract tourists, but these are appreciated for the scenery to either side, rather than interest in the roads themselves, or the associated roadscape. Perhaps the day will come when arterial routes such as the Great West Road, or early motorways such as the M45, will be designated for their intrinsic historical importance.

Presenting the heritage of motoring to the public has depended largely on private enthusiasm. Only a small number of England's many motor museums are national in scope, attempting to tell the story of motoring in a comprehensive manner. Many are simply collections of motor cars. The Motoring Memories Museum at Colyford in east Devon is unique as the only *in situ* petrol station to have been turned into a museum (pl. 169). Its displays are devoted to the history of the filling station, with a large collection of pumps and other artefacts. While carriages are frequently displayed at country houses, and some sites make an effort to depict stable life and work, motor cars are seldom presented in this way – though examples are put on show at some National Trust properties, such as Bateman's and Dunham Massey. With the exception of Sandringham House, where the motor house is devoted to a display of royal cars, cars are rarely shown in the setting of a garage, or alongside information on their role in country house living. In fact, motor houses are often regarded as expendable outbuildings, which are swept aside to make way for up-to-date visitor facilities. With the modern emphasis on 'downstairs' living, and fashionable interest in service areas such as kitchens and laundries, the neglect of motoring as an integral part of country house history is inexplicable.

Futuristic Visions

The car stimulated futuristic visions from its earliest days (pl. 427). Thus, around 1900 H. G. Wells and others began to envisage motorways. Lord Montagu speculated on future developments in 1906, and many of his predictions, based on his belief in the future of 'dustless motor ways', have come to pass. 'Populations', he declared, 'will gradually tend to become less concentrated and be diffused over wider areas.'[7] Land in the countryside would become more valuable, due to greater ease of access. He hinted that railway shareholders should jettison their holdings, and predicted that 'in most places motor carriages conveying the public will kill the trams'. Farming would change too, since crops such as oats, grown to feed horses, would not be wanted.

Not all visions of the future proved so accurate. In a rather contrived literary conceit, published in 1922, the journalist and author Leonard Henslowe awakened from a 'dream' of 1950, noting that 'the only place where horses were to be seen was in the Zoological Gardens'.[8] He reported: 'fuel . . . was of trifling cost, whether petrol, paraffin, alcohol, or electricity . . . for private vehicles electricity was largely used'.[9] To make this possible, there were recharging stations in every street.[10] Henslowe's predictions were less accurate than Lord Montagu's, since the popular acceptance of the electric car – especially outside London – remains a dream in 2012.

Architects and planners were inspired by the car to produce ever more dramatic schemes that might reshape the world, or at least stimulate debate. These projects were usually designed to enhance, rather than restrict, car use. Thus Elcock produced his palatial design for a Motor Centre (pl. 67); engineers invented extraordinary mechanisms to facilitate parking; the motoring press published schemes that would elevate pedestrians above cars, or vice versa; Archigram drew up wild designs for the drive-in house and the plug-in city, and Jellicoe produced Motopia (pl. 418). Motopia sat within an international tradition of car-based visionary planning: in Europe, Le Corbusier's *Plan voisin* (1925) and his plan of Algiers (1932); in America, Frank Lloyd Wright's Broadacre City (presented in 1932) and Norman Bel Geddes's 'Futurama', the General Motors pavilion at the New York World's Fair of 1939. The sheer ambition of schemes seeking to remodel the physical environment to welcome the car fizzled out in the 1970s; planners and designers turned their skills to the calming of traffic and the concealment of cars.

The visionaries of the early to mid-twentieth century did not often see their projects realised, but the influence of Le Corbusier, Jellicoe and others can be glimpsed on occasion on English streets, inevitably in a heavily modified or compromised form, for example, in the fragmentary first-floor walkways of Bristol and the rooftop road that is London's Westway (see pl. 404). Truly futuristic carscapes can be experienced in England on occasion, for example, on the M4 viaduct (see pl. 398) as it approaches west London; but the thrill of such roads palls with familiarity, and is tempered by the less positive experience of those at ground level. In general, the reality of the world as it has been reshaped for the car is disappointingly mundane. Thus everyone is familiar with residential areas where cars are half-parked crookedly on pavements, or shopping centres where bulky retail sheds are beached in an ocean of cars. We have a society that is completely car-dominated, just as certain forecasters thought it would be, but the environment we have created lacks the pizzazz, the wonderment of their schemes.

Exurbia: The Way Forward?

Throughout its existence, the motor car has been a mass of contradictions. Promising freedom, it has imposed severe restrictions on the movements of pedestrians. As an object of pleasure, it has killed and maimed. Presented as a hygienic alternative to the horse, it has generated much of the world's pollution. These contradictions continue. At a time when environmentalists and politicians emphasise the need to cut carbon emissions, to preserve stocks of fossil fuels, and to reclaim the streets for pedestrians, other forces have led people to undertake more and more journeys by car. Drivers now face high parking charges, congestion charges, soaring fuel prices and road taxes – not to mention speed bumps, cameras and clamps – but still they drive. Just why do motorists put up with this? One answer may be that the car allows people to live life to the full: to do more things, more efficiently, at a faster pace. Another is that the impact of the motor car on England has been so profound that most people would be unable to lead their lives without it. Settlements, workplaces, shops and entertainments have become so dispersed – as predicted by Lord Montagu in 1906 – that car use is the only way the infrastructure can function.

It might be argued that society was already primed to reject urbanism, and that the car simply delivered the mechanism to achieve this. So many Victorian buildings were grimy with smoke; so much housing was inadequate for its occupants; dense habitation and the presence of horses made cleanliness difficult, and disease spread with ease. The garden city movement, led by Ebenezer Howard, can be seen as a reaction to the state of the urban environment in the 1890s. By that time factories were relocating to edge-of-town sites in large numbers: something made possible, not by the advent of motor transport, but because labourers could now cycle to work, or use improved public transport systems. The phenomenon of dispersal, with the shift of certain facilities to the clean air and cheap land of the urban fringe, most certainly pre-dates the car.

By the 1930s, however, the creation of new arterial roadways for motor traffic was accelerating this trend towards dispersal, especially around London. For a start, the urban sprawl that followed these roads was on a bigger scale, and of lower density, than the suburban growth of the previous century. The factories lining these routes were not the first to move out of town, yet – by abandoning traditionally preferred sites by railways and canals – they were symptomatic of a more recent growth in road haulage. The first industrial estate had been created at Trafford Park in the 1890s; this was followed by others in the 1920s and 1930s, for example, at Slough; but while Trafford Park had relied on a canal, these new developments depended on roads. The arterial roads also attracted car showrooms, which began to quit their original central sites. The town centre was still the hub of British life, but its character had changed, as its streets struggled to cope with the increase in motor traffic and bristled with controls and restrictions. It became much less pleasant for those on foot.

The comprehensive urban redevelopment that followed the Second World War included new schemes, with underpasses and flyovers, footbridges and subways, that attempted to engineer the safe coexistence of vehicles and people in towns and cities. To a degree this succeeded, though – safety being, largely, uncongenial – it wreaked havoc with the urban fabric and made urban living less palatable. Nevertheless, town centres continued to fulfil their traditional roles into the late 1960s. Their shops, however, soon encountered a new threat, as American and French retailers, such as Woolworths and Carrefour, spearheaded the development of edge-of-town shopping by building large DIY and food superstores for a new generation of car-borne consumers.[11] For around fifteen years, this was restricted by stringent planning controls, but, as a commercial model, it eventually proved irresistible.

It was in the 1980s that consumer services shifted out of town to an unprecedented degree, jeopardising the very status of the urban centre and creating an extra-urban landscape of sprawl. This had happened long before in the U.S.A., where such areas were often termed 'exurbia'. In fact, cultural commentators had been warning against the American model since the late 1950s. The spur came when Margaret Thatcher's Conservative Government introduced a raft of incentives to encourage the development of out-of-town superstores and shopping malls on brownfield sites, served by ample parking.[12] This was conceivable only in an age of mass car ownership, and it was an instant hit. Shoppers got into their cars and flocked to these places, while Thatcher famously declared that nothing could stop 'the great car economy'.[13]

As exurbia became established in England, it became possible to live on the edge – to eat, sleep, work and be entertained – without setting foot in the town centre, with its frustratingly slow road systems, awkward multi-storey car parks, high parking charges and exasperating pedestrian routes. The business traveller, provided with convenient roadside hotels and restaurants in exurbia, had no need to enter the town. Even the car, itself, could be bought, fuelled, serviced and sold outside town. The town – formerly the hub of so much human activity – was in danger of becoming redundant.

Realising the economic damage that exurbia was inflicting on urban centres, where shops and other services were shutting at alarming rates, politicians reversed their policy on out-of-town retail developments in the mid-1990s. Urban regeneration became the new mantra, but this was a case of shutting the garage door after the car had left. Exurbia was, by then, well established, presenting town centres with permanent competition. The policy reversal was not, in any case, absolute. It is true that no gigantic new out-of-town malls have opened since Bluewater in 1999, but numerous smaller shopping, office and leisure parks have been added to the edges of towns, while older developments, like Newcastle's MetroCentre, have been revamped and enlarged. 'Urban regeneration' has proved to be a broadly defined concept.

In more recent years, the exurban landscape – distinguished by large sheds surrounded by roads and car parks – has begun to intrude on the urban realm. In the centres of historic towns the exurban model is modified at the insistence of planners. Thus, at Morrisons superstore in the centre of Letchworth Garden City, the car park is at the back rather than the front, while the frontage is an exercise in façadism, preserving the urban character of the street. In all other respects, this is an out-of-town superstore transplanted to a town centre. More radically, a development grafted onto the north-east corner of Stevenage's pedestrianised centre apes the out-of-town retail-park format, while a Tesco superstore occupies the north-west corner. By facing onto surface car parks, these subvert the principles of the original town plan, in which shops faced onto pedestrian ways, while parking was hidden at the rear. Thus the exurban model is beginning to shake up the relationship between shops, cars and people in the urban sphere. It is up to politicians and the planning system to determine how far this will go in the future, and whether our town centres will increasingly imitate exurbia, on the principle of 'if you can't beat 'em, join 'em'.

One place where exurban characteristics have transformed a large area, perhaps offering a taste of the future, is Holbeck, just south of Leeds city centre (pl. 430). Holbeck is threaded by a series of major roads joining the city centre with the M621 motorway. Because of these excellent communications, the area – once a densely occupied Victorian district – has been redeveloped with low-rise offices, all of which are surrounded by extensive parking lots, while the buildings themselves are set well back from the street. The frontage of each plot comprises either car parks or low foliage, and the area has lost all sense of urbanity. Workers and visitors arrive by car; there are few reasons to walk and it is difficult to cross the many roads. The Crown Point Shopping Park, with more than 800 parking spaces, is located next to the Leeds City Office Park: it draws much of its custom from the availability of free parking, in contrast to the nearby city centre, where parking is limited and expensive. These office

430   Exurbia in England: Holbeck, south of Leeds.

and retail developments in Holbeck, as in many other places throughout England, owe their existence to the car. They have all the benefits of an out-of-town location, yet they lie within the orbit of the city centre.

Parking is responsible for this, just as much as roads. Certainly, it is the need to park conveniently and cheaply that has under-pinned the tendency to isolate buildings in a sea of cars. This phenomenon has had a huge impact on the built environment since the 1980s, but its roots run deeper. Already in the 1920s suburban cinemas were providing adjacent open-air car parks for their customers. But the street line was never threatened by these initiatives, and a preference for secure, covered parking put a brake on this development. In the mid-1930s, when the LCC insisted that large new developments include parking, many hotels, flats and office blocks were built with underground car parks. But this was expensive for developers and inconvenient for drivers: as cars became more secure and weather-proof in the post-war years, the cheapness and flexibility of the surface car park was preferred and, increasingly, permitted. Car showrooms – set behind a forecourt – must have been amongst the very first to adopt this plot layout, followed by superstores, malls and retail parks, and more recently by business and leisure parks. Much of central Milton Keynes was planned and built on this principle, lending the approach some urban credibility, and it has subse-quently spread to other places, generally where land prices are low. The sea-of-cars approach has freed architects from the need to relate structures to their surroundings, whether streets or other buildings. Structures are treated as free-standing objects that fight with one another for attention. An extreme form of this can be seen in some American cities, such as Houston, Texas. Many blocks on the Houston grid are open parking lots; others just contain a single very tall building, surrounded by parking. There is no street line, and none of the variety and interaction that one would experience in a traditional city centre.

•

What Next?

We are living at a time when the car is regarded as environmentally unfriendly, yet we show little sign of embracing alternatives. Awareness of environmental issues has not persuaded drivers to switch, *en masse*, to smaller, greener vehicles; neither has it persuaded people to give up the car for their daily commute. This is commonly identified as selfish individualism, or a reflection of the poor state of public transport, but other factors are at play. One crucial explanation, outlined above, is that the world we live in has been reshaped over the last century to make existence very difficult – even disadvantaged – for those who do not have a car. Having dispersed our infrastructure to such an extent, it seems inconceivable that we can sweep exurbia aside and return to an urban lifestyle that is not predicated on the car.

Trams have been reintroduced to some city centres, such as Manchester, Sheffield and Croydon, but, as has been seen, cars are needed to access the wide array of essential services that now exist beyond the urban realm and are not served by good public transport links. Acknowledging that only the most brutal policies will persuade people to abandon private transport – and realising that rises in the cost of fuel arouse the wrath of the powerful road-haulage lobby, as well as private motorists – politicians have focused on making vehicles greener. Efforts have been made to reduce emissions – the car of today is a great deal cleaner than the car of 1970 – and much debate concerns alternative power sources, with governments encouraging manufacturers to invest in a new generation of electric cars.

Electric cars appeal for another reason: the reliance of this country on foreign oil. This is a major concern, and any step that will reduce this dependency is to be welcomed. The provision, however, of an infrastructure to support electric cars beyond metropolitan centres seems to be as unresolved now as it was in 1910. The erection of recharging stations and the take-up of electric cars appears to be a classic chicken-and-egg situation (pl. 431). But it is not impossible to imagine that some of Henslowe's predictions of 1922 might come to pass belatedly; that there might, eventually, be a recharging point – perhaps with ancillary services for the motorist – on every street; and that the city air might fill with the quiet hum of electric vehicles. The initial investment that this will require, however, is unlikely to be forthcoming in the current (2012) climate of recession and public service cuts. Unavailability of petrol may eventually render this a necessity.

The era of the electric car is taking some time to arrive, and in the meantime some urban centres – rather than go down the path of exurbia – are adopting principles of 'Shared Space' planning, to slow down cars, give priority to pedestrians, and generally improve the urban realm. Shared Space – the antithesis of

431 A recharging point for electric cars at the entrance of the Park Lane underground car park in central London. When the car park first opened in 1962, this was the site of a BP filling station.

the car-based planning of fifty years ago; indeed, the antithesis of exurbia – is basically a sophisticated refinement of old-fashioned, and perhaps rather crude, traffic-calming measures, which started with sleeping policemen and straightforward pedestrianisation in the late 1960s. The new approach – with a 20mph speed limit, high-quality paving materials and courtesy crossings – is becoming mainstream. It is likely that it will be adopted widely throughout England. As urban planners continue to study Continental developments, however, and as this type of planning is made safer for the elderly and disabled, it is bound to require refinement and adjustment.

Having emphasised how our dispersed society depends on the car, it seems contradictory to speculate on a future without cars. But lurking in the background is the notion of 'peak car', the idea (or, perhaps, hope) that traffic – which rose rather less than forecast in recent years – has reached saturation point, just as rail travel peaked around 1920, and buses around 1950.[14]

Saturation point does not, however, mean decline. The decline, or even demise, of the car probably lies far ahead. But already some academics are thinking the unthinkable and hypothesising about a car-free future. What if – for example – long-distance commuting and road haulage collapsed and the motorway network became redundant? People might find new ways to use and enjoy roads. Some commentators have imagined stretches of motorway being kept open by enthusiasts, driving cherished vehicles from past eras: this was even the subject of BBC News Online's 2006 April Fool feature about Britain's quietest motorway, headlined 'M45 to be listed as heritage road'.[15] Alternatively, motorways might become high-capacity public transport corridors for some future transit system, or more of a leisure facility, reclaimed like redundant railway lines and canals for walking, cycling and recreation. Disused motorways could provide space

432   The northern end of the M23 was never used, and has been reclaimed by nature.

for human-powered vehicles, perhaps with solar or wind assistance, or for launching and landing personal flying machines. As enthusiasts for bungee-jumping from bridges show, human ingenuity in exploiting infrastructure for new physical challenges knows few limits. However, ensuring continued use would be expensive and challenging – perhaps prohibitive. Motorway foundations are up to 1.5 metres thick, but, without active use and vegetation clearance, weeds would become established in five to ten years. An abandoned motorway could, within a few decades, turn into an impenetrable thicket used only by wildlife. As a case in point, the northern end of the M23 in Surrey, constructed in the early 1970s, was never used and is now heavily overgrown with encroaching scrub and trees (pl. 432).

Other aspects of the motoring heritage may come to be cherished, perhaps before they become redundant. After all, fifty years ago the idea of listing a multi-storey car park or a motorway bridge would have seemed laughable. Many car-related buildings from the 1950s, 1960s and 1970s are currently being remodelled or demolished. When we are ready to appreciate these structures we will have to consider preserving the best of what survives, not the best examples that were ever built. We might regret the structures we have let go, such as Owen Luder's Brutalist car parks, and we might open our eyes to the historical interest of Bristol's aerial walkways (see pl. 417) or Leeds's mechanical car park (see pls 265–7). Much of the heritage of the car, however, is so ephemeral that it is bound to pass almost without notice.

APPENDIX:
STATISTICS OF CAR OWNERSHIP:
ENGLAND AND GREAT BRITAIN

IN 1908 AND 1911 LORD MONTAGU NOTED how difficult it was to discover the correct total of vehicles in Britain, due to disparities in the returns of different local authorities, various exemptions and other complicating factors.[1] From 1903 cars were registered by local authorities, and annual licences were issued to drivers. In 1920 the registration authorities began to keep a file for each vehicle. A centralised computerised licensing centre was set up in Swansea in 1969, but some local record keeping endured for a further decade. Because record keeping and category definitions have changed so much over the years, the figures presented here inevitably contain anomalies and must be regarded as estimates. Nevertheless, they convey an overall picture of how vehicles have multiplied on British roads since the first figures were collected in 1904.

Vehicle Licence Statistics, 1904–2010

Date	Car licences England	Car licences Great Britain	Vehicle licences England	Vehicle licences Great Britain
April 1904	13,302*	14,887	28,073*	31,421
1908		46,500		102,500
1911	133,959*	145,133	236,316*	255,825
1913	201,469*	218,556	376,289*	407,671
1920		187,000		591,000
1924		474,261		1,255,530
August 1930		1,042,258		2,251,142
September 1935	1,303,919	1,477,378	2,266,201	2,581,027
September 1938	1,715,737	1,944,394	2,723,491	3,093,884
September 1946	1,558,517	1,769,952	2,729,721	3,112,930

'A sight for traffic-weary eyes' (*Country Fair*, September 1957): a long, straight country road devoid of cars, near Stamfordham, Northumberland.

Date	Car licences England	Car licences Great Britain	Vehicle licences England	Vehicle licences Great Britain
September 1950	1,984,571	2,257,873	3,853,525	4,413,833
September 1955	3,106,251	3,525,858	5,629,610	6,411,740
September 1960		4,900,000		8,512,000
September 1965		7,732,000		11,697,000
September 1970		9,971,000		13,548,000
September 1975		12,526,000		16,511,000
December 1980		14,660,000		19,199,000
December 1985		16,454,000		21,159,000
December 1990	17,741,000	19,742,000		24,673,000
December 1995	18,211,679	20,505,000		25,369,000
December 2000	21,014,662	23,196,000		28,898,000
December 2005	23,427,786	26,208,000		32,897,000
December 2010	24,095,536	27,018,000		34,120,100

*including Wales

Sources:

1904: motor cars and cycles registered, *The Times*, 30 August 1904, 2.

1908: *Car Illustrated*, 9 December 1908, 189.

1911: *Car Illustrated*, 13 December 1911, 184.

1913: *Car Illustrated*, 10 December 1913, 190.

1924: *The Autocar*, 13 February 1925, 256.

1920 and 1922–57: Ministry of Transport, 'Mechanically-Propelled Road Vehicles, Returns.'

1955–2010: www.dft.gov.uk/pgr/statistics/datatablespublications/vehicles/licensing/ (accessed 7 September 2011).

NOTES

INTRODUCTION

1 Jellicoe 1961; Wollen and Kerr 2002.
2 Such as O'Connell 1998, Brandon 2002, Wollen and Kerr 2002, Merriman 2007 and Moran 2009.

1:   MAKING CARS

1   Collins and Stratton 1993, 35; Wood 2010, 5.
2   Nicholson 1982, 336–7; Thorold 2003, 7–8.
3   In fact, the first steam-powered road vehicles appeared at the end of the eighteenth century. In 1803 Richard Trevithick built a ten-seater steam carriage, which ran in London for some months. More successful steam coaches ran from the 1820s. The requirements of the Locomotive Act of 1865 discouraged such initiatives.
4   Montagu 1906, 3–12; Johnson n. d., 22–3. Evelyn Ellis and David Salomons imported cars in July and October 1895, respectively (*The Autocar*, 22 February 1896, 200). Henry Hewetson – a tea merchant who later became a Benz dealer (see Chapter 2) – claimed to have imported a Benz 'about the end of the year 1894' (Montagu 1906, 54), but company records show that his first Benz left the factory on 29 November 1895 (information from Malcolm Jeal).
5   *The Times*, 21 May 1896, 6.
6   The New Beeston Cycle Co. made De Dion-type motor tricycles at its Quinton Works in Coventry. It was reported to be putting up new works in October 1896 (*The Autocar*, 3 October 1896, 587).
7   The offices of the Motor Car Club, the Daimler Motor Co. and the Great Horseless Carriage Co. were at 40 Holborn Viaduct, London.

8   *The Times*, 1 December 1896, 17; *The Autocar*, 6 March 1897, 150; Nicholson 1982, 364.
9   Arnold manufactured about twelve Benz-type cars between 1896 and 1898.
10 By January 1896 L'Hollier, Gascoine & Courtois were adapting works for the manufacture of Roger carriages at Maidstone. In July 1897, however, the works of the Anglo-French Motor Carriage Co. was established in Digbeth, Birmingham, under Gascoine's management (*The Autocar*, 3 July 1897, 421).
11 The Yeovil Motor Car & Cycle Co.'s new premises were reported by *The Autocar*, 21 November 1896, 666. This was possibly P. W. Petter's manufactory at Reckleford, Yeovil (*PO Directory*, Somerset, 1897, 511).
12 Richardson and O'Gallagher 1977, 17–19. Selwyn F. Edge, former manager of the Dunlop Tyre Co. and sales agent for Napier cars (see Chapter 2), tried to carry on Lawson's monopoly scheme through the British Motor Traction Co. and took unsuccessful action against Charles Friswell of the Automobile Mutual Protection Association (see note 26) for infringement of a Maybach patent in 1901.
13 *The Times*, 25 August 1865, 6.
14 *The Times*, 17 February 1896, 7; *The Autocar*, 22 February 1896, 197; Johnson n. d., 32–4. The Prince of Wales was given his first ride on a motor car by Evelyn Ellis at this event.
15 *The Times*, 2 May 1896, 11; 4 May 1896, 14. Despite warning notices, a woman visiting the exhibition was knocked down by a Roger-Benz, receiving fatal injuries (Nicholson 1982, 429; *The Times*, 21 August 1896, 6). *The Autocar* (9 May 1896, 333) deemed this exhibition a failure.
16 For contemporary accounts of this, see *Manchester Weekly Times*, 18 October 1895, 4; *The*

Autocar, 2 November 1895, 10–12. This was not the first time a horseless carriage had been exhibited in England: for example, a Serpollet steam carriage was demonstrated in London in 1891 (information from Malcolm Jeal, citing *Engineering*, 13 March 1891, 315).
17 Lawson and his associates were members for a short period (Nicholson 1982, 383).
18 *The Autocar*, 9 November 1895, 18; 9 May 1896, 333. This car is now in the National Motor Museum at Beaulieu, Hampshire. The Elliot Reliance Works still exist.
19 The Light Locomotives on Highways Order, regulations issued by the Local Government Board to local authorities, came into force on the same day as the Act, and stated that the speed limit must not exceed 12mph. Local authorities had the power to set lower speed limits.
20 A commemoration run, usually held annually, started in 1927.
21 In September 1897 it was claimed that private motor cars of English construction were to be found in more than forty British towns: 'there must be close on fifty autocars of one kind or another in use in London, and there are at least six in Blackpool' (*The Autocar*, 4 September 1897, 561).
22 Richardson and O'Gallagher 1977, 21.
23 Richardson and O'Gallagher 1977, 129.
24 The Motor Union merged with the Automobile Association (AA) in 1911.
25 Richardson and O'Gallagher 1977, 170.
26 Not to be confused with Friswell's Automobile Mutual Protection Association, 1 Prince's Road, Holland Park Avenue, London, established in June 1898 (see Chapter 2).
27 Information from Malcolm Jeal, citing *The Autocar*, 23 June 1900, 599.
28 *Car Illustrated*, 22 November 1905, 41. The

Motor Exchange taught its students how to maintain a car, as well as how to drive it.

29 From 1937 until 1976 the motor show was held at Earls Court, before moving to the National Exhibition Centre (NEC), Birmingham, in 1978. In 2006 the show returned to London, taking place at ExCeL in London Docklands.

30 According to Richardson and O'Gallagher 1977, 53 and 56.

31 For example, *The Times*, 22 March 1905, 11; 15 November 1906, 12.

32 Saul 1962–3, 24.

33 Collins and Stratton 1994, 69.

34 Sites in Cheltenham and Birmingham were also considered (Saul 1962–3, 29).

35 The difficulties encountered by Daimler in its first year were set out at a shareholders' meeting by Henry Sturmey in March 1897 (*The Autocar*, 13 March 1897, 171–3). On the same occasion the foundation stone of the 'works extension' was laid.

36 See, for example, *Pall Mall Gazette*, 25 February 1897, 4; 3 March 1897, 4.

37 *The Autocar*, 6 March 1897, 150–54.

38 Collins and Stratton 1994, 16. According to Saul 1962–3, 23, fifty-nine firms were making motor cars in Britain by 1900.

39 Saul has argued that it was the car manufacturers' preference for traditional engineering methods that was at fault, not the unwillingness of component makers to enter mass production (Saul 1962–3, 37).

40 Collins and Stratton 1993, 11; Collins and Stratton 1994, 67.

41 *The Autocar*, 9 January 1897, 19. The Great Horseless Carriage Co. evidently made bodies, frames and wheels, as did its successor, the Motor Car Co.. In 1901 its department for making wheels and carriage bodies occupied the top floor of the Mill, while painting and upholstery were located on the second floor (*The Observer*, 30 June 1901, 7).

42 *The Times*, 11 July 1907, 11, with an account of the Napier factory.

43 For Napier, see Collins and Stratton 1993, 127; for Austin, see Richardson and O'Gallagher 1977, 116; and for Daimler, see *Car Illustrated*, 9 May 1906, 364; Nicholson 1982, 470.

44 *Motor Trader*, 25 April 1906, 152.

45 *Car Illustrated*, 18 March 1908, 197; *Motor Trader*, 18 March 1908, 680; *The Motor*, 17 March 1908, 188–90; *Car Illustrated*, 7 August 1912, 425–6.

46 Saul 1962–3, 23.

47 *The Times*, 16 November 1905, 10.

48 Collins and Stratton 1993, 165.

49 Hildebrand 1974, 27–43; Collins and Stratton 1993, 43.

50 *The Autocar*, 22 March 1902, 304; Wood 2010, 14 (with elevation drawing of the new building).

51 Collins and Stratton 1993, 235. Both the Dennis and Star factories have been listed, Grade II.

52 *Motoring Illustrated*, 19 April 1902, 168–70. This factory was demolished *circa* 2007.

53 Collins and Stratton 1993, 38, illus.

54 Buchanan 1958, 43.

55 Nixon 1949, 43. The Wolseley Sheep-Shearing Machine Co. had come under the Vickers umbrella, and this new company was formed in 1901.

56 Working in Australia, Austin began to manufacture parts for the Wolseley Sheep-Shearing Machine Co., then joined the company in 1892 as a manager. A year later he returned home to England as manager of the Wolseley operation, with a factory on Broad Street, Birmingham. Because of the difficulties in obtaining high-quality parts from suppliers, he brought all manufacturing in-house, with a new factory, the Sydney Works, Alma Street, Aston, in 1895. The firm manufactured items other than sheep shears, including bicycles.

57 Another noteworthy survival comprises the extensions to Lanchester's factory at Armourer Mills, Sparkbrook, Birmingham, begun in 1911 and designed by J. L. Ball.

58 Morriss 2005, 220–22.

59 *Cooper's Vehicle Journal* [Special Institute Number], 1911, 27; *Automobile Engineer*, 13 August 1914, 244.

60 A technique borrowed from railway works.

61 Rolls-Royce had started in Manchester in 1904 and produced the Silver Ghost from 1906.

62 Taking a different approach, Rover bought the coachbuilder Hawkins & Peake in 1907 (Thoms and Donnelly 1985, 49).

63 Collins and Stratton 1993, 194.

64 *The Motor*, 16 January 1906, n. p. Austin made similar claims; see Church 1979, 24.

65 *The Motor*, 16 January 1906, n. p.

66 *Motor Trader*, 18 March 1908, 684.

67 *Car Illustrated*, 7 August 1912, 425.

68 In 1905 it was claimed that 'comparatively few drivers are turned out of our motor factories, for the simple reason that it is a risky and often expensive thing to train a novice in a haphazard way, such as must obtain in any factory where the testing of cars is the work of a small number of skilled drivers who are not at all anxious to see others coming into their sphere' (*Motor Trader*, 1 August 1905, 356).

69 *Motor Trader*, 20 December 1911, 964.

70 *Cooper's Vehicle Journal* [Special Institute Number], 1911, 27.

71 Collins and Stratton 1993, 183.

72 Fraser and Kerr 2007, 74. See also Morriss 2005, 222; Parkinson-Bailey 2000, 128.

73 *Journal of the Royal Institute of British Architects*, 21 February 1938, 410 (obituary of Charles Heathcote).

74 Nevins 1954, 408.

75 Nevins 1954, 452–3.

76 Collins and Stratton 1993, 21–2.

77 Hildebrand 1974, 51, 91.

78 *The Autocar*, 13 March 1897, 174.

79 See tirade on this issue in *The Motor*, 16 January 1906, n. p.

80 *Car Illustrated*, 8 April 1908, 308.

81 Nicholson 1982, 370; Walker 2007, 175.

82 Walker 2007, 147; *Coach Builders', Wheelwrights' & Motor Car Manufacturers' Art Journal*, May 1907, 127.

83 *The Times*, 5 May 1913, 4.

84 Thorold 2003, 75.

85 *Motor Trader*, 29 March 1911, 695–9.

86 *Motor Trader*, 10 May 1911, 289–90; 29 November 1911, 773–7; *Car Illustrated*, 26 June 1912, 227–8.

87 G. F. Milnes & Co. had manufactured some private cars at the Castle Car Works from 1901 to 1902. For an illustration of this factory, see Ware 1976, fig. 13.

88 The pneumatic tyre was invented by R. W. Thompson in 1843, and reinvented by J. B. Dunlop in 1888, while the first detachable pneumatic tyre was introduced by Michelin. Replacing solid rubber tyres, these vastly improved the design of the bicycle, and then the motor car, quickly becoming standard.

89 The Alma Street factory was built in 1894 for Singer and acquired in 1896 by Dunlop. The Manor Rubber Mills at Aston Cross was bought by Harvey Du Cros's Rubber Tyre Manufacturing Co. Ltd (purchased by Dunlop, 1901) in 1896 (*The Times*, 13 June 1896, 8). For Fort Dunlop, see *The Times*, 2 December 1919, 23.

90 Gibbings also designed London car parks (see Chapter 6) and was probably related to Du Cros, whose second wife was named Florence Gibbings.

91 Church 1979, 43.

92 Bardsley and Corke 2006, 34.

93 Collins and Stratton 1993, 25.

94 Richardson and O'Gallagher 1977, 105; Thoms and Donnelly 2000, 76.

95 A former military vehicle dump at Slough became the second industrial estate of any significance in England after the First World War. This was preceded by Trafford Park and followed by Park Royal and Wembley.

96 *Light Car and Cyclecar*, 25 March 1927, 467.

97 For example, through the article 'Secret of the Ford Output', *The Motor*, 19 May 1920, 721.

98 Wood 2001, 9; *The Motor*, 11 February 1920, 87–8.

99 *The Motor*, 26 January 1921, 1303. By 1927 Standard had installed chain-driven chassis lines in this shed (Collins and Stratton 1993, fig. on p. 20).

100 Church 1979, 117.

101 Church 1979, 48–9.

102 Engelbach 1927–8, 508.

103 *The Autocar*, 22 March 1929, 572–6.

104 *Motor Trader*, 2 November 1927, 157–8.

105 *The Autocar*, 8 July 1932, 83–8; Fraser and Kerr 2007, 111–12.

106 Skinner 1997, 251–3. Ford absorbed Briggs Motor Bodies Ltd in 1953, and the Kelsey-Hayes Wheel Co. in 1947.

107 *Automobile Engineer*, October 1934, 359–65; *The Motor*, 3 July 1934, 955.

108 Richardson and O'Gallagher 1977, 116.

109 Priestley 1997, 73.

110 *The Motor*, 14 November 1933, 809; *Motor Trader*, 15 November 1933, 237.

111 Fraser and Kerr 2007, 109.

112 Priestley 1997, 20.

113 For John Charles & Co., see *The Autocar*, 26 January 1934, 150; *Motor Trader*, 26 June 1935, 353. The factory was converted into an Alvis service station when John Charles relocated in 1934, shortly before going out of business (Walker 2007, 93–4). For the Firestone Tyre & Rubber Co., see Skinner 1997, 114–28.

114 Buchanan 1958, 47.

115 Collins and Stratton 1993, 27.

116 Collins and Stratton 1993, 27, with illustration.

117 Collins and Stratton 1993, 28 and 64.

118 *The Times*, 9 December 1948, 2; 17 June 1949, 2.

119 Collins and Stratton 1993, 28.

120 'Assembly at Cowley', n. d. (factory tour brochure, *circa* 1959).

121 *Architects' Journal*, 17 April 1952, 489–92.

122 *The Times*, 11 December 1956, 3.

123 For example, at Ford Rouge, begun in 1916, and more recently at the Chevrolet plant at Baltimore, completed in 1937 (Hildebrand 1974, 93ff; Collins and Stratton 1993, 49).

124 Harry Weedon & Partners also designed factories for Rootes and Pressed Steel, both at Linwood, Scotland, 1960, and BMC's factory at Bathgate.

125 Weedon had also designed the Collier Filling Station at Sheldon, Birmingham, in 1936 (Jeremiah 2004, 178–9, fig. 102). This was a circular filling station with a snack bar.

126 *The Motor*, 11 April 1962, 345. Issigonis briefly left BMC for Alvis, 1952–5.

127 Collins and Stratton 1993, 122–3.

128 Collins and Stratton 1993, 229.

129 Collins and Stratton 1993, 30.

130 *The Motor*, 20 November 1957, 634–5. This had the earliest flyover junction in Bedfordshire.

131 Midland-based manufacturers such as Jaguar and Aston Martin are said to have tested their high-performance cars on the M1 until the 70mph speed limit was introduced in 1965 (Moran 2009, 175).

132 *The Times*, 15 October 1969, x.

133 *The Times*, 9 December 1969, 17.

134 *The Times*, 5 September 1980, 1.

135 Collins and Stratton 1993, 80.

136 Thoms and Donnelly 2000, 11.

137 In 2010 Jaguar Land Rover announced heavy investment in research to develop new models at its British design centres, at Whitley and Gaydon, in 2010–15 (*Sunday Times*, 4 April 2010, Business section, 3).

138 As well as those mentioned in the text: Bentley, now owned by Volkswagen, which – with its Mulliner Park Ward subdivision – occupies the former shadow factory at Crewe; Caterham (as its name implies, at Caterham), Lotus (at Hethel, Norfolk) and Morgan (at Malvern, Worcestershire).

139 *The Times*, 23 January 1912, 12; 1 June 1912, 6.

140 *The Times*, 13 March 1914, 12.

141 Brittain-Catlin 2010, 99.

2: SELLING CARS

1 Morrison 2006, 291.

2 Hobhouse 1976, 188–9.

3 *Pall Mall Gazette*, 12 November 1896, 4; *The Times*, 18 November 1896, 13.

4 Building Control Plans, Tyne & Wear Archive Service T186/1738, dated 12 March 1897.

5 *Automotor Journal*, 17 March 1897, 225. J. D. Rootes and Cuthbert Venables were threatened with legal action by Harry Lawson's British Motor Syndicate in 1897 for patent infringement.

6 In December 1895 L'Hollier received a summons for driving a 'locomotive' that was not preceded, at a distance of at least 20 yards, by a person on foot; he was fined 1s. plus costs (*The Autocar*, 8 February 1896, 176–8). In August 1896 L'Hollier Gascoine & Co. and Emile Roger & Co. were taken over by the Anglo-French Motor Carriage Co. (*Bristol Mercury*, 10 August 1896, 4; *Pall Mall Gazette*, 10 August 1896, 5). Gascoine was retained as a manager, and the works moved to Digbeth. The company was liquidated in 1899.

7 *The Times*, 26 June 1896, 4; *Freeman's Journal*, 26 June 1896, n. p. Charles Friswell & Co., cycle manufacturers and salesmen, was established at 97 Newgate Street in 1893. In 1896 the company had another two premises, a shop at 3 Holborn Viaduct (in the London Cycle Mart) and a repair depot at 19–20 Old Bailey. By 1899 the main shop was Friswell's 'Elite Cycles' at 18 Holborn Viaduct, which was lined by French cycling posters, and stocked Mors, Benz and de Dion cars (*The Autocar*, 18 February 1899, n. p.).

8 *British Medical Journal*, 16 May 1896, 1211.

9 Edge 1934, 22–3. Lawson's offices and the Motor Car Club were based at 40 Holborn Viaduct.

10 *The Autocar*, 25 July 1896, 458.

11 *The Standard*, 17 December 1897, 5.

12 They had previously run the 'Motor Car Emporium' from the same address (information from Malcolm Jeal). See *Automotor Journal*, July 1898, 388.

13 *The Autocar*, 24 February 1900, 197.

14 *The Autocar*, 16 March 1901, 256. Friswell had sold the stock of the Automobile Association Ltd 'by order of the liquidator' in February 1901 (*The Autocar*, 2 February 1901, 28, advertisement).

15 *The Times*, 22 April 1903, 2.

16 Andrew Minney, 'The Cars and Career of Daniel Weigel', *Aspects of Motoring History*, vol. 6 (2010), 16.

17 Edge 1934, 69.

18 For Perry's early career, see Nevins 1954, 358–9. For an illustration of Perry's agency, at 117 Long Acre, see *Motor Trader*, 26 June 1907, 782. Initially called the American Motor Car Co., Perry's agency was renamed the Central Motor Car Co. in 1905.

19 The shop and shopfront survive. For an obituary of Gordon Stewart, see *The Times*, 23 January 1952, 6.

20 *Motoring Illustrated*, 2 August 1902, 226.

21 *The Motor*, 11 March 1913, 274.

22 Saul 1962–3, 39.

23 O'Connell 1998, 16.

24 *Car Illustrated*, 7 June 1905, xii; *Motorist and Traveller*, 21 June 1905, 800.

25 *Motor Trader*, 3 November 1909, 236; Nevins 1954, 362. By 1910 more than sixty subdealers were selling Ford cars under Perry's management (Nevins 1954, 362).

26 *Automotor Journal*, 16 March 1907, 372. Rover established its repair garage on Theobald's Road.

27 *Car Illustrated*, 1 May 1907, 501.

28 *Car Illustrated*, 12 June 1907, 179.

29 See, for example, an illustration of Jarrott & Lett's showroom at 45 Great Marlborough Street (which sold De Dietrich cars), with a lift in action (*Car Illustrated*, 23 May 1906, xxi).

30 *Motor Trader*, 1 July 1908, 17–18.

31 *The Motor*, 16 June 1908, 572.

32 *The Autocar*, 7 April 1900, 331.

33 *Car Illustrated*, 11 October 1905, 252; *The Autocar*, 25 November 1905, lvii.

34 *Car Illustrated*, 23 January 1907, 509; *Motor Trader*, 23 January 1923, 204; *Automotor Journal*, 26 January 1907, 116. Edge had contracted with Napier for three cars to be sold through his Motor Vehicle Company in 1900; 396 had been supplied by 1904 (Richardson and O'Gallagher 1977, 38).

35 *Motor Trader*, 29 June 1927, 361.

36 *The Autocar*, 25 November 1905, lvii; *Car Illustrated*, 20 September 1911, 171; *The Builder*, 4 October 1912, 393–4.

37 *Car Illustrated*, 9 October 1912, 289. For Austin's campaign for the home market, see Jeremiah 2007, 151.

38 List Description 901–1/2/686.

39 *Motor Trader*, 31 October 1906, 224–5; 21 November 1906, 412.

40 *Motor Trader*, 28 March 1928, 360. This building survives, known as Lightbox.

41 In addition, Rosebery Buildings, 89–91 John Bright Street, is sometimes cited as an early car showroom or factory. It was built *circa* 1902 and was later occupied by the Mobile Motor & Engineering Co. Ltd and Heron Motor Co. Ltd.

42 *Motor Trader*, 1 February 1911, 242.

43 *Building News*, 28 February 1913, 297.

44 Marshall & Tweedy designed other showrooms, for example, Watkins Ltd, St Mary Abbot's Terrace, Kensington, 1932 (*The Builder*, 8 April 1932, 638).

45 *Motor Trader*, 20 July 1910, 371.

46 *Car Illustrated*, 22 February 1911, 56.

47 Balfour 1992, 12.

48 Balfour 1992, 12 and 25; *Motor Car Journal*, 15 August 1903, 465.

49 *The Motor*, 16 June 1908, 572; *Car Illustrated*, 3 June 1908, 128. Warwick Wright obtained exclusive rights to the Vanden Plas name in England and changed the name of his associate coachbuilding firm, Théo Masui, to Vanden Plas (England) Ltd (Walker 2007, 177).

50 *Motor Trader*, 7 November 1905, 254. No. 366 was formerly occupied by Lawson.

51 *Car Illustrated*, 8 July 1914, xi.

52 Not 1893, as claimed by the firm: *Light Car and Cyclecar*, 26 September 1924, 24; *The Autocar*, 24 February 1933, 309.

53 *Motor Trader*, 10 May 1911, 309.

54 *The Motor*, 29 July 1913, 1215; *Car Illustrated*, 30 July 1913, xi.

55 *Car Illustrated*, 22 July 1914, 405.

56 *The Times*, 14 June 1906; *Car Illustrated*, 11 March 1908, 157; *The Motor*, 17 March 1908, 155; *The Motor*, 11 May 1909, lxviii; *Motor Trader*, 11 March 1911, 595–6.

57 Sir Frank Elgood was the favoured architect for the Howard de Walden estate, and carried out extensive work in Marylebone.

58 *Building News*, 21 August 1914, 242; *Car Illustrated*, 15 October 1913, xix.

59 O'Connell 1998, 49–51.

60 *Car and Golf*, February 1923, 14. Rover's building is now part of Fenwick's department store.

61 *Architects' Journal*, 4 January 1922, 58.

62 *Motor Trader*, 29 September 1926, 340; 6 October 1926, 22; *Motor Commerce*, 9 October 1926, 360.

63 *Motor Trader*, 6 October 1926, 22.

64 *Architect and Building News*, 25 April 1930, 540–43; 10 July 1931, 48–50.

65 *Motor Trader*, 18 May 1921, 233.

66 Michael Worthington-Williams, 'Warren Street and the London Motor Trade', *Aspects of Motoring History*, vol. 6 (2010), 36.

67 *The Motor*, 5 November 1929, 770.

68 *The Motor*, 14 November 1933, 809.

69 *The Autocar*, 11 May 1928, 70–71; *Architect and Building News*, 24 August 1928, 249.

70 *The Motor*, 16 April 1929, 524.

71 *The Motor*, 13 May 1924, 642.

72 *Motor Trader*, 16 February 1927, 177.

73 *Motor Commerce*, February 1930, 63.

74 *Architect and Building News*, 13 January 1928, xx.

75 *Architect and Building News*, 22 November 1929, 651.

76 *The Motor*, 9 October 1928, 486; *Architect and Building News*, 2 November 1928, 570; *Motor Trader*, 31 October 1928, 162–3. Vincent's previous showroom had two tiers of display windows.

77 *Motor Trader*, 24 July 1929, 103.

78 *Motor Trader*, 31 July 1929, 131.

79 Photographs in *Motor Commerce*, July 1931, 68–9.

80 *Motor Trader*, 2 April 1930, 17.

81 *The Times*, 18 October 1929, 11.

82 An example by Sage is H. & J. Quick, Manchester, *circa* 1926.

83 *Motor Trader*, 14 September 1927, 5.

84 *Motor Trader*, 14 September 1927, 287.

85 *Motor Trader*, 1 June 1927, 240.

86 James Edward Tuke of the Yorkshire Motor Car Co., Bradford, intended to offer motor cars on a deferred payment system in August 1897 (*The Autocar*, 28 August 1897, 552). See also advertisement for William Lea of Birkenhead in *The Autocar*, Supplement, 6 June 1903, iii: 'some of our large stock of second-hand cars can be purchased on easy terms'. In 1919 the General Motors Acceptance Corporation was set up to finance motor sales, taking the burden off individual dealers. See Genat 1999, 9.

87 O'Connell 1998, 18.

88 Church 1979, 91.

89 O'Connell 1998, 25.

90 O'Connell 1998, 26.

91 *Motor Trader*, 2 April 1930, 9; *The Builder*, 11 April 1930, 710–11; *Ford Times*, no. 66 (May 1930), 388–411.

92 Morrison 2003, 60–61; *Motor Trader*, 13 January 1932, 39.

93 *Motor Trader*, 29 January 1936, 109.

94 *Garage and Motor Agent*, 8 June 1935, 306.

95 *Garage and Motor Agent*, 20 March 1937, 1166. This was the old Western Bazaar.

96 *The Builder*, 25 January 1929, 196.

97 *The Motor*, 30 January 1923, 1230.

98 *Motor Trader*, 18 November 1925, 245.

99 *Garage and Motor Agent*, 17 September 1932, 814–16; *The Times*, 25 April 1932, 16.

100 Another garage clearly borrowing aspects of Burton's house style was Barton's in Plymouth, a Morris garage that was opened by Sir William Morris on 31 March 1931.

101 *Motor Trader*, 5 April 1933, 16.

102 *Garage and Motor Agent*, 21 March 1936, 1022.

103 For an earlier car dealership here, see *The Motor*, 1 July 1930, 63.

104 *Architects' Journal*, 19 July 1934, 85–6; 4 October 1934, 493–6; 8 August 1935, 201–3; Holme 1935, 174–5.

105 Holme 1935, 174.

106 *Architects' Journal*, 19 July 1934, 87.

107 *Motor Commerce*, November 1936, 52–3; *Garage and Motor Agent*, 18 July 1936, 648.

108 *The Motor*, 12 April 1938, 489; 22 March 1938, 342; *Garage and Motor Agent*, 9 April 1938, 1384.

109 *The Builder*, 2 August 1935, 7.

110 *Motor Commerce*, August 1936, 38.

111 *Motor Trader*, 26 May 1954, 260.

112 For example, North Midland Motors, Market Drayton, by W. H. Wainwright, using a system introduced by Coseley Buildings Ltd of Wolverhampton (*Garage and Motor Agent*, 12 March 1960, 1586).

113 *Motor Trader*, 1 July 1964, 14.

114 For Plymouth, see *The Builder*, 28 August 1959, 103–4; Stratton 1997, 120. For Northwich, see *Motor Trader*, 5 June 1963, 418.

115 *The Builder*, 3 March 1961, 400–01. Similar to this was Clifton's Service Station, Eltham, south London (1964) (*Motor Trader*, 26 February 1964, 320).

116 *Architect and Building News*, 4 February 1959, 12–13; *The Builder*, 28 August 1959, 103–4.

117 *The Builder*, 28 January 1966, 177.

118 *Motor Trader*, 22 July 1964, 138; *The Builder*, 30 October 1964, 923.

119 *Motor Trader*, 2 February 1955, 151.

120 *Motor Trader*, 27 June 1962, 376; 19 December 1962, 567.

121 Westwood and Westwood 1952, 52.

122 Examples of inclined windows include: Taylor's, Eastern Avenue, Gloucester, 1957 (*Motor Trader*, 18 December 1957, 373); Gordon Motors, Southampton Road, Portsmouth, 1958, by Ernest J. Thomas, Jolly & Grant (*The Builder*, 15 August 1958, 260; 3 March 1961, 401).

123 *Motor Trader*, 28 January 1959, 108.

124 *Motor Trader*, 15 July 1964, 102.

125 *The Builder*, 19 December 1958, 1043.

126 *Motor Trader*, 20 May 1964, 372.

127 *Motor Trader*, 17 April 1968, 131.

128 *Motor Trader*, 21 July 1965, 102.

129 *Motor Trader*, 24 January 1962, xii.

130 *Motor Trader*, 30 August 1972, 1.

131 *The Times*, 1 January 1971, 16.

132 Davies 1988, 64; Fraser and Kerr 2007, 305. Fraser and Kerr described high tech as 'a British dream of what US post-war architecture could have become' (p. 323).

133 http://www.scaramangadesign.com (accessed 4 March 2011).

134 *Observer Review*, 7 October 2007, 3.

135 http://www.ribaproductselector.com/Docs/7/12287/external/COL712287.pdf?ac (accessed 3 May 2011).

3: KEEPING THE CAR AT HOME

Part of this chapter, dealing with the pre-1914 motor house, is based on Minnis 2010.

1 *Car Illustrated*, 28 May 1902, 8.

2 *The Builder*, 15 February 1908, 175.

3 *The Autocar*, 6 June 1896, 379.

4 *The Autocar*, 7 October 1899, 897–9.

5 Salomons 1902; Minnis 2009.

6 Ellis's riverside house 'Rosenau' was burnt down in the 1930s and rebuilt as 'Woolacombe', Southlea Road, Datchet.

7 Hissey was one of the earliest writers to produce books based on motor touring, illustrated with his own photographs. The garage or 'motor car stables' is referred to as being 'the only noticeable addition' to Trevin Towers in a letter dated 7 March 1899 from Hissey to 'Bentley' (letter in collection of John Hissey, grandson of J. J. Hissey).

8 This section is based on research by Pete Smith. For fuller details, see Smith 2010.

9 Dates derived from list description.

10 *Car Illustrated*, 10 October 1906, 317–18. The article describes it as a model motor house and includes a detailed description with plans.

11 Aslet 1982, 330. *Academy Architecture*, vol. 1 (1904), 46–7, 49; *Architectural Review*, vol. 16 (August–September 1904), 80–85, 117, 122–5; *Building News*, 9 December 1904, 829.

12 'Tylney Hall: The Home of Mr Lionel Phillips' [Cars and Country Houses XXVI], *Car Illustrated*, 18 February 1903, 437.

13 This information is recorded on the surviving foundation stone.

14 *The Builder*, 23 March 1923, 480.

15 Leonard Willoughby, 'The Homes of Motorists, 1: Sandringham House', *Motorist and Traveller*, 8 February 1905, 17–18.

16 National Trust, *Great Chalfield Manor Guide Book*, 2007.

17 The first two garages were built before 1905. *Motorist and Traveller*, 22 February 1905, 90–92; 1 March 1905, 135–7. The four later garages were built before 1919.

18 Leonard Willoughby, 'Somerleyton Hall' [The Homes of Motorists], *Motorist and Traveller*, 16 December 1905, 257.

19 *Car Illustrated*, 22 October 1902, 280.

20 Redbridge Local Studies and Archives, Building Regulations Plan 2589.

21 Redbridge Local Studies and Archives, Building Regulations Plan 2918.

22 Redbridge Local Studies and Archives, Building Regulations Plan 2918A.

23 The motor house was designed by Essex, Nicol & Goodman for J. D. Prior. Birmingham City Libraries, Building Regulations Plan 1759.

24 Portable Building Co. Catalogue, n. d. [*circa* 1909].

25 *Motoring Illustrated*, 16 May 1903, 328.

26 *The Motor*, 4 March 1903, advertising supplement, n. p.

27 *Car Illustrated*, 20 December 1905, 193.

28 Jackson 1991, 108.

29 *The Builder*, 27 October 1906, 483–4; 15 February 1908, 175–83.

30 *The Builder*, 15 February 1908, 182.

31 *Motoring Illustrated*, 20 September 1902, 68.

32 *Car Illustrated*, 10 February 1909, 565–7.

33 *Car Illustrated*, 18 June 1902, 120.

34 *Car Illustrated*, 17 June 1914, 203–4.

35 *The Motor*, 23 January 1912, supplement ix. Asbestos was evidently still a novelty two years later because a garage in Warlingham, Surrey, constructed of Poilite, an asbestos material, was featured in *The Autocar* (10 January 1914, 48). Its fireproofing was somewhat compromised by the thatched roof and the panel gaps being covered by deal slats in imitation of half-timbering.

36 The requirements for cyclecars are dealt with in 'Cheaper Housing for the Cyclecar', *The Cyclecar*, 25 December 1912, 133–4.

37 *Car Illustrated*, 23 July 1913, 369.

38 'Les garages à la campagne', *La vie automobile*, 22 July 1911, 453–5; 'Private Garages and Repairs', in *Cyclopedia of Automobile Engineering*, Chicago, 1913, 211–34.

39 Goat 1989.

40 *The Motor*, 5 May 1920, 619.

41 *The Motor*, 5 May 1920, 645.

42 *The Autocar*, 3 August 1923, 186.

43 'Choosing a House', *Ideal Home*, June 1928, 509–22.

44 *Ideal Home*, March 1929, 279.

45 *The Autocar*, 3 August 1923, 187.

46 E. G. Heathcote, 'The Home Garage', *The Autocar*, 13 May 1927, 798.

47 '*Solving a Motor Problem*': Sectional Houses for Motor Cars and Motor Cycles, Boulton & Paul Ltd Catalogue A118/4, February 1925, 10–11.

48 *The Motor*, 13 December 1920, 1021–4.

49 'Housing the Car at Home', *The Autocar*, 15 May 1925, 853–6.

50 *The Autocar*, 16 January 1925, 117.

51 *The Autocar*, 23 January 1925, 139.

52 *The Motor*, 24 June 1924, 895–6.

53 *Ideal Home*, July 1935, 55.

54 *The Autocar*, 27 April 1928, 839.

55 *The Motor*, 23 October 1923, 505.

56 Jackson 1991, 108.

57 *The Motor*, 3 March 1920, 232–3; 5 February 1924, 37.

58 Barron 1929 incorporates a chapter on garages (pp. 201–6), in which he deplores 'a ghastly erection of corrugated iron . . . painted a vicious green'. Captain Barron was a journalist who contributed monthly articles, usually of a humorous or sporting nature, to the *Motor Owner* from its inception in 1919 until the mid-1920s. He then wrote for a wide variety of publications on architectural and motoring topics, much of this material being used in *The House Desirable*. For more on Barron and the context in which he was writing, see Gavin Stamp, 'Neo-Tudor and its Enemies', *Architectural History*, vol. 49 (2006), 13–14.

59 [P. A. Barron], 'Garages that Charm', *The Motor*, 24 December 1929, 1060–63.

60 P. A. Barron, 'Making the Garage Part of the Picture', *Popular Motoring*, May 1933, 18–19.

61 *Architects' Journal*, 22 April 1937, 682.

62 C. S. Watkinson, 'Measure Up Your Car!', *The Autocar*, 8 April 1938, 640–42.

63 'Why Let Your Garage be an Eyesore?', *Light Car and Cyclecar*, 1 January 1932, 154.

64 Jackson 1991, 108–10.

65 *Municipal Review*, February 1937, 54.

66 *Motor Commerce*, November 1936, 36–7.

67 'Garage Planning for the Future', *The Motor*, 19 May 1936, 691–4.

68 *The Times*, 20 April 1922; 6 June 1922.

69 *The Motor*, 13 December 1932, 891.

70 *The Autocar*, 24 June 1932, 1034.

71 Southern Railway, *Southern Homes: Surrey and Hampshire*, London, n. d. [1937].

72 Reproduced as 'The Motorist's House' in *The Autocar*, 1 November 1935, 855–9.

73 'Ideal Garages of the Future', *The Autocar*, 15 June 1934, 1010–11.

74 'The Metamorphosis of the Mews', *Architect and Building News*, 6 January 1928, 56–9.

75 'The Metamorphosis of the Mews', *Architect and Building News*, 6 January 1928, 56–9.

76 *The Builder*, 11 January 1929, 94, 95, 98 and 107.

77 'Eltham Palace, London', *Country Life*, 9 November 1995, 69.

78 Le Corbusier, *Towards a New Architecture* [1923], Oxford, 1993, 140–41.

79 Fraser and Kerr 2002, 317.

80 Yorke 1944. The second edition of 1944 includes sixteen additional houses to the first edition of 1937.

81 *Architects' Journal*, 23 November 1932, 680–82.

82 *Architect and Building News*, 17 February 1928, 251–3, 262.

83 *Architect and Building News*, 13 September 1929, 312–14.

84 *Architect and Building News*, 20 March 1931, 406–9.

85 *The Builder*, 3 December 1937, 1022–3.

86 *The Motor*, 8 March 1938, 230.

87 *Architectural Design and Construction*, 7 December 1936, 56.

88 *The Autocar*, 15 June 1934, 1011.

89 *The Builder*, 8 November 1935, 828–33.

90 *Car Illustrated*, 9 December 1908, 207.

91 Earls Court Motor Garage brochure, n.d., in the library of the Veteran Car Club of Great Britain (VCCGB).

92 *Light Car and Cyclecar*, 28 August 1925, 441.

93 *The Times*, 16 May 1924, 19.

94 *Motor Trader*, 14 August 1929, 178.

95 *The Autocar*, 18 November 1927, 1092.

96 *The Motor*, 21 May 1912, 699–700.
97 *The Motor*, 17 March 1920, 306.
98 *The Autocar*, 7 February 1920, 236.
99 *The Motor*, 28 April 1920, 611.
100 *The Autocar*, 21 November 1924, 1086.
101 *The Autocar*, 30 March 1928, 651.
102 *Motor Trader*, 27 August 1930, 224.
103 *Motor Commerce*, January 1929, 51.
104 Westminster Archives Drainage Plans, Box 1451(25).
105 Rosoman 1987; for Banbury, see *The Autocar*, 29 August 1952, 1063.
106 *The Autocar*, 4 September 1959, 152–3.
107 *The Autocar*, 4 September 1959, 152–4; *The Motor*, 29 August 1962, 144–6.
108 Ministry of Health, *Housing Manual 1949*, 38.
109 Womersley 1961.
110 Fifteenth and Sixteenth Annual Reports, Welwyn Garden City Development Corporation, 1963–4.
111 Brierley 1972, 203.
112 Gibberd et al. 1980, 173. Details of dates and architects of the various Harlow neighbourhoods are derived from this source.
113 See Simms 2006.
114 *The Times*, 17 March 2009.
115 English Partnerships, *Car Parking: What Works Where*, n. d., 14.
116 A sale at this price was recorded in 2002. *Sunday Times*, 21 April 2002, London section, 15.
117 *The Observer*, 21 April 2002, Property section, 8–9.
118 *The Times*, 11 January 1966, 11; 20 January 1966, 7; 23 November 1967, 2.
119 *The Times*, 22 February 1966, 3.
120 Royal Horticultural Society, *Gardening Matters: Front Gardens*, n. d. Official guidance is in Department for Communities and Local Government, *Guidance on the Permeable Surfacing of Front Gardens*, London, 2008; revised edition, 2009.

4: MAINTAINING THE CAR

1 *Motor Trader*, 5 June 1912, 689.
2 Sheffield Archives, Building Regulations Plan CA206/20274.
3 Douglas and Humphries 1995, 128.
4 *Motor Trader*, 24 May 1911, 401–5.
5 *Cooper's Vehicle Journal*, vol. 33 (April 1912), 69.
6 *Car Illustrated*, 24 September 1913, 227. The building is used today by Westminster City Council refuse department.
7 *Catalogue of Humber Cars, 1911*. We are indebted to John Tarring for bringing these premises to our attention.
8 *Car Illustrated*, 22 July 1914, 372–3.
9 Hitchmough 1995.
10 *Cooper's Vehicle Journal (Motor Supplement)*, vol. 32 (July 1911), 137; Cherry and Pevsner 1999, 540.

11 *The Dunmow Centenary Book, 1894–1994*, Dunmow, 1994.
12 *Garage and Motor Agent*, 21 May 1932, 136.
13 *Motor Trader*, 11 August 1926, 147.
14 *Motor Trader*, 1 January 1930, 12.
15 *Architect and Building News*, 24 August 1928, 240.
16 *Motor Trader*, 11 January 1928, 37.
17 *Motor Trader*, 4 May 1921, 133–4.
18 Judge n.d., frontispiece.
19 *Motor Trader*, 11 May 1921, 194–6.
20 *The Builder*, 22 December 1933, 986, 991, 996.
21 *The Builder*, 5 July 1929, 22, 27.
22 Stewart & Ardern Ltd brochure, n. d. [*circa* 1930].
23 *Motor Trader*, 30 November 1927, 393.
24 For the many other companies mentioned, see *Light Car and Cyclecar*, 18 March 1927, 452–4; for Daimler, see *The Motor*, 10 July 1928, 1111.
25 *The Builder*, 11 May 1923, 770.
26 For Charles Heathcote (1850–1938) and his work for Ford, see Chapter 1.
27 *The Motor*, 2 June 1920, 829–31.
28 *Motor Trader*, 11 October 1933, 69.
29 *Garage and Motor Agent*, 21 May 1938, 238, 240.
30 *Garage and Motor Agent*, 12 February 1938, 916–18.
31 *Garage and Motor Agent*, 4 March 1939, 994.
32 *Garage and Motor Agent*, 29 October 1932, 16.
33 *Garage and Motor Agent*, 9 May 1936, 120, 122; 16 October 1937, 1440, 1442.
34 *Garage and Motor Agent*, 24 July 1937, 734, 736.
35 *The Motor*, 22 March 1938, 342; 12 April 1938, 489.
36 It is significant that the garage originally had a broad canopy across the façade, believed to enable it to form the basis of a cinema if the garage failed. The present clock, lettering and windows date from a refurbishment *circa* 1999. Information from Philip Heath, Heritage and Conservation Officer, South Derbyshire District Council.
37 *Motor Trader*, 11 October 1933, 69–71.
38 *Motor Commerce*, March 1933, 38–41.
39 Brooks and Pevsner 2007, 754.
40 *Morris Owner*, October 1932, 832–3.
41 Plymouth and West Devon Record Office, Building Regulations Plan, ACL 2901 13966 pt (unlisted).
42 *Morris Owner*, February 1938, 1158.
43 *Garage and Motor Agent*, 30 November 1935, 320.
44 *Garage and Motor Agent*, 22 July 1933, 544–5.
45 The architects were Elsworth & Knighton of Exhibition Road, London SW7.
46 Advertisement, *Motor Trader*, 27 June 1934, 19.
47 *Motor Trader*, 4 August 1965, 210–11.
48 *Concrete Quarterly*, January–March 1960, 11–12.
49 *Garage*, 24 July 1965, 694–5.

5: FILLING UP

1 An account of the early years of petroleum manufacture and distribution is given in Richardson and O'Gallagher 1977, 198–224, on which this account is partly based. David Jeremiah's accounts of the early years of petrol distribution in Jeremiah 1995 and in Jeremiah 2007, 45–52, are also invaluable. Russell 2007 gives a detailed account of the development of the American filling station, together with useful commentary on brands and international developments.
2 See letter from William Leonard of Carless, Capel & Leonard: *Automotor Journal*, January 1899, 221. We are indebted to Malcolm Jeal for this reference.
3 *Automotor and Horseless Vehicle Journal*, May 1898, 315–16; April 1899, 386–8.
4 Jeremiah 2007, 47.
5 Richardson and O'Gallagher 1977, 202.
6 *Motor Trader*, 18 June 1930, 333.
7 Russell 2007, 2–3; Barty-King 1980, 135.
8 *The Autocar*, 1 November 1929, 956.
9 *Motor Trader*, 8 January 1930, 32; *Motor Commerce*, March 1930, 66–7 (photograph); Jeremiah 1995, 100.
10 Jakle and Sculle 1994, 132.
11 Barty-King 1980, 134.
12 Aldermaston cost a total of £850 and the remainder an average of £660 each. Dates of opening were as follows: Aldermaston, 2 March 1920; Coombe Hill, 21 June 1920; Mere Corner, 31 July 1920; Yarcombe, 4 August 1920; Stump Cross, 2 October 1920; Blue Boar Corner, 4 January 1921. Memos dated 5 March 1937 and 30 August 1943, AA Public Relations Department Garages file, Hampshire Record Office 73M94/G1/13/11.
13 *The Motor*, 10 March 1920, 256; 29 June 1921, 914; Barty-King 1980, 135.
14 Perspective drawings of designs with and without covered way by Forbes & Tate, 97 Jermyn Street, London SW1, survive in the AA archives, Hampshire Record Office 73M94/G1/13/11. For Percy White, see *The Motor*, 15 December 1920, 1023.
15 These details are given in a letter dated 27 October 1975 from A. F. Ward, a former AA patrolman, who had worked at the Stump Cross station. Hampshire Record Office 73M94/G1/13/11.
16 Owen John, 'On the Road', *The Autocar*, 17 July 1920, 105. Owen John Llewellyn (b. 1870) contributed regular articles under this heading on different facets of motoring from 1905 until the 1920s – see note in *Aspects of Motoring History*, vol. 6 (2010), 60.
17 *The Autocar*, 11 June 1921, 1057.
18 See Russell 2007, 94–108.
19 *The Motor*, 4 February 1920, 8.
20 Ferrier 1982, 487–8.
21 *The Autocar*, 4 March 1922, 345.
22 *The Motor*, 27 April 1921, 523; *Motor Trader*, 29 June 1921, 423.

23 *Motor Trader,* 14 July 1926, 48.

24 Ian Patience, 'A Country Garage', *The Automobile,* February 1992, 42–4.

25 *Motor Trader,* 30 June 1926, 318.

26 *The Autocar,* 11 May 1923, 790.

27 *The Autocar,* 18 May 1928, 964.

28 *Motor Trader,* 13 December 1933, 353.

29 The winning design by R. L. Gould was illustrated in *The Builder,* 12 April 1929, 689.

30 *Motor Trader,* 15 October 1930, 69; 16 March 1932, 284.

31 *Motor Trader,* 22 May 1929, 218–19; 23 July 1930, 83.

32 *Motor Trader,* 22 June 1927, 334.

33 *Motor Trader,* 23 August 1933, 201.

34 *The Builder,* 2 November 1928, 710.

35 'Beauty and the Pump', *The Autocar,* 20 March 1931, 505–6; John Dower, 'Architecture and the Filling Station', *The Motor,* 19 May 1931, 650–51; *Architect and Building News,* 6 March 1931, 348–51.

36 *The Autocar,* 6 September 1929, 461.

37 'Planning the Petrol Station: Roadside Object Lessons in a Growing Problem of Today', *Architect and Building News,* 5 October 1928, 435–8.

38 *Motor Trader,* 9 August 1933, 154.

39 *The Builder,* 28 June 1928, 1165.

40 *The Motor,* 12 April 1932, 447.

41 *The Autocar,* 1 January 1932, 7.

42 *The Builder,* 4 January 1929, 56; *Light Car and Cyclecar,* 7 February 1930, cover.

43 'Fill up here with . . .', *Architectural Review,* vol. 66 (December 1929), 273–6.

44 *Motor Trader,* 9 May 1934, 165.

45 *Motor Commerce,* May 1934, 42–3.

46 *The Autocar,* 1 September 1933, 338–9.

47 *The Autocar,* 10 July 1931, 64; McMinnies 1936, 267.

48 *The Motor,* 20 February 1934, 111.

49 Margolies 1993, 34–5.

50 *Motor Trader,* 21 August 1929, 206.

51 *The Autocar,* 4 November 1931, 1085; *Motor Commerce,* January 1932, 47.

52 *The Autocar,* 4 April 1930, 627–8.

53 *Architectural Review,* vol. 66 (December 1929), 276.

54 Design and Industries Association Annual Report, 1931. The DIA received back many letters from the garages complaining that they were not to blame; it was the large companies whose products were advertised on the enamelled signs emblazoned on their premises that were responsible.

55 Design and Industries Association, *The Village Pump: A Guide to Better Garages,* London, 1930, 2.

56 *Garage and Motor Agent,* 9 February 1935, 687.

57 *Garage and Motor Agent,* 8 April 1939, 1280.

58 The photographs are available on www.leodis.org.

59 *The Autocar,* 31 October 1930, 936; *Motor Trader,* 1 February 1933, 13.

60 Bamberg 2000, 229–30.

61 Dixon 1962, 45; Bamberg 2000, 231.

62 Ministry of Transport: Technical Committee on Petrol Stations, *Petrol Stations,* London, 1949.

63 *Architects' Journal,* 10 July 1952, 48, 36–8, 63.

64 *Architects' Journal,* 29 August 1957, 314–16, 331–7; 5 September 1957, 348–9; 8 April 1964, 821–6.

65 Shell-Mex & BP, *Service on the Way,* 1955; *The Builder,* 15 July 1955, 91–3; *Architects' Journal,* 16 June 1955, 810.

66 *Architectural Record,* September 1937, 69–72. See also Lohof 1974, which examines the filling stations of the Marathon Oil Company.

67 Bamberg 2000, 229.

68 BP New Look brochure, 1957. The work of transforming the garages began in 1958 on an experimental basis and in 1959–60 nationwide; see *BP Progress,* October 1959, 4–5.

69 Figures from the Monopolies Commission report on petrol supply, 1965, quoted in Sedgwick 1969, 5.

70 Bamberg 2000, 232.

71 The earliest of the type to be recorded was at Tewkesbury Road, Cheltenham, opened in December 1959. *BP Progress,* February 1961, 1.

72 *Motor Trader,* 6 December 1967, 609.

73 *Motor Trader,* 13 November 1968, 442.

74 *Motor Trader,* 6 November 1963, 351.

75 *Motor Trader,* 19 December 1962, 564.

76 *Motor Trader,* 28 June 1967, 622.

77 *Concrete Quarterly,* April–June 1961, 12–13.

78 *Architects' Journal,* 6 February 1958, 230.

79 *Garage and Motor Agent,* 9 January 1960, 1057–8; *The Builder,* 19 February 1960, 348–9.

80 *Motor Trader,* 9 October 1963, 68.

81 Russell 2007, 188.

82 The kiosk was designed by Bribex Ltd; *Architect and Building News,* 6 July 1966, 28; *Motor Trader,* 4 August 1965, 203.

83 *Architect and Building News,* 6 May 1964, 811–13; *Motor Trader,* 5 June 1968, 520.

84 *The Autocar,* 22 July 1927, 191.

85 *Motor Trader,* 24 April 1963, 134.

86 *Motor Trader,* 24 April 1963, 134–5.

87 *Motor Trader,* 21 August 1963, 275.

88 *Motor Trader,* 22 January 1964, 128–9.

89 *Motor Trader,* 10 June 1964, 542.

90 *Motor Trader,* 20 January 1965, 86.

91 *Motor Trader,* 20 August 1969, 294.

92 Mobil advertisement, *Motor Trader,* 10 December 1969, xv.

93 *Motor Trader,* 9 October 1968, 81.

94 *Motor Trader,* 21 June 1967, 561.

95 *Motor Trader,* 15 May 1968, 355.

96 *Motor Trader,* 4 September 1968, 399; *Service Station Manual,* eleventh edition, London, 1974, 77.

97 *Motor Trader,* 15 May 1968, 350.

98 Russell 2007, 122–4.

99 Russell 2007, 125.

100 *Motor Trader,* 20 January 1971, 6; 15 September 1971, 4.

101 *Motor Trader,* 26 May 1971, 1–2.

102 *Motor Trader,* 16 March 1966, 503.

103 *Motor Trader,* 3 December 1969, 17.

104 *Service Station Manual,* eleventh edition, 1974, 9.

105 The initial Canopus station had modular buildings at one end. A Gulf advertisement shows a station of this type: *Motor Trader,* 8 December 1971, iii.

106 *Motor Trader,* 14 February 1973, 19.

107 North Watford is described in *Architects' Journal,* 14 December 1995, 27–35.

108 *Coventry Telegraph,* March 2002.

109 www.ukpia.com (accessed 25 November 2010).

110 Giles Worsley, 'Is Banality Inevitable?', *Country Life,* 20 September 1990, 140–43.

111 *Building Design,* 10 September 2010, 1.

6: PARKING, 1896–1939

1 Edge described this as 'the old Holborn skating rink' (Edge 1934, 35).

2 Edge 1934, 31.

3 *The Autocar,* 24 October 1896, 614.

4 *Automotor and Horseless Vehicle Journal,* April 1899, 387.

5 This had stabled motor cars from 1897 (*The Autocar,* 9 October 1897, 652).

6 *Lloyd's Weekly Newspaper,* 25 November 1900, 23. It has been claimed that the first 'recognised temporary car park' was set up at the Henley Regatta in 1898 (Morriss 2005, 233).

7 According to the *Oxford English Dictionary,* the earliest occurrence of 'garage' was in January 1902, when the *Daily Mail* reported that Mr Harrington Moore had founded a 'garage' with accommodation for eighty cars (*Daily Mail,* 11 January 1902, 6–7). The term was introduced in 1900, however, and had become current by the end of 1901.

8 In 1901 the Lord Justice Clerk of Scotland suggested 'car-house' as the English equivalent to the French 'garage'. *The Autocar* attempted to introduce the word 'carage'. See *The Observer,* 10 November 1901, 3.

9 *Car Illustrated,* 28 May 1902, 8; *The Times,* 1 March 1902, 4.

10 *The Times,* 12 August 1933, 12.

11 *Car Illustrated,* 28 May 1902, 29.

12 *Automobile Club Journal,* 20 August 1903, 193–5, with illustrations. In later years this became the Universal Motor Engineering Co. (*RAC Yearbook,* 1913, 112); later still University Motors (*The Times,* 12 January 1922, 13).

13 Morriss 2005, 233; *The Times,* 1 July 1903, 18.

14 Sims 1903, 192.

15 Sims 1903, 192–3.

16 Another example was the Gracile Motor Car Co., Great Russell Street (*Car Illustrated,* 6 February 1907, 611).

17 *Motor-Car Journal* (20 June 1903), xxi; Morris 1985, 28.

18   *The Motor*, 11 May 1909, 541.
19   An advertisement of 1907 for Medway's lifts listed examples at the King's Cross Carriage Works and the Eagle Carriage Works (*Coach Builder etc.*, June 1907, 60). An advertisement of 1911 for the same lift illustrated a motor car rather than a carriage, and cited the Automobile Club, Argyll Motors, Ford Motors and the Motor House on Euston Road amongst its clientele (*Cooper's Vehicle Journal*, January 1911, xxi).
20   *Car Illustrated*, 4 May 1904, xvii. One of the first examples of a turntable in a multi-storey garage is thought to have been the three-storey, reinforced concrete Park Square Garage, Boston, of 1905 (McDonald 2007, 141–2).
21   *Car Illustrated*, 6 February 1907, 611; *Motor Trader*, 30 January 1907, 260. This garage was later replaced by a cinema on the same site. The garage seems to have been positioned behind a showroom, with accommodation for forty cars in the basement and the usual dressing rooms for customers going to the theatre. Illustrations show that the garage was an iron-and-steel structure, with jack-arch floors. Another example of a unified turntable-lift was the Iris showroom on Bird Street (*Car Illustrated*, 1 May 1907, 501).
22   The disadvantages of the lift turntables were discussed in *Motor Commerce*, August 1929, 71.
23   Jeremiah 2004, 167, illus.
24   *RAC Journal*, 21 November 1907, 568.
25   *Car Illustrated*, 4 December 1907, 147. Many electric cars were hired on annual contracts, with the supplier responsible for battery charging and maintenance.
26   Examples include the Argyll Garage and the Bryanston Garage: see *The Builder*, 15 February 1908, 181, and *The Motor*, 11 May 1909, 540, respectively.
27   Illustrated in *The Motor*, 11 May 1909, 500.
28   For the addition of the ramp, see *The Times*, 20 October 1927. For the façade at this date, see *Architect and Building News*, 17 August 1928, 213.
29   *The Motor*, 11 May 1909, 501.
30   Daimler established its hiring department in 1907 in small premises in Marylebone. The business outgrew this site, and in 1914 moved to a larger building on Store Street, where 250 cars were garaged (*Car Illustrated*, 20 May 1914, 60).
31   *The Garage*, 7 March 1914, 12.
32   One purpose-built garage opened in James Street, Kensington, in December 1905, with three floors, including accommodation for 200 cars on the ground and first floors, and private lockers and dressing rooms for ladies and gentlemen, largely for residents of the area (*The Motor*, 19 December 1905, 564).
33   Westminster Archives Drainage Plans, Box 705 (15); *Car Illustrated*, 27 August 1913, 87.

34   The ticket hall was photographed by Bedford Lemere in 1888 (NMR).
35   *Car Illustrated*, 18 June 1902, 139; 4 February 1903, 374, advertisement.
36   McDonald 2007, 14–15.
37   Nixon 1949, 62–6. Vickers, Wolseley's parent company, took over The Siddeley Co. in 1905. Siddeley's offices and showrooms were at 79–80 York Street, across the road from Niagara Hall, which was bought from the Electric Carriage Co. Wolseley's head staff were transferred here from Birmingham. In 1909, in another reorganisation, Niagara Hall became the London Sales Depot and Garage, managed by J. E. Hutton (see also Chapter 2). Like many large garages of the period, it had a sizeable hire department.
38   *RAC Journal*, 31 March 1911, 235; 8 September 1911, 185. The former RAC garage on Brick Street (run by the Motor Supply Co.) remained open to 'Associates' of the RAC.
39   *Car Illustrated*, 22 March 1911, 192.
40   *The Motor*, 28 May 1912, 731. See illustration in the *RAC Journal*, 8 September 1911, 186.
41   *The Motor*, 11 May 1909, 540–41. Each ground-floor lock-up in the Garage Ponthieu in Paris had its own lockable cupboard (*Architectural Review*, vol. 24, September 1908, 136).
42   *Car Illustrated*, 24 September 1913, 227.
43   *The Motor*, 11 May 1909, 540, with illustration on p. 539. Illustration of frontage in the *Car Illustrated*, 30 August 1911, 76.
44   *Motoring Illustrated*, 6 September 1902, 24; *Car Illustrated*, 3 September 1902, 68.
45   *The Autocar*, 22 May 1925, 899.
46   *Motoring Illustrated*, 30 August 1902, 339. According to http://www.visitworthing.co.uk/aboutworthing/blueplaques/ (accessed 9 March 2011), Warne promoted his hotel as 'the Motorists' Mecca', and the garage was demolished in 1947.
47   *Automobile Club Journal*, 22 October 1903, 402, 405.
48   Borsay 2000, 273.
49   *Car Illustrated*, 12 April 1911, 293.
50   *The Motor*, 2 October 1923, 367.
51   *Motor Trader*, 23 January 1929, 93–4.
52   London Metropolitan Archives, AR/BR/06/060122.
53   J. E. Connor, *London's Disused Underground Stations*, Harrow Weald, 2001, 68, with illustration.
54   *Municipal Review*, May 1933, 171.
55   For a plea for garages at Underground stations for commuters, see *Car and Golf*, January 1924, 3.
56   *Motor Trader*, 23 February 1927, 217; *The Autocar*, 4 February 1927, 196; Minutes of Morden Station Garage Ltd, London Metropolitan Archives, ACC/1297/MSGA.
57   Getty Images: RAI.STAT.(BRI).WELWYN K2044-M.

58   Westminster Archives Drainage Plans, Box 908 (5).
59   For an illustration of a turntable here, see *The Motor*, 9 February 1921, 85. For another illustration of the interior, see *Car and Golf*, April 1924, 24.
60   Illustrated in *Car and Golf*, August 1924, 34.
61   *The Motor*, 17 March 1920, 318; London Metropolitan Archives, COL/SVD/PL/01/2913.
62   *The Motor*, 24 June 1924, 903.
63   There were crucial differences between hydraulic and electric lifts. Hydraulic lifts were cheaper, but more expensive to operate. Installation costs (excavation for a hydraulic ram or erection of a lift cage) were on a par. Hydraulic power depended on the proximity of high-pressure water mains, whilst electricity was widely available in English towns by the 1920s. Electric lifts had at least one blind side, whilst hydraulic lifts could be accessible on all four sides (though it was expected that their exemption from the need to provide gates and guards on every floor would be terminated eventually). Electric lifts had heavy overhead gears, unlike hydraulic lifts. The choice was finely balanced: see *Motor Commerce*, August 1929, 72, which concluded that hydraulic lifts were better for connecting just two floors.
64   *The Motor*, 10 March 1925, 241. Shaw & Kilburn was formed after the First World War when the dealer Drysdale Kilburn was joined by Captain H.O.N. Shaw (Walker 2007, 171). Shaw & Kilburn was the main Vauxhall dealer for London, and an importer.
65   In 1929 *Motor Commerce* recommended lifts of 50 cwt, with a platforms 20 ft by 9 ft. *Motor Commerce*, August 1929, 70.
66   *Motor Owner*, June 1925, 26.
67   McDonald 2007, 30.
68   *Garage and Motor Agent*, 29 January 1921, 710, with illustration. The ramp had a ridged surface. Many photographs of early twentieth-century coachworks show impermanent wooden ramps – often just planks – going up to first-floor loading bays.
69   *Motor Commerce*, September 1929, 58.
70   London Metropolitan Archives, E/NOR/L/05/002, plans dated February 1922; Clerkenwell District Surveyor's Returns, February 1922 and December 1922; *The Builder*, 14 December 1923, 926–7.
71   *The Times*, 16 May 1924, 19.
72   Westminster Archives Drainage Plans, Box 309 (26).
73   The surviving turntable was manufactured by Francis Theakston and is dated 1933.
74   *The Motor*, 24 July 1922, 1060.
75   Westminster Archives Drainage Plans, Box 1086 (12); Jeremiah 2004, 173.
76   *Motor Trader*, 7 October 1925, 33; *The Motor*, 8 September 1925, 255. This provided garag-

ing as well as parking, including basement lock-ups accessed by a 'slow incline'.

77   Stated in *The Times*, 5 July 1928, 24. The Lex Garage built in Bayswater in 1930 also followed this house style (see *Motor Trader*, 5 February 1930, 154).

78   *The Times*, 5 July 1928, 24; *Architect and Building News*, 21 June 1929, 819–21; *Motor Trader*, 12 June 1929, 308.

79   *The Times*, 12 March 1929, xxvii.

80   H. E. Meacock, 'Off-Street Parking', *Journal of the Institution of Highway Engineers*, vol. 55 (October 1958), 275.

81   Westminster Archives Drainage Plans, Box 841 (13).

82   *Architecture*, May 1928, 76–7.

83   *The Motor*, 22 April 1924, 490.

84   *The Motor*, 9 October 1929, 486, with illustration of ramps.

85   *The Builder*, 22 June 1928, 1057; *RIBA Journal*, 27 April 1929, 492. A competition for a petrol-station design was announced at the prize-giving ceremony. Another competition was held for a City Garage in connection with the Manchester Building Exhibition in 1931 (*The Builder*, 1 May 1931, 805).

86   *Architect and Building News*, 12 April 1929, 478–81; *Architects' Journal*, 24 April 1929, 652. The winner of the 1928 RIBA competition adopted a staggered floor with 'tandem' ramps, a variation on the straight-run system.

87   Also moderne was the 'Large Public Garage' designed by architectural student A. L. McMullen and published in February 1929, some months before the results of the RIBA competition were announced (*The Builder*, 8 February 1929, 286, 297). A more audacious vertical Art Deco design with close-set projecting fins was produced by Mewès & Davis for a site on the corner of Rossmore Road and Park Road, London (i.e., at the top of Gloucester Place), in 1931; it was never built, but the block of flats on the site incorporates a corner petrol filling station: see Chapter 3.

88   *The Times*, 23 March 1929, 19; *The Motor*, 26 March 1929, 398; *Architect and Building News*, 12 April 1929, 475–94; Westminster Archives Drainage Plans, Box 741 (1).

89   McDonald 2007, 31–2, 222; Mary Beth Klatt, 'Car Culture', *Preservation Online*, National Trust for Historic Preservation, 1.

90   *The Autocar*, 18 November 1927, 1092.

91   *Architect and Building News*, 21 August 1931, 209–12. The garage stored Daimler-owned cars on the upper floor, and had a basement car park for privately owned cars.

92   *The Motor*, 9 December 1930, 965.

93   *Architect and Building News*, 9 June 1939, 266. This was Sir Owen Williams's only significant pre-war parking garage, other than the Cumberland Garage.

94   McDonald 2007, 21.

95   A speech by the Director-General of Roads, reported in the *Garage and Motor Agent*, 28 November 1925, 284.

96   *Motor Trader*, 19 March 1930, 314.

97   Thorold 2003, 106–7.

98   *The Autocar*, 17 April 1920, 721.

99   *Blackpool Gazette and Herald, Fylde News and Advertiser*, 10 March 1928, 14.

100 *Blackpool Gazette and Herald, Fylde News and Advertiser*, 24 July 1928, 12.

101 *Blackpool Gazette and Herald, Fylde News and Advertiser*, 7 May 1932, 5.

102 *Motor Trader*, 23 May 1934, 225.

103 Tyne & Wear Archives Service T186/A3161. Information from Grace McCombie.

104 *Architects' Journal*, 15 June 1932, 801; *Motor Trader*, 23 March 1932, 332. For a slightly earlier development by Seal & Hardy, just down the road from Motor Mac's, see Jeremiah 2004, 180.

105 J. Drake, 'Municipal Works of Blackpool', 66th Annual Meeting of the Institution of Municipal and County Engineers, Blackpool, 15–17 June 1939, 34–6.

106 Armando Silvestri, 'Le garage à étages de Venise', *La technique des travaux*, June 1936, 305–11.

107 *Architect and Building News*, 12 August 1932, 189.

108 Lift garages were still being built, for example, the City of London garage on Wilson Street, Finsbury Square (1932, with five floors served by two lifts; *Garage and Motor Agent*, 10 December 1932, 305).

109 *Architects' Journal*, 13 December 1934, 879–83, 887–8; *Architect and Building News*, 14 December 1934, 329–33; *Garage and Motor Agent*, 9 February 1935, 666; *Architectural Record*, February 1935, 98–100; Lydia Wilson, 'Cumberland Garage', Report by The Architectural History Practice Ltd, 2005. It has been claimed that the Cumberland Garage was 'the first split-level parking garage structure in the world', and the design has been assessed as being 'without precedent' (Stamp 1986, 22 and 166). The precise basis of these claims is unclear.

110 *The Builder*, 31 October 1937, 1197–9.

111 *Architect and Building News*, 6 January 1939, 17–20. This survives intact.

112 *Motor Trader*, 11 January 1933, 40; *Architectural Design and Construction News*, November 1937, 523; *The Builder*, 18 June 1937, 1280.

113 Information from Peter Guillery, to be published in the forthcoming Survey of London volume on Woolwich.

114 *Garage and Motor Agent*, 2 February 1935, 620.

115 Photograph dated 1958 in Getty Archive; Westminster Archives Drainage Plans, Box 1086 (14).

116 *Garage and Motor Agent*, 18 March 1933, 902–4; 25 March 1933, 950–51.

117 *The Times*, 20 September 1938, 10.

118 Other examples included Arlington House, next to the Ritz Hotel (1936), and Dorset House, Marylebone Road (T. P. Bennett with Joseph Emberton, 1936).

119 This was published in *The Builder*, ARP Supplement, 24 February 1939, xvi.

120 *The Motor*, 16 March 1921, 301.

121 See, for example, *The Times*, 11 March 1926, 20; 30 August 1929, 8.

122 *Motor Owner*, May 1922, 26.

123 *Motor Trader*, 2 April 1924, 7.

124 This led to the creation of the London and Home Counties Traffic Advisory Committee.

125 'Report on Parking Places', London and Home Counties Traffic Advisory Committee, Ministry of Transport, 1927 (chairman: Henry P. Maybury), 7.

126 Hansard HC Deb, 20 April 1932, vol. 264, CC1458–60: http://hansard.millbanksystems.com/commons/1932/apr/20/parked-cars-locking#S5CV0264P0_19320420_HOC_45 (accessed 10 March 2011).

127 *The Times*, 25 May 1925, 17; *The Motor*, 21 March 1933, 256; *The Motor*, 23 June 1925, 963. Harrods aped Debenham's innovation in April 1926, advertising 'a large, covered enclosure, providing free accommodation for 150 cars', near the store (*The Times*, 26 April 1926, 11). Debenhams Ltd had acquired Marshall & Snelgrove in 1919. The stores were located close to one another (Wigmore Street and Oxford Street respectively).

128 *The Times*, 9 March 1926, 24.

129 Jakle and Sculle 2004, 48.

130 *The Motor*, 13 October 1920, 483.

131 *Blackpool Gazette and Herald, Fylde News and Advertiser*, 19 May 1921, 7.

132 *Light Car and Cyclecar*, 18 March 1932, 474.

133 Walton 2000, 80.

134 *Light Car and Cyclecar*, 8 January 1932, 173. This was followed by a car park at the Orpheum Theatre in 1932.

135 *Garage and Motor Agent*, 18 March 1933, 918; 10 June 1933, 297.

136 *Light Car and Cyclecar*, 4 March 1932, 415.

137 *The Motor*, 6 July 1937, 1024.

138 *Motor Trader*, 9 January 1924, 48.

139 *The Autocar*, 4 July 1924, 37. This patent was not granted.

140 *Motor Trader*, 17 April 1929, 74.

141 *Motor Commerce*, May 1929, 48–9.

142 *Architect and Building News*, 23 March 1928, 445; 31 August 1928, 1.

143 *The Autocar*, 18 July 1930, 140.

144 *Motor Trader*, 6 April 1932, 13; *The Autocar*, 16 November 1934, 961. In 1934 a working model was displayed at the Building Centre Ltd, 158 New Bond Street. Another American system, the Car-Rak, was published in *The Autocar*, 25 November 1932, 1031.

145 McDonald 2007, 115–16.

146 *The Autocar*, 18 January 1935, 82.

147 *The Motor*, 26 July 1932, 1063.

148 McDonald 2007, 163.

149 *The Times*, 14 April 1925, 8; *The Autocar*, 10 April 1925, 653.

150 *Garage and Motor Agent*, 18 March 1933, 903.

151 *The Autocar*, 27 December 1929, 1367; *Light Car and Cyclecar*, 4 December 1931, 32; *Municipal Review*, January 1932, 3; *The Autocar*, 8 February 1935, 198.

152 *Municipal Review*, July 1936, 259–60.

153 Information from Clare Hartwell.

154 *Blackpool Gazette and Herald, Fylde News and Advertiser*, 20 October 1934, 24.

155 *Municipal Review*, March 1937, 102.

156 *Light Car and Cyclecar*, 23 December 1932, 116.

157 *Architects' Journal*, 15 October 1930, 580–82.

158 *The Autocar*, 15 June 1934, 1011. This was bombed during the Second World War and rebuilt along original lines.

159 *The Autocar*, 1 June 1934, 924–5

160 *The Times*, 15 November 1935, 13.

161 *The Autocar*, 8 February 1935, 198.

162 *Evening News*, 29 March 1935, n. p.

163 *Architects' Journal*, 11 July 1935, 37.

164 McDonald 2007, 117.

165 *The Motor*, 7 February 1939, 28.

166 *The Builder*, 6 January 1939, 8–9.

167 *The Autocar*, 10 February 1939, 236; Coe and Reading 1981, 162–8.

168 *L'Illustration*, 9 March 1929.

169 *The Times*, 8 June 1937, 18; *The Builder*, 21 October 1938, 794–5.

170 *The Builder*, 12 April 1940, 449. Further information from Allan Adams.

7: PARKING SINCE 1945

1 *The Builder*, 11 January 1946, 57. By the late 1960s such stipulations – which varied between different local authorities – were falling out of favour, since they encouraged urban car use.

2 *The Times*, 3 August 1946, 5; 'Report on the Road Fund for 1946–47', Ministry of Transport, 1948, 9; 'Report on the Road Fund for 1947–48', Ministry of Transport, 1949, 11. Most sites were gradually handed back to their owners.

3 The National Archives, MT 95/121; *Daily Telegraph*, 18 June 1958.

4 Jakle and Sculle 2004, 36.

5 *The Times*, 26 June 1956, 9.

6 For the Samuels Report on parking in Paris, see *The Times*, 31 January 1958, 8.

7 *Parking – The Next Stage: A New Look at London's Parking Problem*, HMSO, London, 1963.

8 This had risen to 8,500 by 1967, and the revenue had financed six public garages, with arrangements in hand for another eight.

9 For the 'Pink Zone' experiment in enforcing parking regulations at Christmas 1959, see Starkie 1982, 22–3.

10 *Municipal Review*, September 1965, 528. By 1963 Bristol had been followed by Manchester, Southend, Brighton and Birmingham.

11 By 1963 Woolwich had been followed by Croydon (October 1961) and Kingston upon Thames (October 1962).

12 *The Times*, 20 March 1965, 14.

13 Brierley 1972, 7.

14 *The Times*, 18 October 1957, 5.

15 Only a semblance of control: nationally, 89 per cent of car commuters parked free of charge at or near their place of work in 1964 (Tetlow and Goss 1968, 72).

16 *The Builder*, 11 January 1946, 57.

17 This was the Cage Garage, Boston, Massachusetts, built in 1933 and demolished in 1985 (Kitching 1957, 2; McDonald 2007, 39–40 and 139).

18 *The Times*, 16 March 1955, 4 (submission for planning permission); *Concrete Quarterly*, April–June 1959, 2–4; *Garage and Motor Agent*, 2 July 1960, 838–40.

19 *Official Architecture and Planning*, May 1961, 229; *The Builder*, 28 February 1964, 439–40.

20 One was built in Detroit in 2003.

21 *Architectural Review*, vol. 134 (August 1963), 86–90. Klose 1965, 222–3: 'It is doubtful whether this rather laborious system . . . will have much of a future.'

22 *The Builder*, 10 November 1961, 860–61; Klose 1965, 128–31; *The Motor*, 26 July 1961, n. p.

23 *The Builder*, 28 December 1962, 1249–50. Forty had prepared plans for the City of London during the Second World War. These featured a ring road within the City boundary, with roundabouts at junctions. After the war, a different plan was drafted by consultants C. H. Holden and W. G. Holford, who included through routes and dropped Forty's ring road except for a 'Northern Boundary Route' (Buchanan 1970, 34).

24 For Moor Street, Birmingham, see *The Builder*, 16 September 1955, 468; 7 October 1955, 592. For Exeter, see *Official Architecture and Planning*, February 1960, 177.

25 Lewison and Billingham 1969, 42.

26 *The Builder*, 8 April 1960, 694–6; Klose 1965, 207–11.

27 *The Motor*, 20 September 1961, 254.

28 At one time it was suggested, erroneously, that this was the oldest MSCP in Britain (Hudson 1983, 79).

29 *The Builder*, 17 March 1961, 521; *Municipal Review*, May 1961, 316–17 and 331.

30 *Motor Trader*, 1 April 1964, 29; Brierley 1972, 209; *The Times*, 10 June 1965, 9. While the 'Tempark' was a MSCP with level floors accessed by straight, external, superimposed ramps, the 'Wheelwright Arch' had three superimposed arching floors that could be entered from ground level.

31 *The Builder*, 18 September 1964, 587.

32 The Yield Hall car park (Manning & Clamp, with Jan Bobrowski & Partners) opened in 1967. The same design was used for a second car park in Reading, on Chatham Street, which opened in 1969 (*Building*, 7 April 1967, 95; *Municipal Review*, February 1969, 68–70).

33 For Pydar Street, Truro, see Henley 2007, 89.

34 *Municipal Review*, August 1969, 380.

35 *Concrete Quarterly*, January–March 1961, 16–17; *Official Architecture and Planning*, May 1961, 227.

36 *Municipal Review*, November 1969, 546.

37 *Municipal Review*, February 1968, 69.

38 *Municipal Review*, May 1969, 227.

39 For example, *The Builder*, 25 January 1929, 190.

40 McDonald 2007, 35.

41 *The Builder*, 16 December 1960, 1106–9; *Concrete Quarterly*, October–December 1960, 23–4; Klose 1965, 152–4.

42 A circular continuous ramp garage designed by Maurice H. J. Bebb was proposed for a site in Hemel Hempstead in 1962 but was never built (*The Builder*, 19 June 1962, 1338).

43 *Architects' Journal*, 24 March 1960, 467; Klose 1965, 154.

44 *Architects' Journal*, 18 January 1967, 187.

45 *The Times*, 26 October 1970, 14.

46 Klose 1965, 244–7; Henley 2007, 13; McDonald 2007, 71–6.

47 *The Builder*, 26 August 1960, 384; *The Motor*, 20 September 1961, 254.

48 *Municipal Review*, May 1968, 224; February 1969, 72–3.

49 *Municipal Review*, February 1966, 88–90; Brierley 1972, 174.

50 In 1966 a second car park was built on Church Street, Watford (*Municipal Review*, February 1967, 94). This also had ramped floors and a projecting rapid-exit ramp. Two more car parks of similar type were later built at Sutton Road (1971, by the Borough Engineer, R. H. Brand, with Holst & Co.) and on Beechen Road.

51 Henley 2007, 42.

52 The first in the world, according to the *Municipal Review*, April 1970, 171.

53 *The Builder*, 11 January 1946, 57.

54 A prototype was in operation at Fraser & Chalmers Engineering Works, Erith, in 1947 (The National Archives, MT 95/121, extract from *The Engineer*, 31 January 1947). A sleeker, electrical version of this, the Plymoth Plate, was taken up in Germany and Scandinavia, but not in England: see Brierley 1972, 218–19.

55 *The Builder*, 22 February 1946, 187.

56 *The Builder*, 9 November 1956, 796–7.

57 Brierley 1972, 220–21. This was rebuilt in 2007.

58 Brierley 1972, 226–7.

59 *The Times*, 10 June 1965, 9.

60 Brierley 1972, 216.

61 McDonald 2007, 123.

62 *The Builder*, 16 September 1955, 468; 5 April 1957, 628–9; Brierley 1972, 219–20.

63 Illustration: H. E. Meacock, 'Off-Street Parking', *Journal of the Institution of Highway*

Engineers, vol. 55 (October 1958), 281. For an account of the Zidpark, see Klose 1965, 74–5.

64 *The Builder*, 15 February 1957, 322.
65 *The Times*, 5 April 1957, 7; Klose 1965, 76–7.
66 *Interbuild*, December 1959, 8; *The Times*, 12 February 1960, 6.
67 For Bristol, see *Motor Trader*, 19 February 1958, 212. For Liverpool, see *Architects' Journal*, 11 July 1962, 111.
68 *Impulse*, December 1957, 31–3; *Interbuild*, December 1959, 9.
69 *The Builder*, 1 February 1963, 227–30; *Surveyor and Municipal and County Engineer*, vol. 119, no. 3530 (30 January 1960), 110–11. Parcar was owned jointly by Mitchell Engineering Ltd and the Unit Construction Co. Ltd.
70 *Building*, 21 July 1967, 97–9.
71 For the Burlington Garage, see *The Builder*, 21 January 1966, 116–20. For Rochester Row Car Park, see *Building*, 8 November 1968, 111–14; Brierley 1972, 221–3.
72 *Concrete Quarterly*, July–September 1970, 15.
73 *Yorkshire Evening Post*, 31 March 1970, 7.
74 *The Times*, 13 March 1953, 4.
75 McDonald 2007, 166.
76 *The Times*, 13 March 1953, 4.
77 *The Builder*, 20 March 1953, 442; *The Motor*, 8 April 1953, 316–17. Grey Wornum presented alternatives: a car park for 700 cars that would involve felling the trees, and one for 420 cars that would save some trees.
78 *The Times*, 24 June 1954, 6.
79 *The Times*, 26 September 1957, 6; 24 March 1959, 7; 8 July 1959, 4.
80 *The Times*, 30 May 1959, 10.
81 Klose 1965, 172–3.
82 The National Archives, MT 113/39.
83 *The Builder*, 26 October 1962, 819–21; Klose 1965, 182–3; Westminster Archives Drainage Plans, 2/796/1.
84 *Municipal Review*, March 1966, 134–5; July 1967, 386; Brierley 1972, 232–3.
85 *The Builder*, 11 December 1964, 1255; *Architects' Journal*, 26 July 1972, 199.
86 Henley 2007, 171–3.
87 McDonald 2007, 63.
88 *The Builder*, 21 November 1958, 872.
89 Kitching 1957, 3; *Concrete Quarterly*, January-March 1959, 16–17; *The Times*, 17 September 1957, 7.
90 *Municipal Review*, July 1965, 408.
91 *Building*, 5 January 1968, 80–81.
92 *Building*, 5 January 1968, 80–81; Brierley 1972, 199–201.
93 *Architects' Journal Information Library*, 6 May 1970, 1129–41.
94 *Architects' Journal*, 15 October 1930, 580.
95 Burt and Grady 1994, 234.
96 Tetlow and Goss 1968, 208.
97 *Yorkshire Evening Press*, 8 July 1957 ('Unwins Motor Show Supplement').
98 *The Times*, 15 August 1966, 1.
99 *The Times*, 16 June 1964, 7; 11 June 1965, 24.
100 *The Times*, 15 December 1969, III. Coventry contemplated a scheme of this kind in 1968 (Starkie 1982, 85).
101 'City of Oxford Report on Pilot Operational Study of Abingdon Road Park and Ride Scheme', Department of Transport, Traffic Advisory Unit, 1974.
102 'The Nottingham Zones and Collars Experiment. Summary Report', Department of Transport, Traffic Advisory Unit, 1978.
103 *Municipal Review*, June 1975, 68–70. The four sites were: Western Boulevard, Trowell Road, University Boulevard and Queen's Drive. See plan in Starkie 1982, 86.
104 Groves 1978, 73–4.
105 'The Nottingham Zones and Collars Experiment. Summary Report', Department of Transport, Traffic Advisory Unit, 1978.
106 *The Times*, 7 April 1971, 4.
107 By D. Tomkinson, the City Architect. *The Times*, 21 February 1968, 4; Brierley 1972, 190.
108 Clark and Cook 2009, 23.
109 *Hitchin, Letchworth and Baldock Advertiser*, 6 January 2010, 2.

8: SCRAPPING THE CAR

1 Motoring enthusiasts have long been fascinated by scrapyards because they were, until recent years, a source of interesting old vehicles and parts. W. H. Charnock wrote a fine essay, the 'Valley of Old Bones', on Voake's yard at Adversane in Charnock 1954.
2 Aerial photographs were published in *Motor Commerce*, July 1936, and *The Motor*, 27 October 1936. Charles Trent Ltd is now a major vehicle dismantling company with sites in six counties and a staff of 140.
3 Car Dumps General file, Museum of English Rural Life, SR CPRE C/1/63/22.
4 *The Guardian*, 7 August 1965, 3.
5 Brierley 1972, 326–9.
6 Information from the website of Sims Metal Management: http://uk.simsmm.com (accessed 10 January 2012).

9: ON THE ROAD

1 The first in the series was 'To the Great North Road', *Car Illustrated*, 28 March 1902, 31.
2 *The Times*, 18 May 1900, 7.
3 Wells 1902, 61.
4 Patent GB 189600285 (A).
5 *The Autocar*, 25 January 1896, 146.
6 *Automotor and Horseless Carriage Journal*, December 1901, 111.
7 *Nineteenth Century*, August 1902, 305–8; *Car Illustrated*, 8 October 1902, 218; 4 November 1902, 327–8. Merriman 2007, 25.
8 *London Gazette*, 21 November 1905, 7898–7900; *The Car*, 25 October 1905, 302; Baldwin and Baldwin 2004, 37–8 (including map of route), 401; Merriman 2007, 26. This scheme was revived in 1914 by the London, Brighton & South Coast Road Syndicate Ltd (*Car Illustrated*, 27 May 1914, 82).
9 *Surveyor and County Engineer*, 15 November 1901, 576–7.
10 *The Car*, 27 November 1907, 75.
11 *The Car*, 18 December 1907, 261.
12 *The Times*, 28 December 1907, 6; 7 February 1908, 14.
13 Jeremiah 2007, 128.
14 Captain George S. C. Swinton, 'A Garden Road', *Fortnightly Review*, 1909, 514–25; George S. C. Swinton, 'A Garden Road', *Car Illustrated*, 30 June 1909, 277–8.
15 *The Car*, 17 July 1907, 417–18; *The Autocar*, 22 May 1920, 949; Kroplick and Velocci 2008.
16 Charlesworth 1987, 4–5. For an account of the Road Board, see Jeffreys 1949, 22–83.
17 *The Car*, 21 February 1912, 53.
18 *Car Illustrated*, 20 October 1909, 407; *The Times*, 29 September 1909, 8; *The Motor*, 18 April 1911, 444.
19 The very first reinforced concrete bridges are said to be those built at Chewton Glen, Hampshire, 1901, and Satterthwaite, Cumbria, 1902 (Morriss 2005, 182). Crompton claimed, in 1912, that he had built a highway across Essex to Thames Haven, with reinforced concrete bridges (Crompton 1928, 203). The first concrete surfaced country road in America was probably Woodward Avenue, Detroit, in 1908, but by 1913 about 800 miles of concrete surfacing existed in the U.S.A. (Nevins 1954, 484). For the first concrete-surfaced streets in England, see Chapter 12.
20 *The Times*, 8 August 1916, 3.
21 The National Archives, MT 39/38, MT 39/41 and MT 39/295; *The Times*, 5 March 1923, 9; *The Motor*, 13 November 1923, 762–3; Merriman 2007, 28–9.
22 'A Bill to facilitate the construction of motorways and the granting of powers in relation to such ways and to traffic thereon', presented by Mr Clynes (Leader of the House of Commons), 15 November 1923. A second Bill without mention of the Coventry–Salford section was introduced by Sir Leslie Scott on 9 April 1924. The first attempt to obtain the necessary powers was the Light Railways (Motorways) Bill drafted in July 1923. See The National Archives, MT 39/41.
23 *The Times*, 18 April 1925, 7; Baldwin and Baldwin 2004, 115.
24 Jeremiah 2007, 131.
25 *The Motor*, 10 July 1923, 976–7; 28 April 1925, 575–6.
26 Charlesworth 1987, 9.
27 For example, H. C. Lafone, 'Aerial Overways', *The Autocar*, 14 December 1934, 1092–3.
28 *The Times*, 18 November 1937, 19; 27 January 1938, 9.

29 Charlesworth 1987, 12–13; Baldwin and Baldwin 2004, 169; Barty-King 1980, 172.
30 Merriman 2007, fig. 2.2.
31 Drake 1969, 37.
32 *The Times*, 13 December 1922, 9.
33 *The Autocar*, 15 January 1921, 110–13.
34 'Arterial Roads and the Unemployed', *The Autocar*, 15 January 1921, 110–13.
35 See photograph of the Great West Road in 1927, *The Autocar*, 3 June 1927, 948. Compare photograph in *The Motor*, 28 July 1936, 1136.
36 Tripp 1942, 40.
37 It had been planned with two 24ft carriageways, with a 20ft central reservation, 8ft verges and 8ft footways (*The Motor*, 15 May 1928, 727; 2 February 1937, 23).
38 *The Times*, 22 August 1934, 12.
39 *The Motor*, 11 December 1934, 910; *The Times*, 28 May 1936, 17; *The Motor*, 21 February 1939, n. p.
40 *The Autocar*, 23 July 1921, 172.
41 *The Motor*, 26 February 1924, 143.
42 *The Times*, 1 June 1925, 11. In fact, these had been installed in 1924 (*Commercial Motor*, 29 June 1924, 741). Many of these lights were repositioned in the 1930s, as ideas evolved.
43 *The Times*, 27 October 1925, 11.
44 *The Motor*, 18 December 1940, 428. There may have been earlier instances of white lines, for example, at Ashford, Kent (Morriss 2005, 127).
45 *The Autocar*, 17 August 1923, 299.
46 *The Times*, 8 December 1925, 8.
47 'White Lines on the Highway', Ministry of Transport Circular, 29 January 1926; *The Times*, 30 January 1926, 7.
48 Buchanan 1958, 124. 'Report on the Road Fund, 1934–35', Ministry of Transport, 1936, 57.
49 *The Autocar*, 7 June 1929, 1142. This is probably the 'historic motor mirror' that was replaced by the Chinese Pagoda filling station in 1929 (*The Motor*, 23 July 1929, 1192).
50 The first reflecting road studs in England were Follsain Gloworm studs, installed in Market Harborough in 1934. The first of Percy Shaw's Catseyes were installed near Bradford a few weeks later (Morriss 2005, 128). The Ministry of Transport is said to have trialled ten makes of luminous stud in 1937–9, and found that Shaw's performed best: www.storyoflondon.com/modules (accessed 19 January 2011).
51 *Architects' Journal*, 24 November 1926, 646–51.
52 *The Autocar*, 29 March 1929, 653; Stamp 1986, 44–5. Until 1929 traffic on the A1 had to cross the narrow seventeenth-century bridge in Wansford village. Today, this operates a single-lane system. The bridge of 1929 now carries northbound traffic only, since the bypass was dualled, with a second bridge, in 1975.
53 Illustrated in *The Motor*, 30 April 1929, 598.
54 Whiteley 1998, 225–6.

55 *The Motor*, 24 July 1934, 1072.
56 *The Motor*, 6 September 1938, 225.
57 *The Times*, 26 October 1937, 11.
58 *The Times*, 20 March 1934, 11.
59 *The Times*, 11 September 1935, 7.
60 Tripp 1942, 39.
61 *The Times*, 30 May 1925, 13.
62 The town of Brackley in Northamptonshire claimed to have originated the idea of flanking service roads in the treatment of its main street, dating from 1901, by the Borough Surveyor, A. A. Green (*The Motor*, 22 September 1936, 314).
63 Tripp 1942, 103.
64 *The Times*, 6 April 1925, 15.
65 *The Autocar*, 2 August 1929, 235.
66 *The Times*, 7 June 1934, 11; 15 December 1934, 9. These experimental concrete cycle paths were separated from the main carriageway by grass verges. Another experimental cycle path, this time in asphalt, was laid by Buckinghamshire County Council on the A422 (Wolverhampton to Stony Stratford) in the same year. See 'Report on the Road Fund, 1934–35', Ministry of Transport, 1936, 11.
67 *The Times*, 10 September 1938, 12. Burgin was then the Minister of Transport.
68 For example, at Osterley: *The Motor*, 29 November 1938, 800.
69 *The Motor*, 12 January 1937, 1097. The reconstruction of 1937 included cycle paths.
70 *The Autocar*, 9 September 1938, 446–7.
71 *Light Car*, 16 September 1938, 537.
72 *The Motor*, 10 December 1935, 895–6.
73 *Road Architecture, 1939: Handbook to the Exhibition Organised by the RIBA*, London, 1939; *The Motor*, 14 March 1939, n. p. By the 1950s the BRF largely represented road construction firms.
74 *The Motor*, 17 March 1925, 315.
75 *Architects' Journal*, 14 November 1928, 665.
76 'Roads of Remembrance as War Memorials' [pamphlet], 1919. See also Law 2010.
76 Law 2010, 69.
77 *The Times*, 2 August 1919, 7.
78 *The Autocar*, 12 April 1919, 521–2.
79 *The Times*, 2 July 1920, 19.
80 *The Times*, 26 July 1928, 11. There are detailed accounts of the Association and its relationships with bodies such as the CPRE and the Institute of Landscape Architects in Merriman 2007 and Law 2010. The Association continued in being until 1965.
81 *The Times*, 1 November 1928, 11.
82 *The Autocar*, 10 August 1928, 271; *The Times*, 18 August 1928, 13.
83 *The Autocar*, 13 December 1929, 1244.
84 *The Times*, 12 May 1930, 10.
85 *The Times*, 22 November 1930, 15.
86 *The Motor*, 19 March 1929, 303.
87 *The Times*, 31 October 1934, 10.
88 *The Times*, 9 November 1934, 10.
89 *Manchester Guardian*, 26 September 1947, 4.

This criticism was made by Clough Williams-Ellis, anticipating the more scathing attacks launched on municipal planting by Ian Nairn in the 1950s.
90 Merriman 2007, 55–6.
91 Hall 2002, 35; Williams-Ellis 1928, 161–6.
92 Williams-Ellis 1928, 165; Davis 2008, 40.
93 The use of the term 'parkway' goes back to 1870, when Olmsted and Vaux designed Jamaica Parkway in Brooklyn. It was only in the motoring age that 'parkway' acquired a special meaning. See Newton 1971, 596–8.
94 *Manchester Guardian*, 3 September 1929, 13. Princess Parkway was opened by the Minister of Transport on 1 February 1932.
95 *Manchester Guardian*, 4 May 1931, 11.
96 Crowe 1960, 43 and 87.
97 *The Autocar*, 6 June 1930, 1090–93.
98 *The Motor*, 4 March 1930, 103 (advertisement).
99 *The Autocar*, 30 March 1928, 608; Barty-King 1980, 155.
100 *The Motor*, 30 September 1930, 396.
101 Subsequently, their number declined rapidly, with only about forty left in 1989 and twenty-two in 1999 (undated manuscript notes, letter dated 6 June 1989 from M. D. Tuckfield, Head of Public Relations Information, AA Public Relations Department, Telephone Boxes and Telephone Boxes General Correspondence Files, Hampshire Record Office, 73M94/G1/13/126–7).
102 *The Motor*, 24 March 1931, 314.
103 *The Times*, 17 October 1930, 12.
104 *The Motor*, 10 April 1934, 417.
105 Whiteley 1998, 227.
106 Tripp 1942, 7.
107 Baldwin and Baldwin 2004, 72–7, 107–25; Merriman 2007, 45–6.
108 Advertisement in *The Times*, 7 December 1943, 3; Merriman 2007, 57.
109 Curnock 1944, 22.
110 Baldwin and Baldwin 2004, 91; Merriman 2007, 62.
111 Consolidated with the Trunk Roads Act in the Highways Act of 1959.
112 Charlesworth 1987, 27 and 35; Yeadon 1998, 248–61.
113 The hard shoulders were paved in red asphalt in 1963 and third lanes were added to the carriageways in 1966. The hard shoulder remained discontinuous at bridges until the 1990s, when eleven bridges were replaced (McCoubrey 2009, 261–2; *The Motor*, 2 January 1957, 912–15).
114 Smith 1996, 444, fig. 20.
115 McCoubrey 2009.
116 Quoted by Moran 2009, 10.
117 Charlesworth 1987, 98–129.
118 The bridge design was borrowed for use on the St Albans Bypass (M1/M10), which had a concrete road surface.
119 For a detailed account of this criticism, see Merriman 2007, 83–7.

120 Charlesworth 1987, 124–5.

121 *The Times*, 3 November 1959, 8; Merriman 2007, 154.

122 The computer centres at Coleshill and West-houghton dealt with all telephone calls from motorways in the 1970s and were superseded in 1988 by a strategic control centre at Perry Barr.

123 *The Times*, 2 December 1958, 10. Britain's motorways formed part of a European network agreed in 1949: the M1 would be part of route E31.

124 *The Times*, 17 November 1966, 10. The first remotely controlled signs were set up on the M4.

125 *The Times*, 28 March 1972, 5.

126 *The Times*, 15 December 1969, 2.

127 *The Times*, 25 May 1972, 30.

128 Buchanan 1958, 145.

129 The Ministry of Transport stopped its annual subsidy to the Roads Beautifying Association in 1949.

130 Charlesworth 1987, 67.

131 *The Appearance of Bridges*, Ministry of Transport, HMSO, 1964.

132 *The Appearance of Bridges*, Ministry of Transport, HMSO, 1964, n. p.

133 The first pre-stressed railway bridge in England was the Adam Railway Viaduct, Wallgate, Wigan, of 1946, now listed Grade II. The first pre-stressed road bridge was the small Nunn's Bridge, Fishtoft, Lincolnshire (1948; L. G. Mouchel & Partners). For further historical context, see Smith 1996, 432–3.

134 *Concrete Quarterly*, April–June 1965, 9–12.

135 *Concrete Quarterly*, January–March 1969, 15.

136 *The Autocar*, 8 January 1965, 48, 57.

137 McCoubrey 2009, 286. Williams 1974, 15.

138 Quoted in Moran 2009, 47; Merriman 2007, 2.

139 *The M25 Orbital Motorway*, Department of Transport, 1986.

140 Buchanan 1970, 30.

141 *The Times*, 27 October 1961, 15.

142 Less obtrusive tensioned wire rope barriers are suitable for sensitive landscapes: they are used widely on 'A' roads through the Scottish Highlands, and on the A1 in north-east England.

143 The first section with lighting along its length was the M4 from Slough (Charlesworth 1987, 131).

144 *The Appearance of Bridges and other Highway Structures*, Highways Agency, HMSO, 1996, 142.

145 This was £6 billion more than existing schemes. It was augmented a year later by 'Trunk Roads, England: Into the 1990s', February 1990.

146 'Roads for Prosperity: The Archaeological Impact', English Heritage, 1990, 5.

147 Baldwin and Baldwin 2004, 295.

148 The end result was admired by the landscape historian W. G. Hoskins (see Merriman 2007, 215).

149 *The Times*, 27 April 1962, 11.

150 *The Times*, 9 May 1964, 6.

151 *The Times*, 5 March 1970, 2.

152 *The Times*, 8 February 1973, 17.

153 Fasham and Whinney 1991, 95–6.

154 The results were published as K. E. Walker and D. E. Farwell, *Twyford Down, Hampshire: Archaeological Investigations of the M3 Motorway from Bar End to Compton, 1990–93*, Hampshire Field Club Monograph 9, 2000.

155 A Public Inquiry in 1976 rejected the first preferred route, more or less along the existing Winchester Bypass. Mott, Hay & Anderson designed a new route, through a chalk cutting, which was opposed at a Public Inquiry in 1985. This reconvened from 1986 to 1988.

156 http://www.schnews.org.uk/sotw/twyford-down-plus10.htm (accessed 4 November 2010).

157 *The Guardian*, 9 July 1993, 18.

158 Schofield 2009, 87–98.

159 Moran 2009, 253.

160 *The Times*, 3 August 1946, 6.

161 Three of the original metal collars at Cobham, Surrey, survive: http://www.cobham heritage.org.uk/events-memorial-unveil-apr09-report.html (accessed 6 June 2011).

162 *The Times*, 4 May 1956, 4; Starkie 1982, 4–5.

163 Charlesworth 1987, 60.

164 McCoubrey 2009, 177. The viaduct was listed in 1998.

165 *Official Architecture and Planning*, March 1959, 117.

166 Morriss 2005, 255. *Traffic Signs Regulations and General Directions*, 1994, provided specifications for new fingerpost signs for the first time since 1965. In June 2005 the Department for Transport and English Heritage issued advice that 'all surviving traditional fingerpost direction signs should be retained *in situ* and maintained on a regular basis. They should be repainted every five years in traditional black and white livery' (Traffic Advisory Leaflet 6/05).

167 *The Times*, 21 August 1982, 3; McCoubrey 2009, 39.

168 McCoubrey 2009, 57.

169 Charlesworth 1987, 34; Baldwin and Baldwin 2004, 96.

170 *The Times*, 8 October 1962, 20.

171 *The Times*, 28 December 1962, 8.

172 Tripp 1942, 98–9.

173 Bell 2001, 99.

174 Bell 2001, 15.

10: THE CAR AND THE COUNTRYSIDE

1 Standard advertisement quoted in Hardy and Ward 1984, 22.

2 'Motoring and its Pleasures', *The Motor*, 19 March 1912, 273.

3 Margaret Montague Jackson, 'Welcome to Winter', *The Motor*, 17 October 1933, 627.

4 The literature on the subject is considerable. Martin J. Wiener, *English Culture and the Decline of the Industrial Spirit, 1850–1980*, Cambridge, 1980, provides the initial thesis. Alun Howkins, 'The Discovery of Rural England', in *Englishness: Politics and Culture, 1880–1920*, ed. Robert Colls and Philip Dodd, London, 1986, 62–88, persuasively sets out the 'rural myth' argument and allies it specifically to southern England. For an account of the impact of the car on Sussex, the epitome of the South Country, see Peter Brandon, *The Discovery of Sussex*, Andover, 2010. Ben Knights, 'In Search of England: Travelogue and Nation between the Wars', and Stephan Kohl, 'Rural England: An Invention of the Motor Industries', in *Landscape and Englishness*, ed. Robert Burden and Stephan Kohl, Amsterdam, 2006, argue that car touring articles and guides provided a conservative, reassuring assertion of the old ways in response to the onset of modernism. Peter Mandler, 'Against Englishness: English Culture and the Limits to Rural Nostalgia, 1850–1940', *Transactions of the Royal Historical Society*, vol. 7 (1997), 155–75, sets out the counter-argument, pointing to the small membership of The National Trust and the Society for the Protection of Ancient Buildings (SPAB) in the 1920s as evidence of how these traditionalist views were held by a tiny minority, while David Matless, *Landscape and Englishness*, London, 1998, explores the extent to which those associated with the preservationist cause in the CPRE and the DIA were opposed to the myth of rural nostalgia in their emphasis on 'fitness for purpose' and openness to modern design in the creation of a new, re-planned England.

5 For an examination of the role of the motoring press and motor advertising in the modernisation of the countryside in the inter-war years, see Jeremiah 2010.

6 A comprehensive selection of his work is in Bacon 1995.

7 T. Lovat Williams, 'Spring in England', *The Autocar*, 27 March 1931, 537.

8 H. Massac Buist, 'Spring, Space and Speed', *The Autocar*, 30 March 1928, 597.

9 A. B. Heckstall-Smith, 'The Open Road', *The Autocar*, 30 May 1930, 1048–9.

10 An analogy made by John Lowerson in Lowerson 1980, 264.

11 'Exploring an Old English Village', *Light Car and Cyclecar*, 15 April 1927, 576–7.

12 'Missed by Most of Us', *Light Car and Cyclecar*, 27 May 1927, 740–41.

13 Owen John, 'On the Road', *The Autocar*, 10 October 1924, 689.

14 'Athos', 'Are You Tired of Guide-books?', *Light Car and Cyclecar*, 31 March 1933, 553. 'Antiquarian Prejudice' was delivered as a lecture in 1937 and reprinted in John Betjeman, *First and Last Loves*, London, 1952.

15 Owen John, 'On the Road', *The Autocar*, 17 June 1922, 1005.

16 Edgar Stewart, 'A New Sightseeing', *Popular Motoring*, September 1932, 37.

17 Stephen Spender, *The Pylons* in Skelton 1964; 99, Quennell and Quennell 1935.

18 Arthur Nettleton, 'The Car and the Countryside', *Popular Motoring*, November 1932, 29.

19 Austin advertisement, rear cover, *Light Car and Cyclecar*, 10 April 1931.

20 *The Autocar*, 1 January 1932, front cover.

21 *The Motor*, 26 April 1932, pp. 503–4; *The Autocar*, 31 May 1935, 980–82.

22 Mandler 1997, 252.

23 Mandler 1997, 247–53.

24 'Historic Mansions Now Open to Motorists', *The Motor*, 26 May 1936, 734–6.

25 Articles appeared regularly in the motoring press encouraging motorists to visit National Trust properties. See, for example, Vagrant, 'Down Zummerzet Way', *The Autocar*, 21 June 1935, 1103–4, for Montacute and Muchelney.

26 Thorold 2003, 93.

27 See Mandler 1997, 369–88, for an account of how country houses were turned into visitor attractions.

28 Clive Holland, 'Curio Hunting by Car', *The Autocar*, 14 April 1933, 604–6.

29 Rhoads 1986, 135.

30 For Shell Guides, see Heathcote 2011.

31 *The Motor*, 26 July 1910, 947.

32 *The Motor*, 25 March 1913, 361.

33 *The Motor*, 20 August 1912, frontispiece.

34 *The Motor*, 26 June 1923, 897.

35 *The Motor*, 24 July 1923, 1080–81.

36 *The Autocar*, 15 October 1926, 631. For other examples of Owen John's comments on advertising in the countryside, see *The Autocar*, 13 May 1922, 782–3; 1 July 1922, 21–3.

37 *The Motor*, 29 December 1925, 1088.

38 *The Autocar*, 25 March 1922, 496–7.

39 *The Autocar*, 24 May 1929, n.p.

40 'Preserve England's Beauty', *The Motor*, 7 August 1923, 15.

41 'Safeguarding our Countryside', *The Autocar*, 20 November 1925; 24 May 1929, title page.

42 *The Motor*, 7 September 1926, 211–12. For a balanced account of the conflicting pressures on the countryside, see Lowerson 1980.

43 Advertisement on rear cover of G. L. Pepler, *The Country Town and its Rural Setting: A Paper To Be Read at the 4th National Conference for the Preservation of the Countryside*, London, 1931.

44 *The Times*, 22 February 1930, 7; *The Motor*, 4 March 1930, 185–6.

45 Sheila Kaye-Smith, 'Laughter in the South-East', in Williams-Ellis 1938, 34.

46 Sir William Beach Thomas, 'The Home Counties', in Williams-Ellis 1938, 209.

47 C. E. M. Joad, 'The People's Claim', in Williams-Ellis 1938, 73.

48 Owen John, 'On the Road', *The Autocar*, 15 October 1926, 632.

49 Charles Houghton, 'Wayside Eyesores', *The Autocar*, 22 June 1928, 1273.

50 Sharp 1937, 4.

51 See, for example, Stevenson 1984, 130, 390.

52 Neve 1988, 49.

53 For plotland development, see Hardy and Ward 1984.

54 *The Star*, 22 June 1932, quoted by Hardy and Ward 1984, 147.

55 'La vie au grand air', *The Motor*, 26 September 1933, 396.

56 *The Motor*, 14 August 1923, 56.

57 *The Times*, 17 August 1925, 16.

58 Lindley Searle, 'Not on Sundays', *The Motor*, 7 September 1937, 201–3.

59 Major A. Livingstone-Oke, 'The Open-Air Life', *The Motor*, 23 June 1925, 923.

60 *The Motor*, 26 September 1933, 396.

61 *The Motor*, 26 September 1933, 924.

62 Major D. D. Milne, 'All about Motor Caravanning', *The Motor*, 25 May 1921, 691.

63 For caravanning, see Jenkinson 1998.

64 Jenkinson 1998, 34.

65 *The Autocar*, 7 April 1933, 589.

66 P. A. Barron, 'Ideal Homes for Motorists', *The Autocar*, 6 December 1929, 1200–03; Wells's obituary, *The Times*, 18 July 1951, 8.

67 West Chiltington Village Design Statement Steering Group, *West Chiltington Village Design Statement*, 2003, 12–13; E. P. Beaumont, 'The Intriguing Mr Wells', Storrington and District Museum, *Times Past*, no. 14 (Spring 2003); 'The Roundabout Area', Storrington and District Museum, *Times Past*, no. 21 (summer 2005), 5–7.

68 *The Times*, 13 July 1929, 25.

69 'New Towns Built for Motorists', *The Motor*, 8 April 1930, 481–4.

70 For an account of the changes taking place in the country, as they affected agricultural workers and incomers from the towns, see Howkins 2003, 163–86.

11: HOSPITALITY FOR THE MOTORIST

1 *Car Illustrated*, 19 August 1903, 396.

2 *Licensing World*, quoted in the *Car Illustrated*, 19 November 1902, 432.

3 *The Motor*, 15 May 1928, 717–18.

4 *The Autocar*, 8 April 1922, 573; 15 December 1922, 1225; *The Motor*, 18 March 1924, 243.

5 'The New Tea-house Vogue', *The Motor*, 27 March 1928, 329–31.

6 *The Motor*, 14 August 1928, 49.

7 *The Autocar*, 20 August 1926, 292.

8 *The Motor*, 27 March 1928, 330.

9 McMinnies 1936, 252–3.

10 *The Motor*, 9 September 1930, 228–9.

11 The distinction is made forcefully in Gutze 2005.

12 *Riley Record*, May 1934, 28.

13 *Morris Owner*, April 1932, 132.

14 McMinnies 1936, 7. McMinnies wrote on motoring subjects and had raced at Brooklands as a young man.

15 Hayward & Maynard were the architects. *The Builder*, 18 May 1928, 859.

16 *The Autocar*, 20 January 1928, 103–4.

17 *The Autocar*, 8 April 1932, 574.

18 *The Autocar*, 8 April 1932, 574.

19 For the new club room, see *Architectural Review*, vol. 73 (May 1933), 186–7. The interior was filmed for Pathé News for two newsreels: *Roadhouse Nights (Filmed on the Kingston Bypass, Hot Nights and Cool Waters)* (1932) and *London's Famous Clubs and Cabarets – The Ace of Spades Club* (1933). Both are available on www.britishpathe.com (accessed 2 September 2008). The films give a good idea of the atmosphere of a roadhouse.

20 *Flight*, 6 July 1933, 672.

21 Harold A. Albert, 'This Country Club Idea', *Popular Motoring*, October 1932, 36–7.

22 *The Autocar*, 29 December 1933, 1196.

23 McMinnies 1936, 246–7, 280–81.

24 Alec Davies, 'The Buildings We Deserve: The Motorist and the Architect', *Standard Car Review*, vol. 4, no. 9 (n.d.), 410.

25 Oliver 1947, 37–8.

26 *Architects' Journal*, 16 November 1933, 633–6.

27 Betjeman 1970, 23.

28 *Morris Owner*, July 1937, 463.

29 *The Builder*, 18 March 1938, 543–4.

30 Oliver 1947, 132–3, 137–8.

31 *The Motor*, 24 February 1925, 141.

32 *Design for Today*, June 1933, 48–9.

33 Clough Williams-Ellis, 'The Roadhouse', *Design for Today*, June 1933, 43.

34 For the Knights, see *The Motor*, 11 July 1933, 980; *The Autocar*, 14 October 1932, 674; 17 February 1933, 246.

35 *The Motor*, 2 May 1933, 524.

36 *The Autocar*, 29 December 1933, 1196.

37 *The Autocar*, 3 September 1921, 426; *The Times*, 15 September 1921, 5.

38 *The Times*, 24 July 1924, 16.

39 *The Autocar*, 10 April 1931, 639.

40 Albert, 'This Country Club Idea', *Popular Motoring*, October 1932, 37.

41 Motor camps in England had been proposed by Owen John of *The Autocar* on several occasions between 1921 and 1924. He saw them as rest camps, something like the dak-bungalows of India, with cubicled huts, a common mess room, plain cooking and an opportunity for a wash, and thought that the Automobile Association was a suitable candidate for running them. Nothing came of the idea, which was perhaps too spartan for the well-heeled British motorist. See Owen John, 'On the Road', *The Autocar*, 8 October 1921, 621–3; 29 October 1921, 795–7; 18 July 1924, 102–4.

42 For the early development of the motel, see Belasco 1979.

43 Belasco 1979, 168.

44 Described as 'fugitive suburbia' with their

45 *The Motor*, 16 October 1934, 591; *The Autocar*, 11 March 1955, 307–8.

46 *The Motor*, 28 June 1938, 991; *The Times*, 29 April 1939, 26.

47 The architects were Sydney H. Jones and J. Arnold Parker of Coventry. Vahlefield and Jacques 1960, 198.

48 *The Motor*, 2 July 1952, 717–18.

49 Obituary, *The Times*, 23 April 1963, 15.

50 *Architects' Journal*, 9 July 1953, 46–7. See also 'British Motels Have a Future', *The Autocar*, 11 March 1955, 306–8, which reviews the four then in existence.

51 C. John Main, 'The Motel Concept', *Architect and Building News*, 16 April 1970, 41.

52 The information on Watney Lyon motels is derived from Mauger 1959, 82–5, and McMinnies 1965.

53 *Manchester Guardian*, 20 April 1957, 4.

54 *Architect and Building News*, 15 September 1965, 501–6.

55 For the totals, see manuscript list dated September 1961, AA Public Relations Department Motels file, Hampshire Record Office 73M94/G1/5/41; *The Motor*, 3 April 1963; *The Times*, 18 February 1965. The *Signpost* guide lists twenty-two motels in England in the 1965 edition (McMinnies 1965).

56 The Angel was converted by Maxwell Joseph in 1959: *The Autocar*, 13 March 1959, 393.

57 *The Times*, 31 July 1962. Descriptions of the motel are in the *Architect and Building News*, 17 October 1962, 579–81; and the *Architects' Journal*, 27 March 1963, 683–8.

58 *Morning Advertiser*, 23 March 1962.

59 Belasco 1979, 171; and see Rhoads 1986.

60 *The Times*, 4 March 1969, 21.

61 *Building*, 22 November 1968, 89–93.

62 *Motor Trader*, 4 September 1963, 356.

63 *Concrete Quarterly*, October–December 1968, 6–9.

64 *The Times*, 29 October 1969, 21.

65 *The Times*, 15 January 1968, 13, and information from Simon Bradley, Pevsner Architectural Guides.

66 See www.travelodgedevelopment.co.uk (accessed 16 June 2009).

67 *The Times*, 16 September 1960, 5; *The Observer*, 18 September 1960, 9.

68 *Motor Trader*, 1 April 1964, ii–iii.

69 *Motor Trader*, 28 July 1965, 145.

70 *Motor Trader*, 25 August 1965, 333.

71 The section on Little Chef is based on research undertaken by Hannah Waugh.

72 'Lessons at the Roadside', *Architectural Research Quarterly*, vol. 8, no. 1 (2004), 32.

73 Lawrence 2010, 118.

74 'Square Meals for the Motorist', *BP Progress*, no. 70 (October 1964), 3.

75 'A Wider Choice for Roadside Customers', *Popular Foodservice*, May 1987, 33.

76 Lawrence 2010, 124–5.

77 For a comprehensive account of the major chains of drive-through restaurants and roadside catering in the U.S.A., see Jakle and Sculle 1999.

78 www.caterersearch.com (accessed 31 March 2011).

79 Lawrence 2002, 97–111, discusses the models for the British motorway service area. The principal example is the bridge restaurant of 1958 at Vinita, Oklahoma, which was the inspiration for the subsequent 'Oases' bridge restaurants on the Illinois State tollways and those on the Italian Autostrada del Sole.

80 The section on MSAs is based on research undertaken in the Moto archives by Katie Carmichael and Matthew Whitfield.

81 Lawrence 2002. This section is heavily indebted to this and to David Lawrence's other writings on the subject: Lawrence 1999a, Lawrence 1999b, Lawrence 2004 and Lawrence 2010.

82 Lawrence 2002, 177.

83 *Building*, 13 October 1967, 125–30.

84 Lawrence 1999b, 27.

85 *Architectural Review*, vol. 131 (May 1962), 306.

86 *Building*, 20 May 1966, 106–8; Dan Cruickshank, 'Masterclass: Forton Services', *RIBA Journal*, April 1996, 49–55.

87 Depicted in Lawrence 1999b, 40.

88 The report was prepared by the Bartlett School of Architecture and was kept secret at the time, although some of the findings were published in contemporary articles by Bev Nutt, who was responsible for much of its content. See Lawrence 2002, 200–14.

89 *Architectural Review*, vol. 158 (August 1975), 99–102.

90 *Architectural Review*, vol. 151 (June 1972), 382.

91 *Architectural Review*, vol. 151 (June 1972), 384.

92 Lawrence 1999b, 66–7, 91, 108.

93 *Architects' Journal*, 6 May 2004, 36–41.

12: TRAFFIC IN TOWNS, 1896–1939

1 Edge 1934, xvi.

2 Bird 1973, 134; Barker and Robbins 1975, 1ff.

3 Barker and Robbins 1974, 178ff. Fragments of early electric tram systems are still in use, such as Volk's Electric Railway, which was laid along the Brighton seafront in 1883, and the Blackpool Tramway, which opened in 1886.

4 Barker and Robbins 1975, 66 and pls 12 and 25. See also *The Times*, 15 August 1856, 9.

5 Much feed for horses was imported. It cost 10s. a week to feed a town horse in the 1890s.

6 Gordon 1893, 187.

7 For a history of the Road Car Co., see Herbert J. Reinohl, 'No Surrender to the Frenchies: The Story of the London Road Car Company', in *Buses Annual, 1966*, ed. R. A. Smith, London, 1965.

8 For example: Birmingham (London & Birmingham Railway, one- to two-storey horse-shoe-shaped stables with ribbed ramps, *circa* 1840), Sheffield (Castle House, multi-storey stables for John Henry Bryars, 1899–1900) and Sunderland (North Eastern Railway, one- to two-storey stables, 1883–4).

9 Peter Darley, 'Stables Complex and Underground Features in Former Camden Goods Depot, Historic Area Assessment', English Heritage, April 2010.

10 In addition, a site on Kingsland Road, Hackney, originated as a carriers' depot. The almshouses that previously occupied the site were sold for redevelopment in 1906 (*The Times*, 17 February 1906, 17); the new building was advertised for sale to jobmasters and carriers in 1908 (*The Times*, 30 May 1908, 24).

11 Gordon 1893, 12. Demolished; now the site of Putney Exchange. For London General, see Barker and Robbins 1975, 69ff.

12 Horses were often bred and reared in Ireland or in the East Riding of Yorkshire.

13 Gordon 1893, 16. Tram horses lasted only four years.

14 Gordon 1893, 19.

15 Rosen and Zuckermann 1982, 10ff.

16 *The Times*, 16 February 1909, 4.

17 Turvey 1996.

18 The use of granite setts increased from the 1830s, as the machinery to cut this hard stone was introduced, and railways facilitated its distribution.

19 *The Times*, 4 January 1890, 12.

20 Turvey 1996, 141–3.

21 'Report on an inquiry concerning the Nuisances arising during the transport of Manure from Towns to Agricultural Districts and the means available for their prevention or mitigation, by Dr Parsons', Annual Report of the Medical Officer of the Local Government Board, 1891–2, 80–83.

22 Turvey 1996, 147.

23 Knight was General Manager of the London Brighton & South Coast Railway.

24 *The Autocar*, 22 November 1929, 1097; Morriss 2005, 261.

25 One of the earliest references to refuges dates from 1841, and reveals that some already existed (Ishaque and Noland 2006, 129).

26 Edge 1934, 5.

27 Edge 1934, 8.

28 The club moved from its first home, 4 Whitehall Court, to 119 Piccadilly, formerly Lord Palmerston's home, in 1902 (Brendon 1997, 80–81).

29 *Architectural Review*, vol. 29 (April 1911), 247–64. The steelwork was designed by Sven Bylander.

30 Barty-King 1980, 151, 155.

31 Wildman and Crawley 2003, 131. This club was founded in 1906.

32 Bridges 1995, 10.

33 Many roads in Kent were tarred between 1903 and 1914 (Morriss 2005, 123).

34 Mechanical tests on stone used for road purposes were undertaken by the National

Physics Laboratory for the Road Board (from *circa* 1910), and then by the Ministry of Transport (from 1919).

35 Jeffreys 1949, 146. In the U.S.A., also, the first concrete surfaces for traffic were streets rather than country roads. The first were in Bellefontaine, Ohio, in 1898 (Nevins 1954, 484).

36 Circular Letter, Local Government Board, 10 March 1904; *The Times*, 28 January 1904, 13.

37 For illustration, see Hands 2005, 7.

38 Circular Letter to County Councils other than the London County Council, Local Government Board, 16 October 1907.

39 The four warning signs adopted by the Congress were for crossroads, level crossings, bends and obstructions. See Lay 1992, 190; *The Times*, 27 October 1908, 14.

40 *The Times*, 18 August 1908, 5.

41 *Automobile Club Journal*, 17 September 1903, 296.

42 Wells 1914, 70.

43 *Car Illustrated*, 30 August 1905, 53.

44 *Automobile Club Journal*, 17 September 1903, 295.

45 *Car Illustrated*, 9 October 1907, 320.

46 The junction at Sollershott Circus was not shown as a circle on Parker and Unwin's original plan of Letchworth, dated 1904, although a similar feature was positioned north of the railway line on the same axis. Two drawings of 1908, by Barry Parker, show the circus with a central island, but no indication of traffic flow. A letter published in *The Citizen* on 1 February 1963 (n. p., cutting in Letchworth First Garden City Museum) recounts a childhood memory of an experiment in gyratory flow, carried out *circa* 1909 with the participation of invited vehicles. This has not been corroborated by documentary evidence.

47 Unwin 1909, 240–41.

48 Letter from Barry Parker to the Secretary, First Garden City Ltd, dated 21 November 1923 (copy in Letchworth First Garden City Museum).

49 *The Citizen*, 19 February 1932 (n. p., cutting in Letchworth First Garden City Museum).

50 Fifth Annual Report of the London Traffic Branch of the Board of Trade, 1912.

51 For example: www.rigb.org (accessed 21 August 2011).

52 Fifth Annual Report of the London Traffic Branch of the Board of Trade, 1912.

53 *The Times*, 17 December 1912, 13. Street maps show that this was still in place in the 1920s.

54 *Car Illustrated*, 29 January 1913, 442.

55 *The Times*, 16 November 1899, 8, address to the Society of Arts.

56 Buchanan 1970, 8.

57 *The Times*, 19 March 1904, 17.

58 Not long after this, in 1909, D. Barclay Niven suggested a ring road 10 miles from the centre of London, 110ft wide, smoothly paved for fast traffic, with a sunken railway to one side and a strip of parkland to the other. Furthermore, 'each outside edge would be occupied by a service road, macadamised, for heavy slow traffic' (*The Times*, 8 February 1910, 16).

59 *Architectural Review*, vol. 29 (April 1911), 239–44; Crouch 2002, 177–9; Fraser and Kerr 2007, 70.

60 *The Times*, 6 October 1913, 4.

61 *The Motor*, 17 March 1908, 169.

62 Jeremiah 2007, 131.

63 *The Motor*, 21 May 1912, 700.

64 *Car Illustrated*, 17 June 1914, 203.

65 For a discussion of statistics relating to the demise of the horse, see Thomson 1976.

66 *The Autocar*, 9 September 1927, 457–8.

67 *The Autocar*, 6 March 1920, 440–41.

68 *The Autocar*, 6 March 1920, 440–41.

69 Collins 1995, 73 and 76.

70 'Recommendations for the Standardisation of Road Direction Posts and Warning Signs', Ministry of Transport, 28 February 1921.

71 *The Autocar*, 8 January 1921, 55–6; 12 March 1921, 472.

72 *The Times*, 13 June 1929, 13.

73 *The Times*, 23 June 1952, 4.

74 Five warning signs agreed by most European nations at an International Convention held in Paris in 1926 were ratified by Great Britain in 1929. These were 'sharp turn', 'crossroad', 'guarded level crossing', 'unguarded level crossing' and 'uneven road'. In Britain, the 'sharp turn' sign was used for 'double bend', and the 'uneven road' sign was seldom used.

75 Report of the Departmental Committee on Traffic Signs', Ministry of Transport, 1933.

76 *The Autocar*, 7 July 1933, 25.

77 *The Motor*, 12 December 1933, 975.

78 *The Times*, 20 August 1935, 12.

79 *The Times*, 2 April 1935, 32.

80 *The Autocar*, 15 March 1935, 461.

81 For example, *The Autocar*, 8 February 1935, 216–17.

82 Ashley 2002, 70–73, illustrates surviving examples, for instance at Horsted Keynes Station, Sussex (recently restored), Ludlow, Shropshire, and Glastonbury, Somerset.

83 Silex 1931, 158–9.

84 Lay 1992, 187.

85 These were made by the Gas Accumulator Co. Ltd, which manufactured marine navigation lights (*The Times*, 4 March 1924, 11).

86 *The Times*, 19 January 1926, 9; 23 July 1926, 11; 27 July 1926, 12. This colour combination, of red, yellow and green, had first been used in this country on the London & North Eastern Railway between Marylebone and Neasden in 1923.

87 For Manchester, see *The Times*, 18 October 1929, 16. For a list of installations by 31 March 1930, see 'Report on the Road Fund, 1929–30', Ministry of Transport, 1931, Appendix 22 (map).

88 *The Motor*, 30 July 1929, 1205–7; *The Times*, 14 September 1929, 7; 'Traffic Control by Light Signals', Memo No. 297 (Roads), Ministry of Transport, September 1929 (notably, this recommended lenses of 8in. diameter, although some installations, particularly in Birmingham and the Midlands, had lenses of 12in.; it also decreed that posts should be painted with white and black bands). For Oxford Street, see *The Times*, 4 June 1929, 11.

89 Lay 1992, 188.

90 *The Times*, 24 July 1935, 16: in a census, 6,125 people crossed when the signal indicated 'Cross Now', and 13,292 when it indicated 'Don't Cross'.

91 *The Times*, 3 April 1933, 11.

92 The first of these was not built before the 1930s. Similarly, the Central Circus laid out in front of Hendon Underground Station in 1923 – which, like Sollershott Circus, has a central island – probably did not enforce a gyratory system at the outset.

93 *The Times*, 5 January 1926, 12, with diagram. See photograph in *The Times*, 5 January 1926, 16, showing arrows and policemen.

94 For The Mall, see *The Times*, 26 January 1926, 14, with diagram. For Hyde Park Corner, see *The Times*, 23 March 1926, 16, with diagram; *The Autocar*, 26 March 1926, 550. For Trafalgar Square, see *The Times*, 23 April 1926, 11, with diagram. For Piccadilly Circus, see *The Times*, 6 July 1926, 11.

95 *The Times*, 12 August 1924, 9.

96 For an example of an earlier sign, see *Light Car and Cyclecar*, 5 August 1927, 268.

97 For the Pedestrians' Protection Association (secretary, N. Glasson), see *The Times*, 23 June 1925, 12. For the Pedestrians' Association (secretary, T. Foley), see *The Times*, 14 August 1929, 8: this was formed at a meeting of cycling and rambling clubs, held at Essex Hall, London, on 13 August 1929.

98 *The Times*, 18 December 1926, 7. These must have been considered experimental. According to the 'Report on the Road Fund, 1930–31', Ministry of Transport, 1931, 67, 'the first permanent signs indicating pedestrian crossing places have been erected on the Embankment by the London County Council'.

99 *The Times*, 18 December 1926, 7.

100 See, for example, *The Motor*, 6 November 1934, 703.

101 *The Times*, 3 October 1933, 9; Moran 2006, 479.

102 'Report on the Road Fund, 1934–35', Ministry of Transport, 1936, 53.

103 *The Autocar*, 16 November 1934, 922.

104 Charlesworth 1987, 106. By some accounts the first zebra crossings had blue and yellow stripes, but contemporary accounts (e.g., *The Times*, 29 March 1949, 2) state that white lines were painted on the road surface.

105 Thorold 2003, 207; *The Motor*, 6 November 1934, 702.

106 *The Autocar*, 17 August 1934, 249.

107 *The Times*, 11 March 1935, 9; 'Report on the

Road Fund, 1934–35', Ministry of Transport, 1936, 53.

108 *The Times*, 2 October 1935, 11; 'Report on the Road Fund, 1936–37', Ministry of Transport, 1937, 15: in the first year there had been no 'material reduction' in the number of accidents.

109 *The Times*, 18 June 1935, 14.

110 *The Times*, 21 March 1934, 11; 18 June 1935, 14.

111 *The Times*, 6 July 1938, 13.

112 *The Times*, 29 June 1938, 9; 31 March 1939, 8; Moran 2006, 483.

113 *The Motor*, 27 October 1936, 650.

114 *The Motor*, 3 July 1923, 935.

115 *The Motor,* 17 December 1935, 943. A similar idea was being put forward in 1935 by Lt Col. A.W.C. Richardson.

116 *Architectural Review*, vol. 81 (April 1937), liii; Morrison 2003, 253.

117 *The Motor*, 22 March 1938, 324–5, with illustration.

118 'Report on the Road Fund, 1924–1925', Ministry of Transport, 1925, 49.

119 *Architect and Building News*, 3 January 1930, 14.

120 *The Motor*, 11 September 1934, 236.

121 *The Motor*, 14 December 1937, 906.

122 Letter from Coventry City Council to SPAB, 17 September 1914 (Coventry file, SPAB Archive).

123 Letter from A. R. Powys, Secretary of SPAB, to *Country Life*, dated 17 May 1935 and published 1 June 1935 (Coventry file, SPAB Archive).

124 Letter from Coventry City Council to SPAB, 12 April 1935 (Coventry file, SPAB Archive).

125 Letter from Coventry City Council to SPAB, 12 April 1935 (Coventry file, SPAB Archive).

126 *The Motor*, 11 September 1934, 236.

127 The idea of urban roads in tunnels was put forward by Lord Ashfield (of the Underground 'Combine') in 1920. *The Motor* (21 January 1920, n. p.) commented: 'we think, however, the problem of dispersing the fumes will present some difficulty'. Lord Montagu proposed elevated roads served by lifts (*The Motor*, 16 June 1920, 909; *The Times*, 21 August 1924, 11). Sir Alfred Yarrow proposed 'flying junctions' at major London crossings, such as Piccadilly Circus (*The Times*, 21 August 1924, 11).

128 See *Car Illustrated*, 6 January 1904, 211.

129 *The Times*, 16 December 1916, 8. Presented by Mr G. A. T. Middleton to the Society of Architects, inspired by the high-level railway bridge running from Cannon Street to Charing Cross. *The Autocar*, 14 December 1934, 1092–3.

130 'Report on the Road Fund for 1934–35', Ministry of Transport, 1936, 13.

131 *The Times*, 14 September 1934, 9.

132 See Sharples 2004, 161–2; *Architectural Review*, vol. 75 (June 1934), 202–4; *Building*, May 1934, 172–82.

133 Edwin Lutyens and Charles Bressey, 'Highway Development Survey, Greater London, 1937', May 1938 (the 'Bressey-Lutyens Report'). *The Autocar*, 20 May 1938, 922–3; *The Motor*, 24 May 1938, 744–6.

134 Buchanan 1970, 24.

13: TRAFFIC IN TOWNS SINCE 1945

1 In June 1955 the *Architectural Review* published an influential edition titled *Outrage*, in which the architectural critic Ian Nairn expressed his fears for a future in which the rural and urban landscape would merge into a uniformly bland 'Subtopia'.

2 *The Times*, 4 June 1943, 2. The kerb drill ('At the kerb halt; look right, look left, look right again; then if all clear, quick march!') was superseded by the Green Cross Code in 1971.

3 As expressed, for example, in the House of Lords in February 1941 (*The Times*, 27 February 1941, 2).

4 Tripp 1942, 11.

5 The Barlow Report ('Report of the Royal Commission on the Geographical Distribution of the Industrial Population') was followed by the Scott Report on land use in rural areas (1941) and the Uthwatt Report on compensation (1942). These resulted in the appointment of a Minister of Planning in 1943, and the Reith Report into New Towns (1946).

6 For a detailed and accessible account of the planning context of reconstruction plans, see Larkham and Lilley 2001.

7 Abercrombie already had wide experience of urban and regional planning, having devised plans for Sheffield, Doncaster, East Kent, Bristol, Bath and Cumberland between the wars.

8 'London Replanned', The Royal Academy Planning Committee's Interim Report, October 1942; Buchanan 1970, 24.

9 An unplanned example of this is Westway in London. There are also enclosed units beneath Silvertown Way in London.

10 *The Motor*, 16 April 1929, 493–5.

11 Tripp 1942, 61–2, 82. Tripp proposed elevated ring roads, but mentioned a successful sunken road in the U.S.A.: the Express Highway in St Louis.

12 Tripp 1942, 112.

13 Abercrombie's 'Greater London Plan' of December 1944 suggested five ring roads, including 'D', 12 miles from the centre of London.

14 'Road, Rail and River in London', The Royal Academy Planning Committee's Second Report, July 1944; Buchanan 1970, 32.

15 Buchanan 1970, 32 and 35; Thomson 1970, 101.

16 Curnock 1944, 14.

17 'Design and Layout of Roads in Built-up Areas', Ministry of War Transport, 1946 (Report of Departmental Committee appointed 1943).

18 Superseded by *Roads in Urban Areas*, Ministry of Transport, 1966.

19 Starkie 1982, 20.

20 Starkie 1982, 71; Charlesworth 1987, 38; *The Times*, 18 September 1956, 13.

21 The Moat Street and Hill Cross Flyovers were completed around 1965.

22 Buchanan 1963, 172.

23 Stamp 2007, 17. The possibility of an inner ring road had been mooted in Birmingham since the early twentieth century (see Chapter 12).

24 *The Times*, 1 October 1959, 6.

25 *The Times*, 23 January 1960, 8.

26 *The Times*, 10 December 1959, 6.

27 Charlesworth 1987, 130. The western ramp of the Chiswick Flyover had to be modified to form a continuation of the new elevated road. Evidence of this can still be seen in its brickwork.

28 *The Autocar*, 28 March 1958, 487.

29 McCoubrey 2009, 296.

30 *The Times*, 18 August 1964, 11; 14 February 1967, 3. A very similar flyover survives nearby, at Lodge Avenue Junction.

31 Admittedly this 7-mile stretch of the M1 ('Hendon Urban Motorway'), which ran from Elstree to Staples Corner on the North Circular Road (A406), followed a railway line for most of its route. It caused some disruption at its southern end, where a flyover was erected over Edgware Road.

32 *The Times*, 29 July 1970, 3.

33 The North Kensington Play Space Group had already, in 1968, campaigned for an adventure playground under six bays of the motorway (*The Times*, 29 July 1968, 7).

34 Bell 2001, 75.

35 Starkie 1982, 80.

36 Starkie 1982, 90; *The Times*, 19 January 1973, 3.

37 In central London this was followed by the conversion of the Kingsway Tramway (from Kingsway to Waterloo Bridge, under the Strand and Aldwych) into an underpass in 1963–4 and the construction of the Euston Road Underpass in 1964–6.

38 McCoubrey 2009, 224.

39 McCoubrey 2009, 158–9.

40 Winskell 2004, 101.

41 Morrice 2006.

42 Simmons 1974, 86.

43 Simmons 1974, 88.

44 Simmons 1974, 88–9.

45 *The Times*, 2 June 1932, 11.

46 Proposed by Thomas Sharp and named 'Merton Mall'. Sharp 1948, 113–20; Plowden 1971, 58–78.

47 Starkie 1982, 72.

48 Starkie 1982, 77–8.

49 Fraser and Kerr 2007, 165–8.

50 Fraser and Kerr 2007, 163.

51   Brendon 1997, 286, unreferenced quote.
52   *Official Architecture and Planning*, July 1960, 311.
53   Burt and Grady 1994, 234.
54   In 1970 independent candidates fought seats in the GLC election with the slogan 'homes before roads', proposing scrapping the Greater London Development Plan with its ringway system, and devoting the money saved (estimated £1,700 million) to housing. The campaign claimed that the ringways risked turning central London into 'an American-style disaster area' (*The Times*, 24 March 1970, 5). They failed to win seats, but focused attention on the issue.
55   Public inquiries were held in 1983, 1987 and 1988 (McCoubrey 2009, 35).
56   McCoubrey 2009, 35.
57   The spelling 'drive-thru' was in use in the U.K. – to describe a car wash – in 1969 (*The Times*, 1 August 1969, 16).
58   *The Times*, 12 January 1959, 6.
59   *The Times*, 2 February 1959, 5.
60   *The Times*, 12 April 1960, 18; 30 August 1961, 12. Coutts laid plans for a drive-in bank in 1963 (*The Times*, 11 January 1963, 7). The Westminster opened their fifth drive-in in Long Eaton, Derbyshire, in 1964 (*The Times*, 22 January 1964, 18).
61   *Official Architecture and Planning*, February 1960, 84; *The Times*, 12 December 1959, 10.
62   *The Times*, 2 February 1960, 3.
63   *The Times*, 10 May 1969, 21.
64   Morrison 2003, 251.
65   In the Introduction to Tripp 1942, 6.
66   Tripp 1942, 66.
67   Lewison and Billingham 1969, 34–5.
68   Tetlow and Goss 1968, 215.
69   *The Times*, 4 October 1973, 2.
70   'Streets for All, East of England', English Heritage, 2005, 53.
71   Buchanan 1963, 166; Tetlow and Goss 1968, 76.
72   *The Times*, 29 November 1961, 8.
73   *Architects' Journal*, 23 March 1961, 419–20.
74   Jellicoe 1961.
75   Buchanan 1970, 45.
76   *The Guardian*, 17 July 1996, B4.
77   *The Guardian*, 15 May 1995, 6.
78   *The Guardian*, 15 July 1996, 7; 17 July 1996, B4.
79   http://rts.gn.apc.org/ (accessed 22 March 2011).
80   'Report of the Departmental Committee on Traffic Signs 1944', HMSO, 1946. European signs had been agreed at three international conferences: 1909 and 1926 in Paris, and 1931 in Geneva. These were not adopted in their entirety in Great Britain, but were influential in the long run.
81   Hands 2005, 11–12.
82   *The Times*, 9 February 1957, 4.
83   For example in Reading, see Starkie 1982, 55–7.
84   As far as one can tell, the first new-style signs in England were erected in Dereham,

Norfolk, on 9 December 1964, but could not be unveiled until 1 January 1965 (*The Times*, 10 December 1964, 8).
85   *The Motor*, 22 December 1936, 970.
86   Jeffreys 1949, 146. This red asphalt has gone.
87   These were suspended yet again during the Suez Crisis of 1956.
88   Earlier experiments with striped crossings had been made in Hornsey and Leicester; Charlesworth 1987, 106; *The Times*, 29 March 1949, 2.
89   Moran 2006, 486.
90   *The Times*, 15 June 1961, 6; 3 April 1962, 12.
91   *The Times*, 8 September 1964, 6.
92   *The Times*, 23 February 1967, 2.
93   *The Times*, 26 July 1968, 2.
94   The National Physics Laboratory at Teddington undertook surface testing for the Road Board from 1913. In 1930 the Ministry of Transport opened its Experimental Station at Harmondsworth, with an experimental road surface on the nearby Colnbrook Bypass. The Experimental Station became the Road Transport Laboratory in 1933. See Charlesworth 1987, 1 and pl. 2.
95   Charlesworth 1987, 65.
96   Charlesworth 1987, 138.
97   F. C. Blackmore, 'Priority at Roundabouts', *Traffic Engineering and Control*, vol. 5, no. 2 (1963), 104–6; *The Times*, 26 April 1963, 17; 3 November 1966, 1.
98   See F. C. Blackmore, 'Capacity of Single-Level Intersections', Road Research Laboratory Report 356, 1970.
99   Information in tribute from Anna Blackmore (daughter of Frank Blackmore): www.mini-roundabout.com/tribute (accessed 15 August 2010).
100   F. C. Blackmore and M. Marlow, 'Improving the Capacity of Large Roundabouts', Transport and Road Research Laboratory Report 677, 1975.
101   *Concrete Quarterly*, April–June 1972, 6.
102   *The Times*, 3 May 1973, 4.
103   *The Times*, 29 July 1976, 27.
104   *The Times*, 15 April 1981, 9.
105   *Car Illustrated*, 26 May 1909, 56.
106   Amanda Delaney, Heather Ward and Max Cameron, 'The History and Development of Speed Camera Use', A Report for Monash University Accident Research Centre, 2005, 31.
107   *Sunday Times*, 3 October 2010, 3.
108   *The Times*, 2 April 2011, 37.
109   Indeed, since 2007 it has not been compulsory for cameras to be yellow or visible from 200ft (60m).
110   *The Times*, 21 May 1982, 3.
111   Bell 2001, 124.
112   The west London Congestion Zone was abolished at the end of 2010 by the new Mayor, Boris Johnson. Saddler Street in Durham was subjected to a congestion charge in 2002. Subsequent proposals for congestion charges in other British cities

(such as Edinburgh and Manchester) have been defeated in referendums.
113   *The Times*, 23 February 1951, 3.
114   For road pricing and 'area licensing', see Starkie 1982, 42–8 and 96.
115   For example, English Historic Towns Forum Seminar on Traffic Signing and Calming in Historic Areas, 2–3 April 1992; 'Traffic in Townscape: Ideas from Europe', Civic Trust and English Historic Towns Forum, 1994.
116   'Streets for All', English Heritage, 2004.
117   In particular, the yellow no parking 'at any time' sign is no longer deemed necessary, yellow lines being sufficient to enforce the restriction. 'Streets for All: East of England', English Heritage, 2005, 67.
118   *Evening Standard*, 27 August 2010, 4.
119   'Sight Lines', CABE, October 2010.
120   CABE, *Street Design and Placemaking: Case Study 1, Gun Wharf, Plymouth*, n. d.
121   Moran 2009, 114, based on 2008 obituary notices; *The Times*, 11 January 2008: http://www.timesonline.co.uk/tol/comment/obituaries/article3167372.ece (accessed 18 August 2010). See also Eleanor Besley (for the Parliamentary Advisory Council for Road Safety, or PACTS), *Kerb Your Enthusiasm*, 2010, 3; Hamilton-Baillie 2008.
122   *Evening Standard*, 4 March 2010, 24.

CONCLUSION

1   *English Journey*, 1934 (see Priestley 1997), quoted in Merriman 2007, 48.
2   See Mike Berry, *Petroleum Collectables*, Princes Risborough, 2008; Alan Chandler, *Petroliana: The Hunt*, n. p., 2008.
3   Blake 1964.
4   National Scenic Byways were established by U.S. Congress in 1991, and are administered by the Federal Highway Administration.
5   Intimated in Merriman 2007, 48.
6   'Carchitecture', coined by Bell 2001.
7   Montagu 1906, 123.
8   Henslowe 1922, 72.
9   Henslowe 1922, 74.
10   Henslowe 1922, 75.
11   Morrison 2003, 291.
12   Morrison 2003, 291–305.
13   *The Guardian*, 24 May 1990, 24.
14   Phil Goodwin, 'What About 'Peak Car': Heresy or Revelation?', *Local Transport Today*, 25 June 2010 and 8 July 2010: http://www.transportxtra.com/magazines/local_transport_today/opinion/?id=23221 (accessed 25 March 2011).
15   Moran 2009, 37.

APPENDIX

1   *Car Illustrated*, 9 December 1908, 189 29 November 1911, 79.

BIBLIOGRAPHY

Inexplicably, there is no comprehensive bibliography for motoring, unlike, for example, railways, where there are the three massive volumes of George Ottley's *Bibliography of British Railway History* to consult. The nearest thing to such a work is Charles Mortimer, *The Constant Search: Collecting Motoring and Motorcycling Books*, Sparkford, 1982, but this is by no means complete and, as its title suggests, is more of a book collector's guide with a bias towards individual makes of car and motor sport. The Railway & Canal Historical Society publishes annual transport bibliographies that pick up some of the journal articles and are especially useful for material on roads.

Journal articles and websites cited are in full in the notes, with the exception of substantial articles in journals, which are in the main bibliography. To simplify cross-referencing between notes and bibliography, published and unpublished authored works are listed alphabetically in a single sequence below.

WEBSITES

The Motorway Archive:http://www.motorwayarchive.ihtservices.co.uk

Motorways: http://www.cbrd.co.uk/motorway

Oil company road maps: http://www.ianbyrne.free-online.co.uk

Old Birmingham garages: http://www.obgt.pwp.blueyonder.co.uk

Old Manchester garages: http://www.images.manchester.gov.uk

Roads: http://www.sabre-roads.org.uk

AUTHORED WORKS (PUBLISHED AND UNPUBLISHED)

Abercrombie 1944
Patrick Abercrombie, *Greater London Plan*, London, 1944

Adeney 1988
Martin Adeney, *The Motor Makers: The Turbulent History of Britain's Car Industry*, London, 1988

Ashley 2002
Peter Ashley, *Hard Furnishings: Street Furniture*, London, 2002

Aslet 1982
Clive Aslet, *The Last Country Houses*, New Haven and London, 1982

Bacon 1995
Roy Bacon, ed., *The Golden Age of British Motoring*, London, 1995

Badminton Library 1902
Alfred C. Harmsworth, ed., *Motor Cars and Motor Driving*, Badminton Library, London, 1902

Baldwin and Baldwin 2004
Sir Peter Baldwin and Robert Baldwin, eds, *The Motorway Achievement*, vol. 1: *The British Motorway System: Visualisation, Policy and Administration*, London, 2004

Balfour 1992
Michael Balfour, *Alfred Dunhill: One Hundred Years and More*, London, 1992

Bamberg 2000
James Bamberg, *British Petroleum and Global Oil, 1950–1975*, Cambridge, 2000

Bardsley and Corke 2006
Gillian Bardsley and Colin Corke, *Making Cars at Longbridge: 100 Years in the Life of a Factory*, Stroud, 2006

Bardsley and Laing 1999
— and Stephen Laing, *Making Cars at Cowley*, Stroud, 1999

Barker and Robbins 1974
T. C. Barker and Michael Robbins, *A History of London Transport*, vol. 2: *The Twentieth Century to 1970*, London, 1974

Barker and Robbins 1975
— and —, *A History of London Transport*, vol. 1: *The Nineteenth Century*, London, 1975

Barron 1929
P. A. Barron, *The House Desirable*, London, 1929

Barty-King 1980
H. Barty-King, *The AA: A History of the First 75 Years of the Automobile Association, 1905–1980*, Basingstoke, 1980

Beazley 2006
Ben Beazley, *Postwar Leicester*, Stroud, 2006

Belasco 1979
Warren J. Belasco, *Americans on the Road: From Autocamp to Motel, 1910–1945*, Cambridge, Mass,, 1979

Bell 2001
Jonathan Bell, *Carchitecture: When the Car and the City Collide*, Basle and London, 2001

Berry 2004
Mike Berry, *Petroleum Collectables*, Princes Risborough, 2004

Betjeman 1970
John Betjeman, *John Betjeman's Collected Poems*, third edition, London, 1970

Beveridge and Rocheleau 1998
C. E. Beveridge and P. Rocheleau, *The Papers of Frederick Law Olmsted: Designing the American Landscape*, New York, 1998

Bird 1973
Anthony Cole Bird, *Roads and Vehicles*, London, 1973

Blake 1964
Peter Blake, *God's Own Junkyard: The Planned Deterioration of America's Landscape*, New York, 1964

Boddy 1965
William Boddy, 'Garages Fit for Motor Cars', *Veteran and Vintage Magazine* (September 1965), 8–9 and 32

Borsay 2000
Peter Borsay, *The Image of Georgian Bath*, Oxford, 2000

Brandon 2002
Ruth Brandon, *Automobile: How the Car Changed Life*, London 2002

Brendon 1997
Piers Brendon, *The Motoring Century: The Story of the Royal Automobile Club*, London, 1997

Bridges 1995
John F. Bridges, *Early Country Motoring: Cars and Motorcycles in Suffolk, 1896–1940*, Little Waldingfield, 1995

Bridle and Porter 2002
Ron Bridle and John Porter, eds, *The Motorway Achievement*, vol. 2: *Frontiers of Knowledge and Practice*, London, 2002

Brierley 1972
John Brierley, *Parking of Motor Vehicles*, second edition, London, 1972

Brittain-Catlin 2010
Timothy Brittain-Catlin, *Leonard Manasseh & Partners*, London, 2010

Brooks and Pevsner 2007
Alan Brooks and Nikolaus Pevsner, *The Buildings of England: Worcestershire*, New Haven and London, 2007

Bryan 1996
Barbara Bryan, *Twyford Down: Roads, Campaigning and Environmental Law*, London, 1996

Buchanan 1958
Colin Buchanan, *Mixed Blessings: The Motor in Britain*, London, 1958

Buchanan 1963
—, ed., *Traffic in Towns: A Study of the Long Term Problems of Traffic in Urban Areas*, Ministry of Transport, London, 1963 [Report of the Steering Group and Working Group appointed by the Minister of Transport]

Buchanan 1970
C. M. Buchanan, *London Road Plans, 1900–1970*, London, 1970

Burns 1967
W. Burns, *Newcastle: A Study in Replanning at Newcastle upon Tyne*, London, 1967

Burt and Grady 1994
Steven Burt and Kevin Grady, *Illustrated History of Leeds*, Derby, 1994

Calladine and Morrison 1998
Tony Calladine and Kathryn Morrison, 'Road Transport Buildings: A Report by RCHME for the English Heritage Post-1939 Listing Programme', January 1998

Charlesworth 1987
George Charlesworth, *A History of the Transport and Road Research Laboratory, 1933–1983*, Aldershot, 1987

Charnock 1954
W. H. Charnock, *Mind over Motor*, London 1954

Cherry and Pevsner 1999
Bridget Cherry and Nikolaus Pevsner, *The Buildings of England: London, 3: North West*, London, 1999

Church 1979
R. Church, *Herbert Austin: The British Motor Car Industry to 1941*, London, 1979

Church 1994
—, *The Rise and Decline of the British Motor Industry*, Cambridge, 1994

Clark and Cook 2009
Celia Clark and Robert Cook, *The Tricorn: The Life and Death of a Sixties Icon*, Portsmouth, 2009

Coe and Reading 1981
Peter Coe and Malcolm Reading, *Lubetkin and Tecton: Architecture and Social Commitment*, Bristol, 1981

Collins 1995
Paul Collins, *The Tram Book*, Shepperton, 1995

Collins and Stratton 1993
— and Michael Stratton, *British Car Factories from 1896: A Complete Historical, Geographical, Architectural and Technological Survey*, Godmanstone, 1993

Collins and Stratton 1994
— and —, 'A Survey of Coventry Car Factories', unpublished report for Coventry City Council, November 1994

Croft 1999
Catherine Croft, ed., *On the Road: The Art of Engineering in the Car Age*, Architecture Foundation exhibition catalogue, London, 1999

Crompton 1928
R. E. Crompton, *Reminiscences*, London, 1928

Crosby 1998
Alan Crosby, ed., *Leading the Way: A History of Lancashire's Roads*, Preston, 1998

Crouch 2002
Christopher Crouch, *Design Culture in Liverpool, 1880–1914*, Liverpool, 2002

Crowe 1960
Sylvia Crowe, *The Landscape of Roads*, London, 1960

Curnock 1944
George C. Curnock, *New Roads for Britain: A Plan for the Immediate Future*, The British Roads Federation, December 1944

Davies 1988
Colin Davies, *High Tech Architecture*, London, 1988

Davis 2008
Timothy Davis 'The Rise and Decline of the American Parkway', in *The World beyond the Windshield*, ed. Christof Mauch and Thomas Zeller, Athens, Ohio, 2008, 35–58

Dixon 1962
Donald F. Dixon, 'The Development of the Solus System of Petrol Distribution in the United Kingdom, 1950–1960', *Economica*, n. s., vol. 29, no. 113 (February 1962), 40–52

Douglas and Humphries 1995
Priscilla Douglas and Pauline Humphries, *Discovering Hitchin*, Baldock, 1995

Drake 1969
James Drake with H. L. Yeadon and D. I. Evans, *Motorways*, London, 1969

Dunnett 1980
P.J.S. Dunnett, *The Decline of the British Motor Industry*, London, 1980

Edge 1934
S. F. Edge, *My Motoring Reminiscences*, London, 1934 [republished 1972]

Engelbach 1927–8
C. R. F. Engelbach, 'Some Notes on Re-organising a Works to Increase Production', *Proceedings of the Institution of Automobile Engineers*, vol. 22 (1927–8), 496–514

Esher 1983
Lionel Esher, *A Broken Wave: The Rebuilding of England, 1940–80*, Harmondsworth, 1983

Evans and Self 1972
Hazel Evans and Peter Self, eds, *New Towns: The British Experience*, London, 1972

Fasham and Whinney 1991
P. J. Fasham and R.J.B. Whinney, *Archaeology and the M3*, Hampshire Field Club Monograph 7, 1991

Ferrier 1982
R. W. Ferrier, *The History of the British Petroleum Company*, vol. 1: *The Developing Years, 1901–1932*, Cambridge, 1982

Filson-Young 1904
A. B. Filson-Young, *The Complete Motorist*, London, 1904

Foreman-Peck, Bowden and McKinlay 1995
J. Foreman-Peck, S. Bowden and A. McKinlay, *The British Motor Industry*, Manchester, 1995

Fraser and Kerr 2002
Murray Fraser and Joe Kerr, 'Motopia: Cars, Cities and Architecture', in Wollen and Kerr 2002, 315–26

Fraser and Kerr 2007
— with —, *Architecture and the 'Special Relationship': The American Influence on Post-War British Architecture*, London and New York, 2007

Genat 1999
Robert Genat, *The American Car Dealership*, Osceola, Wis., 1999

Georgano 1995
Nick Georgano, ed., *Britain's Motor Industry: The First Hundred Years*, Sparkford, 1995

Gibberd et al. 1980
Frederick Gibberd et al., *Harlow: The Story of a New Town*, Stevenage, 1980

Goat 1989
Leslie G. Goat, 'Housing the Horseless Carriage: America's Early Private Garages', *Perspectives in Vernacular Architecture*, vol. 3 (1989), 62–72

Goodman 2001
Bryan Goodman, *Motoring around Surrey*, Stroud, 2001

Gordon 1893
W. J. Gordon, *The Horse World of London*, London, 1893

Greenland 2005
Charles Greenland, 'Conservation of Historic Garages', unpublished MSc. dissertation, Oxford Brookes University, 2005

Groves 1978
F. P. Groves, *Nottingham City Transport*, Glossop, 1978

Gutze 2005
David W. Gutze, 'Improved Pubs and Road Houses: Rivals for Public Affection in Interwar England', *Brewery History*, no. 119 (2005), 2–9

Hall 1963
Peter Hall, *London 2000*, London, 1963

Hall 2002
—, *Urban and Regional Planning*, fourth edition, London and New York, 2002

Hamilton-Baillie 2008
Ben Hamilton-Baillie, 'Shared Space: Reconciling People, Places and Traffic', *Built Environment*, vol. 34, no. 2 (2008), 161–80

Hands 2005
Stuart Hands, *Road Signs*, Princes Risborough, 2005

Harding 2004
Tim Harding, *Motoring around Sussex: The First Fifty Years*, Stroud, 2004

Harding and Goodman 2009
— and Bryan Goodman, *Motoring around Kent: The First Fifty Years*, Stroud, 2009

Hardy and Ward 1984
Dennis Hardy and Colin Ward, *Arcadia for All: The Legacy of a Makeshift Landscape*, London, 1984

Heathcote 2011
David Heathcote, *A Shell Eye on England: The Shell County Guides, 1934–1984*, Faringdon, 2011

Henley 2007
Simon Henley, *The Architecture of Parking*, London, 2007

Henslowe 1922
Leonard Henslowe, *Motoring for the Million*, London, 1922

Hildebrand 1974
Grant Hildebrand, *Designing for Industry: The Architecture of Albert Kahn*, Cambridge, Mass., 1974

Hitchmough 1995
Wendy Hitchmough, *The Michelin Building*, revised edition, London, 1995

Hobhouse 1976
H. Hobhouse, *Lost London*, London, 1976

Holden 2003
Len Holden, *Vauxhall Motors and the Luton Economy, 1905–2002*, Woodbridge, 2003

Holliday 1973
John Holliday, ed., *City Centre Redevelopment*, London, 1973

Holme 1935
C. G. Holme, ed., *Industrial Architecture*, London, 1935

Howkins 2003
Alun Howkins, *The Death of Rural England*, London, 2003

Hudson 1983
Kenneth Hudson, *Archaeology of the Consumer Society*, London, 1983

Huggett 1979
F. E. Huggett, *Carriages at Eight*, Guildford, 1979

Ishaque and Noland 2006
Muhammad M. Ishaque and R. B. Noland, 'Making Roads Safe for Pedestrians or Keeping Them Out of the Way? An Historical Perspective on Pedestrian Policies in Britain', *Journal of Transport History*, 3rd series, vol. 27, no. 1 (2006), 115–37

Jackson 1991
Alan A. Jackson, *The Middle Classes, 1900–1950*, Nairn, 1991

Jakle and Sculle 1994
John A. Jakle and Keith A. Sculle, *The Gas Station in America*, Baltimore, 1994

Jakle and Sculle 1999
— and —, *Fast Food: Roadside Restaurants in the Automobile Age*, Baltimore, 1999

Jakle and Sculle 2004
— and —, *Lots of Parking: Land Use in a Car Culture*, Charlottesville and London, 2004

Jarrott 1906
Charles Jarrott, *Ten Years of Motors and Motor Racing*, London, 1906

Jeffreys 1949
William Rees Jeffreys, *The King's Highway: An Historical and Autobiographical Record of the Development of the Past Sixty Years*, London, 1949

Jellicoe 1961
Geoffrey A. Jellicoe, *Motopia: A Study in the Evolution of Urban Landscape*, London, 1961

Jenkinson 1998
Andrew Jenkinson, *Caravans: The Illustrated History, 1919–1959*, Dorchester, 1998

Jeremiah 1995
David Jeremiah, 'Filling Up: The British Experience, 1896–1940', *Journal of Design History*, vol. 8, no. 2 (1995), 97–116

Jeremiah 2004
—, 'Architecture for the Motor-Car', in *The Architecture of British Transport in the Twentieth Century*, ed. Julian Holder and Steven Parissien, Studies in British Art 13, New Haven and London, 2004, 161–88

Jeremiah 2007
—, *Representations of British Motoring*, Manchester and New York, 2007

Jeremiah 2010
—, 'Motoring and the English Countryside', *Rural History*, vol. 21, no. 2 (2010), 233–50

Joad 1938
C. E. M. Joad, 'The People's Claim', in *Britain and the Beast*, ed. Clough Williams-Ellis, London, 1938, 64–85

Johnson n. d.
Claude Johnson, *The Early History of Motoring*, London and Cheltenham, n. d. [?1927]

Judge n. d.
A. W. Judge, *The Modern Motor Engineer*, vol. 1, London, n. d. [?1930]

Kennard 1902
Mrs Kennard, *The Motor Maniac*, London, 1902

Kilham and Hopkins
Walter Kilham and James Hopkins, *Garages Country and Suburban*, New York, 1911

Kitching 1957
E. G. Kitching, 'Multi-Storey Parking Garages', *Truscon Review*, no. 19 (1957), 1–8

Klose 1965
Dietrich Klose, *Multi-Storey Car Parks and Garages*, London, 1965

Kroplick and Velocci 2008
Howard Kroplick and Al Velocci, *The Long Island Motor Parkway*, Charleston, S.C., 2008

Lambert and Baldwin 1998
Julie Anne Lambert and Nick Baldwin, *Motoring in Britain, 1895–1940*, London, 1998

Larkham and Lilley 2001
Peter J. Larkham and Keith D. Lilley, *Planning the 'City of Tomorrow': British Reconstruction Planning, 1939–1952: An Annotated Bibliography*, Pickering, 2001

Law 2010
Michael John Law, '"Stopping to Dream": The Beautification and Vandalism of London's Interwar Arterial Roads', *London Journal*, vol. 35, no. 1 (March 2010), 58–84

Lawrence 1999a
David Lawrence, 'Motorway Service Areas: A Report for the English Heritage Post-1939 Listing Programme', unpublished, 1999

Lawrence 1999b
—, *Always a Welcome: The Glove Compartment History of the British Motorway Service Station*, Twickenham, 1999

Lawrence 2002
—, 'A Bit of Town Dumped Down in the Country: Investigating the Circumstances of the Conception, Design and Operation of the British Motorway Service Area, 1948–2002', unpublished Ph.D. thesis, University of Westminster, 2002

Lawrence 2004
—, 'The Motorway Service Station', in *The Architecture of British Transport in the Twentieth Century*, ed. Julian Holder and Steven Parissien, Studies in British Art 13, New Haven and London, 2004, 219–44

Lawrence 2010
—, *Food on the Move: The Extraordinary World of the Motorway Service Area*, 2010

Lay 1992
M. G. Lay, *The Ways of the World: A History of the World's Roads and of the Vehicles that Used Them*, New Brunswick, N.J., 1992

Levitt 1909
Dorothy Levitt, *The Woman and the Car*, London, 1909

Lewison and Billingham 1969
Grant Lewison and Rosalind Billingham, *Coventry New Architecture*, Warwick, 1969

Lohof 1974
Bruce A. Lohof, 'The Service Station in America: The Evolution of a Vernacular Form', *Industrial Archaeology*, vol. 11, no. 2 (Spring 1974), 1–13

Lord 1994
Thomas Lord, 'The Development of the Petrol Filling Station, 1895–1939', MSc. dissertation, Birmingham University, 1994

Lowerson 1980
John Lowerson, 'Battles for the Countryside', in *Class, Culture and Social Change*, ed. Frank Gloversmith, Brighton, 1980, 258–75

Mandler 1997
Peter Mandler, *The Fall and Rise of the Stately Home*, New Haven and London, 1997

Manson 1958
Grant Carpenter Manson, *Frank Lloyd Wright to 1910*, New York, 1958

Margolies 1993
John Margolies, *Pump and Circumstance*, New York, 1993

Marshall 1995
James Marshall, *The History of the Great West Road*, Hounslow, 1995

Mauger 1959
Paul Mauger, *Buildings in the Country*, London, 1959

McCarter 1997
Robert McCarter, *Frank Lloyd Wright, Architect*, London, 1997

McCoubrey 2009
William James McCoubrey, ed., *The Motorway Achievement*, vol. 3: *Building the Network*, London, 2009

McDonald 2007
Shannon Sanders McDonald, *The Parking Garage: Design and Evolution of a Modern Urban Form*, Washington, D.C., 2007

McMinnies 1936
W. G. McMinnies, *Signpost*, second edition, London, 1936

McMinnies 1965
—, *Signpost*, 26th edition, London, 1965

Merriman 2003
Peter Merriman, '"A Power for Good or Evil": Geographies of the M12 in Late Fifties Britain', in *Geographies of British Modernity*, ed. David Gilbert, David Matless and Brian Short, Oxford, 2003, 115–31

Merriman 2007
—, *Driving Spaces: A Cultural-Historical Geography of England's M1 Motorway*, Oxford, 2007

Merriman 2008
—, '"Beautified" is a Vile Phrase': The Politics and Aesthetics of Landscaping Roads in Pre- and Postwar Britain', in *The World Beyond the Windshield*, ed. Christof Mauch and Thomas Zeller, Athens, Ohio, 2008, 168–86

Minnis 2009
John Minnis, *Sir David Salomons' Motor Stables, Broomhill, Southborough, Tunbridge Wells, Kent*, English Heritage Research Department Report Series, No. 7-2009

Minnis 2010
—, 'Practical yet Artistic: The Motor House 1895–1914', in *Living Leisure and Law: Eight Building Types in England 1800–1914*, ed. Geoff Brandwood, Reading, 2010, 73–88

Montagu 1906
Lord Montagu of Beaulieu, ed., *A History of Ten Years of Automobilism, 1896–1906*, London, 1906

Moran 2006
Joe Moran, 'Crossing the Road in Britain, 1931–1976', *Historical Journal*, vol. 49, no. 2 (2006), 477–96

Moran 2009
—, *On Roads: A Hidden History*, London, 2009

Morrice 2006
Richard Morrice, 'Anthony Swaine and Conservation in East Kent', *Twentieth Century Architecture*, 7 (2006), 33–42

Morris 1985
Lynn E. Morris, *The Country Garage*, Aylesbury, 1985

Morrison 2003
Kathryn A. Morrison, *English Shops and Shopping*, New Haven and London, 2003

Morrison 2006
—, 'Bazaars and Bazaar Buildings in Regency and Victorian London', *Georgian Group Journal*, vol. 15 (2006), 281–302

Morriss 2005
Richard K. Morriss, *Roads, Archaeology and Architecture*, Stroud, 2005

Mumford 1938
Lewis Mumford, *The Culture of Cities*, London, 1938

Neve 1988
Kenneth Neve, *A Bit Behind the Times*, London, 1988

Nevins 1954
Allan Nevins with Frank Ernest Hill, *Ford: The Times, the Man, the Company*, New York, 1954

Newton 1971
Norman T. Newton, *Design on the Land: The Development of Landscape Architecture*, Cambridge, MA, 1971

Nicholson 1982
T. R. Nicholson, *The Birth of the British Motor Car, 1769–1897*, vol. 3: *The Last Battle, 1894–97*, London and Basingstoke, 1982

Nixon 1948
St John C. Nixon, *Daimler, 1896–1946*, London 1948

Nixon 1949
—, *Wolseley: A Saga of the Motor Industry*, London, 1949

O'Connell 1998
Sean O'Connell, *The Car in British Society: Class, Gender and Motoring, 1896–1939*, Manchester, 1998

Oliver 1947
Basil Oliver, *The Renaissance of the English Public House*, London, 1947

Oliver 1962
George A. Oliver, *A History of Coachbuilding*, London, 1962

Parkinson-Bailey 2000
John J. Parkinson-Bailey, *Manchester: An Architectural History*, Manchester, 2000

Pemberton 1907
Max Pemberton, *The Amateur Motorist*, London, 1907

Penrose 2007
Sefryn Penrose, *Images of Change: An Archaeology of England's Contemporary Landscape*, Swindon, 2007

Platt 2000
Edward Platt, *Leadville: A Biography of the A40*, London, 2000

Plowden 1971
William Plowden, *The Motor Car and Politics in Britain*, London, 1971

Priestley 1997
J. B. Priestley, *English Journey* [1934], Folio Society, London, 1997

Purdom 1925
C. B. Purdom, *The Building of Satellite Towns*, London, 1925

Quennell and Quennell 1935
Marjorie Quennell and C.H.B. Quennell, *The Good New Days*, London, 1935

Rhoads 1986
William B. Rhoads, 'Roadside Colonial: Early American Design for the Automobile Age, 1900–1940', *Winterthur Portfolio*, vol. 21, no. 2–3 (summer–autumn 1986), 133–52

Richardson 1972
Kenneth Richardson, *Twentieth Century Coventry*, Coventry, 1972

Richardson and O'Gallagher 1977
— and C. N. O'Gallagher, *The British Motor Industry, 1896–1939: A Social and Economic History*, London, 1977

Ritter 1964
Paul Ritter, *Planning for Man and Motor*, Oxford, 1964

Robson 1979
Graham Robson, *Motoring in the 1930s*, Cambridge, 1979

Rolt 1959
L.T.C. Rolt, *The London–Birmingham Motorway*, London, 1959

Rosen and Zuckermann 1982
Barbara Rosen and Wolfgang Zuckermann, *The Mews of London*, Exeter, 1982

Rosoman 1987
Treve Rosoman, 'The Motor House', *Traditional Homes*, March 1987, 11–16

Russell 2007
Tim Russell, *Fill 'er up! The Great American Gas Station*, St Paul, Minn., 2007

Salomons 1902
David Salomons, 'The Motor Stable and its Management', in *Motors and Motor-driving*, ed. Alfred C. Harmsworth, London, 1902

Saul 1962–3
S. B. Saul, 'The Motor Industry in Britain to 1914', *Business History*, vol. 5 (1962–3), 22–44

Schofield 2009
John Schofield, *Aftermath: Readings in the Archaeology of Recent Conflict*, New York, 2009

Sedgwick 1969
J. R. E. Sedgwick, *The Valuation and Development of Petrol Filling Stations*, revised by R. W. Westbrook, London, 1969

Setright 2002
L. J. K. Setright, *Drive On! A Social History of the Motor Car*, London, 2002

Sharp 1937
Thomas Sharp, *Town and Countryside*, Oxford, 1937

Sharp 1948
—, *Oxford Replanned*, London, 1948

Sharples 2004
Joseph Sharples, *Pevsner Architectural Guide: Liverpool*, London, 2004

Silex 1931
Karl Silex, *John Bull at Home*, London, 1931

Simmons 1974
Jack Simmons, *Leicester Past and Present*, London, 1974

Simms 2006
Barbara Simms, ed., *Eric Lyons & Span*, London, 2006

Sims 1903
George R. Sims, *Living London*, 1903

Sinclair 2002
Iain Sinclair, *London Orbital: A Walk Around the M25*, London, 2002

Skelton 1964
Robin Skelton, ed., *Poetry of the Thirties*, Harmondsworth, 1964

Skinner 1997
Joan S Skinner, *Form and Fancy: Factories and Factory Buildings by Wallis, Gilbert and Partners, 1916–1939*, Liverpool, 1997

Smith 2010
Peter Smith, *The Motor Car and the Country House*, English Heritage Research Department Report Series, No. 94-2010

Smith 1996
W. J. R. Smith, 'U.K. concrete bridges since 1940', *Proceedings of the Institution of Civil Engineers, Structures and Buildings*, no. 116 (August–November 1996), 432–48

Stamp 1986
Gavin Stamp, ed., *Sir Owen Williams, 1890–1969*, London, 1986

Stamp 2007
—, *Britain's Lost Cities*, London, 2007

Starkie 1982
David Starkie, *The Motorway Age: Road and Traffic Policies in Post-war Britain*, Oxford, 1982

Statham 1988
Margaret Statham, *The Book of Bury St Edmunds*, Buckingham, 1988

Stevenson 1984
John Stevenson, *British Society, 1914–45*, London, 1984

Stratton 1997
Michael Stratton, ed., *Structure and Style: Conserving 20th Century Buildings*, London, 1997

Stratton and Trinder 2000
— and Barry Trinder, *Twentieth Century Industrial Archaeology*, London, 2000

Sutcliffe 1981
A. Sutcliffe, *Towards the Planned City*, Oxford, 1981

Sutcliffe and Smith 1974
— and R. Smith, *History of Birmingham*, vol. 3: *Birmingham, 1939–1970*, London and New York, 1974

Tetlow and Goss 1968
John Tetlow and Anthony Goss, *Homes, Towns and Traffic*, second edition, London, 1968

Thoms and Donnelly 1985
David Thoms and Tom Donnelly, *The Motor Car Industry in Coventry since the 1890s*, London and Sydney, 1985

Thoms and Donnelly 2000
— and —, *The Coventry Motor Industry: Birth to Renaissance?*, Brookfield, 2000

Thomson 1976
F. M. L. Thomson, 'Nineteenth-Century Horse Sense', *Economic History Review*, n. s., vol. 29, no. 1 (February 1976), 60–81

Thomson 1970
J. Michael Thomson, ed., *Motorways in London: Report of a Working Party*, London, 1970

Thorold 2003
Peter Thorold, *The Motoring Age: The Automobile and Britain, 1896–1939*, London, 2003

Tripp 1942
Sir Herbert Alker Tripp, *Town Planning and Road Traffic*, London, 1942

Tritton 1985
Paul Tritton, *John Montagu of Beaulieu*, London, 1985

Turvey 1996
R. Turvey, 'Street Mud, Dust and Noise', *London Journal*, vol. 21, no, 2 (1996), 131–48

Unwin 1909
Raymond Unwin, *Town Planning in Practice*, London, 1909

Vahlefield and Jacques 1960
R. Vahlefield and F. Jacques, *Garages and Service Stations*, London, 1960

Vickers 1994
Robert Vickers, 'Coachbuilding in London', *London's Industrial Archaeology No. 5*, Greater London Industrial Archaeology Society, 1994

Vincent 1907
J. E. Vincent, *Through East Anglia in a Motor Car*, London, 1907

Walker 2007
Nick Walker, *A–Z British Coachbuilders, 1919–1960* [1997], revised edition, Beaworthy, 2007

Walton 2000
John K. Walton, *The British Seaside: Holidays and Resorts in the Twentieth Century*, Manchester, 2000

Waugh 2010
Hannah Waugh, *West Hill Works, West Hill, Hitchin, Herts*, English Heritage Research Department Report Series, No. 11-2010

Ware 1976
Michael E. Ware, *Making the Motor Car, 1895–1930*, Buxton, 1976

Webb and Webb 1913
Sidney Webb and Beatrice Webb, *The Story of the King's Highway*, London, 1913

Weightman and Humphries 1984
G. Weightman and S. Humphries, *The Making of Modern London, 1914–1939*, London, 1984

Wells 1902
H. G. Wells, *Anticipations of the Reaction of Mechanical and Scientific Progress upon Human Life and Thought*, London, 1902

Wells 1914
—, *The World Set Free: A Story of Mankind*, Leipzig, 1914

Westwood and Westwood 1952
B. Westwood and N. Westwood, *The Modern Shop*, London, 1952

Whiteley 1998
John Whiteley, 'The Beginning of the Motor Age, 1880–1940', in Crosby 1998, 183–239

Wildman and Crawley 2003
Richard Wildman and Alan Crawley, *Bedford's Motoring Heritage*, Stroud, 2003

Williams 1974
O. T. Williams, 'Some Considerations in the Design and Operation of Multi-Level Interchanges', *Highway Engineer: Journal of the Institution of Highway Engineers*, vol. 22, no. 5 (May 1974), 12–24

Williams-Ellis 1928
Clough Williams-Ellis, *England and the Octopus*, London, 1928

Williams-Ellis 1938
—, ed., *Britain and the Beast*, London, 1938

Winskell 2004
Cyril Winskell, 'Newcastle upon Tyne, 1945–2003', in *The Heroic Period of Conservation*, ed. Elain Harwood and Alan Powers, Twentieth Century Architecture 7, London, 2004, 101–10

Winter 1993
James H. Winter, *London's Teeming Streets, 1840–1913*, London, 1993

Witzel 2006
Michael Karl Witzel, *The American Diner*, Osceola, 2006

Wollen and Kerr 2002
P. Wollen and J. Kerr, *Autopia: Cars and Culture*, London, 2002

Womersley 1961
J. L. Womersley, 'Housing the Motor Car', *Journal of the Town Planning Institute*, September–October 1961, 238–44

Wood 2001
Jonathan Wood, *The Bean*, Princes Risborough, 2001

Wood 2010
—, *The British Motor Industry*, Princes Risborough, 2010.

Worthington-Williams 2001
Michael Worthington-Williams, 'The Motor House', *The Automobile*, December 2001, 48–51

Yeadon 1998
Harry Yeadon, 'The Motorway Era', in Crosby 1998, 240–84

Yorke 1944
F. R. S. Yorke, *The Modern House in England*, London, 1944

ILLUSTRATION CREDITS

© English Heritage.NMR. Mike Hesketh-Roberts: page i, 141, 226, 282

Reproduced by permission of English Heritage.NMR: frontispiece, 2, 3, 56, 58, 123, 160, 195, 204, 211, 237, 245c, 279, 280, 331, 336, 354, 355, 360, 362, 363, 365, 409, 422, 428, 433

© English Heritage.NMR. Derek Kendall: 1, 10, 19, 57, 59, 61, 79, 118, 121, 122, 129, 133, 136, 137, 144, 146, 167, 175, 176, 198, 213, 214, 217, 218, 225, 238, 240, 241, 246d, 246e, 249, 269, 271, 339, 340, 383, 387, 390, 398, 400, 405, 411, 425, 426, 431

© Lord Nuffield: 4, 11, 29

© English Heritage. Andy Donald: 5, 21, 27, 34, 50, 53, 60, 65a, 65b, 99, 100, 108, 109, 134, 145, 149, 179, 194, 196, 203, 212, 215, 219, 220, 263 (based on Brierley 1972, 139), 293a–d, 303a–d, 402

Collection of Malcolm Jeal: 6, 157, 368

The Veteran Car Club of Great Britain: 7, 26, 30, 54, 55, 82, 89, 90, 91, 96, 98, 105, 120, 197, 201, 205, 206, 229, 231a–c, 232, 283, 284, 292, 301, 318, 321, 326, 328, 330, 344, 345, 371, 384

Photo Ron Baxter: 9, 78, 119, 161, 207 230, 287a–d, 289, 297, 357, 370, 375a–d and g, 412

© English Heritage.NMR. Damian Grady: 12, 23, 24, 28, 31, 32, 35, 40, 41, 43, 44, 200, 254, 256, 260, 270, 274, 275, 309, 312, 316, 349, 394, 395, 404, 410, 419, 423, 424, 432

Collection of John Tarring: 14

National Motor Museum, Beaulieu: 15, 18, 42, 47, 127, 148, 152, 170, 180, 285 296, 319, 320, 334

British Motor Industry Heritage Trust, Gaydon: 16, 36, 38, 93, 178

Vauxhall Heritage Archive: 17

Ford Motor Company Limited: 20

© English Heritage.NMR. Steve Cole: 22, 71, 72, 85, 107, 110, 111, 124, 128, 132, 138, 147, 151, 187, 191,

224, 245b, 248, 257, 258, 261, 265, 266, 267, 268, 290, 291, 306, 311, 315, 317, 332, 347, 351, 352, 353, 358, 367, 374, 375e, 375f

Collection of Jonathan Wood: 25

© English Heritage.NMR. Aerofilms Collection: 33, 323, 325, 327, 333, 385

© English Heritage.NMR. James O. Davies: 37, 46, 70, 74, 76, 169, 171, 208, 243, 247, 429

© English Heritage.NMR. Dave MacLeod: 39, 155, 273

Rolls-Royce: 45

Photo Kathryn A. Morrison: 49, 75, 239

Collection of Bryan Goodman: 51, 52

Collection of Tony Clark: 62, 210

NMR. Sydney Newbery: 63

© English Heritage.NMR. Patricia Payne: 64, 77, 112, 114, 242, 245e, 245f, 253, 262

Cambridge University Library: 66, 228, 281, 288, 366, 373, 389, 427

Dell & Wainwright / Architectural Press Archive / RIBA Library Photographs Collection: 68, 69, 102, 104

© English Heritage.NMR. Bob Skingle: 73, 83, 88, 116, 135, 251, 300, 307, 314, 356, 430

© English Heritage.NMR. Alun Bull: 80, 117, 131, 142, 143, 173, 244, 245a, 245d, 246a, 250, 272, 388, 407

Collection of Mike Worthington-Williams: 81, 97

Salomons Centre: 84

Collection of John Minnis: 86, 177, 199, 202, 322, 324, 337, 343, 364, 391, 392, 416

Photo Peter Smith: 87

Photo John Minnis: 92, 94, 95, 113, 162, 193, 278, 393, 408

© English Heritage.NMR. Peter Williams: 101, 106, 115, 139, 172, 222, 233, 235, 246b, 246c, 252, 255, 310, 313, 341, 348, 417

Getty Images: 103, 190, 227, 236, 277, 286, 299, 302, 329, 338, 376. 377, 378, 379, 380, 381, 382, 397, 403, 413, 421

CPRE Archive, Museum of English Rural Life, University of Reading: 125, 163, 164, 166, 182, 186, 192

Courtesy P. Mitchell: 130

John Maltby / Architectural Press Archive / RIBA Library Photographs Collection: 150

© English Heritage.NMR. Nigel Corrie: 153

BDP / Architectural Press Archive / RIBA Library Photographs Collection: 154

Architectural Press Archive / RIBA Library Photographs Collection: 156, 168, 223, 264, 342, 350

Hampshire Record Office: 158, 159, 346

Collection of Neil Parkhouse: 174

Hugh de Burgh Galway / Architectural Press Archive / RIBA Library Photographs Collection: 181

BP Archive: 183, 185

Collection of Leigh Travail: 184

E. S. Saunders: 188

© English Heritage.NMR. Keith Buck: 189, 221

London Transport Museum: 209

Courtesy of John Barker, www.austinmemories.com: 259

Courtesy Charles Trent plc: 276

Collection of Kathryn A. Morrison: 294, 305, 386, 396, 399, 401, 406, 415, 418, 420

Liverpool Record Office: 295, 372

First Garden City Heritage Museum: 298, 369

Lancashire County Council: 304

© English Heritage. Philip Sinton: 308a–d

Courtesy Delia Gaze: 335

INDEX

Illustrations are shown as page numbers in *italics*.
London boroughs and streets are listed under London.